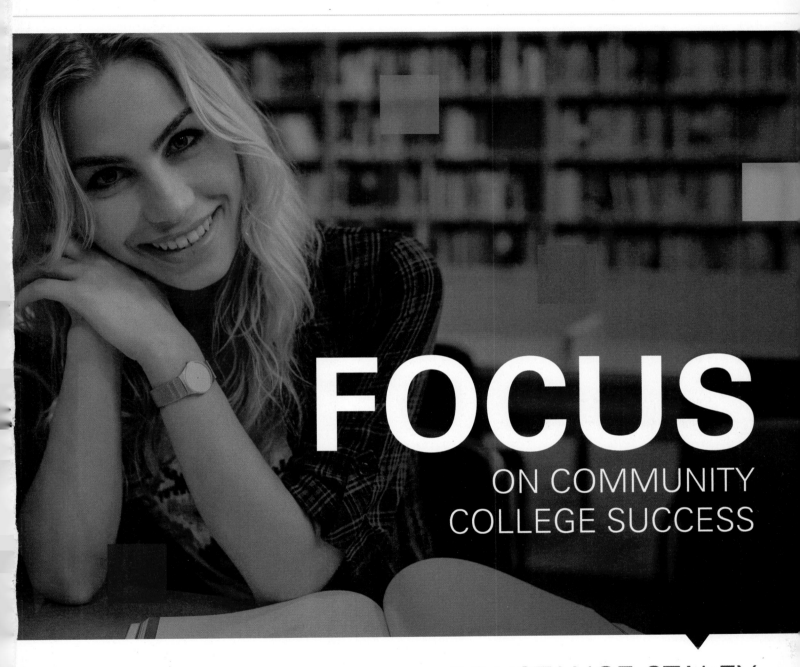

FOCUS
ON COMMUNITY
COLLEGE SUCCESS

CONSTANCE STALEY
UNIVERSITY OF COLORADO, COLORADO SPRINGS

CENGAGE

Australia • Brazil • Mexico • Singapore • United Kingdom • United States

***FOCUS on** Community College Success,*
Fifth Edition
Constance Staley

Product Director: Lauren Murphy

Product Manager: Sarah Seymour

Content Developer: Courtney Triola

Product Assistant: Emily Wiener

Marketing Manager: Allison Moghaddasi

Content Project Manager: Aimee Bear

Manufacturing Planner: Douglas Bertke

IP Analyst: Ann Hoffman

IP Project Manager: Kathryn Kucharek

Production Service: MPS Limited

Compositor: MPS Limited

Art Director: Diana Graham

Cover Designer: Diana Graham

Cover Image: wavebreakmedia/Shutterstock.com

> For product information and technology assistance, contact us at
> **Cengage Customer & Sales Support, 1-800-354-9706.**
>
> For permission to use material from this text or product, submit all requests online at **www.cengage.com/permissions.**
> Further permissions questions can be emailed to
> **permissionrequest@cengage.com.**

Library of Congress Control Number: 2017938977

Student Edition:
ISBN: 978-1-337-40612-3

Loose-leaf Edition:
ISBN: 978-1-337-40602-4

Annotated Instructor's Edition:
ISBN: 978-1-337-40611-6

Cengage
20 Channel Street
Boston, MA 02210
USA

Cengage is a leading provider of customized learning solutions with employees residing in nearly 40 different countries and sales in more than 125 countries around the world. Find your local representative at **www.cengage.com.**

Cengage products are represented in Canada by
Nelson Education, Ltd.

To learn more about Cengage platforms and services, visit **www.cengage.com.**

To register or access your online learning solutions or purchase materials for your course, visit **www.cengagebrain.com.**

Printed in the United States of America
Print Number: 01   Print Year: 2017

5e

FOCUS

ON COMMUNITY COLLEGE SUCCESS

CONSTANCE STALEY

University of Colorado, Colorado Springs

BRIEF CONTENTS

CONTENTS

1 Starting Strong, Building Resilience 1

2 Becoming Mindful, Setting Goals 31

3   Learning Styles and Studying   55

4   Managing Your Time, Energy, and Money   87

5 Thinking Critically and Creatively 117

6 Learning Online 139

7 Engaging, Listening, and Note-Taking in Class 169

8 Reading, Writing, and Presenting 197

11 Choosing a College Major and Career 287

12 Creating Your Future 307

ACKNOWLEDGMENTS

It's been said that "Achievement is a *we* thing, not a *me* thing, always the product of many heads and hands." There are so many people to thank that this acknowledgments section could be as long as a chapter of *FOCUS*! However, here I'll at least mention those who have contributed the most, including all the students over the last forty-plus years who have taught me more than I've ever taught them.

Family   Let me start at the center of my life. My deepest thanks go to Steve, my Sean-Connery-look-alike husband (How do I put up with it?), who has almost forgotten what I look like over the last few years. As I *FOCUS*ed away in my loft office day after day and night after night, he brought me too many cups of coffee to count. I cherish his devotion. My daughters, Shannon and Stephanie, helped bring some much-needed balance to my life, and aside from being the sharpest teenagers on the planet, my grandtwins, Aidan and Ailie, have been a living learning laboratory for me. As they've grown up, they truly have taught me about of the pure joy of learning. And to my beautiful Mother to whom I finally said goodbye not long ago, I miss you.

Reviewers   The list of reviewers who have contributed their insights and expertise to *FOCUS on Community College Success* is long. I'd like to especially thank Regina Lewis of Pikes Peak Community College for her willingness to serve as the original consulting editor of *FOCUS on Community College Success*. And my heartfelt thanks to the reviewers who helped inform the fifth edition revisions:

Angie Anderson, Tennessee College of Applied Technology; Karen Baracskay Tri-County Technical College; Sharon Barnes Tennessee College of Applied Technology; Anitre Bell, Community College of Beaver County; Jenny Billings, Rowan-Cabarrus Community College; Tony Boyd, Maysville Community and Technical College; Annette Bui, Santa Ana College; Carolyn Coulter, Atlantic Cape Community College; Christie Cruse, Bloomfield College; Delphine Davis, Henry Ford College; Hester Furey, Georgia State University at Perimeter College; Tanya Harris-Rocker, Lake-Sumter State College; Angela Jackson, Georgia State University; Lois Kahl, Suffolk Community College; Shauna Moser, Rowan-Cabarrus Community College; Angie Smith, Georgia State University; Tammara Walker, Rowan-Cabarrus Community College; Keron Ward-Myles, Mountain View College; Carol Williams; Drexel University

I'd be remiss to ignore the valuable input gained from reviewers of the previous editions of *FOCUS on Community College Success* that helped shape this book: Germaine Albuquerque, Essex County College; Jenny Billings Beaver, Rowan-Cabarrus Community College; Mary Ellen Beres, Westmoreland County Community College; Lynda Bennett, Blue Mountain Community College; Liz Boyd, Jefferson Community & Technical College; Beverly Brucks, Illinois Central University; Susannah Chewning, Union County Community College; Ann Marie Coons, Corning Community College; Colleen Courtney, Palm Beach State College; Myra Cox, City Colleges of Chicago, Harold Washington; Traci-Dale Crawford, Thomas Nelson Community College; Jean M. Davis, Florida Community College at Jacksonville; Melanie Deffendall, Delgado

Community College; Mark Deitrick, Community College of Beaver County; Anne Dickens, Lee College; Gregory Dieringer, University of Akron; Michael Discello, Pittsburgh Technical Institute; Sammie Dortch, City Colleges of Chicago, Harold Washington; Shirley Flor, San Diego Mesa College; Maria Galyon, Jefferson Community & Technical College; Wendy Grace, Holmes Community College; Evelyn Green, City Colleges of Chicago, Harry Truman; Laurene M. Grimes, Lorain County Community College; Anne M. Gupton, Mott Community College; Amy Harrell, Nash Community College; William Hysell, Mohawk Valley Community College; Cynthia S. Johnson, Palm Beach Community College; Benjamin G. Kramer, New River Community College; Joseph Kornoski, Montgomery County Community College; Judy Kronenberger, Sinclair Community College; Carol Kushner, Dutchess Community College; Christine Landrum, Mineral Area College; Lois Lawson-Bridell, Gloucester County College; Amelia Leighton, Jackson Community College; Jeanine Long, Southwest Georgia Technical College; Marian Macbeth, J. Sargeant Reynolds Community College; Sandra Mahon, Community College of Allegheny County; Michael G. McCreary, Florida Community College at Jacksonville; Cherie Meador, Daley College; Mark A. Mills, Florida Community College at Jacksonville; Jennifer D. Morrison, J. Sargeant Reynolds Community College; Amber Morgan, Greenville Technical College; Mita Noor, Los Angeles Pierce College; Bob Noyes, Tidewater Community College; Bonnie Tamra Ortgies-Young, Georgia Perimeter College; Porter Pajka, Luzerne County Community College; Kate Pandolpho, Ocean County College; Patricia Parma, Palo Alto College; Richard Patete, Keiser University; Gail Platt, South Plains College; Mary Poole, Madisonville Community College; Carlos Rivera, Essex County College; Cristina Rodriguez, Los Angeles Pierce College; Rebecka Sare, Polk State College; René Sawyer, Greenville Technical College; Lynnae Selberg, Grand Rapids Community College; Janet Sims, Cleveland Community College; Camilla Swain-Ledoux, Ivy Technical College; Claudia Swicegood, Rowan-Cabarrus Community College; Ivanhoe Tejeda, City Colleges of Chicago, Harold Washington; Karla Thompson, New Mexico State University Carlsbad; Carrie Tomko, University of Akron; Susan Todd, Jefferson College; Kirstin Wiley, Bluegrass Community and Technical College; Janice Woods, Mohave Community College.

The Cengage Team   No book, of course, gets very far without a publisher, and *FOCUS* has had the best publishing team imaginable: the best-in-the-industry, innovative, energetic Sarah Seymour, Product Manager; the meticulous, multitalented Courtney Triola, Content Developer; the creative, gifted, Diana Graham, Senior Designer; true professionals who combed pages and probably did more than I'll ever know, Aimee Bear, Content Project Manager; and Lori Hazzard, Project Manager at MPS North America. And heartfelt thanks to Annie Mitchell and Sean Wakely, who believed in this project from the very start at Cengage.

Other Contributors   I'd like to thank my colleagues at UCCS who have helped me develop many of the ideas in this book, whether they know it or not—all the Freshmen Seminar faculty past and present. I also can't go without thanking the many authors who granted me permission to use their work, and two essential scholars who allowed me to use, apply, and extend their instruments throughout the book, including Brian French and John Bransford. And thanks to my expert student research assistants: Phil Wilburn, Sarah Snyder, Jessica Smith, and Lindsey McCormick, and my best buddy Liz for all her encouraging words. I'd like to give a special thanks to Aren Moore, who worked closely with me to create *FOCUS* Points, the interactive, multimedia Power-Point designed for *FOCUS*. And finally, I'd like to thank Matt McClain, the comedy writer who brought his innovative humor to the learning process through the original podcast summaries of the chapters and television scripts for the website TV shows. He took the "big ideas" from *FOCUS* chapters and made them memorable to students by using their own best-loved media.

Above all, *FOCUS* has taught me truly to focus. Writing a book takes the same kind of endurance and determination that it takes to get a college degree. My empathy level for my students has, if anything, increased—and I am thankful for all I've learned while writing. It has been a cathartic experience to see what has filled each computer screen as I've tapped, tapped, tapped away. Ultimately, what I have chosen to put into each chapter has told me a great deal about who I am, what I know (and don't), and what I value. There's no doubt: I am a better teacher for having written this book. May all my readers grow through their *FOCUS* experience, too.

MEET THE CAST

The *FOCUS* cast is based on real students who've taken a course very similar to the one that you're in right now. While we've used photos of different people, the information about the cast, what they've learned and advice they want to share is passed on directly from these students.

mimagephotography/Shutterstock.com

CHAPTER 1 Carson Reed

HOMETOWN: Highlands Ranch, Colorado

MAJOR: Business

LESSONS LEARNED: Carson realized that he had to learn how to motivate himself, especially when it came to studying, because no one was telling him he had to do it. He also realized how important it is to get to know people in his classes. "This helps because if you can't show up to class … you can always get the notes from a friend, and you can gather your friends to make study groups to help ace those tests."

TOUGHEST FIRST-YEAR CLASS: World Politics. In every other class, Carson had some prior knowledge about the subject, but everything about World Politics was brand new. Carson says this made the class enjoyable!

ADVICE TO NEW STUDENTS: "Take good notes. Your test grade does in fact reflect your note-taking capability. If just taking bullet point notes isn't your style, try using different note-taking techniques."

FREE TIME: Play basketball, go to the gym, play video games, hang with friends

ESB Professional/Shutterstock.com

CHAPTER 2 Sylvia Sanchez

HOMETOWN: I've lived all over Colorado. I consider the whole state to be my hometown!

MAJOR: Nursing with a minor in psychology

LESSONS LEARNED: Sylvia is still learning lessons about college. She keeps growing and discovering new things about herself and has made lifelong friends. She plans to remember college as the best years of her life!

TOUGHEST FIRST-YEAR CLASS: Anatomy … It was hard to study *all* the time.

ADVICE TO NEW STUDENTS: "Listen to your heart; it will lead you to the right place. Take every opportunity that comes to you because college is about finding out who you are and what you want from life."

CHAPTER 3 Tammy Ko

HOMETOWN: Manitou Springs, Colorado

MAJOR: Marketing

LESSONS LEARNED: Juggling a part-time job while in school, Tammy loved meeting new people, but she regretted not talking to other students about which instructors and courses to take toward her marketing major. In order to succeed, she says, you've "gotta give it all you've got!"

TOUGHEST FIRST-YEAR CLASS: Microeconomics because it wasn't like high school courses that just required memorizing a lot of facts.

ADVICE TO NEW STUDENTS: "Talk to other students to learn about the best instructors, and make sure you are studying something that you are interested in."

CHAPTER 4 Derek Johnson

HOMETOWN: Colorado Springs, Colorado

MAJOR: Communications/Recording Arts

LESSONS LEARNED: Even though he's not married and has no children, Derek and his case study character have much in common—too much to do and too little time! Derek felt his biggest mistake in college was not asking enough questions in class. He knows now he should have asked for clarity on content or assignments he didn't understand.

TOUGHEST FIRST-YEAR CLASS: English because he and his instructor had differing opinions, but he communicated through the tough spots and earned an "A."

ADVICE TO NEW STUDENTS: "Surround yourself with positive people. As the saying goes, 'You are the company you keep.' I've seen many of my friends drop out because the people they called friends were holding them back from their full potential."

FREE TIME: Composing music and producing films

CHAPTER 5 Desiree Moore

HOMETOWN: Colorado Springs, Colorado

MAJOR: MA Communication

LESSONS LEARNED: Organization, time management, study groups, and note cards

TOUGHEST FIRST-YEAR COURSE: Psychology because in this class I had to be very organized to keep my notes in order. There were only two exams in this class during the entire semester. I did not organize my notes or my time very well.

ADVICE TO NEW STUDENTS: "Get to know your professors, ask questions, and have a study buddy."

FREE TIME: In my free time, I work out at the gym. I also spend quality time with my son.

CHAPTER 6 Dario Jones

HOMETOWN: Fountain, Colorado

MAJOR: MA, Communication

LESSONS LEARNED: Start strong, work hard, and finish strong

TOUGHEST FIRST-YEAR COURSE: Math 099

ADVICE TO NEW STUDENTS: "Get to know your instructors and fellow classmates. Ask questions in class when you're not sure about something."

FREE TIME: What free time? To relax, I listen to jazz or classical music, or I'll channel surf until I find something interesting to watch.

CHAPTER 7 Rachel White

HOMETOWN: Denver, Colorado

MAJOR: Philosophy

LESSONS LEARNED: Go to class!

TOUGHEST FIRST-YEAR COURSE: Intro to Geography (it might have been easier if I'd gone to class).

ADVICE TO NEW STUDENTS: "Balance fun and schoolwork, so you don't get burned out on either one!"

FREE TIME: Acting and improv

CHAPTER 8 Katie Alexander

HOMETOWN: Colorado Springs, Colorado. Because she went to college in her hometown, Katie really enjoyed the opportunity college provided to meet new people.

MAJOR: Nursing

LESSONS LEARNED: Spending her free time with her friends watching movies, going bowling or dancing, and just hanging out, Katie found that like her *FOCUS* Challenge Case character, she, too, would make up excuses to get out of studying and doing her homework. She quickly learned the importance of reading and taking notes. "As weird as it may sound, reading cuts your end study time by more than half. Reading the material ahead of time helps you understand everything so much better."

ADVICE TO NEW STUDENTS: "Stay motivated. College is going to *fly* by! If you stay motivated and get good grades, it really will be over before you know it."

CHAPTER 9 Kevin Baxter

HOMETOWN: St. Paul, Minnesota

BACKGROUND: Portraying a student returning to school after fifteen-plus years in the working world, Kevin is currently a professor of chemistry at University of Colorado at Colorado Springs.

COLLEGE MEMORIES: Kevin remembers how much he liked the different social environment college provided after graduating from high school.

TOUGHEST FIRST-YEAR COURSE: English Composition, because writing wasn't exactly his forte.

ADVICE TO NEW STUDENTS: "Study hard, and use your time wisely."

FREE TIME: Woodworking, hiking, and climbing

CHAPTER 10 Serena Jackson

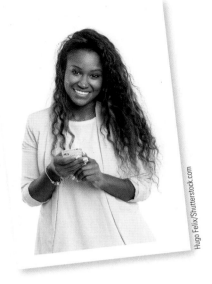

HOMETOWN: Denver, Colorado

MAJOR: Nursing

TOUGHEST FIRST-YEAR COURSE: Biology, because the way the class was taught in college (lecture-based) was very different than the way classes were taught in high school. She had to learn on her own what material was most important to study.

LESSONS LEARNED: Serena wishes she had gone to more study groups and devoted more of her time to subjects that she struggled with in order to be more successful. She also would have asked for help from professors since she now realizes they are fully ready to help a student become better in their class.

ADVICE TO NEW STUDENTS: "Make the most out of your college years. Make new friends because they could be great resources in the future. Also, if your professor tells you to read something, make sure you read the entire thing and you are able to teach it back to them because that will help your grade."

FREE TIME: Hanging out with friends, participating in club events, and volunteering

HELPFUL STUDY APPS: Quizlet, Learnsmart, and Study Blue help Serena study for upcoming quizzes and exams.

CHAPTER 11 Ethan Cole

HOMETOWN: Fort Morgan, Colorado

MAJOR: Sociology

LESSONS LEARNED: Like his *FOCUS* Challenge Case character, Ethan noticed that he, too, didn't always push himself to reach his potential. But he learned through his first-year seminar course that he is responsible for himself and that instructors aren't like high school teachers. They will let you fail a class if you don't do what you need to. It's up to you.

ADVICE TO NEW STUDENTS: "Not only did getting involved on campus help me have more fun in school, but it has also helped me academically. It taught me how to manage my time and has made it so much easier for me to partici-pate with confidence in class. Just make sure you get what you need to do done, and you will enjoy your college experience so much more."

FREE TIME: "Free time? What's that?! I'm too busy to have free time!" (But he secretly admits he snowboards, plays guitar, draws, and spends time with friends.)

CHAPTER 12 Anthony Lopez

Luna Vandoorne/Shutterstock.com

HOMETOWN: Aguascalientes, Mexico

MAJOR: Spanish with an emphasis on secondary education

LESSONS LEARNED: Anthony is extremely involved on campus and within his community—he is President of the Association of Future Teachers, sings with his church choir, plays intramural soccer, and works for the Air Force on weekends. Anthony thinks one mistake he made in his first term was that he procrastinated with homework because his new freedom let him think he could have fun first and study later, but he quickly learned he was wrong.

ADVICE TO NEW STUDENTS: "Be smart and be involved, but always do your homework first. If you are involved on campus, you will meet people that will help make your college experience easier and more fun."

MEET THE AUTHOR

Constance Staley

HOMETOWN: Pittsburgh, Pennsylvania (Although she never actually lived there. Instead, she lived all over the world and went to ten schools in twelve years.)

BACKGROUND: Connie has taught at the University of Colorado at Colorado Springs for more than 40 years after getting a bachelor's degree in education, a master's degree in linguistics, and a Ph.D. in communication.

COLLEGE MEMORIES: Connie remembers loving her public speaking class as a first-year student and having tons of friends, but being extremely homesick for her family.

ADVICE TO NEW STUDENTS: "Earning a college degree is hard work, takes a long time, and requires a substantial investment of your time, energy, and resources. But it's the best investment you can make in your own future—one you'll never regret."

FREE TIME: Spending time with her husband, her two daughters, and her boy/girl grandtwins; relaxing at her cabin in the mountains; and traveling around the country to speak to other professors who also care about first-year students and their success.

INTRODUCTION TO STUDENTS

Dear Reader,

This book is different. It won't coerce, coddle, caution, or coax you. Instead, it will give *you* the tools you need to coach yourself. Ultimately, this book is about you, your college career, and your career beyond college. It's about the future you will create for yourself.

FOCUS on Community College Success stars a cast of twelve students, like a stage play. One student "actor" is featured in each chapter's opening case study. All twelve cast members reappear throughout the book, so that you'll get to know them as you read. I've been teaching for more than 40 years now and worked with thousands of students. Each case study is about a real student (with a fictitious name) that I've worked with or a mixture of several students. You may find you have some things in common with them. But whether you do or not, I hope they will make this book come to life for you.

I love what I do, and I care deeply about students. I hope that comes through to you as a reader. You'll see that I've inserted some of my personality, had a bit of fun at times, and tried to create a new kind of textbook for you. In my view, learning should be engaging, personal, memorable, challenging, and fun.

Most importantly, I know that these next few years hold the key to unlock much of what you want from your life. And from all my years of experience and research, I can tell you straight-forwardly that what you read in this book works. It gets results. It can turn you into a better, faster learner. *Really?* you ask. Really! The only thing you have to do is put all the words in this book into action. That's where the challenge comes in.

Becoming an educated person takes time, energy, resources, and focus. At times, it may mean shutting down the six windows you have open on your computer, and directing all your attention to one thing in laser-like fashion. It may mean disciplining yourself to dig in and stick with something until you've nailed it. Can you do it? I'm betting you can, or I wouldn't have written this book. Invest yourself fully in what you read here, and then decide to incorporate it into your life. If there's one secret to college success, that's it.

So, you're off! You're about to begin one of the most fascinating, liberating, challenging, and adventure-filled times of your life. I may not be able to meet each one of you personally, but I *can* wish you well, wherever you are. I hope this book helps you on your journey.

READINESS: FOCUS ENTRANCE INTERVIEW

Although you may not have experienced life as a new college student for long, we're interested in how you expect to spend your time, what challenges you think you'll face, what strengths you can build on, and your general views of what you think college will be like. Please answer thoughtfully.

INFORMATION ABOUT YOU

NAME _____

STUDENT NUMBER _____ COURSE/SECTION _____

INSTRUCTOR _____

GENDER _____ AGE _____

YOUR BACKGROUND

1. Ethnic Identification (check all that apply):

___ American Indian or Alaska Native ___ Native Hawaiian or Other Pacific Islander ___ Asian

___ Hispanic/Latino ___ Black or African American ___ White

___ Mixed Race (for example, one Caucasian parent and one Asian) ___ Prefer not to answer

2. Is English your first (native) language?

___ yes ___ no

3. Did your parents graduate from college?

___ yes, both ___ yes, father only ___ yes, mother only ___ neither ___ not sure

YOUR HIGH SCHOOL EXPERIENCE

4. If you are entering college soon after completing high school, on average, how many total hours per week did you spend studying outside of class in high school?

___ 0–5 ___ 6–10 ___ 11–15 ___ 16–20 ___ 21–25
___ 26–30 ___ 31–35 ___ 36–40 ___ 40+ ___ I am a returning student and attended high school some time ago.

5. What was your high school grade point average when you graduated?

___ A+ ___ A ___ A− ___ B+ ___ B
___ B− ___ C+ ___ C ___ C− ___ D or lower
___ I don't remember. ___ I earned a GED.

INFORMATION ABOUT THIS SEMESTER/QUARTER

6. How many credit hours are you taking this term?

_____ 6 or fewer _____ 7–11 _____ 12–14 _____ 15–16 _____ 17 or more

7. Where are you living this term?

_____ in campus housing _____ with my immediate family _____ with a relative other than my immediate family

_____ on my own _____ other (please explain)

WORKING WHILE IN COLLEGE

8. In addition to going to college, do you expect to work for pay at a job (or jobs) this term?

_____ yes _____ no

9. If so, how many hours per week do you expect to work?

_____ 1–10 _____ 11–20 _____ 21–30 _____ 31–40 _____ 40+

10. If you plan to work for pay, where will you work?

_____ on campus _____ off campus _____ at more than one job

YOUR COLLEGE EXPECTATIONS

YOUR REASONS AND PREDICTIONS

11. Why did you decide to go to college? (Check all that apply.)

_____ because I want to build a better life for myself. _____ because I want to build a better life for my family.

_____ because I want to be well-off financially in the future. _____ because I need a college education to achieve my dreams.

_____ because my friends were going to college. _____ because my family encouraged me to go.

_____ because it was expected of me. _____ because I want to prepare for a new career.

_____ because I want to continue learning. _____ because the career I am pursuing requires a degree.

_____ because I was unsure of what I might do instead. _____ other (please explain)

12. How do you expect to learn best in college? (Check all that apply.)

_____ by looking at charts, maps, graphs _____ by writing papers

_____ by listening to instructors' lectures _____ by engaging in activities

_____ by reading books _____ by looking at symbols and graphics

_____ by going on field trips _____ by talking about course content with friends or roommates

_____ by looking at color-coded information _____ by taking notes

_____ by listening to other students during in-class discussions _____ by actually doing things

13. The following sets of opposite descriptive phrases are separated by five blank lines. Put an X on the line between the two that best represent your response, like this: For me, high school was easy ____:__X__:____:____:____ hard

I expect my first term of college to:

challenge me academically	____:____:____:____:____	be easy
be very different from high school	____:____:____:____:____	be a lot like high school
be exciting	____:____:____:____:____	be dull
be interesting	____:____:____:____:____	be uninteresting
motivate me to continue	____:____:____:____:____	discourage me
be fun	____:____:____:____:____	be boring
help me feel a part of this campus	____:____:____:____:____	make me feel like an outsider

14. How many total hours per week do you expect to study outside of class for your college courses?

____ 0–5   ____ 6–10   ____ 11–15   ____ 16–20   ____ 21–25

____ 26–30   ____ 31–35   ____ 36–40   ____ 40+

15. What do you expect your grade point average to be at the end of your first term of college?

____ A+   ____ A   ____ A–   ____ B+   ____ B

____ B–   ____ C+   ____ C   ____ C–   ____ D or lower

YOUR STRENGTHS, PERSONALITY, AND INTERESTS

16. Please identify your *strengths*—personal characteristics that will contribute to your college success. (Check all that apply.)

____ a. I am good at building relationships.

____ b. I can usually convince others to follow my plan.

____ c. I like to win.

____ d. I work toward future goals.

____ e. I like to be productive and get things done.

____ f. I have a positive outlook on life.

____ g. I'm usually the person who gets things going.

____ h. I enjoy the challenge of learning new things.

____ i. I am focused.

____ j. I can usually look at a problem and figure out a plan of action.

____ k. I work to keep everyone happy.

____ l. I'm a take-charge kind of person.

____ m. I help other people develop their talents and skills.

____ n. I'm a very responsible person.

____ o. I can analyze a situation and see various ways things might work out.

____ p. I usually give tasks my best effort.

17. How confident are you in yourself in each of the following areas? (1 = very confident, 5 = not at all confident)

____ overall academic ability

____ mathematical skills

____ leadership ability

____ reading skills

____ public speaking skills

____ study skills

____ technology skills

____ physical well-being

____ writing skills

____ social skills

____ emotional well-being

____ teamwork skills

18. For each of the following pairs of descriptors, which set sounds most like you? (Choose between the two options on each line and place a check mark by your choice.)

____ Extraverted and outgoing   or   ____ Introverted and quiet

____ Detail-oriented and practical   or   ____ Big-picture and future-oriented

____ Rational and truthful   or   ____ People-oriented and tactful

____ Organized and self-disciplined   or   ____ Spontaneous and flexible

19. *FOCUS* is about twelve different aspects of college life. Which are you most interested in applying to yourself in your academic work? (Check all that apply.)

____ Starting strong, building resilience   ____ Engaging, listening, and note-taking in class

____ Becoming mindful, setting goals   ____ Reading, writing, and presenting

____ Learning styles and studying   ____ Developing memory, taking tests

____ Managing your time, energy, and money   ____ Communicating in groups, valuing diversity

____ Thinking critically and creatively   ____ Choosing a college major and career

____ Learning online   ____ Creating your future

YOUR CHALLENGES

20. Of the twelve aspects of college life identified in the previous question, which do you expect to be most challenging to apply to yourself in your academic work? (Check all that apply.)

____ Starting strong, building resilience   ____ Engaging, listening, and note-taking in class

____ Becoming mindful, setting goals   ____ Reading, writing, and presenting

____ Learning styles and studying   ____ Developing memory, taking tests

____ Managing your time, energy, and money   ____ Communicating in groups, valuing diversity

____ Thinking critically and creatively   ____ Choosing a college major and career

____ Learning online   ____ Creating your future

21. Which one of your current classes do you expect to find most challenging this term and why?

Which class? (course title or department and course number) _____

Why? _____

Do you expect to succeed in this course?   ____ yes   ____ no   ____ Perhaps (please explain): _____

22. Please mark your *top three areas of concern* relating to your first term of college by placing 1, 2, and 3 next to the items you choose (with 1 representing your top concern).

____ I might not fit in.   ____ I might have difficulty making friends.

____ I might not be academically successful.   ____ My grades might disappoint my family.

____ I'm not sure I can handle the stress.   ____ I may have financial problems.

____ I might overextend myself and try to do too much.   ____ I might cut class frequently.

____ I might not reach out for help when I need it.   ____ I might tend to procrastinate on assignments.

_____ I might not put in enough time to be academically successful.

_____ I might be tempted to drop out.

_____ I might not be organized enough.

_____ I may be distracted (for example spend too much time online).

_____ Other (please explain). _____

_____ My professors might be hard to communicate with.

_____ I might be homesick.

_____ I might be bored in my classes.

_____ My job(s) outside of school might interfere with my studies.

YOUR FUTURE

23. How certain are you now of the following (1 = totally sure, 5 = totally unsure)?

_____ Finishing your degree

_____ Choosing your major

_____ Deciding on a career

_____ Completing your degree at this school

_____ Transferring to a four-year school

_____ Continuing on to work toward an advanced degree after college

24. What are you most looking forward to in college?

25. Describe the best outcomes you hope for at the end of this first semester/quarter. Do you expect to achieve them? Why or why not?

UPDATED FOR
THE FIFTH EDITION

This edition has an increased emphasis on the topics of mindfulness, financial literacy, new presentation e-tools, and career planning.

New research. The research on today's students—their characteristics, learning styles, strengths, and challenges—is continually evolving. New studies appear in online and print journals daily. This edition of *FOCUS* contains updated research in every chapter to keep abreast of the prolific material available on the scholarship of teaching and learning and the practical world of careers—a primary reason why students come to college today. Specific areas of new research that are crucial to success include the specific effects of being distracted by technology interruptions, (like the time it takes to "reboot" after interrupting a task), the essential roles of mindfulness and grit on college success, and the role a college degree plays in living a better life.

This edition has **new content on mindfulness and grit, and increased content on financial literacy and career planning.** Managing money with rising tuition and tempting credit-card excesses is a challenge. *FOCUS* provides hands-on activities and real-world examples to drive these principles home. Additionally, many students believe they should have their futures defined as soon as they enter college. *FOCUS* includes the newest strategies to help students understand themselves and what they have to offer over a continually-evolving future career.

New FOCUS Challenge Case design allows students to immediately connect each student's story to their own needs and experiences.

Up-to-date technology. In a world in which new technologies are introduced every day, *FOCUS* is spot on. For example, *FOCUS* now contains **infographics called "Quick Study"** in each chapter to capture students' attention and aid comprehension. Staley's own engagement in the latest technologies comes through in her message to students.

Life Hacks. Life hacks are brief pointers, often technology-based, to save readers time and help them increase productivity. These short tips are placed in the margins for quick discovery. Without disrupting Staley's unique voice, this edition contains streamlined, yet robust, content for today's busy reader.

WIIFM. Every chapter contains a new feature called **WIIFM?**, or What's in It for Me? Launched with a pertinent quote from a famous community college attendee or graduate, WIIFM?s accentuate the relevance of the chapter topic and its importance to students in building connections between what they're learning and their lives, including academically, professionally, and personally.

New overall contemporary design streamlines content, yet retains the interactive tone, visual interest, and compelling features that students need in a first-year seminar textbook.

New Readiness and Reality Check design and content allows students to immediately connect the material in the chapter to their own lives.

The updated quote and photo design plugs into student engagement by offering photos of college students like readers themselves, stimulating students' interest and appealing to visual learners.

Sharpen Your Focus is now offered exclusively in MindTap for *FOCUS on Community College Success.*

Numerous interactive, in-class activities that you're familiar with from the fourth edition of *FOCUS on Community College Success* have been moved to an updated Instructor's Manual, available online.

Throughout the instructor edition, Application Idea, Activity Selection, and Teachable Moment annotations provide useful instructor ideas.

CHAPTER LEVEL REVISIONS

CHAPTER 1: STARTING STRONG, BUILDING RESILIENCE

Chapter Content

> **NEW QUICK STUDY:** "Why Our Brains Crave Infographics" illustrates reasons why information PLUS graphics are processed quickly and efficiently.

Features

> **NEW WIIFM:** "What's in It for Me?" (WIIFM?) is not just sassy, it's smart, especially in today's fast-paced, information-overloaded world. In short (reading time included) articles, each chapter of *FOCUS* will include reasons why the chapter content is worth reading—with both in college and on the job applications.

> **NEW** Exercise on resiliency—"How Resilient Are You?" has been replaced with "Grit Scale," popularized in Angela Duckworth's book, *Grit: The Power and Passion of Perseverance,* and originating from her published research on grit.

CHAPTER 2: BECOMING MINDFUL, SETTING GOALS

Chapter Content

> **NEW** Chapter 2 has a new focus on "The Three Ms of College Success": mindfulness, mindset, and motivation. FOCUS makes a strong case for "psychological readiness," "emotional intelligence," or "soft skills" as the foundation for learning.

> **NEW QUICK STUDY:** "How to Focus When It's Next to Impossible" paints an overview of how to zero in and study when tempting distractions bombard from both inside and outside.

Features

> **NEW** Exercise 1.2 "Chocolate Mindfulness Meditation" illustrates the benefits of mindfulness, while teaching students to learn how to become more mindful in a simple and satisfying way.

> **NEW WIIFM:** Mindfulness is important for college students so that they can clear the deck for learning, but it's also the key to productivity on the job. Many employers now provide mindfulness training, but why wait? Start learning about mindfulness now.

> **NEW** "Curiosity: *Presence*: Can Your Body Change Your Mind?" discusses the compelling story of Amy Cuddy, who overcame the odds and teaches students how to leverage the power they hold within themselves.

CHAPTER 3: LEARNING STYLES AND STUDYING

> **NEW** Figure 3.2 "Learning Style Preferences: Would you rather...?" illustrates the differences between visual, auditory, read/write, and kinesthetic learning preferences.

> **NEW QUICK STUDY:** "How to Focus in College by Really Trying" depicts some key personal "to do's" that can help ensure college success.

Features

> Exercise 3.3 "Interpreting Your VARK Preferences" helps students understand their VARK assessment scores.

> **NEW WIIFM:** VARK provides insights into learning in college *and* building a productive superior-subordinate relationship on the job.

CHAPTER 4: MANAGING YOUR TIME, ENERGY, AND MONEY

Chapter Content

> **NEW QUICK STUDY:** "8 Secrets for Mastering Time Management" gives helpful ideas for saving and managing time.

> "How Time Flies" has been updated with recent research on how Americans spend their time.

Features

> **NEW WIIFM:** Getting a handle on time management helps students get college assignments in by due dates. But time management on the job is a "job-saver," so begin busting some common myths *now*.

> Box 4.2 "Top Ten Financial AID FAQs" has been updated with **NEW** questions.

> Exercise 4.9 "How Do You 'Spend' Your Time?" was moved from Chapter 2 to Chapter 4.

CHAPTER 5: THINKING CRITICALLY AND CREATIVELY

Chapter Content

> **NEW QUICK STUDY:** "How to Let Your Creative Juices Flow" illustrates eight ways to liberate natural creativity.

Features

> **NEW WIIFM:** Critical thinking is what college is all about. But "critical thinking" references in job ads have doubled since 2009. Just how important is critical thinking on the job?

CHAPTER 6: LEARNING ONLINE

Chapter Content

> Chapter 6 includes updated references to current technology.

> Content on types of software, search engines, learning management systems, and other class-related possibilities from former Exercise 6.2 "How Tech-Savvy Are You?" is now part of the section "Use Technology to Your Academic Advantage."

> **NEW QUICK STUDY:** "Do Paraphrase; Don't Plagiarize" shows ways to "translate" so that intentional and unintentional plagiarism are avoided.

Features

> **NEW WIIFM:** Technology skills aren't just increasingly important in college. They help "future-proof" other job-related skills if they're continually upgraded.

> Exercise 6.5 "Plagiarism or Not?" has a new example passage to review.

CHAPTER 7: ENGAGING, LISTENING, AND NOTE-TAKING IN CLASS

Chapter Content

> **NEW QUICK STUDY:** "The Ultimate Guide to Note-Taking in Class" illustrates what's important in taking productive notes *before*, *during*, and *after* class.

Features

> **NEW WIIFM:** Note-taking skills are important in college, naturally. But note-taking on the job is equally important—to carry through on an assignment and to help others who can benefit.

CHAPTER 8: READING, WRITING, AND PRESENTING

Chapter Content

> **NEW QUICK STUDY:** "9 Ways to Hack Your Speaking Anxiety" illustrates that anxiety is natural and suggests what to do about it.

Features

> Former Exercise 8.8 "Paper Submission Checklist" is now Box 8.1 "Paper Submission Checklist" for students to go back to when writing papers throughout college.

> **NEW WIIFM:** Simply put: Those who know how to put words together in college and on the job come out ahead.

CHAPTER 9: DEVELOPING MEMORY, TAKING TESTS

Chapter Content

> "Twenty Ways to Master Your Memory" is now grouped into five categories and is renamed as "Five Major Ways to Master Your Memory."

> **NEW QUICK STUDY:** "5 Major Ways to Master Your Memory": Make It Stick, Make It Meaningful, Make It Mnemonic, Manipulate It, Make It Funny.

Features

> **WIIFM:** Tests are a reality in college. But tests on the job—or tests in order to *get* a job—are real, too. Preparing now can help big-time.

CHAPTER 10: COMMUNICATING IN GROUPS, VALUING DIVERSITY

Chapter Content

> **NEW QUICK STUDY:** "The Top 10 Rules of Responsible Team Membership" portrays key areas of obligation to be a member of a productive team.

Features

> **NEW WIIFM:** It's obvious that knowing more about teamwork will help with group projects in class or online. But teamwork on the job is more prevalent now than ever before.

CHAPTER 11: CHOOSING A COLLEGE MAJOR AND CAREER

Chapter Content

> **QUICK STUDY:** "Designing Your Life" depicts the five steps involved in Design Thinking applied to designing your life: Be curious, try stuff, reframe problems, know it's a process, and ask for help.

Features

> **NEW** Exercise 11.1 "The Four P's: Passion, Purpose, Practicality, and Promise" encourages students to explore their future through the lens of the four P's.

> **NEW WIIFM:** Polls say that most Americans are not engaged in their work. Make the most of your major and career choices and maximize your happiness.

CHAPTER 12: CREATING YOUR FUTURE

Chapter Content

> "Write the Right Résumé" has been updated to "Write the Right Résumé and Cover Letter," and now includes five suggestions for writing a strong cover letter.

> **NEW QUICK STUDY:** "Interviewing Etiquette" provides a valuable snapshot of what TO do and what NOT to do during interviews.

Features

> Exercise 12.1 "What If… A Crystal Ball for Careers?" has been updated with the top-paying twenty-seven career fields that require a two-year degree or less.

> **NEW WIIFM:** Creating the future is a job that starts now. Devote present attention to future goals.

intostock/Shutterstock.com

STARTING STRONG,
BUILDING RESILIENCE | 1

HOW THIS CHAPTER RELATES TO YOU

1. When it comes to starting strong and building resilience, what are you most unsure about, if anything? Put check marks by the phrases that apply to you or write in your answer.

   ☐ Whether college is right for me
   ☐ What academic professionalism means
   ☐ What different instructors expect
   ☐ What it takes to succeed in college
   ☐ How to deal with hurdles along the way
   ☐ _____

2. What is most likely to be your response? Put a check mark by it.

   ☐ I'll check with my instructors.
   ☐ I'll ask my classmates.
   ☐ I'll see how things go and adjust.
   ☐ I'll wait and eventually figure it out.

3. What would you have to do to increase your likelihood of success? Will you do it this quarter or semester?

HOW YOU WILL RELATE TO THIS CHAPTER

1. What are you most interested in learning about? Put check marks by those topics.

   ☐ Who goes to community college and why
   ☐ How to display academic professionalism
   ☐ How campus resources can support you
   ☐ Why college success courses are important
   ☐ What resilience is and why you need it

YOUR READINESS FACTOR

1. How motivated are you to learn more about starting strong and building resilience in college? (5 = high, 1 = low)

2. How ready are you to read now? (If something is in your way, take care of it if you can. Zero in and focus.)

3. How long do you think it will take you to complete this chapter? If you start and stop, keep track of your overall time. ____ Hour(s) ____ Minute(s)

© 2019 Cengage Learning, Inc. May not be scanned, copied or duplicated, or posted to a publicly accessible website, in whole or in part.

Carson Reed

A week after his high school graduation, the nudges and nagging began. "Hey, you'd better get on it," his Dad kept saying to him. His Mom warned, "Classes are filling up at the community college! I called to check." But Carson wasn't that sure about things. Was college really right for him? And was it right for him *now*? Why not wait a while? For now, he was doing just fine. He had a good-enough job, and he was constantly on the go. After a summer of tense discussions, it was decided; he'd start classes at the local community college in the fall and see how things went. Hopefully, he could get some financial aid.

Carson and his family were close. They texted back and forth all day, talked on the phone frequently, and posted on each other's Facebook pages, even though they lived in the same house! Strangely enough, the family member he was closest to was Allie, his sister. Even though she was five years younger, they were good buddies—hanging out together sometimes on weekends, watching movies, popping popcorn, or finishing off a tub of ice cream late at night. Allie was one of the reasons why he'd decided to stay at home and go to college right in his hometown. When he finally agreed to give college a try, his Mom and Dad were overjoyed. "Nobody gets anywhere without a college degree," his Dad pronounced several times a week, as if he were some kind of expert.

Stockbyte/Getty Images

Although the decision about college was confusing, at least Carson was a confident, optimistic person. He was a bit of a rock star at home, and his parents liked to brag about him whenever they could. School had never been his strong suit particularly, but his bedroom was lined with wall-to-wall trophies for playing sports. He hadn't actually won any awards, but he had earned trophies for taking part. In fact, in a lot of ways, Carson was just an average guy—except that he had more friends than most people. He always slept with his phone beside him and checked it literally 150 times a day. His parents were always on his case about spending so much time on his phone, but, honestly, they were just as bad.

Deep down, Carson figured college would just be "grade 13," and he'd be able to get by. High school had been a breeze, and he never even cracked a book. His college classes got off to a decent start, especially his developmental English class, the one he didn't think he needed but was the most worried about. The classes were easy, in fact, just reviews of what he had learned in high school.

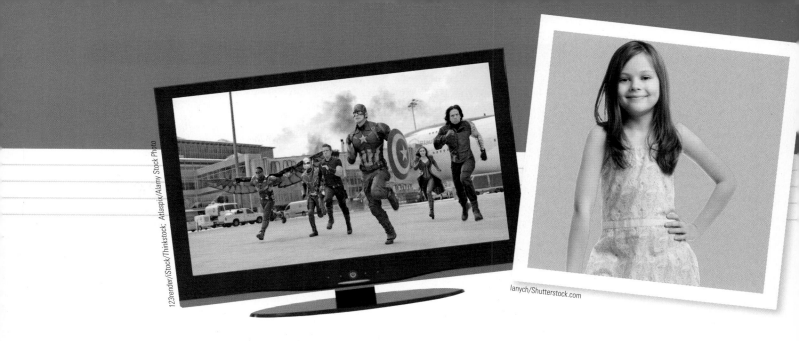

He was meeting a few people, but for the most part, he just drove to campus for classes and then drove home. He worked as a server three days a week and every weekend at a local chain restaurant to help pay his bills, so finding study time was a challenge. But he was confident that everything would work out as it always had. Anyway, he figured that being able to say that he was in college probably sounded impressive.

But as the weeks went by, Carson noticed that the pace was picking up quickly in his classes. Sooner or later, he'd have to buckle down and think about what kind of job he wanted after college, if he could even find a good job after he graduated. But overall, he even liked his instructors more than he expected to. "hey prof Allen how'd i do on my first essay in ur class" he fired off in an e-mail the second week. After he hit the send button, he wondered if that kind of informal writing would fly in college. Carson was used to texting; that's how he usually wrote.

The weeks rolled by, but around the middle of the semester, Carson got a shocking reality check. It came in the form of an F on his third developmental English paper. He couldn't believe it. He'd gotten a B on the first one, a C+ on the second one, and now an F. An F! Some students hadn't even turned a paper in; at least he should get some credit for that. He would have in high school! Carson had never gotten an F in his life—on any assignment in any class—ever. The F on his English paper made him begin to wonder about his grades in all his classes. He was right: he got a D on his history midterm, and his algebra

professor had mentioned the words "early alert," which meant that he was turning in Carson's name to the Student Support Center because his grade was at risk. He had been trying to slide by like he had in high school, and now things were totally out of control. What was strange was how quickly it had happened! Major stress!

Carson was stunned. He'd never expected anything like this to happen. He had always thought of himself as a winner, but now he was beginning to feel like a loser, and he didn't like the feeling at all. He had to face the music, and more importantly, face his parents, who were helping him out financially as much as they could. He felt guilty and angry with himself for letting things go wrong. The questions began to mount: Did he belong in college? Was he smart enough? Should he drop his English class? And why did he have to take classes like history and biology anyway? What would they possibly have to do with his future? Should he tell his parents he wanted to quit school? Or should he just wait and see and keep quiet for now? College was much more stressful than he expected, and he was tempted to give up. Right now, Carson wasn't sure it was worth the stress or the money.

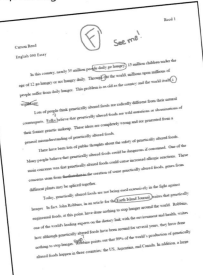

1. Why aren't things going the way Carson expected in college? Identify three reasons and explain them.

2. What should Carson do to get his college career on track? If he were your friend, what advice would you give him?

3. In your view, will Carson be successful in college? Why or why not?

4. It seems that Carson doesn't know much about being a college student. What is he missing? Can you describe what it takes to be a "professional" college student?

YOU'RE
IN COLLEGE NOW

"First say to yourself what you would be; and then do what you have to do."

Epictetus, Greek philosopher (55–135 A.D.)

Congratulations! You're in college. You've just started a new chapter of your life! As the saying goes, "The first step toward getting somewhere is to decide that you are not going to stay where you are." In choosing to go to community college, that's what you've decided. You're *not* going to stay where you are. Your journey has begun.

As a new college student, you may be feeling competing emotions: excitement and anxiety, happiness and sadness, exhilaration and fear. That's natural; your life is about to change forever. But as motivational speaker Tony Robbins says, "Change is inevitable." But, he quickly adds, "Progress is optional." Progress, specifically progress toward the future you want for yourself, is your goal, and that's what *FOCUS* is about—helping you make actual, steady, undeniable progress. This chapter will launch you on your journey by discussing essential elements of college that make or break many students. You'll read about starting strong and keeping your focus, even when challenges present themselves. This text and this class can make all the difference, but only on one condition: *You* have to keep *your* part of the bargain.

If you're like most students, there will be times along the way when you're tempted to throw in the towel. Some students do. You may wonder if college was a good decision for you or if it's worth all the effort. Having those thoughts from time to time isn't unusual.

But you can't go wrong by investing in your own future. A college education has the power to create a better life for you, and in the opinion of many people who look back on theirs, it's possibly the best thing they've ever done. If you read this text carefully and follow its advice, you will become the best student you can possibly be. You will learn practical tools to help you manage your life, and the advice here will take you beyond college into your career. That is this text's challenge to you as you begin your college experience.

Why do people go to community college? Generally, people go to a community college to improve their skills or gain completely new ones. Many community college students differ from four-year college students in ways like these: they attend school part-time, support themselves, work full-time, are single parents, waited to go on to college, or got their high school degrees in nonstandard ways.[1] (In fact, if you don't yet have a high school diploma or GED, your community college may be able to help you with that.)

GED stands for **g**eneral **e**ducation **d**evelopment; passing these tests is an alternative to earning a traditional high school diploma

➤ **Reason 1: Transitioning from High School to College.** If you just finished high school, you may see college as the obvious next step. Like Carson, you'll find college to be a very different game. Think of it this way: Carson arrived at college, playing what he thought was a decent game of checkers. But he quickly discovered that his instructors expected him to play chess. He'd been successful in high school, and to the inexperienced eye, college looked like the same game board. After all, school is school, right? Wrong! Carson quickly discovered that college is a new game with different rules!

Other students you know may have gone off to college somewhere else. But you considered things like cost and convenience and chose a college in your own community. A community college is a *real* college— a marketplace of ideas, where you can try out all kinds of new things. According to one study, more community college students than students at four-year schools report opportunities to speak in class and get to know their instructors. A community college that focuses on teaching— and on you—can be a good place to be.[2]

A community college can also be a great place to test the waters. Before plunging into a university setting (often with higher tuition rates), you want to see if college is right for you. After you get into the rhythm of your classes, you may decide you've made a good decision. Or you may decide to wait until your life is less complicated or your head is in the right place.

Ultimately, the decision is up to you. But if you consider dropping out sometime during your first semester, do your homework first. Make the decision for the right reasons, not because you failed a test, dislike a class, or ran out of steam.

Think about it: A college education is one of the best investments you can make. Someone can steal your car or walk away with your cell phone, but once you've earned a college degree, no one can ever take it from you. Your choice to go to college will pay off in many ways.

marketplace of ideas a place where many ideas are exchanged freely

Oscar Calero/iStock/Thinkstock

"Speed has never killed anyone, suddenly becoming stationary … that's what gets you."

Jeremy Clarkson, British racing broadcaster and star of the television show Top Gear

➤ **Reason 2: Going Back to School after a Break.** Perhaps you've tried college before and quit. But now you've decided to get back on the road to success. Maybe you're absolutely committed to making it this time, so you're more motivated. Something may have changed in your life, or you worked to save up for college for a while, or you've been a stay-at-home parent, or you have an employer now who will help foot your tuition bill.

One of the most interesting things about community colleges is the amazing mix of students from all walks of life. You're just as likely to be sitting beside a grandmother who's decided it's her turn now, a soldier who's just come back from overseas, or an employee gaining credentials for a promotion. Adult community college students are practical, self-directed learners who want to build on their past experiences and apply what they learn to their everyday lives. Does that describe you?[3]

Or perhaps you're returning to school to gear up with a select course or two. For example, maybe you have a new job that requires giving presentations, and the thought of it terrifies you. So you take a course to help you overcome your fear of public speaking. You don't necessarily want a degree; you just want to take a course or two. There's probably no better place than a community college to meet those kinds of focused needs.

Who goes to community college? Take a look at these statistics:

- 45 percent of all college students nationwide attend community colleges.
- twenty-eight years old is the average age.
- 57 percent are female.
- 4 percent are veterans.
- 17 percent are single parents.
- 36 percent are the first in their families to go to college.
- 85 percent work full- or part-time.
- 46 percent are Hispanic, African American, Asian/Pacific Islander, or mixed race students, with the Latino population increasing most rapidly.[4]

WIIFM?

 2 MINUTE READ

WIIFM? It's not exactly a radio station, although everyone listens to it. Instead, it's that still, not-so-small, oh-so-practical voice in your head that whispers, "What's in It for Me?" It's so well known that it even has its own acronym (pronounced *whiff' em*). In fact, it comes up anytime anyone asks you to do anything. It's not just *sassy*; it's *smart*. We're all part of today's new "Attention Economy"; we have to make minute-by-minute choices about where to direct our attention. Information has never been more readily available, but we only have so much attention to go around, so it's natural to wonder, *WIIFM*? Why should I pay attention to this particular item when I'm literally drowning in a sea of possibilities?

Here's a concrete example. "Exactly why should I buy this car?" you might ask on the showroom floor, with "WIIFM?" as your motivation. (*What's in it for me? Will this guy give me the deal of the century?*) Salespeople know about "WIIFM?" In order to sell, they're taught to turn a product's *features* into *benefits*. "This car goes from 0 to 60 mph in six seconds" is a feature. But "This car's pick-up will help you merge safely onto the crazy freeways around here" is a benefit.[5] See?

So that you know exactly why everything that's included in this text is worth doing, every chapter will have a "WIIFM?" feature. Eventually, as you read, you may come up with some "WIIFM?" ideas of your

own. But the point is: College success IS worth paying attention to. It has real, quantifiable benefits. And every chapter of *FOCUS*, based on its specific contents, will try to convince you why in just a couple of minutes. (Check how long it will take you to read each "WIIFM?" right up top.)

Take getting an associate's degree in the first place, for example. Why not get a four-year bachelor's degree? That's a good question, and you may, in fact, want to transfer to a university and pursue a four-year degree. But let's face it: Getting an associate's degree is downright smart—less time and resources are required to get a return on your investment. You can launch a very good career in less time for less money. Did you know that many careers require an associate's degree (rather than a four-year bachelor's degree), and that their starting salaries are impressive? Air traffic controllers are among the highest paying careers that don't require a bachelor's degree. The average air traffic controller earns $122,950 per year, and there are expected to be 7,500 openings through 2024. Dental hygienists earn $72,330 on average, and 70,300 positions will be filled by 2024. Web developers make an average of $64,970, and you may be one of the 58,600 hired.[6]

Carson Reed wondered about whether college was worth it, and eventually he

Tinseltown/Shutterstock.com

"I went to college because I didn't have anywhere else to go and it was a fabulous hang. And while I was there I was exposed to this world that I didn't know was possible."

Tom Hanks, *actor, attended Chabot College, Hayward, California, and transferred to California State University, Sacramento*

worked his way through his challenges by making use of campus resources that were created with students like him in mind. So, when it comes to finishing what you've started in college, what's in it for you? Potentially, everything—especially, preparing yourself for a successful career and opening up real possibilities for a better life.

WE'D LIKE TO GET TO KNOW YOU …

Take a few minutes to finish the following statements. Think about what each sentence says about you. Use your responses to introduce yourself to the class, or form pairs, talk over your responses together, and use your partner's answers to introduce him or her to the class.

1. I'm happiest when _____

2. If I had an extra $100, I'd _____

3. The thing I'm most proud of is _____

4. Once people get to know me, they're probably surprised to find I'm _____

5. I've been known to consume large quantities of _____

6. I'd rather be _____ than _____

7. My best quality is _____

8. My worst quality is _____

9. The academic skill I'd most like to develop is _____

10. One thing I'd like to figure out about myself is _____

People go to a community college like yours at a particular point in their lives for a variety of reasons. As you discuss this exercise in class, explore these additional questions: What is your background and why are you here?

EARNING A
TWO-YEAR DEGREE

If you're in college to earn a degree, an associate's degree will prepare you to go one of two ways in a relatively short amount of time: (1) into a career or (2) on to further education. If you want a career-oriented associate's degree, in two years you can train for one of the fastest-growing jobs in the economy by taking approximately twenty classes. The five best jobs for the future requiring a two-year degree include becoming an air traffic controller, nuclear medicine technician, dental hygienist, funeral service director, and diagnostic medical sonographer.[6] If you prefer hands-on coursework and a career like one of these is your goal, a community college is exactly the right place for you. (It's also quite possible that you couldn't prepare for some of these specific degrees at a four-year institution.)

Instead of a career-oriented associate's degree, you may want to earn a fairly general two-year degree to apply toward a bachelor's degree at a university. Part of the coursework you'll complete to get an associate's degree will consist of core requirements or general education courses, like writing and speaking, that apply to any career field. If those are your plans, you'll leave your community college with transferable courses when the time comes.[7]

Perhaps instead of a two-year associate's degree, you want to specialize even further and finish your coursework sooner, so instead you opt for a certificate.

Certificates generally require fifteen to as many as fifty credits, and you'll most likely only take courses that apply specifically to the career field you're preparing for. You set your sights on a target and finish your certificate program in as little as one year, sometimes less.[8]

One of the biggest differences between an associate's degree and a certificate is that the courses you take for an associate's degree usually transfer to a four-year school and include core requirements, general courses like speaking, writing, and math.[9] That may not be true of certificate programs. So if you think you may want to earn a bachelor's degree at some point, choose an associate's degree. It's up to you. How soon do you need a job? What interests you? How hands-on do you want your course of study to be?[10] Whatever degree you choose, getting off to a strong start will be key to your success.

ACADEMIC PROFESSIONALISM:
WHAT INSTRUCTORS WILL EXPECT FROM YOU

The way to start strong in college can be summed up in these two words: Academic Professionalism. Here's what the term means, and using a comparison may help explain it. Imagine this: You've just landed a new job, and it's one you really wanted. How do you know what to do and how to act? What will your boss expect from you? Should you just show up whenever it's convenient, take on this job on top of others you already have, and start firing off casual e-mails and texts about business? ("what up with the johnson report i thought max was gonna write that") Probably not—at least not if you want to be successful. You'll want to display workplace professionalism by noting how professionalism is defined in your new organization, and then start doing those things right away. The same thing is true in college: If you want to be successful, you must display academic professionalism. It's a set of behaviors you start now and carry with you into your career.

Hiring experts in the workplace identify three areas in which they believe college graduates are not as well prepared as they should be. They expect college graduates to have **oral and written communication skills, a positive attitude and strong work ethic**, and the ability **to work in groups and teams**.[11] You'll see that these three things, among others, are emphasized throughout *FOCUS*. You may be thinking, *"But wait a minute…I just started college!"* True, but considering how competitive the job market is these days, why not start preparing for it *now*? You'll gain a major advantage over other applicants—college graduates, or not. The academic professionalism you learn early in your college career can translate into career professionalism later. Or if you decide to continue for a bachelor's degree, all the academic strengths you begin building from your first year on will serve you well when further schooling requires even more of you.

So how is academic professionalism defined, specifically, and what's required? If you asked college instructors across the country, they'd give you advice like this:

1. **Don't just pile on.** Ever see the winning team "pile on" after a big football game? When one too many players jumps on top of the one unfortunate person at the bottom, the whole pile collapses. Some students hope they'll

"Let us not look back in anger, nor forward in fear, but around in awareness."

James Thurber, American author (1894–1961)

be able to just add college to an already-long list of obligations. But when they add one more thing, the entire stack crumbles. College isn't just "one more thing" to fit into the daily agenda of your life. Like many students, you may have to work to afford tuition, or you may want to keep up the demanding social life you had before college. But being successful in college may mean that you must give something up (like the temptation to OD on Netflix or Facebook) to give school the attention it needs. Something in your life will need adjusting to make room for college classes. You may have to cut back on your hours at work once you get a sense of your academic workload, or tell your sister who has to miss class because she has the flu that you can't stay and keep her company because you have class, too. Put college at the top of your list of obligations.

2. *Choose* **to go to class.** Let's face it: life is complicated. It involves overlapping demands and minute-by-minute decisions. Your boss wants a piece of you, your friends want your attention while you try to study, your romantic partner wants to go to the movies the night before your midterm exam, the bills keep mounting—and on and on. Some students choose to miss class to pick up a relative at the airport or shop with a friend who's in town, for example. Sometimes true emergencies in your personal life will interfere with your academic life. If you're ill, for example, call or e-mail your instructor beforehand, if for no other reason than to be courteous. But your instructors will expect you to plan nonemergencies around your already scheduled (and paid-for!) classes. Many things in your life are important—it's true—but while you're in school, going to class and doing your coursework should be at the top of your to-do list.

3. **Don't be an ostrich!** Some students develop "the Ostrich Syndrome." If reading or homework assignments seem too hard or feel like busywork, they just don't do them. Instead, they bury their heads in the sand and pretend like nothing's at stake. Somehow they may even think that they can't get a bad grade if they don't turn in an assignment for the instructor to grade. It goes without saying (but here it is, anyway) that "ostriching" is the opposite of academic professionalism, and your instructors will *not* be impressed. Always do your best work and submit it on time. If the assignment is due on October 1, it's due on October 1. Familiarize yourself with each syllabus since it will outline what's due and when for every one of your classes. Honest-to-goodness realism and continuous upkeep in your courses work wonders in college, just as they do in the workplace.

4. **Show respect.** One thing instructors dislike is getting a sense from students that school isn't a top priority. Dress like you're a serious student who's there to learn. Leave the muscle tanks and halter tops for truly informal occasions. You're not in college to score fashion points, draw attention to your tattoos, or define your personality with your baseball cap. That doesn't mean you can't be yourself, but it does mean that you should use good judgment. And when you breeze in late or sneak out early, you're communicating that you don't value school, your instructor, and your classmates, whether you realize it or not. If you criticize a classmate or your instructor in public—even if you think it's constructive—that's disrespectful, too. And when you whip out your cell phone to see how many

Juniors Bildarchiv/AGE Fotostock

"An ostrich with its head in the sand is just as blind to opportunity as to disaster."

Anonymous

"likes" you have in response to your latest Facebook post, or text your boyfriend about where to go for dinner, everyone knows where your head is. When you're in class, be in class.

5. **Know the rules.** Your college and your professors have policies you need to know about up front. What constitutes cheating? How can you avoid plagiarism? Who should you talk to if you have a concern about your grade? Do instructors accept texts and calls on their cell phones? What kind of writing will they expect in e-mails? Even when it comes to every-day things—like weather cancellations—your college and instructors have policies and procedures to guide you. Don't leave yourself in the dark when it comes to important rules that affect you.

6. **Take charge.** When it comes right down to it, who is responsible for your success? None other than you! Even though you may be afraid to speak up or not want to admit that you're fuzzy about something, your instructors will rely on *you* to let them know that. They aren't mind readers. Do what you need to do: get help, take advantage of instructors' office hours, or hire a tutor. Don't sit idly by while success drifts away.

7. **Invest enough time.** In high school you may have done well without trying very hard. A teacher may have forgiven a late assignment, provided opportunities for extra credit, or graded on a curve so that everyone passed. But college is different. In college, it's important to get ready for class beforehand by reading and doing assignments, and then jump in once you're there. Bring your books, notebook, and pen, and sit up straight, too, just like mom always used to say. College isn't a place to just slide by or wing it. It's a place to put your best foot forward. That may mean rewriting a paper three times or rereading a textbook chapter more than once. Academic professionalism requires you to invest as much time as it takes.

8. **Learn to work in groups.** Your instructors know the value of teamwork later in your career, so they'll expect you to work with your classmates in class, outside of class, or online. They may even think it's important enough to assign points for group projects in the course syllabus. Even though you may prefer to work alone, teamwork skills are highly valued in today's workplace, and you'll learn things from other students that you might not learn from your instructor.

9. **Check your e-mail regularly.** Sure, you can talk to an instructor in person or on the phone, or text a classmate with a question about an assignment. But the primary means of communication in college is e-mail. Most colleges will send all "official correspondence" (like bills) this way, and many professors will use campus e-mail to communicate with you. If you never check your school e-mail account, but instead only use your personal account, you'll miss important information. ("What? The instructor's sick today? I broke my neck to get here!") Your campus IT department or an online helpsheet can tell you how to forward one e-mail account to the other so that you're always up to speed. Believe it or not, this one simple thing trips up more students than you would ever imagine!

life hack #1

To maximize your productivity, get chummy with Siri. Use more voice commands for school reminders via your cell phone: "Siri, remind me to start my algebra homework at 7 P.M." She'll do it. Or you can use Google Now with Android.

"No one can whistle a symphony. It takes a whole orchestra to play it."

H. E. Luccock, professor, Yale Divinity School (1885–1961)

Hiroyuki Ito/Hulton Archive/Getty Images

10. **Engage!** Students who soak up all they can enjoy college most. When they're in class, they're tuned in. Sure, Professor Whoever may not be quite as funny as your favorite late-night TV comedian, and going to class isn't like going to see the latest box office smash hit. But college is about becoming an *educated* person, not an *entertained* one.

If you follow all the advice offered in these ten recommendations, you'll display academic professionalism and reach your goal—to start strong.

ACADEMIC PROFESSIONALISM:
HOW TO HELP YOURSELF SUCCEED

Any time you start something new, there's a learning curve involved. The best thing to do is to admit it, decide what to do, and start climbing! Beyond conducting yourself as a professional student, what other things will help you succeed? Here are some additional responsibilities.

DEVELOP A DEGREE PLAN AND PLAN YOUR COURSEWORK

In some ways, college is like a journey with parts of the itinerary planned for you. You can't just hitchhike wherever you like. It's more like a guided tour planned by experts in the areas you'd like to explore. You can choose to go left or right at particular moments, but much of the trip is planned in advance.[12] If you'd like to become a nurse, for example, your coursework will be prescribed for you. However, everyone appreciates the focused knowledge of nurses when they need one!

Some courses will count toward your major or area of concentration, and some will satisfy core requirements. Core requirements often make students wonder: "I'm never going to be another Stephen King. Why do I have to suffer through writing courses I'll never use?" The key words in that last sentence are *never use*. You'll speak and write and think and solve problems in any career. And even though you're in college to prepare for a career, becoming a more knowledgeable person in general should be a big part of your mission.

Most community colleges will ask you to fill out an academic or degree plan up front. You'll plan your coursework for each semester or quarter from now until you've finished. Not only do you end up taking the right courses, but you can watch your progress as you go.

If you decide to transfer to a four-year institution later to get a bachelor's degree, it's likely you can bring many of your associate's degree credits (up to 60 credit hours or half the credits you'll need for a four-year degree) from your community college courses with you. That wouldn't be true unless community colleges were considered to be **real** colleges and coursework was seen as equivalent. However, it is your responsibility to know what courses will transfer to the particular transfer institution you may have in mind. Do some digging on your own by calling an advisor at that school for information that will help you with your planning now. Find out **exactly** which courses will transfer into the major you're considering. And remember that there's a difference between whether a course will **transfer** (for general credit) or **count** (toward a specific degree).

learning curve a measure of how long it takes you to learn something and how hard it is

"If you don't know where you are going, you might wind up someplace else."

Yogi Berra, major league baseball player and manager (1925–2015)

concentration focused effort; specialization

core basic

BOX 1.1   **SAMPLE DEGREE PLAN**

Here is a road map, or a sample degree plan, for Carson, assuming he decides to get a general Associate of Arts Degree at his community college. (The requirements at your community college will be different from this example.)

GREAT BLUFFS COMMUNITY COLLEGE

DEGREE TRACKING WORKSHEET

NAME_____Carson Reed_____   EMAIL ADDRESS_____creed5@gbcc.edu_____

STUDENT NUMBER_____123-45-6789_____   PHONE_____555-9876_____

GENERAL STUDIES

Associate of Arts Degree

Program Course #	Course Title	Term (to be) Taken	Term Hours	Grade A = 4 B = 3 C = 2 D = 1 F = 0	Notes
ENGL 090	English Composition I	Fall 2018	3	?	
HIST 103	United States History I	Fall 2018	3		
	Foreign Language		3		
GBCC 100	College Success		3		
SPE 115	Public Speaking	Fall 2018	3	?	
ENGL 102	English Composition II		3		
HIST 104	United States History II		3		
	Foreign Language (must be the same language)		5		
	Humanities		3		
PSC 205	United States Government		3		
	Literature		3		
	Visual and Performing Arts		3		
SOC 103	Introduction to Sociology		3		
	Mathematics		3		
	Humanities		3		
PSC 206	State and Local Government		3		
BIO 100	Natural Science I	Fall 2018	3–4		
	Natural Science II		3–4		
	Unrestricted Elective		3		
	Unrestricted Elective		3		

Many community colleges, yours included, use a worksheet or degree plan, like this one of Carson's to help you stay on course and track your progress as you earn your degree. Check with an advisor to see what aids like this your campus provides.

In the "Notes" column, Carson can keep track of his thoughts about each course and things to keep in mind when registering for the next term.

The courses with department abbreviations and numbers listed are required for Carson's degree plan. The open categories are places where he can choose from a list of possible courses. His advisor will help him know his options.

Source: Adapted from Austin Community College website. Available at https://www6.austincc.edu/cms/site/www/awardplans
/awardplan.php?year=2017&type=CC&group=@0004&apid=3855

BE ADVISED! ADVISING MISTAKES STUDENTS MAKE

One of the most important relationships you'll have as a community college student is the one you build with your academic advisor. On your campus, this person may be an advisor, a counselor, or a faculty member who can steer you toward courses you can handle and instructors you can learn best from. An advisor can keep you from taking classes that bog you down academically or unnecessary ones that take you extra time to earn your degree. Here's a list of advising mistakes students make, from real advisors who work with college students every day.

1. **Not using the campus advising office or your faculty advisor.** If you don't get regular advice from an advisor, counselor, or a designated faculty member who's serving as your advisor, your degree may take longer and cost more money. It's that simple. It's your college career, after all, and it's important that you and your advisor work as partners.

2. **Not planning ahead.** Some students walk into the advising office or e-mail an advisor and expect help right away, and sometimes that works. However, planning ahead is a better option. Planning ahead includes making an appointment, looking through the course offerings, making a list of questions to ask, and thinking in advance about which days you can attend classes based on your work schedule, how many classes you can take, and on which days of the week. And, if you're leaving your advisor a voice mail, remember to include all of this important information. What's wrong with this message? "Hi, this is Tony. I have a question about my schedule. Please call me back, OK?" Tony who? And what's his phone number? Or how about an e-mail like this from hotchick13@email.com? "Do I need to take English 090? Please let me know." Exactly who is "hotchick13"?

3. **Procrastinating.** It's important not to put off advising appointments. To drop a class, you may need to meet a deadline. Or you may need help from an advisor to solve a problem with a faculty member, but by the time you get around to it, the instructor has already left campus for the summer. If you deal with problems right away, while they're small, they may be reversible. (And it's always a good idea to discuss dropping a class with the instructor first.)

4. **Skipping prerequisites.** Some students want to skip the required prerequisites. They think they can handle the work. They think prereqs are a waste of time and money when, actually, they're in place because hundreds of students before you have shown that these classes help you succeed. And in some cases, students who haven't taken a prereq are actually disenrolled from the course that requires it.

5. **Choosing the wrong major.** Sometimes students lock on to a major because someone else thinks it's a good idea or because a particular career field pays well, not because they enjoy the subject and are suited for it. Staying motivated is hard when you're not interested in something. Advisors can help you figure out which major is right for you.

6. **Taking too many credits or too few.** Some students are overly optimistic and think they can handle a heavier course load than the other factors in their lives will permit. Other students may underestimate the number of

---

life hack #2

On average, cell phone users check their phones 150 times a day. Why? What are they looking for? Beware: Technology can become an unproductive procrastination habit!

prerequisites courses that you need to take before advancing on to other ones courses they should take, which increases the time it takes them to finish school. An advisor can help you stay on target.

7. **Ignoring problems.** If you run into difficulty and end up on academic probation, for example, an advisor or college official will work with you to get you back on track. But you must agree to that bargain and accept the help, possibly by signing a contract of steps you must take to reverse the situation.

8. **Being afraid to drop a course.** Sometimes, when you've tried everything (for example, tutoring, extra help sessions, and the campus learning center), but you're still not succeeding in a class, the best thing to do may be to drop the course by filling out a drop form (online or on paper) and submitting it. Then retake the class later. That option is better than just not going to class and assuming that by not coming, you've dropped the course. Colleges require deliberate action from you. It's always best to know your school's rules and talk with your instructor first. *And beware that dropping a course may affect your financial aid.*[13]

MAKE THE GRADE: COMPUTING YOUR GPA

GPA an average of all your grades for a single semester or a running average across all your coursework

One of the most important things to learn as a new college student—and fast—is what grade point averages (GPAs) are and how they work. Your GPA is an indication of how well you're doing, and you keep track of it over time, term by term. Your academic record will follow you for the rest of your life! Some students don't realize how grade points add up. They end up on academic probation, even if they only have one failing grade. Let's say you're taking four courses this term, and you earn the following grades:

COURSE	CREDITS	FINAL GRADE	GRADE POINT VALUE
English Composition	3 credits	C (2 points)	6
College Algebra	3 credits	F (0 points)	0
College Success	3 credits	B (3 points)	9
Public Speaking	3 credits	D (1 point)	3
TOTAL	**12 credits**		**18 grade points**

You may look at this record and think, *Not bad. I passed three of my four courses.* But divide that Grade Point Value column total (18) by the total number of credits (12), and you get 1.5.

GPA = Grade Point Value ÷ Total Number of Credits

At most schools, a 1.5 GPA puts you on academic probation, and eventually, you may be facing suspension. That can be a discouraging way to start, and digging yourself out of a GPA hole once you're there takes a very long time, like paying off credit card debt.

Not only is it important to keep track of your grades over the whole term, but it's also important to keep track of your grade in each course. If you stop going to your math class because it's too hard or because you don't like the teacher, your grade will suffer. If an assignment is worth 25 percent of your grade, and you don't turn it in, the highest grade you can possibly earn, even if you do everything else perfectly, is a 75 percent or "C." You may think, *but it's only one assignment*. It is only one assignment, but it counts as one-quarter of your grade. In college, everything counts. The typical grading scale in college is:

A = 90–100%   B = 80–89%   C = 70–79%
D = 60–69%   F = 59% and below

REALIZE THE VALUE OF DEVELOPMENTAL COURSES

As a rule, community colleges have what's called an open-door admissions policy. That means that anyone who wants to get an education is invited in. You don't have to get a certain score on the SAT or ACT standardized national tests, and you don't have to have a particular GPA in high school to be admitted. That's a good thing. As a nation, we are opening the doors of education to everyone, and our society as a whole benefits in many ways. Education improves the quality of life.[14]

But when restrictions are removed, more variety is a natural result, right? Think of it this way: If every student at your community college had to be over six feet tall to be admitted, then you and all your classmates would tower over the general public. But if anyone of any height could attend, you'd see a range from very short to very tall. Some people would need steps to reach high places, and others would have to duck under low ceilings. But variety presents challenges. Community colleges are characterized by variety, and they've devised ways to make it work. Here's how.

New community college students bring standardized test scores or take placement tests that help schools know where to *place* them. If you're "short" on some necessary skills for success, like reading, writing, or math, they'll place you in a developmental (sometimes called *remedial*) class to help you catch up fast. Some students see these courses negatively, thinking they're a waste of time or money. At your particular college, you may be allowed to opt out of developmental classes or take them online at your own pace, but generally speaking, they're insurance that you will grow into the skills you'll need.

If you're enrolled in a developmental class, you're in good company. In one study of 35 community colleges that were all part of a proposal to increase student success, 37 percent of incoming students required one remedial course, 26 percent required two courses, and 22 percent required three courses—for a total of 85 percent. And note this piece of good news: In a related study, students who earned a C or better in a developmental course during their first semester were, from that point forward, more likely to stay in school and succeed than students who weren't required to take a developmental course in the first place![15] In another study, students who took a developmental writing course earned higher English grades in later courses and higher GPAs overall than students who did not.[16] If you're enrolled in a developmental class, perhaps you're beginning to see its value *now*. If you don't see the value yet, chances are you'll greatly appreciate what it did for you *later*.

MASTER THE SYLLABUS

You'll get a syllabus (or course schedule) for most of the college classes you'll take. If the syllabi (plural of syllabus) for your courses are available online,

iStock.com/Photoservice

"Problems are only opportunities in work clothes."

Henry J. Kaiser, American industrialist (1882–1967)

developmental designed to develop or improve a skill

iStock.com/rjmiz

"Your current safe boundaries were once unknown frontiers."

Anonymous

BOX 1.2 **ANALYZING A SYLLABUS**

Take a look at this example of a syllabus to see what you think. What is this professor like? Do you get a sense of her standards and values from her syllabus? Will this be a challenging course? Take a close look at a syllabus from one of your current classes. Analyze it, just as this one has been analyzed, and make a list of things you learn about specific aspects of the syllabus that can help you be successful.

> Some community colleges have a syllabus template or standard format so that your syllabus for each class will look basically the same and contain similar kinds of information.

> Send the instructor an e-mail the first week of class, introducing yourself and discussing your thoughts about how this class will help you. Remember, however, that in college, you must use good grammar and correct spelling in ALL your writing, including e-mails.

GREAT BLUFFS COMMUNITY COLLEGE
COURSE SYLLABUS

Course ID: SPE 115
Term: Fall 2018
Instructor: Regina Lewis
Office: Vail Hall 501
Office Hours: MW 10:00–11:00 A.M., TR 2:00–3:00 P.M., by appointment only

> It's appropriate to ask the instructor what she prefers to be called: Regina, Ms. Lewis, Professor Lewis, and so on.

Course Title: Public Speaking
Credit Hours: 3
E-mail Address: regina.lewis@gbcc.edu
Office Phone: 555–1234

> Pay attention to the course description. It's a summary of what you can expect.

Course Description: This course combines the theory of speech communication with oral performance skills. Emphasis is on researching, organizing, and preparing speeches and analyzing the needs and interests of your particular audience. Although this is primarily a performance class, you will also build your writing and researching skills.

Prerequisites/Corequisites: ENG 090, REA 090

> You can buy the textbook from your college bookstore or order it online. But often textbooks are "customized" with portions inserted from different books or material that pertains to your own campus. You must buy those books from your campus bookstore. You can also rent textbooks or you can buy or rent an e-version of the text. Even though textbooks cost money, they are a critical investment. Trying to get by without one puts you at a disadvantage right from the start.

Course Text: *Public Speaking:* Concepts and Skills for a *Diverse Society*, 2016. Cengage Learning.

Professional Conduct in Class: Students are responsible for knowing and abiding by the "Standards of Conduct" listed in the 2018–2019 GBCC Catalog (beginning on page 10). Your cell phone should be turned off, set to vibrate only, or left at home. Eating, sleeping, social discussions, or doing reading or homework for other classes are distracting behaviors and communicate indifference and disrespect for this learning environment and subject matter. Children should not be brought to class. Getting up and coming in and out during class (unless you are sick, of course) is distracting to your classmates. These activities are unacceptable in academic environments and qualify as examples of inappropriate conduct in class, which may result in your academic withdrawal from the class.

> The instructor has devoted a substantial portion of the syllabus to this topic, and she has spelled out her expectations in detail. Professional conduct must be important to her.

Online Learning Management System (LMS): e-CC (pronounced EASY). All students have access to the materials posted on the LMS website through the internet from a campus computer lab or from home.

Attendance: If you must miss a class for an emergency, you must still submit assigned work by the due date. Please provide documentation to indicate that the absence was due to a situation beyond your control. There are no excused absences without documentation. In order to receive credit for attendance, you must attend the ENTIRE class period. IF YOU MISS A CLASS, IT IS YOUR RESPONSIBILITY TO CONTACT A CLASSMATE FOR NOTES AND ASSIGNMENTS. NO MAKEUP WORK IS ALLOWED.

Grading: Assignments must be turned in on time and speeches must be presented on schedule. Grades for makeup speeches are automatically reduced by 20 percent. Only one makeup day will be scheduled for speeches missed due to emergencies! THERE ARE NO MAKEUP EXAMS OR WRITTEN ASSIGNMENTS.

Americans with Disabilities Act (ADA): Any student eligible for academic accommodations because of a learning or physical disability should speak with the instructor during the first week of class and contact the Office of Support Services.

Speeches: You will be required to give a minimum of five speeches.

> This syllabus actually continues on for several more pages and includes three other things: (1) a campus statement about academic honesty and plagiarism, (2) due dates for each assignment, and (3) specific information on how speeches will be graded.

- SP 1: Informative 5 mins. (+ or –1 min.) (1 visual aid) Prep and speaking outline required.
- SP 2: Career (Impromptu) Speaking on the spot!
- SP 3: Ceremonial 3 mins. (+ or –1 min.) (1 quote) Prep and speaking outline required.
- SP 4: Persuasive 7 mins. (+ or –1 min.) (2 visual aids and 2 sources) Prep and speaking outline required. You must have a partner for the opposition.
- SP 5: Public Speaking Outside the Box 10 mins. (+ or –2 mins.) (Poster, flyer, 2 visual aids) Presented in TV studio.

Source: Regina Lewis, Pikes Peak Community College. Used by permission.

check them often to keep up with any changes in the schedule or new assignments. If you have a hard copy, keep it handy and refer to it often. Think of a syllabus as:

> - a preview of what to expect during every class
> - a road map for where the course will take you
> - a contract between you and your instructor
> - a summary of all the assignments and how much they count toward your grade
> - a tool that lists reading and homework to help you prepare for class
> - evidence of an instructor's standards, grading system, and values

AVOID THE PCP SYNDROME: USE CAMPUS RESOURCES

The convenience of community college can also be a drawback. Because you're going to college in your own community, it's easy to develop a drive-through mentality. You show up for classes and then hightail it for work or home right away. Some experts describe this phenomenon as the "PCP Syndrome: Parking Lot, Class, Parking Lot." What's wrong with that? you ask. When you've finished grocery shopping, you get back in your car and go home, right? You don't cruise the aisles and hang around.

But going to college is very different from shopping for groceries. Your campus has many things available for you to take advantage of: student clubs, special presentations, musical events, and learning resource centers, for example. You may never find out about these "free samples" if you're not there. You won't make new friends or get to know your instructors, two practices that are essential to your success.[17] The danger is that when the going gets rough, which can happen during exam time, you may be tempted to retreat to what you're most familiar with—your life before college—and abandon your efforts. Whatever the problem, there's a place to go for help on campus. Even if your campus doesn't have every possible kind of support center right there, your advisors or instructors can always direct you to services off campus.

Remember that "HELP" is not a four-letter word. Getting help when you need it isn't shameful; it's smart. Take this example: In 2013, at 64 years old, Diana Nyad became the first person to swim nearly 53 hours nonstop from Cuba to Florida. But it took a crew of 35 trainers and handlers in five boats moving alongside her to help her reach her goal (guides to check winds and currents, divers to look for sharks, and crew members to provide food and water during the 112 mile swim).[18] In college, you have a "crew," to help you too. Your campus has all kinds of resources available for the taking, but you must take them. They won't come to you. Here are some of the FAQs new college students often ask:

> - **How can I meet other students?** Take advantage of favorite gathering spots on campus. If you're finding it hard to meet people, could it be because you're not around? To meet people, it helps to be where they are.
>
> - **What if I need help with a challenging course?** Many campuses have support centers: a science learning center or a math learning center, for example. Or particular courses may offer what's called supplemental instruction, extra help beyond class sessions with basic course materials or homework assignments. You may be able to work with a tutor, too—a

student who's extra-good at math, for example. Check out whatever options are available to you, and use them, rather than struggle on your own if you're not getting results.

➤ **I'm thinking of dropping a class. How do I do it?** The Office of the Registrar or Office of Admissions and Records is where to go. They also help with things like transferring credits and getting transcripts if you've attended college somewhere before or plan to transfer. Or you may be able to drop a class online, but think through the results. Will doing so change your financial aid status, for example?

➤ **What if I need a counselor?** College is a time of change. Your relationships may be affected or you may suffer from symptoms of stress. If your campus has a counseling center and you need to use its services, do so. And if you find yourself in the middle of a real crisis, call the campus hotline for immediate help.

➤ **How can I find out if I have a learning disability?** Check to see whether your campus has a learning center or a special office that helps with learning disabilities. You can work with a specialist there who can help. If you've been diagnosed with a learning disability before, bring your documentation to that office for their records and let your instructors know. They can help, too.

➤ **What if I have a technology crisis?** Your campus probably has a computer help desk, where techies can often solve what seems like a complicated problem with simple advice. Also, use the campus computer labs. They may have better computers than yours at home, and you can make good use of blocks of time between classes.

➤ **Are health services available to students?** Many campuses have a student health center where you can find a range of free or inexpensive services—everything from flu shots to strep throat tests to birth control advice if you're sexually active.

➤ **What do I want to be when I grow up?** Thinking ahead to a career when you finish college is sometimes hard when so much is going on at the moment. What do you like to do? What people skills do you have? Visit your campus's career center. Experts there can help you discover a major and career that will work for you.

➤ **Is child care available?** Many campuses have inexpensive child care available. Being able to drop off a child in the morning right on campus and pick him up after your classes are over can be a real help.

➤ **Where can I buy my text?** Texts are a big investment these days, and it's important to buy the right editions for your classes. Should you buy them from your campus bookstore or order online? Buying texts online may save you money, although you'll have to wait for shipment. The bookstore is a much quicker option, and it's a good idea to find out where it is, no matter where you buy your books. You'll most likely need it for other school supplies. Renting your books or buying an e-book that you can download immediately may be an option, too.

➤ **Where can I get other pieces of information I may need?** Try your campus website, the school bulletin or catalog, the student handbook, or the school newspaper.

"One hundred percent of the shots you don't take don't go in."

Wayne Gretzky, called the greatest ice hockey player of all time

iStock.com/walik

TOP TEN RESOURCES YOUR CAMPUS OFFERS

Make a list of ten resources your campus offers that can help you succeed in your coursework. For example, does your campus have a health center, a day care center, or a learning center? Visit each location, and identify specific ways you will use each office or service.

	Name of office/service	Contact information	How will I use this resource?
1.			
2.			
3.			
4.			
5.			
6.			
7.			
8.			
9.			
10.			

➤ **What if I need the help of Campus Security?** If you feel unsafe walking to your car late at night or you need information about parking permits on campus, check with the Campus Security or Public Safety Office. They're there for your protection.

What's the bottom line? Get to know your campus and its full range of offerings—and take advantage of everything that's in place to help you be as academically successful as possible.

Your instructor and your classmates will contribute a great deal to what you learn. So will *FOCUS* and its special features, like a "Quick Study" infographic like this one (Figure 1.1) in every chapter.

FIGURE 1.1

Quick Study: Why Our Brains Crave Infographics

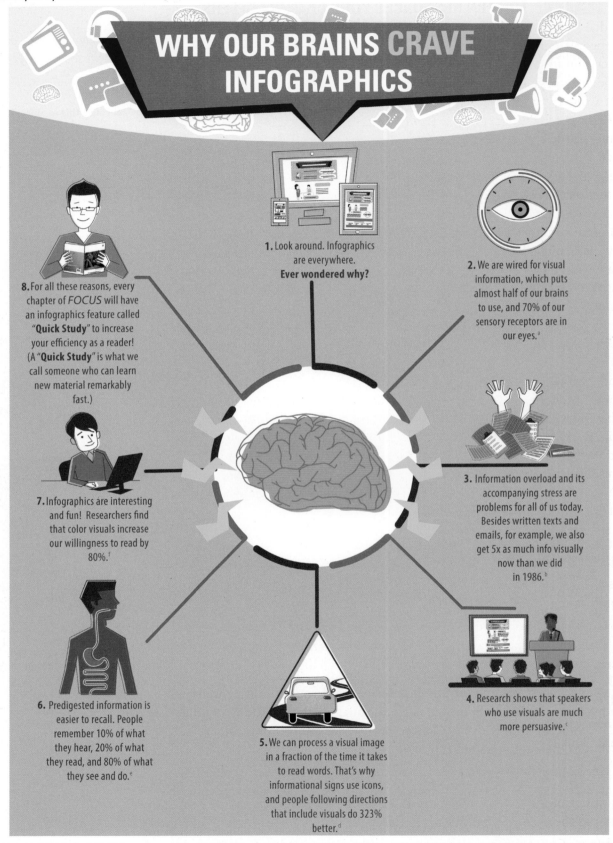

WHY OUR BRAINS CRAVE INFOGRAPHICS

1. Look around. Infographics are everywhere. **Ever wondered why?**

2. We are wired for visual information, which puts almost half of our brains to use, and 70% of our sensory receptors are in our eyes.[a]

3. Information overload and its accompanying stress are problems for all of us today. Besides written texts and emails, for example, we also get 5x as much info visually now than we did in 1986.[b]

4. Research shows that speakers who use visuals are much more persuasive.[c]

5. We can process a visual image in a fraction of the time it takes to read words. That's why informational signs use icons, and people following directions that include visuals do 323% better.[d]

6. Predigested information is easier to recall. People remember 10% of what they hear, 20% of what they read, and 80% of what they see and do.[e]

7. Infographics are interesting and fun! Researchers find that color visuals increase our willingness to read by 80%.[f]

8. For all these reasons, every chapter of *FOCUS* will have an infographics feature called "**Quick Study**" to increase your efficiency as a reader! (A "**Quick Study**" is what we call someone who can learn new material remarkably fast.)

Sources: (a) Merieb, E. N. & Hoehn, K. (2007). *Human Anatomy & Physiology* 7th Edition, Pearson International Edition; (b) Alleyne, R. (11 Feb 2011). Welcome to the information age—174 newspapers a day. *The Telegraph*; (c) Wharton School of Business. 'Effectiveness of Visual Language'; (d) Levie, W. J. & Lentz, R. (1982). Effects of text illustrations: A review of research, *Educational Communication and Technology*; (e) Lester, P. M. (2006). *Syntactic Theory of Visual Communication*; (f) Green, R. (1989). *The Persuasive Properties of Color, Marketing Communications*.

TOUGHING IT OUT:
WHAT COLLEGE TAKES

What does it mean to succeed? Actually, success is difficult to define, and different people define success differently. Right now in college, you may think of success in terms of the money you'll make after you finish. But is success just about money? Is it about fame? Status? According to motivational author Robert Collier, "Success is the sum of small efforts, repeated day in and day out." Perhaps to you, success is somewhere off in the distant future, and it happens more or less suddenly, like winning the lottery.

Actually, success begins right now. You should be the one to define what success will look like in your life, but generally, success is *setting out to do something that means something to you, and then being fully engaged while doing it.* It's that simple. And it applies to your college experience as well. It starts now.

In order to understand your own definition of success in college, first you need to ask yourself why you're here. Why *did* you come—or return—to college, anyway? Do you want to develop into a more interesting, well-rounded, educated human being? Are you working toward a degree that leads to a specific career? Do you have children and want an education in order to give them a better life? This text will provide you with an honest look at what that takes, including plenty of opportunities to ask yourself questions about these things. It will also offer you tools you can use throughout your college courses and in your life beyond college.

Some students think going to college is like any other financial transaction: buying a gallon of milk, for example. You pay the cashier the money, and the milk now belongs to you. They think if they pay tuition, the college credits should be theirs. Not so. There's much more to it than that. A college education requires more than a financial commitment. It requires you to invest your ability, your intellect, your drive, your effort—and yourself. College has to do with more than the brain matter found between your ears.

THE GOOD NEWS AND THE BAD NEWS
(BENEFITS AND OBSTACLES)

What's the good news about going to college? The benefits are wide-reaching and long-lasting. Think about how this list applies to you.

1. **Higher earning potential.** College increases your potential to earn money. It's that simple. On average, people with associate's degrees earn $798 per week, compared to $678 per week for those with a high school diploma only.[19] Experts say that by 2020, 65 percent of all jobs in the U. S. economy will require some education after high school.[20]

2. **Lower unemployment rates.** College decreases your risk of unemployment. This is especially helpful when the economy takes a downturn. According to one major study, getting an associate's or bachelor's degree is a much better personal investment today than the stock market.[21]

3. **Insight.** College students have the opportunity to understand themselves better as they learn different ways of doing things.

4. **Wisdom.** College gives you opportunities to gain understanding about many things—politics, people, and current affairs to name a few. Beyond

iStock.com/LuisPortugal

"Always bear in mind that your own resolution to succeed is more important than any one thing."

Abraham Lincoln, 16th
President of the United States
(1809–1875)

theories, facts, and dates, well-educated people know how to think critically, contribute to society, and manage their lives.

5. **Lifelong learning.** According to research, getting a college degree—even for a career that doesn't require one—leads to a happier, healthier life.[22] College students are prepared to become lifelong learners. It's not just about grades. It's about becoming the best student-learner you can be—inside or outside of the classroom. This one benefit will stay with you through the rest of your life.

What's the bad news? What obstacles may stand in your path? Carson Reed isn't quite sure why he's in college. Will he be successful? It depends, doesn't it? Here's some evidence on what "it" consists of.

Of first-time college students who enrolled in a community college in the fall of 2009, 38.1 percent earned a credential from a two- or four-year institution within six years.[23] But who goes, who finishes later, and who transfers to another school are hard things to track. The risk factors for dropping out of college include working more than thirty hours per week, going to school part-time, being a single parent or having children at home, and being a first-generation college student.[24] However, more than 70 percent of community college students have at least one of these characteristics, and half have two or more.[25] It's true that going to college is "A Whole 'Nother World," as one major report's title says. Juggling a job, family, friends, transportation, tuition, and all the things that are impacted by the energy and effort it takes to go to college can be overwhelming. If you're a first-generation college student, you may not have a role model at home who can help you, because your parents didn't go to college. (That's why it's important to make connections with your classmates, instructors, and advisors who can guide you.)[26] Even though college may be more challenging for first-generation students, you can still be highly successful. Perhaps the most famous recent example is Michelle Obama, who went from first-generation college student to First Lady.[27]

The important thing to keep in mind as you think about risk factors is that they alone cannot determine your ultimate level of success. Don't throw in the towel now if you had a child at age sixteen or are working thirty-five hours per week. These factors are presented merely as information to assist you on your journey. They are simply predictors—not *determiners*. Only you can determine your outcomes in life, and that includes college.

Plenty of people who have achieved great things in their lives got their start at a community college. Look at this impressive list:[28]

> Queen Latifah, rapper, actress, talk show host
> Aaron Rogers, quarterback, Green Bay Packers
> Billy Crystal, actor and comedian
> Tom Hanks, actor
> Calvin Klein, designer
> Clint Eastwood, actor
> Sarah Palin, former governor of Alaska and vice presidential candidate
> Halle Berry, actress and Oscar winner
> Walt Disney, entertainment genius

predictors something that indicates something in the future may happen

Marian Lopez Ojeda/Shutterstock.com

I am only one,
But still I am one.
I cannot do
everything,
But still I can do
something;
And because I cannot
do everything
I will not refuse to do
the something that I
can do.

Edward Everett Hale,
American author (1822–1909)

Your effort, attitude, and willingness to get any help you need to succeed are all vital.

THE BOTTOM LINE: RESILIENCE

Although there are both costs and benefits associated with college, let's face it: Life Happens. Some bumper stickers may substitute another less polite word for "life," but it's true. Everyone faces tough challenges, and college students aren't exempt. In fact, sometimes life's challenges are more than bumps in the road. They're major setbacks, personal tragedies, or even natural (or unnatural) disasters. If someone's home on the beach is destroyed by a hurricane, or the family dog is diagnosed with a terrible disease, devastation is a natural response. Some students only find out about their parents' plans to divorce after they start, and the shock sends them reeling.[29] Veterans who recently served in combat may have witnessed unforgettable things and still feel the effects. Serious circumstances like these cause great distress, and one possible reaction is to think "Why me? I feel like a helpless victim in a cruel world." You can probably think of examples in your own life before college—times when you faced shock, grief, or a major disappointment. Bad things happen—it's true—but what's important is how you handle them.

Interestingly, people handle tough situations differently. Some people show signs of "give-up-itis" immediately. But after the same initial reaction, eventually, other people see disasters as challenges. You may not believe the following paragraph, and if you don't already know who it's about, you may not be able to guess:

> A five-year-old boy watched helplessly as his younger brother drowned. In the same year, glaucoma began to darken his world, and his family was too poor to afford the medical help that might have saved his sight. Both of his parents died during his teens. Eventually he was sent to a state institution for the blind. Because he was an African American he was not permitted access to any activities, including music. Given the obstacles he faced, one could not have predicted that he would someday become a world-renowned musician.[30]

Ray Charles endured more challenges than anyone could possibly imagine, yet he overcame the odds. Although resilience is a term we usually reserve for people like Ray Charles, it applies to all of us. Psychologists don't fully understand why people react differently, but two words come to mind: "True Grit." Besides being the title of a famous novel and award-winning movie, what does it have to do with you as a new college student? Fill out the instrument in Exercise 1.3 to begin thinking about your own resilience potential in college.

HOW CAN YOU "GROW" YOUR GRIT?

If you look up the word *grit*, you'll find this definition: "firmness of character; indomitable spirit; pluck."[31] People with grit have what it takes to hang in there. They tough things out, despite huge obstacles that get thrown in their way. They bounce back stronger than before. If someone you know says you have true grit, that's a compliment. "Grit is a willingness to commit to long-term goals, and to persist in the face of difficulty. Studies show that gritty people obtain more education in their lifetime, and earn higher college GPAs. Grit predicts which cadets will stick out their first grueling year at West Point. In fact, grit even predicts which round contestants will make it to at the Scripps National Spelling Bee."[32]

> "Strength does not come from winning. Your struggles develop your strengths. When you go through hardships and decide not to surrender, that is strength."
>
> **Arnold Schwarzenegger,** *actor, former politician, activist, philanthropist, attended Santa Monica College*

Aflo Relax/Masterfile

> There's a crack in everything. That's how the light gets in.
>
> **Leonard Cohen,** *Canadian singer-songwriter, poet, and novelist (1934–2016)*

> "Always focus on the front windshield and not the rearview mirror."
>
> **Colin Powell,** *American statesman, retired four-star General, and 65th U.S. secretary of state*

Following are twelve statements that may or may not apply to you. There are no right or wrong answers. Just answer honestly, considering how you compare to most people you know. At the end, you'll tabulate a score and find out what it means. Put a checkmark or "X" next to the phrase that best describes you.

1. I have achieved a goal that took years of work.
   _____ Very much like me
   _____ Mostly like me
   _____ Somewhat like me
   _____ Not much like me
   _____ Not like me at all

2. I have overcome setbacks to conquer an important challenge.
   _____ Very much like me
   _____ Mostly like me
   _____ Somewhat like me
   _____ Not much like me
   _____ Not like me at all

3. I finish whatever I begin.
   _____ Very much like me
   _____ Mostly like me
   _____ Somewhat like me
   _____ Not much like me
   _____ Not like me at all

4. Setbacks don't discourage me.
   _____ Very much like me
   _____ Mostly like me
   _____ Somewhat like me
   _____ Not much like me
   _____ Not like me at all

5. I am a hard worker.
   _____ Very much like me
   _____ Mostly like me
   _____ Somewhat like me
   _____ Not much like me
   _____ Not like me at all

6. I am diligent.
   _____ Very much like me
   _____ Mostly like me
   _____ Somewhat like me
   _____ Not much like me
   _____ Not like me at all

7. I often set a goal but later choose to pursue a different one.
   _____ Very much like me
   _____ Mostly like me
   _____ Somewhat like me
   _____ Not much like me
   _____ Not like me at all

8. New ideas and new projects sometimes distract me from previous ones.
   _____ Very much like me
   _____ Mostly like me
   _____ Somewhat like me
   _____ Not much like me
   _____ Not like me at all

9. I become interested in new pursuits every few months.
   _____ Very much like me
   _____ Mostly like me
   _____ Somewhat like me
   _____ Not much like me
   _____ Not like me at all

10. My interests change from year to year.
    _____ Very much like me
    _____ Mostly like me
    _____ Somewhat like me
    _____ Not much like me
    _____ Not like me at all

11. I have been obsessed with a certain idea or project for a short time but later lost interest.
    _____ Very much like me
    _____ Mostly like me
    _____ Somewhat like me
    _____ Not much like me
    _____ Not like me at all

12. I have difficulty maintaining my focus on projects that take more than a few months to complete.
    _____ Very much like me
    _____ Mostly like me
    _____ Somewhat like me
    _____ Not much like me
    _____ Not like me at all

Now tally your responses using this scoring system for items 1–6:

Very much like me = 5

Mostly like me = 4

Somewhat like me = 3

Not much like me = 2

Not like me at all = 1

Total for items 1–6 _____

Next, add up your responses using this scoring system for items 7–12:

Very much like me = 1

Mostly like me = 2

Somewhat like me = 3

Not much like me = 4

Not like me at all = 5

Total for items 7–12 _____

Then combine your total for items 1–6 and your total for items 7–12 to find your grand total _____.

Grand total _____ divided by 12 _____ = Final Grit score _____

Generally speaking, the higher your Final Grit score, the more grit or resilience you consider yourself to have at this point in your life. How does your score relate to other people's scores? If your final grit score was on the low end at 2.5, you'd have more grit than 10 percent of the population. If your grit score was in the middle at 3.8, you'd have more grit than 50 percent of the population. And if your grit score was high, say 4.5, you'd have more grit than 90 percent of the population.[34] Think about where your score falls. Is it general low (in the twos), medium (in the threes), or high (in the fours)?

Grit can increase or decrease based on experiences and life events; however, increasing your grit in college is a good goal to have. Grit or resilience equips you to push through, recharge and recover, and bounce back when the going gets tough.[35] For more information on grit, read Angela Duckworth's best-selling book *Grit: The Power and Passion of Perseverance*.

Think of it this way: in college, grit explains the difference between three students who fail the same math test but respond very differently. One decides to drop out of college: "I knew this was a bad idea. I just can't hack it, and I might as well admit it now." One throws the exam in the trash can on the way out of the classroom and refuses to ever crack open the textbook again. The other vows to study differently and spend more time doing it. "I'm not going to let calculus *get the better of me*. I'm going to take control of my learning so that it gets the *best from me*!" See the difference? After college, in the workplace, grit has to do with how you react to being treated unfairly or badly—like being shocked because you're laid off just when you thought your job was going especially well. Some people give up; others dig in to beat the challenge.

Psychologists have been interested in grit (also called *resilience* or *hardiness*) for years, going back to a major study done when the government deregulated the telephone business. Half of the employees at AT&T were laid off. Two-thirds of these people simply couldn't cope. They died of heart attacks or strokes, engaged in violence, got divorces, or suffered from mental health issues. The lives of the other third actually improved. They got better jobs, deepened their relationships, and launched highly successful lives. When all was said and done, psychologists believed that it had to do with three "Cs": <u>c</u>ommitment, <u>c</u>ontrol, and <u>c</u>hallenge.[36] They were <u>c</u>ommitted to turning a bad situation around, they took <u>c</u>ontrol of their lives, and they saw adversity as a <u>c</u>hallenge to overcome. The good news is that if you're short on grit, you can get more. Increasing your self-awareness, especially with help from experts, is the way to start. Also consider these five suggestions:

1. **Cultivate "realistic optimism."** "Realistic optimism" isn't blind faith or false hope; it's looking for the best in things and then working to make them happen. It's accepting what's going on around you, but at the same time admitting what needs to be changed. It's about resilience, "getting back on the horse," and trotting on. It's a productive pattern of thinking. If a particular course isn't going well for you, realistic optimism means

admitting it and moving ahead full throttle to reverse the situation. Some students just throw up their hands and decide a particularly challenging course is a waste of their time. Instead, invest *more* time to show you can do it.

2. **Fail forward.** Have you ever thought about the good things that can come from tough challenges? "J.K. Rowling described to a Harvard graduating class a perfect storm of failure—broken marriage, disapproving parents, poverty that bordered on homelessness—that sent her back to her first dream of writing because she had nothing left to lose. 'Failure stripped away everything inessential,' she said. 'It taught me things about myself I could have learned no other way.'"[37] *Dilbert* cartoonist Scott Adams says, "If you're taking risks, and you probably should, you can find yourself failing 90% of the time. The trick is to get paid while you're doing the failing and to use the experience to gain skills that will be useful later. I failed at my first career in banking. I failed at my second career with the phone company. But you'd be surprised at how many of the skills I learned in those careers can be applied to almost any field, including cartooning … failure is a process, not an obstacle."[38] Many people picture failures as "crash and burn" scenarios. Try picturing failure as "forward progress." When you trip and fall, can you come out ahead in the long run?

3. **Realize that becoming resilient is a process.** Some people think that the natural response to a stressful event is depression. Depression is a possible response, but it's only part of the picture. Becoming resilient is a process that involves passing through other emotional states like shock, guilt, anger, even blame. But the healthiest among us have enough reserves within us (or we can get them from others who care) to achieve positive change. Think back to a time in your life when you showed resilience during a difficult situation and remember the emotional process you went through. You don't just decide to "get over it"; you work through it. The same process applies to tough challenges you will face in college. It's important to realize that a particular academic setback is temporary, and that you *can* work your way through it.

4. **Recognize how you contribute to your own need for resilience.** You can't snap your fingers and control everything. But you *are* the author of your own life—not your parents or teachers or even your friends. If you run into bureaucratic red tape in college, find out how to cut through it and pursue answers yourself. If you tend to procrastinate with a capital "P," take command and get your work done. If the temptation of technology overwhelms you, zero in and focus. If you'd like to improve your performance in a course, find a resource to help you. Leaving problems to someone else to solve for you (like your Mom) or hoping they'll resolve on their own can cause your stress level (and your need for resilience) to skyrocket.[39]

self-absorption only thinking about yourself and your own problems

contracts shrinks

5. **Look around.** Daniel Goleman, expert on emotional intelligence, says this, "Self-absorption in all its forms kills empathy, let alone compassion. When we focus on ourselves, our world contracts as our problems and preoccupations loom large. But when we focus on others, our world expands."[40]

Sometimes reaching out to someone else who is also dealing with hard times puts things in perspective, and helping someone else develop resilience helps you develop more.

So when unexpected challenges come up—and they surely will—remember the earlier quote: "There's a crack in everything. That's how the light gets in." Cracks are just cracks. They don't have to become breaks. And they can shed light on an otherwise dark situation. It's not the challenge itself that counts; it's how you respond to it. When hard times strike, remember the three "C's," see the light, and get truly gritty.

THIS COURSE HAS A PROVEN TRACK RECORD

If you're reading this text, there's a good chance you're enrolled in a first-year seminar course, called something like First-Year Seminar, First-Year Experience, College Success, Learning Community, or any of a host of other names. These courses are designed to introduce you to college life, familiarize you with your own campus, and help you improve your academic skills. Do they work? According to experts, the answer is yes! Of course, you have to keep your part of the bargain, but in general, community college students who complete first-year seminars are much more successful.

According to one study, community college students who took an orientation or college success course were seventy-two times more likely to graduate than students who didn't.[41] And take a look at the results of another major study in Figure 1.2. Students who completed a college success course that encouraged them to apply their new skills were more likely to stay in school, succeed academically, and complete more credits. That's what this course is about: your success. Your instructor and your classmates are rooting for you. Now it's up to you!

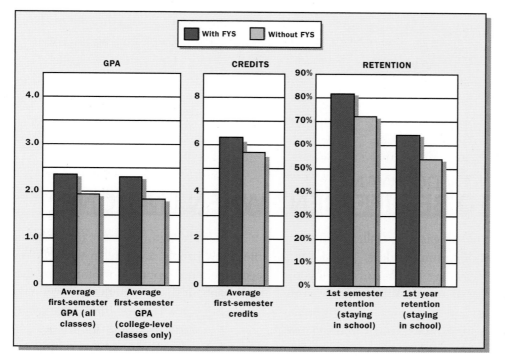

FIGURE 1.2

Comparing Community College Students Who Completed a First-Year Seminar Course with Those Who Did Not

Source: Adapted from Karp, M. M., Raufman, J., Efthimiou, C., & Ritze, J. (2017). Revising a college 101 course for sustained impact: Early outcomes. *Community College Journal of Research and Practice 41*(1), 42–55.

BOX 1.3 **GENERATION 1: FIRST IN THE FAMILY?**

Did both your parents graduate from college? If not, you are a "first-generation college student." Quite an impressive title, isn't it? Being first at something has some definite pros. You're a trailblazer, a pioneer, someone to be looked up to. "Imagine, our son Dion with a college degree! Isn't that something?" But along with pros come potential challenges. Who will you go to for advice? Will your family understand what it takes? Will they support your efforts? At moments when your confidence is shaken, you may wonder: *Can* a first-generation student be successful? The answer? Of course! (Your author is a first-generation college graduate!) In the end, your success is up to you. As you begin your college career, take these suggestions to heart:

1. **Communicate with your family.** Research shows that the *quality* and *quantity* of communication about college that you engage in with your family is key to your success. Although they can't empathize because they haven't "been there and done that," they can listen and encourage you. Talk to them openly about your college experience.[42]

2. **Keep your stress level in check.** If your family puts extra pressure on you to perform, your stress level may increase dramatically. But stress isn't the best motivator. This is something you want to do, so hone in and hunker down. Pay particular attention to your instructors, keep track of due dates, and focus. All you can do is your best. Think of it this way: you're "demystifying" college. You may just inspire Mom or Dad or your little brother to go to college one day, too.[43]

3. **Get going.** Remember this: when the going gets tough, the tough get going. Sometimes first-generation students are tempted to drop out, scale back (from four classes to three, for example), avoid assessment (thinking, oddly, "If I don't turn my paper in, I can't get a bad grade on it"), or lower their own expectations ("I was hoping for a 4.0 GPA, but maybe a 2.0 will do"). Although sometimes these options may be the right ones, sabotaging your own efforts is

never a good idea. Keep your eye on the prize—that degree you'll be the first one to earn in your family.[44]

4. **Find a true mentor.** Look for a particular professor or advisor to serve as a mentor—someone you can go to for advice and support. Just knowing that someone cares can be a powerful motivator. Ask this person to help you through rough patches or go to her to get recharged when your "academic batteries" are low.

5. **Get involved.** College may feel like a "foreign" culture to you. You may have conflicting emotions: excitement, confusion, and anxiety. You may not understand what instructors expect, how to fit in, or how to get it all done. But you won't learn these things if you aren't around. If you breeze in for your classes and bolt afterward, it will be harder to adjust to your new role. Ease into the campus culture and take full advantage of what it means to be in college. Make friends and feel the beat of campus life.[45]

If you follow this advice, you *can* be successful! If you're a first-generation college student, dog-ear or bookmark this page, and refer back to it whenever you need to.

Ryan McVay/Stockbyte/Getty Images

Though no one can go back and make a brand new start, anyone can start from now and make a brand-new ending.

Carl Bard

HOW DO I WANT
TO BE DIFFERENT WHEN I'M DONE?

One thing is sure: College will change you. Most every high-intensity experience full of opportunities does. Take advantage, meet new people, and stretch yourself. You may notice that as a result of your college experience, your old relationships may "fit" differently. Your romantic partner may brag about you or secretly envy you. Your family may praise your efforts or hardly notice. But you will. If you finish what you've begun, you will watch yourself become a more sophisticated, more knowledgeable, more confident person. You can't help but be. Ask yourself now, at the beginning of your college experience, just how you'd like to change, and make it happen.

BOX 1.4 **HOW TO READ A CASE STUDY**

Each chapter of *FOCUS* will begin with a case study about a real student, portrayed by a member of the *FOCUS* cast. (You'll see the cast members in photos throughout the text—and will perhaps almost feel you know them all by the end.) As you read the case, you may think: *Hmmm . . . this is an interesting story, but what does it have to do with me?* Make the most out of these case studies by following these suggestions:

- **Make a connection.** Although you may be a different age, gender, or ethnicity, look at the issues beneath the surface. Actually, you may have some things in common with the case study character, or you may know someone else who does. Are you tempted to make some of the mistakes Carson is making? Is your best buddy worried about similar issues? Did your sister, who was in college before you, struggle with her writing class, as Carson does?

- **Get engaged.** The case studies are designed to be a fully interactive and visual experience for you. You can gain a complete picture of the case study students by reading their story *and* looking closely at the photos and visual examples. Learn even more about the students by looking at sample e-mails, notes, text messages, Facebook profiles, and other key visual examples of their lives.

- **Think critically.** Imagine yourself in a conversation with the case study students. What advice would you give them? How would you help them solve their problems? Becoming an active reader and critical thinker will help you build skills that will contribute to your success as a college student.

- **Prepare to learn.** The case study will preview all the topics you'll read about in the chapter. The chapters will provide you with strategies to deal with these challenges. Make sure you read each case thoroughly, watch for things you will learn in the chapter, and then answer the Reaction questions that follow.

If you follow them through the text, these featured students will lead you into a rich, "FOCUSed" learning experience!

WRITE YOUR OWN CASE STUDY

Everyone has a story. This is your opportunity to tell yours! Start by flipping through FOCUS and skimming the other Challenge Cases. Perhaps your biggest challenge will be something like those facing Katie Alexander or Derek Johnson, or maybe your particular challenge doesn't appear in this text. (If you expect everything to be "smooth sailing" for you, you may prefer to write about a friend or relative beginning college, and that's acceptable too.) This exercise will allow you to personalize what you will learn in this class and identify possible issues that may interfere with your success in college early on. Here are the steps you will follow:

1. First, write your story. Your instructor will give you specific guidelines, but in general, write a two-page case study that highlights your previous learning experiences, your expectations for college, key pieces of your life outside of college that may interfere with your success, and the top challenges you are facing right now in college. You should write your story in the third person, and you may give yourself a fictional (but real-sounding) name. You may write, for example, "It was her first day of college, and the temperature outside had reached a record high. She rushed into the building from the parking lot so that the air conditioning would start cooling her down right away. But she had more than the temperature outside on her mind. She was nervous. No one from her family had ever gone to college, and suddenly she felt pressure to impress them"—or whatever was true for you. Remember to leave things up in the air at the end of your case study, just like the cases in *FOCUS*, so that someone else can read it and think about what would help you succeed.

2. Choose personalized images to surround your story—a photo of you, other photos of people in the story, images that relate to the case, whatever you wish—and place them around the story. (Go to an online site that has free images you can choose from or download photos from your Facebook page, if you have one.) Your case should look something like one of the ones in *FOCUS*. You may use whatever e-tool you wish to create your case (PowerPoint or Word, for example), but your instructor may want you to turn in a paper copy. This part of the assignment should be two (facing) pages.

3. Write three to five questions to go along with your case. Start by thinking about issues where you need the most advice, and build your questions around those. You may want to ask your reader, "What's the primary challenge facing

(continued on next page)

this new student? Describe it in your own words." or "Why is this issue (whatever it is) something that could interfere with college success?" Your instructor may ask you to answer these questions yourself or swap your case with a classmate and answer his or her questions. At the end of this course, you will look back at your beginning case study and write about the learning that has taken place for you along the way.

INSIGHT: *NOW* WHAT DO YOU THINK?

At the beginning of this chapter, Carson Reed faced a series of challenges as a new college student. Now after learning from this chapter, would you respond differently to any of the questions you answered about the "FOCUS Challenge Case"? Using what you learned in the chapter, write a paragraph ending to Carson's case study. What are some of the possible outcomes for Carson?

ACTION: YOUR PLANS FOR CHANGE

1. Identify one new thing you learned in reading this chapter. Why did you select the one you've selected? How will it affect what you do in your college classes?

2. Why are you going to community college? How do you see your college experience impacting your future?

3. How do you plan to increase your resilience and tackle tough challenges that come up in college?

4. How do you want college to change you? Why?

BECOMING MINDFUL, SETTING GOALS | 2

HOW THIS CHAPTER RELATES TO YOU

1. When it comes to becoming mindful and setting goals, what are you most unsure about, if anything? Put check marks by the phrases that apply to you or write in your answer.

   ☐ What it means to be mindful
   ☐ How mindset and motivation fit in
   ☐ What I really want to do with my life
   ☐ Whether my dreams are achievable
   ☐ How to set realistic goals

2. What is most likely to be your response? Put a check mark by it.

   ☐ I'll keep thinking about it.
   ☐ I'll ask for guidance from an expert on campus.
   ☐ I'll see which courses really interest me.
   ☐ I'll figure it out on my own.

3. What would you have to do to increase your likelihood of success? Will you do it this quarter or semester?

HOW YOU WILL RELATE TO THIS CHAPTER

1. What are you most interested in learning about? Put check marks by those topics.

   ☐ What mindfulness is and why it's important
   ☐ What role the "Three Ms of College Success" play
   ☐ How this text will help you learn
   ☐ How positivity helps you succeed
   ☐ How hope helps
   ☐ How to understand your values, dreams, and goals
   ☐ How to develop *goals* to help you achieve your *dreams*

YOUR READINESS FACTOR

1. How motivated are you to learn more about becoming mindful and setting goals? (5 = high, 1 = low)

2. How ready are you to read now? (If something is in your way, take care of it if you can. Zero in and focus.)

3. How long do you think it will take you to complete this chapter? If you start and stop, keep track of your overall time. ____ Hour(s) ____ Minute(s)

ESB Professional/Shutterstock.com

Sylvia Sanchez

Her own apartment—finally! As Sylvia opened the new package of turquoise sheets for her bed, she felt excited but at the same time, amazingly calm. Frankly, she couldn't believe her parents had agreed to it. But their response to the idea had been, "Sure, if you're willing to pay your own rent, we'll find plenty of uses for your room. But don't even think about taking Charlie with you! Get your own dog!" they had said, in a surprisingly serious tone.

So Sylvia had been counting off the days all summer, and frankly, it felt good to be on her own. No younger brothers and sisters squawking, no parents breathing down her neck, no grandparents living right next door, and no lame boyfriend thinking he could just hang around all the time. A fresh start—that's what she wanted. She stopped to check her cell phone—four new texts, probably all from him. And all those pictures of her he had posted on Facebook this morning! She wanted to write back and tell him to get over it, but she thought she'd better wait awhile for that. *Let's just see what college has to offer. That's smarter*, she admitted. Her three high school friends—soon to be roommates—hadn't arrived yet, so naturally Sylvia claimed the best bedroom. *They'd probably have done the same thing*, she reassured herself. *They should have gotten here earlier.*

Sylvia had always been smart—not brilliant, but smart enough to know how to play the game. She was always rushing around, doing a hundred things at once. Focusing wasn't her strong point, and multitasking didn't always get her the best grades. But truthfully, she'd never even cracked a book during her senior year and still passed all her classes. She always did her homework in front of the TV (that is, when she did any) while she played with the dog, texted her friends, played some addictive online game, and checked her Facebook page. College, she imagined, would be a slightly harder version of high school. It couldn't be as hard as her parents had warned. She remembered their threats when she brought home a bad grade in high school: *You just wait until you start college!* How would they know? They'd never even been to college themselves. If all that propaganda from parents and high school teachers were really true, no one would go to college! *How hard can it possibly be?* she asked herself. Her parents said they'd help financially when they could, but she wasn't expecting much. "And we're not paying for anything below a B!" her father had insisted. She just had to keep her grades up enough to hold onto her financial aid, and if she could manage to impress her parents, that wouldn't hurt, either. Her track record in school had never been all that great, but maybe—just maybe—she could change that in college.

Of her four new college courses, Sylvia was least worried about her college success class. *Automatic A*, she predicted. *Everyone knows how to study. It's just common sense*, she thought to herself. But did she *really* know the best ways to study? Did she actually know how much to study to "live up to her potential"? Those were different questions. The thought of writing an essay every week for her English Composition class brought on major dread; in fact, she wasn't all that excited about any of her classes. There might be other, more compelling pursuits that took up her time

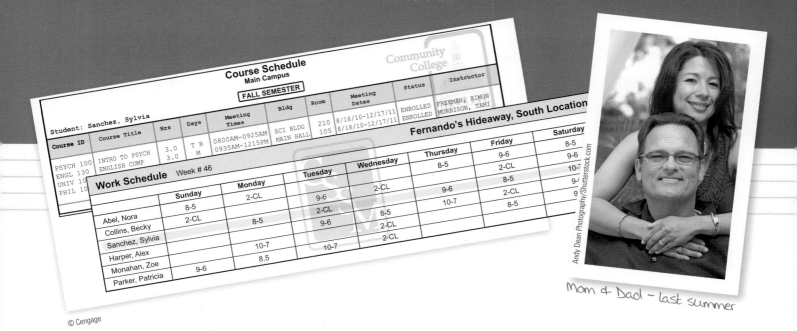

Course Schedule
Main Campus

FALL SEMESTER

Community College

Student: Sanchez, Sylvia								Status	Instructor
Course ID	Course Title	Hrs	Days	Meeting Times	Bldg	Room	Meeting Dates		
PSYCH 100	INTRO TO PSYCH	3.0	T R	0800AM-0925AM	SCI BLDG	210	8/18/10-12/17/11	ENROLLED	FREEMAN, SIMON
ENGL 130	ENGLISH COMP	3.0	M	0935AM-1215PM	MAIN HALL	105	8/18/10-12/17/11	ENROLLED	MORRISON, TAMI
UNIV 10									
PHIL 10									

Fernando's Hideaway, South Location

Work Schedule Week # 46

	Sunday	Monday	Tuesday	Wednesday	Thursday	Friday	Saturday
		2-CL	9-6	2-CL	8-5	9-6	8-5
Abel, Nora	8-5		2-CL		9-6	2-CL	9-6
Collins, Becky	2-CL	8-5	9-6	8-5	10-7	8-5	10-7
Sanchez, Sylvia				2-CL		2-CL	9-
Harper, Alex		10-7		2-CL		8-5	
Monahan, Zoe		8.5	10-7	2-CL			
Parker, Patricia	9-6						

© Cengage

Mom & Dad – last summer

Andy Dean Photography/Shutterstock.com

---

in college, like meeting interesting people and finishing her demo CD.

The one thing Sylvia knew for sure was that she desperately wanted to make it in the music industry, and her parents desperately wanted her to major in business. "How many people actually become famous musicians?" they would ask. Her Dad grilled her regularly on the subject. "There are all kinds of possible careers if you earn a business degree, but how many people actually make it as musicians—even if they're good? What are the odds? College is the way to go, and a certificate in business makes sense. Your mother and I never had the chance; don't blow this opportunity!" "Yeah, whatever . . ." was her usual retort.

But all Sylvia really wanted in life was to be behind a microphone in front of an audience. And the bigger the audience, the better. Someday— she just knew it—she'd sign a recording contract with a major record label. All her friends told her how good she was. They'd even encouraged her to try out for a TV singing competition. Imagine— fame and fortune. *Sylvia Sanchez, recording artist* . . . even her name had the right ring to it and eventually, everyone would recognize it. They'd download her top hits, and she'd have the clothes,

hair, make-up, and money she'd always wanted. As she stood at the foot of the bed, admiring her new sheets, Sylvia caught a glimpse of herself in the mirror on the wall. "Looking good!" she whispered. Was she referring to how her new bedroom was shaping up or how she'd made the right decision on what to wear?

Suddenly, Sylvia heard laughter in the hallway and realized it was her new roommates. They had hung out together in high school, but how would she like actually living with them? Would they start getting on one another's nerves? Deep down, Sylvia realized, she really did want to be successful in college. But she also wanted to live her own life and do her own thing. Still, she rationalized, *If this whole college thing doesn't work out, I'll move back home, pick up where I left off, work retail for a while, and wait for the future I really want.*

Artmim/Shutterstock.com

1. Is Sylvia sufficiently motivated to succeed in college? Why or why not?

2. Describe Sylvia's beliefs about her intelligence. Does she think college is mostly about effort or about ability? Is Sylvia a *learner* or a *performer*?

3. Is Sylvia's vision of becoming a famous singer a goal or a dream? Why?

4. Identify three things that show focus and might help Sylvia make good life management choices.

5. Are any elements of Sylvia's situation similar to your own college experience thus far?

WHO ARE YOU?
AND WHAT DO YOU WANT?

PhotostoGO.com PhotoObjects.net/Jupiter Images

"What is important is to keep learning, to enjoy challenge, and to tolerate ambiguity. In the end there are no certain answers."

Matina Horner, former
President of Radcliffe College

Imagine this voicemail greeting: "Hi. At the tone, please answer two of life's most important questions. Who are you? And what do you want?" Beep. Can you answer these questions right now? How much do you really know about yourself and what you want from this life of yours?

Don't worry. These aren't trick questions and there are no wrong answers. But there are some answers that are more right for you than others. College is a great time to think about who you are and what you want. In addition to learning about biology or history or business, college will be a time to learn about yourself: your motivation, values, dreams, and goals. You may make some of the most important choices of your life. Which major will you choose? Which career will you aim for? From this point on, it's up to you. Have you ever heard this phrase with 10 two-letter words: "If it is to be, it is up to me"? It's true. So even if you aren't sure exactly how you want to spend the rest of your life right now, you can't go wrong by investing in your future.

Of course, some people achieve success without a college degree, but by and large, they're the exception. Even movie billionaire Steven Spielberg, winner of Academy Awards for his movies *Schindler's List* and *Saving Private Ryan*, felt the need to finish the college degree he had started more than thirty years before. "I wanted to accomplish this for many years as a 'thank you' to my parents for giving me the opportunity for an education and a career, and as a personal note for my own family—and young people everywhere—about the importance of achieving their college education goals," he said. "But I hope they get there quicker than I did. Completing the requirements for my degree thirty-three years after finishing my principal education marks my longest post-production schedule."[1]

This text starts with the big picture: managing your life. Notice the phrase is "managing your life"—not *controlling* your life. Let's face it: Many things in life are beyond our control. But you can manage your life by making smart choices, setting goals you can work toward, paying attention to your time and energy, and motivating yourself. As the title of this text states boldly, it's about focus. If you read this text carefully and follow its advice, it will help you become the best student you can possibly be. It will give you practical tools to help you manage your life. It will take you into your next level of education or into your career. And most of all, it will encourage you to become a true learner. That is this text's challenge to you as you begin your college experience.

WHAT DOES IT TAKE
TO SUCCEED IN COLLEGE? THE "THREE Ms" OF COLLEGE SUCCESS

What does it mean to succeed? Is success about money, fame, status? According to motivational author Robert Collier, "Success is the sum of small efforts, repeated day in and day out." Perhaps when you think about it, success seems off somewhere in the distance—something that appears out of nowhere. But, actually, you are the person who will define success in your life, and it starts now.

Success in college will require both academic skills and what are typically called "soft skills." Naturally, reading writing, and presenting will be critical skills to have in place. But if your moods, attitudes, or feelings get in the way, it may be harder to achieve success in college. We'll start in this second category first by discussing the "Three Ms" of college success. Read on for new insights that apply to your future!

MINDFULNESS: GETTING READY TO LEARN

Do you remember when you were a kid in elementary school? Every morning, the teacher called "roll." When your name was called, you would usually say, "here." But if you wanted to feel really special that day, you might say "present," which sounded much more sophisticated. Then, being present just meant that you were there; it wasn't a guarantee that you'd pay attention. *Mindfulness*, however, *is* about "being present"; it's about your attention. It means paying attention to your attention so that you can gain better control of it. Now there's an idea!

In today's crazy, busy world, mindfulness doesn't come naturally. We're constantly on the go, and everything and everyone want our attention. Information floods our screens nonstop. A Twitter feed can change drastically in just a few seconds, and a Facebook page takes ages to go through if you've been away for a while. Our work lives are equally frantic; the average American employee "is interrupted or switches tasks every three minutes and five seconds." No wonder our lives feel so hectic at times![3]

Many of us are "on" 24/7. "We want to connect and be connected. We want to effectively scan for opportunity and optimize for the best opportunities, activities, and contacts, in any given moment. To be busy, to be connected, is to be alive, to be recognized, and to matter."[4] In fact, nowadays when people ask, "How are you?" or "How's it going?," instead of "fine" or "OK," people often respond by saying "Busy!" In today's society, "busyness" has become a status symbol. Being busy must mean we are "in demand." "Everybody wants a piece of us," and that supposedly gives us prestige.[5]

But truthfully, instead of giving us prestige, busyness increases our anxiety and stress. We are so connected that it's hard to slow down long enough to process what's really going on inside us and around us. What's easy is going through

lightwavemedia/Shutterstock.com

Slow down and enjoy life. It's not only the scenery you miss by going too fast— you also miss the sense of where you are going and why.

Eddie Cantor, *American singer and songwriter (1892–1964)*

the motions and speeding through life, but *mindlessness* can take its toll. Our minds are full of distractions, and we may neglect the romantic partner who just wants a sympathetic ear, the child tugging on our jeans, the teammate with the ball, the soldier next to us, the patient lying in the hospital bed, or the instructor at the front of the classroom. What can we do about it?

The best antidote for a hectic lifestyle is not just slowing down, it's learning to control our attention. The hottest new word in the world of careers right now is *mindfulness*, a word that used to make people think of monks on Himalayan mountain tops, Buddhist chants, and Zen meditation. Now mindfulness experts are training employees in all kinds of organizations—Google, Apple, Aetna, HBO, Target, and Bank of America, professional sports teams, the military, healthcare workers—even the Pentagon and the U.S. House of Representatives. According to some estimates, at least 40 percent of Fortune 500 employees will receive training on mindfulness in the coming years.[6] As a new college student learning to *FOCUS*, why not get a head start by learning to practice mindfulness <u>now</u>?

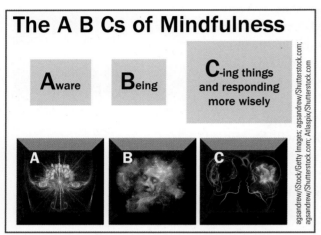

The A B Cs of Mindfulness

Aware

Being

C-ing things and responding more wisely

A

B

C

agsandrew/iStock/Getty Images; agsandrew/Shutterstock.com; agsandrew/Shutterstock.com; Atlaspix/Shutterstock.com

So what is mindfulness, exactly? An easy explanation to remember is based on the letters A, B, C: being **A**ware—really aware—of what's going on inside you and around you, **B**eing—just being in the present—not regretting the *past* or worrying about the *future*. And thirdly, seeing (**C**-ing) things or being observant so that you respond more wisely.[7]

Think of it this way: Often we just let go with a quick "automatic" response when we feel wronged, for example, and we snap back to a family member, "You are *such* a jerk!" Instead, being mindful might help you pause for a moment and think about your response by considering the other person's point of view. Perhaps your family member is distracted by a bigger problem, working through a sticky situation on the job, or dealing with bad news. You don't really know, so if you're mindful, you'll be more likely to respond neutrally or even with empathy instead of "going off" on him.

Mindfulness typically includes meditation, which isn't necessarily sitting cross-legged on the floor with fingers and thumbs touching, nor does it require converting to Buddhism. You can meditate by quietly concentrating on something specific like your breath going in and out, in and out, and noticing sensations and thoughts. Or meditation can be doing something as simple as closing your eyes and "regrouping" at your desk for a few minutes at the start, middle, or end of the day. Your mind will wander; that's natural. Just gently pull it back and refocus your attention to where it was when you started. While you're meditating, it's important to monitor what's going on in your head, but remember: "Thoughts and feelings (including negative ones) are transient" almost as if they're on a conveyor belt in your mind. "They come and go, and ultimately, you have a choice about whether to act on them or not."[8] Just because you think or feel a certain way doesn't mean it's true or real. And you don't need to worry about whether you're meditating incorrectly. If your thoughts drift away, just gently pull them back and focus on your breathing again.

transient passing, brief, momentary

TZIDO SUN/Shutterstock.com

To some people, reflecting quietly is a challenge; being on the go is the norm, and stopping to look inward and think about yourself, your values, and your life seems hard. It's supposed to be hard—that's normal—and meditation isn't just "one more thing to do."[9] In fact, as you're reading right now, you may be thinking, "I'm just starting college, and I should be thinking about my classes" or "I'm not a spiritual person, and besides, I don't have time for mindfulness!" These are common reactions, but experts believe that mindfulness actually *saves* time. Grabbing a few moments of solitude and reflection isn't just one more thing on a to-do list, and it's not necessarily "religious." In fact, "The busier you are, the more you need mindfulness."[10] It's deliberately doing *nothing* in order to reap the benefits, like being available to focus on your work when

| EXERCISE 2.1 | **CHOCOLATE MINDFULNESS MEDITATION** |

In today's world, enthusiasm for mindfulness is spreading to many different arenas besides the workplace—mindful parenting, mindful commuting, mindful relationships—you name it. One area that's a particularly good introduction to the topic is mindful eating. Instead of "inhaling" our food or chowing down, which many of us do, try slowing down to totally "experience" your food. If you're a fan of chocolate, try this meditation exercise. (If you're not or you're allergic, use a pistachio in the shell or some other "wrapped," non-messy food, or even a raisin.) Peppermint patties work especially well because the mint stimulates your sense of smell. Set your phone stopwatch, and do this exercise as s-l-o-w-l-y as you can, instead of ripping open the package and popping the whole candy in your mouth. Follow these general steps:

iStock.com/evemilla

- Leave what you're doing and take several deep breaths to clear your mind and focus.

- First, look at the candy wrapper more carefully than you ever have before. What color is it? What's its texture? What writing appears on it? What kind of font marks the brand? Be as thorough as possible in noticing everything about it. Bring the wrapped candy to your ear, and listen to the wrapper as you wriggle it. See if you can smell anything before you unwrap it.

- Now unwrap the mint. Smell it. Look at its surface. How is it shaped? Is the surface smooth, or are there dips and rough patches? Rub your fingers over both sides of the mint in order to find out.

- Take a small bite. Don't chew it; let the mint dissolve slowly in your mouth. Feel the smell of mint hit your sinuses. Enjoy the taste and texture of the chocolate and filling on the roof of your mouth and sides of your cheeks. Is it creamy and sweet? Is the mint taste strong or mild?

- Continue eating the mint very slowly, one small bite at a time, until you finish it.

You have just engaged in a mindful eating exercise. How long did it take you? What did it feel like? It may have been hard to resist popping the whole mint in your mouth, and you may have felt impatient, but you were fully focused on what you were doing—eating mindfully.

Now apply what you learned to other aspects of your life—times when slowing down might help you experience something more fully. What other areas of your life might improve by slowing down? If it involves another person, what might be the results? Try slowing down and focusing all your attention on one particular thing and report the results in class or online.

Source: Based on Mindful chocolate-eating in 5 easy steps. *headspace.com*. Retrieved from https://www.headspace.com/blog/2015/04/21/mindful-chocolate-eating-in-5-easy-steps/

Mat Hayward/Shutterstock.com

Mindfulness, you may be thinking, *WIIFM?* It sounds like a good idea, but so are lots of things. For example, *I should walk my dog regularly to get more exercise. I should take cooking lessons to broaden my diet beyond mac and cheese for dinner.* But how does mindfulness actually benefit people, and more specifically, how can it benefit me? To put it simply, if everyone else is "device-happy," constantly playing on their cell phones, and you're paying attention—now and on the job—you come out ahead. That's obvious, but let's look at some specific instances in which mindfulness can benefit you, both in your eventual career and now.

Steve Jobs, a strong believer in mindfulness and a regular meditator, used mindfulness to get Apple employees' creative juices flowing. Taking mindful moments allows people to see things as they *could* be—"stories of the future"—so that they can envision potential positive outcomes. "Pessimism narrows our focus, whereas positive emotions widen our attention and our receptiveness to the new and unexpected."[11] That's good for business!

So exactly how does mindfulness help you? Mindfulness reduces stress, lowers blood pressure, and improves your ability to monitor emotions. In the corporate world, mindfulness training has produced big-time results. Take Google and Twitter, for example, companies that have trained thousands of employees who don't just want to survive the workday and then feel better on the weekends. They want work-life balance and improved "soft skills," a better quality of life in both their work and home lives.[12] Google's mindfulness programs teach emotional intelligence, which helps people communicate better, increase their resilience, and improve mental focus. Participants say that mindfulness training has helped them be calmer, more patient, more skilled at handling their emotions, and better listeners.[13] Over one-quarter of Aetna's 50,000 employees have taken part in a company-sponsored mindfulness course. In addition to being better able to focus, employees reported that their stress levels dropped by 28 percent, their sleep quality improved 20 percent, and whatever pain they had been experiencing dropped by 19 percent.[14]

Okay, maybe benefits like these are for later, after you've launched your career. But what about now? What does all this have to do with you as a new college student? It may not be true for you, but research reports that today's college students are more distracted than ever.[15] (Perhaps everyone is.) It's hard to learn when your attention is splintered off in many different directions at once, and you're constantly being interrupted. However, there's mounting evidence that mindfulness doesn't just affect your attitude, it can literally change your brain: "Research has found that it [mindfulness] increases density of gray matter in brain regions linked to learning, memory, emotion regulation, and empathy." The trick, of course, is that to reap the genuine benefits of mindfulness, you actually have to practice it—regularly.[16] Most importantly, as a new college student, mindfulness can help you clear the deck for learning: "If your car [or in this case, your brain] is ready to go, you can leave faster than if you have to turn on the engine."[17]

> "If I can slow it down in my mind, things will be fine."
>
> **Aaron Rodgers,** *Green Bay Packers quarterback, attended Butte College, Oroville, California, and transferred to the University of California at Berkeley*

you need to, and noticing the world and people around you—not to mention living your life to the fullest, right now, in the present moment.

MINDSET: RECOGNIZING THE VALUE OF EFFORT

Successful people have several things in common: they love learning, look for challenges, value effort, and keep going even when things get tough.[18] They demonstrate both *ability* and *effort.* These two things are ingredients in any recipe for success.

Some people think ability is more important than effort, and when it comes to ability, they think that the bad news is: either you have it or you don't. Whoa! In fact, new students often worry about whether they're smart enough for college.[19] If you wonder about that from time to time, just realize that these self-doubts are normal—actually not only for college students but people in various stages of life. ("Am I smart enough for this new job?" "Will my co-workers figure out that I have no idea what I'm doing?")

But here's a new way of thinking about the question of ability versus effort. Take the notion of genius, for example. Experts used to think that a genius was someone born with extraordinary talent, like Mozart. From an early age, geniuses demonstrate exceptional natural abilities, they thought. But experts have changed their thinking: "What Mozart had, we now believe, was … the ability to focus for long periods of time. The key factor separating geniuses from the merely accomplished is not a divine spark.… It's deliberate practice. Top performers spend more hours (many more hours) rigorously practicing their craft."[20] A master violinist once said, "I practice the violin eight hours a day for 40 years, and they call me a genius?" Effort counts much more than you might think. Actor Will Smith, who's won a Grammy award and been nominated for an Oscar, obviously has ability. But he says this: "I've never viewed myself as particularly talented. Where I excel is ridiculous, sickening work ethic. I will not be outworked, period."[21]

That said, think about some of the possible combinations of ability and effort. If you have high ability and put forth great effort, you'll most likely succeed. If you have high ability and put forth only a little effort, and still succeed, you've just proved how smart you must be! But if you have high ability and put forth only a little effort and fail, you can always claim you didn't have the time to invest or you didn't really care, right? You can always say that you could have done well if you'd tried harder. Rationalizing like this can become a dangerous self-handicapping strategy, one that hurts you in the long run."[22]

Some college students actually don't work very hard in school, perhaps because they have no confidence in themselves or because they're afraid they'll fail, and then they rationalize when they don't do well. "See? I just proved that I'm not smart enough for college," they might say.

Research by Carol Dweck and her colleagues at Stanford shows that what you *believe* about your own intelligence—your *mindset*—can make a difference in how successful you'll actually be in college. At first glance this statement seems absurd. What does what you believe about intelligence have to do with how smart you really are? The scaled questions in Exercise 2.2 demonstrate

"When I was in grade school, they told me to write down what I wanted to be when I grew up. I wrote down happy. They told me I didn't understand the assignment. I told them they didn't understand life."

John Lennon, singer/ songwriter (1940–1980)

self-handicapping hurting your own chances to succeed

EXERCISE 2.2 **THEORIES OF INTELLIGENCE SCALE**

What is intelligence? Are people born with a certain amount? Or can it be cultivated through learning? Using the following scale, write in the number that corresponds to your opinion in the space next to each statement. There are no right or wrong answers.

1	2	3	4	5	6
Strongly Agree	Mostly Agree	Agree	Disagree	Mostly Disagree	Strongly Disagree

1. _____ You have a certain amount of intelligence, and you can't really do much to change it.

2. _____ You can learn new things, but you can't really change your basic intelligence.

3. _____ You can always substantially change how intelligent you are.

4. _____ No matter how much intelligence you have, you can always change it quite a bit.

"Don't tell me how talented you are. Tell me how hard you work."

Arthur Rubinstein, Polish-American pianist (1887–1982)

performer someone who is driven to appear smart

learner someone who is driven to learn, even by making mistakes

Don't think of it as failure. Think of it as time-released success.

Robert Orben, professional comedy writer and speechwriter

that there are two basic ways to define intelligence. Some of us are *performers*, who agree with statements 1 and 2, while others of us are *learners*, who agree more with statements 3 and 4. What did you find when you tried responding to these four short statements on your own?

The first two statements indicate the extent to which you see yourself as a *performer*. Performers believe that everyone is given a set amount of intelligence; it's fixed. You can't get any more; you're stuck with what you've got. The second two statements indicate that you believe in a growth mindset as a *learner*. Learners believe you can grow your intelligence if you take advantage of opportunities to learn. Whenever you tackle a tough challenge, you learn from it. Whenever you fail, you figure out how to improve from your mistakes. The more you learn, the more intelligent you can become. Understanding which view of intelligence you support (although the scale actually represents more of a continuum than an either-or choice) will make a difference in how you approach your college classes, as well as the outcomes—both positive and negative—that you'll achieve.

To *learners*, academic challenges are opportunities for growth; to *performers*, academic challenges are threats that might reveal their shortcomings. Performance is about measuring ability. In poker terms, it's "trying to convince yourself and others that you have a royal flush when you're secretly worried it's a pair of tens."[23] Learning is about investing the effort needed to grasp new things: "Why waste time proving over and over how great you are, when you could be getting better?"[24]

Sometimes students who are highly confident are *performers*. They've always been told they're smart, and they have an image to protect. When they come to a tough course, they may think, "If I have to work hard at this, I must not be very good at it." But if they believe they can develop their intelligence through learning, they have a very different view: "If I have to work hard at this, eventually I'll become *very* good at it." It's not the case that everyone is equally intelligent. That's not true, but people can boost their intelligence with effort and guidance. Think of college as an opportunity to build up the muscle called your brain, just like you'd bulk up your pecs at the gym. According to Dweck, just learning about the importance of mindset can make a difference. Truly grasping something challenging takes continued effort; performing can simply be going through the motivations. Learners are more likely to be self-motivated; performers love the "cheering of the crowd"—external approval. If you don't do well in a class, as Carol Dweck says, work on shifting your mindset. ("Are you doing well in your composition class?" If you aren't, instead of a pessimistic "no!" shift your mindset to "not yet," and keep working at it.) Mindset matters, perhaps more than you've ever even considered.

Let's admit it: We live in a performance-based society. Getting good grades is what it's all about, we're told. We all want to do well, look good, appear smart, and impress others. Did your previous schooling emphasize the performance mindset? Do you come from a family that overemphasizes grades? Is your family putting extra pressure on you because they never had the chance to go to college? Are you from an underrepresented population on campus and because of this you feel performance pressure to succeed?[25] That's normal, but your view of intelligence can be changed, and changing it may be your key to academic success. There is evidence that students who are taught the value of a *growth mindset* over a *fixed mindset* can actually achieve more than students who aren't.[26]

Of course, a growth mindset isn't just about effort, and it's not about any old effort. But it is about giving the best effort you can, expanding your set of effective strategies, and realizing you need to get help when you're stuck.[27]

Regardless of what you believe about your precise intelligence level, the fact is this: *Intelligence can be cultivated through learning. And people's beliefs about their intelligence can be shifted.* That's where the answer to the "Am I smart enough to be here?" question can be found. The real question is this: Can I grow my intelligence and give college my best effort?

MOTIVATION: WANTING TO LEARN

Let's get serious. When it comes right down to it, motivation is a huge factor in any type of success. In general, motivation is your drive to give something a go, even when the going gets rough. The word *motivation* comes from Medieval Latin, *motivus*, meaning moving. What *moves* you to learn?

There are many ways to define motivation, and different people are motivated by different things.

To get right to the point, whose job is it to motivate you in college? Your instructor's? Your parents'? This text's? Yours? *Can* anyone else besides you motivate you? This text will ask you: How motivated *are* you to succeed in college? And *how* are you motivated? To begin answering these questions, take a moment to fill out Exercise 2.3, Academic Intrinsic Motivation Self-Assessment now.

If your overall score on the AIMS in Exercise 2.3 was 100–125, you're intrinsically motivated at a high level. If you scored between 75 and 99, you're intrinsically motivated at a moderate level, but increasing your intrinsic motivation may help you achieve more. If you scored below 75, a lack of intrinsic motivation could interfere with your college success. If your score is below 75, you may need a reality check about why you're in college in the first place, or at the very least, a bit of an attitude adjustment. But here's another thing to remember: Motivation is something you can grow and develop *while* you're in college. You needn't have everything figured out up front; you just have to be willing to stick with it.[28]

When it comes to success in college, it's important to understand the difference between *extrinsic* and *intrinsic* motivation.[29] Students who are extrinsically, or externally, motivated learn in order to get a grade, earn credits, or complete a requirement, for example. They are motivated by things outside themselves, including other people, like parents, who insist they go to college no matter what.

People who are intrinsically, or internally, motivated learn because they're curious, fascinated, challenged, or because they truly want to grasp a subject. They are motivated from within. Let's be realistic, however. Extrinsic motivation is real and important. You need a particular number of credit hours to earn an associate's degree. You'd rather get As than Fs. But how intrinsically motivated you are in college will have a great deal to do with just how successful you are. The motivation to become truly educated must come from within you.

> Ability is what you're capable of doing. Motivation determines what you do. Attitude determines how well you do it.
>
> *Lou Holtz, former college football coach and ESPN sports analyst*

extrinsically outside yourself

intrinsically inside yourself

ACADEMIC INTRINSIC MOTIVATION SELF-ASSESSMENT

How intrinsically motivated are you? Read each of the following statements and select the number beside each statement that most accurately represents your views about yourself.

	Completely Not True	Somewhat Not True	Neutral	Somewhat True	Completely True
1. I have academic goals.	1	2	3	(4)	5
2. I am confident I can complete my degree.	1	2	3	4	(5)
3. I determine my career goals.	1	2	3	4	(5)
4. I enjoy solving challenging, difficult problems.	1	2	3	(4)	5
5. I work on an assignment until I understand it.	1	2	3	(4)	5
6. I am confident I will finish a degree or certificate.	1	2	3	4	(5)
7. I determine the quality of my academic work.	1	2	3	4	(5)
8. I am pursuing college because I value education.	1	2	3	(4)	5
9. I feel good knowing that I determine how my academic career develops.	1	2	3	4	(5)
10. I have high standards for academic work.	1	2	3	4	(5)
11. Staying in college is my decision.	1	2	3	(4)	5
12. I study because I like to learn new things.	1	2	3	(4)	5
13. I enjoy doing outside readings in connection to my future coursework.	1	2	3	(4)	5
14. I am intrigued by the different topics introduced in my courses.	1	2	3	(4)	5
15. I study because I am curious.	1	2	3	(4)	5
16. I look forward to going to class.	1	2	3	(4)	5
17. I am excited to take more courses within my major.	1	2	3	4	(5)
18. I enjoy learning more within my field of study.	1	2	3	4	(5)
19. I like to find answers to questions about material I am learning.	1	2	3	(4)	5

	Completely Not True	Somewhat Not True	Neutral	Somewhat True	Completely True
20. I enjoy studying.	1	2	③	4	5
21. I have pictured myself in a career after college.	1	2	3	4	⑤
22. I am excited about the job opportunities I will have later.	1	2	3	④	5
23. I have pictured myself being successful in my chosen career.	1	2	3	4	⑤
24. I believe I will make a substantial contribution to my chosen profession.	1	2	3	4	⑤
25. I feel good knowing I will be a member of the professional community in my area of study.	1	2	3	4	⑤

Total each column, then add your scores across.

____0____ + ____0____ + ____3____ + ____48____ + ____60____ =

_III_____ OVERALL SCORE

Source: French, B. F., & Oakes, W. (2003). Measuring academic intrinsic motivation in the first year of college: Reliability and validity evidence for a new instrument. *Journal of the First Year Experience, 15(1)*, 83–102.

Look at Figure 2.1 and select the three boxes (and only three) that most accurately describe your overall current motivation to attend college. When you think about why you're in college, are you generally on the extrinsic side or

Extrinsic Motivation

Grades · Credits · Pay · Parents

Intrinsic Motivation

Curiosity · Mastery · Fascination · Challenge

FIGURE 2.1

Extrinsic versus Intrinsic Motivation

the intrinsic side—or both? Your instructor may wish to generate a discussion about these questions in class or online.

You completed the Academic Intrinsic Motivation Scale (AIMS) in Exercise 2.3, which is designed to measure your intrinsic, or internal, motivation to succeed in college in terms of four C-Factors. You'll see that these C-Factors are built into *FOCUS* to boost your intrinsic motivation:

CURIOSITY Read cutting-edge mini-articles that are related to college success. These short pieces may make you curious to read more somewhere else.

CONTROL Apply what you are learning to a challenging task this term. It may help with your toughest class, a challenging part of your job outside school, or some other difficult situation.

CAREER OUTLOOK Check out highly useful career advice you can start putting into practice now and carry with you into your new career after college. As you read these short articles, think about how they may apply to your future, and ask yourself whether you have the interest and motivation required to start using some of these techniques now. As Yogi Berra supposedly once said, "In theory there is no difference between theory and practice. In practice there is." It's time to start practicing for your career now!

CHALLENGE Think about whether your college coursework challenges you appropriately. Too much challenge can cause you to become frustrated and give up. Not enough challenge can cause you to lose interest.[30]

Adjusting the level of challenge to one that's right for you is key to keeping yourself motivated to learn, and that's up to you. No one else. Test the level of challenge by working through the Reality Check questions at the end of the *FOCUS* chapters and seeing how well you do.

THE BOTTOM LINE: SELF-MOTIVATION WORKS BEST

Imagine this: Two students volunteer to take part in an experiment: Student A and Student B. Both are tasked with learning some new material in fifteen minutes. Student A reads and rereads the material until it's virtually memorized. Student B tries to figure out what the material means by looking for patterns, connections, and themes. Both students use their fifteen minutes, but Student B totally outscores Student A on a test that follows. Why? Student B was motivated to actually learn the material; Student A was motivated to get through the experiment. Even though you could say that the two students came to the task with roughly the same *amount* of motivation, the *type* of motivation they each had was very different. To better understand motivation, think about these two factors—amount and type.[31]

Think, too, about these three additional factors that explain how and why people are motivated—autonomy (Is it *your* idea?), value (Is it *worth* it?), and competence (Do you have *what it takes*?).[32] Let's take a look at what these terms mean, especially as they relate to you as a college student.

AUTONOMY ["Is it something I want to do?"] When all is said and done, the kind of motivation that gets the best from you has to *come from you*. Remember this old fable? If you want your stubborn donkey to move, you can do one of

"People often say that motivation doesn't last. Well, neither does bathing—that's why we recommend it daily."

Zig Ziglar, American motivational speaker and author

two things: dangle a *carrot* in front of him or beat his back side with a *stick*. Heads or tails. These two options relate to positive or negative reinforcement, and the donkey will usually move either way.

Now think about that analogy in terms of human beings. Your parents agree to pay double tuition for any course in which you earn an "A" (a "carrot" approach) or refuse to pay for any course in which you earn lower than a "B" (a "stick" approach). You might be motivated by either of these two strategies, but, typically, the motivation would be short-lived in the first case and stressful in the second. Autonomy means asking: Can I generate the energy required for action on my own? If *you* are motivated to do something, you're eager and energetic. If someone else wants you to do something, especially something you really don't particularly care about, you're bothered and bored. The truth is, the best motivation for doing excellent work in college must come from you. To the extent you're able, choose assignments that fire you up or a major in which you have real interest.[33] If you don't know what that is yet, be on the lookout. You'll find it.

"There's more to motivation than carrots and sticks."

Anonymous

VALUE ["Is it worth it to me?"] It's much easier to motivate yourself if you think whatever you need to do is worthwhile. Picture two men. Both are picking up bits of paper along a highway. One is doing community service after getting a DUI; the other is looking for a winning lottery ticket that blew out of the car window. The difference in value is probably obvious, especially to them.

In college, you may think to yourself, *What? An essay every week?* Interestingly, we don't respond the same way to other stiff requirements, *What? Three meals every day?* The difference, of course, is that food is vital; essays aren't, or so we seem to think. If you didn't eat for four weeks, you might die. If you didn't write essays for four weeks, you'd have more time for flag football. But essays are, in fact, essential for several reasons: they give us an opportunity to reflect and record what we think. They give us practice in a life skill that—believe it or not—may make or break our careers. But the value is s-t-r-e-t-c-h-e-d out. In college, your instructors will value everything they ask you to read or write about. They'll value every class or online session; otherwise, they wouldn't include these things in the course. You, on the other hand, may have to search for value or focus on recognizing it.

Make a list of all the reasons college assignments are important. Convince yourself to look for the value in every individual course, and remind yourself continually of the long-term value of your overall college degree. It's your future, after all, and you want to be ready for it.

COMPETENCE ["Can I do it well—or learn to?"] It's easier to find motivation when you think you're good at something than when you think you aren't. Picture this ridiculous example: you challenge yourself to swim the English Channel when you can barely dog paddle. But if you've put in countless hours refining your swimming skills and you've developed confidence based on that hard work, you might just give it (or something like it) a go. The same thing is true in college. The more you work to develop your math skills, the better you get at doing math, and the more motivated you are to keep getting better. In your introductory courses, commit to working hard, so that when the challenges really hit later, you've already developed the abilities you need to do well.

life hack #2

When you're feeling overloaded, try this micro-meditation strategy. Just S.T.O.P. Here's what it stands for: (STOP)
S (Hit the pause button).
T (Take a few deep breaths to regain your composure.)
O (Observe what's going on with your body, mind, and emotions).
P (Proceed with what you were doing, now with some insight about what you should do next).[34]

FIGURE 2.2

Quick Study: How to Focus When It's Next to Impossible

How to Focus
When It's Next to Impossible

← Most people struggle to focus these days →

Bring healthy food.
Keeping your blood sugar at a good level helps you focus.

Put your phone in another room.
You can still hear an emergency call, but you won't be tempted by apps.

Be ergonomically correct.
Back and neck pain can be distracting. Google what's best for your posture.

Make a list and check off items.
This is an easy way to get a real sense of accomplishment.

Time yourself.
When the timer bings, you get a buzz!

Turn it off if you don't need it.
You may think music helps you study, but if it makes you want to sing along or get up and dance, it's more likely a distraction.

Declutter your desk.
Mess can cause stress.

Use headphones to block out noise.
Putting on white noise may help you zero in.

Finish History Paper by Wednesday at 6:00 PM.

Frame your goal
and look at it often.

Bring your pet along.
Their devoted attention can help you focus yours.

Reward yourself.
Go to a movie, have a friend over— do something to celebrate success.

Yay!

GIVE YOURSELF AN
ATTITUDE ADJUSTMENT

There's a difference of opinion on the subject of attitude. Some people say attitude is not all that important. Attitude-schmattitude, they say. Others say that *attitude* is more important than aptitude. What do you think?

In research studies conducted by Rick Snyder at the University of Kansas, students who scored high on a measure of hope got higher grades. Snyder explained that students with high hopes set themselves higher goals and know how to work hard to attain them.

Quick quiz. How many times a day do you catch yourself saying "Whatever . . .," and rolling your eyes? Whatever-ness—an attitude of boredom and impatience—takes a lot less effort than staying positive. Whether you realize it or not, whatevers chip away at your motivation, and they can cause you to give up on your dreams and goals. When it comes to your college education, one good thing you can do for yourself is to delete the word *whatever* from your vocabulary. Your education is much too important for whatevers—and so are you.

"You must motivate yourself EVERY DAY!"

Matthew Stasior, motivational speaker

FIVE WAYS TO ADJUST YOUR ATTITUDE

The good thing about attitude is that you can change it yourself. As you think about benefits of fine-tuning your attitude, keep these five recommendations in mind:

1. **Know that you always have choices.** Regardless of circumstances—your income, your background, or your academic experiences—you always have a choice, even if it's limited to how you choose to view your current situation.

2. **Take responsibility for your own outcomes.** Coach Vince Lombardi used to have his players look in a mirror before every game and ask themselves, "Am I looking at the person who is helping me win or the one who is holding me back?" Blaming others simply diminishes your own power to work toward constructive responses to challenges.

3. **Turn down your negativity meter.** "Can't" and "won't" are two of the biggest obstacles to a healthy attitude. Also pay attention to how you describe things. Is the cup half empty or half full? State things in the positive rather than the negative (for example, "stay healthy" rather than "don't get sick"). Paying attention to positive role models whose traits you admire is also a great way to boost your outlook.

EXERCISE 2.4 **THE IDEAL STUDENT**

Create your own personal top-ten list of the characteristics (attitudes and actions) of an ideal student. Bring your completed list to your next class session so that all students can read their lists and create a master list that everyone can agree on. Put your initials next to each of the ten items on the master list that you promise to do throughout the term. Your personal top-ten list, which your instructor may discuss with you individually at a later time, will become your own list of goals for the course.

4. **Turn learning points into turning points.** Have you ever watched someone do something so badly that you've said to yourself, "I'm never going to do that! I'm going to do it differently!"? You can also choose to learn from your own mistakes and setbacks. They all offer some sort of lesson, even if it takes a bit of distance from the event to see what you can learn.

5. **Acknowledge your blessings.** Taking time at the end of each day to recognize and feel gratitude for the blessings in your life—no matter how large or small—is a great way to develop a positive attitude.

WHAT DRIVES YOU?
VALUES, DREAMS, AND GOALS

value something you think is important

goals something you make specific plans to achieve

dreams something you wish for

The "Three Ms" of College Success lead right back to our opening questions in this chapter: Who are you? And what do you want? Other questions to explore are: What do you value? What are your goals? Where will your dreams take you?

VALUES AT THE CORE

What do you value in life? By taking time to examine your personal values, managing your life will become easier and make more sense. Values can be things you can't exactly see or touch, like love or respect, or things that are visible and real, like family or money. Understanding how they motivate you isn't as simple as it might seem. Values can change as you go through life. For example, if you're single now, you may value the freedom to meet a variety of potential romantic partners. Later, however, you may want a committed relationship because you want stability in your life. For this reason, it's important to look at your values from time to time and rethink them.

Another complicating factor is that values can conflict with one another. Suppose that you value honesty and kindness, and you are at a party and a friend asks you what you think of her new hair color. You honestly think it's hideous, but telling her so would hurt her feelings, thus violating your value of being kind. How do you respond? That would depend on which value is a

"You are never given a wish without the power to make it come true. You may have to work for it, however."

Richard Bach, from Illusions

What are your core values? What's most important to you—deep down inside? Review the following list and mark the items that you value. Don't spend too much time thinking about each one; just go with your initial gut reaction. For each item, ask yourself, "Is this something that's important to me?"

_____ Health	_____ Physical Appearance	_____ Financial wealth
_____ Fitness/Physical strength	_____ Independence	_____ Commitment
_____ Loyalty	_____ Honesty	_____ Compassion
_____ Academic achievement	_____ Children	_____ Leisure time
_____ Success	_____ Leadership	_____ Balance
_____ Happiness	_____ Family	_____ Friendship
_____ Social life	_____ Marriage/Partnership	_____ Recognition
_____ Athletics	_____ Spirituality	_____ Status
_____ Creativity	_____ Variety	_____ Wisdom
_____ Meaningful work	_____ Challenge	_____ Time spent alone
_____ Adventure	_____ Personal growth	_____ Other (list here)

Now review all of the items you marked, and select the five that are most important to you at this point in your life, ranking them with number one as your top priority.

Top Five Values

1. _____
2. _____
3. _____
4. _____
5. _____

Finally, take stock. Is this the person you want to be? Is there anything about your values that you would like to change? If so, what's keeping you from making this change?

higher priority for you. You have to make an on-the-spot decision about which value to use. Once you define your values, however, they can help you make everyday choices as well as big decisions, like which major to pursue in college. For example, if academic achievement is one of your top values, the next time you have the urge to cut class, consider what that choice says about your value system. There is a great inner satisfaction that comes from living a life tied to core values.

DREAMS VERSUS GOALS

Do you agree or disagree with this statement: "I can be anything I want to be"? You've probably heard this statement frequently. Your family and teachers all want you to have positive self-esteem, and certainly there are many career options available today. But is it true? Can you be *anything* you want to be? What's the difference between a dream and a goal?

As a student, you may dream of being a famous doctor or a famous athlete or just plain famous. That's the beauty of dreams—you can imagine yourself doing anything. When you're dreaming, you don't even have to play by the rules of reality. Dreams are fantasy-based—*you* in a perfect world. But when it's time to come back to reality, you discover that there are rules, after all. You may have dreamed of becoming a top-earning NBA player or a top fashion model when

Philipp Schmidli/Getty Images Entertainment/Getty Images

"Self-knowledge is far more important than self-confidence."

Simon Cowell, *judge from* American Idol, America's Got Talent, *and* The X Factor, *and author of* I Don't Mean to Be Rude, But . . .

What drives you? Values, dreams, and goals   **49**

Flying Colours Ltd/Getty Images

"What you get by achieving your goals is not as important as what you become by achieving your goals."

Zig Ziglar, motivational speaker, writer, and trainer

you were a child, but you have grown up to be the same height as Uncle Al or Aunt Sue—and that's not tall enough.

Dreams alone are not enough when it comes to creating your future. As professional life coach Diana Robinson says, "A dream is a goal without legs." And without legs, that goal is going nowhere. Dreaming is the first step to creating the future you want, but making dreams come true requires planning and hard work. Sylvia Sanchez wanted to become a famous singer because she likes music people always told her she was good. As she continues through college, however, she will come to understand herself better. The music industry might be challenging to break into, but that doesn't mean she should abandon her dream. She must find a realistic way to help her turn her dreams into goals. Just dreaming isn't enough. Dreams are exciting; you can let your imagination run wild. Goals are real; you must work out how to actually achieve your dreams.

Goal setting is an important part of the life management skills this text will help you develop. Your goals may not seem at all clear to you right now, but the important thing is to learn that there's a right way and a wrong way to set your goals. The best way to ensure that the goals you set will serve you well is to make sure you *FOCUS*. Here's a brief overview of what that means.

F Fit. Your goal must fit your values, your character, and who you are as a person. Goals that conflict with any of these things will not only be difficult to accomplish, but they just won't work. If your goal is to become a writer for a travel magazine because you love adventure, but flying in planes terrifies you, you're in trouble.

O Ownership. Own your goal: See it, taste it, want it! It must be your goal, not someone else's goal for you. Ask yourself: Does the thought of achieving this goal get me fired up? Do I genuinely own this goal or do I feel I ought to have this goal because it sounds good or makes someone else happy?

C Concreteness. For any goal to be effective, it must be real. In other words, you must be able to describe your goal in detail: "To run a mile in less than six minutes by March 4th" is much more concrete than "to eventually run faster." The more concrete, the better.

U Usefulness. Goals must be useful. They must serve a purpose, and that purpose should be tied to your long-term vision of the person you want to become. For example, if you want to work for an international hotel some day, it would be useful to begin studying a foreign language now.

S Stretch. In the business world, people talk about stretch goals. These are goals that require employees to stretch beyond their usual limits to achieve something more challenging. Goals must be based in reality, but also offer you a chance to grow beyond the person you currently are.

Your goals should include both short- and long-term goals. Once your long-term goals are set (though they may shift over time as *you* shift over time), you will then want to set some short-term goals, which act as in-between steps to achieving your long-term goals.

LONG-TERM GOALS WHAT DO I WANT TO ACCOMPLISH...	SHORT-TERM GOALS WHAT DO I WANT TO ACCOMPLISH...
In my lifetime?	This year?
In the next twenty years?	This month?
In the next ten years?	This week?
In the next three to five years?	Today?

HOW *FOCUS* WILL HELP:
SPENDING TIME "IN THE SYSTEM"

Spending time "in the system"? No, being in college isn't like being in jail—far from it. "The system" is the approach used in this text to help you learn: the Challenge → Reaction → Insight → Action system. It is based on the work of Dr. John Bransford and his colleagues, who together wrote an influential book called *How People Learn*.

Bransford believes learning is a chain reaction that might look something like this:

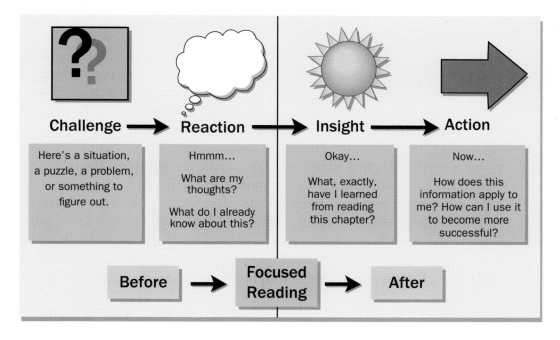

FIGURE 2.3

CRIA System: How People Learn
Source: Based on J. Bransford, et al. (2000). *How People Learn: Brain, Mind, Experience, and School*. Washington, DC: National Academy Press.

This Challenge → Reaction → Insight → Action learning chain reaction is integrated into *FOCUS* to help you learn. Each chapter takes you through "the system" by walking you through four activities:

Challenge

Whenever you're learning something new, the best place to start is by identifying what you think you already know. For example, each chapter's "Readiness Check" will ask you how this chapter will relate to you and how you'll relate to it. Then you'll continue by reading a case study about a new college student who's facing problems related to the topics in the chapter. Research shows that people generally learn more from examples of things going wrong than they can from examples of things going right. The challenges are real ones many students face. Perhaps you (or a classmate you know) are facing similar issues yourself. Read the case studies carefully and think about solutions that would help these students—before you read the chapter's content. Every chapter begins with a challenge as the first step of the learning chain reaction.

deep learner someone who learns everything they can about a topic

take stock evaluate your progress

"Surround yourself with people who take their work seriously, but not themselves, those who work hard and play hard."

Colin Powell, former U.S. secretary of state

Reaction

After you read the case study, you are asked for your reaction by answering a few questions about it. What is the student in the case study doing wrong or right? What should the student do differently? Your instructor may ask you to discuss your reaction in class or answer the questions in writing. This step of the learning process shows you how much you already know—before you begin reading. It also shows you what you don't know and what you can learn by reading. The goal of this text is help you become a deep learner, as opposed to someone who skims the surface and simply rushes on to the next assignment and the next course. It will ask you to pause, take stock, focus, and think.

Insight

At the end of each chapter, you'll be asked to revisit some of the questions you were asked in the chapter's opening Reaction. Rethinking your responses to the Challenge case will help you gauge how much you've learned. For example, Sylvia Sanchez dreamed of becoming a famous singer, a dream that could have become reality if things fell into place for her. But after reading about it in the chapter, you might decide that you really hadn't thought about it very deeply and there's more to it than you originally thought. The difference between Reaction (your immediate reaction) and Insight (the new insights you've gained from reading) demonstrate that you've learned! After reading the chapter and discussing it with your class, you'll know some research on the subject, the chapter's suggestions, examples you can apply, and your instructor's thoughts about how the case study student handled the challenges. You'll also gain some insights about yourself, if you face any of these issues, too.

Action

The final activity in this learning chain reaction is about action. What have you learned that will change how you face similar challenges? Learning takes place when it relates to you personally, and insights have no impact unless they lead to change. The bottom line is: You must use your insights to take action. Think of this comparison. One day you feel tired, you notice that your clothes are tight, and you are suddenly aware that you're out of shape. You realize that you must eat healthier food and exercise more. But if you don't take action, it won't happen. To become real, new knowledge must lead to personal insights that result in action. What you learned by reading relates to you, and you must use it!

If you follow the system built into this text and use it as you read for all your classes, the learning chain reaction will become automatic for you.

"I am larger, better than I thought, I did not know I held so much goodness."

Walt Whitman, *American poet (1819–1892)*

As a nineteen-year-old college student, Amy Cuddy woke up in a hospital bed, surrounded by cards and flowers. She later learned that while she and her college friends were driving overnight to get back to campus in Boulder, Colorado, she was thrown out of the car during a horrific accident. The front right side of Amy Cuddy's brain slammed into the highway, and she suffered a traumatic brain injury. She awoke a different person. Always known for being smart, she was told by doctors that her IQ had dropped by 30 points, and that college would not be a part of her future. *You'll have to find something else to do*, they said, because (in essence), you're not smart anymore.[36] Imagine what a shock that must have been!

Amy did finish college, though. It took guts and perseverance, and it also took her longer than it did her former classmates. Eventually, she earned graduate degrees and began a career in higher education, entering the job market in 2004, even though she "felt like a fraud." Amy was worried that others would discover that she wasn't smart enough. Dr. Cuddy, now a professor at Harvard Business School, tells her story in a TED Talk, which has become one of the most-watched TED Talks of all time.

Now in her book, *Presence: Bringing Your Boldest Self to Your Biggest Challenges*, Professor Cuddy writes about having people in research studies assume confident "power poses" right before challenging situations. When people feel powerful, their bodies expand so that they take up more space. When they feel powerless, they "shrink," almost as if trying to become invisible. See the difference?

Amy Cuddy's book asks "How can we be our strongest selves in life's most challenging situations? We often approach these situations—job interviews, difficult conversations, speaking up for ourselves—with anxiety and leave them with regret."[37] But we don't have to. Presence, as she calls it—part confidence, part comfort level and part enthusiasm—is something we can cultivate.

Cuddy says our minds control our bodies, which most of us already realize, so we know that to some extent, emotions control behavior. When we're feeling depressed, our shoulders droop and we hang our heads. When we're feeling victorious, we raise our arms above our heads and make a "V." But, can the opposite be true? Can assuming the power poses first make us actually feel more powerful? Her research says yes. Our *bodies* can control our *minds*. We can actually *become* more powerful by displaying powerful body language. If an important job interview is coming up, for example, go somewhere private (like the rest room) and assume an expansive "power pose" (like Wonder Woman's) for two minutes beforehand. In her research, people who assume power poses in private before stressful or nerve-wracking events are much more confident and successful. Their bodies have changed their minds.

Amy Cuddy's recommendation to anyone in college who sometimes feels like a fake ("Am I smart enough?") isn't just the standard suggestion, "fake it 'til you make it." Her advice is, "fake it until you *become* it." It's almost as if she's saying, "If I did it, you can, too!" Our bodies can convince our minds to not only display, but to *achieve* and *own*, the presence needed for success.

iStock.com/g-stockstudio

iStock.com/4x6

iStock.com/wickedpix

At the beginning of this chapter, Sylvia Sanchez faced a series of challenges as a new college student. Now after learning from this chapter, would you respond differently to any of the questions you answered about the "FOCUS Challenge Case"? Using what you learned in the chapter, write a paragraph ending to Sylvia's case study. What are some of the possible outcomes for her?

1. Identify one new thing you learned in reading this chapter. Why did you select the one you've selected? How will it affect what you do in your college classes?

2. Do you have some of the same questions Sylvia does about your own level of motivation to achieve in college? How could you increase your motivation? How important might that be?

3. How do your own goals and dreams differ? How do you plan to turn your dreams into goals?

CHALLENGE: REALITY CHECK

How much did you learn? At the beginning of this chapter, you filled out a "Readiness Check" that asked how you thought this chapter would relate to you, and how you would relate to it. Now, fill out this "Reality Check" to find out.

1. How do people learn?

2. What is the difference between intrinsic and extrinsic motivation?

3. What's the difference between being a learner and being a performer?

4. How are dreams and goals different?

5. How long did it take? _____ hours _____ minutes. Before you began this chapter, you were asked to predict how long it would take you to complete it (total time, even if you read it in more than one sitting). Was your estimate on target, or will you revise it for the next chapter you'll read? _____

LEARNING STYLES AND STUDYING | 3

READINESS CHECK

HOW THIS CHAPTER RELATES TO YOU

1. When it comes to learning and studying in college, what are you most unsure about, if anything? Put check marks by the phrases that apply to you or write in your answer.

   ☐ Whether I can find enough time
   ☐ Whether I really know how
   ☐ How I learn best
   ☐ How to study different subjects
   ☐ How to make myself study when I don't want to
   ☐ _____

2. What is most likely to be your response? Put a check mark by it.

   ☐ I'll ask my instructors for suggestions.
   ☐ I'll ask my classmates what they do.
   ☐ I'll see how things go and adjust.
   ☐ I'll probably just figure it out somehow.

3. What would you have to do to increase your likelihood of success? Will you do it this quarter or semester?

HOW YOU WILL RELATE TO THIS CHAPTER

1. What are you most interested in learning about? Put check marks by those topics.

   ☐ How learning changes your brain
   ☐ How people are intelligent in different ways
   ☐ How you learn through your senses
   ☐ How your personality type can affect your learning style
   ☐ What metacognition is and how it can help you
   ☐ How to apply your learning style to your study style
   ☐ How to become an intentional learner and make a master study plan

YOUR READINESS FACTOR

1. How motivated are you to learn more about learning styles and studying in college? (5 = high, 1 = low)

2. How ready are you to read now? (If something is in your way, take care of it if you can. Zero in and focus.)

3. How long do you think it will take you to complete this chapter? If you start and stop, keep track of your overall time. _____ Hour(s) _____ Minute(s)

Darren Baker/Shutterstock.com

TAMMY KO

As she walked out of her "Introduction to Criminology" class, she texted her new boyfriend Sam, who had taken the course with Professor Caldwell the previous term. "I can't believe that guy," she wrote. "I know he's smart, but why does he have to make the class so hard?" It was obvious to Sam that Tammy and their professor lived in different worlds. Hers was filled with people and excitement. His was filled with dull PowerPoint slides and complex theories in books.

Tammy was a first-semester student at a large community college an hour from her tiny hometown, where she'd been a popular high school student. If you went through her high school yearbook, you'd see Tammy's picture everywhere. There Tammy had been a big fish in a small pond, but now it was the other way around.

Even though she found college life at the large community college somewhat overwhelming, Tammy was excited about her major, forensic chemistry. The crime shows on TV were her favorites. She watched them all each week, and now she had Sam hooked on some of them, too. She rationalized how much time it took by thinking of it as career development. The fun was picturing herself as an investigator

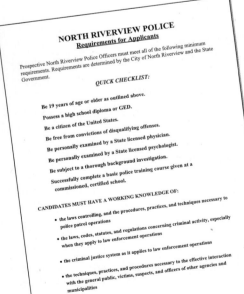

solving headline cases: "Man Slain, Found in City Park" or "Modern Day 'Jack the Ripper' Terrorizes Las Vegas." She could envision herself hunched over laboratory equipment, testing intently for fibers or DNA, and actually breaking the case.

When she registered for classes, her academic advisor had told her that taking an "Introduction to Criminology" course from the sociology department would be a good idea. "It'll teach you how to think," he'd said, "and it'll give you the background you need to understand the criminal mind. At the end of this class," he said, "you'll know if you really want to pursue a career in forensics." *Maybe it would teach me how to think,* Tammy thought to herself now that the term was underway, *if only I could understand the professor. Forget understanding the criminal mind—I'd just like a glimpse into his!* Most of the time, Sam agreed with her just to keep the peace although Sam always aced everything.

Professor Caldwell was quiet and reserved, and he seemed a bit out of touch. He dressed as if the word "jeans" wasn't in his vocabulary. In class, he was very articulate, knowledgeable, and organized with his handouts neatly piled on the desk, and he covered each day's material methodically point by point. Tammy wished

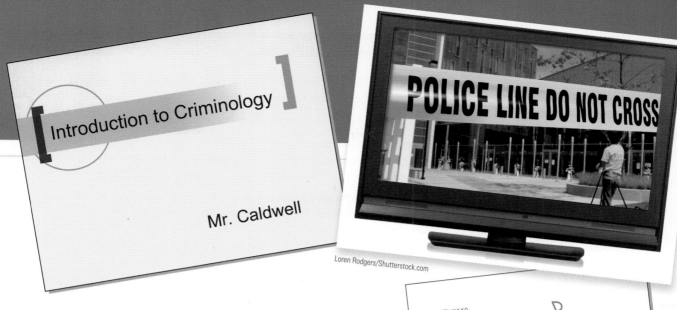

Introduction to Criminology

Mr. Caldwell

POLICE LINE DO NOT CROSS

Loren Rodgers/Shutterstock.com

Name: TAMMY KO

ESSAY TEST
INTRO TO CRIMINOLOGY
Mr. CALDWELL

65% D

QUESTION: COMPARE AND CONTRAST TWO THEORIES OF CRIMINOLOGY DISCUSSED IN CLASS THUS FAR

Classical Theory was first developed by Cesar Beccaria in the X century. Classical theory says that people engage in a social deal. They must balance between freedom and happiness. Classical theory also describes special and general deterrence. General deterrence is punishing a person for a crime. Special deterrence is making examples of people so that others don't do the same thing. Neoclassical theory was developed in the X century and includes the concepts of free will and penitentiaries. These systems are the basis for the US Government system of justice. The positivist approach includes the ideas of free will and determinism. It says that there is a fundamental difference between criminals and non-criminals. It also says that there are many factors that contribute to crime. The positivist approach also suggests that there is subjectivity in social science. In other words social science is based on the viewpoint of each individual. NO specific facts or data. Finally the biological theories suggest that criminals are biologically superior to non-criminals.

he'd leave his notes occasionally to explore fascinating, related tangents. Tammy had always preferred teachers who created exciting things to do in class over teachers who went completely by the book.

Tammy's biggest complaint about Professor Caldwell was that he only talked about *theories* of criminology. When was he ever going to get to the hands-on part of the course? She couldn't help thinking, *When will we stop talking about theories and start working on real cases—like the ones on all those TV shows?*

To make matters worse, learning from lectures was not Tammy's strong suit. She hadn't done well on the first exam because she'd had to resort to memorizing things that didn't make much sense to her, and her D grade showed it. The exam consisted of one question: "Compare and contrast two theories of criminology discussed in class thus far." Tammy hated essay tests. She was at her best on tests with right or wrong answers, like true-false or multiple-choice questions. Making sense out of spoken words that go by very quickly during a lecture and trying to psych out professors' preferred answers on essay tests were challenges to her.

But her "Introduction to Criminology" class was far from hands-on. In fact, Tammy had noticed that many of her teachers preferred talking about things to doing things. They seemed to take more interest in theories than in the real world. *Too bad*, she thought. *The real world is where exciting things happen*. Although she hated to admit it, sometimes Tammy couldn't wait for her college career to be over so that she could begin her real career.

A few of Tammy's friends from her other courses had taken Professor Caldwell's classes, too. "Just try and memorize the stuff; that's all you can do," they'd advised her. Regardless of what they happened to be talking about, somehow the conversation always came around to stress, Professor Caldwell, and how impossible it was to learn in his classes.

1. Do you have anything in common with Tammy? If so, how are you managing the situation so that you can be successful?

2. Is Tammy smart? If so, in what ways? What is she particularly good at?

3. What sensory modality does Tammy prefer for taking in information? Does she learn best by viewing information through charts and graphs, for example, or by talking and listening, by reading and writing, or by actually doing things?

4. Tammy says straightforwardly that she doesn't know how to study and dislikes doing it. In your view, what, specifically, should she do to succeed, not only in this class but also in college?

GO TO THE HEAD OF THE CLASS:
LEARNING AND THE BRAIN

EXERCISE 3.1   **WHAT IS LEARNING?**

The following statements represent common student views on learning. Think about each statement, and mark it true or false based on your honest opinion.

1. _____ Learning is often hard work and really not all that enjoyable.

2. _____ Memorization and learning are basically the same thing.

3. _____ The learning done in school is often gone in a few weeks or months.

4. _____ In college, most learning takes place in class.

5. _____ Learning is usually the result of listening to an instructor lecture or reading a textbook.

6. _____ The best way to learn is by working alone.

7. _____ Most students know intuitively how they learn best.

8. _____ Teachers control what students learn.

9. _____ Learning only deals with subjects taught in school.

10. _____ The learning pace is controlled by the slowest learner in the class.

You probably noticed that many of these statements attempt to put learning in a negative light. How many did you mark true? This chapter will help you understand more about learning as a process and about yourself as a learner. As you read, your goal should be to use the insights you gain to become a better learner.

In one of his most famous plays, Shakespeare wrote, "O this learning. What a thing it is!" He was right. The fact that human beings can learn throughout their lives is an amazing characteristic. We learn language, numbers, and concepts right from the very start, and we keep learning until we draw our last breaths. But how do we do it, and more specific to this chapter, how do we learn at our best? In this chapter, you'll learn a great deal about yourself and your learning preferences, and you'll discover new ways to study so that you can learn more productively and efficiently. That kind of knowledge can definitely give you an advantage!

Let's start our exploration of the learning process close to home—in our own heads. What's going on up there, anyway? While your hands are busy manipulating test tubes in chemistry lab or your eyes are watching your psychology instructor's PowerPoint presentation, what's your brain up to? The answer? Plenty.

USE IT OR LOSE IT

The human brain consists of a complex web of connections between neurons or nerve cells. This web grows in complexity as it incorporates new knowledge. But if the connections are not reinforced frequently, you lose them. As you learn new things, you work to hardwire these connections, making them less likely to deteriorate. When your instructors repeat portions of the previous week's lecture or assign homework so you can practice material covered in class, they're helping you to form connections in your brain by using and reusing them—or, in other words, helping you to learn. Repetition is vital to learning. You must use and reuse information in order to hardwire it.

American humorist Will Rogers once said, "You know, you've got to exercise your *brain* just like your muscles." He was right. Giving your brain the exercise it needs—now and in your years after college—will help you form connections between neurons that, if you keep using them, will last a lifetime. From a biological point of view, that's what being a lifelong learner means. The age-old advice "use it or lose it" is true when it comes to learning.

ASK QUESTIONS AND HARDWIRE YOUR CONNECTIONS

Your instructors have been studying their disciplines for years, perhaps decades. They have developed extensive hardwired connections between their brain neurons. They are *experts*.

By contrast, you are a *novice*, or newcomer, to whatever discipline you're studying. You've not yet developed the brain wiring that your instructors have developed. That can lead to a potential problem. Sometimes instructors are so familiar with what they already know from years of traveling the same pathways in their brains that what you're learning for the first time seems obvious to them. Without even realizing it, they can expect what is familiar to them to be obvious to you. Think of how challenging it is when you try to teach something that you understand thoroughly to another person who doesn't, like teaching someone who has never used a computer before how to upload an assignment.

Because you're a novice, you may not understand everything your instructors say. Ask questions, check, clarify, probe, and persist until you do understand. Sometimes your confusion is not due to a lack of knowledge, but a lack of the *correct* knowledge. For example, you may study for a test by doing only one thing—reading and rereading the textbook. Actually, it's important to be familiar with many different ways to study and then choose the ones that work best for you.

Think of it this way. Some of the brain wiring you brought with you to college is positive and useful, and some actually hurts more than it helps. When

"When we come to know something, we have performed an act that is as biological as when we digest something."

Henry Plotkin, Darwin **Machines and the Nature of Knowledge** *(1994)*

prerequisite something that must be completed before something else

you learn, you not only add new connections, but you rewire some old connections. While you're in college, you're under construction![1]

TAKE CHARGE AND CREATE THE BEST
CONDITIONS FOR LEARNING

Throughout this discussion, we've been talking about processes inside your brain. *Your* brain, not anyone else's. The bottom line is this: Learning must be *internally initiated*—by you. It can only be *externally encouraged*—by someone else. You're in charge of your own learning. Learning actually changes your brain.

Let's look at food as an analogy: If learning is a process that is as biological as digestion, then no one can learn for you, in the same way that no one can eat for you. The food in the refrigerator doesn't do you a bit of good unless you walk over, open the door, remove it, and start eating. It's there for the taking, but you must make that happen. To carry the analogy further, you eat on a daily basis, right? "No thanks, I ate last week" is a silly statement. Learning does for your brain what food does for your body. Nourish yourself!

Brain researchers tell us the best state for learning has many dimensions. Let's look at some of the most important ones.

1. **You're intrinsically motivated (from within yourself) to learn material that is appropriately challenging.**

   • **Examine where your motivation to learn comes from.** Are you *internally* motivated because you're curious about the subject and want to learn about it or *externally* motivated to get an A or avoid an F? Can you generate your own internal motivation? This text has built-in reminders to boost your intrinsic motivation. Use them to your advantage as a learner.

   • **Adjust the level of challenge yourself.** If you're too challenged in a class, you become nervous. Make sure you're keeping up with the workload and that you've completed the prerequisites. In many classes, you must know the fundamentals before tackling more advanced concepts. If you're not challenged enough, you can become bored and tune out. Your instructor will provide one level of challenge for everyone in the class. But it's up to you to fine-tune that challenge for yourself. Get extra help if you aren't quite up to the task, or bump up the challenge a notch or two if you're ahead of the game so that you're continually motivated to learn.

2. **You're appropriately stressed, but generally relaxed.**

   • **Assess your stress.** According to researchers, you learn best in a state of *relaxed alertness,* a state of high challenge and low threat.[3] Although relaxed alertness may sound impossible, it can be achieved. No stress at all is what you'd find in a no-brainer course. Some stress is useful; it helps you learn. Stress can heighten your alertness and help you focus. How stressed are you—and why—when you get to class? Are you overstressed because you've rushed from your last class, you're late because you missed your bus, or because you haven't done the reading and hope you won't be called on? Prepare for class so that you're ready to jump in. Or instead of too much stress, are you understressed because you don't value the course material? Consider how the information can be useful to you—perhaps in ways you've never even thought of. Here's the vital question to ask yourself: How much stress do I need in order to trigger my best effort?

- **Pay attention to your overall physical state.** Are you taking care of your physical needs so that you can stay alert, keep up with the lecture, and participate in the discussion?

3. **You're curious about what you're learning, and you look forward to learning it.**

- **Get ready to learn by looking back and by looking ahead.** When you're about to cross the street, you must look both ways, right? Keep that image in mind because that's what you should do before each class. What did class consist of last time? Can you predict what it will consist of next time?

- **Focus on substance, not style.** Part of Tammy's bias against Mr. Caldwell focused on his appearance. Despite society's obsession with attractiveness, grooming, and fashion, a student's job is to ask, "What can I learn from this person?" Deciding an instructor isn't worth paying attention to because he doesn't dress well or because his hair style is outdated is just an excuse not to learn.

4. **You search for personal meaning and patterns.**

- **Ask yourself: What's in it for me?** Why is knowing this important? How can I use this information in the future? Instead of dismissing material that appears unrelated to your life, try figuring out how it *could* relate. You may be surprised! That's why every chapter of FOCUS has a "WIIFM?" feature.

- **Think about how courses relate to one another.** How does this new knowledge relate to things you're learning in other courses? Does sociology have anything to do with history? Psychology with economics?

5. **Your emotions are involved, not just your mind.**

- **Evaluate your attitudes and feelings.** Do you like the subject matter? Do you admire the teacher? Remember your high school teacher, Mr. Brown, whose class you just couldn't stand? Not every class will be your favorite. That's natural. But if a class turns you off as a learner, instead of allowing your emotions to take over, ask why and whether your feelings are in your best interest.

- **Make a deliberate decision to change negative feelings.** Fortunately, feelings can be changed. Hating a course or disliking a professor can only build resentment and threaten your success. It's possible to do a 180-degree turn and transform your negative emotions into positive energy.

6. **You realize that as a learner you use what you already know in constructing new knowledge.**[4]

- **Remember that passive learning is impossible.** When it comes to learning, you are the construction foreman, building on what you already know to construct new knowledge. You're not just memorizing facts

"It is not the answer that enlightens, but the question."

Eugene Ionesco, Romanian and French playwright (1909–1994)

Take charge and create the best conditions for learning   **61**

"It is what we think we know already that often prevents us from learning."

Claude Bernard, French physiologist (1813–1878)

someone else wants you to learn. You're a full partner in the learning process!

- **Remind yourself that constructing knowledge takes work.** No one ever built a house by simply sitting back or just hanging out. Builders work hard, but in the end they have something to show for their efforts. In your college courses, identify what you already know, and blend new knowledge into the framework you've built in your mind. By constructing new knowledge, you are building yourself into a more sophisticated, more polished, and most certainly more educated person.

7. **You're given a degree of choice in terms of what you learn, how you do it, and feedback on how you're doing.**

- **Make the most of the choices you're given.** College isn't a free-for-all in which you can take any classes you like toward earning a degree. However, which electives you choose will be up to you. Or in a particular course, if your instructor allows you to write a paper or shoot a video, choose the option that will be more motivating for you. When you receive an assignment, select a topic that fires you up. It's easier to generate energy to put toward choices you've made yourself.

- **Use feedback to improve, and if feedback is not given, ask for it.** It's possible to get really good at doing something the wrong way. Take a golf swing or a swimming stroke, for example. Without someone intervening to give you feedback, it may be difficult to know how to improve. Your instructors will most likely write comments on your assignments to explain their grades. Evaluating your work is their job; it's what they must do to help you improve. Take their suggestions to heart and try them out.

"The purpose of learning is growth, and our minds, unlike our bodies, can continue growing as long as we live."

Mortimer Adler, American philosopher, educator, and editor (1902–2001)

All of us are already good learners in some situations. Let's say you're drawn to technology, for example. You're totally engrossed in computers and eagerly learn everything you can from books, classes, and online sources—and you sometimes totally lose yourself in a flow state as you're learning. No one has to force you to practice your technology skills or pick up an issue of *Wired* or *PC World*. You do it because you want to. In this case, you're self-motivated and therefore learning is easy. This chapter provides several different tools to help you understand your own personal profile as a learner so that you can try to learn at your best in *all* situations.

MULTIPLE INTELLIGENCES:
HOW ARE YOU SMART?

Have you ever noticed that people are smart in different ways? Consider the musical genius of Mozart, who published his first piano pieces at the age of five. Olympic Gold Medalist Lindsey Vonn started skiing when she was two years old. Not many of us are as musically gifted as Mozart or as physically gifted as Lindsey Vonn, but we all have strengths. You may earn top grades in math, and not-so-top grades in English, and your best friend's grades may be just the opposite.

According to Harvard psychologist Howard Gardner, people can be smart in the eight different categories you can see in Exercise 3.2. Most schools focus on particular types of intelligence, linguistic and logical-mathematical intelligence, reflecting the three R's: reading, writing, and 'rithmetic. But Gardner claims there are many different types of intelligence that can't be measured by traditional one-dimensional standardized IQ tests and represented by a three-digit number: 100 (average), 130 (gifted), or 150 (genius). Gardner defines intelligence as "the ability to find and solve problems and create products of value in one or more cultural settings."[5] One recent study showed that the three primary intelligences of community college students are intrapersonal, interpersonal, and bodily-kinesthetic.[6] What are yours?

EXERCISE 3.2   **MULTIPLE INTELLIGENCES SELF-ASSESSMENT**

Are people smart in different ways? How so? Put check marks next to all the statements in this self-assessment that best describe you.

Linguistic Intelligence: The capacity to use language to express what's on your mind and understand others ("word smart")

_____ I'm a good storyteller.

_____ I enjoy word games, puns, and tongue twisters.

_____ I'd rather listen to the radio than watch TV.

_____ I've recently written something I'm proud of.

_____ I can hear words in my head before I say or write them.

_____ When riding in the car, I sometimes pay more attention to words on billboards than I do to the scenery.

_____ In high school, I did better in English, history, or social studies than I did in math and science.

_____ I enjoy reading.

_____ TOTAL check marks

Logical-Mathematical Intelligence: The capacity to understand cause/effect relationships and to manipulate numbers ("number/reasoning smart")

_____ I can easily do math in my head.

_____ I enjoy brainteasers or puzzles.

_____ I like it when things can be counted or analyzed.

_____ I can easily find logical flaws in what others do or say.

_____ I think most things have rational explanations.

_____ Math and science were my favorite subjects in high school.

_____ I like to put things into categories.

_____ I'm interested in new scientific advances.

_____ TOTAL check marks

Spatial Intelligence: The capacity to represent the world visually or graphically ("picture smart")

_____ I like to take pictures of what I see around me.

_____ I'm sensitive to colors.

_____ My dreams at night are vivid.

_____ I like to doodle or draw.

(continued on next page)

_____ I'm good at navigating with a map.

_____ I can picture what something will look like before it's finished.

_____ In school, I preferred geometry to algebra.

_____ I often make my point by drawing a picture or diagram.

_____ TOTAL check marks

Bodily-Kinesthetic Intelligence: **The capacity to use your whole body or parts of it to solve a problem, make something, or put on a production ("body smart")**

_____ I regularly engage in sports or physical activities.

_____ I get fidgety (tap my foot, etc.) when asked to sit for long periods of time.

_____ I get some of my best ideas while I'm engaged in a physical activity.

_____ I need to practice a skill in order to learn it; rather than just reading or watching a video about it.

_____ I enjoy being a daredevil.

_____ I'm a well-coordinated person.

_____ I like to think through things while I'm doing something else like running or walking.

_____ I like to spend my free time outdoors.

_____ TOTAL check marks

Musical Intelligence: **The capacity to think in music; hear patterns; and recognize, remember, and perhaps manipulate them ("music smart")**

_____ I can tell when a musical note is flat or sharp.

_____ I play a musical instrument.

_____ I often hear music playing in my head.

_____ I can listen to a piece of music once or twice, and then sing it back accurately.

_____ I often sing or hum while working.

_____ I like music playing while I'm doing things.

_____ I'm good at keeping time to a piece of music.

_____ I consider music an important part of my life.

_____ TOTAL check marks

Interpersonal Intelligence: **The capacity to understand other people ("people smart")**

_____ I prefer group activities to solo activities.

_____ Others think of me as a leader.

_____ I enjoy the challenge of teaching others something I like to do.

_____ I like to get involved in social activities at school, church, or work.

_____ If I have a problem, I'm more likely to get help than tough it out alone.

_____ I feel comfortable in a crowd of people.

_____ I have several close friends.

_____ I'm the sort of person others come to for advice about their problems.

_____ TOTAL check marks

Intrapersonal Intelligence: **The capacity to understand yourself, who you are, and what you can do ("self-smart")**

_____ I like to spend time alone thinking about important questions in life.

_____ I have invested time in learning more about myself.

_____ I consider myself to be independent minded.

_____ I keep a journal of my inner thoughts.

_____ I'd rather spend a weekend alone than at a place with a lot of other people around.

_____ I've thought seriously about starting a business of my own.

_____ I'm realistic about my own strengths and weaknesses.

_____ I have goals for my life that I'm working on.

_____ TOTAL check marks

Naturalistic Intelligence: The capacity to discriminate between living things and show sensitivity toward the natural world ("nature smart")

_____ Environmental problems bother me.

_____ In school, I always enjoyed field trips to places in nature or away from class.

_____ I enjoy studying nature, plants, or animals.

_____ I've always done well on projects involving living systems.

_____ I enjoy pets.

_____ I notice signs of wildlife when I'm on a walk or hike.

_____ I can recognize types of plants, trees, rocks, birds, and so on.

_____ I enjoy learning about environmental issues.

_____ TOTAL check marks

Which intelligences have the most check marks? Write in the three intelligences in which you had the most number of check marks.

_____ _____ _____

Although this is an informal instrument, it can help you think about the concept of multiple intelligences, or MI. How are you smart?

Based on Armstrong, T. (1994). _Multiple intelligences in the classroom_. Alexandria, VA: Association for Supervision and Curriculum Development, pp. 18–20.

So instead of asking the traditional question "How smart are you?" a better question is "How are you smart?" The idea is to find out how, and then apply this understanding of yourself to your academic work in order to achieve your best results.

USE INTELLIGENCE-ORIENTED STUDY TECHNIQUES

Do you sometimes wonder why you can't remember things for exams? Some learning experts believe that memory is intelligence-specific. You may have a good memory for people's faces but a bad memory for their names. You may be able to remember the words of a country-western hit but not the dance steps that go with it. The Theory of Multiple Intelligences may explain why.[7]

Examine your own behaviors in class. If your instructors use their linguistic intelligence to teach, as many do, and your intelligences lie elsewhere, do you get frustrated? Instead of zeroing in on the lecture, do you fidget (bodily-kinesthetic), doodle (spatial), or socialize (interpersonal)? You may need to translate the information into your own personal intelligences, just as you would if your instructor speaks French and you speak English. This strategy might have worked for Tammy Ko from the "FOCUS Challenge Case."

Mr. Caldwell's most developed intelligence is linguistic, whereas Tammy's are bodily-kinesthetic (manipulating test tubes) and interpersonal (interacting with people). Tammy's learning problems are partially due to her inability to translate from one set of intelligences (his) to another (hers). Creating flash cards, for example, or talking over the lectures with Sam might have really helped her. Take a look at Figure 3.1, a chart of possible intelligence-oriented study options:

FIGURE 3.1

Studying Using the Theory of Multiple Intelligences

Linguistic ---->	1. Rewrite your class notes. 2. Record yourself reading through your class notes, and play the recording as you study. 3. Read the textbook chapter aloud.
Logical Mathematical ---->	1. Create hypothetical conceptual problems to solve. 2. Organize chapter or lecture notes into a logical flow. 3. Analyze how the textbook chapter is organized and why.
Spatial ---->	1. Draw a map that demonstrates your thinking on course material. 2. Illustrate your notes by drawing diagrams and charts. 3. Mark up your textbook to show relationships among concepts.
Bodily–Kinesthetic ---->	1. Study course material while engaged in physical activity. 2. Practice skills introduced in class or in the text. 3. Act out a scene based on chapter content.
Musical ---->	1. Create musical memory devices by putting words into well-known melodies. 2. Listen to music while you're studying. 3. Sing or hum as you work.
Interpersonal ---->	1. Discuss course material with your classmates. 2. Organize a study group that meets regularly. 3. Meet a classmate before or after class for coffee and class conversation.
Intrapersonal ---->	1. Keep a journal to track your personal reactions to course material. 2. Study alone and engage in internal dialogue about course content. 3. Coach yourself on how to best study for a challenging class.
Naturalistic ---->	1. Search for applications of course content in the natural world. 2. Study outside (if weather permits and you can resist distractions). 3. Go to a physical location that exemplifies course material (for example, a park for your geology course).

DEVELOP YOUR WEAKER INTELLIGENCES

It's important to cultivate your weaker intelligences. Why? Because life isn't geared to one kind of intelligence. It's complex. A photo journalist for *National Geographic,* for example, might need linguistic intelligence, spatial intelligence, interpersonal intelligence, and naturalistic intelligence. Being well-rounded, as the expression goes, is truly a good thing. Artist Pablo Picasso once said, "I am always doing that which I cannot do, in order that I may learn how to do it."

Use your multiple intelligences to multiply your success. Remember that no one is naturally intelligent in all eight areas. Each individual is a unique blend of intelligences. But the Theory of Multiple Intelligences claims that we all have the capacity to develop all of our eight intelligences further. That's good news!

HOW DO YOU
PERCEIVE INFORMATION?

Style—we all have it, right? What's yours? Baggy jeans and a tee shirt? Sandals, even in the middle of winter? A signature hairdo that defies gravity? When it comes to appearance, you have your own style. You know it, and so does everyone who knows you.

Think about how your mind works. For example, how do you decide what to wear in the morning? Do you turn on the radio or check the weather app on your phone for the forecast? Stick your head out the front door? Ask someone else's opinion? Throw on whatever happens to be clean? We all have different styles, don't we?

So what's a learning style? A learning style is defined as your "characteristic and preferred ways of gathering, interpreting, organizing, recalling, and thinking about information."[8]

Here's one way of looking at things. The way you prefer to receive information is based in part on your senses. Which senses do you prefer to use to take in information—your eyes (visual-graphic or visual-words); your ears (aural); or all your senses, using your whole body (kinesthetic)? Which type of information sinks in best? Which type of information do you most trust to be accurate?

To further understand your preferred sensory channel, let's take this hypothetical example. Assume a rich relative you didn't even know leaves you some money, and you decide to use it to buy a new car. You must first answer many questions: What kind of car do you want to buy—an SUV, a sedan, a sports car, a van, or a truck? What are the differences between various makes and models? How do prices, comfort, and safety compare? Who provides the best warranty? Which car do consumers rate highest? How would you go about learning the answers to all these questions? It turns out we all have preferences in terms of how we'd like to have our information "delivered."

What would you do? Eventually, as you're deciding which vehicle to buy, you might do all these things, and do them more than once. But learning style theory says we all have preferences for how we **perceive** and perhaps

"Learning how to learn is life's most important skill."

Tony Buzan, memory expert

perceive become aware of

FIGURE 3.2

Learning Style Preferences: Would
You Rather...?

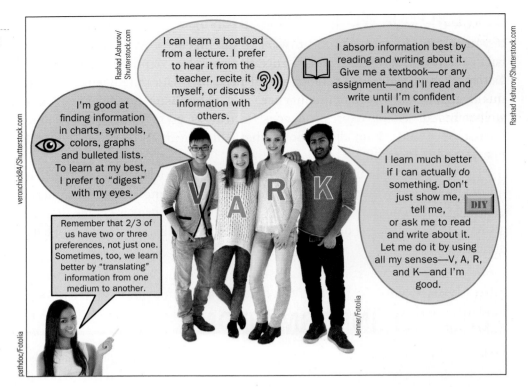

even process information. Perhaps this infographic (Figure 3.2) will help you think about your own preferences in terms of the letters VARK.

You probably have a gut feeling about your own style after reading the car buying decision and looking over the four different preference possibilities. But stop for a moment and take the VARK questionnaire online at http://vark-learn.com/the-vark-questionnaire/ and your results will be tabulated for you. After you see what the instrument says about your learning preferences, reflect on your results in Exercise 3.3.

EXERCISE 3.3   INTERPRETING YOUR VARK PREFERENCES

Scoring the VARK

Place your four VARK scores here after completing the instrument online.	Visual	Aural	Read/Write	Kinesthetic

What is or are your VARK preferences? Could you have predicted them? Did anything surprise you? Can you explain how and why they are what they are? How will you capitalize on your preferences to learn at your best?

Now that you've calculated your scores, do they match your perceptions of yourself as a learner? Could you have predicted them? The VARK's creators believe that you are best qualified to verify and interpret your own results.[9] Try the "just-in-time" VARK IT! suggestions that appear alongside as you read this text. They will help you apply your preferred VARK strategies and learn at your best.

USING YOUR SENSORY PREFERENCES

Knowing your preferences can help you in your academic coursework. If your highest score (by 4 or 5 points) is in one of the four VARK modalities, that particular learning modality is your preferred one.[10] If your scores are more or less even between several or all four modalities, these scores mean that you don't have a strong preference for any single modality. A lower score in a preference simply means that you are more comfortable using other styles. If your VARK results contain a zero in a particular learning modality, you may realize that you do indeed dislike this mode or find it unhelpful. You might want to reflect on why you don't like to use this learning modality.

Most college classes emphasize reading and writing; however, if your lowest score is in the read/write modality, don't assume you're academically doomed. VARK can help you discover alternative, more productive ways to learn the same course material. You may learn to adapt naturally to a particular instructor or discipline's preferences, using a visual modality in your economics class to interpret graphs and a kinesthetic modality in your chemistry lab to conduct experiments.

However, you may also find that you need to deliberately and strategically reroute your learning methods in some of your classes, and knowing your VARK preferences can help you do that. Learning to capitalize on your preferences and translate challenging course material into your preferred modality may serve you well. Remember these suggestions about the VARK, and try them out to see whether they improve your academic results.

1. **VARK preferences are not necessarily strengths.** However, VARK is an excellent vehicle to help you reflect on how you learn and begin to reinforce the productive strategies you're already using or select ones that might work better.

2. **If you have a strong preference for a particular modality, practice using it in many different ways.** Reinforce your learning by doing many things in that column.

3. **An estimated 60 percent of people are** multimodal. In a typical classroom of 30 students (based on VARK data):

   • 17 students would be multimodal (and many of these would contain a "K")

   • 1 student would be visual,

   • 1 student would be aural,

   • 5 students would be read/write,

   • 6 students would be kinesthetic,

   and the teacher would most likely have a strong read/write preference![11]

multimodal preferring to use more than one sensory channel

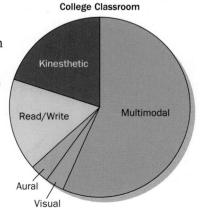

Learner Preferences in the Average College Classroom

4. **If you are multimodal, as most of us are, it may be necessary to use several of your modalities to boost your confidence in your learning.** Practice the suggestions for all of your preferred modalities.

5. **While in an ideal world, it would be good to try to strengthen lesser preferences, you may wish to save that goal for later in life.** Some experts suggest that college isn't the place to experiment. Grades count, and your continuing success will depend on how well you do. You may decide it's better to try to strengthen your current preferences now and work on expanding your lesser preferences later. This text will give you an opportunity to practice your VARK learning preferences—whatever they are—in each chapter. Ultimately, learning at your best is up to you.

Gaining the insights provided in this chapter and acting on them have the potential to greatly affect your college success. Understand yourself, capitalize on your preferences, build on them, focus, and learn!

WIIFM?

🕐 **3.5-MINUTE READ**

Let's project into the future. You've launched your career, and you're on the job as a newbie. You've been working on a huge project for your boss, and you've finally written up all your results in what turned out to be a lengthy report. You make an appointment to meet with her, eager to hand off your report, literally bursting with pride. Honestly, you think it represents some of your best work ever. When you get there and give her the massive, bound document, she says, "Thanks, but I don't have time to read all of this. Just give me a verbal summary. That's all I need." You're aghast! *What?*

She didn't want a written report? I spent days on this! You've just made a classic error. Like countless others new to a job and a fresh employee-supervisor relationship, you didn't think about whether your boss is a listener or a reader. You guessed and missed the mark.

In short, what you didn't consider was your boss's VARK preferences. Maybe you can't ask her to go online and fill out the VARK Learning Styles Questionnaire like you did, but you could easily ask her how she prefers to receive information:

"Change is such hard work."

Billy Crystal, Nassau Community College, Garden City, New York, transferred to New York University

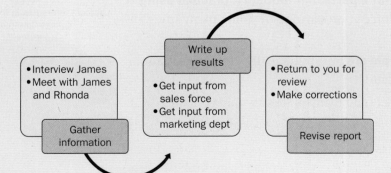

- Interview James
- Meet with James and Rhonda

Gather information

Write up results

- Get input from sales force
- Get input from marketing dept

- Return to you for review
- Make corrections

Revise report

V "After I finish the project, would you like me to create a chart to take you through the process I went through?"

A "Would you like me to summarize my work to you verbally so that you can listen and then we can talk it over?"

R "Would you like me write up a report so that you can read all the details and can add your own written comments?"

K "Would you like me to use an e-tool like Pikto-chart to create an info-graphic that summarizes everything I've done on the project and the conclusions I've come to?"

VARK is one way to explain communication problems on the job. According to one expert, "One of the biggest problems that occurs between bosses and employees is a mismatch in their communication styles. When you speak and the boss doesn't hear you, or vice versa, it can greatly hurt your chances of career success. And I've recently been working on research that shows that when bosses and employees have different communication styles, the employee can be 20-30% less engaged at work."[12] Not good.

Instead of making assumptions (like, my boss probably likes to receive information the way I do), wouldn't finding out early on have saved you a lot of time and grief? Did you know that the biggest predictor of your future job satisfaction isn't how much money you earn or how many vacation days you get? It's all about the quality of your relationship with your boss.[13] And it's *your* job to do all you can so that your communication isn't at cross purposes. Ideally, you need to be on the same page.[14]

Of course, if your boss is indecisive, insecure, or a know-it-all, you may have to work harder to build a relationship, but it can be done, and it's still *your* responsibility.[15] Here are four important points to remember about communicating with your boss (besides finding out his or her VARK preferences):

1. **Bring solutions to your boss, not problems**. Instead of running to your boss with a problem at the drop of a hat, bring potential solutions. Discuss the pros and cons of each "fix," and ask for his recommendation. That kind of approach demonstrates initiative on your part and shows the boss that you can think for yourself.[16]

2. **Clarify expectations up front.** When you take on a new assignment, discuss all the specifics with your boss. "Do you want me to get to this when I can, or is it a top priority?" "If you'd like me to run this project, can you assign someone else to help me with my other big task?" "I'm thinking I could get you a draft by Wednesday, October 5. Will that work?" Nailing down specifics up front is much better than backtracking later.

3. **Learn to "listen between the lines."** When your boss says something, what does he *really* mean? Here's an example.

An "open-door policy" can have different definitions to different bosses. To one boss, it might mean "Interrupt me any time you need to." To another it may mean, "Generally, I'm open to questions except when I'm too busy with my own work." No boss would ever say, "I have a closed-door policy," but the exact meaning of an "open-door" policy is open to interpretation.[17] If you're not sure of what your boss means about something, it's better to ask.

4. **Help your boss recognize your good work**. Bosses are busy; they have their own jobs to do. It's not enough for you to do a good job and hope your boss notices. You need to bring the quality of your work to her attention by discussing your projects and their outcomes. "You are responsible for making your boss appreciate the good work that you do."[18] And while you're at it, ask for regular feedback from your boss, not just at your annual or semi-annual performance review. Getting hit in January with news about a performance problem that you could have fixed in July can be extremely demotivating. Get in front of performance issues so that your work *is* good, consistently.

WIIFM? you ask. As Billy Crystal says, change *is* very hard work. But remember that your hard work to improve your communication skills now, while you're still in college, *will* most certainly enhance your future success.

WHAT ROLE DOES YOUR
PERSONALITY PLAY?

One of the best things about college is having a chance to meet so many different types of people. At times you may find these differences intriguing. At other times, they may baffle you. Look around and listen to other students, and you'll start to notice. Have you heard students saying totally opposite things such as those listed here?

"There's no way I can study at home. It's way too noisy."

"There's no way I can study in the library. It's way too quiet."

"I'm so glad I've already decided on a major. Now I can go full steam ahead."

"I have no idea what to major in. I can think of six different majors I'd like to choose."

"My sociology instructor is great. She talks about all kinds of things in class, and her essay tests are actually fun!"

"My sociology instructor is so confusing. She talks about so many different things in class. How am I supposed to know what to study for her tests?"[19]

VARK IT

Visual: Draw four horizontal lines across a piece of paper. On the left end of the four lines, list E, S, T, and J, one letter per line. On the opposite side of the four lines, list I, N, F, and P, one letter per line. Now that you've made a chart, place an X along the line, where you think *you* belong on the MBTI scales—closer to one side or somewhere in the middle.

You're likely to run into all kinds of viewpoints and all types of people, but differences make life much more interesting! We're each unique. Perhaps your friends comment on your personality by saying, "She's really quiet," or "He's a party animal," or "He's incredibly logical," or "She trusts her gut feelings." What you may not know is how big a role your personality plays in how you prefer to learn.

The Myers-Briggs Type Indicator® (MBTI) is the most well-known personality assessment instrument in the world. Each year, approximately 2 million people worldwide get a look into their personalities, their career choices, their interaction with others, and their learning styles by completing it. If you are able to complete the full Myers-Briggs Type Indicator in the class for which you're using this text, or through your college counseling center or learning center, do so. You'll learn a great deal about yourself.

The Myers-Briggs Type Indicator shows you your preferences in four areas:

E or I **What energizes you and where do you direct energy?** Do you get energy from other people (Extravert) or do you go within yourself to find strength (Introvert)?

S or N **How do you gather information and what kind of information do you trust?** Do you trust your senses and factually based information (Sensor) or do you trust your gut feelings (iNtuition)?

T or F **How do you make decisions, arrive at conclusions, and make judgments?** Do you think things through logically (Thinker) or do you care about how others react and feel (Feeler)?

J or P **How do you relate to the outer world?** Do you prefer organization and structure (Judging) or do you like spontaneity and going with the flow (Perceiver)?

If you take the Myers-Briggs Type Indicator, you should realize that it isn't about what you can do. It's about what you prefer to do. Here's an illustration. Write your name on a piece of paper. Now put the pen in your other hand, and try writing your name again. What was different the second time around? For most people, the second try takes longer, is messier, probably feels strange, and requires more concentration. But could you do it? Yes. It's just that you prefer doing it the first way. The first way is easier and more natural; the second way makes a simple task seem like hard work! It's possible that you might have to try "writing with your other hand" in college—doing things that don't come naturally.

Hugo Felix/Shutterstock.com; Vibrant Image Studio/Shutterstock.com

"Each person is an exception to the rule."

Carl Jung, psychiatrist (1875–1961)

In the "FOCUS Challenge Case," Tammy was described as outgoing (Extraverted) and hands-on (Sensing), whereas Mr. Caldwell was described as reserved (Introverted) and theoretical (iNtuitive). It's unlikely that Mr. Caldwell will change his teaching style, and even if he did, students in his class have a variety of learning styles. Whose style would he try to match? Both Tammy's personality and Mr. Caldwell's are similar to the most common types of students and instructors found in college classrooms. Although you couldn't be sure without looking at actual MBTI scores, you'd expect Tammy to be an ESFP. ESFP's are outgoing, like facts as opposed to theories, pay attention to the feelings of others, and prefer exploring options to following a structure. Based on the clues in the "Focus Challenge Case," you'd also expect Mr. Caldwell to be an INTJ—the opposite.

This chapter has covered learning from several different perspectives, and you now know more about yourself as a learner than you did before you read it. But you may be wondering: So how do Multiple Intelligences, VARK preferences, and personality traits (MBTI) work together to produce a unique learner? Although the three perspectives aren't intended to connect, let's look at this example to help you understand how each one would explain how people learn.

Let's say the person you sit by in your math class always asks you whether you want to join his study group. Based on what you've learned in this chapter, you'd be more likely to say yes if you:

1. **MI:** have *interpersonal* (or social) intelligence
2. **VARK:** are an *aural* learner who likes to discuss things
3. **MBTI:** are *extraverted* (you get energy from other people).

The three perspectives don't overlap; they're different. That's why this chapter presents all three. Each perspective explains how people learn in a different way.

Although simply knowing about these three perspectives is good, it's important to go further and act on that knowledge. As a single learner in a larger class, you will need to adjust to the teaching style of your instructor in ways such as the following:

> **Translate for maximum comfort.** The way to maximize your comfort as a learner is to find ways to translate from your instructor's preferences to yours. If you know that you prefer feeling over thinking, and your instructor's style is based on thinking, make the course material come alive by personalizing it. How does the topic relate to you, your lifestyle, your family, and your future choices?

> **Make strategic choices.** Although learning preferences can help explain your academic successes, it's also important not to use them to rationalize your nonsuccesses. An introvert could say, "I could have aced that assignment if the instructor had let me work alone! I hate group projects." Become the best learner you can be at what you're naturally good at. But also realize that you'll need to become more versatile over time. In the workforce, you will not always be able to choose what you do and how you do it. Actively choose your learning strategies rather than simply hoping for the best. Remember: No one can learn for you, just as no one can eat for you.

BOX 3.1   **LEARNING DISABILITY? FIVE WAYS TO HELP YOURSELF**

Perhaps you were diagnosed with Attention-Deficit/Hyperactivity Disorder (ADHD) or dyslexia as a young child. If you're beginning your college career with a learning disability (LD), you're not alone. "The National Center for Learning Disabilities reported in 2014 that among high school students with learning disabilities, 54 percent planned to attend a two-year or four-year college."[20] More than 200,000 entering college students have a learning disability of some type.[21] Does a learning disability mean all the odds are against you? No, but there are some important steps you must take to help yourself. Successful college students with LDs recognize, understand, and accept these steps, and develop compensating strategies to offset their LDs.

1. **If you've been previously diagnosed with a learning disability, bring a copy of your evaluation or Individualized Education Plan (IEP) with you to campus.** Some schools require documentation in order to use the institution's support services.

2. **Locate the support services office on your campus and use it.** These services are free and can make all the difference in your success.

3. **Learn more about your specific LD.** Read about it. Visit credible websites. Understanding the ins and outs of what you're up against is important.

4. **If you need special accommodations such as taking exams somewhere other than the classroom, schedule an appointment with your instructors early in the term to let them know.** Having a learning disability doesn't mean you're required to do less work, but you'll get the support you need in order to do your best.

5. **Remember that the advice in this text, which is helpful to all college students, can be even more useful to anyone with a learning disability.** Time management strategies and study skills tailored to your specific LD are key.

Don't let fear of failure immobilize you. Instead, keep your eye on the goal and take charge of your own learning.[22]

> "A year from today, you will wish you had started today."
>
> *Karen Lamb, American author*

> **Take full advantage.** College will present you with an extensive menu of learning opportunities. You will also build on your learning as you move beyond your general, introductory classes into courses in your chosen major—and across and between classes. Don't fall victim to the temptation to make excuses as some students do ("I could have been more successful in college if . . . I hadn't had to work so many hours . . . I hadn't had a family to support . . . my instructors had been more supportive. . . ." If, if, if. College may well be the most concentrated and potentially powerful learning opportunity you'll ever have. Ultimately, learning at your best is up to you.

METACOGNITION:
TAKE CHARGE OF HOW YOU STUDY

life hack #2

How much time do you spend in a "focused" state? Consider using a wearable device that monitors your breathing and helps you achieve a sense of control over your emotions, your learning, and your life.

Talk about needing to use a dictionary! What does the word *metacognition* mean? *Meta* is an ancient Greek prefix that is often used to mean *about*. For example, metacommunication is communicating *about* the way you communicate. ("I feel humiliated when you tease me in front of other people. Can you *not* do that?")

Because cognition means thinking and learning, metacognition is thinking about your thinking and learning about your learning. It's about identifying your learning goals, monitoring your progress, backing up or getting help when you're stuck, forging ahead when you're in the groove, and evaluating your results. Metacognition is about knowing yourself as a learner and about your ability (and motivation) to control your own learning. Some things are easy for you to learn; others are hard. What do you know about yourself as a learner, and do you use that awareness *intentionally* to learn at your best?[23]

DO YOU KNOW HOW TO STUDY?

To what extent do these ten statements apply to you? Read the following statements and mark each of them according to the 1 through 5 scale with the number that describes you best.

Never		Sometimes		Always
1	2	3	4	5

1. _____ I keep going with things I have to learn rather than skipping over what I don't understand.

2. _____ When I'm studying something difficult, I realize when I'm stuck and ask for help.

3. _____ I make a study plan and stick to it in order to master class material.

4. _____ I quiz myself as I'm studying to see what I understand and what I don't.

5. _____ I talk through my learning challenges to help me understand things while I study.

6. _____ After I study something, I think about how well it went.

7. _____ I know when I learn best: morning, afternoon, or evening, for example.

8. _____ I know how I study best: alone, with one other person, in a group, etc.

9. _____ I know where I study best: at home, at the library, at my computer, etc.

10. _____ I believe I'm in control of my own learning.

Now tally your scores on this informal instrument. If you scored between 40 and 50 total points, you have excellent metacognitive skills. If you scored between 30 and 40 points, your skills are probably average. However, note any items you rated down in the 1 to 2 range, and then read the metacognition section of the chapter carefully.

These questions may seem simple, but how do you know:

1. When you've finished a reading assignment?

2. When your paper is ready to turn in?

3. When you've finished studying for an exam?

When you're eating a meal, you know when you're full, right? But when it comes to academic work, how do you know when you're done? Some students resort to answers like these to the question "How do you know when you're done?" Look at the range of students' answers:

> I just do.

> I trust in God.

> My eyelids get too heavy.

> I've been at it for a long time.

> My mom tells me to go to bed.

> I understand everything.

> I can write everything down without looking at the textbook or my notes.

Dmitry Kalinovsky/Photos.com

"Striving for success without hard work is like trying to harvest where you haven't planted."

David Bly, Minnesota politician

> ➤ I've created a practice quiz for myself and get all the answers right.

> ➤ When my wife or girlfriend drills me and I know all the answers.

> ➤ When I can teach my husband everything I've learned.

> ➤ When I've highlighted, recopied my notes, made flash cards, written sample questions, tested myself, and so on.

You can see that their answers become increasingly reliable as you progress down the list.[24]

Metacognition is about having an "awareness of [your] own cognitive machinery and how the machinery works."[25] It's about knowing the limits of your own learning and memory capabilities, knowing how much you can accomplish within a certain amount of time, and knowing what learning strategies work for you.[26] Know your limits, but at the same time, stretch.

APPLY YOUR LEARNING STYLE
TO YOUR STUDY STYLE

Now that you've gained some insight into how you prefer to learn, it's time to apply those preferences to how you study. Are you the kind of student who re-reads a textbook page five times without having the information sink in? Do you procrastinate when it comes to reading assignments for your classes? If so, through this chapter, you may have discovered why. Perhaps your linguistic intelligence is relatively low. Perhaps Read/Write is your least preferred VARK modality. Perhaps your off-the-charts extraverted personality enjoys the company of others, not a book.

Metacognition means thinking about your thinking and learning about your learning—taking charge of your own learning—and maybe that's exactly what you need to do. Early on, this chapter advised you about creating "the Best Conditions for Learning." Monitoring how you study and how well it's working is at the top of the list. Use Figure 3.3 as your guide, and note the results. You may just see an improvement!

BECOMING AN INTENTIONAL LEARNER:
MAKE A MASTER STUDY PLAN

"Parents should play an inestimable role in children's learning to read and learning to love to read."

—*Barbara Swaby, Literacy expert*

What's your favorite class this term? Or let's turn the question around: What's your least favorite class? Becoming an educated person may well require you to study things you wouldn't *choose* to study. Considering all you have to do, including your most and least favorite classes, what would making a master study plan look like? You've "been there, done that" all through your schooling, but do you *really* know how to study?

To begin, think about what you have to think about. What's your goal? Is it to finish your English essay by 10:00 P.M. so that you can start your algebra homework? Or is it to write the best essay you can possibly write? If you've allowed yourself one hour to read this chapter, but after an hour you're still not finished, you have three choices: keep reading, finish later, or give up entirely. What's in your best interest, honestly? See whether you find the following planning

Maria Evseyeva/Shutterstock.com

		Everyday Study Strategies	Exam Preparation Study Strategies
iStock.com/Marcela Barsse	**VISUAL**	• Convert your lecture notes to a visual format. • Study the placement of items, colors, and shapes in your textbook. • Put complex concepts into flowcharts or graphs. • Redraw ideas you create from memory.	• Practice turning your visuals back into words. • Recall the pictures you made of the pages you studied. • Use diagrams to answer exam questions, if your instructor will allow it.
Johanna Goodyear/ Dreamstime.com	**AURAL**	• Read your notes aloud. • Explain your notes to another auditory learner. • Ask others to "hear" your understanding of the material. • Record your notes or listen to your instructors' podcasts. • Realize that your lecture notes may be incomplete. You may have become so involved in listening that you stopped writing. Fill your notes in later by talking with other students or getting material from the textbook.	• Practice by speaking your answers aloud. • Listen to your own voice as you answer questions. • Opt for an oral exam if allowed. • Imagine you are talking with the teacher as you answer questions.
iStock.com/Nadezda Firsova	**READ/WRITE**	• Write out your lecture notes again and again. • Read your notes (silently) again and again. • Put ideas and principles into different words. • Translate diagrams, graphs, etc., into text. • Rearrange words and "play" with wording. • Turn diagrams and charts into words.	• Write out potential exam answers. • Practice creating and taking exams. • Type out your answers to potential test questions. • Organize your notes into lists or bullets. • Write practice paragraphs, particularly beginnings and endings.
iStock.com/Pascal Genest	**KINESTHETIC**	• Recall experiments, field trips, etc. Remember the real things that happened. • Talk over your notes with another "K" person. • Use photos and pictures that make ideas come to life. • Go back to the lab, your manual, or your notes that include real examples. • Remember that your lecture notes will have gaps if topics weren't concrete or relevant for you. • Use case studies to help you learn abstract principles.	• Role-play the exam situation in your room (or the actual classroom). • Put plenty of examples into your answers. • Write practice answers and sample paragraphs. • Give yourself practice tests.

strategies helpful, and check out the suggestions in this chapter's Quick Study, "Figure 3.4, How to Succeed in College by Really Trying."

1. **Make sure you understand your assignments.** Understanding is critical to making a master plan. You can actually waste a great deal of time trying to read your instructor's mind after the fact: "Did she want us to *analyze* the play or *summarize* it?" When you have work to do, make sure you're clear on what's been assigned.

FIGURE 3.4

Quick Study: How to Succeed in
College by Really Trying

How to Succeed in College by Really Trying

Let's be clear on one thing. You're in school to succeed—not to squander your time on frivolous activities.

Nerd is the new cool,

and studying is nerdy (they say), so do it!

Rise and Shine!

Sleeping in can become a tiresome habit that causes you to skip breakfast, miss classes, be late for exams, and lose out on a lot. It's a luxury, perhaps, but one you can't afford on a regular basis. Of course, getting up at a reasonable time assumes you went to bed at one, too.

Get to know your instructors.

They're not your enemies; they want you to succeed, and they're there to help you make that happen. Some will even give you their cell phone numbers, and all of them are on email regularly. But **you** have to reach out first.

Check your email at least once a day.

Many people prefer to text these days because it's quicker, but it's likely that email will be your best bet in college. If you prefer your personal account, make sure your college email is forwarded to it.
A general rule: Use technology wisely.

Make sure your head is screwed on.

In order for your study session to be truly effective, your head has to be with you. If you left it at your boyfriend's house or somewhere else, you're not really "on the clock," so to speak. And start with the hardest task first, while you're fresh.

Develop a routine.

Breakfast, class (*and skipping class is the worst idea ever*), studying, lunch, more studying, working out, club meeting, more studying. Squeeze as much productive time as you can out of the day.

2. **Schedule yourself to be three places at once.** Making a master plan requires you to think simultaneously about three different time zones:

The past: Ask yourself what you already know. Is this a subject you've studied before? Have your study habits worked well for you in the past? How have you done your best work—in papers, on exams, on projects?

The present: Ask yourself what you need to learn now. How interested are you in this material? How motivated are you to learn it? How much time will you devote to it?

The future: Ask yourself how you'll go about learning it. Will you learn it using the strategies that work best for you? Which learning factors will you control? Will you do what you can to change what's not working?[27]

3. **Talk through your learning challenges.** There's good evidence that talking to yourself while you're studying is a good thing. Researchers find it helps you figure things out: *Okay, I understand the difference between a neurosis and a psychosis, but I'm not sure I can provide examples on my psychology test.* Once you've heard yourself admit that, you know where to focus your efforts next.[28] Or consider the possibility on "talking online" to other students worldwide at brainly.com.

4. **Be a stickler.** Sticklers pay attention to details. They want to make sure everything is absolutely right. Have you ever thought about how important accuracy is? For example, if you were 99 instead of 100 percent accurate, that would mean that:

   • 500 airplanes in U.S. skies each day wouldn't be directed by air traffic controllers.[29] Disastrous!

   As you read and study, remember this example. Be thorough. Read the entire assignment. Pay attention to details. If you make a mistake, for example in solving a math problem, figure out exactly what went wrong so that you don't hold on to a bad academic habit. Rework the problem at least twice, write a few sentences describing the right way to solve it, and try another problem similar to it to see whether you really understand.[30] Accuracy counts!

5. **Take study breaks.** The human attention span is limited, and according to some researchers, it's shrinking, rather than expanding.[31] Plan to take brief scheduled breaks to stretch, walk around, or grab a light snack every half hour during study sessions. Of course, it's important to sit down and get back to work again. Don't let a quick study break to get a snack multiply into several hours of television viewing that wasn't in the plan.

6. **Mix it up.** Put a little variety into your study sessions by switching from one subject to another or from one mode of studying—for example, reading, self-quizzing, writing—to another. Variety helps you fight boredom and stay fresh (unless, of course, you're on the verge of a breakthrough). Even changing locations from time to time, rather than always studying in one place, stimulates your brain to reboot.[32]

7. **Estimate how long it will take.** Before starting an assignment, estimate the amount of time you will need to complete that assignment (just as you do at the start of each chapter of this text), and then compare that estimate

"No one can become really educated without having pursued some study in which he took no interest."

T. S. Eliot, American-born poet (1888–1965)

Becoming an intentional learner: Make a master study plan **79** with the actual amount of time the assignment took to complete. Getting into this habit helps you develop realistic schedules for future projects.

8. **Vary your study techniques by course content.** Studying productively is more than just learning a few general rules that apply to any type of subject matter. You need to zoom in on whatever subject or discipline it is that you're studying. Look over the pages of your textbook. Does the material synch with your learning style? Is it text-heavy (read/write)? Do graphs or charts explain the text and seem important? Is color-coding or bulleting used to call your attention to particular items (visual)? If the material isn't presented as you'd prefer, what can you do to "translate"? For example, if you prefer to learn kinesthetically can you make flash cards? Can you create and complete practice tests? If you prefer to learn by listening, can you read the material aloud (aural)? And finally, what kind of exam (multiple-choice, essay, problem sets, etc.) does the material lend itself to? What are you likely to need to know, and what will you be asked to do on an exam? When you study math, it's important to do more than read. Working problem sets helps you actually develop the skills you need. When you study history, you study differently. You might draw a timeline of the events leading up to World War I, for example.[33]

9. **Study earlier, rather than later.** Whenever possible, study during the daytime, rather than waiting until evening. Research shows that each hour used for study during the day is equal to one and a half hours at night. Another major study showed that students who study between 6:00 P.M. and midnight are twice as likely to earn A's as students who put off their studying until after midnight.[34] And simply getting enough sleep can help you rachet up your GPA more than you'd expect.

10. **Create artificial deadlines for yourself.** Even though your instructors will have set deadlines for various assignments, create your own deadlines that precede the ones they set. Finish early, and you'll save yourself from any last minute emergencies that may come up, like crashed hard drives or empty printer cartridges.

iStock.com/Jacob Wackerhausen

11. **Treat school as a job.** If you consider the amount of study time you need to budget for each hour of class time, and you're taking 12–15 credits, then essentially you're working a 36–45 hour/week job on campus. Arrive at "work" early and get your tasks done during "business hours" so you have more leisure time in the evenings.

12. **Show up.** Once you've decided to sit down to study, really commit yourself to showing up—being present emotionally and intellectually, not just physically. If you're committed to getting a college education, then give it all you've got! Get help if you need it. If you have a diagnosed learning disability, or believe you might, find out where help is available on your campus. One of the best ways to compensate for a learning disability is by relying on metacognition. In other words, consciously controlling what isn't happening automatically is vital to your success.[35]

Assume you are taking three classes this term: calculus, psychology, and music. For the three textbook pages here, describe how you would go about studying the material, based on what the content in these three subjects requires. Among other things, which particular VARK learning style preferences should be used: V, A, R, and/or K? Fill in specifics about how you would study each subject's textbook page. It's also important to annotate as you read, as shown here. Make notes to yourself in the margins or on sticky notes, reacting, explaining, or summarizing what you've learned or what is still fuzzy. In doing so, you'll be interacting with the material and personalizing it. Make connections; don't just let information float by and hope that something sticks. After you're done, compare notes with your classmates.

WEIRD LOOKING DUDE! BUT SMART!

POINT PLOTTING THIS GRAPH REALLY HELPS ME UNDERSTAND THE DEFINITION OF PARABOLA. MAYBE THAT'S BECAUSE MY LEARNING PREFERENCE IS VISUAL.

---

2   **Chapter P**   Preparation for Calculus

P.1 Graphs and Models

- Sketch the graph of an equation.
- Find the intercepts of a graph.
- Test a graph for symmetry with respect to an axis and the origin.
- Find the points of intersection of two graphs.
- Interpret mathematical models for real-life data.

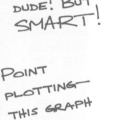

RENÉ DESCARTES (1596–1650)

Descartes made many contributions to philosophy, science, and mathematics. The idea of representing points in the plane by pairs of real numbers and representing curves in the plane by equations was described by Descartes in his book *La Géométrie*, published in 1637.

iStock.com/Georgios Kollidas

The Graph of an Equation

In 1637 the French mathematician René Descartes revolutionized the study of mathematics by joining its two major fields—algebra and geometry. With Descartes's coordinate plane, geometric concepts could be formulated analytically and algebraic concepts could be viewed graphically. The power of this approach was such that within a century of its introduction, much of calculus had been developed.

The same approach can be followed in your study of calculus. That is, by viewing calculus from multiple perspectives—*graphically*, *analytically*, and *numerically*—you will increase your understanding of core concepts.

Consider the equation $3x + y = 7$. The point $(2, 1)$ is a **solution point** of the equation because the equation is satisfied (is true) when 2 is substituted for x and 1 is substituted for y. This equation has many other solutions, such as $(1, 4)$ and $(0, 7)$. To find other solutions systematically, solve the original equation for y.

$$y = 7 - 3x \qquad \text{Analytic approach}$$

Then construct a **table of values** by substituting several values of x.

x	0	1	2	3	4
y	7	4	1	-2	-5

Numerical approach

From the table, you can see that $(0, 7)$, $(1, 4)$, $(2, 1)$, $(3, -2)$, and $(4, -5)$ are solutions of the original equation $3x + y = 7$. Like many equations, this equation has an infinite number of solutions. The set of all solution points is the **graph** of the equation, as shown in Figure P.1.

NOTE en though we refer to the sketch shown in Figure P.1 as the graph of $3x + y = 7$, it really represents only a *portion* of the graph. The entire graph would extend beyond the page. ■

In this course, you will study many sketching techniques. The simplest is point plotting—that is, you plot points until the basic shape of the graph seems apparent.

EXAMPLE 1 Sketching a Graph by Point Plotting

Sketch the graph of $y = x^2 - 2$.

Solution   First construct a table of values. Then plot the points shown in the table.

x	-2	-1	0	1	2	3
y	2	-1	-2	-1	2	7

Finally, connect the points with a *smooth curve*, as shown in Figure P.2. This graph is a **parabola.** It is one of the conics you will study in Chapter 10. ■

Graphical approach: $3x + y = 7$
Figure P.1

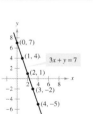

The parabola $y = x^2 - 2$
Figure P.2

How would you study this? Calculus, 9th Edition, by Ron Larson and Bruce H. Edwards.

(continued on next page)

studies of the brain. Case studies lack formal control groups. This, of course, limits the conclusions that can be drawn from clinical observations.

Survey Method

Sometimes psychologists would like to ask everyone in the world a few well-chosen questions: "Do you drink coffee? How often per week?" "What form of discipline did your parents use when you were a child?" "What is the most dishonest thing you've done?" Honest answers to such questions can reveal much about people's behavior. But, because it is impossible to question everyone, doing a survey is often more practical.

In the **survey method,** public polling techniques are used to answer psychological questions (Tourangeau, 2004). Typically, people in a representative sample are asked a series of carefully worded questions. A **representative sample** is a small group that accurately reflects a larger population. A good sample must include the same proportion of men, women, young, old, professionals, blue-collar workers, Republicans, Democrats, whites, African Americans, Native Americans, Latinos, Asians, and so on as found in the population as a whole.

A *population* is an entire group of animals or people belonging to a particular category (for example, all college students or all single women). Ultimately, we are interested in entire populations. But by selecting a smaller sample, we can draw conclusions about the larger group without polling each and every person. Representative samples are often obtained by *randomly* selecting who will be included (▶▶ Figure 1.11). (Notice that this is similar to randomly assigning participants to groups in an experiment.)

How accurate is the survey method? Modern surveys like the Gallup and Harris polls are quite accurate. The Gallup poll has erred in its election predictions by only 1.5 percent since 1954. However, if a survey is based on a biased sample, it may paint a false picture. A *biased sample* does not accurately reflect the population from which it was drawn. Surveys done by magazines, websites, and online information services can be quite biased. Surveys on the use of guns done by *O: The Oprah Magazine* and *Guns and Ammo* magazine would probably produce very different results—neither of which would represent the general population. That's why psychologists using the survey method go to great lengths to ensure that their samples are representative. Fortunately, people can often be polled by telephone, which makes it easier to obtain large samples. Even if one person out of three refuses to answer survey questions, the results are still likely to be valid (Hutchinson, 2004). **LIKE ME!**

Internet Surveys

Recently, psychologists have started doing surveys and experiments on the Internet. Web-based research can be a cost-effective way to reach very large groups of people. Internet studies have provided interesting information about topics such as anger, decision making,

[Handwritten margin note:] THERE'S LOTS OF PHONE POLLING DURING A PRESIDENTIAL ELECTION YEAR TO GET SOME IDEA OF WHO WILL WIN. . . . It's IMPORTANT THAT THE SAMPLE IS REPRESENTATIVE AND NONBIASED. I LIKE TO LEARN KINESTHETICALLY, SO MAYBE I SHOULD LOOK UP SOME WEBSITES ON POLLING. . . .

Survey method The use of public polling techniques to answer psychological questions.

Representative sample A small, randomly selected part of a larger population that accurately reflects characteristics of the whole population.

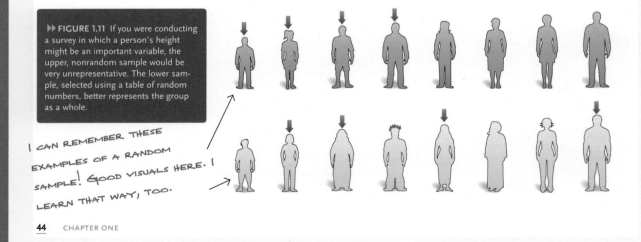

▶▶ **FIGURE 1.11** If you were conducting a survey in which a person's height might be an important variable, the upper, nonrandom sample would be very unrepresentative. The lower sample, selected using a table of random numbers, better represents the group as a whole.

[Handwritten margin note:] I CAN REMEMBER THESE EXAMPLES OF A RANDOM SAMPLE! GOOD VISUALS HERE. I LEARN THAT WAY, TOO.

44   CHAPTER ONE

How would you study this? *Psychology: A Journey, 4th Edition, by Dennis Coon and John O. Mitterer.*

Exercise 3.5 Continued

Measures

As you performed the different meters, you may have lost your place momentarily. Even if you didn't, you can see that it would be difficult to play a long piece of music without losing one's place. For this reason, music is divided into **measures** with vertical lines called **bar lines**.

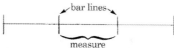

A bar line occurs immediately before an accented pulse. Thus, duple meter has two pulses per measure, triple meter has three pulses per measure, and quadruple meter has four pulses per measure. The following example shows the common meters again, this time with bar lines included. Notice how much easier it is to read and perform the meter when it is written this way.

I REMEMBER LEARNING ABOUT PITCH AND RHYTHM AS A KID IN MY PIANO LESSONS WITH MRS. SAUERBRATEN— OR WHATEVER HER NAME WAS! MAYBE BEING AN AURAL LEARNER HELPED ME FAKE MY WAY THROUGH ALL THOSE LESSONS MY PARENTS PAID FOR!

duple meter

triple meter

quadruple meter

Double bar lines have a special meaning: Their two most common uses are to signal the beginning of a new section in a large work and to mark the end of a work. Put double bar lines at the end of any exercises or pieces you write.

MUSIC IN *Action* | **Hearing Pulse and Meter**

As members of the class listen, clap a steady pulse without any noticeable accents. Slowly change the pulse to duple, triple, or quadruple meter. You may want to have a contest to see how quickly members of the class can detect the shift to a measured pulse.

Note Values

Learning to read music involves mastering two different musical subsystems: pitch notation and rhythmic notation. Pitch is indicated by the placement of a note on a five-line staff (the higher the note on the staff, the higher the pitch). You will learn about that later in this chapter. Rhythm, on the other hand, is written with

How would you study this? A Creative Approach to Music Fundamentals, 10th Edition, by William Duckworth.

Finally, what have you learned about studying and about yourself as a learner by completing this exercise?

SPRINTING TO THE FINISH LINE:
HOW TO STUDY WHEN THE HEAT IS ON

"Education is learning what you didn't even know you didn't know."

—Daniel J. Boorstin, American historian, 1914–2004

Let's be realistic. Planning is important, but there will be the occasional time when you'll have to find some creative ways to survive the onslaught of all you have to study. You'll need to prioritize your time and make decisions about what to study. When you do need to find a way to accomplish more than is humanly possible, keep these "emergency preparedness" suggestions in mind:

1. **Triage.** With little time to spare, you must be efficient. Consider this analogy: If you're the physician on duty in the ER, and three patients come in at once, who will you take care of first: the fellow with strep throat, the woman with a sprained wrist, or the heart attack victim who needs CPR? Making decisions about priorities is called triage. Of all the material you need to study, ask what is most important, moderately important, and least important. For example, if you are earning an A− in art history, a B+ in geography, and a C− in math, you know which course most needs your attention. Evaluate the material and ask yourself which topics have received the most attention in class and in the textbook. Then focus your study time on those topics, rather than trying to study everything.

2. **Use every spare moment to study.** If flashcards work for you, take your flashcards with you everywhere, like on your daily bus ride or to the laundromat, for example. Organize your essay answer in your head while you're filling up at the pump. It's surprising: Small amounts of focused time do add up.

3. **Give it the old one-two-three-four punch.** Immerse all your senses in the precious little amount of time you have to study: *read, write, listen,* and *speak* the material.

4. **Get a grip on your gaps.** Honesty is the best policy. Rather than glossing over what you don't know, assess your knowledge as accurately as possible, and fill in the gaps.

5. **Cram, but only as the very last resort.** If you're ultrashort on time due to a real emergency, and you have studying to do for several classes, focus on one class at a time. Be aware: If you learn new information that is similar to something you already know, the old information can interfere. So if you're studying for a psychology test that contains some overlap with your sociology test, separate the study sessions by a day. Studies also show that cramming up to one hour before sleeping can help minimize interference.[36] Nevertheless, continually remind yourself: What's my goal here? Is it to just get through twenty-five pages or is it to truly understand?

A FINAL WORD ABOUT
STUDYING AND LEARNING

Albert Einstein said this: "Never regard study as a duty, but as the enviable opportunity to learn . . ." Studying and learning are what college is all about. Take his advice: Consider the opportunities before you to become an educated person, and take advantage of them all.

CONTROL: YOUR TOUGHEST CLASS

Reflect on yourself as a learner in your toughest class this term. How optimal are the conditions for learning? Put a check mark in the box if any of the following conditions are present.

COURSE TITLE: _____

SEVEN CONDITIONS FOR OPTIMAL LEARNING

☐ 1. You're intrinsically motivated to learn material that is appropriately challenging.
☐ 2. You're appropriately stressed, but generally relaxed.
☐ 3. You're curious about what you're learning, and you look forward to learning it.
☐ 4. You search for personal meaning and patterns.
☐ 5. Your emotions are involved, not just your mind.
☐ 6. You realize that as a learner you use what you already know in constructing new knowledge.
☐ 7. You're given a degree of choice in terms of what you learn, how you do it, and feedback on how you're doing.

If no boxes are checked, identify specific strategies discussed in this chapter that you could you use to create the best conditions for learning.

INSIGHT: *NOW* WHAT DO YOU THINK?

At the beginning of this chapter, Tammy Ko faced a series of challenges as a new college student. Now, after learning from this chapter, would you respond differently to any of the questions you answered about the "FOCUS Challenge Case"? Using what you learned in the chapter, write a paragraph ending to Tammy's case study. What are some of the possible outcomes for her?

ACTION: YOUR PLANS FOR CHANGE

1. How will you put the information from this chapter to good use, not only in this class but in any others you're enrolled in this term?

2. List your learning and personality preferences as you discovered them in this chapter here:

   Multiple Intelligences _____

   VARK _____

   MBTI _____

   What do you think these preferences reveal about you and how you learn?

3. If you apply your learning style to your study style, what will you actually change? Over the course of this term, note whether it helps you become more successful.

HOW MUCH DID YOU LEARN?

At the beginning of this chapter, you filled out a "Readiness Check" that asked how you thought this chapter would relate to you, and how you would relate to it. Now, fill out this "Reality Check" to find out.

1. What does the term *multiple intelligences* mean? Can you name three different types of intelligences?

2. What does VARK stand for? Can you identify the letters as they relate to students' preferences for taking in information?

3. What's the definition of the word *metacognition*?

4. What can you do to become a more intentional learner? Identify three study habits you use now that you could change in order to study at your best.

5. How long did it take? _____ hours _____ minutes. Before you began this chapter, you were asked to predict how long it would take you to complete it (total time, even if you read it in more than one sitting). Was your estimate on target, or will you revise it for the next chapter you'll read?

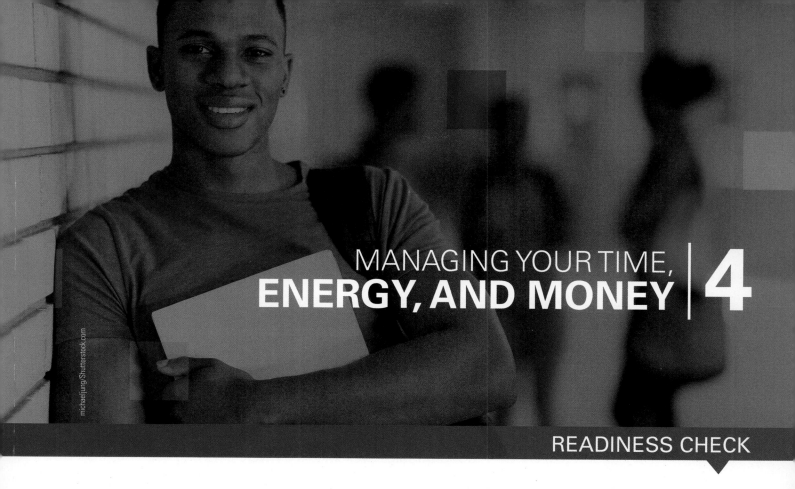

michaeljung/Shutterstock.com

MANAGING YOUR TIME, ENERGY, AND MONEY | 4

HOW THIS CHAPTER RELATES TO YOU

1. When your time is limited, and you should be using it to study, what is most likely to derail you, if anything? Put check marks by the phrase(s) that apply to you or write in your answer.

   ☐ People needing my attention
   ☐ My job getting in the way
   ☐ Spending time online
   ☐ Watching TV or movies
   ☐ Having responsibilities at home
   ☐ _____

2. What is most likely to be your response? Put a check mark by it.

   ☐ I have strong will power and focus no matter what.
   ☐ Even though it's hard, eventually I settle in and focus.
   ☐ I try to focus, but I can't seem to do it for long.
   ☐ I give in to the urge to do something else and procrastinate.

3. What would you have to do to increase your likelihood of success? Will you do it?

HOW YOU WILL RELATE TO THIS CHAPTER

1. What are you most interested in learning about? Put check marks by those topics.

   ☐ Why time management alone doesn't work
   ☐ How time management differs from energy management
   ☐ How to schedule your way to success
   ☐ How the P word can derail you
   ☐ How to realistically balance work, school, and your personal life
   ☐ How to manage your money

YOUR READINESS FACTOR

1. How motivated are you to learn more about managing your time, energy, and money in college? (5 = high, 1 = low)

2. How ready are you to read now? (If something is in your way, take care of it if you can. Zero in and focus.)

3. How long do you think it will take you to complete this chapter? If you start and stop, keep track of your overall time. ____ Hour(s) ____ Minute(s)

michaeljung/Shutterstock.com

Derek Johnson

As Derek Johnson walked out of his World History class on Wednesday evening, he felt panicked. The instructor had just assigned a twelve-page paper, due one month from today. How could she? Derek thought. *Doesn't she realize how busy most community college students are?* The syllabus had mentioned a paper, but twelve pages seemed downright excessive. He sent a tweet complaining about it from his phone on his way to his next class. Twitter was quickly becoming Derek's favorite way to communicate. His twin sister, Danielle, tweeted right back, "@DerekJ I hear ya!" Dani and Derek had been good buddies ever since they were kids, and even more so now that they were in their twenties.

When Derek had decided to go back to college five years after he graduated from high school, he hadn't quite realized what a juggling act it would require. First, there was his family—his wife, Justine, his four-year-old daughter, Taura, and another baby due before winter break. Then there was his job, which was really quite demanding for what he earned. He hoped that an associate's degree in accounting would help him get a job as an accounting assistant and possibly even move into the management ranks, where salaries were higher. Money was tight, and they always seemed to run out before payday. Add to that singing in his church choir, coaching the youth soccer league, competing in cycling races, and working out every morning at the gym. Derek had been a high school athlete, and physical fitness was a priority for him. And then there was his twin sister Dani, who decided to start college at the same time and always seemed to want to talk about some college course or other.

His head began to swim as he thought about all his upcoming obligations: his mother's birthday

next week, his dog's vet appointment, his sister's frequent drop-in visits, the training class he was required to attend for work. Something had to go, but he couldn't think of anything he was willing to sacrifice to make time for a twelve-page paper. Maybe he'd have to break down and actually do some planning like the *compulsive* students he knew—Dani included.

Still, the paper was to count as 25 percent of his final grade in the course. He decided he'd try to think of a topic for the paper on his way home. But then he remembered that his wife had asked him to stop at the store to pick up groceries. Somewhere on aisle 12, between the frozen pizza and the frozen yogurt, Derek's thoughts about his research paper vanished.

The following week, the instructor asked the students in the class how their papers were coming along. Some students gave long descriptions of their research progress, the amazing number of sources they'd found, and the detailed outlines they'd put together. Derek didn't raise his hand. Somehow, he never seemed to have enough time

Twitter/Cengage®/ Khomulo Anna/Shutterstock.com

Tweet

Derek
@DerekJSon

Heading to world history class. I have a 12 page paper due in a few weeks! This isn't fair!!

1:07 PM · 30 May 17

VIEW TWEET ACTIVITY

Tweet your reply

Studio 10ne/Shutterstock.com

to plan—and therefore nothing ever seemed to get done.

A whole week has gone by, Derek thought on his way back to his car after class. *I have to get going!* Writing had never exactly been Derek's strong suit. In fact, it was something he generally disliked doing. Through a great deal of hard work, he had managed to earn a 3.8 GPA in high school—a record he planned to continue. A course in World History—a general education class that was not even a part of his major—was *not* going to ruin things! The week had absolutely flown by, and there were plenty of good reasons why his paper was getting off to such a slow start. Derek didn't waste time, except for occasionally binge-watching his favorite TV shows while he studied and caught up on e-mail. Regardless, he rarely missed his nightly study time from 11:00 P.M. to 1:00 A.M. Those two hours were reserved for homework, no matter what. The problem, of course, was keeping other things from crowding in.

At the end of class two weeks later, Derek noticed that several students lined up to show the instructor the first drafts of their papers. *That's it!* Derek thought to himself. *The paper is due next Wednesday. I'll spend Monday night, my only free night of the week, in the library. I can get there right after work and stay until 11:00 A.M. or so. That'll be five hours of concentrated time. I should be able to write it then.* Despite his good intentions, Derek didn't arrive at the library until nearly 8:00 P.M., and his work session wasn't all that productive. As he sat in his library stall, he found himself obsessing about things that were happening at work. His boss was offering him more hours. Considering that he really did want a degree, should he take on more, even though he didn't really like the job? Finally, when he glanced at his watch, he was shocked to see that it was already midnight! The library was closing, and he'd only written three pages. Where had the time gone?

On his way out to the car, his cell phone rang. It was Justine, wondering where he was. Taura was running a fever, and his boss had called about an emergency meeting at 7:00 A.M. *If one more thing goes wrong . . .,* Derek thought to himself. His twelve-page paper was due in two days.

MAKE TO-DO LIST!?

Hintau Aliaksei/ Shutterstock.com

REMEMBER TO BUY MOM A BIRTHDAY GIFT!!!

blackpixel/ Shutterstock.com

REMEMBER:

COMPUTER TRAINING CLASS FOR WORK ON WEDNESDAY!

fotorro/Shutterstock.com

Focus challenge case **89**

1. What do you have in common with Derek? What time, energy, or money management issues are you experiencing in your life right now?

2. Describe the time-wasters that are a part of Derek's schedule. Do you think procrastination is an issue for Derek? What's behind his failure to make progress on his paper?

3. Suggest three realistic ways for Derek to balance work, school, and personal life.

TIME MANAGEMENT
REQUIRES FOCUS

Before diving into the details of time management skills, let's clarify one important point. There's a sense in which the phrase *time management* is misleading. Let's say you decide to spend an hour reading an assigned short story for your literature class. You may sit in the library with your book propped open in front of you from 3:00 to 4:00 P.M. on the dot. But you may not digest a single word you're reading. You may be going through the motions, reading on autopilot. Have you managed your time? Technically, yes. Your planner says, "Library, short story for Lit 101, 3:00–4:00 P.M." But did you get results? Time management expert Jeffrey Mayer asks provocatively in the title of his book: *If You Haven't Got the Time to Do It Right, When Will You Find the Time to Do It Over?*. Now that's a good question!

Time management is not just about managing your time, it's about managing your attention. Attention management is the ability to focus your attention, not just your time, on a designated activity so that you produce a desired result. And that's a big challenge, because research shows that the human mind wanders about half the time.[1] Time management may get you through reading a chapter of your textbook, but attention management will make sure that you understand what you're reading. It's about *focus*. If you manage your attention during that hour, then you've managed your time productively. Without attention management, time management is pointless. And the good thing is that we can train our brains to focus.

Succeeding in school, at work, and in life is not just about what you do. It's about what gets done. You can argue about the effort you put into an academic assignment all you want, but it's doubtful your professor will say, "You know what? You're right. You deserve an A just for staying up late last night working on this paper." Activity and accomplishment aren't the same thing. Neither are quantity and quality. Just because the assignment asked for five pages and you turned in five, doesn't mean that you automatically deserve an A. Results count. So don't confuse being busy with being successful. Staying busy isn't much of a challenge; being successful is.

Here's a list of preliminary academic time-saving tips. However, remember that these suggestions won't give you a surefire recipe for academic success. To manage your time, you must also manage yourself: your energy, your behavior,

"In truth, people can generally make time for what they choose to do; it is not really the time but the will that is lacking."

Sir John Lubbock, British banker, politician, and archaeologist (1834–1913)

your attention, your attitudes, *you*. Once you know how to manage all that, managing your time begins to work.

> Have a plan for your study session; include suggested time limits for each topic or task.

> Pay attention to what gets you off track. If you come to understand your patterns, you may be better able to control them.

> Turn off your phone or tell other people you live with that you don't want to be disturbed if something relatively unimportant comes up. Let them know what time you'll be available again.

> If you're working on your computer, work offline whenever possible. If you must be online to check sources, don't give in to the temptation to check your social networking account or e-mail every five minutes. According to a recent survey of over one million people, willpower is the one virtue human beings are least likely to recognize in themselves.[2] Whether it's resisting the third cupcake or staying on task to write a paper, willpower is sometimes hard to muster. But it can be cultivated by continually monitoring ourselves so that we're making decisions that are in our own best interest.

> Take two minutes to organize your workspace before beginning. Having the resources you need at your fingertips makes the session go much more smoothly, and you won't waste time searching for things you need.

> Focus. You can't do anything if you try to do everything. Multitasking may work for simple matters, such as scheduling a doctor's appointment while heating up a snack in the microwave. But when it comes to tasks that require brainpower, such as studying or writing, you need single-minded focus. Remember that the more you multitask, the less able you are to focus. Believe it or not, multitasking actually slows you down. It may sound like the solution to time management, but it's not![3]

> Actually use a timer. Forty minutes is thought by some experts to be the optimum amount of time to focus on something before taking a break. It takes 30 minutes to really get in gear, and then you arrive at another 10 minutes of optimal productivity. If you aim for more than that, tedium can set in. And use a real, physical countdown timer. When you hear the "ding," you get a real feeling of accomplishment and a bit of relief from stress. Online timing tools can get buried under layers of other software applications, and your cell phone brings the potential to delay what you're working on for "just a few quick texts." An actual timer can force you to face the challenge.[4]

> Monitor how your life works. There are different ways to manage time, and different ways work best for different people. Think of this analogy: Is time like ice or like water? A hard copy planner is a day-by-day record of solid blocks of time. But in today's world, solid blocks can melt away in seconds as events around us change. Managing time may be less like moving around ice cubes and more like "going with the flow." Many dynamic e-tools are available to help you on a minute-by-minute basis, if you stay on top of how time flows in your life.[5] Whether it's an automatic, audible reminder from something you've entered into your Google calendar or an electronic "personal assistant" like Siri via your iPhone, these reminder systems can help you manage your obligations.[6]

> "Don't confuse activity with accomplishment. 'Time = Success' is a myth."
>
> *Dr. Constance Staley, University of Colorado at Colorado Springs*

VARK IT!

Read/Write: Make a list of all the things that are distracting you the next time you sit down to study. Simply acknowledging them may help you set them aside for a while.

multitasking doing two or more tasks at one time

"To do two things at once is to do neither."

Publius Syrus, Maxim 7, 42 B.C.

Time management? WIIFM? Really—isn't it obvious? Who would ever even *ask* that question? But just in case you have any lingering doubts at all, let's take on the WIIFM question by busting some common myths about time management. At the very least, maybe your attitude—and, in fact, your actual behavior—needs tweaking, if not now, then certainly when you launch your career. Take a look:

Myth 1: I'm crazy busy; therefore, I *must* be productive. Hold on—not so fast! Just because you go through your workday at breakneck speed doesn't mean you actually accomplish all that much. You could be running in circles, and at the end of the day, you haven't really gotten very far. As you've read in this chapter, *activity* and *accomplishment* aren't the same thing.[7]

Myth 2: I can multitask like a champ. Research shows that unless you're super-human, you're probably not very good at multitasking. Virtually no one is; human beings aren't wired that way. And interestingly enough, those who think they're best at multitasking are actually worst at it. Ouch![8]

Myth 3: Workaholics are heroes. Some employees come in early, leave late, and take work home with them.

However, "working more doesn't mean you care more or get more done. It just means you work more."[9] Spending more time working doesn't guarantee the best results. In fact, workaholics' physical and mental well-being often suffer,[10] and their children are more likely to show signs of depression.[11] The quality of your work and the outcomes you achieve are what count, and working "smarter" by following the time management advice in this chapter can make all the difference.

Myth 4: Deadlines are the enemy. If you dread deadlines, don't. "Deadlines are a done-for-you prioritization tool that tells you a given project is important to focus on since its deadline is earlier."[12] They also help you figure out how much time you have to spend on each task and plan ahead. And when you meet a deadline, you get a natural high. Score!

Myth 5: Being tired is a badge of honor. Dragging ourselves around because we've said yes to too much, work too much, and have too many obligations hardly makes for superheroes in the workplace. In fact, just the opposite is true. "Sustained exhaustion is not a rite of passage. It's a mark of stupidity. Literally. Scientists have suggested that scores on IQ tests decline on each successive

> "My favorite things in life don't cost any money. It's really clear that the most precious resource we all have is time."
>
> *Steve Jobs (attended De Anza Community College, Cupertino, California)*

day you sleep less than you naturally would. It doesn't take long before the difference is telling."[13] Aetna CEO Mark Bertolini pays employees for sleeping (at night, not on the job). His perspective? "If they [employees] can prove they get 20 nights of sleep for seven hours or more in a row, we will give them $25 a night, up to $500 a year." (Employees use Fitbits, for example, to track their sleep.) Sleep is "really important. Being present in the workplace and making better decisions has a lot to do with our business fundamentals."[14]

No matter what your major or your eventual career, making time work for you instead of the other way around will do wonders to combat stress and anxiety, boost your "soft skills," and help you rise to the top as an exceptional employee. That's WIIFY!

ENERGY, OUR MOST PRECIOUS RESOURCE

"We live in a digital time. Our rhythms are rushed, rapid-fire and relentless, our days carved up into bits and bytes. . . . We're wired up but we're melting down." So begins the bestselling book *The Power of Full Engagement: Managing Energy, Not Time, Is the Key to High Performance and Personal Renewal*. The authors, Jim Loehr and Tony Schwartz, have replaced the term *time management* with the term *energy management*. Their shift makes sense. Because most of us are running in overdrive most of the time, energy is our most precious resource.

Energy management experts say you can't control time—everyone has a fixed amount—but you can manage your energy. And in fact, it's your responsibility to do so. Once a day is gone, it's gone. But your energy can be renewed.

It's clear that some things are energy *drains*: bad news, illness, interpersonal conflict, time-consuming hassles, a heavy meal, rainy days. Likewise, some things are energy *gains* giving you a surge of freshness: a new job, good friends, music, laughter, fruit, coffee. It's a good idea to recognize your own personal energy drains and gains so that you know how and when to renew your supply.[15] Energy management experts say it's not just about *spending time*, it's about *expending energy:*

> ➤ physical energy
> ➤ emotional energy
> ➤ mental energy
> ➤ spiritual energy

Of the four dimensions of energy, let's take a closer look at the first two. To do your very best academically, it helps to be *physically* energized and *emotionally* connected. Physical energy is measured in terms of *quantity*. How much energy do you have—a lot or a little? Emotional energy, on the other hand, is measured by *quality*. What kind of energy do you have—positive or negative? If you put them together into a two-dimensional chart with *quantity* as the vertical axis and *quality* as the horizontal axis, you get something like Figure 4.1.

When you're operating in the upper right quarter of the chart, with high, positive energy, you're most productive, which makes sense. The question is, How do you get there? How do you make certain you're physically energized and emotionally connected so that you can do your best academically?

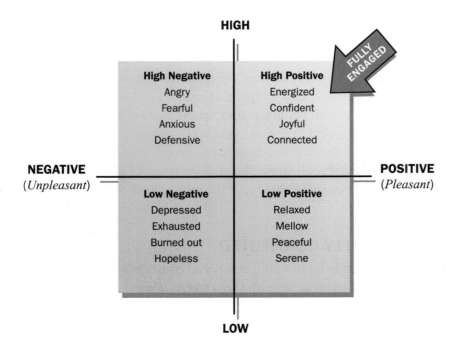

FIGURE 4.1

The Dynamics of Energy [16]

GET PHYSICALLY ENERGIZED

To make sure you're physically energized, try these suggestions.

1. **Snap to your body's rhythm.** Have you noticed times of the day when it's easier to concentrate than others? Perhaps you regularly crash in the middle of the afternoon, for example, so you go for a chocolate fix or a coffee pick-me-up. Everyone has a biological clock. Paying attention to your body's natural rhythms is important. Plan to do activities that require you to be alert during your natural productivity peaks. That's better than plodding through a tough assignment when the energy just isn't there. Use low energy times to take care of mindless chores that require little to no brainpower.[17]

2. **Up and at 'em.** What about 8:00 A.M. classes? Don't use your body's natural rhythms as an excuse to sleep through class! ("I'm just not a morning person. . . .") If you're truly not a morning person, don't sign up for early morning classes. If you are coming off working a night shift, you may need some rest first. Sleeping through your obligations won't do much for your success—and you'll be playing a continual game of catch-up, which takes even more time. Some experts advise that you start your day as early as possible. Marking six items off your to-do list before lunch can give you a real high.[18]

3. **Sleep at night, study during the day.** Burning the midnight oil and pulling all-nighters isn't the best idea either. It only takes one all-nighter to help you realize that a lack of sleep translates into a drop in performance. Without proper sleep, your ability to understand and remember course material is impaired. Research shows that the average adult requires seven to eight hours of sleep each night. If you can't get that much for whatever reason, take a short afternoon nap. Did you know that the Three Mile Island nuclear meltdown in Pennsylvania in 1979 and the Chernobyl disaster in the Ukraine in 1986 took place at 4 A.M. and 1:23 A.M., respectively? Experts believe it's no coincidence that both these events took place when workers would normally be sleeping.[19]

4. **"Burn premium fuel."** You've heard it before: Food is the fuel that makes us run. The better the fuel, the smoother we run. It's that simple. A solid diet of carbs—pizza, chips, and cookies—jammed into the fuel tank of your car would certainly gum up the works! When the demands on your energy are high, such as exam week, use premium fuel. If you don't believe this, think about how many people you know who get sick during times of high stress. Watch how many of your classmates are hacking and coughing their way through exams—or in bed, missing them altogether.

GET EMOTIONALLY CONNECTED

Physical needs count, to be sure, but emotional connections are part of the picture, too. See whether you agree with these suggestions.

1. **Communicate like it matters.** Sometimes we save our best communicating for people we think we have to impress: teachers, bosses, or clients,

---

VARK IT!

Multimodal: Set your phone alarm for the same three times each day—for example, 10 A.M., 3 P.M., and 8 P.M.—for one to two weeks. Each time the alarm goes off, write down your energy level (from 1 = low to 10 = high) and what you're doing. This mini-experiment will show you when your energy level is highest and which tasks energize you.

---

for example. But what about the people we care about most in our lives? Sometimes these people get the leftovers after all the "important" communicating has been done for the day. Sometimes we're so comfortable with these people that we think we can let it all hang out, even when doing so is *not* a pretty sight. Communicate as if everything you said would actually come true—"Just drop dead," for instance—and watch the difference! Communicating productively with people we care about is one of the best ways to replenish our energy.

2. **Choose how you renew.** Finish this comparison: Junk food is to physical energy as _____ is to emotional energy. If you answered "TV," you're absolutely right. Many people use television as their primary form of emotional renewal, but, like junk food, it's not that nutritious and it's easy to consume too much. Try more engaging activities that affirm you: singing or reading or playing a sport.[20]

3. **Let others renew you.** Remember that people don't just make demands on your time; they also provide emotional renewal. There's pure joy in a child's laugh, a friend's smile, a father's pat on the back. These small pleasures in life are priceless—prize them!

We've focused on physical and emotional energy here, but remember that all four dimensions of energy—physical, emotional, mental, and spiritual—are interconnected. If you subtract one from the equation, you'll be firing on less than four cylinders. If you are fully engaged and living life to the fullest, all four dimensions of your energy equation will be in balance.

"I'LL STUDY IN MY FREE TIME" …
AND WHEN IS THAT?

EXERCISE 4.1   **WHERE DID THE TIME GO?**

How do you spend your time? Complete this self-assessment to get some insights. Fill in the number of hours you spend doing each of the following, then multiply your answer by the number given (7 or 5 to figure weekly amounts) where appropriate. Some items may overlap, which is to be expected. Just fill in your numbers, accordingly, as best you can.

	Number of hours per day
Sleeping:	_____ × 7 = _____
Personal grooming (for example, showering, shaving, putting on makeup):	_____ × 7 = _____
Eating (meals and snacks; include preparation or driving time):	_____ × 7 = _____
Commuting Monday through Friday (to school and work):	_____ × 5 = _____
Doing errands and chores:	_____ × 7 = _____
Spending time with family (parents, siblings, children, or spouse):	_____ × 7 = _____
Spending time with boyfriend or girlfriend:	_____ × 7 = _____

(continued on next page)

	Number of hours per week
At work:	_____
In classes:	_____
At regularly scheduled functions (church, clubs, etc.):	_____
Socializing, hanging out, watching TV, talking on the phone, etc.:	_____

Now add up all the numbers in the far right column, and subtract your total from 168, the number of hours in a week.

168 − _____ = _____. This is the total number of hours you have remaining in your week for that ever-important task of studying. You may wish to revise how much time you spend on other activities of your life, based on whether you're already short on hours without studying factored in.

VARK IT!

Kinesthetic: Try writing each item from your schedule today on sticky notes and arrange them in chronological order. Then try moving the sticky notes around to make the best use of your time and energy.

VARK IT!

Visual: Think back over your day yesterday and draw it as a pie chart in PowerPoint. Look at this student's chart as a model. Subtracting the percentage of time for sleep, note that a considerable amount of his day was spent on social activities and there is no sector labeled as schoolwork. Are *you* using your time well?

My Week on Wednesday

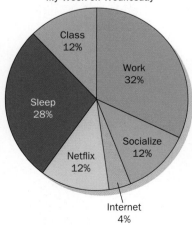

Class 12%
Work 32%
Sleep 28%
Socialize 12%
Netflix 12%
Internet 4%

Ask ten students when they study, and chances are at least eight will reply, "In my free time." The strange thing about this statement is that if you actually waited until you had free time to study, you probably never would. Truthfully, some students are amazed at how easily a day can race by without their ever thinking about cracking a book. This is why you should actually *schedule* your study time, but to do that, you should first be aware of how you're currently spending those twenty-four hours of each day.

Notice that Exercise 4.1 places studying at the bottom of the list, even though it's vital to your success in college. The exercise reflects a common attitude among college students, namely, that studying is what takes place after everything else gets done. Where does schoolwork rank on *your* list of priorities?

If succeeding in college is a top priority for you, then make sure that you're devoting adequate time to schoolwork outside the classroom. Most instructors expect you to study two to three hours outside of class for every hour spent in class. If it's a particularly challenging class, you may need even more study time. You can use the following chart to calculate the total number of hours you ought to expect to study—effectively—each week:

Credit hours for less demanding classes: _____ × 2 hours = _____ hours

Credit hours for typical/average classes: _____ × 3 hours = _____ hours

Credit hours for more challenging classes: _____ × 4 hours = _____ hours

Expected total study time per week = _____ hours

Remember, just putting in the time won't guarantee that you'll truly *understand* what you're studying. You need to ensure that your study time is productive by focusing your attention and strategically selecting study techniques that work best for you. Take a look at the following Quick Study for a visual preview of some of the primary time management ideas presented in this chapter.

FIGURE 4.4

Chapter 4 Quick Study: Master Time Management in 8 Steps

Master TIME MANAGEMENT in 8 Steps

1. Streamline

Get rid of what you don't need—in your e-mail inbox, on your to-do list, on top of your desk, and in your life. "Stuff happens," but you don't have to leave it there.

2. Plan

Start the day by planning. What's on the docket for the day? Planning first can save a boatload of time later.

3. Prioritize

A key part of planning is prioritizing. What absolutely HAS to get done today, and which tasks will take longer? What should you do first, second, third, etc.? It may seem easy, but sometimes we do what we like first. Then what needs to get done suffers.

4. Slow down to speed up

Effectiveness should be your goal, rather than speed. Mistakes cost time, and doing things over isn't always an option.

5. Focus

Rather than going wide, go deep. You'll be surprised how much you can accomplish!

6. Stay on task

Tedium can set in when you've been working on something for a long time. Hang in there and "just do it." Leaving many things hanging is stressful.

7. Say no to procrastination

Procrastination is tempting, but don't do it! Pay now or pay later, but remember that paying later costs more in remorse or missed opportunities!

Later

8. Stay organized

Once you get organized, stay there. It's easy to let chaos slowly rear its ugly head again!

SCHEDULE YOUR
WAY TO SUCCESS

TIME MONITOR

Can you remember how you spent all your time yesterday? Using the following Time Monitor, fill in as much as you can remember about how you spent your time yesterday, for the complete twenty-four-hour period. Be as detailed as possible, right down to thirty-minute segments. If you were multitasking, put down your primary activity, and put an asterisk beside that time block. When you're finished, note how many asterisks are on your chart, and assess your overall productivity.

12:00 A.M. _____	8:00 _____	4:00 _____
12:30 _____	8:30 _____	4:30 _____
1:00 _____	9:00 _____	5:00 _____
1:30 _____	9:30 _____	5:30. _____
2:00 _____	10:00 _____	6:00 _____
2:30 _____	10:30 _____	6:30 _____
3:00 _____	11:00 _____	7:00 _____
3:30 _____	11:30 _____	7:30 _____
4:00 _____	12:00 P.M. _____	8:00 _____
4:30 _____	12:30 _____	8:30 _____
5:00 _____	1:00 _____	9:00 _____
5:30 _____	1:30 _____	9:30 _____
6:00 _____	2:00 _____	10:00 _____
6:30 _____	2:30 _____	10:30 _____
7:00 _____	3:00 _____	11:00 _____
7:30 _____	3:30 _____	11:30 _____

Now monitor how you use your time today (or tomorrow if you're reading this at night), or your instructor may have you complete this Time Monitor for a several days. Again, be very specific. At the conclusion of your record-keeping for this exercise, go back to Exercise 4.1, and check to see how accurate your estimates were.

There is no one right way to schedule your time, but if you experiment with the system presented in this text, you'll be on the right path. Eventually, you can tweak the system to make it uniquely your own. Try these eight steps to schedule your way to success!

STEP 1: Fill out a "Term on a Page" Calendar. Right up front, create a "Term on a Page" calendar that shows the entire school term on one page. (See Exercise 4.3.) This particular activity works best on a chart like this—a month-by-month cell phone calendar won't let you see an entire term in detail at once, while the calendar in Exercise 4.3 allows you to see the big picture. You will need to have the syllabus from each of your classes and your school's course schedule to do this step properly. The following items should be transferred onto your "Term on a Page" calendar:

> Holidays when your school is closed

> Exam and quiz dates from your syllabi

> Project or paper deadlines from your syllabi

> Relevant administrative deadlines (e.g., registration for the next term, drop dates)

> Birthdays and anniversaries to remember

> Important out-of-town travel

> Dates that pertain to other family members, such as days that your children's school is closed or that your spouse is out of town for a conference—anything that will impact your ability to attend classes or study

"Take care of your minutes, and the hours will take care of themselves."

Lord Chesterfield, British statesman and diplomat (1694–1773)

STEP 2: Invest in a Planner. Although it's good to have the big picture, you must also develop an ongoing scheduling system that works for you. Using the "It's all right up here in my head" method is a surefire way to miss an important appointment, fly past the deadline for your term paper without a clue, or lose track of the time you have left to complete multiple projects.

Although your instructor will typically provide you with a class syllabus that lists test dates and assignment deadlines, trying to juggle multiple syllabi—not to mention your personal and work commitments—is enough to drive you crazy. You need *one* central place for all of your important deadlines, appointments, and commitments. This central place is a planner—a calendar book with space to write in each day. Most every successful person on the planet uses some kind of planner, whether paper or electronic.

TERM ON A PAGE

Take a few minutes right now to create your own Term on a Page, using the charts in Figure 4.2.

Term _____ Year _____

	Sunday	Monday	Tuesday	Wednesday	Thursday	Friday	Saturday
Month:							

FIGURE 4.2

Term on a Page

	Sunday	Monday	Tuesday	Wednesday	Thursday	Friday	Saturday
Month:							

	Sunday	Monday	Tuesday	Wednesday	Thursday	Friday	Saturday
Month:							

	Sunday	Monday	Tuesday	Wednesday	Thursday	Friday	Saturday
Month:							

	Sunday	Monday	Tuesday	Wednesday	Thursday	Friday	Saturday
Month:							

When you go planner shopping, remember that you don't have to break the bank unless you want to. Many new college students find that an ordinary paper-and-pencil daily calendar from an office supply store works best. Having a full page for each day means you can write your daily to-do list right in your planner (more on to-do lists later), and that can be a huge help. Using an online calendar, like Google calendar or Outlook, can work, too. But remember that unless you have a smart cell phone with internet access, an online calendar won't be portable, and you'll have to remember to enter events later.

STEP 3: Transfer Important Dates. The next step is to transfer important dates for the whole term from your "Term on a Page" overview to the appropriate days in your planner. It's important to be able to see all of your due dates together to create a big picture, but it's equally important to have these dates recorded in your actual planner because you will use it more regularly—as the final authority on your schedule.

STEP 4: Set Intermediate Deadlines. After recording the important dates for the entire academic term, look at the individual due dates for major projects or papers that are assigned. Then set intermediate stepping-stone goals that will ultimately help you accomplish your final goals. Working backward from the due date, choose and record deadlines for completing certain chunks of the work. For example, if you have a research paper due, you could set an intermediate deadline for completing all of your initial research and other deadlines for the prewriting, writing, and rewriting steps for the paper.

STEP 5: Schedule Fixed Activities for the Entire Term. Next, you'll want to schedule in all fixed activities throughout the entire term: class meeting times and reading assignments, religious services you regularly attend, club meetings, and family activities. It's also a great idea to schedule brief review sessions for your classes. Of course, sometimes you'll be going directly into another class, but ten-minute segments of time before and after each class to review your notes help prepare you for surprise quizzes and improve your comprehension.

STEP 6: Check for Schedule Conflicts. Now, take a final look at your planner. Do you notice any major scheduling conflicts, such as a planned business trip smack dab in the middle of midterm exam week? Look for these conflicts now, when there's plenty of time to adjust your plans and talk with your instructor to see what you can work out.

STEP 7: Schedule Flextime. In all the scheduling of important dates, checking and double-checking, don't forget one thing. You do need personal time for eating, sleeping, exercising, and other regular activities that don't have a set time frame. Despite your planner, life will happen. If you get a toothache, you'll need to see a dentist right away. Several times each week, you can count on something coming up that will offer you a chance (or force you) to revise your schedule. The decision of how high the item ranks on your priority list rests with you, but the point is to leave some wiggle room in your schedule. One other good idea is to follow the "two-minute" rule. Do any work items that can be completed in two minutes right then, on the spot. Doing so will free you from nagging details as you plan for bigger items.[21]

"Nothing is so fatiguing as the eternal hanging on of an uncompleted task."

William James, American psychologist and philosopher (1842–1910)

STEP 8: Monitor Your Schedule Every Day. At this point, you've developed a working time management system. Now it's important to monitor your use of that system on a daily basis. Each night, take three minutes to review the day's activities. How well did you stick to your schedule? Did you accomplish the tasks you set out to do? Do you need to revise your schedule for the rest of the week based on something that happened—or didn't happen—today? This simple process will help you better schedule your time in the future and give you a sense of accomplishment—or of the need for more discipline—for tasks completed, hours worked, and classes attended.

TO DO OR NOT TO DO?
THERE *IS* NO QUESTION

Part of your personal time management system should be keeping an ongoing to-do list. Although the concept of a to-do list sounds relatively simple, here are a few tricks of the trade.

Before the beginning of each school week, brainstorm all the things that you want or need to get done in the upcoming week. Using this random list of to-do items, assign a priority level next to each one. The A-B-C method is simple and easy to use:

A = must get this done; highest priority

B = very important, but not absolutely necessary to get done immediately

C = not terribly important, but should be done right away (time-sensitive)

The two factors to consider when assigning a priority level to a to-do item are *importance* and urgency, creating four time zones. Use Figure 4.3 as a guide.[22]

After you've assigned a time zone to each item, review your list of A and B priorities and ask yourself:

1. **Do any of the items fit best with a particular day of the week?** For example, donating blood may be a high priority task for you, yet you don't want to do it on a day when you have a sports event planned. That might leave you with two available days in the upcoming week that you can donate blood.

2. **Can any items be grouped together to make things easier?** For example, you may have three errands to run downtown on your to-do list, so grouping them together will save you from making three separate trips.

3. **Do any A and B priorities qualify as floating tasks that can be completed anytime, anywhere?** For example, perhaps you were assigned an

urgency in need of immediate attention

FIGURE 4.3

Time Zones

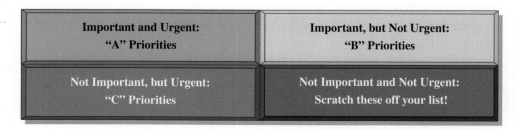

Important and Urgent: "A" Priorities	Important, but Not Urgent: "B" Priorities
Not Important, but Urgent: "C" Priorities	Not Important and Not Urgent: Scratch these off your list!

SO MUCH TO DO—SO LITTLE TIME

Assume this is your to-do list for today (Monday). Assign each item one of the four time zones described earlier: A, B, and C (and strike through any items that are not urgent and not important). Finally, renumber the items to indicate which you would do first, second, and so forth.

Start time: 9:00 A.M., Monday morning, during the second week of the fall term.

1. _____ Respond to Professor Jordan's e-mail before class tomorrow. He sent you a message saying he wants to talk to you before class about some problems with the assignment you turned in.

2. _____ Pick up your paycheck and get to the bank before it closes at 5:00 P.M. this afternoon.

3. _____ Call your mother to find out how grandma is doing in the hospital.

4. _____ Start figuring out how to go about your new assignment at work. Your boss seems nervous about it.

5. _____ Call or Facetime your favorite aunt. She lives overseas in a time zone seven hours ahead of yours. Today is her fiftieth birthday.

6. _____ Stop by the Health Center to take advantage of free meningitis vaccinations today only.

7. _____ Listen to the new music you downloaded yesterday.

8. _____ Leave a note asking your boy- or girlfriend/sibling/child to please stop leaving messes everywhere. It's really aggravating.

9. _____ Read the two chapters in your history textbook for the in-class quiz on Wednesday.

10. _____ Watch the season premiere of a TV show you've been waiting for at 9 P.M. tonight.

11. _____ Write a rough draft of the essay due in your composition class on Thursday.

12. _____ Invite an out-of-town friend to spend the weekend.

13. _____ Return the three library books that are a week overdue.

14. _____ Call your math Teaching Assistant and leave a message asking for an appointment during her office hours to get help with the homework due on Wednesday. Nearly everyone is confused about the assignment.

15. _____ Meet your best friend for dinner for his or her birthday at 6 P.M.

Outline the criteria you used for making your decisions. For example, did you base your answers on personal priorities, locations (combining tasks based on where you need to be to do them), urgency/importance, or some other principle? (Note that this exercise asks you to put these tasks in order, according to whatever principles from this chapter you choose—not to figure out how to multitask and accomplish several at once!) If you choose to call your aunt (5) while writing your essay (11), chances are she'll hear the tapping of the keys and the breaks in the conversation and know exactly what you're doing. It's important to base your choices not only on what's quick or convenient, but also on how much people and priorities mean to you.

extra-long reading assignment for one of your classes. It's both important and urgent, an A priority item. Bring your book to read while waiting at the dentist's office for your appointment, a B priority. Planning ahead can really help save time.

4. **Do any priorities need to be shifted?** As the days pass, some of your B priorities will become A priorities due to the urgency factor increasing. Or maybe an A priority will become a C priority because something changed about the task. This is normal.

Items you've marked with a C must be decided on a case-by-case basis. But don't let their urgency convince you that you should do them before you accomplish items on your A and B lists. As for those not important and not urgent to-do items, scratch them off the list right now. Life is too short to waste time on unimportant tasks. Give yourself permission to focus on what's important. Because time is a limited resource, one of the best ways to guarantee a successful college experience is to use it wisely. If you don't already use these tools on a regular basis, give them a shot. What do you have to lose except time?

HOW TIME FLIES!

According to published informal calculations, in a lifetime, the average American will spend:

> 1.5 years in the bathroom

> 3.66 years eating

> 1.1 year cleaning

> 2 years in meetings

> 3 months in traffic

> 25 years sleeping

> 2.5 years cooking

> 9.1 years watching TV[24]

What a waste of time! We can't do much about some of these items, but what *can* we do about other time-wasters? Plan—schedule—organize! Think about the issue of control in time management, and come up with examples for the following:

1. Things you think you can't control, and you can't.

2. Things you think you can't control, but you can.

3. Things you think you can control, but you can't.

4. Things you think you can control, but you don't.

5. Things you think you can control, and you can.

Perhaps you came up with something like *medical emergencies* for (1). You could have said *family or friends bothering you while you study* for (2). For (4), maybe you could control how much *time you waste online*, but you don't. And for (5), perhaps you thought of *your attention*. You're absolutely right. But what about (3)? Did anything fit there? Are there things you think you can control, but you can't? Try to think of something that would fit into (3), and then think of creative ways you really could control this situation if you tried.[25] Have you ever thought about how much the issues of control and time management are related?

"We cannot waste time. We can only waste ourselves."

George Matthew Adams, newspaper columnist, (1878–1962)

According to experts, there are four kinds of common problematic time management "P's" in the world. When it comes to time management, control is generally a good thing. You take control and become more productive. But take a look at these four "P's." They exert control in ways that can bring counterproductive results!

➤ **The Preemptive.** Preemptives believe they are doing their best; in fact, they are continuously ahead of the game. They constantly, compulsively play "beat the clock." They're always way ahead of schedule. So what's wrong with that? Sometimes, nothing. But preemptives can gain a reputation of being non–team players, only out for themselves. They look like they're trying to impress everyone—or someone in particular, like the boss or teacher.

➤ **The People Pleaser.** People pleasers have the best of intentions, but they take on too much and sabotage their own effectiveness by trying to make others happy. Always saying yes to everyone may mean that there's no time left for their own work. Over time, they can even come to resent the very people they're trying to please and vice versa.

➤ **The Perfectionist.** Nothing is ever good enough for perfectionists. In effect, what they do is make other people play a waiting game while they continue to tinker with their projects to make them into some ideal they may never reach. They're control freaks, and they lead anxiety-ridden lives.

➤ **The Procrastinator.** Procrastinators are adrenaline junkies. They put things off until the 11th hour and then make a mad dash for the finish line, trailing a long list of excuses. Often, the root cause of procrastination is fear. Although the perfectionist will only accept an A+, the procrastinator is secretly afraid of not ever being able to achieve an A+. If she doesn't turn in an assignment, she can't find out just how good (or not) she is.[26]

EXERCISE 4.5

ARE YOU A PREEMPTIVE, PEOPLE-PLEASING, PERFECTIONISTIC PROCRASTINATOR?

Do you know people who fit into each of these four problematic time management "P" categories? Do you fit into one of these categories? Brainstorm ways of helping these people improve their time management skills. What advice would you give each type?

Preemptive

People Pleaser

Perfectionist

Procrastinator

THE "P" WORD. READ THIS SECTION *NOW!* ... OR
MAYBE TOMORROW ... OR ...

Picture this: You sit down to work on a challenging homework assignment. After a few minutes, you think, *Man, I'm thirsty,* so you get up and get a soda. Then you sit back down to continue your work. A few minutes later, you decide that some chips would go nicely with your soda and you head to the kitchen. Again, you sit down to face the task before you, as you concentrate more on eating than on working. Ten minutes go by and a nagging thought starts taking over: *Must do laundry.* Up you go again to throw a load of clothes in the washer. Before long you're wondering where all the time went. Because you only have an hour left before class, you think, *Why bother getting started now? Doing this project will take much more time than that, so I'll just start it tomorrow.* Despite good intentions at the beginning of your work session, you've just succeeded in accomplishing zip, nada, nothing.

EXERCISE 4.6   ## WHO, ME? PROCRASTINATE?

Procrastination is a habit. It may show up as not getting around to doing your homework (if you don't turn it in, you can't get a bad grade on it—which almost guarantees that you'll get a bad grade on it), not vacuuming the carpet because it takes too much energy to lug the machine around, or not getting to work on time because your job is boring. What about you? Think about the following ten situations, and put a check mark next to each one to indicate the degree to which you normally procrastinate:

	Always	Sometimes	Never
1. Doing homework	_____	_____	_____
2. Writing a paper	_____	_____	_____
3. Studying for tests	_____	_____	_____
4. Reading class material	_____	_____	_____
5. Meeting with your academic advisor	_____	_____	_____
6. Texting/e-mailing a friend	_____	_____	_____
7. Playing a game/hanging out	_____	_____	_____
8. Going to see a movie you've heard about	_____	_____	_____
9. Meeting someone for dinner at a restaurant	_____	_____	_____
10. Spending social/personal time online	_____	_____	_____

If you are like many students, you checked "always" or "sometimes" more often for the first five items than you did for the last five. But procrastination isn't as simple as not procrastinating when you want to do something and procrastinating when you don't. You may actually hate vacuuming but decide to vacuum the entire house so that you don't have to face studying for a test. There are "layers" of procrastination and many reasons why people procrastinate. Which of these apply to you?

_____ Avoiding something you see as unpleasant

_____ Feeling overwhelmed by all you have to do

_____ Being intimidated by the task itself

_____ Fearing failure

_____ Fearing success

_____ Not realizing how important the task is

_____ Reacting to your own internal conflict

_____ Protecting your self-esteem

_____ Waiting for a last-minute adrenaline rush

_____ Just plain not wanting to

Congratulations! You—like thousands of other college students—have just successfully procrastinated! Researchers define procrastination as "needlessly delaying tasks to the point of experiencing subjective discomfort."[27] And according to researchers, 70 to 95 percent of college students admit to procrastinating on their assignments.[28]

You may be in the majority, but alas, in this case, there's no safety in numbers! Academic procrastination is a major threat to your ability to succeed in college. And procrastination in the working world can actually bring your job, and ultimately your career, to a screeching halt. Plenty of people try to rationalize their procrastination by claiming that they work better under pressure. However, the challenge in college is that during some weeks of the term, every class you're taking will have an assignment or test due, all at once, and if you procrastinate, you'll not only generate tremendous anxiety for yourself, but you'll lower your chances of succeeding at any of them.

Before you can control the procrastination monster in your life, it's important to understand *why* you procrastinate. Think about all the instances in which you don't procrastinate: meeting your friends for dinner, returning a phone call from a friend, going to the store. Why are those things easy to do, but getting started on an assignment is difficult until you feel the jaws of a deadline closing down on you?[29] The reasons for procrastinating vary from person to person, but once you know your own reasons for putting things off, you'll be in a better position to address the problem from its root cause.

The next time you find yourself procrastinating, ask yourself why. Procrastination hurts your chances for success and gives you ready-made excuses if you don't succeed: "It's like running a full race with a knapsack full of bricks on your back. When you don't win, you can say it's not that you're not a good runner, it's just that you had this sack of bricks on your back."[30] In addition to understanding why you procrastinate, try these ten procrastination busters to help you kick the habit.

1. **Keep track (of your excuses).** Write them down consistently, and soon you'll be able to recognize them for what they are. Own your responsibilities—in school and in the rest of your life.

2. **Break down.** Break your project into its smaller components. A term paper, for example, can be broken down into the following smaller parts: prospectus, thesis, research, outline, small chunks of writing, and bibliography. Completing smaller tasks along the way is much easier than facing a threatening monster of a project.

3. **Trick yourself.** When you feel like procrastinating, pick some aspect of the project that's easy and that you would have to do anyway. If the thought of an entire paper is overwhelming you, for example, work on the bibliography to start. Start with something—*anything*—that will get you into the rhythm of the work.

4. **Resolve issues.** If something's eating away at you, making it difficult to concentrate, take care of it. Sometimes you must deal with a bossy friend, your kids vying for your attention, or something equally intrusive. Then get down to work.

5. **Get real.** Set realistic goals for yourself. If you declare that you're going to finish a twelve-page paper in five hours, you're already doomed. Procrastinators

Shalom Ormsby/Blend Images/Getty Images

"Things which matter most should never be at the mercy of things which matter least."

Johann Wolfgang von Goethe, German writer and scholar (1749–1832)

> "One look at an e-mail can rob you of fifteen minutes of focus. One call on your cell phone, one tweet, one instant message can destroy your schedule, forcing you to move meetings, or blow off really important things, like love, and friendship."
>
> *Jacqueline Leo, magazine editor and media producer*

are sometimes overly optimistic. They underestimate how much time something will take. Make it a habit to keep track of how long assignments take you in all your courses so that you can be increasingly realistic over time. And be specific. Instead of writing, "Finish Chapter 10" in your planner, write exactly what you need to do: "Finish reading Chapter 10, answer the discussion questions at the end, and e-mail my responses to my instructor."

6. **Capture killer B's.** You're working on Task A when Task B presents itself—perhaps it's a text or an e-mail, something that seems important at the time. Immediately capture the threatening "Killer B" by writing it in a paper notebook that's always by your side. Why paper? If you use an online journal, you'll be tempted to wander further online. You may end up in Timbuktu.com and make countless stops along the way.[31]

7. **Make a deal with yourself.** Even if it's only spending fifteen minutes on a task that day, do it so that you can see progress.

8. **Overcome fear.** Many of the reasons for procrastinating have to do with our personal fears. We may fear not doing something perfectly, or failing completely—or even the responsibility that comes with success to keep succeeding. But as Susan Jeffers, author and lecturer, states, "Feel the fear, and do it anyway!"

9. **Get tough.** Sometimes projects simply require discipline. The best way to complete a tough task is to just dig in. Become your own taskmaster; "crack the whip" and force yourself to focus on those things that are high priorities, but perhaps not your idea of fun.

10. **Acknowledge accomplishment.** We're not talking major shopping sprees at Neiman Marcus here. We're talking reasonable, meaningful rewards that match up with how much effort you invested. Go buy yourself a small treat, call your best friend in another state, take a relaxing soak in the bathtub, or do something to celebrate your accomplishments—big and small—along the way. Acknowledgment, from yourself or others, is a great motivator for tackling future projects.

BEYOND JUGGLING: *REALISTICALLY* MANAGE WORK, SCHOOL, AND PERSONAL LIFE*

Your personal time management needs depend on who you are and how many obligations you have. Today's college students are more diverse than ever. Increasing numbers of college students are also parents, part-time employees or full-time professionals, husbands or wives, community volunteers, soccer coaches, or Sunday school teachers. How on earth can you possibly juggle it all?

The answer? You can't. According to work–life balance expert Dawn Carlson, juggling is a knee-jerk coping mechanism—the default setting when time gets tight and it seems that nothing can be put on the back burner. If you, like millions of others, feel overworked, overcommitted, and exhausted at every turn, you may have already learned that you can't juggle your way to a balanced life. It's impossible.[32]

*Adapted from Sandholtz, K., Derr, B., Buckner, K., & Carlson, D. (2002). *Beyond juggling: Rebalancing your busy life*. San Francisco: Berrett-Koehler Publishing.

Now for the good news. Balance among work, school, and personal life is possible. All of us have three primary areas of our lives that should be in balance, ideally—meaningful work (including school), satisfying relationships, and a healthy lifestyle. In addition to work and relationships, we all need to take care of ourselves. See what you think of these five rebalancing strategies. The idea is you can't have it all, but you can have it better than you do now.

ALTERNATING

If you use this strategy, your work–life balance comes in separate, concentrated doses. You may throw yourself into your career with abandon, and then cut back or quit work altogether and focus intensely on your family. You may give your job 110 percent during the week but devote Saturdays to physical fitness or to your kids or to running all the errands you've saved up during the week. Or you save Tuesdays and Thursdays for homework and go to classes Mondays, Wednesdays, and Fridays. People who use this strategy alternate between important things, and it works for them. An alternator's motto is "I want to have it all, but just not all at once."

OUTSOURCING

Outsourcing, or paying someone else to do something for you, is another solution. An outsourcer's motto might be "I want to have it all, not do it all." This strategy helps you achieve work–life balance by giving someone else some of your responsibilities—usually in your personal life—to free up time for the tasks you care about most. If you have enough money, hire someone to clean the house or mow the lawn. If you don't, trade these jobs among family, friends, or neighbors who band together to help each other. Of course, there are ways this strategy could be misused by college students. Don't even think about outsourcing your research papers by having someone else write them or downloading them from the internet with a charge card! Warning: This practice will definitely be hazardous to your academic health! In fact, your college career may be over!

BUNDLING

Bundling is efficient because it allows you to "kill two birds with one stone." Examine your busy life and look for areas in which you can double dip, such as combining exercising with socializing. If your social life is suffering because you have too much to do, take walks with a friend so that you can talk along the way. A bundler's motto is "I want to get more mileage out of the things I do by combining activities."

> "The bad news is time flies. The good news is you're the pilot."
>
> *Michael Altshuler,*
> *motivational speaker*

TECHFLEXING

Technology allows us to work from almost anywhere, anytime, using technology. If you telecommute from home several days a week for your job, you might get up early, spend some time on e-mail, go out for a run, have breakfast with your family, and then get back on your computer. In the office, you use instant messaging to stay connected to family members or a cell phone to call home while commuting to a business meeting. Chances are you can telecommute to your campus library and do research online, register for classes online, and pay all your bills online, including tuition. Use technology, and the flexibility it gives you, to your advantage to merge important aspects of your life.

SIMPLIFYING

People who use this strategy have decided they don't want it all. They've reached a point where they make a permanent commitment to stop the craziness in their lives. The benefit of simplifying is greater freedom from details, stress, and the rat race. But there are trade-offs, of course. People may have to take a significant cut in pay in order to work fewer hours or at a less demanding job. But for them, it's worth it.[33]

These five strategies, used separately or in combination, have helped many people who are dealing with work, school, and family commitments at the same time. They all require certain trade-offs. None of these strategies is a magic solution.

But the alternative to rebalancing is more stress, more physical and emotional exhaustion, more frustration, and much less personal satisfaction. If you focus on rebalancing your life—making conscious choices and course corrections as you go—small changes can have a big impact. Work–life balance isn't an all-or-nothing proposition. It's an ever-changing journey. So take it one step at a time.

"Don't tell me where your priorities are. Show me where you spend your money and I'll tell you what they are."

James W. Frick, former vice president, University of Notre Dame

TIME IS
MONEY!

EXERCISE 4.7   ## HOW FISCALLY FIT ARE YOU?

Have you ever heard the phrase "Time is money"? Before leaving the subject of time and energy management, let's look at how you manage your money as well. How good are you at managing your finances? Check one of the three possible responses for each statement, to get a sense of how financially savvy you are.

	Always true of me	Sometimes true of me	Never true of me
1. At any given moment in time, I know the balance of my checking account.	_____	_____	_____
2. I use my credit card for particular types of purchases only, such as gas or food.	_____	_____	_____
3. I pay off my bills in full every month.	_____	_____	_____
4. I know the interest rate on my credit cards.	_____	_____	_____
5. I resist impulse buying and only spend when I need things.	_____	_____	_____
6. I have a budget and I follow it.	_____	_____	_____
7. I put money aside to save each month.	_____	_____	_____
8. When I get a pay raise, I increase the proportion of money I save.	_____	_____	_____
9. I keep track of my spending on a daily or weekly basis.	_____	_____	_____
10. I don't allow myself to get pressured by others into buying things I don't really need.	_____	_____	_____

Look over your responses. If you have more checks in the "Never true of me" column than you do in either of the two others, you may be able to put the information you're about to read to good use!

It's true that "time is money." If you're so efficient with your time that you can call more customers or sell more products, then time does equal money. If your company is the first to introduce a hot new kind of cell phone or a zippy fuel-efficient car, you win. Even if better models come out next year, they may fall flat because people have already invested. Both time management and money management are key to your college success.

For example, studies show that working too many hours at a paid job increases your chances of dropping out of college.[34] Many students find themselves working more so that they can spend more, which in turn takes time away from their studies. They may take a semester off from college to make a pile of money and then never come back. Although there's evidence that working a moderate amount can help you polish your time and energy management skills, the real secret to financial responsibility in college is to track your habits and gain the knowledge you need to make sound financial decisions.

VARK IT!

Kinesthetic: Try a free online budget tool such as Mint.com, or create an Excel spreadsheet to track your monthly budget. Look for opportunities to cut your spending.

EXERCISE 4.8 CREATE A SPENDING LOG

Take a look at this student's spending log, then complete one for yourself. Money has a way of slipping through our fingers. Choose one entire day that is representative of your spending, and use the chart on the next page to keep track of how you spend money. Write down everything from seemingly small, insignificant items to major purchases, and explain why you made each purchase. Your log may look something like this student's:

TIME	ITEM	LOCATION	AMOUNT	REASON
8–9 A.M.	coffee and bagel	convenience store	$5.50	overslept!
9–10 A.M.	computer paper	office supply store	$4.25	English paper due
10–11 A.M.	gas fill-up	gas station	$33.75	running on fumes!
11 A.M.– 12 P.M.	burger and fries	fast-food restaurant	$6.00	lunch on the run
12–1 P.M.	toiletries, etc.	drugstore	$21.00	out of stock
1–2 P.M.	energy drink	convenience store	$2.95	forgot to bring
2–3 P.M.	supplies	bookstore	$29.25	forgot to get earlier
3–7 P.M.	WORK			
7–8 P.M.	pizza	pizza place	$9.00	meet friends
8–9 P.M.	week's groceries	grocery store	$43.30	cupboard is bare!
9–10 P.M.	laundry	laundromat	$8.00	washer broken
10–11 P.M.	STUDY TIME			
11 P.M.– 12 A.M.	weekend movie, online tickets, DVDs, smartphone apps	internet retail websites, app store	$195.00	friend's recommendations, need games

This student has spent $368 today without doing anything special! When you analyze his expenditures, you can find patterns. He seems to (1) forget to plan so he (1) spends money continuously throughout the day, (2) spends relatively

(continued on next page)

large amounts of money online, (3) be particularly vulnerable late at night, and (4) spends money grabbing food on the run. These are patterns he should be aware of if he wants to control his spending. He could pack food from home to save a significant amount of money, for example. Now create your own chart.

TIME	ITEM	LOCATION	AMOUNT	REASON
8–9 A.M.				
9–10 A.M.				
10–11 A.M.				
11 A.M. – 12 P.M.				
12–1 P.M.				
1–2 P.M.				
2–3 P.M.				
3–4 P.M.				
4–5 P.M.				
5–6 P.M.				
6–7 P.M.				
7–8 P.M.				
8–9 P.M.				
9–10 P.M.				
10–11 P.M.				
11 P.M.–12 A.M.				

What patterns do you notice about your spending? What kinds of changes will you try to make to curb any unnecessary spending?

THE PERILS OF PLASTIC

Credit cards—those attractive, little pieces of plastic that make spending money so convenient and so easy. Why go out of your way and make repeated trips to the ATM to get cash when you can just whip out your credit card instead? Now you can even customize your own with a personal photo of you and your beloved Cocker Spaniel, Rusty, or whatever your heart desires. You can spend, spend, spend until you max out. Many students today find debit cards less tempting because they tap your bank account immediately and help you keep track of your spending. But if you already have a credit card or plan to get one, keep this general advice in mind.

1. **Think about the difference between needs and wants.** You may think you need particular things so that your friends will like you ("Hey, let's stop for a burger"), so that you have a new item (like a new car you can't afford), or so that you look fabulous (like pricey manicures). Here's a rule

of thumb: If buying something simply helps you move from acceptable to amazing, it's not an emergency. Do you really need a mocha latté every day?

2. **Leave home without it.** Don't routinely take your credit card with you. Use cash and save your credit card for true emergencies or essentials, like gas and groceries. Do you really want to risk paying interest on today's ice cream cone years from now?

3. **Don't spend money you don't have.** Only charge what you can pay for each month. Just because your credit card limit is $2,000 doesn't mean you need to spend that much each month. One piece of good advice is to "live like a student while you are in school so you don't have to live like a student after you graduate."[36]

If you buy one $4 coffee beverage every day, you will be spending:

$28 a week

$120 a month

$1,460 a year

$7,300 over five years

If you had invested that money, you would have earned (assuming a generous 9% return on your investment):

Approximately **$9,300** over 5 years

Approximately **$16,000** over 10 years

Approximately **$240,000** over 30 years

Approximately **$630,000** over 40 years!

In 40 years, your coffee habit could generate an income of *more than $2,600 a month!*

Now THAT'S something to think about!

Source: Branden Williams and Jevita Rogers, University of Colorado, Colorado Springs. Used with permission. Based on http://finance.yahoo.com/news/what-your-starbucks-habit-really-costs-you.html

4. **Understand how credit works.** It's important to know the basics. According to one source, "Only 15% [of college students] have any idea how much their interest rate is, and fewer than one in 10 students know their interest rate, late fee and over-limit fee amounts."[37]

Here are some terms you need to know:

• **Credit reports.** Your credit history is based on (1) how many credit cards you owe money on, (2) how much money you owe, and (3) how many late payments you make. Bad grades on your credit report can make your life difficult later.

• **Fees.** Credit card companies charge you in three ways: (1) annual fees (a fee you must pay every year to use the card); (2) finance charges (a charge for loaning you the money you can't pay back when your bill is due); and (3) late fees (for missing a monthly payment deadline). Think about what's most important to you—no annual fee, frequent flyer miles, or a lower interest rate—and shop around!

• **The fine print.** How can you learn more? Read your credit card contract carefully. Credit card companies must give you certain important

BOX 4.2

TOP TEN FINANCIAL AID FAQs[38]

Financial aid. Like all good things, you have to know how it works. You can think of financial aid as complicated and time-consuming, or it can be the one thing that keeps you in school. Take a look at these questions students often ask about the mysteries of financial aid. Most students need financial help of some kind to earn a college degree. Here is some information to help you navigate your way financially.[39]

1. **Who qualifies for financial aid?** Almost everyone! You may not think you qualify for financial aid, but it's a good idea to apply anyway. You won't know until you apply, and some types of aid are based on criteria other than your income and assets.

2. **What does FAFSA stand for?** FAFSA stands for Free Application for Federal Student Aid. You apply online at fafsa.gov, or you can get a copy of the application by calling 1-800-4-FED-AID.

3. **What types of financial aid exist?** You can receive financial aid in the form of scholarships, fellowships, loans, grants, or work-study awards. Generally, scholarships and fellowships are for students with special academic, artistic, or athletic abilities; students with interests in specialized fields; students from particular parts of the country; or students from minority groups. Typically, you don't repay them. Loans and grants come in a variety of forms and from several possible sources, either federal or state government or private organizations. Loans must be repaid, but there are many loan programs to pay down your student loans if you pursue fields such as teaching, nursing, or public service. In addition, if you qualify for a need-based work-study job on or off campus, you can earn an hourly wage to help with your educational expenses.

4. **When should I apply?** You can apply for financial aid any time after October 1 of the year before you intend to go to college, but be mindful of your school's priority filing date to ensure you meet that deadline, as grant funds are limited. The FAFSA requires tax information from the previous two years. Remember, you must be enrolled by the start of classes to receive funds.

5. **Do I have to reapply every year?** Yes. Your financial situation can change over time. Your brothers or sisters may start college while you're in school, for example, which can change your family's status. If you experience any financial or household changes from what is listed on your FAFSA,

make sure you contact the financial aid office, and they will be able to help you file an appeal to take your change of circumstances into account.

6. **How can I keep my financial aid over my college years?** Assuming your financial situation remains fairly similar from year to year, you must demonstrate that you're making progress toward a degree in terms of credits and a minimum GPA. Remember that if you drop courses, your financial aid may be affected based on whether you're considered to be a full-time or part-time student.

7. **Who's responsible for paying back my loans?** You are. Others can help you, but ultimately the responsibility is yours and yours alone. If your parents forget to make a payment or don't pay a bill on time, you will be held responsible. Loan repayment begins once you are no longer enrolled at least half-time or you graduate. Most loans will have a grace period of six or nine months before you must begin repayment. You can request a forbearance or deferment if you need to postpone payments beyond your grace period.

8. **If I get an outside scholarship, should I report it to the Financial Aid office on campus?** Yes. Most of the time an additional scholarship does not change the amount of financial aid you have been awarded, but if it does, your Financial Aid office will adjust your financial aid package if necessary. Also, the rules require that scholarships must be processed through the financial aid office. In most instances when financial aid awards are adjusted, the loans a student is offered are adjusted before any grants are applied.

9. **Where can I find out more?** Your best source of information is in the Office of Financial Aid right on your own campus. Or you can get information online at studentaid.ed.gov. Or call the Federal Student Aid Information Center at 1–800–433–3243, and ask for free copies of student guides to financial aid from the U.S. Department of Education.

10. **When it comes to money matters and college, is there "an app for that?"** Yes! Check out mint.com, goodbudget.com, or easyenvelope.com. (But be aware of using apps that may be collecting personal information that could put you at risk. Identify theft is a reality!) The best advice is to start with your own Financial Aid Office! They have a wealth of information to share!

information, which is often on their website. Go to the Federal Reserve website for vital, bottom-line information, and search online to find out more.

5. **Track your expenses.** All kinds of tools—technology-based and otherwise—can help you discover where your money actually goes. To control your spending, use a credit card with caution or use a debit card. Remember, too, that your bank is tracking your expenses, and they'll alert you if

someone is on a spending spree with the help of *your* credit card! Banks take credit card fraud very seriously, and you should, too.

6. **If you're already in financial trouble, ask for help.** Talk to an expert who can help you figure out what to do.

HOW DO YOU "SPEND" YOUR TIME[40]

Add up the cost of going to college for an entire term: tuition for one semester/trimester/quarter, the total estimated cost of all the gas you will use to get to and from class for the term, books and supplies, a computer you may have bought, and child care or any other expenses related to your going to school. Put down everything you can think of.

Total Cost = _____

Divide that grand total by the number of hours you are in school (number of weeks class is in session multiplied by the number of hours you are scheduled to be in class). For example, if you are taking two 3-hour classes for a sixteen-week semester, the number you will divide your grand total by is 96 (= 6 hours × 16 weeks).

Total Cost Divided by Hours = _____

Completing this exercise will show you how much money each class session costs you—and the cost of missing class! Compare your "hourly rate" with that of your classmates and discuss the results as a group.

CURIOSITY: *CHOOSE TO CHOOSE!*

Have you ever thought about how many dozens, if not hundreds, of choices you make each day? Psychologist and Professor Barry Schwartz, in his book *The Paradox of Choice: Why More Is Less*, believes that making nonstop choices can actually cause us to "invest time, energy, and no small amount of self-doubt, and dread." Choosing a new cell phone plan can take some people weeks while they research models of cell phones, minutes available, quotas of text messages, and internet access, not to mention the fine print. Although being flooded with choices may feel luxurious, it can be stressful and even unrewarding. Paralysis, anxiety, and stress, rather than happiness, satisfaction, and perfection, can be the result of too much "more." Some of us, Schwartz says, are "maximizers"; we don't rest until we find the best. Others of us are "satisficers"; we're satisfied with what's good enough, based on our most important criteria. Of

course, we all do some "maximizing" and some "satisficing," but generally, which are you? Here are Schwartz's recommendations to lower our stress levels in a society where more can actually give us less, especially in terms of quality of life:

1. **Choose to choose.** Some decisions are worth lengthy deliberation; others aren't. Be conscious of the choices you make and whether they're worth the return on your investment. "Maximize" when it counts, and "satisfice" when it doesn't.

2. **Remember that there's always greener grass somewhere.** Someone will always have a better job than you do, a nicer apartment, or a more attractive romantic partner. Regret or envy can eat away at you, and second-guessing can bring unsettling dissatisfaction.

3. **Regret less and appreciate more.** Although green grass does

abound, so do sandpits and bumpy roads. That's an important realization, too! Value the good things you already have going for you.

4. **Build bridges, not walls.** Think about the ways in which the dozens of choices you've already made as a new college student give you your own unique profile or "choice-print": where you live, which classes you take, clubs you join, campus events you attend, your small circle of friends, and on and on. Remember that, and make conscious choices that will best help you succeed.[41]

Think about the last decision you made. How much time and energy did you spend making the decision? Did you maximize or satisfice? What was the outcome?

_____

_____

_____

At the beginning of this chapter, Derek Johnson, a frustrated and disgruntled student, faced a challenge. Now after reading this chapter, would you respond differently to any of the questions you answered about the "FOCUS Challenge Case"? Using what you learned in the chapter, write a paragraph ending to Derek's case study. What are some of the possible outcomes for Derek?

ACTION: YOUR PLANS FOR CHANGE

1. What's the most important thing you learned in reading this chapter?

2. How will you apply the information you've learned to yourself to improve your time, energy, and money management?

CHALLENGE: REALITY CHECK

HOW MUCH DID YOU LEARN?

At the beginning of this chapter, you filled out a "Readiness Check" that asked how you thought this chapter would relate to you, and how you would relate to it. Now, fill out this "Reality Check" to find out.

1. This chapter discusses time management, attention management, and energy management. How are they different, and what do they have in common?

2. What is the A-B-C method for prioritizing tasks? What does each letter represent, and how is the system used?

3. What percentage of college students admit to procrastinating on assignments? Why do they procrastinate? Does the fact that procrastination is so widespread (Everybody's doing it . . .) excuse it?

4. What percentage of college students with credit cards know how much interest they pay on their credit card bills?

5. How long did it take? _____ hours _____ minutes. Before you began this chapter, you were asked to predict how long it would take you to complete it (total time, even if you read it in more than one sitting). Was your estimate on target, or will you revise it for the next chapter you read?

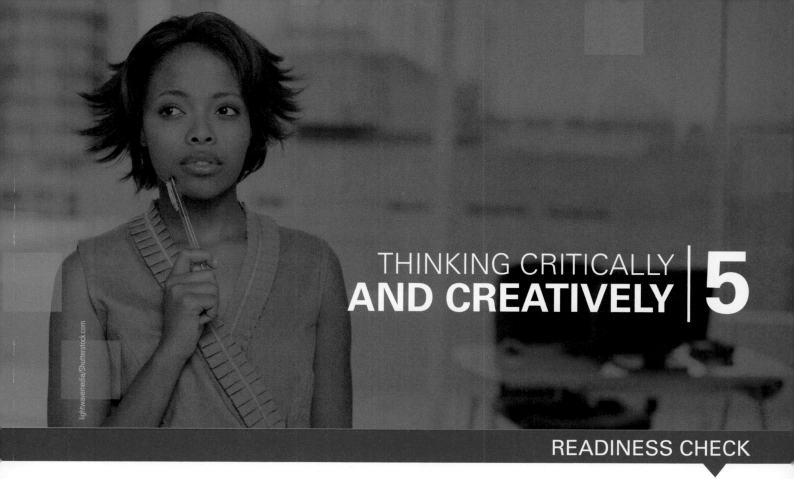

lightwavemedia/Shutterstock.com

THINKING CRITICALLY AND CREATIVELY | 5

HOW THIS CHAPTER RELATES TO YOU

1. When it comes to thinking critically and creatively in your college classes, what do you find most challenging, if anything? Put check marks by the phrase(s) that apply to you or write in your answer.

   ☐ Understanding what critical thinking is
   ☐ Preferring to just Google quick answers
   ☐ Solving problems
   ☐ Making decisions
   ☐ Seeing myself as a creative thinker
   ☐ _____

2. What is most likely to be your response? Put a check mark by it.

   ☐ I'll try to learn more about critical and creative thinking.
   ☐ I'll wait and see how much of this chapter I understand.
   ☐ I'll actively look for ways to improve my own critical and creative thinking.
   ☐ Eventually, I'll just figure it out.

3. What would you have to do to increase your likelihood of success? Will you do it this quarter or semester?

HOW YOU WILL RELATE TO THIS CHAPTER

1. What are you most interested in learning about? Put check marks by those topics.

   ☐ How critical thinking and creative thinking are defined
   ☐ How a four-part model of critical thinking works
   ☐ How to analyze arguments, assess assumptions, and consider claims
   ☐ How to avoid mistakes in reasoning
   ☐ How to become a better critical thinker
   ☐ How to become a more creative thinker

YOUR READINESS FACTOR

1. How motivated are you to learn more about critical and creative thinking in college? (5 = high, 1 = low)

2. How ready are you to read now? (If something is in your way, take care of it if you can. Zero in and focus.)

3. How long do you think it will take you to complete this chapter? If you start and stop, keep track of your overall time. ____ Hour(s) ____ Minute(s)

© 2019 Cengage Learning, Inc. May not be scanned, copied or duplicated, or posted to a publicly accessible website, in whole or in part.

lightwavemedia/Shutterstock.com

DESIREE MOORE

Simply put: Desiree Moore was a perfectionist. Her friends said she was "detail oriented." Her family said she was compulsive. Truthfully, though, she hadn't been all that successful in high school; her assignments were always turned in late, if at all, because they were never "finished." She'd always ask her teachers how long a paper should be and what topic she should write about. She wanted to get things right. Her teachers always advised her to stop "tweaking": "You spend so much time revising your assignments that nothing ever gets done." But she found it hard to take their advice.

High school had been so stressful that when she graduated, she took the first job that came along, as a receptionist for a small law firm. When the two lawyers announced they were going to retire, she started to job hunt immediately. She found another job as a telemarketer, which didn't pay much, but at least the money helped her keep her gym membership. Along with her other obsessions, Desiree was a total fitness enthusiast.

But being hung up on all day wasn't all that much fun, so eventually she quit. She tried waiting tables and cleaning houses, but those jobs didn't hold much appeal either. Before she knew it, several years had gone by, and Desiree realized she didn't have much to show for it. She needed more specialized skills in order to get a better job. When she thought back over all the jobs she'd had since high school, she realized that working with the two lawyers had been her favorite. So, Desiree decided to become a paralegal by earning a two-year degree at the big community college in town. She would be the first person in her family to go to college! It was a pretty good career field, she read online, and she could investigate legal cases, draft documents, and do research working alongside an attorney.

Her first semester consisted of two night classes: "Introduction to Paralegal Careers" and "Paralegal Ethics." But "Paralegal Ethics" was a very challenging course. The instructor, Mr. Courtney, a retired lawyer himself, had announced on the first day of class that he believed in the Socratic method of teaching, by asking questions of students instead of lecturing. "Socrates, perhaps the greatest philosopher of all time," he announced the first day," is the 'father' of critical thinking. In this class, you'll learn to think critically. *Learning to think* is what college is all about." Mr. Courtney began every class session with a hypothetical story, and he always randomly chose a student to respond. His openings went something like this:

An attorney has just finished law school and opens a law office. He hires a legal assistant, just

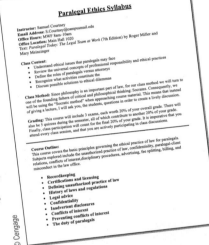

out of college. He is eager to begin his new career, but he is also nervous because he's starting from scratch.

The lawyer's specialty is civil law, and several weeks go by before the phone even rings. His first potential client has a big problem. He wants to sue his next-door neighbor for keeping old cars, junk, and trash in his front yard. When he's asked the neighbor nicely to clean up his property, the neighbor has refused in threatening tones. The teenage sons who live in the home have ties to local gangs, and other neighbors are afraid. They all suspect the teenage boys of a series of unsolved robberies in the neighborhood. The neighborhood is getting a bad reputation, and home values in the area have fallen dramatically.

The lawyer, who desperately needs the work, decides to take the case. However, when the client fills out the contract, his legal assistant notices that the client's zip code is the same as her boss's. In fact, she recognizes the street name as one that's in the subdivision where the lawyer himself lives. Is this a problem? Would you say the lawyer has a "conflict of interest"? What should our legal assistant do?

One student responded with, "Yes, the lawyer lives in the same neighborhood as his client. He doesn't want his own property value to fall. According to our textbook, that's a conflict of interest." Another student said, "But the legal assistant should keep quiet and just do her job. She

needs a paycheck. She shouldn't tell her boss what to do. It's none of her business." Mr. Courtney continued, "But what if the new client discovers that he and his lawyer live in the same neighborhood? Would the client see that as a possible conflict of interest? Could this damage the lawyer's legal career? What would *you* do if the legal assistant were you?" Mr. Courtney's questions seemed endless. Desiree's best friend suggested that she look up his ratings online, but when she did, she found that students wrote about how much they had learned from him.

"What's important in college is thinking through problems," he said. "There aren't always clear right and wrong answers. The process of learning to think can be just as important as the answer itself."

Frankly, that explanation didn't sit well with Desiree. *If there aren't right answers, why go to college? The instructor knows the right answers. Why doesn't he just tell us?* Perfectionists like Desiree were always most comfortable when things were straightforward. Without fail, she always left Mr. Courtney's class with a headache from thinking so hard.

1. Do you have anything in common with Desiree, like an instructor who teaches in a way you find difficult to understand? What specific steps are you taking to help yourself succeed?

2. Why does Desiree's instructor say that "learning to think is what college is all about"? What does he mean, and do you agree?

3. Do you agree with Mr. Courtney's statement that "there aren't always right answers"? If that's true, why is getting a college education so important?

4. Identify three things Desiree should do to get the most from Mr. Courtney's class.

RETHINKING
THINKING

Thinking is a natural, ongoing, everyday process we all engage in. In fact, we can't really turn it off, even if we try. We're always on. Everyone thinks all the time. We talk to ourselves in our heads. However, some experts say school teaches us how to just regurgitate what we've memorized, not how to think. Learning to think is what counts, and *focused thinking*—thinking critically and creatively—is what this chapter is about.

Picture this: You're in the library. It's late, and you're tired. You're supposed to be studying for your political science test, but instead of thinking about foreign policy, your mind begins drifting toward the vacation you took last summer, the great food you ate, and how much fun it was to be with your friends or family.

Would the mental process you're engaging in while sitting in the library be called *thinking*? For our purposes in this chapter, the answer is no. Here thinking is defined as a focused mental activity you engage in on purpose. You direct your thoughts toward a particular topic. You're the *active* thinker, not the *passive* daydreamer who is the victim of a wandering mind. Focused thinking involves zeroing in and managing your attention. It's deliberate, not accidental. You choose to do it for a reason.

Focused thinking is like a two-sided coin. Sometimes when you think, you *produce* ideas. That's what this chapter calls *creative thinking*, and that's something we'll deal with later. The other side of thinking requires you to *evaluate* ideas—your own or someone else's. That's *critical thinking*. The word *critical* comes from the Greek word for *critic* (*kritikos*), meaning "to question or analyze." You focus on something, sort through the information, and decide which ideas are most sensible, logical, or useful. When you're thinking critically, you're asking questions, analyzing arguments, assessing assumptions, considering claims, avoiding mistakes in reasoning, problem solving, decision making, and all the while, thinking about your thinking.

aslysun/Shutterstock.com

"'Knowledge is power.' Rather, knowledge is happiness. To have knowledge, deep broad knowledge, is to know truth from false and lofty things from low."

Helen Keller, American author, activist, and lecturer (1880–1968)

WIIFM?

Critical thinking. You ask: WIIFM? The bottom line? Quite possibly, a good job.

Critical thinking skills are something today's employers want desperately in new hires; however, they worry that college graduates don't really have them. In one recent study by *PayScale* and *Future Workplace,* 87 percent of college graduates reported they're ready to "hit the ground running" in the workplace, but only 50 percent of employers agree.[1]

Underdeveloped critical thinking and problem-solving skills top employers' lists of concerns. "Graduates need strong communication and problem-solving skills if they want to interview well and succeed in the workplace, because effective writing, speaking, and critical thinking enables you to accomplish business goals and get ahead," writes Dan Schawbel, author of *Me 2.0* and research director at *Future Workplace.* "No working day will be complete without writing an email or tackling a new challenge, so the sooner you develop these skills, the more employable you will become."[2]

Meanwhile, references to the term "critical thinking" have more than doubled in job ads since 2009, according to Indeed.com, the job search website giant. At one point in their research, Indeed.com found references to critical thinking in 21,000 healthcare and 6,700 management postings.[3] Critical thinking skills are in high demand no matter what the type of career you'll be entering, partly because we live in frantic technology-driven times, experts say. "People do not spend enough time thinking through issues.

Critical thinking is left by the wayside."[4] True critical thinkers know how to read between the lines, dig deeper, show skepticism when appropriate, and come prepared.[5]

But here's one sticky issue: Employers themselves aren't quite sure how to define critical thinking. Or let's say this: There are many different ways employers define it. Is it "forming your own opinion from a variety of different sources"? Is it "thinking about your thinking, while you're thinking, in order to improve your thinking"? However, it's defined, employers "know it when they see it," and they know how to test job candidates' critical thinking skills during interviews.[6]

One way interviewers test for critical thinking skills is by asking problem-solving questions ("How would you handle conflict on your team?") or even "off the wall" questions, like "How many pieces of pizza are eaten in the United States every year?" Trick questions don't have specific answers; they're off the wall. But the interviewer wants to see a) whether you get rattled and b) how you think. The best way to answer an off-the-wall question would be to say, "We'll let's see. I eat pizza about once a week, and I usually have three pieces. That's roughly a dozen pieces of pizza a month—times 12 months in a year for one person. Now, multiply that figure by the population of the United States, ages four and up." The question is silly, but the interviewer can see by your answer that you go about solving problems logically.

> "What are all the experiences and problems that I have to learn about and master so that what comes out at the other end is somebody who is ready and capable of becoming a successful CEO? "
>
> *Nolan Archibald, once the youngest Fortune 500 CEO (Black & Decker) (attended Dixie Community College, St. George, Utah, transferred to Weber State University, and earned an MBA from Harvard Business School)*

So just how important are critical thinking skills to employers? Mark Cuban, the billionaire investor of *Shark Tank* fame, takes the claim even further. He believes that technology will eventually "outsmart" itself, and that tech jobs will be replaced by computers and robots. What will be left? If not now, then soon, he says, tech skills will take a back seat to good, old-fashioned "soft skills," like communication, teamwork, and critical thinking. "Cuban believes that employers will soon be on the hunt for candidates who excel at creative and critical thinking."[7] That statement could well affect *you!* The more critical thinking skills you can show during a job interview, the more highly you'll be rated as a candidate. "WIIFM?" is really that simple.

WHAT IS
CRITICAL THINKING?

Critical thinking is a particular kind of focused thinking. It is purposeful, reasoned, and goal-directed. It's thinking that aims to solve problems, calculate likelihood, weigh evidence, and make decisions.[8] In that sense, movie critics are

"What we need is not the will to believe, but the will to find out."

Bertrand Russell, British philosopher, logician, and mathematician (1872–1970)

critical thinkers because they look at a variety of standards (screenplay, acting, production quality, costumes, and so forth) and then decide how a movie measures up. When you're thinking critically, you're not just being critical. You're on the lookout for both faults and strengths. You're looking at how things measure up.[9]

Critical thinkers develop standards they can use to judge advertisements, political speeches, sales pitches, movies—you name it.[10] Critical thinking is not jumping to conclusions; buying arguments lock, stock, and barrel; accepting controversial ideas no matter what; or ignoring the facts.

Unfortunately, some people are noncritical thinkers. They may be biased or closed-minded. Other people are *selective* critical thinkers. When it comes to one particular subject, they shut down their minds. They can't explain their views, they're emotional about them, and they refuse to acknowledge any other position. Why do they believe these things? Only if they understand the *why*, can they explain their views to someone else or defend them under fire. The importance of *why* can't be overstated. Some people, of course, have already thought through their beliefs, and they understand their positions and the reasons for them very well. Arriving at that point is the goal of anyone who wants to become a better critical thinker.

A FOUR-PART MODEL
OF CRITICAL THINKING

Now that we've defined critical thinking, let's ask an important related question: How do you do it? We'll look at the four primary components of critical thinking, and later in this chapter, we'll use a realistic news story, one that could take place near any community college campus, to allow you to apply what you've learned through a memorable example.

Take a look at Figure 5.1 to preview the four-part model of critical thinking. You'll see right away that your reasoning skills underlie everything. They are the foundation upon which your problem-solving and decision-making skills rest,

FIGURE 5.1

Critical Thinking Is Focused

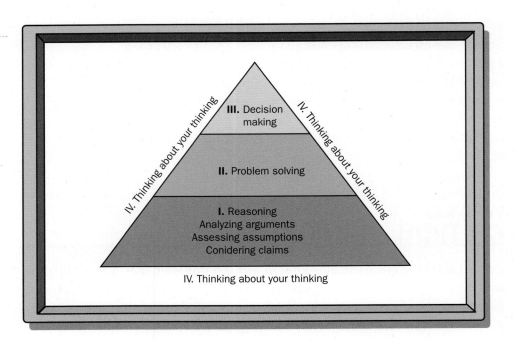

and your metacognitive skills, or thinking about your thinking, surround all the focused thinking you do.

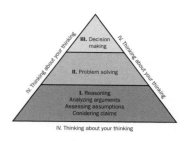

I. REASONING: THE FOUNDATION OF CRITICAL THINKING

Reasoning, the foundation of critical thinking, is the ability to reach a conclusion from one or more arguments. A strong argument is convincing because it offers evidence to back up its claim. If no one would disagree with what you're saying, it's not an argument. It's obvious. "Grass is green" is not an argument. But "Cows that are grass-fed make the best meat" is (if supporting evidence is provided). Do you see the difference?

evidence reasons why something is true, based on statistics, expert testimony, or examples

Think about your reasoning skills. How good are you at creating a sound argument? Let's say that you're trying to convince your friend that her cell phone conversation is making it difficult for you to study for a major exam. What evidence would you use to convince her? What's the likelihood of your success? Or how about this: How good are you at evaluating someone else's argument? For example, you're trying to decide whether an online discount is really a good deal. Would you take the advertiser's word for it, or would you compare prices on your own?

Throughout the rest of this chapter, ask yourself: Are there ways I can improve my reasoning skills? As you think about your own skills, consider these reasoning nuts and bolts that are essential parts of creating and evaluating arguments.

Analyzing Arguments

Have you ever seen the *Monty Python Flying Circus* "Argument Clinic" sketch? In this bizarre skit a man comes to an "argument clinic" to buy an argument. The two arguers—"professional" and customer—engage in a long, "yes, it is"/"no, it isn't" squabble.

contradictory two people saying opposite things

proposition a point

Critical thinking is about arguments. But most of us think of an argument as a back-and-forth disagreement. In the middle of the "Argument Clinic" sketch, however, the customer actually makes an important point. He says that they're not really arguing; they're just contradicting each other. He continues, "An argument is a connected series of statements intended to establish a proposition." That's the kind of argument that's related to critical thinking.

Critical thinking is about an argument that *one* person puts forth, not a squabble between two people. An op-ed piece in the newspaper contains an argument. (Op-ed stands for the page "opposite the editorial page" that features signed articles expressing personal viewpoints.) Both attorneys—prosecution and defense—put forth their closing arguments at the end of a trial.

Arguments are said to be inductive or deductive. *Inductive* arguments go from specific observations to general conclusions. In criminal trials, the prosecution puts together individual pieces of evidence to prove that the defendant is guilty: eyewitnesses put him at the scene, the gun store salesman remembers selling him a pistol, and his fingerprints are on the weapon. Therefore, the prosecutor argues that the defendant is guilty. Other arguments are said to be *deductive*, meaning they go from broad generalizations to specific conclusions. All serial killers have a particular psychological profile. The defendant has this psychological profile. Therefore, the defendant is the killer.

A four-part model of critical thinking **123**

life hack #1

"I think therefore, I am" said philosopher Rene Descartes. But *what* do you think, especially about yourself? Negative self-talk ("I'm not good enough" or "I'll never be successful," for example) can affect your actions more than you might think.[11]

What do arguments do? They propose a line of reasoning. They try to persuade. Arguments contain clear reasons to believe someone or something. Arguments say A plus B equals C. Once you understand what an argument is, you must also understand that arguments can be sound or unsound. If I tell you that two plus two equals four, chances are good that you'll believe me. If, on the other hand, I tell you two plus two equals five, you'll flatly deny it. If I say "Cats have fur. Dogs have fur. Therefore dogs are cats," you'll tell me I'm crazy—because it's an unsound argument.

The standard we use to test the soundness of arguments is logic, which is a fairly extensive topic. Let's just say for our purposes here that arguments are sound when the evidence for them is reasonable, more reasonable than the evidence against them. The important point is that a sound argument provides at least one good reason to believe. Let's look at an example:

I don't see why all students have to take an introductory writing course. It's a free country. Students shouldn't have to take courses they don't want to take.

Based on our definition, is this example an argument? Why or why not? Is the statement "It's a free country" relevant? What does living in a free country have to do with courses that community college students are required to take? Nothing. *Relevancy* is a condition needed for a sound argument.

Now look at this example:

I don't see why all first-year students have to take an introductory writing course. Many students have developed good writing skills in high school, and their entrance test scores are high.

Is this second example an argument? Why or why not? The first example doesn't give you a good reason to believe the argument; the second example does. A true argument must contain at least one reason for you to believe it.

Here's another warning. Not everything that sounds like an argument is one. Look at this example:

Everyone taking Math 100 failed the test last Friday. I took the test last Friday. Therefore, I will probably get an F in the course.

Is that a sound argument—or is something missing? Even though all three statements may be true, when you put them together they don't make a sound argument. What grade has this student earned on earlier math tests? How many tests are left in the course? What other assignments figure into students' grades? The information present may not be adequate to predict an F in the course. *Adequacy* is another condition needed for a sound argument. This alternative, on the other hand, is a sound argument:

Everyone taking Math 100 failed the test last Friday. I took the test last Friday. Therefore, I earned an F on the test.

When you're assessing the soundness of an argument, you must look for two things: *relevance* and *adequacy*.[12]

Not all arguments are sound. Have you ever heard this story? A scientist came up with a new study to find out what makes people drunk, using himself in the experiment. The study went like this. On Monday night, he drank three tall glasses of scotch and water, mixed in equal amounts. The next morning, he recorded his results: intoxication. On Tuesday night, he drank three tall glasses of whiskey and water. On Wednesday night, he drank three tall glasses of rum and water. On Thursday night, he drank three tall glasses of vodka and water. Each morning, his recorded results were the same. He had become drunk. His totally wrong conclusion? Water makes people drunk.

Not only is it important to be able to construct sound arguments, but it's also important to be able to recognize them. As a consumer in today's information society, you must know when to buy into an argument, and when not to.

Assessing Assumptions

When you're thinking critically, one of the most important kinds of questions you can ask is about the *assumptions* you or someone else is making, perhaps without even realizing it. Assumptions are things you take for granted, and they can limit your thinking. Consider this well-known puzzle, and afterward examine how the assumptions you brought with you interfered with solving it.

> *One day Kerry celebrated her birthday. Two days later her older twin brother, Harry, celebrated his birthday. How could that be?*

You may have solved this puzzle if you were willing to question the underlying assumptions that were holding you back. (The answer is at the bottom of this page.)

People reveal their basic assumptions in what they say. If you listen carefully, you can uncover them. "Go on for a bachelor's degree after I finish here? No way! As soon as I get my associate's degree, I'm done!" This student's underlying assumption is that college itself isn't as important as what comes afterward (like making money). This student may sit through her classes without getting engaged in the subject matter, and she checks off requirements as quickly as she can. Too bad.

Considering Claims

Evaluating claims is one of the most basic aspects of reasoning. A claim is a statement that can be true or false, but not both. This is different from a fact, which cannot be disputed. What's the difference between a *fact* and a *claim*? Facts can't be disputed; claims can be true or false, but they must be one or the other, not both.

> *FACT: Ronald Reagan, Bill Clinton, and Barack Obama were presidents of the United States who each served two full terms.*

> *CLAIM: Bill Clinton was the most popular American president in recent history.*

The fact is obvious. The claim needs evidence to support it. As a critical thinker, it's important to use your reasoning skills to evaluate the evidence. Generally speaking, be wary of claims that

> ➤ are supported by unidentified sources ("Experts claim . . . ").

> ➤ are made by a person or company who stands to gain ("Brought to you by the makers of . . .").

> ➤ come from a single person claiming his experience as the norm ("I tried it and it worked for me!").

"And how is education supposed to make me feel smarter?"

Homer Simpson, television cartoon character, The Simpsons

"Great minds discuss ideas. Average minds discuss events. Small minds discuss people."

Eleanor Roosevelt, First Lady of the United States (1884–1962)

Kerry and Harry are not twins. Harry and his brother are twins, and they are older than Kerry.

> use a bandwagon appeal ("Everybody's doing it.").

> mislead with statistics ("over half" when it's really only 50.5 percent).

On the other hand, we must also keep an open mind and be flexible in our thinking. If you get good evidence to support a view that contradicts yours, be willing to change your ideas. One way to evaluate the validity of claims is to use the Critical Thinking Pyramid (Figure 5.2). Consider claims by asking these four key questions: "Who?" "What?" "Why?" and "How?" Figure 5.2 shows how the questions progress from level 1 to 4.

FIGURE 5.2

The Focused Thinking Pyramid

Source: Adapted from Hellyer, R., Robinson, C., & Sherwood, P. (1998). *Study skills for learning power.* New York: Houghton Mifflin, 18.

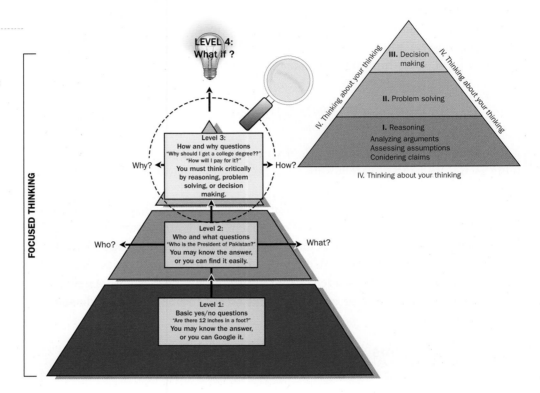

Avoiding Faulty Reasoning

Although we can certainly improve our critical-thinking skills, it's impossible to be perfect critical thinkers 100 percent of the time. As thinkers, we make mistakes, and sometimes others try to trick us with bad arguments. It's important to cultivate both types of critical thinking skills: your *productive* skills, which you use as a speaker and writer when you "produce" ideas, and your *receptive* skills, which you use as a reader and listener when you "receive" others' ideas. As responsible communicators, we must understand what a sound argument is and know how to construct one ourselves. We must also understand what a defective argument is so that we avoid getting sucked in when we shouldn't.

Here is a top-ten list of logical fallacies, or false logic strategies, we can slip into—or others can use against us—if we're not careful. For each of the ten types, read through the example and then see whether you can come up with one of your own.

1. **False cause and effect** (assuming one cause for something when other causes are possible, too)

   I moved back home from my own apartment last month. I've failed every exam I've taken since. Living at home is blowing my GPA!

2. **Personal attack** (reacting to a challenge by attacking the challenger)

   How could anyone believe Mr. Courtney's views on ethics? We all know he's a very poor teacher.

3. **Unwarranted assumption** (taking too much for granted without evidence)

   You say community colleges give women equal opportunities. I say they don't. Reply: It's true. I read it on a website.

4. **Emotional appeal** (appealing to someone's feelings in order to gain acceptance of an argument)

   If you care about all the people hurt in this tragic accident, you'll dig deep into your pockets and send in a donation now.

5. **False authority** (attributing your argument to someone else in a supposed position of power to get you off the hook)

   I'd really like to be able to change your grade, but my Department Chair doesn't like me to do that.

6. **Hasty conclusion** (jumping to a conclusion when other conclusions are possible)

   I'm sure that guy next to me in class stole my textbook when I wasn't looking. He's too cheap to buy his own.

7. **Straw man** (attempting to "prove" an argument by overstating, exaggerating, or oversimplifying the arguments of the opposing side)

   We should let students have more say in which courses they take. Reply: You actually want students to take any courses they want to? Oh, right, why don't we all just have a free-for-all instead?

8. **Shifting the burden of proof** (shifting the responsibility of proving an assertion to someone else because you have no evidence for what you assert)

   The policy forbidding any alcohol at campus events is working. Reply: No, it's not. Reply back: Oh yeah? Prove it.

9. **Oversimplification/overgeneralization** (reducing a complex issue to something very simple or stereotyping)

   College teachers have it made. They teach a couple classes a week for a few hours, and then they have free time the rest of the week. That's the kind of job I want!

10. **Either/or thinking** (taking only an extreme position on an issue when other positions are possible)

    Either we ban dating between students or we will be facing sexual harassment lawsuits.

> "Too often … we enjoy the comfort of opinion without the discomfort of thought."
>
> *John F. Kennedy, 35th president of the United States (1917–1963)*

II. PROBLEM SOLVING: THE BASIC HOW-TO'S

When you have to solve a problem, your critical thinking skills should move front and center. Perhaps you need to find a way to earn more money. You run short each month, and the last few days before payday are nerve-racking. What should you do? Use a shotgun approach and try many different strategies at once, or come up with a more precise way to get the best results? See whether the following steps make sense to you and seem like something you might actually do.

A four-part model of critical thinking **127**

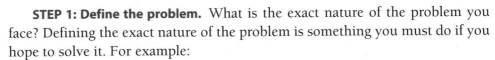

STEP 1: Define the problem. What is the exact nature of the problem you face? Defining the exact nature of the problem is something you must do if you hope to solve it. For example:

➤ Is it that you don't meter your spending and run out of money long before the next paycheck?

➤ Is it that you don't have a budget and you spend money randomly?

STEP 2: Brainstorm possible options. List all of the possible solutions you can come up with. For example:

➤ Pack food from home instead of hitting the fast-food joints so often.

➤ Stop ordering in pizza four nights a week when you get the munchies at midnight.

➤ Ask your boss for a raise. You've been doing a good job.

➤ Look for a job that pays more. Tips at the Pancake House where you work don't really amount to much.

➤ Capitalize on your particular skills to earn extra money. If you're a whiz at math, you could sign on as a math tutor on campus.

STEP 3: Set criteria to evaluate each option. For example:

➤ *Distance* is important. Your car isn't very reliable, so it would be good to find a job you can walk or ride your bike to.

➤ *Good pay* is important. In the past, you've always had low-paying jobs. You need whatever solution you arrive at to be worth your while.

➤ *Time* is important. You're taking a challenging load of classes, and you need to keep up your grades to keep your scholarship.

STEP 4: Evaluate each option you've proposed. For example:

➤ Pack food from home. (This is a good idea because you've already paid for that food, regardless of which solution you choose.)

➤ Stop ordering pizza when the munchies hit at midnight. (This is also a good option because unplanned expenses like this can mount up fast.)

➤ Ask your family to borrow money. (You'd really like to avoid this option. You don't want to seem like you're trying to take advantage of them.)

➤ Get a job that pays more. (Unfortunately, your campus is half an hour from the center of town where all the posh restaurants are.)

➤ Capitalize on your particular skills to earn extra money. (Tutors are paid more than minimum wage, and getting a job on campus would be convenient.)

STEP 5: Choose the best solution. In this case, it looks like getting a job on campus could fit the bill!

STEP 6: Plan how to achieve the best solution. When you talk with your advisor about applying for a job as a math tutor, you discover that you need a letter of recommendation from a math instructor. You e-mail your math instructor and set up a meeting for later in the week. When the letter is ready, you make an appointment to schedule an interview, and so forth.

"Everyone is entitled to their own opinion, but not their own facts."

Senator Daniel Patrick Moynihan (1927–2003)

"Education is nothing more, nor less, than learning to think!"

Peter Facione, professor, administrator, author, consultant, and critical thinking expert

Great Bluffs Herald

Saturday, September 22, 2018

Start of School + Parties = Recipe for Death

Great Bluffs, Colorado It's that time of year again. The fall semester began last month at Great Bluffs Community College, and again this year, a student died of alcohol poisoning within the first three weeks of classes. Dante Lewis, a resident of an apartment complex near the school, Aspen Commons, was found dead yesterday morning. The body of the collapsed GBCC student was found in a third-floor apartment. An anonymous call to 9-1-1 came in at 6:15 A.M.: "We've got a guy here. We can't wake him, and we know he drank way too much last night." Lewis was pronounced dead on arrival at Great Bluffs General Hospital. The incident represented the second death from alcohol poisoning at Aspen Commons in as many years. Roland Bishop, GBCC's new president, is said to deeply mourn the loss of another new student. "No student should die during his first few weeks of college—what should be one of the most exciting times of his life. It's insane and very, very sad."

The Aspen Commons Apartment Complex has been warned that student parties among underage residents, where alcohol is served, should be discouraged.

President Bishop will convene a cross-college panel of faculty, staff, and students to investigate the incident and decide if any action should be taken by GBCC. Professor Juan Cordova, Sociology Department Chairperson, will head the new committee. A report with specific recommendations to President Bishop is expected by the end of the term. Alcohol is to blame for the deaths of 1,825 college students per year, according to figures from the National Institute on Alcohol Abuse and Alcoholism. About 599,000 students between the ages of 18 and 24 are injured annually while under the influence of alcohol, more than 696,000 are assaulted by another student who has been drinking, and more than 97,000 students are victims of alcohol-related sexual assault or date rape.

The average age of students at Great Bluffs Community College has dropped from 28 to 20 in recent years. Although many community college students live at home, many others live on their own in the community. Because it is within walking distance to GBCC, Aspen Commons is a popular choice. President Bishop's office indicates that it may enter into negotiations with the Colorado Housing Authority and with Clifford Industries, owners of Aspen Commons, about banning alcohol in the complex and requiring tenants to sign a no-alcohol agreement.

After this article appeared in the Great *Bluffs Herald,* many readers sent letters to the editor on September 23 and 24. Examine the following excerpts.

Trevor Ryan, GBCC Student: "My first few weeks at GBCC have been awesome, and living at Aspen Commons has been totally cool—one of the highlights of my life so far. I'd do it all over again tomorrow. But I didn't want to live at Aspen Commons just for the parties everyone talks about. It's a great place to live. All the students who live there say so."

Carlos Garcia, GBCC Student: "This whole incident has been very hard on me. Dante was my roommate. We've known each other since we were kids, and we moved into an apartment right after we graduated from high school last spring. I still can't believe this happened to him. Yeah, I was drinking at the party where he got totally wasted, too. But I lost track of him when I went to bed around midnight. If I had just stayed around, I'll bet I could have prevented what happened."

Ross Riley, Building Manager, Aspen Commons: "As building manager, I've seen my fair share of parties over the years. Sometimes things get out of control. I get a call in the middle of the night and end up calling the cops. Other residents complain about the noise. But it's not the apartment complex's problem. We just put a roof over people's heads. They make their own decisions about how to live."

Dr. Ruby Pinnell, ER Physician, Great Bluffs General Hospital: "As a doctor, I see all the damage today's young people are doing to themselves. The national study I spearheaded last year found that 31 percent of college students meet the clinical criteria

(continued on next page)

for alcohol abuse, and 6 percent could be diagnosed as being alcohol-dependent. They don't realize that binge drinking could be risking serious damage to their brains now and actually cause increased memory loss later in adulthood. Many college males consume as many as 24 drinks in a row. These are very sad statistics."

Rufus Unser, Aspen Commons resident: "I've lived at Aspen Commons for 12 years now, and I'm just about to move into an assisted living facility because I'm 78 and my health is failing. I'm sick of rowdy parties, loud music late at night, and residents who run up and down the halls. I don't mind all the younger people who live in this complex, but I'd really like to get some sleep once in a while."

Sergeant Rick Fuller, Great Bluffs Police Department: "Over the 15 years I've worked for the Great Bluffs Police Department, I've seen a dramatic rise in alcohol-related violence, crimes, and accidents. GBCC needs to do something. Their students are part of the problem, and they need to assume some responsibility."

Now that you've read the story from the *Great Bluffs Herald* and the excerpts from letters to the editor, answer the following questions:

1. What are the facts relating to the death of GBCC student Dante Lewis? How do you know they are facts and not claims?

2. Do you see logical fallacies in any of the letters to the editor of the *Great Bluffs Herald*? If so, which can you identify? What assumptions do the letter writers hold—right or wrong?

VARK IT!

Visual: Using different colored highlighters or sticky notes, identify the facts versus the claims in the Aspen Commons case study. Doing so may help you better understand the difference.

STEP 7: Implement the solution and evaluate the results. A month or two after you take on the tutoring job, you evaluate whether this solution is really the best one. You may need to request more hours or different days. Or you may find that this job leads to a better one on campus. At any rate, you've used your critical thinking skills to solve a problem, systematically, logically, and effectively.

EXERCISE 5.2   PROBLEM SOLVING FOR YOURSELF

Try out the seven-step problem-solving model for yourself. Think of a problem you're facing right now, and fill in your ideas for steps 1 through 7. When you're done, ask yourself whether filling in these steps helped you understand the problem and this problem-solving process better.

STEP 1: Define the problem.

STEP 2: Brainstorm possible options.

STEP 3: Set criteria to evaluate each option.

STEP 4: Evaluate each option you've proposed.

STEP 5: Choose the best solution.

STEP 6: Plan how to achieve the best solution.

STEP 7: Implement the solution and evaluate the results.

III. DECISION MAKING: WHAT'S YOUR STYLE?

The kinds of arguments we're discussing in this chapter lead to decisions, and it's important to make good ones! After you've evaluated an argument, you must often do something about it. Before you know it, you'll be deciding on a major if you haven't already, a career field, a place to live, a romantic partner—you name it.

When you have an important decision to make, your critical thinking skills should kick into action. The more important the decision, the more thoughtful the process of deciding should be. But people make decisions in different ways.

Alan J. Rowe and Richard O. Mason wrote a book called *Managing with Style* about four basic decision-making styles used by managers. Although you may not be a manager now, think about what your style may be when you do have a position of responsibility. Here are the four styles they describe. See which one sounds as if it might describe you.

Hemera Technologies/PhotoObjects .net/Jupiter Images

> **Directive.** This decision-making style emphasizes the here and now. Directives prefer structure and using practical data to make decisions. They look for speed, efficiency, and results, and focus on short-term fixes. Directive decision makers base their decisions on experience, facts, procedures, and rules, and they have energy and drive to get things done. On the downside, because they work quickly, they are sometimes satisfied with simple solutions when something else might work better.

Ian Scott/Shutterstock.com

> **Analytical.** This decision-making style emphasizes a logical approach. Analyticals search carefully for the best decision, and they sometimes get hung up with overanalyzing things and take too long to finally make a decision. They are sometimes considered to be impersonal because they may be more interested in the problem than in the people who have it. But they are good at working with data and doing careful analysis.

Hemera Technologies/PhotoObjects. net/Jupiter Images

> **Conceptual.** This decision-making style emphasizes the big picture. Conceptuals are adaptable, insightful, and flexible, and they look for interesting, new solutions. They are sometimes too idealistic, but they take risks and are very creative.

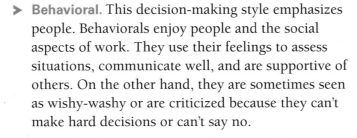

PhotostoGO.com

> **Behavioral.** This decision-making style emphasizes people. Behaviorals enjoy people and the social aspects of work. They use their feelings to assess situations, communicate well, and are supportive of others. On the other hand, they are sometimes seen as wishy-washy or are criticized because they can't make hard decisions or can't say no.

Whether you're in college to prepare for a career field or retool for a new one, eventually, you will have to make important decisions on a daily basis. It's useful to begin thinking about your decision-making style now.

IV. THINKING ABOUT YOUR THINKING

metacognition thinking about your thinking and learning about your learning

IV. Thinking about your thinking

One of the most important aspects of critical thinking is that it evaluates itself. As you're solving problems, for example, you're thinking about how you're thinking. You're assessing your progress as you go, analyzing the strengths and weaknesses in your thinking, and perhaps even coming up with better ways to do it. We call that metacognition.

Novice or new learners don't stop to evaluate their thinking and make revisions. Expert or experienced learners do. Actually, whenever you're faced with learning something new, metacognition involves three elements. Ultimately, these elements should become the foundation of all your learning experiences so that you improve your metacognitive skills as you go.

> ➤ **Before: Develop a plan of action.** Ask yourself what you already know that can help you learn something new. What direction do you want to go in with your thinking? What should be your first task? How much time should you give yourself? Talk through your plan with someone else.

> ➤ **During: Monitor your plan.** While you're working, ask yourself how you're doing. Are you staying on track? Are you moving in the right direction? Should you slow down or speed up? What should you do if you don't understand what you're doing? Keep track of what works for you and what doesn't. Assume responsibility for your own thinking and learning.

> ➤ **After: Evaluate the plan.** How well did you do? Did you do better than expected or not as well as you expected? What could you have done differently? Can you apply what you just did here to future tasks? Give yourself some feedback.[13]

BECOMING A BETTER
CRITICAL THINKER

Sharpening your critical thinking skills is vital because these skills underlie all the others in your academic toolkit. If you think well, you will be a better writer, a better presenter, a better listener, and a better reader. You will be more likely to engage more fully in your academic tasks because you will question, dig, analyze, and monitor yourself as you learn. Here are some suggestions for improving your skills. As you read them, think about yourself and how you learn.

1. **Admit when you don't know.** If you don't know enough to think critically about something, admit it, and then find out more. With the volume of information available in today's world, we can't possibly know everything about anything. But the good news is that information is everywhere. All you need to do is read, listen, point, and click to be well informed on many issues.

2. **Realize you have buttons that can be pushed.** We all have issues we're emotional about. That's normal. It's natural to feel strongly about some things, but it's also important to understand the reasons why so that you can tell your views to someone else. And of course, realize that you're not the only one with buttons. Your teacher, best friend, significant other, boss, and everyone else has them, too.

3. **Learn more about the opposition.** Many times, it's more comfortable to avoid what we don't agree with and reinforce what we already believe. But

"If you have an apple and I have an apple and we exchange these apples, then you and I will still each have one apple. But if you have an idea and I have an idea and we exchange these ideas, then each of us will have two ideas."

George Bernard Shaw, Irish literary critic, playwright, essayist, and the winner of 1925 Nobel Prize for Literature (1856–1950)

part of being a well-educated person means learning about the history, backgrounds, values, and techniques of people you disagree with so that you can anticipate and deal with their arguments more effectively.

4. **Trust and verify.** During the cold war, President Ronald Reagan liked to quote an old Russian saying to his Soviet counterpart, Mikhail Gorbachev: "Doveryay, no proveryay," or "Trust, but verify." Being a good critical thinker means achieving a balance between blind faith and healthy questioning.

5. **Remember that critical thinking is the foundation of all academic achievement.** There's nothing more important than learning to think critically. In college and in life, the skills discussed in this chapter will make you a better college student, a better citizen, a better employee, a smarter consumer, a better relational partner, and a better lifelong learner.

CREATIVITY:
"THINKING OUTSIDE THE … BOOK"

"A mind that is stretched to a new idea never returns to its original dimensions."

Oliver Wendell Holmes, American poet (1809–1894)

Do you believe this statement? *Everyone has creative potential.* It's true. Most of us deny it, however. "Me, creative? Nah!" We're often unaware of the untapped ability we have to think creatively. Try this experiment. Look at the following list of words, and divide the list into two (and only two) different categories, using any rules you create. Take a few moments and see what you come up with.

dog, salad, book, grasshopper, kettle, paper, garbage, candle

Whenever this experiment is tried, people always come up with very creative categories. They may divide the words into things that you buy at a store (dog, salad, kettle, paper, candle), things that move on their own (dog, grasshopper), things that have a distinct smell (dog, candle, garbage), words that have two consonants, and so forth. People never say it can't be done; they always *invent* categories. Interesting, isn't it? Our minds are hungry for the stimulation of a creative challenge.

The fact is that intelligence has more to do with coming up with the right answer, and creative thinking has more to do with coming up with more than one right answer. Often we get so focused on the *right* answer that we rush to find it instead of exploring all the possibilities. Creative thinking is thinking outside the box, or in terms of getting an education, perhaps we should call it thinking outside the book. Going beyond the obvious and exploring possibilities are important parts of becoming an educated person. Employers report that many college graduates today have specific skills, but that what they rarely see "is the ability to use the right-hand side of the brain—creativity, working in a team."[14]

In Figure 5.2, we looked at the Focused Thinking Pyramid. Creative thinking is at the top of the pyramid: What if? It goes beyond critical thinking. It is predictive and multidimensional. It asks "What if . . . ?" questions. Here are some interesting ones: "What if everyone were allowed to tell one lie per day?" "What if no one could perceive colors?" "What if colleges didn't exist?" "If you looked up a word like *squallizmotex* in the dictionary, what might it mean?"[15]

According to creativity expert Alan Rowe, our creative intelligence demonstrates itself in four major styles. Each of us has aspects of all four styles of creativity.

PhotoObjects.net/
Jupiter Images

PhotoObjects.net/
Jupiter Images

PhotostoGO.com

PhotostoGO.com

> **Intuitive.** This creative style is best described as *resourceful*. If you are an Intuitive, you achieve goals, use common sense, and work to solve problems. You focus on results and rely on past experience to guide your actions. Managers, actors, and politicians are commonly Intuitives.

> **Innovative.** This creative style is best described as *curious*. Innovatives concentrate on problem solving, are organized, and rely on data. They use original approaches, are willing to experiment, and focus on step-by-step inquiry. Scientists, engineers, and inventors typically demonstrate the Innovative creative style.

> **Imaginative.** This creative style is best described as *insightful*. Imaginatives are willing to take risks, have leaps of imagination, and are independent thinkers. They are able to visualize opportunities, are artistic, enjoy writing, and think outside the box. Artists, musicians, writers, and charismatic leaders are often Imaginatives.

> **Inspirational.** This creative style is best described as *visionary*. Inspirationals respond to societal needs, willingly give of themselves, and have the courage of their convictions. They focus on social change and the giving of themselves toward achieving it. They are often educators, motivational leaders, and writers.[17]

Which do you think is your predominant style? Think about how you can make the best use of your natural style. How will your creativity affect the major or *career* you choose? Most people have more than one creative style. Remember that motivation, not just intelligence, is the key to creativity. You must be willing to tap your creative potential and challenge yourself to show it.[18] According to *New York Times* best-seller, *A Whole New Mind*, "The future belongs to a very different kind of person with a very different kind of mind—creators and empathizers, pattern recognizers, and meaning makers. These people—artists, inventors, designers, storytellers, caregivers, consolers, big picture thinkers—will now reap society's richest rewards and share its greatest joys." (p. 1)

TEN WAYS TO BECOME A MORE CREATIVE THINKER

Becoming a more creative thinker may mean you need to accept your creativity and cultivate it. Consider these suggestions and those in Figure 5.4, Quick Study, for ideas about ways to think more creatively.

1. **Find new eyes.** Find a new perspective on old issues. Here's an interesting example. Years ago, a group of Japanese schoolchildren came up with a new way to solve conflicts and build empathy for others' positions, called the Pillow Method. Figure 5.3 is an adaptation of it, based on the fact that a pillow has four sides and a middle, just like most problems. The middle, or *mu*, is the Zen expression for "it doesn't really matter." There is truth in

all four positions. Try it: take a conflict you're having difficulty with at the moment, and write down all four sides and a middle.[19]

2. **Accept your creativity.** Many mindsets block creative thinking: "It can't be done!" "I'm just not the creative type." "I might look stupid!" Many people don't see themselves as creative. This perception can become a major stumbling block. If creativity isn't part of your self-image, you may need to change your image. Everyone has creative potential. You may just have to learn how to tap into yours.

3. **Make your thoughts visible.** For many of us, things become clear when we can see them, either in our mind's eye or displayed for us. Even Einstein, a scientist and mathematician, had a very visual mind. Sometimes if we write something down or sketch something out, we generate a new approach without really trying.

4. **Generate lots of ideas.** Thomas Edison held 1,093 patents, still the record. He gave himself idea goals. The rule he set for himself was that he had to come up with a major invention every six months and a minor invention every ten days.

5. **Don't overcomplexify.** In hindsight, many of the most creative discoveries are embarrassingly simple. Biologist Thomas Huxley said, after reading Darwin's explanation of evolution: "How extremely stupid not to have thought of that!" But sometimes the most simple solution is the best one.[20]

6. **Capitalize on your mistakes.** Remember that Thomas Edison tried anything he could think of for a filament for the incandescent lamp, including a whisker from his best friend's beard. All in all, he tried about 1,800 things before finding the right one. Afterward he said, "I've gained a lot of knowledge—I now know a thousand things that won't work."[21]

7. **Let it flow.** Mihaly Csikszentmihalyi, the author of *Flow: The Psychology of Optimal Experience* and many other books on creativity, discovered something interesting. For his doctoral thesis, he studied artists by taking pictures of them painting every three minutes. He was struck by how engaged they were in their work, so engaged that they seemed to forget everything around them. He began studying other "experts": rock climbers, chess players, dancers, musicians, surgeons. Regardless of the activity, these people forgot the time, themselves, and their problems. What did the activities have in common? Clear, high goals and immediate feedback. Athletes call it being in the zone. The zone is described as the ultimate human experience, where mind and body are united in purpose. Csikszentmihalyi's suggestions for achieving flow are these: Pick an enjoyable activity that is at or slightly above your ability level, screen out distractions, focus all your senses and emotions, and look for regular feedback on how you're doing.[22]

8. **Bounce ideas off others.** One good way to become more creative is to use your family or friends as sounding boards. Sometimes just saying something out loud helps you understand more about it. Each person who provides a critique will give you a new perspective, possibly worth considering.

9. **Stop searching for the "right" answer.** This advice doesn't pertain to your upcoming math exam. But it does to apply to situations in which there are many ways to solve a problem. There may be more than one acceptable solution. A fear of making mistakes can hold you back.

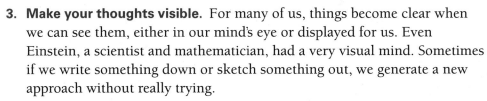

FIGURE 5.3

The Pillow Method

Position 1—I'm right and you're wrong.
Position 2—You're right and I'm wrong.
Position 3—We're both right.
Position 4—We're both wrong.

VARK IT!

Aural: Discuss the Pillow Method with a partner either in class or online and think of a real example of the four "sides" to role play or share.

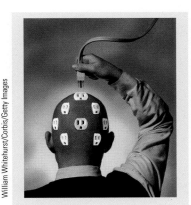

"A hunch is creativity trying to tell you something."

Frank Capra, Italian American film director (1897–1991)

FIGURE 5.4

Quick Study: How to Let Your Creative Juices Flow

HOW TO LET YOUR **Creative** JUICES FLOW

Children often think their creativity comes naturally. Adults often don't.

"I believe this passionately: that we don't grow into creativity, we grow out of it."
~Sir Ken Robinson, education expert

8 EASY WAYS TO BOOST YOUR CREATIVITY

1. ASK THE QUESTION DIFFERENT WAYS

Your first idea may not be your best idea, according to designers, and letting it go can lead to an even better, reframed idea. Henry Ford's eventual idea of moving the product, not the workers, revolutionized manufacturing of all kinds, not just the auto industry.

2. REPURPOSE IDEAS

Many famous inventions actually started out as something else. Duck (yes, duck) tape was originally invented to keep ammunition cases dry during World War II and was a dirty olive-brown color like ducks. Repurposed and recolored years later, "duct" tape is now an all-purpose quick fix to many sticky problems.

3. CHALLENGE YOURSELF

Play beat the clock, take on a dare, bet against the odds. Doing so can stimulate your creative juices. Dr. Seuss wrote *Green Eggs and Ham* after betting he could write a story in under 50 words.

4. KEEP AN IDEA NOTEBOOK or AUDIO NOTE FILE

Jotting ideas down regularly or recording them orally helps you hone your observation skills and notice your creativity.

"Creativity is the power to connect the seemingly unconnected."
~William Plomer, author

5. MULL IT OVER WHILE YOU SLEEP

After a period of sleep, creativity is said to increase by 30 percent. While we're sleeping, our stress levels go down, and we can access information from our subconscious. Director Christopher Nolan says the movie *Inception* came from his own dreams.[a]

6. SPEND TIME OUTDOORS

For thousands of years, famous inventors, scientists, and artists have noted that some of their best ideas came to them while they spent time outdoors. Nature is relaxing and liberating, freeing up our minds for creativity.

"The richness I achieve comes from Nature, the source of my inspiration"
~Claude Monet, painter

7. CHILL

According to brain science, an idle mind is often a more creative one.[b] Over 70 percent of people say they have their best ideas in the shower!

8. BE PATIENT

The more ideas you have, the more likely some are to be useful or productive—and some may even catch on! The Magic 8 Ball, Koosh Ball, and Furby all came from inventors' imaginations. Thomas Edison had a grand total of 1,093 patents and is credited as the most creative inventor in US history. In fact, the light bulb is now the universal icon for creativity.

The only limit to your impact is your imagination and commitment. ~Tony Robbins

Sources: http://www.huffingtonpost.com/2013/11/16/famous-ideas-from-dreams_n_4276838.html; https://www.adobe.com/aboutadobe/pressroom/pdfs/Adobe_State_of_Create_Global_Benchmark_Study.pdf; https://www.scientificamerican.com/article/an-easy-way-to-increase-c/; http://www.creativityatwork.com/2012/03/23/can-creativity-be-taught/; https://www.realsimple.com/health/mind-mood/how-to-be-creative; http://www.bakadesuyo.com/2015/12/how-to-be-creative/; http://www.bakadesuyo.com/2013/07/strokes-of-genius/; https://www.forbes.com/sites/willburns/2013/07/10/multiple-creativity-studies-suggest-creating-our-reality-requires-detaching-from-it/#3dbbe71528e9; https://www.fastcompany.com/3044865/3-ways-to-train-yourself-to-be-more-creative; www.inc.com/christina-desmarais/25-ways-to-be-more-creative.html; https://daringtolivefully.com/ways-to-be-more-creative; https://blog.bufferapp.com/why-we-have-our-best-ideas-in-the-shower-the-science-of-creativity; https://blogs.scientificamerican.com/beautiful-minds/the-real-neuroscience-of-creativity/; http://99u.com/articles/16136/7-ways-to-boost-your-creativity; https://www.helpscout.net/blog/creativity-at-work/; https://www.entrepreneur.com/article/250312; http://www.apa.org/gradpsych/2009/01/creativity.aspx; http://marketeer.kapost.com/productivity-and-creativity-at-work/; http://www.newsweek.com/creativity-crisis-74665. Photo credits: Lyubov Kobyakova/Shutterstock.com; Kaponia Aliaksei/Shutterstock.com; Oleg Bakhirev/Shutterstock.com; Andrey tiyk/Shutterstock.com; Africa Studio/Shutterstock.com; Suslik1983/Shutterstock.com; Golden House Studio/Shutterstock.com; Keith Homan/Shutterstock.com; David S. Baker/Shutterstock.com; Nicescene/Shutterstock.com; Somchai Som/Shutterstock.com

10. **Detach your self-concept.** For most of us, creativity is often linked to self-concept. An idea is your brainchild, and you want it to win people over. You've invested part of yourself in giving birth to it. But there's nothing like self-criticism to shut down your creative juices. Your idea may not succeed on its own, but it may feed into someone else's idea and improve it. Or an idea you have about this problem may inform the next problem that challenges you. In the end, in addition to finding a workable solution, what's important is engaging in the creative process with others.

> "I can't understand why people are frightened by new ideas. I'm frightened by the old ones."
>
> *John Cage, American composer (1912–1992)*

CAREER OUTLOOK: EXAMINE YOUR THINKING

If someone asked you to come up with five adjectives that describe the most memorable boss you've ever had, what words would come to you? Words like *encouraging, smart, visionary, responsive, or supportive*—or words like *hasty, unfair, mean, hypocritical,* or *irrational*? What do all the words you think of have in common? Were they mainly *positive* or *negative*?

When asked this question, most people go in one direction: either entirely positive or negative. No one ever says, "What I really love about my boss is his critical nature. He doesn't miss a single mistake I make."[23] It's natural to lean one way or the other; that's one reason why critical thinking skills are a useful tool in the workplace. They can help you adjust your thinking appropriately and keep you from getting locked into particular patterns, especially negative ones.

In the workplace, the most desirable kind of thinking is "realistic optimism." It's not blind faith or false hope; it's looking for the best in things and then working to make them happen. It's accepting what's going on around you, but at the same time admitting what needs to be changed. It's about resilience, "getting back on the horse," and trotting on. It's a productive pattern of thinking.[24]

If "realistic optimism" sounds like an oxymoron to you, have faith! Remember the words of the environmentalist and founder of Patagonia, the well-known outdoor gear company: "There's no difference between a pessimist who says, 'Oh, it's hopeless, so don't bother doing anything,' and an optimist who says, 'Don't bother doing anything, it's going to turn out fine anyway.' Either way, nothing happens." It's your thinking and your career, and you're in the driver's seat. You want to do things, go places, and make things happen. That's what it's all about.

How does this section apply to your current or a recent job? Can you think of an example of how "realistic optimism" could help you in a real-life scenario from your work experience?

_____

_____

_____

_____

INSIGHT: *NOW* WHAT DO YOU THINK?

At the beginning of this chapter, Desiree Moore, a frustrated student, faced a challenge. Now, after reading this chapter, would you respond differently to any of the questions you answered about the "FOCUS Challenge Case"? Using what you learned in the chapter, write a paragraph ending to Desiree's case study. What are some of the possible outcomes for Desiree?

ACTION: YOUR PLANS FOR CHANGE

1. What's the most important thing you learned in reading this chapter? Why did it have an impact on you?

2. What will you change about the way you try to learn in your classes or perform on the job as a result of reading it?

HOW MUCH DID YOU LEARN?

At the beginning of this chapter, you filled out a "Readiness Check" that asked how you thought this chapter would relate to you and how you would relate to it. Now, fill out this "Reality Check" to find out.

1. What's the difference between thinking and critical thinking?

2. Define *metacognition* in your own words.

3. Identify three specific types of faulty reasoning.

4. What's the difference between critical thinking and creative thinking?

5. How long did it take? _____ hours _____ minutes. Before you began this chapter, you were asked to predict how long it would take you to complete it (total time, even if you read it in more than one sitting). Was your estimate on target, or will you revise it for the next chapter you'll read?

HOW THIS CHAPTER RELATES TO YOU

1. When it comes to online learning, using technology, and doing research for your college classes, what are you most concerned about, if anything? Put check marks by the phrases that apply to you or write in your answer.

   ☐ Having the right technology skills

   ☐ Having enough self-discipline

   ☐ Missing face-to-face classroom interaction

   ☐ Knowing how to conduct research

   ☐ Understanding exactly what plagiarism is

   ☐ _____

2. What is most likely to be your response? Put a check mark by it.

   ☐ I'll be open to learning more about using technology for schoolwork.

   ☐ I'll wait and see how much of this chapter I understand.

   ☐ I'll ask my online or classroom instructor for clarification.

   ☐ Eventually, I'll just figure it out.

3. What would you have to do to increase your likelihood of success? Will you do it this quarter or semester?

HOW YOU WILL RELATE TO THIS CHAPTER

1. What are you most interested in learning about? Put check marks by those topics.

   ☐ How to develop useful strategies for online classes

   ☐ How to use technology to become more academically successful

   ☐ How to cultivate your research skills

   ☐ What information literacy skills are and why they're important

   ☐ What plagiarism is and how to avoid it

YOUR READINESS FACTOR

1. How motivated are you to learn more about learning online, using technology, and doing research in college? (5 = high, 1 = low)

2. How ready are you to read now? (If something is in your way, take care of it if you can. Zero in and focus.)

3. How long do you think it will take you to complete this chapter? If you start and stop, keep track of your overall time. ____ Hour(s) ____ Minute(s)

Dario Jones

Alexander Image/Shutterstock.com

Ever since grade school, Dario Jones had been called a geek. It was a label he hated, but, honestly, most people probably thought of him that way. As a kid, Dario lived for computer games. He played them nearly every waking hour. In high school, he'd shower in record time, throw on whatever clean clothes he could find, and use any spare minutes for computer games. When he got home, he'd log right back on again. His Dad tried threatening him: "You'll lose your eyesight and flunk out of school." Once when he was younger, he faked a sore throat and played Call of Duty at home for a week while his parents were at work. As he got older, his Dad warned: "You'll never get a date." But Dario wasn't worried. Online relationships were enough. Real-life relationships were too much trouble. After high school, he joined the Army, and now that he was finally back from ten months in Afghanistan, his cyber life was much more exciting than ever. Dario spent more time—even sacrificing precious hours of sleep—surfing the Internet, envisioning how he could improve websites, and playing video games with strangers online than he spent talking to anyone in his general vicinity.

Then one day the obvious truth dawned on him. Now that he was a civilian, he was going to have to get a job—plain and simple. He had joined the Army because he really didn't know what he wanted to do next, and he figured he'd gain some skills there. But now that he was home, he wondered how those skills would translate into a different career—and whether he had the right skills.

Eventually, Dario made a decision. He would use his G.I. benefits and go to college. Because he was such a technology fan, maybe being a web designer would be a good field for him. And as he Googled opportunities, he found that he could get an entire degree online! What could be more perfect than that? Sitting in real classrooms with all those college kids didn't appeal to him at all. Besides, now that he was back from some pretty intense experiences while deployed, fighting for parking spots and being in crowded classrooms would just add to his stress, and that was something he didn't need. The images of the past 10 months were still very much alive in his memory. Besides, online courses had to be easier than real classes, and that one thing sealed the deal.

Robert Kyllo/Shutterstock.com

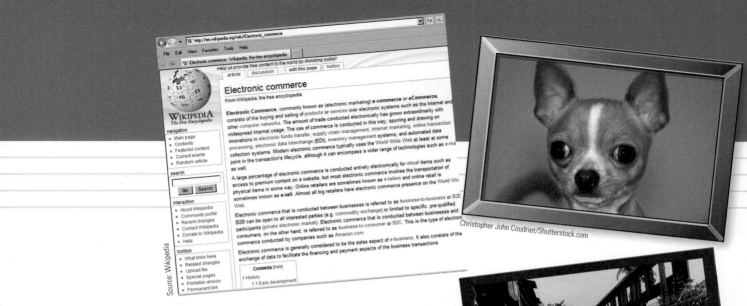

Source: Wikipedia

Christopher John Coudriet/Shutterstock.com

Jamaway/Alamy Stock Photo; 123render/iStock/Thinkstock

But Dario quickly discovered that his considerable tech skills might not be enough. Besides that, all three classes had major assignments that would require a serious time commitment. The first week, he stayed up late, listening to online lectures, downloading handouts, and posting responses on the discussion board. Then before he knew it, he got an e-mail from the instructor in his toughest class, "Fundamentals of Internet Business," reminding him that he needed to post two of his own responses to her questions and respond to two classmates' comments each week. "Your comments need to be substantive, Dario, not just quick entries like, 'I really liked the online lecture for Chapter 6' or 'Good point, Keisha.' And you need to keep up," she wrote. "I didn't hear from you for two weeks." *That kind of criticism is a definite diss*, Dario thought to himself. If he hadn't already paid tuition, he would have been tempted to drop out of the course entirely.

The worst part was that his toughest class required a research paper. The assigned topic was Globalization and Internet Commerce. Even though he had always considered himself to be a technology expert, frankly, he didn't know where to start. *Step one*, Dario thought to himself, *is to Google*. He always Googled everything: the directions to a new Mexican restaurant—his favorite food—or some little-known fact that he wondered about, like how many Chihuahuas were sold in the United States last year. (He had just adopted one from a shelter.) But when he Googled "Internet Commerce," he got 12 million hits. *Better regroup*, he advised himself.

But how? Should he go to a real library or try to do his research online in the comfort of his own apartment? Physically going to a library seemed unnecessary when so much information was available online. Then he had a flash of inspiration: Wikipedia. He found a page on "Electronic Commerce." At least that was a start—that is, until he looked at his instructor's handout on the assignment. Students were discouraged from using Wikipedia as a primary research source. The handout said, "Information literacy is required." He got another idea: He'd close Wikipedia and go back to Googling. This time he'd try "Electronic Commerce." *Uh, oh, 17 million hits this time*. He plugged in "E-Commerce," "E-Business," and "Globalization." He tried "Global Issues," but before he knew it, he found himself knee-deep in articles about "Global Warming." He was so far afield now that he couldn't find his way back to his topic. Should he shut everything down and start over or just give up?

At the last minute, Dario panicked. He found a few useful things online, and cut and pasted from the internet until he'd filled five pages. At least he had something to turn in. He wondered if this was the way to do research and whether he'd broken any rules. *Well, I can always go back into the military*, he thought to himself. But to be honest, he really wanted to make an entirely new life for himself as a civilian.

Focus challenge case **141**

TAKING ONLINE CLASSES:
E-LEARNING VERSUS C-LEARNING

What do an American soldier just back from Afghanistan, a single mother of twin toddlers in California, and a victim of cerebral palsy in New York have in common? All three are taking the same online course in psychology. Instead of c-learning (traditionally, in the classroom), they're engaging in *distance education* or e-learning (electronically, online). E-learning is one kind of technology you may well run into during your time in college.

Of course, most of your college courses are hybrid, or blended, courses: they each have an online component and a classroom component. You e-mail your professor, use software to track your progress, upload assignments and download handouts, but you still go to a physical classroom with classmates once or twice a term, or perhaps even every week. That's why they're called hybrid (like cars: part electricity and part gasoline) or blended (when mediated and face-to-face learning are meshed) classes. If you haven't already, chances are you'll be engaged in distance learning in a totally online environment for at least one of your college classes. According to one large-scale recent study, "in 2010, 66 percent of respondents said their institution offers at least one online degree. Now, virtually all do—92 percent of them. The number of community colleges offering online certificate programs is also on the rise, increasing to 84 percent of respondents from 76 percent last year."[1] However, it's challenging to succeed in online courses, more challenging than you may think.[2] And technology in general will be an essential part of your future career. That's why this chapter is key to your college success, and eventually your career success, too.

What are the differences between e-learning and c-learning? E-learning is sometimes defined as structured learning that takes place without a teacher at the front of the room. If you're an independent, self-motivated learner, e-learning can be a great way to learn, because *you* are in control.

> *You control when you learn.* Instead of that dreaded 8:00 A.M. class—the only section that's open when you register—you can schedule your e-learning when it's convenient for you. If you want to do your coursework at midnight in your pajamas, who's to know?

Hybrid, or blended, courses are part online and part on-ground in varying proportions

> *You control how you learn.* If you are an introvert, e-learning may work well for you. You can work thoughtfully online and take all the time you need to reflect. If you are an extravert, however, you may become frustrated by the lack of warm bodies around. Jumping into threaded discussions and chatting online may satisfy some of those needs, but you may miss real people sitting next to you. If you're a kinesthetic learner, the keyboard action may suit you well. Because you're working independently, you can do whatever you need to do to accommodate your own learning style.

> *You control how fast you learn.* You know for a fact that students learn at different rates. With e-learning, you don't have to feel you're slowing down the class if you continue a line of questioning or worry about getting left in the dust if everyone else is way ahead of you.

E-learning can be a very effective way to learn, but it does require some adjustments. Here are some suggestions for making the best of your online learning opportunities:

1. **Work hard.** Many students think that fully online courses will be easier than going to class. After all, you won't have to shower, get dressed, drive through traffic, and cruise the campus for 15 minutes to find a parking spot. These factors, in and of themselves, should be big time savers. Unless your class requires a webcam (to record yourself for an online public speaking class, for example), you're virtually invisible. But think about it this way: In an online course, you will have to do many of the things that your instructor normally does for you. In a classroom, she may simply walk around and pass out handouts. Online, you'll have to locate them on the course website, download them, and print them out yourself. You'll need to read everything carefully, both the items posted on the course management shell itself (like the course calendar, syllabus, reminder messages, instructions for each assignment) and every document you download. Instead of taking a seat in the classroom to listen to your professor lecture at the front of the room, you will have to get the information yourself by downloading lecture notes, PowerPoint slides, or videos of your instructors' lectures. Some studies show that students work harder and longer online. The belief that online courses are easier is a myth.

2. **Keep up.** Even though you may be "invisible" in online courses, you can't "hide." You'll likely have to keep up by posting regularly to the class blog or online discussion board and comment on your classmates' posts every week. Dario from this chapter's Challenge case received an e-mail from his instructor, asking where he was. If you decide to "take a vacation" in the middle of your online course, your instructor may inquire about your whereabouts, too. Just as you'd do for a face-to-face class, consider setting aside a specific time each week for your online course, like Tuesday and Thursday afternoons, and commit to reserving that time for online coursework.

3. **Get advice from other online students.** The first time you take an online course, ask a friend or classmate who has experience with this type of

course for advice. That person may save you hours of online wandering with a few simple tips. Besides finding out how to navigate the course online, ask what student services are available online, like advising, tutoring, financial aid, enrollment, and tuition payments.

4. **Communicate your needs to your instructor.** If this is your first online course, ask your instructor for a general assessment of how much time he expects you to set aside each week. Think about the three hours or so you usually spend per week in a face-to-face class or lab, and use that as a rule of thumb. (Of course, specifics depend on what else you have going on and your individual learning style preferences. And when you begin to see the grades you earn on the assignments you turn in, you may decide to invest more time on your own.) Remember, too, that your instructor won't be able to see your "huh?" looks when you don't understand something. Take direct action by e-mailing her, for example, instead of hiding behind your computer screen and hoping for the best. "The best" usually doesn't come to you; you'll have to work for it. On the other hand, before you fire off a quick question, reread the assignment. It may be that you just missed something simple, and your question is actually unnecessary.

5. **Stay in touch with other students in the course.** Rather than isolating yourself, which is a mistake, use e-mail to communicate with your cyber classmates to build an online learning community. They may be able to clarify an assignment or coach you through a tough spot.

learning community group of students who help one another learn

6. **Take notes.** When you're sitting through an in-class lecture, you handwrite notes to review later. Likewise, if you're reading lecture notes online, open a Word document and switch back and forth for your own note-taking purposes. Or open an e-tool, like evernote.com, which can work well for note taking.

7. **Keep your antivirus program up to date.** When you upload assignment files, you run the risk of infecting your instructor's computer with whatever viruses your computer may have. Make sure your antivirus software is up to date!

8. **Create a productive learning environment.** Because you'll most likely do your e-learning at home, make sure the environment is right for learning. If your computer is next to the TV or your kids are acting up to get attention, move to another location that's calm, properly lit, and quiet.

9. **Use each login session as an opportunity to review.** Begin each online session by reviewing what you did or how much progress you made last time. Physically logging on can become a signal to take stock before moving forward with new course material.

10. **Organize, organize, organize!** In your face-to-face classes, you can keep courses separate in your mind by remembering where the different classrooms are located, for example, and who your classmates and teachers are. By contrast, in online courses you usually sit down in front of your same computer, and you might never even meet your classmates or teacher. You'll have to find ways to separate and organize materials for each class either physically by using hard copy files or electronically by using folders on your computer or thumb drive.

Larry Harwood Photography. Property of Cengage Learning.

"Any occurrence requiring undivided attention will be accompanied by a compelling distraction."

Robert Bloch, American fiction writer (1917–1994)

11. **Call on your time management skills.** Create a "Term-on-a-Page" master calendar, mark the due dates for each class, and review it at the beginning of every week. If your e-course is self-paced, you'll need to plan ahead, schedule due dates, and above all discipline yourself to make continual progress. For many students, this very thing is the biggest challenge of online courses. The instructor isn't there with you, insisting that you turn in assignments. If you're sharing a computer with other family members, you'll need to create a master schedule of who can use the computer when. Remember that you may need to be online at particular times to engage in class chats or discussions.

12. **Have a back-up plan.** Technology crashes from time to time, and system platforms go down, sometimes just when you need them. If you wait until the last minute to upload an assignment, you may find that your campus technology system is down or your student portal is unavailable because of scheduled maintenance. Get to know your campus tech support staff, and don't hesitate to contact them in an emergency. Work ahead, so that you don't fall behind if the dreaded "blue screen" suddenly appears, signaling a tech failure. Watch for campus emails about system down time for scheduled upgrades, and work around it. In other words, take responsibility. If your paper is late because you left your thumb drive in the car, and your car is at your sister's house, expect to have points deducted. Most online instructors abide by syllabus rules, and they expect you to do the same.[3]

platform the learning (or course) management system (LMS/CMS) your campus uses, like Blackboard or Canvas, sometimes with a title for your school, like GBCConline

---

EXERCISE 6.1 **A DAY IN THE LIFE OF AN ONLINE STUDENT**

You wake up and look out the window. It's a beautiful day, and—lucky you—it's your day off from work! While having your morning coffee, you log on to Facebook. You see a few new interesting posts and some new pictures from last weekend. You check your e-mail and find a tempting new Groupon, a few e-mails from friends, and an e-mail from the instructor of your online class. *Oh no,* you think. *I haven't done anything for my online class in a while, and there's a big assignment due tomorrow!* With a sigh you glance out the window one more time. It looks like you won't be able to spend the day relaxing outside like you thought.

Assume this is what your day looks like. For each entry in your hypothetical schedule, look at the obstacles that may get in your way, and describe how you'll address them.

8:00 A.M.

You pour yourself another cup of coffee and sit down to work on your online course, but you start to wander, electronically. Maybe you should see how many of your friends "like" the new photos you uploaded to your Facebook page. Before you know it, an hour and a half has gone by and you get up to get a snack.

SOLUTION:

_____

_____

10:00 A.M.

You successfully get yourself back on task, but you've hit another snag. You have the syllabus somewhere, and you have lots of questions about the assignment. Your instructor gave you her contact info, but you can't afford to wait very long for a response.

(continued on next page)

SOLUTION:

_____

_____

10:30 A.M.

Now that you have clarification on the assignment, you dig into your work. You need to find four different sources for your research, but you're not having much luck. You try one Google search after another, but the websites don't seem to have what you're looking for.

SOLUTION:

_____

_____

11:00 A.M.

You've finally located some reliable and useful resources for your assignment. As you continue to work, you find yourself copying and pasting a useful word here and there into your paper. Pretty soon, you're clicking and dragging phrases, then sentences into your assignment. *Am I plagiarizing?* you wonder.

SOLUTION:

_____

_____

12:00 P.M.

You're working hard, finding good resources, and using them ethically. Your phone rings. It's one of your friends, inviting you to lunch and a movie this afternoon. You glance at your watch. You've been working on this project for a couple of hours now; haven't you earned a little break?

SOLUTION:

_____

_____

7:00 P.M.

Looking back on the day, you've accomplished a lot. You've coped with understanding the assignment clearly, finding good resources and using them well, and managing your time. You're pretty happy with your work, but you wish there was a way to get some feedback on the assignment before you upload it to be graded.

SOLUTION:

_____

_____

11:00 P.M.

Turn in for the night. Tomorrow is a new "Day in the Life of an Online Student."

TECHNOLOGY SKILLS:
WIRELESS, WINDOWED, WEBBED, AND WIKIED

Ah, technology . . . Does it make our lives simpler or more complicated? Like Dario, are you pulled into video games, even though you know there's something else you *should* be doing? Do you live to text? Do you check Facebook on your phone repeatedly throughout the day? Or, on the other hand, do you hate the thought of facing your e-mail after you haven't had access for awhile? Did you find yourself answering "yes" to any of these questions—or maybe answering "yes" to all of them?

Many of us have a love–hate relationship with technology: We love the convenience but hate the dependence. But in college, your techno-skills will be another key to your success. You'll need to know things like how to produce an essay in Microsoft Word, how to give a PowerPoint presentation, and how to use learning management systems like Blackboard. "Whoa! Wait a minute," you say. "I'm no expert at all of that!" You don't have to be an expert, but you do need to know the basics and be willing to learn more. It's easier to be "device-savvy"—an expert on your phone, for example—than it is to be truly tech-savvy. Dario considered himself to be a technology expert, but his expertise was more about *entertainment* than *education*. In college, you'll be using technology to enhance your education.

Your community college may have invited you to enroll with a Twitter or Facebook invitation. Your school will provide you with an e-mail account and send you official college documents, like your tuition bill and weather alerts, over e-mail. It may "nudge" you with reminders about deadlines or campus events. You will take entire courses or parts of courses online so that you can learn on your own time at your own pace. Many of your instructors will use learning management systems, YouTube clips, streaming video, and websites in the classroom to increase your learning. (And the good news is that many college students say it helps.)[4] So the time to start building your skills is now! Just how useful is the internet to college students? The answer is that just like anything else, the internet has pros and cons.

THE INTERNET: THE GOOD, THE BAD, AND THE UGLY
The Good

A full 98 percent of 18- to 29-year-old Americans own a cell phone.[5] Now we can stay in touch by phone call or text with anyone in our personal networks. For many of us, the internet via our phones, tablets, or laptops is how we get our news, our research, our entertainment, and our communication. When it comes to all the potential benefits of the internet, think about advantages like these:

> **Currency.** While some of the information posted on the internet isn't up to date, much of it is current. This is especially important during a crisis or a national emergency, for example, when it's important to get news fast. Reports, articles, and studies that might take months to publish in books or articles are available on the web as soon as they're written.

ArtFamily/Shutterstock.com

"Technology should improve your life... not become your life."

Billy Cox, speaker and writer

currency   timely

arek_malang/Shutterstock.com

"Technology is nothing. What's important is that you have a faith in people, that they're basically good and smart, and if you give them tools, they'll do wonderful things with them."

Steve Jobs, founder of Apple Computers (1955–2011)

VARK IT!

Visual: Go through this chapter, and highlight everything that relates specifically to you. Or create your own system—yellow for things you do currently, blue for things that are good ideas, and green for things you will defintely try.

VARK IT!

Kinesthetic: Find the browsing history on your web browser. How many of the websites are time-wasters and how many were used for work or school?

> **Availability.** The internet never sleeps. If you can't sleep at 2:00 A.M., the internet can keep you company. It can be a good friend to have. Unlike your real instructor, who teaches other classes besides yours and attends marathon meetings, Professor Google is always in. For the most part, you can check your e-mail or log onto the internet from anywhere, any time.

> **Scope.** You can find out virtually anything you want to know on the internet, from the recipe for the world's best chocolate chip cookie to medical advice on everything from Athlete's Foot to Zits. (Of course, real human beings are usually a better option for serious questions.)

> **Interactivity.** Unlike other media, the internet lets you talk back. You can write a letter to the editor of a newspaper and wait for a reply, or you can push buttons on your phone in response to an endless list of menu questions ("If you want directions in English, press 1 . . .") and finally get to a real-live human being. But the internet lets you communicate instantly and constantly. You can instant message to your heart's content, if you want to; add to your Facebook page daily; or edit a Wikipedia entry whenever you like.

> **Affordability.** The number of internet users worldwide is approaching 4 billion; 287 million Americans are on the Net today.[6] For most of us, when it comes to the internet, the price is right. After you buy a computer and pay a monthly access fee, you get a great deal for your money.

The Bad

Too much of a good thing—anything—can be bad. When something becomes that central to our lives, it carries risks. Here are some internet dangers worth thinking about:

> **Inaccuracy.** Often we take information presented to us at face value, without questioning it. But on many internet sites, the responsibility for checking the accuracy of the information presented there is yours. Bob's Statistics Home Page and the U.S. Census Bureau's website are not equally valid. Not everything published online is true or right.

> **Laziness.** It's easy to allow the convenience of the internet to make us lazy. Why go through the hassle of cooking dinner when you can just stop for a burger on the way home? The same thing applies to the internet. Why not just do what Dario did and find information somebody else has already posted on the internet, and use it? What's wrong with that? For one thing, if you don't give the rightful author credit, that's plagiarism, which can give you a zero on an assignment or even cause you to fail a course. But another thing worth considering is that the *how* of learning is as important as the *what*. If all you ever did was cut, paste, and download, you wouldn't learn how to do research yourself. College helps you learn skills you will need later—critical thinking, research, and writing skills, for example—in your career. You may never have to give your boss a five-page paper on the humor of Mark Twain—as you might your literature instructor—but you may need to write a five-page report on your customers' buying trends over the last six months.

> **Overdependence.** A related problem with anything that's easy and convenient is that we can start depending on it too much. National studies report that many of us lack basic knowledge. We can't name the Chief Justices of the Supreme Court or the capitals of all 50 states. Without even realizing it, we may think: Why bother learning a bunch of facts when you can just check quickly online? Are we so dependent on the internet that we're relying on it for information we should learn or know?[7]

The Ugly

The internet can be used in foul ways. Spam, viruses, spyware, and phishing costs American consumers billions of dollars in damage, affecting 40 percent of U.S. households.[8] Take a look at one student's social networking page in Figure 6.1 to see whether you can guess where things are headed.

"For a list of all the ways technology has failed to improve the quality of life, please press three."

Alice Kahn, technology author

Like the hypothetical Victoria Tymmyns (or her online name, VicTym) featured in Figure 6.1, some students publish inappropriate, confidential, and potentially dangerous information on their social media pages. Victoria has posted her address, phone numbers, and moment-by-moment location. Look at the final entries on her page to find out what potential threat she may be facing. Aside from the risk of serious harm, other types of "danger" can result from bad judgment, too. What some students post just for fun can later cost them a job opportunity. If your web page has provocative photos of you or descriptions of rowdy weekend activities that you wouldn't want your grandmother to see, remove them! (Employers regularly check these sources for insider information on applicants.) "Living out loud," as social networking is sometimes called, requires constant vigilance so that the details of your life aren't on display. Some recent research indicates that younger users are more sensitive to keeping things offline than older users.[9] To avoid "social insecurity," keep these five useful suggestions in mind:

1. Use a password with at least eight letters and numbers, like FO34$&CuS.

2. Don't include your full birth date. Identity thieves can use this information.

3. Take advantage of privacy controls. Use the options provided to you, like choosing the "Friends Only" option. Be sure not to check the box for "Public Search Results." Search engines can find your social media profiles if you do.

4. You wouldn't put a "No One's Home" sign on your door, so don't post it as your status.

5. Don't post your child's name in a caption. If someone else does, remove it.[10]

What does all of this have to do with you? Everything! It's important to remember that the internet itself is neutral. It can be used constructively or destructively, based on the choices you make. It can be an exciting, invigorating, essential part of your college experience. Use it wisely!

USE TECHNOLOGY TO YOUR ACADEMIC ADVANTAGE

Despite the pros and cons, technology plays a big role in all of our lives, especially the lives of college students. The truth of the matter is that technology skills are increasingly important in all academic disciplines—as well as any profession.[11] "Eight in 10 college students surveyed said that the use of tech improves their grades (81 percent), lets them spend more time studying

FIGURE 6.1

Fictional Ispy.com page

Companion, M. (2006). Victoria Tymmyns Ispy.com. Used with permission.

ISpy.com GBCC

View More Photos of Me

Status   edit

Doin' shots at Annie Oakley's!

RMSU Friends

425 friends at GBCC   See All

Seymore Bonz   N.O. Body

Friends in Other Networks

Cal (12)
UF (40)
CMU (6)
KSCC (7)
GBCC (425)

Basic Info [edit]
Name: Victoria Tymmyns
Looking For: A Good Time
Residence: 456 Pine Valley
Birthday: June 12, 1996

Contact Info [edit]
Email: VicTym@gbcc.edu
AIM Screenname   VicTym
Mobile: 719.111.1112
Current Address: 123 Fake St.
                        Great Bluffs, CO 80900

Personal Info [edit]
Activities: Drinkin' at "Annie Oakley's" every Fri. night.
                        Karaoke at "All That Jazz" every Sat. night.

Favorite Music: Adele, Carrie Underwood, Pentatonix
Favorite Movies   Office Space, Star Wars, Harry Potter

Work Info [edit]
Company: Common Grounds Coffee Shop
Schedule: Work M – F 7AM –2PM

 N.O. Body wrote: at 11:00am August 1, 2018
Saw u dancing at Annie Oakley's!! Whatta hottie! We should meet.

 N.O. Body wrote: at 1:00pm August 1, 2018
Aw come on! U know u want to meet me!

 N.O. Body wrote: at 3:02pm August 1, 2018
Still no response? What's up? Do u wanna play or not?

 Seymore Bonz wrote: at 4:27pm August 1, 2018
R we still hookin up w/the gang at Annie Oakley's tonight?
Meet you guys at the front door at 10.

 N.O. **Body** wrote: at 5:20pm August 1, 2018
Sounds fun. Maybe i'll see u there.

 Bay-Bee Face wrote: at 10:17pm August 2, 2018
Can you believe how we much we rocked last night? What was the deal with that guy
who kept staring at us? He gave me the creeps!! You switched shifts w/Mary right?
Working at 4?

 N.O. Body wrote: at 12:39pm August 2, 2018
Gee, BTW u were dressed, I just assumed u liked being stared at… U looked really
cute at work.

 N.O. Body wrote: at 2:21pm August 3, 2018
What's the matter sweetheart? U looked unhappy to see me at work today. Why
didn't u talk to me? BTW, nice house u got. Who knew you lived in such a nice neighborhood.

 N.O. Body wrote: at 12:57pm August 5, 2018
Nice dog u have. Ur parents must be outta town—no one's been home all night.

 N.O. Body wrote: at 7:26pm August 5, 2018
U never showed up for ur shift today. I waited all day for u. Saw your friends.
They said somebody poisoned your dog. That's a shame—such a yappy
little thing. I hate stuck-up women. Guess I'll just have to find u in person…

by increasing the accessibility they have to their materials (82 percent) and improves their efficiency (81 percent). A comparable number (80 percent) said they find that their instructors are 'effectively' integrating digital learning tech into their courses."[12]

What academic benefits does technology provide? In one major study, students noted that it helps them:

> Access resources and information.

> Simplify administrative tasks (enrolling for classes, paying tuition bills, etc.).

> Track progress in classes.

> Commuicate with instructors and classmates.

> Make learning more engaging and relevant.[13]

Let's look at some specific technology applications you'll need to know in college, including types of software, search engines, learning management systems, and other class-related possibilities.

> **Top-Level Domains (TLD).** The part of the URL (Uniform Resource Locator) after the period describes where websites come from:

- .gov = U.S. government (such as www.irs.gov, the Internal Revenue Service [or IRS])

- .edu = education (such as www.gbcc.edu, Great Bluffs Community College)

- .org = organizations or businesses (such as www.democratic.org, the Democratic Party, or nonprofit organizations, like www.americanheart .org, American Heart Association)

- .mil = military (such as www.defenselink.mil, U.S. Department of Defense)

- .com = commercial, buying and selling (such as www.realtor.com, National Association of Realtors)

- .net = network or internet provider (such as www.earthlink.net)

- .int = international organizations (such as Interpol, Council of Europe, or NATO)[14]

> **Software.** College will require you to use several standard software applications to do your academic work:

- Microsoft Word allows you to type, edit, alphabetize, index, footnote, and do many other things to prepare papers for your classes.

- Microsoft PowerPoint, used as an electronic visual aid for oral presentations, allows you to create an on-screen guide for your listeners (and you, if you glance at it periodically and subtly for clues).

- Microsoft Excel spreadsheets are good for tabulating, record keeping, and organizing.

The industry standard for these applications is generally the Microsoft products listed here, although other possibilities exist. If you need help learning any of these applications, your campus techies, your instructors, or online tutorials (which can easily be found by Googling) can help. If you're a techie yourself, you can venture into other software applications like Flash, Camtasia, or iMovie to make your academic work look even more professional.

"Technology can be our best friend, and technology can also be the biggest party pooper of our lives. It interrupts our own story, interrupts our ability to have a thought or a daydream, to imagine something wonderful, because we're too busy bridging the walk from the cafeteria back to the office on the cell phone."

Steven Spielberg, Academy Award-winning film director, producer, and screenwriter

> **Search Engines.** Different search engines work best for different purposes, but these three are the most popular recommendations:[15]

  - Google (www.google.com) has a well-deserved reputation as the best search engine you can use. Its size is not disclosed anywhere, but it's generally thought to have the largest assets to search and an estimated 1.6 billion unique visitors per month.

  - Bing (www.bing.com), a Microsoft alternative to Google, organizes your responses to help you make better informed decisions. It is used by 400 million unique visitors a month.

  - Yahoo (www.yahoo.com) can also help you get excellent search results, or allow you to use any of the other specialized search features.

> **Wikis.** Wikis are today's online, editable encyclopedias. (The word wiki means "fast" in the Hawaiian language.) Wikipedia is the largest of these sites (at 40 million articles in more than 293 languages), and anyone can add information or change content. On the other hand, be aware that inaccurate information can be added just as easily as accurate information. Never consider Wikipedia to be the final word on anything.

> **Learning Management Systems.** Many of your college classes will be conducted partially or wholly online, using a learning management system, like Blackboard, Canvas, or Moodle. These shells help organize the online component of classes, and most students report having positive experiences with them. How do students use learning management systems?

  - To track grades, assignments, and tests
  - To take sample tests and quizzes (or real ones)
  - To get the course syllabus
  - To turn in assignments online
  - To access readings and other course materials
  - To post to an online discussion[16]

> **Blogs.** Web logs, or blogs, can be thought of as online journals that are typically one person's reactions to current events or cultural issues, for example. Or you can think of them as websites that someone changes every day.[17] Your instructors may post a question or comment and ask you to blog your responses online and to respond to your classmates' blogs. Everyone can get to know you by your online personality, and some students say they become better writers by reading other students' responses to their writing. And professional blogs can be a great way to stay current on the career you go into.

> **YouTube.** YouTube is a video-sharing website where you can upload and watch video clips. You may want to insert one into a presentation you create as a class assignment or post one yourself related to your life as a student.

> **Textbook Courseware.** Textbook courseware, which often accompanies your book, can contain information and activities to enrich your learning experience, like an ebook, videos, quizzes, and iAudio chapter summaries. Use these resources to help you master course material.

BOX 6.1

OTHER NEED-TO-KNOW TECHNOLOGY DEFINITIONS

Gaming and Simulation: Technology is quickly becoming an interactive tool that helps you *experience* learning, rather than just listening to lectures or reading books. Both individually and collaboratively, you can easily use all your senses to learn.[18]

Podcasts: Many professors now record their lectures for you to review later. Or you can listen to *FOCUS on Community College Success* and other textbooks' iAudio summaries for each chapter online.

PDF files: Using Adobe technology, you can create and edit documents that are formatted on your computer screen just as they would appear if they were published. PDFs look very professional, and there may be a time when you are asked to create one for a particular class.

Web 2.0: Web 2.0 is not a new version of the internet. It refers to creative and social uses of it, like Facebook, Wikis, and blogs, where instead of just reading passively, users help create the content.

Viruses, Worms, and Trojan Horses: Pranksters (or vicious cyber attackers, for that matter) can infiltrate campus technology systems and infect individual computers or shut down a campus system entirely. The solution? Don't open attachments with suspicious names or ones from people you don't know. And keep your antivirus software up to date!

Mobile Apps: Apps, short for "applications," are internet-based programs that allow you to work, read, or communicate online from your smartphone or other portable electronic device. In today's world, people are busy and don't stay in one spot. They want to work, learn, and study from anywhere at anytime.

QR Codes: QR (short for "quick response") codes are two-dimensional bar codes that you can scan, for example, from your cell phone (if you download an app). The code will take you to a website immediately for more information.

Virtual/Augmented/Mixed Realities: Technology companies with deep pockets like Google, Apple, and Facebook are researching artificial intelligence (AR, VR, and MR), which has the potential to greatly impact learning in higher education.[19]

Dropbox: Dropbox is a free (or paid) service that lets you store your files on the internet, access them from anywhere, and share them with anyone.

WIIFM?

 3 MINUTE READ

Technology skills—WIIFM? That's almost like asking, "Air? What's in it for me?" The first response to that question, of course, is that you need to breathe in order to stay alive. Technology skills are certainly essential when it comes to keeping your career alive—and to launching it in the first place. IT job fields are hot, hot, hot, and nearly all jobs require tech skills of some kind. End of story? Not quite. Let's get more specific so you're fully versed in the subject.

What kinds of technology skills are employers looking for these days? If you want to work for a tech giant, like Google, Facebook, or Amazon, you'll need some highly advanced tech skills in neural networking, programming languages (like Java, C++, or Python), or software development. But not every employee in these high-end companies works in accelerated tech fields, and not all of them have an elite bachelor's degree—or a degree at all, for that matter.[20] What is absolutely critical to getting a job at Google, for example? Four things: Google wants expertise in whatever particular job they're hiring for (naturally); "the ability to absorb information"; the guts to step in and fix a problem when you see one (and then the grace to step out when you're no longer needed); and cultural fit, or what they call Googleyness: "[which] boils down to intellectual humility. You don't have to be warm or fuzzy. You just have to be somebody who, when the facts show you're wrong, can say that."[21]

You may not be aiming for Google, but *Computerworld Magazine* says that IT jobs in general are definitely hot right now, and there aren't enough skilled applicants to fill them. Here's their forecast of what employers want most in the near future:[22]

"I think everybody in this country should learn to program a computer. Learn a computer language. Because it teaches you how to think."

Steve Jobs (attended De Anza Community College, Cupertino, California)

Source: Computerworld (IDG Enterprise only)

Or consider this perspective: Technology in the right hands solves problems. More than a decade ago, Larry Page, co-founder of Google, walked into the company's kitchen and posted a few pages of search results with ads, writing across the top in big black letters, "THESE ADS SUCK." (Google AdWords are the pay-per-click ads that show up to the right of your search results. They generate income for Google.) In many organizations, after a problem like that is blatantly identified, some executive will routinely "kick butt and take names." Heads would have rolled on the AdWords team. But at Google, this simple, indirect action was seen as an invitation to solve a problem, and within 72 hours a team of search engineers had posted a solution. The technical experts fixed the problem, not employees on the AdWords team, because the tech experts had the right skills and accepted the challenge.[23] So accept the challenge and boost *your* tech skills!

It's clear: Technology know-how gives you a definite leg-up in the workplace. You can *do* more, *access* more (by using the "third lobe" of your brain, as in, a computer), *accomplish* more, and *"publish"* more (including your competence) *as* you work. In fact, technology skills are so important and they evolve so continually and quickly that "retraining and upgrading [them] needs to be a lifetime commitment."[24] "Future proof" your employability by becoming as tech savvy as you can *now*, and stay at it throughout your career![25]

But why you? And why now? You may not want to learn a programming language, as Steve Jobs recommended, or learn how to program a computer, but being tech savvy is important in *all* jobs. Here are a few "WIIFM?" answers you may not have thought about:

For example, technology projects your competence and builds your reputation, no matter which career field you're in. What if your goal is to be on the police force or working toward a career in healthcare? Often, the "engines" that keep most organizations running are powered by technology skills you'll develop in college, including presentation software (like PowerPoint), writing software (like Word), spreadsheet software (like Excel),

and e-mail software (like Outlook). Imagine yourself briefing the police department to profile a criminal with the relevant information in PowerPoint projected onscreen, or compiling a report of recent crimes in Excel, or writing a professional e-mail to all your colleagues or your boss as a newbie on the force. In these cases, think of technology as your "public face." People will develop impressions of you based on how well you represent your thinking via your tech skills. Even before everyone in the organization knows your name, they may read one of your e-mails and make inferences about who you are and what you're like, just from what appears on a screen. You've suddenly "gone viral" within your own organization with just a Tweet or an e-mail.

WRITING EFFECTIVE ONLINE MESSAGES

Being a professional student doesn't just apply to how you act in class, like asking questions if you're unclear or turning in your assignments on time. Online communication has particular rules you must follow. For example, when you're writing discussion board posts in a hybrid or online course, it's important to be civil. "How could anyone ever possibly think that?" as a post to a classmate's entry may be honest, but it's hardly collegial. Instead, why not say, "That's something I hadn't thought of. Can you explain more about it?"? Think about the Golden Rule of online posts: How would you feel if a classmate shot down a good idea of yours? Be respectful.

When classmates post an idea, they're putting their egos on the line—or so it feels. Remember that you can disagree with a classmate online, but never disrespect him or her personally. "I thought we were always supposed to use good grammar on this discussion board. Jerome's posts are full of mistakes." There's no need to put Jerome on the spot. On the other hand, using good grammar and correct spelling will be important to your instructor, so be conscientious in that regard.

Another thing your instructor will insist on is that your posts are sufficiently informative. When you are in a hurry, it's tempting to write as little as possible, like "Alicia is right on target!" as your entire entry. Tell why. Mention parts of her argument you agree with, and explain your endorsement. A discussion board is a place for online, back-and-forth dialogue, not Tweet-like comments for other people to decipher.

Of course Tweets and text messages are used more often in social contexts than academic ones, but some of the same rules apply. Breaking up with your romantic partner by sending a text message would probably be perceived as a cowardly "low blow." Simply put: Certain situations call for certain types of messages.

E-mail that you send your instructor has netiquette (online etiquette) standards you should follow, too. Take a look at these widely accepted rules for academic settings:

1. **Don't send a message you don't want to risk being forwarded to someone else.** Doing so has caused many a fretful night. ("Aaaaakkk! What have I done?")

2. **Don't hit the "send" key until you've given yourself time to cool off, if you're upset.** You may want to edit what you've written.

3. **Don't forward chain e-mails.** At the very least, they're a nuisance, and sometimes they're illegal.

4. **Don't do business over your school e-mail account.** Sending all 500 new students an invitation to your family's restaurant grand opening is off-limits. Besides, sending messages to lots of people at once is called "spam," and it can really gum up the works.

5. **Don't spread hoaxes about viruses or false threats.** You can get into big trouble for that.

6. **Don't type in all CAPS.** That's called SHOUTING, and it makes you look angry.

7. **Don't be too casual.** Use good grammar and correct spelling. Your instructors consider e-mails to be academic writing, and they'll expect professionalism from you. "Hey Prof, this is a heckuva of a cool class!" may sound enthusiastic, but it's not professional. Language that you use for texts and IMs is not appropriate for academic correspondence.

8. **Don't forget important details.** Include everything the reader needs to know. For example, if you're writing to an instructor, give your full name and the name of the course you're writing about. Professors teach more than one class and have many students.

9. **Don't hit the "Reply to All" key when you mean to hit the "Reply" key.** Many e-mail message writers have been horrified upon learning that hundreds or thousands of people have read something personal or cranky that was meant for just one reader.

HOW *NOT* TO WIN FRIENDS AND INFLUENCE PEOPLE ONLINE

All four of these e-mail messages from students violate the rules of netiquette. See whether you can identify the rule number for netiquette in academic settings that's been violated in each case.

From Matt   Rule:_____

> Professor X,
>
> I just looked at the online syllabus for Academic Success 101. Why didn't you tell us that our first paper is due on Monday? I will be very busy moving into a new apartment this weekend. Writing an essay for your class is the last thing I want to have to think about.

From Tiffany   Rule:_____

> Prof X,
>
> i didn't know u were makin us write a paper over the weekend i won't be able to do it. i hop you don't mind

From Xavier   Rule:_____

> PROFESSOR X,
>
> I CAN'T GET MY PAPER DONE BY MONDAY. LET ME KNOW WHAT I SHOULD DO.

From Dameon   Rule:_____

> Hey, Section 3
>
> Can you believe our instructor? She assigns a big writing assignment after only one day of class! Who in their right mind would be remotely interested in sitting in their crummy little room writing a bunch of meaningless junk, when we haven't even learned anything yet? What kind of teacher are we stuck with here? Somebody out there respond to me, OK? I'm totally hacked off!

Discuss your responses in class or online. Do you all agree on which rules were broken in the four examples provided? See whether you can create some new ones that violate other rules.

10. **Don't risk being perceived as rude.** If you're sending an attachment to an instructor, include a brief message along with it. Generally, it's considered discourteous not to include at least a brief message that explains what you're sending and why. It's also seen as rude if you don't acknowledge that you've received an e-mail at all. The sender doesn't know if you ever saw it, so it's important to respond, even if it's only a short message, like "Got it."

RESEARCH SKILLS
AND YOUR COLLEGE SUCCESS

Many of your class assignments in college will require you to conduct research. Why? Aren't you in college to learn from your instructors? Why do they ask *you* to do research on your own?

There are unanswered questions all around us in everyday life. Some questions are simple; others are complex. How much time will it take to get across town to a doctor's appointment during rush hour? What can you expect college tuition to cost by the time your kids are old enough to go? What are the chances that someone you know who has cancer will survive for five years? Research isn't necessarily a mysterious thing that scientists in white coats do in laboratories. Research is simply finding answers to questions, either real questions you encounter every day or questions that are assigned to you in your classes. Doing research on your own can be a powerful way to learn, sometimes even more so than hearing answers from someone else, even if those people are your instructors. Going off to a research expedition in the library may sound like exhausting busywork, but the skills you stand to gain are well worth the effort.

Conducting research teaches you some important things about how to formulate a question and then find answers. And it's not just finding answers so that you can scratch a particular assignment off your to-do list. It's about learning an important process. When you get into the world of work, your instructors won't be there to supply answers, so knowing how to figure things out on your own will be key to your success. So, exactly what is college-level research?

WHAT RESEARCH IS *NOT*	WHAT RESEARCH IS
Research isn't just going on a "search and employ" mission. It's not just seeing what all you can find and then using it to check off an assignment on your to-do list.	**Research starts with a question.** If an assignment is broad, as Dario's was, you must come up with a specific question to research yourself. (More about that later.)
Research isn't just moving things from Point A (the library) to Point B (your paper).	**Research is a process with a plan.** A plan was something Dario lacked. He jumped in without a question—or a plan.
Research isn't random rummaging through real or virtual files to find out something.	**Research is goal-oriented.** You've formulated a question, developed a plan, and now you begin to find answers by using both online sources and ones that sit on your library's shelves.
Research isn't doing a quick internet search. The cutting and pasting Dario did to fill up his five pages is actually plagiarism!	**Research often involves breaking a big question into several smaller ones.**[27]

NAVIGATING THE LIBRARY

You've probably heard this since you were a child: "The library is your friend." As a young child, it was exciting to go to the library, choose a book, check it out with your own library card, and bring it home to read. Now, being "exiled" to the library to do research for a paper may seem like torture that can ruin a perfectly good weekend. But if you look at things differently, it can be a mind-expanding trip into places unknown. The truth is that in college the library should be more than just a friend. It should become your best friend! Beyond navigating the web to find research for your assignments, as many students do, it's important to learn your way around the actual, physical space of the library on your campus. The library has many useful resources, including real, very knowledgeable librarians who are there to help you. Asking a reference librarian for help can save you hours of unproductive digging on your own. Here

"I find that a great part of the information I have was acquired by looking up something and finding something else on the way."

Franklin P. Adams, American journalist and radio personality (1881–1960)

are some of the resources your library offers and how you should use these resources when you're assigned a research project:

> **Card Catalog.** Explore your library's catalog that lists all of the books available to you. Card catalogs used to be actual cards in file cabinet drawers, but now most libraries put all the information about their holdings online. Go to your college's website, and from there you can find your way to your college library's home page. Click the library's catalog button. Let's say Dario follows these instructions and finds this book in his campus library's catalog: *The Global Internet Economy*, edited by Bruce Kogut. Cambridge, MA: MIT Press, 2003. The call number for the book is HC79.I55 G579, based on the Library of Congress classification system, which most college libraries use. (Some libraries, like your community's public library, may use the Dewey Decimal system. One advantage of the Library of Congress system is that books usually have the same number, no matter which library you find them in. That's not always true for the Dewey Decimal system.) The Library of Congress number identifies this item as a book about economics and information technology. Now, after identifying other possible useful books, Dario needs to make his way to campus and find the actual book on the shelf.

> **Databases.** If you go to your library's home page, you can link to the list of online databases it subscribes to. Databases identify articles from academic journals and sometimes contain entire articles online. Generally, different databases exist for different disciplines, for example:

Education	**ERIC** (Educational Resources Information Center)
Psychology	**PsycINFO™**
Business	**Business Source Premier**

But more general databases also exist. Dario might want to search through these:

Academic Search Premier

WilsonWeb OmniFile Full Text Mega

The key to making the most of databases is to find the right search words to plug into the database's search engine. That's where a short coaching session with a real reference librarian can be enormously helpful. You can have productive results or no results at all, just by slightly altering the search words you enter. Also, check Google Scholar online. It will search academic literature, including journal abstracts and articles, dissertations and theses, and books, across many different disciplines.

> **Stacks.** Physically walk through the stacks or collections of books and periodicals (journals, magazines, newspapers, and audiovisual resources, for example). Get to know the stacks in your library, and figure out how to find what you need. Look for the Library of Congress numbers posted on signs at the end of each row of books. When Dario finds the book he's looking for, he's likely to find other books in the library's "HC" section that would also be useful to him. That's why even though doing online research is convenient, there's no substitute for "being there."

INFORMATION LITERACY
AND YOUR COLLEGE SUCCESS

Much of the research you do for your college assignments will take place online. Information literacy is defined as knowing *when* you need information, *where* to find it, *what* it means, *whether* it's accurate, and *how* to use it. Simply put, it's "the ability to use technology to solve information problems." Information literacy includes five components, as shown in Figure 6.2. Think about them as a step-by-step process as we work through Dario's assignment.[28]

STEP 1. DEFINE

Define what the assignment requires of you. Dario was assigned a *research* paper. He wasn't being asked to summarize or *evaluate* a topic. He was asked to *find out about it*. But "Globalization and Internet Commerce" is a huge topic. He must narrow it down and decide which specific research question (or questions) he wants to focus on.

summarize condense a longer work into a few essential statements

---

BOX 6.2

THE TOP FIVE RESEARCH MISTAKES FIRST-YEAR STUDENTS MAKE: ADVICE FROM A REFERENCE LIBRARIAN

Are you guilty of any of these common mistakes first-year students make?

1. **Selecting a topic that is too broad.** Students often start out with a very general topic, and sometimes have a hard time narrowing the focus. Trying to write a paper on "recycling" sets you up for an impossible task. Entire books have been written on that subject. Figuring out which words to use can be tricky, too. If you search Google or databases by entering the word "green," you'll get everything from "lime, mint, olive, and avocado" (meaning shades of green, not foods) to "Kermit, the frog." Brainstorming different search words and noting the usable results is half the battle.

2. **Taking short cuts.** Major search engines are a great place to start, but don't stop there. Just using Google or Foxfire is the equivalent of academic "wimping out," like just grabbing something quick from a vending machine when there's so much more nutritious and satisfying food out there. Libraries buy many different electronic databases that have a wealth of information: articles, books, and book chapters, for example. Learn how to use these library databases and really mine them for information. Finding useful information takes time and patience!

3. **Devoting too little time.** Students frequently underestimate how long the research process will take. There are multiple steps required to doing thorough research. It's not a last-minute process, and procrastination isn't the answer. Even if you write like a pro, you can't complete a research paper in an hour or two. Just getting in materials you've ordered from another library can take several weeks.

4. **Not evaluating sources.** Many students don't look closely enough at the sources they find, and then they end up making poor choices or using the first items that come up in search results. Instead, as you scan your results, look for hints about authenticity and accuracy. Compare your findings with other authoritative sites. Note the domain extension (like .gov, for example). One hit may lead you to another, which leads you to yet another. Evaluate your search results and be selective about what you use. Not all sources are created equal; make sure yours are credible ones that support your argument.

5. **Copying and pasting.** Students sometimes use someone else's work without correct and thorough documentation of the source, especially when time is running out. You can end up plagiarizing unintentionally just because you don't understand how to cite your sources. Or you may intentionally cut and paste to save yourself time and effort. But either way, you're putting your academic success at high risk.

The biggest mistake students make is not asking the reference librarian for help at the beginning of the research process! That's why librarians are there—to provide guidance and help with all of these common mistakes. Continue reading this chapter for more strategies on making the most of your research time.[29]

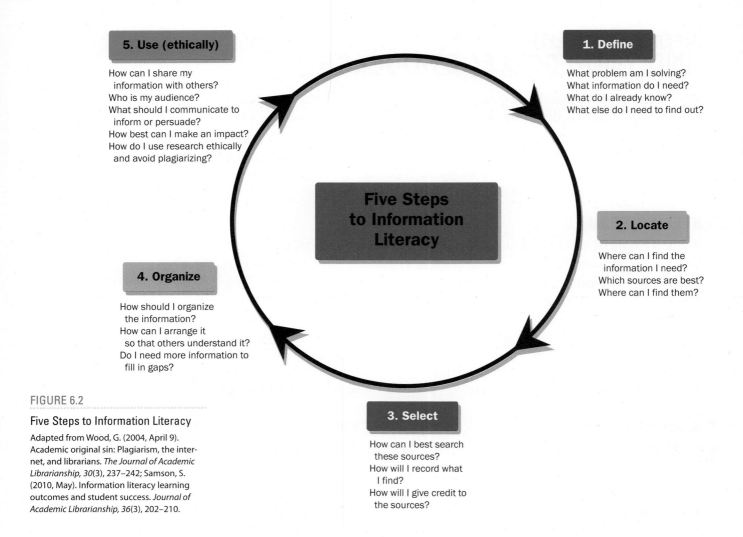

5. Use (ethically)

How can I share my information with others?
Who is my audience?
What should I communicate to inform or persuade?
How best can I make an impact?
How do I use research ethically and avoid plagiarizing?

1. Define

What problem am I solving?
What information do I need?
What do I already know?
What else do I need to find out?

Five Steps to Information Literacy

2. Locate

Where can I find the information I need?
Which sources are best?
Where can I find them?

4. Organize

How should I organize the information?
How can I arrange it so that others understand it?
Do I need more information to fill in gaps?

3. Select

How can I best search these sources?
How will I record what I find?
How will I give credit to the sources?

FIGURE 6.2

Five Steps to Information Literacy

Adapted from Wood, G. (2004, April 9). Academic original sin: Plagiarism, the internet, and librarians. *The Journal of Academic Librarianship, 30*(3), 237–242; Samson, S. (2010, May). Information literacy learning outcomes and student success. *Journal of Academic Librarianship, 36*(3), 202–210.

VARK IT!

Multimodal (Visual/Aural): Think about a current assignment for a class, and use this figure to talk through the questions for each step. Picture how you will actually move from one step to the other.

If you were assigned the paper Dario was assigned, and you knew very little about "Globalization and Internet Commerce," you might start as he did, by Googling your topic to help you define it. But the internet is huge and unstructured. There's really no way to organize that much information into simple, neat categories.[30] And how do you whittle down 12 million hits? According to *Search Engine Journal*, 75 percent of Google users don't look further than the first page of their Google results, regardless of how many hits they get![31]

If you don't know anything about the topic you need to research—absolutely nothing at all—the internet is a great place to start. You can type in "globalization" and "internet commerce," and within the blink of an eye, information appears. The problem is that you now have too much information, and the challenge is knowing what to do next. Your college instructors will insist you go beyond the internet and avoid relying too much on encyclopedias and Wikipedia. College requires you to do more research than you've probably done before, and to do it differently.

Dario could have used the websites that Google brought up to help him *define* a specific research focus, instead of being overwhelmed by the number of hits. Consider these more focused research topics or questions, which Google or Wikipedia could have led him to:

1. **Five Reasons to Go Global with Your Website** (Why is it a good idea?)
2. **Online Retail Businesses Will Explode over the Next Ten Years** (Where will it go in the future?)
3. **Three Problems with Doing E-Business Internationally: Language, Shipping, and Money** (What are the challenges of trying to make it happen?)

Let's take that last focused topic and run with it. Suppose you have an online business and you want to attract customers from around the world to expand it. That's a good idea, but how will you deal with translating what's on your website to other languages? How will you ship your product overseas for a reasonable cost? How will you deal with the exchange rate between the U.S. dollar and the currency used in other countries? Now we've taken a big, broad topic ("Globalization and Internet Commerce") and broken it down into three specific questions or subtopics to research. Your preliminary Google and Wikipedia searches can help you identify what the smaller chunks of your topic could be.

But they can't do *all* the work for you, and you can't stop there, as Dario did. You have to know what to do next. (If you think this process is challenging, you're not alone. In one study, only 35 percent of college students knew how to narrow a Google search!)[32]

STEP 2. LOCATE

If you've identified electronic sources, bookmark them in a file labeled with the name of your project. If they're print resources, physically find them in the library. If they're not available in your own campus library, see whether it participates in an interlibrary loan agreement among libraries. Your own library may be able to borrow the resource from another library. (But be aware that this process may take up to two weeks or so. That's why it's important to start your research projects early!)

bookmark a way to save and organize websites in your web browser

STEP 3. SELECT

The Information Age surrounds us with huge amounts of data of all kinds. With so much information available, how do we know what to believe? Whether or not it's true, we tend to think that if something is on television or in a book or online, it must be important. But in any of these cases, we need to exercise our critical thinking skills and turn them into critical searching skills. Just because information is published doesn't automatically make it right or true. In particular, some of the so-called research you encounter online may be bogus, containing inaccuracies or bias. You must read, interpret, and evaluate research to decide whether to use it. Use these five criteria to evaluate any website you come across:

1. **Currency.** How up to date is the information? Some websites don't list a date at the bottom of the screen (where copyright information is often found). If you don't see one, try using other hints on the site to

Hans Neleman/Corbis/Getty Images

"Don't agonize. Organize."

Florynce Kennedy, American lawyer and African American activist

"I learned the value of hard work by working hard."

—*Margaret Mead, American anthropologist (1901–1978)*

CRITICAL SEARCHING ON THE INTERNET

With these five criteria in mind, choose one of the following two assignments to complete. Each one will ask you to use your critical searching skills.

Assignment 1: Create a list of three websites that pertain to your intended major. (If you're not sure of your major right now, choose one to explore anyway.) Evaluate the websites, using the five criteria, to see which ones seem most useful to you as a student.

Assignment 2: Compare websites with contradictory information. Choose a controversial subject such as abortion, the death penalty, religion, politics, or some other subject of interest. Find three websites on your topic and compare them on the five criteria. Which of the three websites gets the highest marks? Why?

---

life hack #2

The app "Studious" allows you to input your class schedule, and then it silences your cell phone during those times. Check out its other helpful functions, too.

objectivity ability to not take sides, being neutral

"Work is either fun or drudgery. It depends on your attitude. I like fun."

Colleen C. Barrett, President Emeritus and Corporate Secretary, Southwest Airlines

get at how old the information is ("According to a study published in 1995 . . ."). You may find that you need to search for something more up to date.

2. **Accuracy.** How accurate is the information presented? If a website makes an unbelievable claim ("Grow a new head of hair in just six weeks!") or presents shaky statistics to make a case, it's important to be skeptical. Take responsibility to validate the information elsewhere.

3. **Authority.** Does the sponsor of the website have the credentials to post the information you see? Chances are "Steve's Picks" or "myfavoritemovies.com" is a collection of one person's opinions. Compare that to a film reviewer's site with information compiled by a professional film critic for a major newspaper. Which one would you trust more? You may not agree with Steve or the professional film critic, but one has credentials, and the other doesn't.

4. **Objectivity.** Does the website sponsor have a reason to convince you of something, or is it presenting unbiased information? If the site wants you to order something online because it claims to have better products than those you can buy at a store, for example, you should be suspicious.

5. **Coverage.** If a website just presents one side of an issue or a very small piece of a larger picture, check to make sure you're getting all the information you need. If you're left wondering, *But what about . . . ?* you're probably having the right reaction.

STEP 4. ORGANIZE

Now that you have located the information you need, using a variety of sources, and selected those that will be most useful to you in your research project, it's time to organize. Dario's paper will be easier to write now that he has created three subtopics: language, shipping, and money. He should begin taking notes on index cards or highlighting pieces of information he wants to quote word-for-word (giving credit to the author) or paraphrase (putting information

Working with two or three classmates and using PowerPoint, Flash, or iMovie, create a television ad (as professional-looking as possible) for the course for which you're using this text. Use text, images, and music. The advertisement shouldn't be long—two or three minutes, or the length of the song you use—but it should describe what the course is about and why other students should take it. Be as creative as you like! Once you've created your presentation, submit it to your instructor and share it with the class.

into his own words). He can literally put the index cards, printed articles, and photocopied pages from books he found while doing his research into three piles and work from those. Organization is the key to an excellent research paper. To help you keep track of the sources you find, you should follow these suggestions.

Make sure you pay attention to details. Write the name of the book or article, author, place of publication, publisher, date, or URL at the top of an index card with your notes or on a photocopied page of information you plan to use.

If you have ideas of your own that don't come from any book, write them on cards or pages, too, and label them, "My Own Ideas."

Learn how to use Google Docs, if you don't know how. Google Docs can serve as an alternative to index cards in some ways. For example, if you're called away on a trip and you plan to work on a paper for a class while you're away but forget to bring the stack of cards, you're out of luck. Google Docs, on the other hand, can be accessed via the internet from anywhere. Simply create a gmail account for yourself, if you don't already have one, and choose the "Documents" tab. There you'll find all the documents you saved while doing research using your school library's online databases. You can open the articles, categorize them by subtopics, open them, or print them out. It's a great organizational tool for busy students.

STEP 5. USE (ETHICALLY)

You've done your research, and now it's time to share it with the world (or at least your instructor) either through the written word, the spoken word, or both. One of the most important things you can learn as a new student is not only how to *use* your research, but how to use *your* research. Some students think that because the internet is out there, why not just use it? Other people have already made volumes upon volumes of prior research available. They've "been there; done that." Why reinvent the wheel? The reason is because the internet is simply a tool, just like your library's online databases are tools. You must learn how to use the tool—the internet—ethically. If your boss asks you for a report on the job, cutting and pasting from the internet is unlikely to be an option. You must conduct your own research, analyze it, and compile it for a written report or oral presentation. We'll focus on developing speaking and writing skills elsewhere, but learning how to use the internet ethically is a good place to start now.

> "The first principle is that you must not fool yourself, but you are the easiest person to fool."
>
> *Richard P. Feynman (1918–1988), Nobel Prize Winner, Physics, 1965*

VARK IT!

Read/Write: Reread a recent paper you wrote as a class assignment. Did you use your resources ethically, or might you have intentionally or unintentionally plagiarized? If your instructor wishes, bring your paper and source to class for a small group Q & A session.

DOWNLOADING YOUR WORKLOAD:
THE EASY WAY OUT?

One of the trickiest aspects of writing papers for your college courses can be expressed in these three words: *What is plagiarism? You may wonder:* How do I do research methodically in steps so that I don't run out of time, leaving plagiarism as an attractive alternative? Or if an assignment feels a though it's busy work that has nothing to do with my life, is plagiarism really such a bad thing? Or isn't anything published on the internet free, valid, and available to use?[33]

First, you should understand the difference between *intentional* and *unintentional* plagiarism. Intentional plagiarism is deliberately downloading a paper from an online source or cutting and pasting text from a website or book, as Dario did, for example. However, you run the risk of committing unintentional plagiarism if you don't understand what plagiarism is or you forget which book you used, so you don't cite the words you've borrowed from someone else. Intentional plagiarism is cheating, pure and simple. Technology today makes plagiarism all too convenient and easy, but by the same token, finding plagiarism in students' papers has become easy for instructors, too. The bottom line? Follow the guidelines you get from your instructors. And if you don't understand them or your instructor assumes you already know them, ask questions. Both intentional and unintentional plagiarism can hurt you academically. Figure 6.3 (Quick Study) will help.

"Borrowed thoughts, like borrowed money, only show the poverty of the borrower."

Lady Marguerite Blessington, English socialite and writer (1789–1849)

EXERCISE 6.5   **PLAGIARISM OR NOT?**

In your opinion, is the following passage plagiarized? Compare these two examples:

Original passage: One of the worst feelings students can have is receiving a bad grade on an exam, whether it's a test they prepared well for or didn't prepare for at all. The prevalence of video games in today's society helps mitigate some of the effects felt by students from those low test scores by reaffirming their abilities in another area they deem important.

Source: Texas Tech University. (2017, March 9). Video games can mitigate defensiveness resulting from bad test scores, study suggests. *Science Daily.* Retrieved from https://www.sciencedaily.com/releases/2017/03/170309132923.htm

Student paper: One of the worst things students have to deal with is getting a bad grade on an exam, whether they studied or not. Video games can help students feel better because they are something they're often good at.

Has this student committed plagiarism? Why or why not?

FIGURE 6.3

Quick Study: Do Paraphrase; Don't Plagiarize

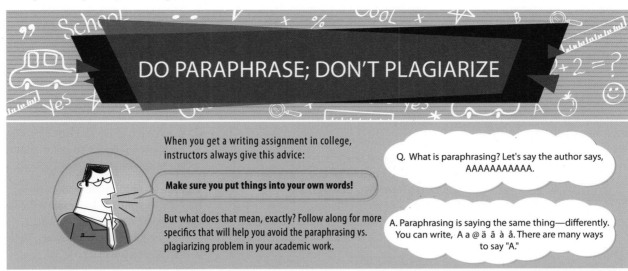

DO PARAPHRASE; DON'T PLAGIARIZE

When you get a writing assignment in college, instructors always give this advice:

Make sure you put things into your own words!

But what does that mean, exactly? Follow along for more specifics that will help you avoid the paraphrasing vs. plagiarizing problem in your academic work.

Q. What is paraphrasing? Let's say the author says, AAAAAAAAAAA.

A. Paraphrasing is saying the same thing—differently. You can write, A a @ ä ä å. There are many ways to say "A."

HOW TO USE YOUR OWN WORDS BUT STILL GIVE CREDIT WHERE CREDIT IS DUE!

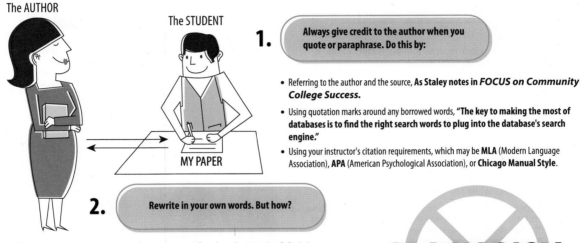

The AUTHOR

The STUDENT

MY PAPER

1. **Always give credit to the author when you quote or paraphrase. Do this by:**

- Referring to the author and the source, **As Staley notes in FOCUS on Community College Success.**
- Using quotation marks around any borrowed words, **"The key to making the most of databases is to find the right search words to plug into the database's search engine."**
- Using your instructor's citation requirements, which may be **MLA** (Modern Language Association), **APA** (American Psychological Association), or **Chicago Manual Style**.

2. **Rewrite in your own words. But how?**

- **Take notes in your own words as you read,** and avoid unintentional plagiarism.
- **Read the original passage, and then describe what you read to a friend.** Write down the words you used and make it more readable. That's your paraphrase!
- **Add new information.** That will make the passage different, assuming it fits the rest of your paper.
- **Make two sentences** out of one longer, complex one.
- **Ensure you don't "hype" your writing.** Write to express, not to impress.
- **Use as many of these techniques as possible.**

PLAGIARISM

DON'T use quotation marks when you use a common term or idea, like learning styles or critical thinking, for example.

OTHER PARAPHRASING TIPS

1. Put the passive voice into the active voice (or vice versa): **As Staley notes...** versus **As noted by Staley...**

2. Change parts of speech: **organize** (verb) versus **organization** (noun).

3. Make passages **l o n g e r** or **shorter.**

4. Use synonyms: **resilience** (or hardiness) (or toughness).

 **BEWARE!**

CAUTION: Use your thesaurus wisely. If you look up every fifth word, for example, and pick a different word via a thesaurus, the passage won't sound like your writing—guaranteed! This technique is a quick route to...getting busted!

Downloading your workload: The easy way out? **165**

Identify your most challenging assignment this term, one that will require you to use your research and information literacy skills. What is the specific assignment? For example, it could be "write a five-page paper in which you take a position on a controversial theme relating to our course topic." On a scale of 1 to 10 (with 10 being extremely difficult), how challenging do you expect this assignment to be? What would make the challenge more manageable? Describe your research assignment here.

Now take a look at the following website and answer the related questions (without Googling):

1. Does this website appear to be authentic? Why or why not?
2. Would this service be useful to a student like you with a challenging research assignment?
3. In your opinion, is this website acceptable for college students to use? Why or why not?
4. Are there differences between the three available options and their degree of acceptability?

5. What's the difference between using these professional services and using the professional services of a campus reference librarian?
6. Do you know students who use "professional" research services? What are their views on the acceptability of these services?
7. If you were a college instructor, what would you tell your students about these services?

Can you identify online resources that might be helpful for your most difficult assignment? What online resources might be more harmful than helpful to your academic success?

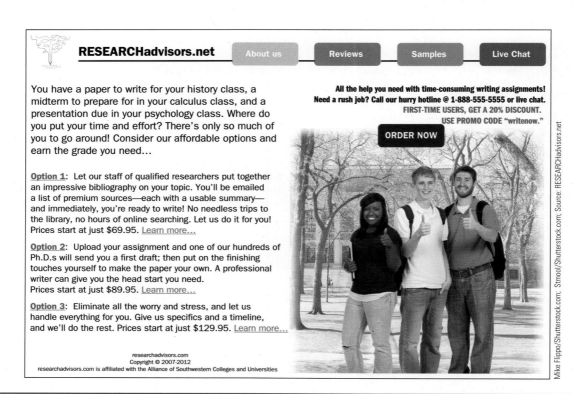

INSIGHT: *NOW* WHAT DO YOU THINK?

At the beginning of this chapter, Dario Jones faced a series of challenges as a new college student taking three online classes. Now after learning from this chapter, would you respond differently to any of the questions you answered about the FOCUS Challenge Case? Using what you learned in the chapter, write a paragraph ending to Dario's case study. What are some of the possible outcomes for Dario?

1. Identify one new thing you learned in reading this chapter. Why did you select the one you've selected? How will it affect what you do in your college classes?

2. How much experience have you had conducting research? What sounds most challenging about the process?

3. How would you describe your technology skills? If you haven't had much experience with technology, how do you plan to increase your skills? If you have technology experience, how will you use your knowledge to your advantage in your college classes?

CHALLENGE: REALITY CHECK

HOW MUCH DID YOU LEARN?

How much did you learn? At the beginning of this chapter, you filled out a "Readiness Check" that asked how you thought this chapter would relate to you, and how you would relate to it. Now, fill out this "Reality Check" to find out.

1. Identify one advantage and one disadvantage of online courses.
2. How would you define research? What steps are involved?
3. What is information literacy?
4. What are the five steps to information literacy?
5. In your own words, define *plagiarism*.
6. How long did it take? _____ hours _____ minutes. Before you began this chapter, you were asked to predict how long it would take you to complete it (total time, even if you read it in more than one sitting). Was your estimate on target, or will you revise it for the next chapter you'll read?

ENGAGING, LISTENING, AND NOTE-TAKING IN CLASS | 7

Maria Evseyeva/Shutterstock.com

HOW THIS CHAPTER RELATES TO YOU

1. When it comes to engaging, listening, and note-taking in your college classes, what do you find most challenging, if anything? Put check marks by the phrases that apply to you or write in your answer.

   ☐ Focusing during lectures

   ☐ Having confidence in my note-taking methods

   ☐ Adjusting how I take notes in different classes

   ☐ Asking questions in class

   ☐ Using my class notes to study

2. What is most likely to be your response? Put a check mark by it.

   ☐ I'll be open to learning more about this subject.

   ☐ I'll wait and see how much of this chapter I understand.

   ☐ I'll ask my instructor for clarification.

   ☐ Eventually, I'll just figure it out.

3. What would you have to do to increase your likelihood of success? Will you do it this quarter or semester?

HOW YOU WILL RELATE TO THIS CHAPTER

1. What are you most interested in learning about? Put check marks by those topics.

   ☐ How to get engaged in class

   ☐ How to listen with focus to different kinds of lecture styles

   ☐ How to take good notes

   ☐ How to adjust your note-taking system and why

   ☐ How to ask questions in class

   ☐ How to use your notes to achieve the best results

YOUR READINESS FACTOR

1. How motivated are you to learn more about listening and taking notes in college? (5 = high, 1 = low)

2. How ready are you to read now? (If something is in your way, take care of it if you can, so you can. Zero in and focus.)

3. How long do you think it will take you to complete this chapter? If you start and stop, keep track of your overall time. _____ Hour(s) _____ Minute(s)

Maria Evseyeva/Shutterstock.com

Rachel White

All she ever wanted to be was a Mom. Rachel White loved kids.
When she was one herself, she helped raise her six younger brothers and sisters. Her parents worked hard to support the family, so Rachel took over her mom's duties. With each new baby, Rachel got better at distinguishing between whiney cries, hurt cries, and hungry cries. It was Rachel who cooked their dinner most nights and took them to the park on Saturdays. It was almost as if they were Rachel's children. In fact, sometimes she pretended they were.

Bondarenko/Shutterstock.com

So as a senior, Rachel dropped out of high school and married her boyfriend, Mike. He loved kids, too, and when they found out they were expecting, he was as happy as she was. But now with another baby on the way, Rachel realized that Mike's income wouldn't be enough. She wanted a big family like the one she'd grown up in, and she knew that getting an education was the best answer. The ideal career for a stay-at-home mom, she thought, would be to open a day care center in her own home. An associate's degree in Early Childhood Development would provide credentials. So she studied at night, earned her GED, and enrolled in two evening classes at her local community college. Mike would be so proud of her.

Despite a 40-minute commute in heavy traffic, Rachel was excited about her first class, Child Development I, as a new college student. But right away, several things caught her off guard. The young instructor was new to teaching, spoke with a foreign accent, and raced through the lecture. Because she'd been out of school for a while, Rachel felt as though she had forgotten how to be a student. As the instructor talked, she tried to take notes as quickly as she could, but how was she supposed to know what was important enough to write down? She looked around: What were other students writing? Was she the only one who couldn't keep up? The lecture began:

Child development is a process every child goes through. This process involves learning and mastering skills like sitting, walking, talking, skipping, and tying shoes. Children learn these skills, called developmental milestones, during predictable time periods. Children develop skills in five main areas of development: First, let's look at cognitive development. This is the child's ability to learn and solve problems. For example, this includes a two-month-old baby learning to explore the environment with hands or eyes or a five-year-old learning how to do simple math problems.

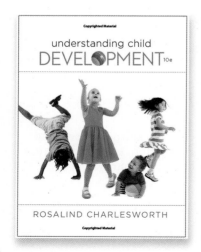

Copyrighted Material

understanding child
DEVELOPMENT 10e

ROSALIND CHARLESWORTH

Copyrighted Material

Maria Evseyeva/Shutterstock.com; Source: Facebook/Cengage® NYgraphic/Shutterstock.com

Second, social/emotional development is the child's ability to interact with others, including helping themselves and self-control. Examples of this type of development would include a six-week-old baby smiling, a ten-month-old baby waving bye-bye, or a five-year-old boy knowing how to take turns in games at school. Third, speech and language development is the child's ability to both understand and use language. For example, this includes a 12-month-old baby saying his first words, a two-year-old naming parts of her body, or a five-year-old learning to say "feet" instead of "foots." Children also learn both fine and gross motor skills. Fine motor skills are the child's ability to use small muscles, specifically their hands and fingers, to pick up small objects, hold a spoon, turn pages in a book, or use a crayon to draw. Gross motor skills, on the other hand, are the child's ability to use large muscles. For example, a six-month-old baby learns how to sit up with some support, a 12-month-old baby learns to pull up to a stand holding onto furniture, and a five-year-old learns to skip.*

Rachel tried to pay attention to the instructor's words and copy down the writing scribbled all over the board, but her mind seemed to drift to the flyers she'd create for her new day-care business, or whether she should call Mike at the break to tell him their toddler seemed to be coming down with a cold. Why was it so hard to focus? Rachel wondered whether she should bring her laptop to take notes that way, but somehow she knew she wouldn't be able to resist the temptation to check her Facebook page every 15 minutes or so. Information seemed to fly out of her instructor's mouth at mach speed, and frankly, she used the foreign accent as an excuse for her troubles. Taking notes that quickly was just plain impossible. She tried giving her instructor quizzical looks to communicate "Slow down, please," but the instructor probably couldn't see Rachel's face in the back of the room.

Because she didn't catch all of what the instructor was talking about, asking questions in class would only prove that she wasn't paying attention. Trying to read and take notes from the textbook chapters *before* class was hard with her active little girl at home. Instead, she tried to look like she was paying attention in class so that no one knew that her brain wasn't really there.

Rachel had thought about trying to stop in during her instructor's office hours sometime, but she hated the thought of rush-hour traffic. She could try making an appointment at another time, but did she really want to discuss how hard it was to concentrate in the course? It was too late in the term to drop the class, and she needed the credits for her degree. Still, she had to figure something out or this course was going to spoil her dream.

Maria Evseyeva/Shutterstock.com; Source: Instagram/Cengage®

*Source: Based on http://www.howkidsdevelop.com/developSkills.html#dev

1. Do you have anything in common with Rachel? If so, how are you managing the situation so that you can be successful?

2. In terms of the title of this chapter—Engaging, Listening, and Note-taking in Class—how is Rachel doing? In your view, is she likely to pass the course? Why or why not?

3. List five mistakes Rachel is making.

4. Now list five things that Rachel should do immediately to improve her childhood development classroom experience.

GET ENGAGED
IN CLASS

engagement emotional and psychological commitment to a task

No, this chapter isn't about buying a ring and getting down on one knee. It's about your willingness to focus, listen, discuss, ask questions, take notes, and generally dive into your classes. It's about being a full participant in your learning, not just a spectator sitting on the sidelines. It's about not just memorizing information for exams and then forgetting it. You see, the secret to college success hinges on this one word: engagement.

Think about this analogy. How did you learn to swim? Did you watch swimming on TV? Did you get advice from your friends about swimming? Did you just Google it? No, you probably jumped in and got wet, right? The same thing is true with your college classes. The more willing you are to jump in and get wet, the more engaged you'll be in the learning process.

FOLLOW THE RULES OF ENGAGEMENT

Just as is the case with most places you can think of, college classrooms have rules about how to behave. You don't find people yelling in church or staring at other people in elevators or telling jokes at funerals. There are rules about how to behave in a variety of contexts, and college classrooms are no exception. In fact, the rules of engagement described here are a part of what this text calls academic professionalism, and preparing for class beforehand is at the top of the list. Despite their best intentions, some community college students "shoot themselves in the foot" without meaning to. They believe they're ready for college and motivated to achieve, but within the first few weeks of the term, they miss class (25%), turn in an assignment late (33%), or don't turn in an assignment at all (24%).[1] Although not all students see the value of academic professionalism and preparation, do more than your classmates—dare to prepare! If you follow these rules of engagement, your classes will be much more enjoyable, enriching learning experiences.

1. **Look ahead.** By checking your course syllabus before class, you'll be prepared for the upcoming topic. You'll also avoid the "oops" factor of sitting down, looking around, and noticing that everyone else knows something you don't about what's supposed to happen today.

2. **Do the assigned reading.** If you have a reading assignment due for class, do it, and take notes as you read. Write in the margins of your textbook or on sticky notes. Or take notes using one of many convenient online

> "When you can do the common things of life in an uncommon way, you will command the attention of the world."
>
> —*George Washington Carver, 1864–1943, horticulturist, chemist, and educator*

note-taking tools while you read. Question what you're reading, and enter into a mental conversation with the author. Having some background on the topic will allow you to listen more actively and participate more intelligently during any discussion: *Yes, I remember the chapter covering that topic*, you'll think when the instructor begins talking about something you recognize. Instead of hearing it for the first time, you'll *strengthen* what you've already read. According to research, as few as 20 to 30 percent of your classmates will have done the assigned reading prior to class.[2] That little-known fact isn't a reason to excuse yourself from reading; instead it gives you insider information on how you can shine in class by comparison.

3. **Show up physically.** Not only is attending class important for your overall understanding of the material, but it may move your grade up a few notches. Even if attendance isn't required by your instructor, require it of yourself. Research says that missing classes is definitely related to your academic performance. And once you give yourself permission to skip one single class, it becomes easier to do it the next time, and the time after that. Studies indicate that on any given day, approximately one-third of your classmates will miss class, and that most students think that several absences during a term is "the standard."[3] Exercise good judgment, even if your classmates don't! Studies show that how often you attend class is the biggest predictor of how well you'll do.[4] Besides the importance of being there, it's essential to be on time and stay for the full class session. Students who arrive late and leave early are annoying not only to the instructor but also to their classmates. To everyone else, it looks like they don't value the other students or the class content. How would you like dinner guests to arrive an hour late, after you'd slaved over a hot stove all day? Your instructors have prepared for class, and they feel the same way. Build in time to find a parking place, hike to the building where class is held, or stop for a coffee. Do everything you can to avoid coming late and leaving early.

4. **Show up mentally.** Showing up means more than just occupying a seat in the classroom. It means thinking about what you bring to the class as a learner on any particular day. Do a mental readiness check when you arrive in class. If you're not ready, what can you do to rally for the cause?

5. **Choose your seat strategically.** Imagine paying $150 for a concert ticket, just like everyone else, and then electing to sit in the nosebleed section as high up and far away from the action as you could get. Sitting in the back means you're more likely to let your mind wander and less likely to hear clearly. Sitting in the front means you'll keep yourself accountable by being in full view of the instructor and the rest of the class. What's the best spot for great concentration? Front and center, literally—the "T zone"! In one study, students who sat at the back of a large auditorium were six times more likely to fail the course, even though the instructor had assigned seats randomly![5]

6. **Bring your tools.** Bring a writing utensil and notebook with you to every class. Your instructor may also ask you to bring your textbook, calculator, a blue book or scantron form for an exam, or other necessary items. If so, do it. Question: How seriously would you take a carpenter who showed up to work without a hammer, nails, and screwdriver? Get the point?

7. **Be aware that gab is not a gift.** In class, talking while others are speaking is inappropriate. And it's certainly not a gift—especially to your instructor. In fact, side conversations while your instructor is lecturing or your classmates are contributing to the discussion are downright rude. If you're seated next to a gabber, don't get sucked in. Use body language to communicate that you're there to learn, not to gab. If that's not enough, politely say something like "I really need to pay attention right now. Let's talk more later, okay?" Don't let other students cheat you out of learning.

8. **Choose to engage.** Engagement isn't something that just happens to you while you're not looking. It's a choice you make, and sometimes it's a difficult choice because the material isn't naturally appealing to you, or the course is a required one you didn't choose, or you're just in a bad mood. Choose to engage anyway. Instead of actively choosing to disengage in class by sleeping through lectures, surfing the internet, or texting friends, choose to engage by leaning forward, listening, finding your own ways to connect to the material, and thinking of questions to ask. For many students, texting during class is particularly tempting. There's a reason why people are asked to turn off their cell phones before concerts, athletic events, or movies. Imagine being in a jam-packed theater trying to follow the film's plot, with cell phones going off every few seconds. You've paid good money to see a film. The same thing goes for your college classes.

9. **Focus.** After sitting down in class each day, take a moment to clear your head of all daydreams, to-do's, and worries. Take a deep breath and remind yourself of the opportunity to learn that lies ahead. Think of yourself as a reporter at a press conference, listening carefully because you'll be writing a story about what's going on. You *will* be writing a "story"—often in response to an essay question on an exam!

10. **Maintain your health.** Being sick can take its toll on your ability to concentrate, listen well, and participate. Prevent that from happening by getting enough sleep, eating well, and exercising. Remember, *energy management* is key to your ability to focus.

LISTENING
WITH FOCUS

Listening with focus is more than just physically hearing words as they stream by. It's actually a complicated process that's hard work. You can't listen well when your energy is zapped, when you've stayed up all night, or when your stomach is growling fiercely. Focused listening means that you are concentrating fully on what's going on in class.

"EASY LISTENING" IS FOR ELEVATORS—FOCUSED LISTENING IS FOR CLASSROOMS

Stores, restaurants, and elevators are known for their programmed, background easy listening music. Chances are you hardly notice it's there. Listening in class, however, requires actual skill, and you'll be doing a great deal of it as a college student. Depending on what your college classes are about and your instructors' preferences, you will spend much of your time listening to lectures in class.[6]

"Every person in this life has something to teach me—and as soon as I accept that, I open myself to truly listening."

John Lahr, drama critic

If you're taking classes online, you will be listening to lectures your instructor has uploaded, as well.

Many of us think that listening is easy. If you happen to be around when there's something to listen to, you can't help but listen. Not so! Did you know that when you're listening at your best, your breathing rate, heartbeat, and body temperature all increase? Just as with physical exercise, your body works harder when you're engaged in focused listening. When all is said and done, listening is really about energy management.

Here are some techniques for improving your listening skills in the classroom. Read through the list, then go back and check off the ones you're willing to try harder to do in class this week.

"Politeness is the art of choosing among one's real thoughts."

Adlai Stevenson II, U.S. Presidential candidate (1900–1965)

> **Calm yourself.** Take a few deep breaths with your eyes closed to help you put all those nagging distractions out of your mind during class time.

> **Be open.** Keep an open mind and view your class as yet another opportunity to strengthen your intellect and learn something new. Wisdom comes from a broad understanding of many things, rather than from a consistently limited focus what's going on in your own world.

> **Don't make snap judgments.** Remember, you don't have to like your instructor's wardrobe to respect his knowledge. Focus on the content he's offering you, even if you don't agree with it. You may change your mind later when you learn more. Don't jump to conclusions about content *or* style.

> **Assume responsibility.** Speak up! Ask questions! Even if you have an instructor with an accent who's difficult to understand, the burden of understanding course content rests with you. You will interact with people with all sorts of accents, voices, and speech patterns throughout your life. It's up to you to improve the situation.

> **Watch for gestures that communicate "Here comes something important!"** Some typical examples include raising an index finger, turning to face the class, leaning forward from behind the lectern, walking up the aisle, or using specific facial expressions or gestures.

> **Listen for speech patterns that subtly communicate "Make sure you include this in your notes!"** For example, listen for changes in the rate, volume, or tone of speech, longer than usual pauses, or repeated information.

> **Uncover general themes or roadmaps for each lecture.** See whether you can figure out where your instructor is taking you *while* he's taking you there. Always ask yourself, "Where's he going with this? What's he getting at? How does this relate to what was already said?"

> **Appreciate your instructor's prep time.** For every hour of lecture time, your teacher has worked for hours to prepare. Although she may make it look easy, her lecture has involved researching, organizing, creating a PowerPoint presentation, and preparing notes and handouts.

LISTEN HARD!

Listening is hard, and although professors now vary their teaching techniques, lecturing is still a common teaching style in colleges and universities everywhere. However, capturing the information as it goes by is a challenge: "One

"You cannot truly listen to anyone and do anything else at the same time."

M. Scott Peck, American author, (1936–2005)

study found that if a professor speaks 150 words a minute, students hear about 50 of them; another study determined that students are tuned out of a fifty-minute lecture around 40 percent of the time."[7] Instructors can speak 2,500–5,000 words during a fifty-minute lecture. That's a lot of words flying by at breakneck speed, so it's important to listen correctly. But what does *that* mean?

Think about the various situations in which you find yourself listening. You often listen to empty chit-chat on your way to class. "Hey, how's it going?" when you spot your best friend in the hallway is an example, right? Listening in this type of situation doesn't require a lot of brainpower. Although you wouldn't want to spend too much time on chit-chat, if you refused to engage in any at all, you'd probably be seen by others as odd, withdrawn, shy, or stuck up.

You also listen in challenging situations, some that are emotionally charged; for example, a friend needs to vent, relieve stress, or verbalize her anxieties. Most people who are blowing off steam aren't looking for you to fix their problems. They just want to be heard and hear you say something like "I understand" or "That's too bad."

Listening to chit-chat and listening in emotionally charged situations require what are called **soft listening skills**. You must be accepting, sensitive, and non-judgmental. You don't have to assess, analyze, or conclude. You just have to be there for someone else.

But soft listening isn't the only kind of listening you need to do. When you're listening to new information, as you do in your college classes, or when you're listening to someone trying to persuade you of something, you have to pay close attention, think critically, and ultimately make decisions about what you're hearing. Is something true or false? Right or wrong? How do you know? When you're listening to a person trying to inform you or to persuade you, you need **hard listening skills**. In situations like these, you must evaluate, analyze, and decide.

One mistake many students make in class is listening the wrong way. They should be using their hard listening skills, rather than sitting back and letting information float over them. Soft listening skills don't help you in class. You must listen intently, think critically, and analyze carefully what you're hearing. It's important to note that

---

EXERCISE 7.1   **PRACTICE YOUR <u>SOFT</u> LISTENING SKILLS**

Listening—really listening—may be the most difficult challenge we face as human beings. Many of us "speak" into cyberspace constantly every day, but is anyone listening? How can we know for sure? Is a quick "like" all we can hope for? According to a study of first-year students, the ability to fully listen is the most important quality of a good communicator.[8] Perhaps what we all need is more focused practice. StoryCorps is a website that features people's fascinating two-minute stories about memorable moments in their lives. Go to StoryCorps.com and listen to the story that interests you most. Then answer the following questions:

1. Who was or were the story-tellers?

2. What was the story's primary point?

3. Was there any wording or idea that particularly impressed you?

4. What aspect of the story could you most relate to?

5. Do you think listening—and practicing more—would make you a better listener in situations that call for soft listening skills?

Hard listening skills—analyzing, evaluating, and deciding—are required for in-class or online learning. Listen to Julian Treasure's TED Talk on "Five Ways to Become a Better Listener," and use one of the note-taking skills described later in this chapter. In particular, use a note-taking style that <u>wouldn't</u> necessarily be chosen by someone with your VARK preferences. Students with Visual preferences might naturally gravitate to mind mapping, for example, and students with Read/Write preferences might gravitate toward the Cornell method. If your preferences are not strong in any one of the VARK learning style types, just choose a note-taking style that seems challenging to you. Listen to the TED Talk, take notes, and then afterwards, write a short summary statement about using a note-taking style that was out of your comfort zone. In retrospect, which note-taking system would have helped you take better notes? After working on your soft versus your hard listening skills, do you see the difference? Do you understand why hard listening skills are needed during in-class or online learning?

neither listening mode is better than the other. They are each simply better suited to different situations. But soft listening won't get you the results you want in your classes. You don't need to be there for your instructor; you need to be there for yourself.[9]

You may find many of your classes to be naturally fascinating learning experiences. But for others, you will need to be convinced. Even if you don't find Intro to Whatever to be the most engaging subject in the world, you may find yourself fascinated by your instructor. Most people are interested in other people. What makes him tick? Why was she drawn to this field? If you find it hard to get interested in the material, trick yourself by paying attention to the person delivering the message. Sometimes focusing on something about the speaker can help you focus on the subject matter, too. And you may just find out that you actually do find this class to be valuable. Although tricking yourself isn't always a good idea, it *can* work if you know what you're doing and why.

GET WIRED FOR SOUND

Increasingly instructors are providing podcasts and videocasts of their lectures so that you can *preview* the lecture in advance or *review* it after class. Some textbooks (like this one) offer chapter summaries you can listen to on the subway, in the gym, at home during a blizzard, or in bed while recovering from the flu, via your computer or digital-audio player.

Regardless of your learning style, recorded lectures allow you to re-listen to difficult concepts as many times as needed. You can take part in the live action in class and take notes later while re-listening to the podcast. In one study, students who re-listened to a lecture one, two, or three times increased their lecture notes substantially each time.[10] Of course, recorded lectures aren't meant to excuse you from attending class, and in order to take advantage of them, you actually have to find time to listen to them. They're supplemental tools to *reinforce* learning for busy students on the go, which is virtually *everyone* these days.[11]

IDENTIFY LECTURE STYLES SO YOU CAN MODIFY LISTENING STYLES

Regardless of how challenging it is to listen with focus, being successful in college will require you to do just that—focus—no matter what class or which instructor. Sometimes your instructors are facilitators, who help you discover information on your own in new ways. Other times they are orators, who lecture

> ### life hack #1
>
> Consider downloading "Meep," a phone app that lets you listen to e-mails and news stories when reading isn't possible. You can create your own listening channels based on your interests.

facilitators guides

orators public speakers

> "The most basic and powerful way to connect to another person is to listen. Just listen. Perhaps the most important thing we ever give each other is our attention."
>
> *Rachel Naomi Remen, physician and author*

Larry Harwood Photography. Property of Cengage Learning

as their primary means of delivering information. If you're not an aural learner, listening with focus to lectures will be a challenge for you.

Chances are you won't be able to change your instructors' lecturing styles. And even if you could, different students react differently to different lecture styles. But what you can do is expand your own skills as a listener—no matter what class or which instructor. Take a look at the lecture styles coming up and see whether you recognize them.

Sophie Louise Davis/ Shutterstock.com

> **The Rapid-Fire Lecturer:** You may have found yourself in a situation like Rachel's with an instructor who lectures so fast it makes your head spin. Listening and taking notes in a class like this are not easy. By the end of class, your hand aches from gripping your pen and writing furiously. Because there'll be no time to relax, you'll need to make certain you're ready for this class by taking all the suggestions in this chapter to heart. Read ahead so that you recognize points the instructor makes. Also take advantage of whatever supplementary materials this teacher provides in the way of audio support, online lecture notes, or Power-Point handouts.

iStock.com/narvikk

> **The All-Over-the-Map Lecturer:** Organization is not this lecturer's strong suit. Although the lecture may be organized in the lecturer's mind, what comes out is difficult to follow. In this case, it will be up to you to organize the lecture content yourself while reviewing after class.

supplementary extra

kuzmafoto/Shutterstock.com

> **The Content-Intensive Lecturer:** This lecturer, determined to cover a certain amount of material in a particular amount of time, is hardly aware that anyone else is in the room. This teacher may use specific language related to the subject, which you will need to learn rapidly to keep up. Prepare yourself for a potentially rich learning environment, but be sure to ask questions right away if you find yourself confused.

Mladen Mitrinovic/ Shutterstock.com

> **The Review-the-Text Lecturer:** This lecturer will follow the textbook closely, summarizing and highlighting important points. You may assume it's not important to attend class, but watch out for this trap! Receiving the same information in more than one format (reading *and* listening) can be a great way to learn.

arka38/Shutterstock.com

> **The Active-Learning Lecturer:** This lecturer may choose not to lecture at all or to alternate between short lectures and activities, exercises, and role plays. Although you may find it easier to get engaged in this type of class, and you'll most

BOX 7.1

LISTENING TIPS IF ENGLISH IS YOUR SECOND LANGUAGE

It's normal to feel overwhelmed in the classroom as a new student, but especially if your first language isn't English. The academic environment in higher education can be stressful and competitive. It's even more stressful if you're also dealing with a new and different culture. You will need to give yourself time to adapt to all of these changes. In the meantime, here are some suggestions for improving your ability to listen well in class:

- **Talk to your instructor before the course begins.** Let her know that English is not your native language but that you're very interested in learning. Ask for any suggestions on how you can increase your chances of success in the class. Your instructor will most likely be willing to provide you with extra help, knowing you're willing to do your part to overcome the language barrier.

- **Try to get the main points of your instructor's lecture.** You don't have to understand every word.

- **Write down words to look up in the dictionary later.** Keep a running list and check them all after class. Missing out on one important term can hurt your chances of understanding something else down the line.

- **Don't be afraid to ask questions.** If you're too uncomfortable to ask during class, make use of your instructor's office hours or e-mail address to get your questions answered. Also, teaching assistants and peer tutors may be available to help you.

- **Use all support materials available for the class.** Find out whether your instructor posts his notes in your LMS or if they are available as handouts. Some instructors offer guided notes or skeleton outlines for students

to fill in throughout the lecture. Some large lectures are videotaped for viewing by students at a later time. Make full use of podcasts of lectures, if they're available, so that you can listen more than once to portions you found confusing in class. Use any tools available to help reinforce lecture content.

- **Team up with a classmate whose native language is English.** Clarify your notes and fill in gaps.

- **Form a study group with other classmates.** Meet on a regular basis so that you can help one another. Remember: Just because your native language isn't English doesn't mean you don't have something to offer the other members of your study group.

- **Be patient.** It will take some time to adjust to the accents of your various instructors. After a few weeks of class, you'll find it easier to understand what is being said.

- **Practice your English comprehension by listening to talk radio or watching television or movies.** You'll hear a variety of regional accents, for example, and broaden your understanding of American culture.

- **Take an English as a Second Language course if you think it would help.** It's important to keep up with the academic demands of college, and further development of your English skills may improve your comprehension and boost your confidence.

- **If you continue to feel overwhelmed and unable to cope after several weeks in school,** find out whether your campus has an International Students Office, and enlist support from people who are trained to help.[12]

likely appreciate the teacher's creativity, remember that you are still responsible for connecting what happens in class to the course material itself. You will need to read, digest, and process the information on your own outside of class.

TURN LISTENING SKILLS
INTO NOTE-TAKING SKILLS

Listening in class is one thing. Taking notes is quite another. You must be a good listener to take good notes, but being a good listener alone doesn't automatically make you a good note-taker. Note-taking is a crucial and complex skill, and doing well on tests isn't based on luck. It's based on combining

HOW WELL DO YOU LISTEN?

Now that you've read about focused listening, see how the following statements apply to you. Check the response that most applies to what you usually do in the classroom. Use this self-assessment to develop a plan for improvement, particularly so that you're listening at your best to take careful, useful notes.

Listening Statements:	Always True of Me	Sometimes True of Me	Never True of Me
1. I stay awake during class so that I can take good notes to use later while studying.	_____	_____	_____
2. I maintain eye contact with the speaker.	_____	_____	_____
3. I don't pretend to be interested in the subject.	_____	_____	_____
4. I understand my instructor's questions.	_____	_____	_____
5. I try to summarize the information in my notes.	_____	_____	_____
6. I look for organizational patterns in the lecture and identify them in my notes (e.g., causes and effects, lists of items).	_____	_____	_____
7. I set a purpose for listening, like trying to capture all the key ideas and examples that explain them.	_____	_____	_____
8. I don't daydream during class, leaving gaps in my notes.	_____	_____	_____
9. I try to predict the lecturer's next main point.	_____	_____	_____
10. I take notes regularly.	_____	_____	_____
11. I don't let external distractions such as loud noises, late-arriving students, and so on, interfere with my note-taking.	_____	_____	_____
12. I try to determine the speaker's purpose.	_____	_____	_____
13. I recognize that the speaker may be biased about the subject, but I don't let that affect my note-taking.	_____	_____	_____
14. I write down questions the instructor poses during class.	_____	_____	_____
15. I copy down main points and examples from the board or screen.	_____	_____	_____
Total check marks for each column:	_____	_____	_____

Add up the check marks in each column to learn the results of your analysis. Pay particular attention to the total in the "Always True of Me" column.

13–15 "Always True of Me": You're probably an excellent listener, both in the classroom and in other situations. Keep up the good work.

10–12 "Always True of Me": You are a good listener, but you need to fine-tune a few of your listening skills.

7–9 "Always True of Me": You need to change some behaviors so that you get more out of your classes.

6 or less "Always True of Me" or 7 or more "Never True of Me": You need to learn better listening skills if you want to achieve academic success in college.[13]

preparation and opportunity—in other words, knowing how to take useful notes in class that work for you.

Actually, one reason that note-taking is so important in the learning process is that it uses all four VARK categories: *visual* (you see your instructor and the screen, if PowerPoint slides are being used), *aural* (you listen to the lecture), *read/write* (you write what you see and hear so that you can read it later to review), and *kinesthetic* (the physical act of writing opens up a pathway to the brain). Have you ever thought about it that way before?

If you look around the typical college classroom, you'll see the majority of students taking notes. That's a good sign, but are these students taking notes correctly, as a result of focused listening? If most college students take notes, why isn't nearly everyone getting straight A's? Research reports several points worth considering:

➤ Students typically only record one-third of the lecture's main content ideas in their notes.[14]

➤ Students often write down key terms, but fail to capture their instructors' examples, which can be confusing later.[15]

➤ A Some students try to take down every word the instructor says without even thinking about what they're writing, especially if they're taking notes on a laptop.[16]

➤ Many students don't know how to take notes, or don't know which system works best for their learning style preferences and the particular subject they're studying.

Does note-taking make a difference? Absolutely.[17] During lectures, it serves two fundamental purposes: It helps you understand what you're learning at the time and it helps you preserve information to study later. In other words, both the *process* of note-taking (as you record information) and the *product* (your notes themselves) are important to learning. There is strong evidence that taking notes during a lecture leads to higher achievement than not taking notes, and working with your notes later increases your chances for academic achievement even more. Studies show that if you take notes, you have a 50 percent chance of recalling that information at test time versus a 15 percent chance of remembering the same information if you didn't take notes.[18]

DIFFERENT STROKES FOR DIFFERENT FOLKS:
NOTE-TAKING BY THE SYSTEM AND SUBJECT

Now that we know just how important listening and note-taking are, let's ask a crucial question. Exactly how do you take *good* notes? Interestingly, when it comes to note-taking, "Different strokes for different folks" is literally true. Different note-taking systems work best for different lecture styles, different learning styles, and different subjects—math versus history, for example. If your instructor uses a "Rapid-Fire" lecture style, you'll need to write quickly, perhaps using abbreviations, no matter which note-taking system you use. If your instructor is an "All-Over-the-Map" lecturer, you may have to create the connections on paper as she talks about all kinds of ideas.

No matter which note-taking strategy you choose to use in a particular situation, an important question to ask is: What constitutes good notes? The answer is: writing an accurate, complete, organized account of what you hear in class (or read in your text, which is discussed later in this chapter). How do you know if your notes are good? Show them to your instructor and get input, or assess your strategy after you see your results on the

---

life hack #2

Research reveals that "the right and left ear each have their own unique strengths! The right ear is superior at processing speech and the left excels in processing musical sounds and tones. So when you are having difficulty hearing what someone is saying, turn your right ear toward the conversation. When you find yourself straining to hear a song, turn your left ear toward the music source."[19]

VARK IT!

Aural: Being an aural learner doesn't necessarily make you a great note-taker. You may be so caught up in listening that you forget to take notes altogether!

first exam. Your note-taking skills should steadily improve as you evolve as a student.[20]

However you decide to take notes in a particular class, it's good to have some general goals:

1. **Capture main ideas.** Listen for an organizing pattern. Has the instructor been covering the subject by major time periods? Has she been listing contributors to the field by specific discoveries? What's her system? Listen for verbal clues your instructor emphasizes or repeats several times, notice what he writes on the board, or watch for major bullets or itemized steps on the screen. In the lecture Rachel was trying to focus on in class, her instructor made it easy to recognize main points by numbering them, "first," "second," and so forth. If portions of the lecture are highlighted verbally, these portions are probably important. Listen for signal words and phrases such as "There are three reasons . . . ," "On the other hand . . . ," "For example . . . ," and "In summary . . . ."

2. **Note whether a handout accompanies lecture materials.** If so, chances are that the information is considered to be important. If the instructor interrupts the lecture to give more detailed examples from a handout, he must consider doing so important enough to take up class time. Keep all handouts, and assume they'll be worth reviewing at exam time.

3. **Write down examples or key words from stories that will help anchor the main points.** If you were a classmate of Rachel's, you might not remember exactly when the social/emotional milestone begins to develop in children, but writing down the instructor's story about something funny her own little girl did may help trigger your memory.

4. **When in doubt, write it down.** If you're not sure whether to write something down, use the motto "Better safe than sorry." If you don't know a word the instructor uses, leave a blank to show you omitted something, or sound it out as you're writing and come back to it later. Put the lecture in your own words for the most part, but write down formulas, definitions, charts, diagrams, and specific facts verbatim. Also, write down good points made by classmates. Not all the words of wisdom in class will come from your instructor. If you've prepared for class by reading the assignment and listened to the lecture, and a classmate makes a point during a discussion that adds new information, write it down! On the other hand, don't confuse quantity with quality. Just because a student has taken pages and pages of notes doesn't mean she understands everything she's copied down. The question is: Did she write down the most important points?[21] When it comes to note-taking, the most critical aspect is completeness—capturing the most important points.[22]

5. **Consider your learning style preferences.** If you're a visual learner, a note-taking system that works well for you may not work particularly well for a classmate who has a different learning style. Drawing all over your paper may help you see connections, whereas a classmate next to you is writing the same information down in a structured outline format. If a note-taking system seems awkward to you

even after you've tried it for awhile, you may be better off trying a different one.

6. **Create a shorthand system that works.** When you're taking notes quickly, as you often do in class, you won't have time to write out every word your instructor utters. Use abbreviations or a shorthand system that you create for yourself. The last thing you want is to look at your notes as you begin to study for an exam and wonder what you meant by a string of letters that makes no sense now. So make an abbreviation "dictionary" for yourself that you use regularly, like in Figure 7.1.

7. **Understand that taking notes electronically can be less effective.** When you type, you tend to take notes verbatim, writing out exactly what's being said during the lecture. When you write by hand, since you can't write as fast as you can type, you have to be selective and choose the most important information to write down. In study after study, this extra mental processing pays off, and students who handwrite their notes achieve higher test scores.[23] Also, know that "pretending" to take notes electronically but actually playing games, shopping, or e-mailing friends can bug your classmates, big-time. In one study, classmates who wandered electronically were identified as other students' biggest pet peeve.[24] And students who were close enough to watch the wandering were as distracted as the students who were actually doing it.[25]

> "When you write down your ideas you automatically focus your full attention on them. Few if any of us can write one thought and think another at the same time. Thus a pencil and paper make excellent concentration tools."
>
> —*Michael Leboeuf, American business author*

SYMBOL	MEANING	EXAMPLE
→	leads to, produces, causes, makes	Practice → perfect.
←	comes from, is the result of	Tsunamis ← earthquakes
↑	increased, increasing, goes up, rises	Taxes ↑ 100 percent last year.
↓	decreased, decreasing, lowering	Salaries ↓ 10 percent this year.
#	number	Retry problem #3.
/	per	25 miles/gallon
p./pp.	page/pages	Read p. 99./Study pp. 99–105
¶	paragraph	Revise ¶ #4.
w/o	without	They revised w/o reading carefully.
w/i	within	There are problems w/i the tax laws.
i.e.	that is	The SAT, i.e., a college entrance exam, is challenging.
e.g.	for example	Professionals, e.g., doctors and lawyers, have advanced degrees.
esp.	especially	Tobacco, esp. cigarettes, causes cancer.
min.	minimum	The min. wage may go up.
max.	maximum	The max. number of people in an elevator is 8.
gov't.	government	The gov't. helped the people.
wrt	write	wrt #3 (write number 3)

Based on http://www.essayzone.co.uk/blog/how-to-take-lecture-notes-quickly-common-abbreviations-and-symbols-for-students/

FIGURE 7.1

Abbreviation Dictionary

life hack #3

Some new electronic tools allow you the best of both worlds. You can handwrite on these e-tablets with a stylus.

So what are the various note-taking methods? What are the steps involved in using each one? Knowing your options, developing your skills, and learning flexibility as a note-taker are keys to your success.

OUTLINING

Outlining is probably the oldest, and perhaps the most trusted form of taking notes. The problem, of course, is that not all instructors speak from an outline. Rachel's instructor probably did, and if Rachel had been able to focus, outlining may have worked well. See Figure 7.2 for what Rachel's notes would have looked like. She'd listen for key points, like the five developmental milestones, and list examples beneath each one, like this.

She's listed the instructor's main points and several examples below each point to help her remember what it's about. At the end of the lecture, she could have included a **summary** of her notes, like in Figure 7.3. Summarizing is an excellent way to make sure you've understood the gist of all the information you've written down.

Of course, if your instructor's lecture is less organized, you can elect to use an informal variation of outlining, like listing bullets, and perhaps even color-coding them so they're easier to remember, as shown in Figure 7.4:

summary a condensed version of the main points

FIGURE 7.2

Sample Outlining

Child Development 1, Week 4

1. Child development involves learning and mastering skills like sitting, walking, talking, skipping, and tying shoes.
   A. Developmental milestones are learned during predictable time periods. ¢
   B. Children develop skills in five main areas of development:
      1. Cognitive development: ability to learn and solve problems.
         a. two-month-old baby learning to explore the environment with hands or eyes
         b. five-year-old learning how to do simple math problems
      2. Social/emotional development: ability to interact with others, including helping themselves and self-control.
         a. six-week-old baby smiling
         b. ten-month-old baby waving bye-bye
         c. five-year-old boy knowing how to take turns in games at school
      3. Speech/language development: ability to both understand and use language.
         a. 12-month-old baby saying his first words
         b. a two-year-old naming parts of her body
         c. a five-year-old learning to say "feet" instead of "foots"

FIGURE 7.3

Sample Summary

Summary:
Children reach developmental milestones in five areas at fairly predictable ages. These five areas are cognitive, social/emotional, speech/language, fine motor skills, and gross motor skills.

FIGURE 7.4

Sample Color-Coded Notes

Child Development 1, Week 4

Child development = learning & mastering skills
- *sitting*
- *walking*
- *talking*
- *skipping*
- *tying shoes*

Children develop skills in five main areas of development:
1. *Cognitive development: ability to learn and solve problems.*
2. *Social/emotional development: ability to interact with others, including helping themselves and self-control.*
3. *Speech/language development: ability to both understand and use language.*

Visual: Color-code a set of class notes to mark important themes (blue highlighter for main points, yellow highlighter for examples, etc.). Or create your own system of symbols to mark items (" " for direct quote from instructor, @ for good comment from classmate, # for video played in class, etc.)

Even if your instructor is flashing PowerPoint slides on the screen, don't count on your memory to do all the work. You have to take notes yourself to help the information stick.

THE CORNELL SYSTEM

The Cornell system of note-taking, devised by educator Walter Pauk, suggests this. On each page of your notebook, draw a line from top to bottom about one and a half inches from the left edge of your paper. (Some notebook paper already has a red line there.) Take notes on the right side of the line. Your notes should include main ideas, examples, short phrases, and definitions, for example—almost like an outline.

Leave the left side blank to fill in later with key words or questions you'd like answered, as Rachel has done in Figure 7.5. After class, as you review your notes, put your hand or a sheet of paper over the right side and use the words or questions you've written on the left side as prompts to see whether you can remember what's on the right side.[26] By doing this to recall the lecture, you can get a good idea of how much of the information you've really understood.

MIND MAPS

An alternative to the Cornell system, or a way to expand on it, is to create mind maps. Mind maps use both sides of your brain: the logical, orderly left side and the visual, creative right side. What they're particularly good for is showing the relationships among ideas. Mind maps are also generally a good note-taking method for visual learners, and even the physical act of drawing one may help you remember the information, particularly if you're a kinesthetic learner. To give mind mapping a try, here are some useful suggestions:

1. **Use extra-wide paper (11 × 17 inches or legal size).** You won't want to write vertically (which is hard to read) if you can help it.

2. **Write the main concept of the lecture in the center of the page.** Draw related concepts coming from the center.

3. **Limit your labels to key words so that your mind map is visually clear.**

4. **Use colors, symbols, and images to make your mind map livelier and more memorable.** See Figure 7.6 for an example.

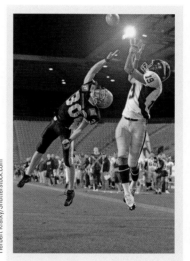

Herbert Kratky/Shutterstock.com

"Luck is what happens when preparation meets opportunity."

Darrell Royal, football coach

Different strokes for different folks: Note-taking by the system and subject **185**

KEY WORDS AND QUESTIONS	SHORT PHRASES, EXAMPLES, DEFINITIONS
Child development	—Every child goes through.
	—learning and mastering skills (sitting, walking, talking, skipping, tying shoes, etc.)
Developmental milestones	— predictable time periods
Five main areas of development	1. Cognitive development
	Ability to learn and solve problems
	—two-month-old baby learning to explore the environment with hands or eyes
	—five-year-old learning to do simple math
~~Was it five main areas or six?~~	2. Social/emotional development
	Ability to interact with others, including helping themselves and self-control
	—six-week-old baby smiling
	—ten-month-old baby waving goodbye
	—five-year-old knowing how to take turns in games at school

FIGURE 7.5

Child Development Milestones: Cornell System Example

5. **Consider using software such as MindManager, MindManuals, Mind-Plugs, MindMapper, or MindGenius, which are all powerful brainstorming and organizing tools.** As you type, these programs will anticipate relationships and help you draw a mind map on screen.

FIGURE 7.6

Child Development Milestones: Mind Map Example

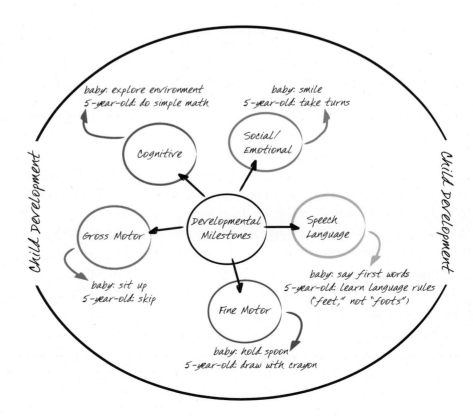

NOTE-TAKING ON INSTRUCTOR-PROVIDED HANDOUTS

PowerPoint Miniatures Some instructors provide full-text lecture notes online or copies of their PowerPoint slides (three or six miniatures on a page). Instructors may hand out PowerPoint miniatures in class before the lecture, so you can follow along; hand them out after the lecture so that you still have to take your own notes but have the print outs of the miniatures as back-up; or e-mail them as attachments (see Figure 7.7). If you have copies of the PowerPoint slides to use during class, write in specifics on the lines provided next to each slide miniature, more or less as you would if you were using the Cornell System. Put down examples that are discussed in class but don't appear on the slide, or a story that will help you remember a main point on a slide. If they're handed out after class, transfer your own notes to the PowerPoint fill-in lines. If they're e-mailed or posted online before or after class, make sure you use them. They're "insurance" that you have access to what appeared in class on the screen. Tools such as these can be a valuable resource if you remember to use them. Don't rely on PowerPoints your instructors provide to the extent that you skip taking notes yourself in class altogether. Although it's helpful to have them available as a tool, you still need to take notes on your own to help you process the information you're listening to in class.

Guided Notes Your instructor may actually help you to pay attention in class by providing what are called "Guided Notes," or copies of lecture outlines or PowerPoint miniatures with key words missing, so that you must listen closely to "fill in the blanks." In one study, students in a college algebra class who used guided notes with problem sets they worked out together in groups liked their math class and did much better than comparable students who weren't using guided notes.[27]

Parallel Note-Taking Because many instructors today provide e-support for lectures, either through web notes, hard copies of onscreen slides, lecture out-lines, or a full transcript, parallel note-taking may be particularly useful, if you go about it in the right way.[28] Here's how it works, ideally.

If they're available, print out lecture notes before class and bring them with you, preferably in a ring binder. As your instructor lectures, use the back (blank)

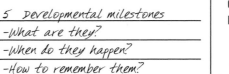

FIGURE 7.7

Child Development Milestones: PowerPoint Miniatures Example

FIGURE 7.8

Child Development Milestones:
Parallel Note-Taking Example

[Fill in the blank page during actual lecture.]
My In-Class Lecture Notes

Every child develops skills like learning to sit up, walk, talk, skip, and tie shoes.

These are called developmental milestones, and they happen to most children around the same age.

Children learn skills in five main areas of development: cognitive, social/emotional, speech/language, fine, and gross motor skills:

[Print out instructor's notes and place in binder.]
Instructor's Lecture Notes

Child development is a process every child goes through. This process involves learning and mastering skills like sitting, walking, talking, skipping, and tying shoes. Children learn these skills, called developmental milestones, during predictable time periods. Children develop skills in five main areas of development: First, let's look at cognitive development. This is the child's ability to learn and solve problems. For example, this includes a two-month-old baby learning to explore the environment with hands or eyes, or a five-year-old learning how to do simple math problems. Second, social/emotional development is the child's ability to interact with others, including helping him or herself and self-control. Examples of this type of development would include a six-week-old baby smiling, a ten-month-old baby waving bye-bye, or a five-year-old boy knowing how to take turns in games at school.

VARK IT!

Kinesthetic: Try cutting up a set of notes into "puzzle pieces" and reassembling them. The more you manipulate your notes, the more the information may stick.

side of each page to record your own notes as the notes from the ongoing, real-time lecture face you. You can parallel what you're hearing from your instructor with your own on-the-spot, self-recorded notes, using a Cornell format on each blank page. It's the best of both worlds! You're reading, writing, and listening at the same time, fully immersing yourself in immediate and longer-lasting learning. Figure 7.8 illustrates how parallel note-taking might look for Rachel in her childhood development class.

VARK IT!

Read/Write: Swap notes for the same lecture with a classmate, and see if his or her notes on the same material make sense to you. You may be able to teach each other something!

NOTE-TAKING BY THE BOOK

So far this chapter has discussed taking notes in class. What about taking notes as you read from a textbook? Is that important, too? The answer: absolutely! It's easy

WIIFM?   ⏱ 3.5 MINUTE READ

The value of note-taking skills in day-to-day life is a no-brainer. With a list, you can whiz through the grocery store in seconds flat. Or you can review your doctor's instructions almost verbatim. And of course, taking good notes in college is a life-saver—no doubt about it. But what about note-taking on-the-job (OTJ)? Will these essential skills from college be useful in the workplace? Probably not, right? After all,

your boss would never say, "Okay, write this down; it's going to be on the final exam."

But career experts say that note-taking skills on the job are one of those subtle career-enhancing strategies that are often overlooked. "Taking notes at work can really boost your productivity. Not only can you prevent having to follow-up later on the same topics with your boss, but it can even be a great source for others who

> "Working hard is very important. You're not going to get anywhere without working extremely hard."
>
> *George Lucas (Star Wars),*
> *attended Modesto Junior College,*
> *Modesto, California (transferred to*
> *University of Southern California)*

are less prepared."[29] Let's run down a few specifics you may not have considered:

Why take notes?

You earn a reputation as a hard worker. If you take notes in on-the-job meetings and others don't, you demonstrate professionalism. *"Does anyone remember what we decided at the last meeting?" "No, but ask Josh; he took notes."* "Taking simple notes during meetings can be invaluable, especially if you jot down action items for yourself and others. Once you do that, it makes following up easier."[30] *"Luisa, I have you down for the scheduling task. How's that coming along? Need any help?"*

You show respect. Taking notes while someone else speaks communicates that what they're saying must be important. *New York Times* best-selling author and popular blogger Gretchen Rubin even takes notes during informal conversations: "I'm a compulsive note-taker, and I used to feel self-conscious about pulling out my little notebook and taking notes during a casual conversation. Then I noticed that people really seemed to enjoy it; the fact that I was taking notes made their remarks seem particularly insightful or valuable. Now I don't hold myself back." (One word of caution, however. If you take notes on your cell phone, make sure your colleagues know you're working, not texting or checking Facebook.)[31]

You see connections. Employees who take notes end up with plenty of data that can help them see patterns, and patterns can stimulate creativity. If you store your notes in the same place, you can refer to them all easily, and you'll "start to see connections between things you otherwise wouldn't have seen and have information that other people don't retain. This is how you'll get great ideas, form new connections, and become the kind of innovator and leader who makes things really happen on your team."[32]

So what do you need to know before you launch this subtle but effective OTJ success strategy? Check out these suggestions about *when* and *how* to take notes in the workplace.

When?

Take notes during important one-on-one conversations with your boss. Besides getting all the details, you may learn things about her communication preferences and work style that are useful later.

Take notes during big conversations. Often after brainstorming sessions, when the whiteboards are filled with suggestions everyone has contributed, people may leave the meeting confused. Even taking a picture of the whiteboards with your phone doesn't help. But if you've taken notes all along, you—and perhaps you alone—know what's up.

Take notes in meetings with clients, customers, contacts, and mentors. You need a record you can refer to later to remember what was said; and besides, whoever takes the notes controls the "real truth" about what went down.

How?

Use whatever tool works best for you—paper, phone, or tablet. If you're taking brief notes, consider using *Simplenote* on your Android or iPhone. For heavy-duty notes, try *Evernote*; or to keep yourself focused on a big task, consider *Dayboard*, a Google Chrome extension.[33] Tech guru Bill Gates states, "Paper is no longer a big part of my day. I get 90 percent of my news online, and when I go to a meeting and want to jot things down, I bring my Tablet PC. It's fully synchronized with my office machine, so I have all the files I need. It also has a note-taking piece of software called OneNote, so all my notes are in digital form."

Be consistent, yet ready to adapt to a better format, based on circumstances. If you have a new boss who "wanders," verbally, mind mapping may work best. Connecting the dots on paper may help you follow along. Regardless of which format you choose, write important information—the date, attendees, and meeting topic—on every page of notes to make sense out of it later. And always review your last set of notes before the next meeting so that decisions and action items are fresh in your mind.

After every important meeting, stop for 30 seconds and summarize the most important things you remember. This practice isn't what we usually think of as note-taking per se, but it will help you become better at listening and asking questions, and it will change the way you pay attention.[34]

The simple truth is this: You may not get fired for not taking notes on the job, but you may lose some respect if your co-workers notice that your memory is short. *"What did you suggest I do next?" "Who are we inviting to the meeting, again?" "Remind me: What did you want me to put in that e-mail?"* Asking the same questions over and over again can become an annoying pattern, especially to your boss. But taking notes can help her see you as the hard-working professional you know you are.

to go on auto-pilot as you read and have no idea what you read afterward! Instead, take notes in the margins, on sticky notes, or better yet, keep a spiral-bound notebook next to you, and fill it with your own words as you read. Jot down questions, summarize main points, or use the Cornell System. Actually, the best thing to do is to read a section, close the book, and write down what you remember. You'll prove to yourself what you absorbed and what you didn't. Then you can dive back into the textbook again and clarify concepts that are still fuzzy.[35]

NOTE-TAKING BY THE SUBJECT

Beyond figuring out which note-taking style seems to "fit" you best, think about times when the subject dictates that you vary your note-taking style. In your American History class, it may make sense to take your notes along a timeline of the beginning of World War II, for example (see Figure 7.9). Because your instructor and your textbook report key events that took place during World War II chronologically, along a time line, you might want your notes to reflect that.

However, in your college algebra class, you may want to take notes very differently. Let's say, for example, that your instructor lectures by working problems on a white board or by projecting them on the screen. Then you are asked to work a problem and then talk it over with a classmate next to you. You may want to divide up your notes into columns by proposing a solution and then showing how you arrived at your answer. Having a record of how

FIGURE 7.9

Timeline Example
Based on http://www.historyplace.com/unitedstates/pacificwar
/timeline.htm

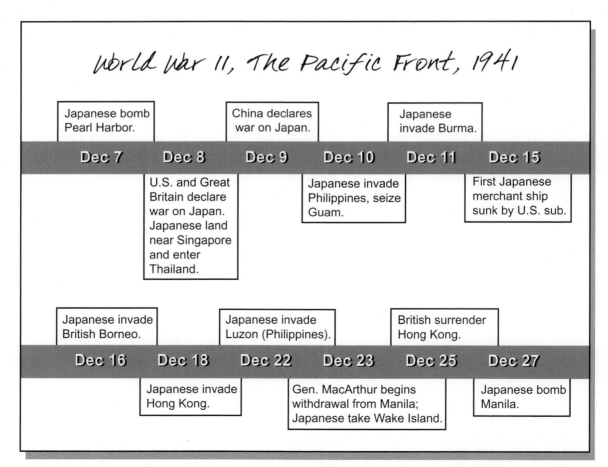

World War II, The Pacific Front, 1941

Japanese bomb Pearl Harbor.		China declares war on Japan.		Japanese invade Burma.	
Dec 7	Dec 8	Dec 9	Dec 10	Dec 11	Dec 15
	U.S. and Great Britain declare war on Japan. Japanese land near Singapore and enter Thailand.		Japanese invade Philippines, seize Guam.		First Japanese merchant ship sunk by U.S. sub.

Japanese invade British Borneo.		Japanese invade Luzon (Philippines).		British surrender Hong Kong.	
Dec 16	Dec 18	Dec 22	Dec 23	Dec 25	Dec 27
	Japanese invade Hong Kong.		Gen. MacArthur begins withdrawal from Manila; Japanese take Wake Island.		Japanese bomb Manila.

Notes, College Algebra 100, Friday, October 5

Determine which of the x values are solutions to the equation

$$x^4 + x^3 - 5x^2 + x - 6 = 0$$

(a) $x = -3$,   (b) $x = -2$,   (c) $x = 1$,   (d) $x = 2$

STEPS TO SOLUTION	CALCULATIONS	RESULTS
(1) Try answer a Substitute –3 into the equation for x and see if the equation is satisfied.	$(-3)^4 + (-3)^3 - 5(-3)^2 + (-3) - 6 \overset{?}{=} 0$ $81 \quad -27 \quad -45 \quad -3 - 6 = 0$ $0 = 0$	YES, because both sides are 0.
(2) Try answer b Substitute –2 into the equation for x and see if the equation is satisfied.	$(-2)^4 + (-2)^3 - 5(-2)^2 + (-2) - 6 \overset{?}{=} 0$ $16 \quad -8 \quad -20 \quad -2 - 6 = 0$ $-20 \neq 0$	NO, because the two sides are unequal.
(3) Try answer c Substitute 1 into the equation for x and see if the equation is satisfied.	$(1)^4 + (1)^3 - 5(1)^2 + 1 - 6 \overset{?}{=} 0$ $1 \quad +1 \quad -5 \quad +1 - 6 = 0$ $-8 \neq 0$	NO, because the two sides are unequal.
(4) Try answer d Substitute 2 into the equation for x and see if the equation is satisfied.	$(2)^4 + (2)^3 - 5(2)^2 + 2 - 6 \overset{?}{=} 0$ $16 \quad +8 \quad -20 \quad +2 - 6 = 0$ $0 = 0$	YES, because both sides are 0.

FIGURE 7.10

Math Note-Taking Example
Based on http://math.armstrong.edu/faculty/hollis/DicksMathTutorial/

you worked a problem can be a valuable aid later when you're studying for a test that will probably contain algebra problems very much like the ones you solve regularly in class. Write everything down, and skip a few lines if there's something you want to fill in later (see Figure 7.10).

Mind mapping, on the other hand, is particularly useful in geology, physiology, biology, psychology, and education courses, where relationships among concepts are important.[36] Some students may make the mistake of thinking that mind maps are "scribbling," but the process of making connections on paper helps you make those same connections in your brain. Successful note-taking does mean "different strokes for different folks"—and different subjects. Be sure to make the right choices about which note-taking system makes the most sense for the course material being presented.

ASK AND YOU SHALL RECEIVE

Even if you listen carefully to every word your instructor utters, it's likely you won't understand them all. After all, your instructor is an expert in the subject you're studying, and you're new to it. At some point or other, you'll need to ask questions. Even though that makes sense, not all students feel comfortable asking questions in class. Why? See whether you've excused yourself from asking questions for any of these reasons:

> I don't want to look stupid.

> I must be slow. Everyone else seems to be understanding.

> I'm too shy.

> I'll get the answer later from the textbook.

> I don't think my question is important enough.

> I don't want to interrupt the lecture. The instructor's on a roll.

> I'm sure the instructor knows what he's talking about. He must be right.

If any of these reasons for not asking questions in class applies to you, the good news is . . . you're in good company. Many students think this way. The bad news, of course, is that your question remains unasked, and therefore unanswered.

The next time you find yourself in a situation where you don't understand something, consider these points.

1. **Remember that you're not in this alone.** Chances are you're probably not the only person in class who doesn't understand. Not only will you be doing yourself a favor by asking, but you'll also be helping someone else who's too shy to speak up.

2. **Ask academically relevant questions when the time is right.** As opposed to "Why do we need to know this?" or "Why did you make the test so hard?" ask questions to clarify information. Don't ask questions designed to take your instructor off on a tangent (to delay the impending quiz, for example). If you're really interested in something that's not directly related to the material being covered, the best time to raise the question would be during your instructor's office hours.

3. **Save _personally_ relevant questions for later.** If your questions relate only to you (for example, you were ill and missed the last two classes), then don't ask in class. Set up an appointment with your instructor. You can also get answers by researching on your own, visiting or e-mailing your instructor, seeking out a teaching assistant or tutor, or working with a study group.

4. **Build on others' questions.** Your instructor isn't the only person who speaks in class. You must apply what you're reading in this chapter to listening to your classmates, too. Listen to the questions other students ask. Use their questions to spark your own. Perhaps another student has a unique way of looking at the issue being discussed that will spark an idea for a follow-up question from you. To your instructor good questions indicate _interest_, not _ignorance_.

Remember, your college education is an investment in your own future. You're here to learn, and asking questions is a natural part of that learning experience. Don't be shy—put that hand in the air!

USING LECTURE
NOTES

Taking good notes is only part of the equation. To get the most value from your notes, you must actually _use_ them. As soon as possible after class, take a few minutes to review your notes. If you find sections that are unclear, take

"He who is ashamed of asking is ashamed of learning."

Danish Proverb

tangent a sudden change of subject

impending upcoming

time to fill in the gaps while things are still fresh in your mind. One instructor found that students who filled in any missing points right after class were able to increase the amount of lecture points they recorded by as much as 50 percent. And students who worked with another student to reconstruct the lecture immediately after class were able to increase their number of noted lecture points even more![37]

See this chapter's Quick Study, Figure 7.11, for suggestions about note-taking before, during, and after class. What to do with notes afterwards is often overlooked, yet it is one of the most helpful steps for learning and recall. If you don't review your notes within twenty-four hours, there's good evidence that you'll end up *relearning* rather than *reviewing*. Reviewing helps you go beyond just writing to actually making sure you understand what you wrote. These three techniques help you get the best use of your notes: manipulating, paraphrasing, and summarizing.

> **Manipulating** involves working with your notes by typing them out later, for example. Some research indicates that it's not writing down information that's most important. Manipulating information is what counts. Work with your notes. Fill in charts, draw diagrams, create a mind map, underline, highlight, organize. Cut a copy of the instructor's lecture notes up into paragraphs, mix them up, and then put the lecture back together. Copy your notes onto flash cards. Manipulating information helps develop your reasoning skills, reduces your stress level, and can produce a more complete set of notes to study later.[38]

> **Paraphrasing** is the process of putting your notes into your own words. Recopy your notes or your instructor's prepared lecture notes, translating them into words you understand and examples that are meaningful to you. Paraphrasing is also a good way to self-test or to study with a classmate. If you can't find words of your own, perhaps you don't really understand the original notes. Sometimes students think they understand course material until the test proves otherwise, and then it's too late! Practice paraphrasing key concepts with a friend to see how well you both understand the material. Or ask yourself, *If I had to explain this to someone who missed class, what words would I use?*

> **Summarizing** is a process of writing a brief overview of all of your notes from one lecture. Imagine trying to take all your lecture notes from one class session and putting them on an index card. If you can do that, you've just written a summary. Research shows that students who use the summarizing technique have far greater recall of the material than those who don't.

Some students think that simply going over their notes is the best way to practice. Research shows that simply reading over your notes is a weak form of practice that does not transfer information into long-term memory.[39] You must actually *work with* the material, rearrange or reword it, or condense it to get the most academic bang for your buck. Active strategies always work better than more passive ones.

"I make progress by having people around me who are smarter than I am and listening to them. And I assume that everyone is smarter about something than I am."

Henry J. Kaiser, American industrialist (1882–1967)

Multimodal: As a multimodal learner, you have an advantage because you are flexible. But you may have to use your two or three preferred modalities in order to be confident that you have learned something. Is this true for you?

FIGURE 7.11

Quick Study "Ultimate Guide to Note-taking in Class"

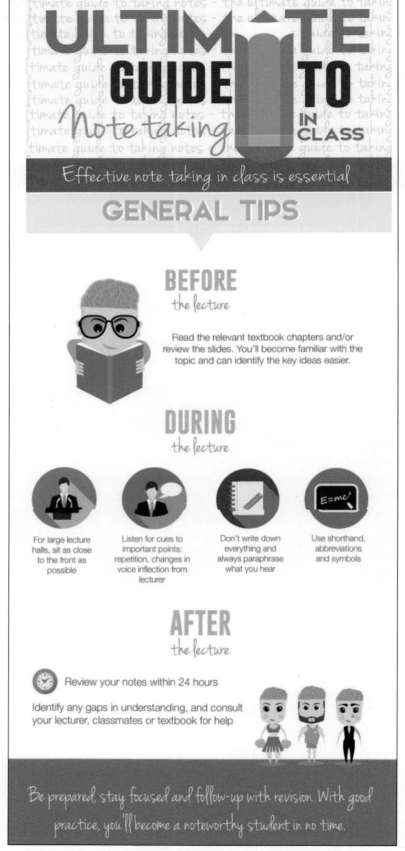

Source: http://wbsa.co.uk/the-ultimate-guide-to-note-taking-in-class-infographic/

CONTROL: YOUR TOUGHEST CLASS

Think about your most challenging course this term. Use the following form to analyze the instructor's lecture style. Be careful not to be too obvious as you listen and analyze his or her style, of course, but after your chart is completed, decide what you can do as a listener to make adjustments in your toughest class. To get an idea of how to fill out the chart, look at what Rachel's entries for her child development class might have been. Filling out this chart may give you some insights about why one particular class is your toughest and help you modify your note-taking skills to what works best for that particular lecture style.[40]

LECTURE CHARACTERISTICS	EXAMPLE: CHILD DEVELOPMENT I	MY TOUGHEST CLASS
EMPHASIS *Content, students, or both?*	Teacher emphasizes content, primarily. She lectures for the full class period with little student interaction.	
ORGANIZATION *Structured or unstructured*	Lectures seem disorganized with notes written all over the board.	
PACE *Fast, slow, or medium?*	Very fast.	
VISUAL AIDS *Used? Useful?*	Board hard to see from the back of the room.	
EXAMPLES *Used? Useful?*	She needs to provide more real examples that students can relate to.	
LANGUAGE *Terms defined? Vocabulary understandable?*	The language isn't too hard, but I can't focus on what she's saying.	
DELIVERY *Animated via body language?*	Delivery style isn't lively and interesting. Instructor doesn't notice when students aren't paying attention.	
QUESTIONS *Encouraged?*	She rarely pauses to take questions.	

Now that you've analyzed your instructor's lecture style, what steps can you take to get more out of lectures in your toughest class?

CHALLENGE: *REALITY* CHECK

HOW MUCH DID YOU LEARN?

At the beginning of this chapter, you filled out a "Readiness Check" that asked how you thought this chapter would relate to you, and how you would relate to it. Now, fill out this "Reality Check" to find out.

1. What does it mean to sit in the "T zone" in class and why is it important?

2. This chapter discusses "hard" and "soft" listening skills. What's the difference between the two and which one is the right one to use in class?

3. Identify three possible formats for taking notes in class.

4. Describe two effective ways of using your lecture notes to study.

5. How long did it take? _____ hours _____ minutes. Before you began this chapter, you were asked to predict how long it would take you to complete it (total time, even if you read it in more than one sitting). Was your estimate on target, or will you revise it for the next chapter you'll read?

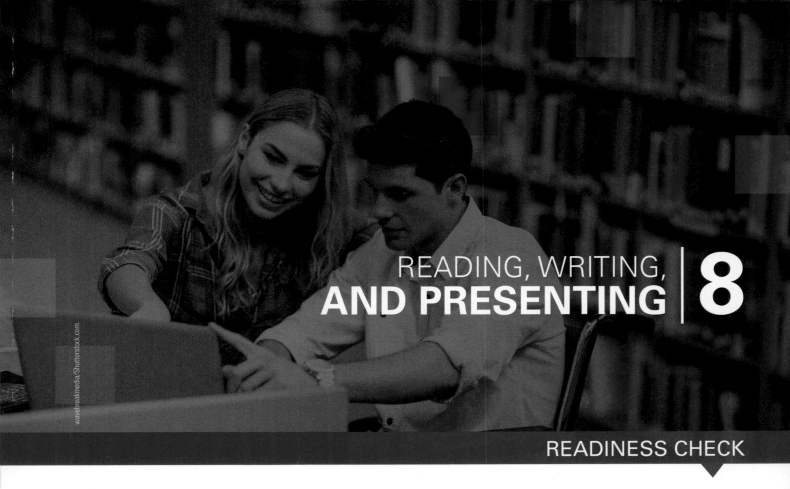

READING, WRITING, AND PRESENTING | 8

HOW THIS CHAPTER RELATES TO YOU

1. When it comes to reading, writing, and presenting in college, what do you find most challenging, if anything? Put check marks by the phrases that apply to you or write in your answer.

   ☐ Understanding what I read
   ☐ Struggling with writing assignments
   ☐ Getting nervous speaking in front of others
   ☐ Procrastinating on these types of assignments
   ☐ Always completing and turning in assignments

2. What is most likely to be your response? Put a check mark by it.

   ☐ I'll be open to learning how to improve my skills.
   ☐ I'll wait and see how much of this chapter I understand.
   ☐ I'll get help from a support center on campus.
   ☐ Eventually, I'll just figure it out on my own.

3. What would you have to do to increase your likelihood of success? Will you do it this quarter or semester?

HOW YOU WILL RELATE TO THIS CHAPTER

1. What are you most interested in learning about? Put check marks by those topics.

   ☐ Why reading is important
   ☐ How to build reading skills
   ☐ How to read right
   ☐ How the writing process works
   ☐ What the seven C's (writing) and seven P's (presenting) are
   ☐ How to make your PowerPoint pop

YOUR READINESS FACTOR

1. How motivated are you to learn more about reading, writing, and presenting in college? (5 = high, 1 = low)

2. How ready are you to read now? (If something is in your way, take care of it if you can. Zero in and focus.)

3. How long do you think it will take you to complete this chapter? If you start and stop, keep track of your overall time. ____ Hour(s) ____ Minute(s)

wavebreakmedia/Shutterstock.com

Katie Alexander

College would be a lot more fun if it weren't for all the reading and writing
required. That was Katie Alexander's take on things. She wasn't much of a student,
actually. She much preferred playing softball or volleyball with her friends to sitting in one spot with a book propped open in front of her. Reading for fun wasn't
something she'd ever even consider doing—at least not reading books. To Katie,
reading 75 text messages a day was necessary; reading books was boring. *Anyway,
why read the book when you can just watch the movie?* she always asked. Katie was
an energetic, active, outgoing person, and "doing" and "socializing" were her things.
Academic pursuits, like reading textbooks, writing papers, and giving presentations,
definitely weren't.

Actually, this was Katie's second attempt at college. She'd gone to a small liberal arts school right
after high school, but the self-discipline required
just wasn't there. A specialist at the college offi-
cially diagnosed dyslexia, a learning disability that
affects reading skills, and Katie became discouraged and dropped out. Working as a server for two
years at a restaurant in her neighborhood helped
her earn enough money to go back to school. She
loved the people part of her waitressing job, and
thought a hospitality degree from the community
college close to home would be the right choice
for her. Besides, how much reading would she
possibly have to do for a career like that?

Because of her dyslexia, reading and writing
papers were hard work for Katie. She was smart
enough to make it in college—she was sure of
that—and this time around, she was more motivated. But reading a long assignment, page by
page, made her fidgety, and after she read something, she found it hard to summarize what it had
been about. Reading took her a long time, so long
that her mind wandered wherever it seemed to
want to go. She found it hard to focus, and things
just didn't seem to stick. Before she knew it, she
was off in some other world, thinking about her

Delihayat/Shutterstock.com

friends, or her schedule at work, or everything
else she had to do. Writing papers was just as
hard, if not harder. And the mere thought of giving a speech was enough to totally freak her out!

Back in grade school, Katie had been labeled
as a slow reader. She was never in the top reading
group, although she resented the label, she didn't
quite know what do to about it. The last time
reading had actually been a subject in school
was sixth grade. Now, eight years later, she was
enrolled in a developmental reading class. Would
it really help her?

Katie's good friend, Jackson, had always
been an excellent student who loved to read,
even more so now that he was in college. Katie
always wondered if Jack's love of reading was
due to the fact that he had been in a wheelchair since a car accident in the third grade. He
couldn't be active or play sports. Katie's classmate, Brittney, however, had a different strategy.
"There's so much required reading in all my
classes that I don't even know where to start,"
Brittney admitted, "so I just don't do it. I go to
class, listen to the lectures, and write down what
the instructor has said on the essay tests. Katie,
just learn to 'play the game'!"

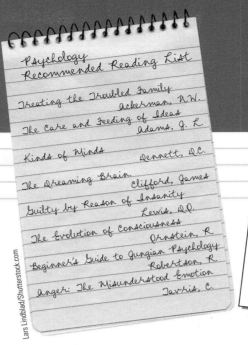

Psychology
Recommended Reading List

Treating the Troubled Family
Ackerman, N.W.
The Care and Feeding of Ideas
Adams, J. L.
Kinds of Minds
Dennett, D.C.
The Dreaming Brain
Clifford, James
Guilty by Reason of Insanity
Lewis, D.P.
The Evolution of Consciousness
Ornstein, R
Beginner's Guide to Jungian Psychology
Robertson, R
Anger: The Misunderstood Emotion
Tavris, C.

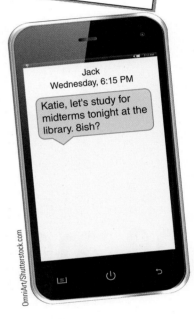

Study Strategies for Students with Dyslexia

- Take advantage of multi-sensory learning methods
  Study diagrams, look at charts
  Listen to the instructor's words
  Combine sensory input to create a more complete picture of the info

- Read through superficially first
  Look at the title page and intro
  Note the major headings and bullets
  Skim through the text to get the main ideas

- Read out loud
  Read out loud while highlighting, then read what you've highlighted
  Listen to your voice as you emphasize important points

- Organize your workspace
  Categorize papers and books for each subject
  Color-code assignments and papers to make organization easier

- Improve your work methods
  Brainstorm at the beginning of a project
  Set priorities and outline your work strategy

- Prepare for tests
  Be sure to attend all classes leading up to the test
  Listen for clues and try to determine the format of the test
  Get a good night's sleep
  Take your time

Besides her developmental reading class, Katie was enrolled in two other classes: history and introduction to psychology. She knew she'd have plenty of reading to do there, and her friend Brittney's strategy definitely wasn't going to work. Professor Harris-Black had assigned a shocking number of chapters to read in their thick psychology textbook for the first exam. She didn't even go over the reading in class, and her lectures were about all sorts of things, much of which wasn't even related to the reading. Whenever Katie sat down to read a chapter, she found what to her were unfamiliar words and long, complicated phrases. The instructor had suggested that students read with a dictionary open online, but who'd ever want to keep stopping to look up words? You'd never finish!

With a midterm exam coming up in her psychology class next week, not to mention a paper and presentation due in her history class, Katie was beginning to panic. She'd only read one of the nine chapters assigned. In fact, she hadn't made it through the first chapter when she got discouraged and gave up. She knew the essay questions would be challenging. Winging it wouldn't work, and choosing to "watch the movie" instead of reading the book wasn't an option. Exactly what did psychology have to do with hospitality, she puzzled, and why did she have to take this course in the first place?

The night before the test, Katie decided to get serious. She sat down at her desk, armed with her yellow highlighter. As she began reading, however, she realized she didn't know exactly what to highlight because she didn't really understand what she was reading. Looking back at the page she had just finished, she saw that she had basically highlighted everything.

Exasperated, Katie told herself that she couldn't go to bed until she'd finished reading everything, no matter when that was. She started with the second chapter, because she'd read the first one, and by morning she'd be as ready as possible. Anyway, whether or not she did well wasn't up to her—it was up to Professor Harris-Black. She was the one making up the test.

Getting a good grade on her Introduction to Psychology midterm exam was probably out of the question, but if she could just manage to pass, Katie knew she would have to settle for that. On the other hand, she secretly hoped that maybe she'd just luck out.

Jack
Wednesday, 6:15 PM

Katie, let's study for midterms tonight at the library. 8ish?

Focus challenge case **199**

1. Do you have anything in common with Katie? If so, in what ways, specifically?

2. Katie is probably an intelligent student, but she has decided that she dislikes reading, so she avoids it. How important will reading be as she continues to pursue a college degree? Is she likely to succeed her second time around?

3. How would you characterize Katie as a student? Identify five specific problems described in this case study that could interfere with her college success.

4. Identify three specific things Katie should do to get her college career on track.

WHO NEEDS
TO READ?

What's so important about reading? Teachers seem to think it's important, but times have changed, haven't they? Now you can just skim predigested information on websites, get the day's news on Facebook, and watch Netflix for entertainment. Who needs to read? Look around the next time you're in a doctor or dentist's waiting room. You'll see some people staring at the TV screen mounted on the wall, others with ear buds plugged in, and still others working with their smart phones. A few may be skimming through magazines, but does anyone ever pick up a book to actually read it cover to cover anymore? Does it matter?

The answer, according to many experts, is a definite yes, it does matter![1] Reading helped create civilization as we know it and taught us particular ways of thinking.

One fairly predictable result of doing anything less often is that eventually you may not do it as well. Practice helps you improve. Even an Olympic athlete who doesn't stick with training gets rusty after a while. As students read less, their reading skills deteriorate, and they don't enjoy doing it. On the other hand, the better you get at reading, the more you may enjoy it. Falling down every ten minutes the first time you get on skis isn't all that much fun, but once you can zip down the mountain like a pro, you begin to appreciate the sport.

Like Katie from the "FOCUS Challenge Case," reading may not be your favorite pastime. You may feel about reading like many people do about eating cauliflower. You know it's good for you, but you'd prefer to avoid it. However, this chapter wouldn't be worth its weight in trees (or room in cyberspace) if it didn't try to convince you otherwise. One aspect of reading Katie particularly dislikes is that reading is not a social or physical activity. You can read with someone else in the room, of course, or talk about what you read afterward with other people, but basically, reading is something you do alone. It's a solitary activity that involves you, words on a page or screen, an invisible author, and your brain. You need to do it with a minimum of physical movement. Reading while playing a game of volleyball would be tough to pull off.

"No matter how busy you may think you are, you must find time for reading, or surrender yourself to self-chosen ignorance."

Confucius, Chinese philospher, 551–479 B.C.

If you enjoy reading, congratulations! When you settle in with an exciting novel, you can travel to the far corners of the Earth, turn back the clock to previous centuries, or fast-forward to a future that extends beyond your lifetime. Whether or not you enjoy reading, it will be one of the primary skills you need to cultivate in college. According to one study, 85 percent of the learning you'll do in college requires careful reading.[2] On average, community college students spend 6 to 10 hours per week preparing for class (studying, reading, writing, doing homework, etc.).[3]

What's more, reading skills go hand in hand with writing and presenting skills, which makes them even more important. The better you get at reading, the more likely you are to achieve academic success. Many of your classes will require intensive reading of complex material, including primary sources by original authors and scholarly research. If you complete reading assignments, and your classmates don't, think about how much ahead of the nonreaders *you* will be! But how do you learn to become a better, college-ready reader?

BUILD YOUR
READING SKILLS

Some people think reading should be second nature since we've all been doing it for many years now. Someone may understand an article they've just read immediately, whereas others ask, "How did you know that?" about something in the same passage. Learning to understand the reading process helps. In this chapter, we will look at some clues to help you become a better reader. It's not always as easy as it looks, especially in college. Books and articles you need to read for your classes are often challenging, and they can require a lot of self-discipline to read. Sometimes you may need to read a section or an entire chapter more than once! Perhaps you're in a developmental reading class to boost your skills. Or perhaps a language other than English is your native tongue. If so, this chapter can be especially useful to you.

RECOGNIZE THE BUILDING BLOCKS OF ENGLISH

One way to become a better reader is by gaining a deeper understanding of how English works. If you've been speaking it all your life, it seems natural. You open your mouth and speak, without pausing to think over every word choice. But even for many people who learned to speak English as children, *reading* English is a bigger challenge. Just what are some of the specific challenges?

Sounds English is spoken as a first or second language by over 1 billion people.[4] Within the United States, English varies somewhat from one region of the country to another. If you live in the South, "pa" (as in "I'll have a slice of apple 'pa'") may be something you eat for dessert; in another part of the country, it's what you call your dad. The sound "tsk" you make when you mean "What a shame . . . " (tsk, tsk . . .) is an actual sound that might be the first sound in a word in other languages. In fact, when you were a 6-month-old baby, you could pronounce most any sound that exists in any language. But as you learn to speak as a young child, you discard sounds that aren't a part of your native language.

Krisztian/Shutterstock.com

life hack #1

If you want to increase your reading rate and comprehension, try www.spreeder.com. Adjust the settings and work toward the results you'd like to achieve. You can actually practice by pasting in a section of text from an online assignment or e-book.

primary sources works written by authors themselves, like the autobiography of Benjamin Franklin (that he wrote himself)

scholarly research articles in academic journals, like the studies about reading and college students, footnoted at the end of the last paragraph

You already know a good deal about English that you're not even aware you know. If you entered a contest to name a new laundry detergent, you'd automatically use the "rules" for how English operates. For example, you know that you can't clump too many consonants together at the beginning of an English word, and you know that some sounds just don't go together, like "f" and "z." You'd never come up with "Buy new Fzuthoox!" People in the supermarket couldn't even pronounce it to ask a stocker, let alone find it on Aisle 9. If you're a new speaker of English, go to a website on English sounds and play the MP3 files. You can hear "pure" English online.[5]

Syllables Things get more complicated when sounds combine into syllables, like prefixes or suffixes. Some syllables are easy to understand, like the difference between the prefixes *pre-* and *post-* in preseason game versus postseason game. Or you know when you see the word *co-presenters*, that more than one person will be speaking. Other times, syllables are just plain puzzling. For example, typically, the prefix "in-" means "not." But why do *flammable* and *inflammable* mean exactly the same thing? Or when someone says your help is *valuable* or *invaluable*, why are both remarks equally complimentary? Go figure. Learning basic prefixes, suffixes, and word roots can help you decipher unfamiliar words you encounter in your reading.

Spelling Here's where many of us get tripped up—and spellcheck isn't always the solution. To make things especially messy, English has many exceptions to its rules. Take a look at the Curiosity box at the end of this chapter to see some humorous examples of just how varied spelling is in English. When you try reading the poem out loud, you'll get the point quickly.

Vocabulary Reading is about words. That's why it's important to put some muscle into your vocabulary. When you study a foreign language, your first task is to learn new vocabulary words so that you have something to say: "What time is it?" or "Where is the train station?" or "How much does this cost?" It's just as important, especially in college, to fill your mind with new words, too.

One of the best things you can do to become a better reader is to make friends with a dictionary. Even though it's annoying to stop every few minutes to look up a word, it's absolutely necessary. Sometimes it's important to break your stride, stop, and look up a word or phrase because what follows in the reading is based on that particular definition. Other times, these strategies might be appropriate:

> Keep a stack of blank index cards next to you, and write down the unknown word or phrase, the sentence it appears in, and the page number. Then when you have a sizable stack, or when you've scheduled a chunk of time, look up the whole stack.

> Try to guess the word's meaning from its context. Remember Lewis Carroll's "Jabberwocky" poem from *Through the Looking-Glass?* Even though the poem contains fabricated words, when you read it, you infer that something was moving around sometime, somewhere, right?
> > '*Twas brillig* ['*twas* usually indicates a time, as in '*twas* daybreak],
> > *and the slithy toves* [we don't know what *toves* are, but *slithy* sounds like a combination of slimy and slithering]

context words, sentences, and/or paragraphs around an unknown word that help you unlock its meaning

EXERCISE 8.1

WORD HUNT

You'll notice that this text defines some words that relate to your college education. That's not only a convenience; they're included to help remind you to stop and look up words as you read assignments for your other courses. Which other words are you looking up on your own as you read FOCUS? Highlight all the additional words you needed to look up in this chapter, and compile them in a list. Once you have your list, share and compare with your classmates.

Often you can infer a word's meaning from how it's used or from other words around it, but not always. Many of your courses will require you to learn precise meanings for new terms. If you can't detect the meaning from the context, use your dictionary—and see it as a friend rather than an enemy.

LEARN TO "READ BETWEEN THE LINES"

We can move beyond the realm of sounds and words into the realm of sentences, inferences and main ideas. Being a good reader is like being a good detective. You have to watch for subtle clues and draw conclusions.

Inferences Combining words into "complete thoughts" gives us sentences, and they can be complicated, too. The mere arrangement of words in a sentence can make a difference. From sentences and paragraphs, we create meaning and make inferences. For example, language experts talk about the difference between active and passive voice, often detectable by how words are arranged. For example:

inference a conclusion reached from hints or clues about something

EXERCISE 8.2

TWO-WAY INFERENCES

Part I. *Find a photo for this quote.*

"The secret of joy in work is contained in one word—excellence. To know how to do something well is to enjoy it."

—*Pearl Buck, Pulitzer Prize-winning American author, 1892–1973*

Part II. *Find a quote for the photo provided and write it here.*

iStock.com/drbimages

Mom (noticing the dent in the front fender): "Did you drive the car?"
You: "Yes, I drove the car." (Active voice, as in "I admit it.")

Compare that answer with "Um, the car was driven [by me]." (Passive voice, as in "the car was practically driving itself . . . ")

Build your reading skills **203**

There's an inference (or conclusion) behind Mom's question, right? The dent is most likely your fault. Even a slight change in intonation or emphasis can make a difference in what two nearly identical sentences mean. Take this sign, for example, hanging in the men's room of a restaurant: "We aim to please. You aim, too, please."

Main Ideas Reading longer sections of text requires that we look beyond sentences, down into the "guts" of a passage. This is where reading becomes interesting. How do you move beyond sounds, syllables, and words—the building blocks of language—toward understanding? The place to start is by finding the main idea. How do you do that?

> Look for hints that identify the topic or subject being discussed.
> Look for words and phrases that are repeated.
> Look for a thesis statement or topic sentence that summarizes the passage.
> Look for evidence of the author's opinion on what's being written about.

How do you know whether the main idea is worth buying into? Where can you find the evidence that supports the idea and makes it believable?

> Look for statistics, testimony from an expert, or examples.

And how do you detect inferences?

> See whether you can uncover a generalization that could be made after reading the passage.
> Ask how the passage overall relates to you.

READ
RIGHT!

What do we know about reading? How *should* you tackle your many reading assignments in college? Consider these twelve essential points:[6] As you read, mark items you see as potential areas of improvement for yourself as a reader.

1. **Understand what being a good reader is all about.** Reading isn't a race. Remember the old children's story about the tortoise and the hare? The turtle actually won the race because he plodded along, slowly and steadily, while the rabbit zipped all over the place and lost focus. The moral of that story applies to reading, too. Reading is a process; understanding is the goal. The point isn't simply to make it through the reading assignment by turning pages every few minutes so that you can finish the chapter in a certain amount of time. Reading requires you to back up occasionally, just like when you back up a movie you're watching at home to catch something you missed: "What did he say to her? I didn't get that."

   Students sometimes mistakenly think that good readers are speed-readers, when it's really about focus.[7] Science fiction writer Isaac Asimov once wrote, "I am not a speed reader. I am a speed understander." On the other hand, reading too slowly can be a problem, too. If you chew (with your eyes) on every word and huff and puff along as you go, your mind can wander. Before you know it, you've let a thousand other thoughts

"Outside of a dog, a book is man's best friend. Inside of a dog, it's too dark to read."

Groucho Marx, American comedian, actor, and singer (1890–1977)

main idea central message a writer is trying to get across

Is there a book you'd really like to read? Perhaps it's a book about which people say, "Oh, the book is much better than the movie!" Perhaps it's an author you've heard about: a famous politician, actor, or singer. Select a book to read for pleasure this month, and keep a reading log of how many pages you read each day and how long you stick with it. After you finish the book, write a letter about the book and the process of reading it to your instructor and classmates. There's evidence that reading something you choose yourself can be an important force in becoming a better reader![8]

intervene, as Katie Alexander did, and you have no idea where you are. The average reader reads at a rate of approximately 250 words per minute, with a 70-percent comprehension rate. Time yourself on an upcoming paragraph in this chapter, and then see whether you can talk through what you've just read and convince yourself that you understand it.[9] The point is to be efficient so that you can actually get all your reading done for all your classes.

2. **Take stock of your own reading challenges.** Which of the following are reading issues for you? Rank order your top five, with 1 as your most difficult challenge.[10]

___ boredom	___ surroundings	___ vision	___ fear	___ speed
___ fluency	___ comprehension	___ fatigue	___ time	___ level
___ amount	___ retention	___ interest	___ laziness	___ motivation
___ vocabulary	___ attitude toward reading	___ finding the main point	___ estimating reading time	___ reading everything the same way

Many people find reading challenging. You may have worked with an impatient teacher as a youngster, or you may have been taught using a method that didn't work well for you—factors that still cause you problems today. Reading involves visually recognizing symbols, transferring those visual cues to your brain, translating them into meaningful signals—recording, retaining, and retrieving information (here's where your memory kicks in)—and finally using these meanings to think, write, or speak. Reading challenges can be caused by *physical factors* (your vision, for example) and *psychological factors* (your attitude). If you want to become a better reader in the future, it's a good idea to assess honestly what's most challenging about the process for you right now.[11]

3. **Adjust your reading style.** You shouldn't read a magazine (flip through and find something interesting) the same way you scan a quick text message or devour a novel that you just can't put down. Reading requires flexibility. Contrast these two situations: reading the menu on the wall at your local fast-food joint and poring over the menu at a fancy, high-end restaurant. You'd just scan the fast-food menu in a few seconds, wouldn't you? You wouldn't read word by word and ask: "Is the beef in that burger

ESB Professional/Shutterstock.com

"Perhaps the most valuable result of all education is the ability to make yourself do the thing you have to do, when it ought to be done, whether you like it or not."

Thomas Henry Huxley, British biologist (1825–1895)

commentary a record of your opinion

from grass-fed cattle?" "What, exactly, is in the 'special sauce'?" If you did, the counter clerk would probably blurt out, "Look, are you going to order something or not?" That kind of situation requires quick skimming. But you'd take some time to study the menu at a pricy restaurant you might go to with friends and family to celebrate a special occasion. It's an entirely different situation, and the information is more complicated. And if it's a fancy French restaurant, you might even need to ask the definitions of some terms like *canard* (duck) or *cassoulet* (a rich, hearty stew). That kind of situation requires slow, considered study, word by word. You're going to pay for what you choose, and you want the best results on your investment. That's true about college, too. You're investing in your college classes, so reading right is important!

You'll face plenty of reading in your combined college classes. The question is, what's fast food (to carry through with the example) and what's fine dining? According to research on reading, good readers know the difference and adjust their reading styles.[12]

Reading a popular new detective novel is something you could whip through, but reading the first chapter of your philosophy textbook would require more concentration. Likewise, some of the reading you'll do in college is fast food. You just need to skim to get the main points and then move on to the next homework item on your agenda. However, much of the reading you'll do in college is fine dining. That's why it's important to devote more time to reading and studying than you think you'll actually need. You'll be able to "digest" what you're reading much better.

4. **Have a "conversation" with the author.** In every book you read, the author is trying to convince you of something. Take this one, for example. We have been engaged in a conversation all the way through. What do you know about me? What am I trying to persuade you to think about or do? Even though I'm not right in front of you in person on every page, you are forming impressions of me as you read, and I'm either convincing you to try the suggestions in this text or I'm not. As you read any book, argue with the author ("That's not how I see it!"), question her ("What makes you say that?"), agree with her ("Yes, right on!"), relate something she said earlier to something she's saying now ("But what about …?"). Instead of just coloring with your yellow highlighter, scribble comments in the margins, or keep a running commentary in a notebook. Reading is an active process, not a passive one in which the words just float by you. In fact, mark up this page right now! How do you decide what's really important? One thing you can do is ask your instructor in this course to show you his or her mark-ups in this text and see whether the two of you agree on what's important.

5. **Dissect the text.** Whether you did it virtually online or physically in a real lab, dissecting or cutting up those little critters in your biology class helped you figure out what was what. The ability to dissect text is important in reading. As you read and make notes in the margins, write "what" and "why" statements. Try it: beside each paragraph on this page, write a one-sentence summary statement, a "what" statement. Put the author's

words into your own words. Then write another sentence that focuses on why the paragraph is included. Does the paragraph contain *evidence* to make a point? Is it an *example* of something? If you can tackle this recommendation, you'll do wonders for yourself when exam time rolls around.

6. **Make detailed notes.** You'll be much more likely to actually master a challenging reading assignment if you keep a notebook beside you and take full-blown notes as you read. Go back and forth, detailing main points and supporting evidence. Or go online and use a note-taking tool like evernote.com. The old rule of thumb still applies: read, close the book, and write down what you remember. Then go back into the book and check.[13] The physical act of writing or typing can help you remember it later.

7. **Put things into context.** Reading requires a certain level of what's called cultural literacy. Authors assume their readers have a common background. They refer to other books or current events, or historical milestones, and unless you know what they're referring to, what you're reading may not make sense to you. An example you might be familiar with is how the television show *Seinfeld* made real words that everyone now knows and uses, out of fake ones: *yada yada yada*, for example. Those words are now part of our cultural literacy that have meaning for you and everyone you know, probably, but may not for people from another culture. They know the literacy of their own culture instead.

8. **Don't avoid the tough stuff.** Much of the reading you'll do in college includes complicated sentences that are difficult to work your way through. When you read complex passages aloud, you may stumble because you don't immediately recognize how the words are linked into phrases. But practicing reading aloud is one way you can become more conversant with difficult language. Many instructors teach their students a common approach to reading and studying called SQ3R:

   Survey—Skim to get the lay of the land quickly.

   Question—Ask yourself "what," "why," and "how" questions. What is this article or chapter about? Why is it included? How might I use this information?

   Read (1)—Go ahead now and read the entire assignment. Make notes in the margins or even create a study guide for yourself.

   Recite (2)—Stop every now and then and talk to yourself. See whether you can put what you're reading into your own words.

   Review (3)—When you've finished, go back and summarize what you've learned.

   Try it right now with this section of the chapter, "Read Right."

   Survey—What is this section of the chapter about, generally? When you preview a chapter or section of a textbook, look for color, highlighting, italics, layout, bullets—anything that communicates, "This is important!"

cultural literacy core knowledge—things that everyone knows—that helps put things into context and give them meaning

VARK IT!

Multimodal (Kinesthetic/ Aural): Use Google images to find an online cartoon to print out and bring to class. If there is time in class, present the specific aspects of cultural literacy behind the humor.

wavebreakmedia/Shutterstock.com

"Reading is to the mind what exercise is to the body."

Joseph Addison, British politician and writer (1672–1719)

Question—What's the point of including it? Why is it here? How can it help you?

Read (1)—Now read the bullets in this section carefully, making "what" and "why" comments in the margins.

Recite (2)—At the conclusion of each bullet, summarize the point out loud, and decide whether this is an item you should put a check mark next to, indicating that it's something you should work on.

Review (3)—When you're finished with the whole section, see whether you can summarize what you've learned from reading it.

9. **Learn the language.** Every discipline has its own perspective and its own vocabulary. In many of the introductory classes you take, you'll spend a good deal of time and effort learning terms to be used in classes you'll take later. In order to study *advanced* biology, everyone has to learn the same language in *introductory* biology. You can't be calling things whatever you want to call them. You call it a respiratory system, but your classmate calls it a reproductive system. In college you will be introduced to various subjects or disciplines as you take what are often called general education or core courses. It's important to get to know a discipline by learning its relevant vocabulary.

10. **Bring your reading to class.** Some of your instructors will infuse the outside course readings into their lectures. They may preview the readings in class, talk about their importance, or create reading worksheets for use in small groups. If they don't, however, it's up to you to integrate them. Bring up the reading in class, ask questions about it, and find out how it relates to particular points in the lecture. Doing so is an important part of being responsible for your own learning.

11. **Ask for a demonstration.** If a textbook reading assignment for a course baffles you, ask your instructor for a mini-lesson in how to proceed. Sometimes all it takes is for the teacher to give the entire class (or just you) some pointers. For example, the instructor may help you come up with "what" and "why" statements or tell you where she would stop to write something in the notebook she keeps beside her.

12. **Be inventive!** Students who are the best readers invent strategies that work for them. Perhaps you're an auditory learner. Reading assignments aloud might drive people you live with crazy (so find a place where you can be alone), but it might be the perfect way for you to learn. If you're a kinesthetic learner, you might make copies of particular passages from your textbook and lecture notes, and build your own scrapbook for a course. Or cut up the instructor's lecture notes into small puzzle pieces and reassemble them. Using what you know about yourself as a learner is a big part of college success, so don't just do what everyone else does or even follow your instructor's advice word for word, if it doesn't work for you. Figure out what does, and then do it!

CHANNEL CHOOSER

Today's wide array of technology options requires that we choose how to communicate on a minute-by-minute basis. Your grandparents used to make long-distance calls (which were expensive) or write snail-mail letters. Besides talking face-to-face, those were the primary options. Today, you can call someone, fire off a text, send an e-mail or Tweet, or post on Facebook, for example. The particular choices you make send a message about you and whether you are a competent communicator. The bottom-line question is this: Is one channel more appropriate than another for a specific message? Look at the following scenarios, decide which particular communication channel you'd choose for each situation, and then explain why. Here's an example:

A student employee who has worked with you for two years wins a prestigious college award. You want to congratulate her. Which channel would you choose, and why?

a. Phone call

b. Text message

c. E-mail

d. Facebook post

e. Written note

f. Face-to-face conversation

g. Tweet

h. Other

E. I'd send her a handwritten note because that's more personal and special.

Now try some on your own. Be prepared to defend your choices during a class discussion.

1. You need your instructor's approval on the thesis statement you've written for your first essay in English class. You're having trouble coming up with something. _____

2. You want to break up with your romantic partner of six months. You just found out something disappointing that makes you feel hurt and angry. _____

3. You want to let other students know about an exciting campus event this weekend. It is free and open to everyone. _____

4. Your last college tuition bill contained a major error. It's a big mess. _____

5. The low grade you earned on your history paper counted for a large portion of your overall grade and may put you on academic probation. You need to ask your instructor to reconsider. _____

6. You want to tell your boss you're not coming in to work today because something came up. _____

7. You want to thank your favorite professor for a great learning experience this term. _____

WRITE
RIGHT!

Although your reading skills will be critical, they are only one of the several types of communication skills you will need in college. Good writing skills will be essential, too. The question we'll explore next is how to build the writing skills you'll need. If you can do that, you're well on your way to successful outcomes.

An old Doonesbury cartoon may very well hang on the wall in the Writing Center on your campus. It shows two college students. One is tapping away at a typewriter and mutters, "Man, have I got a lot of papers due!" as he types the paper's opening: "Most problems, like answers, have finite resolutions. The basis for these resolutions contain many of the ambiguities which conditional man daily

> "It matters, if individuals are to retain any capacity to form their own judgments and opinions, that they continue to read for themselves."
>
> *Harold Bloom, literary critic*

struggles with. Accordingly, most problematic solutions are fallible. Mercifully, all else fails; conversely hope lies in a myriad of polemics.... " The other student is looking over his shoulder and asks, "Which paper is this?" to which the writer replies, "Dunno, I haven't decided yet." Obviously, cranking out college papers just for the sake of getting them done isn't the best idea. But, unfortunately, it happens.

Why do some students put off writing assignments? Is it because they worked with a cranky writing teacher in the past? Are they afraid of producing something less than perfect? Have they been unsuccessful at previous writing projects? Or, like Katie, do they simply dislike writing? As shown in the cartoon dialogue, it's tempting to start with something so general that it could work for literally any paper. Or you may fall into a boring habit, like starting every paper with the dictionary definition for whatever you're writing about. Or perhaps you don't even get that far. You may simply stare at the blank screen until it's time to do something else and move on.

When you have an important writing assignment to do, how do you get started? Many students just sit down at their computers and start typing at midnight the night before the paper is due—hoping for a flash of inspiration— and thereby end up sabotaging themselves. They avoid the upfront work and rationalize that they work better under pressure or they enjoy the adrenaline rush of a tight deadline. But ask yourself this: Would you invite your girlfriend out for dinner before the prom and then just drive around with her until you find a restaurant that looks inviting? Would you start your vacation by going to the airport and wandering around until you see an alluring destination at one of the gates? Of course not! Why then would you sit down at your computer at midnight and just start typing? Sure, eventually you will have filled enough pages to reach the assignment's required length, but it's not just about quantity; it's about quality. Quality writing takes patience, focus, and attention to detail. Writing and critical thinking are linked. When you write, you're thinking on paper. Doing it well will help you become a better critical thinker and learner in all your courses.[14]

EXERCISE 8.5   GETTING STARTED

The mystery writer Agatha Christie once said, "The secret of getting ahead is getting started." Look at the topics that follow and choose one of them. Spend a few minutes writing the first paragraph for an essay on the topic. Set a timer so that you're forced to commit to something. Give it your best effort, and use correct grammar and spelling. The point of the exercise is to practice getting started, which is sometimes the most difficult part of a writing assignment.

A. Why I will (won't) be quitting Facebook

B. Why I love to read (or don't)

C. Why writing is good therapy (or why writing stresses me out)

D. Why public speaking is (or isn't) my strong suit

Now look back at what you have written. Give your paragraph a grade (based on your own standards). What is the grade based on? Does the writing have a topic sentence that can be identified? Is there a clear thesis statement? Spend a few more minutes trying another option. Practicing the art of getting started (when the threat is low because no real grade will be assigned) can be a helpful exercise.

WRITING
AS A PROCESS

How should the writing process work, ideally? It should involve three basic stages: prewriting, writing, and rewriting.

PREWRITING

Think of this analogy: When you speak, you may not know exactly which words will come out, but you have some idea of what you want to say before you open your mouth, right? Just as you prethink what you're going to say, you must prewrite what you're going to put down on paper. In order to do that, you must ask yourself questions like these:

1. **What is the assignment asking me to do?** Let's say one assignment asks you to summarize interviews with three English instructors on campus to find out what makes them effective teachers. And another assignment asks you to compare and contrast teaching English with teaching math. You'd go about these two writing papers differently. Zero in on the verbs in the assignment—*summarize* versus *compare* and *contrast*, in this case. The specifics of the assignment must be crystal clear to you, and if you're given a choice of topic, pick something that really interests you.

2. **Who is my audience, and what do I want them to know or do?** You write differently for different audiences—for your composition class or for your blog on being a college student, for example. If you're writing for your blog readers, you may aim for catchy phrasing, short sentences, and an intriguing title. Once you know who you're writing to or for, then you can ask: *What do I want them to know? Am I trying to inform, persuade, or entertain them?* You'll write differently, depending on your specific purpose.

3. **Can I compose a strong thesis statement?** Your paper's thesis statement should be the specific argument you're making, summarized into one sentence, ideally. For example, in your paper about good teaching, you might begin with a thesis statement like, "Being a good English teacher requires knowledge, patience, and enthusiasm." Formulating a strong thesis is half the battle.

4. **Have I done enough research?** If you've followed the guidelines provided in your instructor's handout about the assignment, ask: Do I have enough support for my thesis? Have I gathered enough statistics, expert testimony, and examples to persuade my reader?

5. **Set in-between target dates for the three stages of writing, even if your instructor doesn't.** Some instructors will ask to see your work at each stage of the writing project. If you try to print your paper at 9:50 A.M. for your 10 A.M. class, you can count on something going wrong, like your printer cartridge shriveling up or your hard drive plummeting to an untimely death. To beat the odds, schedule in-between deadlines for yourself for prewriting, writing, and rewriting to keep the project moving along.

"Start writing, no matter what. The water does not flow until the faucet is turned on."

Louis L'Amour, writer about the American West (1908–1988)

thesis your main points, summed up in a sentence (or two); what you intend to "prove" in your paper

"Finis origine pendet (The end depends on the beginning.)"

Manlius, first century Roman poet

WRITING

Have you ever experienced writer's block, or nowadays, the "tyranny of the blank screen"? You sit down to write and suddenly go blank? Whatever you call it, you'll be relieved to know there are ways around it.

Some professional writers resort to downright weird strategies to get themselves going. Victor Hugo supposedly wrote in his study at the same time every day—naked! His servant was ordered to lock away all Hugo's clothes until he had finished each day's writing.[16] Apparently, the method worked—look at *Les Misérables*. The paperback version has 1,456 pages! But this technique may not be well received by the people you live with. Just write freely about whatever comes into your head, whether it's on target or not. But how do you start doing that? Take a look at these techniques for starting the writing process.

1. **Begin by writing what's on your mind.**

   I'm having trouble starting this paper because there's so much to talk about in terms of good teaching. When I think back over all the English teachers I've ever had, a few really stand out. Mrs. Hampton, in seventh grade, was definitely the worst teacher ever, but Mr. Evans, in eighth grade, was the complete opposite. Just what was it that made him so good? I think it was his knowledge, patience, and enthusiasm. Maybe identifying these three characteristics will help me decide what makes a good English instructor in college.

   Now stop and look at what you've written. Based on your "stream of consciousness," you now have the beginnings of a paper about how being a teacher requires knowledge, patience, and enthusiasm. You're on your way.

2. **Begin with the words, "The purpose of this paper is . . ."** and finish the sentence. You may be surprised by what comes out of your fingertips.

3. **Work with a tutor in your campus Writing Center.** Sometimes talking through the assignment with someone else can help, particularly if that person is a writing expert. Or talk it through with a family member.

4. **Change the audience.** If it helps, assume you're writing your paper to someone who sharply disagrees with you or to a middle school student who just asked you a question. Sometimes thinking about your audience—instead of the topic in the abstract—helps you zero in on the writing task.

5. **Play a role.** Imagine yourself as a nationally-known education guru or a network newscaster deciding what to include on the evening news. Separate yourself from the task, and see it from another perspective.

REWRITING

Rewriting is often called "revision," and that's a powerful term. It means not merely changing, but literally re-seeing, re-en*vision*ing your work. Sometimes students think they're revising when they're actually just editing: tinkering with words and phrases, checking spelling, changing punctuation. But the word revision actually means more than that. It means making major organizational overhauls, if necessary. According to many writing experts, that's what you must be willing to do. You're on a search and destroy mission, if that's what it takes.[17] Try these suggestions for rewriting to see whether they work for you:

1. **Leave it alone.** To help you see your paper as others will see it, set it aside for a while. If you can wait an hour, a day, or a weekend before revising, you'll have distanced yourself long enough to see your writing for what it is, and then improve it. Of course, this suggestion isn't meant to serve as an excuse for a late paper ("I couldn't turn my paper in today because I need to wait before I rewrite."). That won't fly. But coming back later can provide "Aha!" moments. (*What? I wrote that? What was I thinking?*)

2. **Ask for feedback.** One way of discovering how your writing will affect others is simply to ask them. Share your writing before it becomes final.

3. **Edit ruthlessly!** Cutting a favorite phrase or section may feel like lopping off an arm or a leg. But sometimes it must be done. The goal here is to produce the best paper possible, even if it's painful!

4. **Decide on an organizational format.** If you were writing about the three qualities of good English instructors, you'd want to use a *topical* format. Your paper would be organized into three major chunks. If you were writing about the differences between good English instructors and good math instructors, you'd use a *compare and contrast* format. If you were going to present solutions to other instructors about the problems in making English and math classes more exciting, you'd use a *problem-solution* format. Decide how best to present your information, and then follow the format you choose.

5. **Proofread, proofread, proofread!** You may think you have just written an unbelievable essay, but if it's full of mistakes, your instructor may pay more attention to those than to your paper's brilliant ideas. Sometimes it also helps proofread out loud. Somehow, hearing the words, especially if you're an aural learner, makes errors more obvious. Be proud of the document's final appearance—paper clean, type dark and crisp, margins consistent, headings useful, names and references correct, no spelling errors. And remember that spellcheck, for all its convenience, can let you down. If the word you use is an actual one, but not the right on, it will give its approval, regardless. (Did you catch the spelling error in that last sentence? Spellcheck didn't.)

One more tip. Throughout these three stages, be prepared to move fluidly from one to the other at the slightest provocation. If you're rewriting and you come across some prewriting information (as in *new research*) copy it down and fit it in. If in the prewriting stage you think of writing that strikes you as powerful—a good argument or a well-constructed phrase—write it down.[18]

Take a look at this first-year student's essay and offer the writer advice.

Assignment: Describe a problem you have faced as a first-year student and identify a possible solution.

Last summer, I worked for a bank in my hometown to earn money for college. I was told to show up for the interview at 8:30 A.M. I usually don't get up that early, so on Thursday night, I set my alarm clock, my cell phone alarm, and my clock radio to make sure I didn't miss it. Afterward, I thought that I had really hit it off with the interviewer. When I first got the job on a Friday, I was thrilled. Imagine me working for a bank! I thought that sounded like a prestigious job. When I told my Dad about getting the job, he said that he thought banks really shouldn't hire young people because they don't know the value of money. I decided he was probably kidding around.

But after my first week at Citizen's National Bank, I found myself bored stiff. Counting bills and tallying numbers really aren't that interesting. I did meet this girl named Nicole, and she was kind of cool, but everyone else at the bank was a little standoffish, including my supervisor, Ned. I didn't want to have a strained relationship with my boss, so I was friendly with him and serious about getting my work done. But by the following Wednesday, I was ready to quit. I heard about an opening at the coffee shop close to my house that included free food. So that's where I ended up. The moral of this story is to only take a job if you are really interested in the work. And I've definitely decided not to major in accounting.

What's the main problem with this essay? The writer has written about a problem she faced as a first-year student. The essay contains no grammatical errors. But is it likely to earn an A? What is the writer's thesis statement? Instead of telling a story from start to finish, how would the essay change if the writer had asked a question like this: What mistakes do students make when looking for a job to help them pay for college?

BUILD A BETTER PAPER: THE SEVEN C'S

Myron Jay Dorf/Corbis/Getty Images

"I must write it all out, at any cost. Writing is thinking. It is more than living, for it is being conscious of living."

Anne Morrow Lindbergh, American writer and aviation pioneer (1906–2001)

In many ways, writing is like building. But instead of using nails, planks, and sheetrock to construct our communication, we use words, sentences, and paragraphs. Here are seven suggestions—all of which begin with C to help you remember them.[19]

1. **Be Clear.** Unfortunately, the English language gives you endless opportunities to write something quite different from what you mean. You can flip through your thesaurus and use a word that sounds good, but isn't recognizable (as in *profundity*, which follows), or you can write a convoluted sentence that can't be understood. Compare the problems in these two sentences, both of which are unclear:

   ➤ *The profundity of the quotation overtook its author's intended meaning.*

   ➤ *The writing was profound, but on closer examination, not only was it devoid of content but it was also characterized by a preponderance of flatulent words.*

   Yes, many of us will be able to figure out what these sentences mean, though perhaps we'll need to check the dictionary. Sometimes beginning college students decide they must write to *impress* rather than to *express*. They assume instructors like this kind of complicated writing. They think it sounds more academic. Instructors see through that trick. Mean what you say, and say what you mean.

2. **Be Complete.** Ask yourself what your reader needs to know. Sometimes we're so close to what we're writing that we leave out important information, or we fail to provide the background the reader needs to get our meaning. Put yourself in your reader's shoes (or in this case, eyes).

3. **Be Correct.** If your writing has many grammatical, spelling, and punctuation errors, readers may get the sense that you don't know what you're writing about either. If grammar and punctuation aren't your strong points, ask someone you know who's a crackerjack writer to look over your first draft.

4. **Be Concise.** In the past, you may have used tricks like enlarging the font or increasing the margins to fill an assigned number of pages. But college students sometimes face the opposite problem: They find that writing less is more challenging than writing more. Think of this formula: A given idea expressed in many words has relatively little impact. But that same idea expressed in few well-chosen and well-combined words can stick in your memory. You could say:

"Whether or not a penny, or any amount of money, is earned or saved, it has the same or at least a similar value, fiscally speaking, in the long run."

Compare that writer's tendency to "run off at the mouth" with Ben Franklin's concise expression:

"A penny saved is a penny earned."

5. **Be Compelling.** Your writing should be interesting, active, and vivid, so that people want to read what you have to say. Compare these two headlines. Which article would you want to read?

   ➤ *Protests against tuition increases have been led by community college student leaders.*

   ➤ *Student leaders urge campus-wide protests over tuition hikes.*

   The sentences create different images, don't they? The first sentence makes the situation sound like something that happens every day. The second sentence uses the active voice (*leaders urge campus-wide protests*) instead of the passive voice (*protests have been led*), and the second sentence uses a more descriptive verb (*urge* versus *lead*) and noun (*hikes* versus *increases*). Of course, you can go too far (*Campus leaders spearhead fiery student fury over radical tuition upsurge*). But this principle is a good one to remember.

6. **Be Courteous.** Courtesy is important in any kind of writing. E-mail and texts are often places where people are discourteous to one another in writing—perhaps because distance gives them courage or they're just plain cranky. Having a meltdown on paper or your computer screen is rarely the right choice.

7. **Be Convincing.** You'll be a more successful writer if you support your views with solid evidence and credible testimonials. Give specific examples to illustrate your point—anecdotes, testimonials from experts, experiences, analogies, facts, statistics—and your writing will be more persuasive.

> "I am returning this otherwise good typing paper to you because someone has printed gibberish all over it and put your name at the top."
>
> *English Professor, Ohio University*

VARK IT!

Aural: Read the essay in Exercise 8.6 aloud. When you listen to it, is it easier to identify its major problem?

BOX 8.1 **PAPER SUBMISSION CHECKLIST**

Before you turn in a written assignment, make sure you go through this checklist. Consider it to be "insurance" that your paper is fully ready. If you checked the "No" box for any item, explain why. For example, if you checked "no" for item 3 under "Structure," you might write that the assignment required your opinion, rather than research.

STRUCTURE

	Yes	No
1. Did you use a normal-sized font (12-point) and one-inch margins?	☐	☐
2. Did you follow APA or MLA stylesheet rules if doing so was a part of your assignment?	☐	☐
3. Did you include a list of references (bibliography)?	☐	☐
4. Did you number the pages, as instructed, format the title page correctly, and so on?	☐	☐

CONTENT

	Yes	No
1. Reread the assignment. Did you do what the assignment asked you to do?	☐	☐
2. Did you write for the appropriate audience? (Are you writing for your instructor or for another student or group of students, for example?)	☐	☐
3. Does your paper have a clear thesis statement?	☐	☐
4. Did you do enough research?	☐	☐
5. Circle the organizational pattern you used: problem–solution, chronological, topical, cause and effect, other (please explain).		
6. Is your writing clear, complete, correct, concise, compelling, courteous, and convincing? Circle the "C's" that are particularly strong.	☐	☐

PROCESS

	Yes	No
1. Have you received feedback on your paper, either formally from a campus Writing Center tutor or informally from someone you know who is a good writer?	☐	☐
2. Have you edited your paper after reading and rereading it (after allowing some time to pass), or after reading it aloud?	☐	☐

3. Other (as indicated by your instructor): _____

4. Based on the grading criteria your instructor has discussed for this paper, what grade would you assign it? Why? Ⓐ Ⓑ Ⓒ Ⓓ Ⓕ

serpetko/Shutterstock.com

"A C essay is an A essay turned in too soon."

John C. Bean, Professor of English, Seattle University

Keep these seven C's in mind. The secret to learning to think in college is to become a better writer. As you're learning critical thinking skills, you'll also become a more clear, complete, correct, concise, compelling, courteous, and convincing writer.

IN A
MANNER OF SPEAKING . . .

When your assignment involves a presentation, instead of or in addition to, a paper, your public speaking skills will be on the line. You may be thinking something like this: *I'm not going to be a public speaker. I'm going to be a surgeon. I'll spend all my time hunched over an unconscious person lying on an operating table. All I'll need to know how to do is hold a scalpel with a steady hand.* But is that really true? What about the communicating you'll need to do with totally conscious hospital administrators, other doctors, and patients before and after surgery?

Most people think of public speaking as an episode, a one-time event. You stand up to give a speech, and when you're finished, you sit down. But actually, there's a sense in which all the speaking we do is public. By contrast, what would *private* speaking be? Thinking? On the job, you'll communicate with others every day. Unless you join a profession that requires you to take a vow of silence, you'll be speaking publicly all the time!

When you prepare for a presentation in one of your classes, what is your primary goal? To impress your instructor? To amaze your classmates? To get your presentation over with? (If the thought of giving a presentation makes you uneasy, see Figure 8.1, Quick Study: 9 Ways to Hack Your Speaking Anxiety.) How about to give the very best presentation you can give as your goal?

Many of the suggestions in this chapter apply to both writing and speaking. As both a writer and a speaker, you should be clear, complete, correct, concise, compelling, courteous, and convincing. You should choose an organizational pattern and use it to help your audience understand what you're saying. (Unlike reading a written paper, they only have one chance to hear your words go by.) You must have a strong thesis in a speech, just as you must in a paper. But let's examine some other advice that relates primarily to speaking. Use these suggestions to create winning presentations that set you apart in all your courses.[20]

1. **Purpose.** What is the purpose of your presentation? Often the purpose is given to you directly by your instructor: Prepare a five-minute speech *to inform.* . . . But other assignments will allow you to select your own purpose: "The Trials and Tribulations of a Student Mom" (to inform), "Sustainability in an Age of Materialism" (to persuade), "Five Sure-Fire Ways to Flunk Out of College . . . Not!" (to entertain), "How Being in Charge Can Change Your Life" (to inspire). Knowing exactly what you're trying to accomplish helps!

2. **People.** Who will be your listeners? Generally, you'll be speaking to an audience of students in your classes, right? But what are their specific characteristics as they relate to your purpose? For example, if you're addressing parents and friends at graduation, you might create a different speech than the one you'd present to your co-members of a student club.

3. **Place.** Where will you deliver your presentation? The location of your presentation may affect its tone and style. A presentation you might give

> "What's another word for Thesaurus?"
>
> —*Steven Wright, American comedian*

> "There is no greater agony than bearing an untold story inside you."
>
> **Maya Angelou, *I Know Why the Caged Bird Sings* (1928–2014)**

FIGURE 8.1

Quick Study "9 Ways to Hack Your Speaking Anxiety"

9 WAYS TO HACK YOUR SPEAKING ANXIETY

High anxiety—the curse of many a speaker. Doing your best on a writing assignment or business report can certainly generate stress. But when you give a presentation—an even more personal, more immediate look at you and your work—there you are, up front, all eyes on you. By harnessing your anxiety and looking forward to opportunities to speak, you'll build more confidence and you'll get better at doing it. See whether you think these fear-suppressing hacks might work for you.

First ask: Where does your anxiety come from?

The situation?	The audience members?	The stakes?
Did you plan to give a speech? Are you ready?	Sometimes it's harder to give a speech to your peers or co-workers than it is to strangers. Who **are** these people?	Is your presentation for a grade or will it affect your reputation on the job? If the stakes are high, your anxiety may go up accordingly.

Then: Try these strategies.

Admit It

Giving presentations makes most people nervous. That's the honest truth. You're not the exception, so accept the anxiety you're feeling.

To be perfectly honest...

Trick Yourself

On the other hand, tell yourself it's not so much anxiety you're feeling as excitement. You're pumped. This is your chance to show what you know. Introducing yourself to some people before you start can help spark positive energy.

Ready, Set, Go

Being unprepared will cause your anxiety to skyrocket, and winging it won't help your presentation fly! The best antidote to anxiety is to prepare, prepare, prepare!

Dress for Success

Confidence in your physical appearance can increase your confidence overall. Dress up a little—don't just wear a tee shirt. Show the audience they're worth the extra effort!

Find Some Guinea Pigs

To prepare yourself for natural distractions, like people coughing or sneezing, practice in front of your best friend or your family. Research indicates that your grades (or results) are likely to improve.[a]

Lighten Up

Humor can ease tensions, both for your audience and for you. But say something funny that occurs to you at the moment, rather than repeating a joke you read on the internet.

Don't Be a Mannequin

Move around. Use gestures. Look at your audience. Talk as if you were having a conversation with each person in the room individually. Be real, be yourself, and let your personality shine through.

Don't Let a Mistake Throw You

If you make a "tip of the slongue" or there's a technology hitch with your visual aid, remember that how you handle it is what's important. Don't worry; instead, make the most of a few moments of lightheartedness and laugh it off!

Fake It

If you can't shake it, fake it. If your nerves get the better of you, tough it out. Pretend you're confident. Before you know it, your confidence may actually rise to the occasion!

Source: (a) Smith, T. E., & Frymier, A. B. (2006). Get "real": Does practicing speeches before an audience improve performance? *Communication Quarterly*, 54(1), 111–125.

to a group of tourists at a national park would allow you to be informal, and your visual aid would be the scenery around you. But if you gave the same presentation as a geography major to high school seniors, you'd be more formal and scholarly, using a PowerPoint presentation or maps in the classroom.

4. **Preparation.** How should you prepare your speech? Developing the content of a speech is often similar to writing a paper. You'll need to develop a thesis statement and find support for each point by researching examples, statistics, and expert testimonies. Depending on the assignment, you might write out your speech or create a set of PowerPoint slides with talking points. Or you may find it helpful to create a storyboard, a map, or flowchart of your slides on paper before moving to the screen (see Figure 8.2). Then, after you know your basic format, you'll need to come up with an attention-grabbing introduction and a

life hack #3

When you're asked a tough question in public, and you have to give an answer off the top of your head, use the **PREP** formula to structure your answer. Make your **P**OINT, give a **R**EASON for it, provide an **E**XAMPLE, and restate your **P**OINT. It's a quick way to sound organized and intelligent.[21]

FIGURE 8.2

Storyboarding a PowerPoint

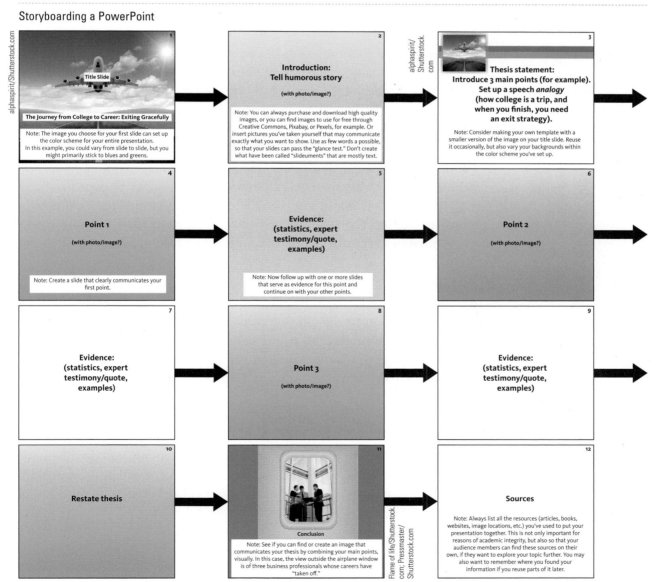

iStock.com/Baran Özdemir

memorable conclusion. Or think about it this way: One of the best ways to prepare is to make sure your presentation is SHARP. SHARP stands for <u>s</u>tories, <u>h</u>umor, <u>a</u>nalogies ("this" is like "that"), <u>r</u>eferences (or quotes), and <u>p</u>ictures/visuals.[22] SHARP is a good formula for a successful presentation, one that your audience will remember. Imagine that you decided to give a presentation about "exiting from college and finding a job." You might start with a horrendous story (S) about a plane trip you just took, where you ran through three airports but missed all three connections (H); compare a plane trip to the journey in college toward a "career destination" (A); include the quote "Map out your future, but do it in pencil. The road ahead is as long as you make it. Make it worth the trip" (Jon Bon Jovi); and include this photo you took with your cell phone camera on the plane.[23] You'd have the makings of a very SHARP presentation.

"The trouble with talking too fast is you may say something you haven't thought of yet."

Ann Landers, syndicated advice columnist (1918–2002)

5. **Planning.** What planning should you do? For example, are visual aids available, or do you need to bring your own? Is there a plug in the room, if you need one? Should you bring a backup of your presentation on a flash drive? Should you test the LCD projector to make any necessary adjustments? Many a speaker has been unnerved at the last minute by some overlooked detail.

6. **Personality.** How can you connect with the audience? How can you demonstrate your competence, charisma, and character to your listeners? Eye contact is important. Look at each person individually, if possible. Inspire trust by telling a story or relating your topic to some aspect of your own experience. Rather than playing a role, act natural and be yourself.

7. **Performance.** This last P relates to delivering your presentation. Rehearsal is important (although too much rehearsal can make your presentation sound singsongy and memorized). Beware of bringing a full written draft to the podium. If you do, you may be tempted to read it, which is the last thing you want to do. Aim for a dynamic delivery, both verbally and nonverbally, that helps keep your listeners listening.

One final thing: After you've finished a paper or presentation, you're not really done. It's time to sit back and think about what you've accomplished. Are you pleased with your work? What have you learned? What will you do differently next time? If you do this every time you finish a project, you'll build your skills over time and take them with you to your other college classes, a university, or the world of work.

If you ask Guy Fieri the "WIIFM" question about why to develop your speaking skills, you're likely to get an earful. He's big, bold, brazen, colorful, and hugely popular in some circles. And not only is he a strong community college advocate, he's also likely to tell you that he's a "talker," and that it has served him well as one of those people who was "born to cook and talk." *Well, he's had some lucky breaks*, you might think. But there's more to it than that.

Unless you were born with a "silver spoon" in your mouth, you have to work at a job to get food to put on the spoon (as well as buy the spoon itself). Everyone has some kind of job, and speaking on the job will take up more time than you can possibly imagine right now. Of course, you'll also be reading (1.4 million books are published each year) and writing (more than 205 billion e-mails are sent each day, which the average worker checks 74 times per day),[24] and sending Tweets (500 million sent each day).[25]

However, beyond engaging in these other communication activities, you may not "talk" on television like Guy, but you can count on speaking informally on a daily basis much of the time, and speaking formally occasionally—maybe even regularly. You may be thinking, *Not me. All this stuff about speaking doesn't really relate to me because of the field I'm going into*. Okay, so honestly, when are you ever going to have to give a real speech later in your eventual career? Probably never! But wait. If you are planning to be a politician, teacher, attorney, or corporate CEO, then you might actually be required to give speeches from time to time. However, most other careers are exempt, right? Why would a nurse, a chef, an automobile mechanic, or a CSI ever need to know how to give a speech?

Actually, it's easy to come up with reasons why people in those professions need

good communication skills. Can you picture a nurse advising a team of doctors about a patient's condition or updating the family after surgery? Can you envision a chef explaining the evening's specials to the wait staff? Can you imagine a mechanic clarifying why a repair bill is so high to a customer? Or a CSI briefing the police about lab results? The fact of the matter is that every day, no matter which career you choose, you'll be making a case to someone about something, and the better your communication skills are, the more successful you'll be. Speaking well is everyone's job. "If you know, or can learn to, effectively convey your ideas to those around you, you'll be more successful. It's really that simple. From the words you choose to the subject lines of your emails, how effectively you communicate can be a benefit or roadblock to your career."[26]

What you may not realize is that any time you're required to speak in front of other people, they will form conclusions about your overall competence based on what you say and how you say it. Beyond daily informal speaking opportunities in most careers, think about this. Successful people in any profession may become spokespersons. Celebrities like Bono, Denzel Washington, Ali G, Sean "Puff Daddy" Combs, and even Kermit the Frog have been invited to give commencement addresses to thousands of people. These performers would hardly consider themselves to be professional speakers. Neither would scientists, activists, and other less known speakers, like Paul Hawkins, environmentalist; Donovan Livingston, graduate student; William Foege, an epidemiologist who helped eradicate smallpox; and Diana Nyad, long-distance swimmer and author. But their success in one arena brought invitations to publicly share their advice. Chances are you'll give plenty of presenta-

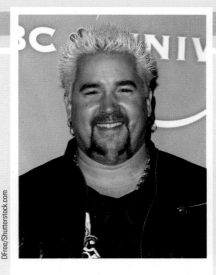

DFree/Shutterstock.com

"Some people are just born to cook and talk."

Guy Fieri, celebrity chef and host of TV's Diners, Drive-ins, and Dives *(attended College of the Redwoods and American River College in California, transferred to University of Nevada, Las Vegas)*

tions later on, regardless of which career field you enter. Think of it that way.

So what makes communication effective or ineffective? On a day-to-day, minute-by-minute basis, you make choices about how to communicate. Sometimes the choices are intentionally thought through, and sometimes they are quick, thoughtless reactions. It's easy to lapse into long-time speaking habits, "like, you know, so, uh whatever," or **BLURT OUT** something before thinking through the possible consequences. The choices you make count.

Knowing how to speak successfully on the job (or off) is a tough challenge, but knowing how brings huge positive results. Having the ability to organize your thoughts, capture other people's attention, and get a message across with clarity and impact is one of the best skill sets anyone can develop. Whether you're speaking publicly to an audience of a thousand or you're communicating privately with your instructor, your BFF, your hair stylist, or your romantic partner, your communication skills are key to your success in life.

Let's look at a few small, everyday examples. Perhaps you'd really like to get your money back on an item, but to have a chance at that, you need to present your best argument to the store clerk. Let's say the purchase you're trying to return is past the 30-day return policy. Can you make it happen? Or consider this: Great hairstylists are more than just "shear" experts; they explain hairstyle options so that customers get the results they're hoping for. The more communication

skills they have, the better. "This isn't the look I was going for at all! I said 'short,' but there's more hair on the floor than there is on my head!" is the last thing a stylist would want to hear. Or assume you're having a room repainted in your house, in which case, you need good communication with your service provider. By specifying "I'd like celery green," you avoid walking into a neon green living room later that week. Your day-to-day life is chock full of examples in which your speaking skills can make or break you.

Good communication is good communication, period. Perhaps you can't look

into a crystal ball now and see yourself giving a presentation in front of a large group of people on the job. Maybe that kind of opportunity is nowhere on your radar, but it just might be later. You may want to (or have to) accept challenges like these when the opportunities present themselves. The more informed you are about making good choices, the more successful you'll become at reaching your goals. Some people say the quality of your communication directly affects the quality of your life. An overstatement? Hardly. WIIFM? In that case, everything!

BOX 8.2

POWERPOINT OR POWERPOINTLESS? FIVE WAYS TO MAKE YOUR POWERPOINT POP

College presentations usually involve visual aids, often electronic ones. These e-tools can serve as helpful cues for you during your presentation. Although you'd never want to simply read your slides to an audience, glancing quickly at a slide can serve as a cue card and remind you of what you want to say. But how professionally your visual aids are created and used can make or break your presentation—and your grade. Your instructor may allow you to use Keynote (for Macs), Prezi (an online tool that moves and shows the relationships between concepts), or PowerPoint, the industry standard. Each of these tools has pros and cons, but the one we'll concentrate on here is PowerPoint. PowerPoint is a neutral tool. How you use it makes all the difference. Bulleted words or phrases with the same PowerPoint background, one after the other, aren't nearly as engaging as SHARP ones, Prezi's (prezi.com), or Keynote presentations delivered from your iPad, using an iPhone app as a slide advancer. Start to perfect your skills now by considering these five ways to make your PowerPoint "pop."

1. **DO use your whole brain.** When it comes to designing PowerPoint presentations, the challenge is to combine useful information with attractive design. Think of it as using both sides of your brain—your logical left hemisphere and your creative right hemisphere. For example, if you're giving a presentation on teaching young children, you might want to use a font that looks like this (children's writing) on your title slide. (Just make sure it's legible from a distance. A good rule of thumb is to use 24-point font size or larger and

keep your fonts simple unless you have a particular reason to change them.) You also might want to include a high-quality graphic like this one here.

ardni/Shutterstock.com

2. **DO use color to your advantage.** Choose an attractive color scheme and stick to it. That doesn't mean that every background on every slide must be the same. In fact, if you do that, your listeners may die of boredom. But if your title slide is blue, orange, and white, then use one, two, or all three of these colors in some hue or shade on every slide. Some speakers create PowerPoint presentations that seem fragmented and messy because the individual slides aren't connected visually.

3. **DON'T crowd your slides with text.** Your listeners won't pay attention to you if they're spending all of their time reading bullets. Be kind, and spare them the trouble by limiting the text on your slides. Some of the most deadly PowerPoint presentations are those in which the speaker turns around, faces the screen, and flies through slide after slide. The only way your listeners can live through that is if oxygen masks drop from the overhead compartments! When it comes to presentations, images can pack more punch than words.

4. **DON'T let your slides steal the show.** Always remember that YOU are the speaker. Your slides shouldn't be so fascinating that your audience ignores you. Gunshots and screaming sirens shouldn't be used as sound effects unless, of course, you're speaking on gun control or ambulance response times. Any special effects should be used sparingly to make a point, rather than to shock your listeners.

5. **DO include a bibliography slide, both for words and images.** Some students assume that plagiarism only pertains to writing papers. Not so! Always give credit where credit is due. List your references, either on individual slides (if you use a direct quote, cite it) or on one slide at the end.

CURIOSITY: HINTS ON PRONUNCIATION FOR FOREIGNERS

I take it you already know
Of laugh and bough and cough and dough?
Others may stumble but not you,
On hiccough, thorough, laugh and through.
Well done! And now you wish, perhaps,
To learn of less familiar traps?

Beware of heard, a dreadful word
That looks like beard and sounds like bird,
And dead: It's said like bed, not bead—
For goodness' sake don't call it "deed"!
Watch out for meat and great and threat
(They rhyme with suite and straight and debt.)

A moth is not a moth in mother
Nor both in bother, broth in brother
And here is not a match for there
Nor dear and fear for bear and pear,
And then there's dose and rose and lose—
Just look them up—and goose and choose,
And cork and work and card and ward,
And font and front and word and sword,

And do and go and thwart and cart—
Come, come, I've hardly made a start!
A dreadful language? Man alive.
I'd mastered it when I was five.

T.S. Watt

Go ahead. Try reading the preceding poem aloud. Even if English is your first language, you probably had to pause and think about how to say a word occasionally. Most anyone would. English isn't exactly the easiest language in the world to learn, non-native English speakers say. It's filled with perplexing irregularities. Think about the raw courage it would take to pursue a college degree by reading and writing in a language other than your native tongue. If English is your first language, could you do it in German or Arabic or Hindi? That being acknowledged, what strategies can ESL (English as a second language) students use to help with challenging reading assignments?

1. Remember that spoken English differs from the written English you'll find in textbooks and academic articles. In casual conversation, you'll hear, "And she's … like, 'Wow!' and I'm . . . like, 'Really?'" If you read that in a book, you'd have no idea what the speakers were communicating about. But if you're standing next to the conversationalists in the hallway, you have a chance of figuring it out. Learning to speak informally in conversation is very different from learning to read scholarly discourse. When you read, there's no body language to rely on or real-live author around to whom you can address questions.

2. Ask your English-speaking friends and instructors to coach you. For example, ESL speakers sometimes struggle with the hundreds of idioms found in English. Idioms are

groups of words with a particular, nonliteral meaning. For example, "I have a frog in my throat" means your voice is hoarse, not that you literally have swallowed a green amphibian. Considering how many idioms English has and how freely English speakers use them without consciously thinking about it, non-native speakers may find learning them all to be a challenge.

3. Use the internet or an online course to improve your language skills. According to one study, international students in an online course made significant gains in their language skills, compared with a control group of students who sat through the same course in a classroom. Online courses provide good exposure and practice for your reading and writing skills via e-mail, web searching, threaded discussions, and online postings.[27]

4. Try explaining what you're reading to someone else. Talking something through while you're reading, especially with a native English speaker, can help you clarify meanings on the spot—and may help the other student achieve better comprehension, too.

5. Mark up the textbook so that you can pursue difficult passages in greater detail later. Insert question marks in the margin. Read with your English–native tongue dictionary in front of you. If you get completely stuck, find another book that may explain the concepts differently.

If you're a native English speaker, what can you learn from strategies intended for ESL students?

At the beginning of this chapter, Katie Alexander, a frustrated and disgruntled student, faced a challenge. Now after reading this chapter, would you respond differently to any of the questions you answered about the "FOCUS Challenge Case"? Using what you learned in the chapter, write a paragraph ending to Katie's case study. What are some of the possible outcomes for Katie?

ACTION: YOUR PLANS FOR CHANGE

1. What, in particular, from this chapter will you put to the test immediately in some other class?

2. In what ways might the information in this chapter help you become more successful in this class? What results are you expecting and how will you achieve them?

CHALLENGE: REALITY CHECK

HOW MUCH DID YOU LEARN?

At the beginning of this chapter, you filled out a "Readiness Check" that asked how you thought this chapter would relate to you, and how you would relate to it. Now, fill out this "Reality Check" to find out.

1. This chapter discusses several reasons why reading skills are important. Can you identify one of them?

2. What does *SQ3R* stand for?

3. Identify the three stages involved in the writing process.

4. List three of the seven "P" items to consider in order to give better presentations.

5. How long did it take? _____ hours _____ minutes. Before you began this chapter, you were asked to predict how long it would take you to complete it (total time, even if you read it in more than one sitting). Was your estimate on target, or will you revise it for the next chapter you'll read?

DEVELOPING MEMORY,
TAKING TESTS | **9**

HOW THIS CHAPTER RELATES TO YOU

1. When it comes to memorizing material for tests and taking exams in college, what do you find most challenging, if anything? Put check marks by the phrases that apply to you or write in your answer.

   ☐ Focusing on test material
   ☐ Developing good memorization strategies
   ☐ Going completely blank when I see the test
   ☐ Not showing what I really know on tests
   ☐ Getting nervous about exams
   ☐ _____

2. What is most likely to be your response? Put a check mark by it.

   ☐ I'll be open to learning how to improve my skills.
   ☐ I'll wait and see if this chapter helps me.
   ☐ I'll get help from a support center on campus.
   ☐ Eventually, I'll just figure it out on my own.

3. What would you have to do to increase your likelihood of success? Will you do it this quarter or semester?

HOW YOU WILL RELATE TO THIS CHAPTER

1. What are you most interested in learning about? Put check marks by those topics.

   ☐ How your memory works like a cell phone camera
   ☐ How to improve your memory, using five major techniques
   ☐ Why you should change your thinking about tests
   ☐ What to do before, during, and after a test
   ☐ What text anxiety is and what to do about it
   ☐ How to take different kinds of tests differently
   ☐ How cheating can hurt your chances for success

YOUR READINESS FACTOR

1. How motivated are you to learn more about developing your memory and taking tests in college? (5 = high, 1 = low)?

2. How ready are you to read now? (If something is in your way, take care of it if you can. Zero in and focus.)

3. How long do you think it will take you to complete this chapter? If you start and stop, keep track of your overall time. ____ Hour(s) ____ Minute(s)

Minerva Studio/Shutterstock.com

Kevin Baxter

As he got ready for work one morning, it finally hit him. He took a long, close look at himself in the mirror, and frankly, he didn't like what he saw. Kevin Baxter was a forty-year-old father of three who was dissatisfied with his life. Yes, he earned a decent income as a construction foreman, and yes, his job allowed him to work outdoors. To Kevin, being cooped up in an office from eight to five every day was something he'd always wanted to avoid. Being outdoors, where you could see the sky, feel the sunshine, and breathe fresh air, was what made him feel alive. The world outside was where he wanted to be, yet at the same time, he knew the world inside his head was withering away. Kevin realized he hadn't really learned much since high school. *I feel brain-dead; that's the best way to describe it*, he frequently thought. *I've run out of options, and I'm stuck.*

Clearly, dropping out of college his first semester twenty-two years ago had been the wrong decision for him. But at the time, he'd convinced himself that he wasn't college material. Besides, college had seemed so expensive, and he desperately wanted to be on his own and begin a life with Carol, his high school sweetheart. Unfortunately, that hadn't worked out well, either. Now he was a single dad whose children lived out of state. He very rarely saw them. Nothing had quite turned out as he had planned.

But in a way, his divorce had jolted him into a midlife crisis. He needed to change things, and going back to college to earn a degree in architecture was the right decision for him now. He was sure of it. Working in construction, he frequently saw flaws in the architects' plans, and he'd often come up with better ideas. *This is a chance to start over again,* he thought to himself, *and I'm going to do it right this time.* So at forty, he quit his construction job and enrolled in his county community college. His first-term courses consisted of Introduction to Architectural Design, Introduction to Philosophy, Introduction to Rhetoric and Writing, and Introduction to Art. For Kevin, college would be an introduction to many new things. Underneath it all, he had to admit that he was proud of himself. *Going back to college at forty takes guts,* he congratulated himself. Who knows? He might even transfer to a four-year school to get an engineering degree before it was all over.

But halfway into the term, Kevin's confidence was shaken. Although he'd been a construction foreman on huge projects, after he got his first midterm exam back, he wondered, *Am I too old to learn new things? I keep up with the reading, come*

Buturlimov Pavlo/Shutterstock.com

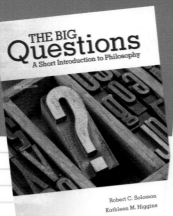

sonya etchison/Shutterstock.com

to every class, do my assignments conscientiously, and study until I'm blue in the face! But things just don't seem to stick. His exam didn't reflect the time he was investing, and frankly, he was embarrassed. Younger students without his years of experience were outperforming him. *That* bothered him. Kevin was getting discouraged about school and his academic capabilities.

Without a doubt, his most challenging class was philosophy. What did Socrates, Plato, Aristotle, Galileo, and Descartes have in common, and what separated them? Philosophy was unlike anything he had ever tried to learn. He'd read a chapter four, five, or six times, and feel sure he knew it, but when he faced the exam, it seemed as if he'd never studied at all. Of course, it didn't help that while he was trying to focus, his kids would call to talk about their problems or text pictures of their sports events. It was getting to the point that exams in any class made him break out in a cold sweat. He just couldn't figure it out. He'd always been known as an unflappable guy, and he never had problems at work remembering details, like ordering materials and managing multiple construction teams. But trying to memorize the differences between Plato,

Aristotle, and Socrates was hard for him, and many of the new terms he was learning didn't really seem to have any relevance to his life. More than once on the exam, he just couldn't come up with a term he thought he had memorized.

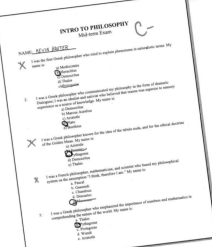

Kevin hated to admit it, but doubts were beginning to creep in. Maybe being a construction foreman was as far as he could ever go in life, and he should have left well enough alone. Maybe college was the last place he should be. Maybe he should have been satisfied with what he'd already achieved, instead of putting everything on the line for more.

Source: Apple Inc./Cengage®, Wallenrock/Shutterstock.com

Course ID	Course Title	Hrs	Days	Meeting Times	Bldg	Room	Meeting Dates	Status	Instructor
ARCH 100	INTRO TO ARCHITECTURAL DESIGN	3.0	T	0500PM-0830PM	SCI BLDG	210	AUG 16 - DEC 16	ENROLLED	FRANKLIN, LAURA
PHIL 101	INTRO TO PHILOSOPHY	3.0	M	0705-1020PM	MAIN HALL	105	AUG 16 - DEC 17	ENROLLED	FREDRICKSON, ALBERT
COMM 180	INTRO TO RHETORIC AND WRITING	3.0	S SU	0800AM-0400PM	MAIN HALL	412	OCT 2 - OCT 23	ENROLLED	WEDDLE, NOE
ART 110	INTRO TO ART	3.0	R	0705-1020PM	MAIN HALL	300	AUG 16 - DEC 17	ENROLLED	DALTON, LEO
	Credit Load:	12.0							

Course Schedule
Community College
FALL SEMESTER
Baxter, Kevin

MEMORY:
THE *LONG* AND *SHORT* OF IT

EXERCISE 9.1 **SUBJECTIVE MEMORY TEST**

How would you rate your memory overall? Please read each of the items below and respond.

A. How often do the following general memory tasks present a problem for you?

	Never		Sometimes		Always
1. Names	1	2	3	4	5
2. Where I've put things	1	2	3	4	5
3. Phone numbers I've just checked	1	2	3	4	5
4. Words	1	2	3	4	5
5. Knowing whether I've already told someone something	1	2	3	4	5
6. Forgetting things people tell me	1	2	3	4	5
7. Faces	1	2	3	4	5
8. Directions	1	2	3	4	5
9. Forgetting what I started to do	1	2	3	4	5
10. Forgetting what I was saying	1	2	3	4	5
11. Remembering what I've done (lock the door, etc.)	1	2	3	4	5

B. How often do the following academic memory tasks present a problem for you?

	Never		Sometimes		Always
12. What I've just been reading	1	2	3	4	5
13. What I read an hour ago	1	2	3	4	5
14. What I read last week	1	2	3	4	5
15. Assignment/exam due dates	1	2	3	4	5
16. Appointments with instructors	1	2	3	4	5
17. Assignment details	1	2	3	4	5
18. Factual information for exams	1	2	3	4	5
19. Theoretical information for exams	1	2	3	4	5
20. Information from readings for exams	1	2	3	4	5
21. Information from in-class lectures for exams	1	2	3	4	5
22. Including everything I should study for exams	1	2	3	4	5

These informal assessments may help you understand your own perception of how well your memory works. The lower your score on each portion, the better you perceive your memory to be. Do your scores for Part A and Part B differ? The general tasks in Part A are presented in the order of concern reported by older adults cited in one study (with the top items perceived as most problematic).[1] Are your priorities similar? Did your numbers drop as you went down the list?

In one study in which college students were asked which aspects of memory they most wanted to improve among general and academic tasks, the top three items were improving schoolwork or study skills, remembering what was read, and remembering specific facts and details.[2] Understandably, the academic aspects of memory were those most personally valued. Is that true for you, too? Are the items in Part B generally higher priorities for you now as a college student?

Most of us may not even realize just how important memory is. We talk about our memories as if they were something we own. We say we have good memories or bad memories, just like we have a crooked smile or a nice one. But no one would ever say, "Hey, that's one nice-looking memory you've got there!" in the same way they'd say, "Wow, you have a really nice smile!" Memory isn't a thing; it's a process. You can't see it or touch it or hold it. Even one specific memory has many different features: You can remember something by what you saw, smelled, heard, or felt. And even within one of these categories, individuals may differ in what they recall. You may be able to hum the movie's theme song, but your friend may remember conversations between the main characters almost word for word.

Don't believe it when someone claims to have a one-size-fits-all, magic formula to help you unlock the secrets of your memory. It isn't that easy. Still, there are techniques that can help you do your best academically. We can only begin to grasp the rich complexities of memory by understanding it as a process. However, it's important to recognize first that mastering memory depends on the answers to several questions like these:[3]

1. **Who is learning?** An algebra instructor and a beginning algebra student would approach memorizing the main points of an article on math differently.

2. **What needs to be learned?** How you learn your lines for a play would differ from how you learn to recognize paintings for your art appreciation test.

3. **How will learning be tested?** Learning information to *recall* uses different memory techniques than learning information to *recognize*. Recognition requires that you select from several possibilities; recall requires that you come up with memorized information on your own.

4. **How long must the information be remembered?** Learning your multiplication tables as a child is something that must remain with you throughout your life. You use it on a daily basis to do routine things like figure how much it will cost you to fill up your gas tank.

mimagephotography/Shutterstock.com

"The existence of forgetting has never been proved: We only know that some things don't come to mind when we want them."

Friedrich Nietzsche, German philosopher (1844–1900)

For a more objective assessment of your memory, try this test. Study the following list of words for up to one minute. Then cover them and see how many you can remember. Write them here.

theory   _____

rehearsal   _____

student   _____

bone   _____

frostbite   _____

camera   _____

rose   _____

calculus   _____

lecture   _____

How many words were you able to remember? Which words did you forget? Unfamiliar words? Words that had no meaning in your life? What memory techniques did you use to help you remember? Specific strategies to help you master your memory are worth learning.

THE THREE R'S OF REMEMBERING:
RECORD, RETAIN, RETRIEVE

Improving your memory is easier if you understand how it works. Memory consists of three parts:

> Your sensory memory

> Your working memory (called short-term memory by some psychologists)

> Your long-term memory

These three parts of the memorization process are connected to these three memory tasks, the "Three R's of Remembering":[4]

> Recording

> Retaining

> Retrieving

We'll compare the three R's of remembering to the process involved when taking pictures with a digital camera: record, retain, retrieve.

YOUR WORKING MEMORY: RECORD

To understand the way your memory works, it may be helpful to use a cell phone camera as a metaphor (Figure 9.1). The first thing you have to do is focus on whatever you want to take a picture of. That's obvious, but it requires that you slow down, clear your mental "deck," and focus. After you've focused your camera on your subject, you're ready to take a picture, right? But with your cell phone camera, you don't just click and walk away. You actually click and then review the picture on the screen to decide whether you want to save it or delete it.

ESB Professional/Shutterstock.com

"I have a photographic memory but once in a while I forget to take off the lens cap."

*Milton Berle, comedian
(1908–2002)*

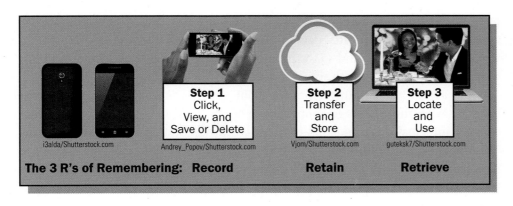

FIGURE 9.1

Your Memory as a Digital Camera

Step 1
Click,
View, and
Save or Delete

Andrey_Popov/Shutterstock.com

Step 2
Transfer
and
Store

Vjom/Shutterstock.com

Step 3
Locate
and
Use

guteksk7/Shutterstock.com

i3alda/Shutterstock.com

The 3 R's of Remembering: **Record** **Retain** **Retrieve**

Similarly, *recording* sensory impressions involves an evaluation process that takes place in your short-term or *working memory*. Your working memory is like a screen, where you review recently acquired sensory impressions. In fact, your working memory is often involved in the focus process.

The problem with working memory is that the length of time it can hold information is limited. You probably don't remember what you ate for dinner last Monday, do you? You'd have to reconstruct the memory based on other clues. Where was I? What was I doing? Who was I with?

The other problem with working memory is that it has limited capacity. It fills up quickly and then dumps what it doesn't need. If you look at a number on a scrap of paper on your desk, you can usually remember it long enough to grab your cell phone, right? A few minutes after you've punched in the number, however, it's gone. Current estimates are that you can keep something in working memory for one to two minutes, giving your brain a chance to do a quick review, selecting what to save and what to delete.[5] Look at these letters and then close your eyes and try to repeat them back in order.

SAJANISMOELIHHEGNR

Can't do it? This task is virtually impossible because the string contains eighteen letters. Researchers believe that working memory can recall only seven pieces of information, plus or minus two.[6] (There's a reason why telephone numbers are prechunked for us.) Chunking these eighteen letters into five units helps considerably. Now look at the letters again and try to recall all eighteen.

SAJA NISM OELI HHEG NR

If we rearrange the letters into recognizable units, it becomes even easier, right?

AN IS MAJOR ENGLISH HE

And if the words are rearranged to make perfect sense, the task becomes simple.

HE IS AN ENGLISH MAJOR

The principle of chunking is also used to move information from your working memory to your long-term memory bank, and it's used in memorization techniques described later in this chapter.

YOUR LONG-TERM MEMORY: RETAIN AND RETRIEVE

Once your camera's memory card or your phone gets full, you probably transfer the photos to your computer, post them online, or you print them out and

VARK IT!

Read/Write: Try another example like the one here to see whether you understand this concept. Can you memorize this list of letters?

HADCEEHISSITHYROESTT

What would make it easier?

put them in photo albums or picture frames. However, before you do that, you generally review the photos, decide how to arrange them, where to put them, whether to print them, and so forth. In other words, you make the photos memorable by putting them into some kind of order or context.

Just as you must transfer photos from your phone to a more permanent location with more storage room (like your laptop or the cloud), you must transfer information from short-term, or working, memory to long-term memory. You retain the information by transferring it, and this transfer takes place if you review and use information in a way that makes it memorable. It is this review process that we use when we study for a test. You transfer information to long-term memory by putting the information into a context that has meaning for you, linking new information to old information, creating stories or using particular memory techniques, or organizing material so that it makes sense. You can frame material you're learning by putting a mental border around it, just as you put pictures into frames.

Your long-term memory is the computer in which you store new knowledge until you need to use it. However, although the memories in long-term memory aren't easily disturbed, they can be challenging to retrieve.[7] Ideally, you'd like your memories to be readily available when you want to retrieve them, just like the pictures or digital images that you have transferred to your laptop, posted online, or put in a photo album. You can click on them to view them again, arrange them into a slideshow, put them on Facebook, Instragram, or Snapchat or send them to your friends as attachments. If you don't do anything or just dump your photos onto your hard drive or print them out and then put them into a box, with no organization or labeling system, how easy will it be to find a specific photo? Difficult, right? Retrieving information from your long-term memory can be equally challenging if you haven't organized your information or created mental labels that will help you retrieve them later. Good recall often depends on having a good storage system. The remainder of this chapter will be about how to *retain* information by transferring it from working memory into long-term memory and how to *retrieve* information when you need to.

"A memory is anything that happens and does not completely unhappen."

Edward de Bono, creative thinking expert and author of Lateral Thinking: Creativity Step by Step

FIVE MAJOR WAYS
TO MASTER YOUR MEMORY

Sometimes it's easy to think that memorization is outdated. If you need information, you just Google it, right? Actually Google isn't always available, and there is information you need to know in school and throughout life, regardless. What can you do to sharpen your memory for the test taking you'll do in college? Try these techniques, grouped into five major categories (to help you remember them), presented in Figure 9.2. As you consider each one, think about what you know about your own learning style preferences. Of course, memorizing means more than simply being able to "regurgitate" back what you've learned. Most exams will supply you with a new problem and ask you to analyze it or apply information you've learned to a new situation. But developing your memory will underlie these tasks, too, so expanding your repertoire of memorization strategies is a major key to doing your best on tests. You can't analyze a new problem if you don't remember how you solved the one you studied.

"Whenever I think of the past, it brings back so many memories."

Stephen Wright, comedian

FIGURE 9.2

Quick Study "Five Major Ways to Master Your Memory"

5 MAJOR WAYS TO MASTER YOUR MEMORY

1. MAKE IT STICK[a]: REHEARSE AND PRACTICE.

- **Rehearse.** Practice makes better. Repeat or reread things.
- **Overlearn.** Practice something so much that it becomes almost second-nature.[b]
- **Space it out.** Instead of studying for multiple hours, break it up. A week before the exam, study an hour a day instead.[c]
- **Separate it.** If you notice two courses have similar content, study one on Mondays and the other on Wednesdays. Or find another way to distinguish the content, like making your own compare and contrast chart.[d]
- **Mind the middle.** People tend to remember what they're introduced to first or last. Information in the middle can get lost unless you pay particular attention to it.[e]

2. MAKE IT MEANINGFUL: ASK "HOW DOES IT RELATE TO ME?"

- **Feel.** Emotions are powerful motivators. If reading a novel for your English class makes you cry or laugh or actually feel fear, your memory can light up.[f]
- **Connect.** Connecting one thing to something you already know helps you know where to "file" it in your brain. "Oh, we talked about this in another class this week. I remember."
- **Personalize.** What does what you're trying to learn have to do with you? Consider how what you're learning relates to your own friendships, people you know, and things you enjoy.

5. MAKE IT FUNNY: BE SILLY AND CREATIVE.

- **Mock it.** Think about how easy it is to remember your favorite comedy scenes. Create a joke about why Shakespeare's tragedies are tragic. To remember the story of Romeo and Juliet, write a silly limerick : *There once was a girl named Cap who fell for a guy and was hap, but her family and his wouldn't stand for the biz so they both ended up playing taps.* Set it to music. Be imaginative. We tend to remember what's bizarre, funny, or even obscene![i]

3. MAKE IT MNEMONIC: USE A PROVEN SYSTEM.

- **Spell.** Acronyms work. RAM stands for your computer's Random Access Memory. The word ASAP, which everyone knows, stands for As Soon As Possible. Shortcuts like these can help us lock in information.
- **Locate.** Sometimes "placing" things can help us remember. If your classmates always sit in the same seats every week, you may learn their names by connecting them with their locations.

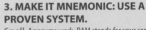

4. MANIPULATE IT: WORK WITH THE MATERIAL.

- **Mark it up.** While reading, write in the margins, highlight things, circle and underline. Actually putting things on paper tells you what you think and feel, instead of ignoring a vague impression.[g]
- **Mark it down.** Sometimes trying to remember something isn't really all that important. In that case, write it down, and then go about your business until you need it.
- **Organize.** You can manipulate and remember information by moving it around. Create a chart or make a timeline, for example.
- **Picture.** Draw a mind map or create an elaborate picture. Visual learners do well with this option.
- **Act.** Put motions to your memorizing. Deliver Martin Luther King's **"I Have Dream"** speech in front of the mirror, as if you were him.
- **Produce.** Put things into your own words.[h] Redeliver the instructor's lecture. Stop while you're reading and explain aloud what you've just read.
- **Test.** Make a practice test for yourself or a classmate. When you do this, you must ask yourself what's important enough to be included. You may just get a preview of the actual test!

Sources: (a) Rozakis, L. (2003). *Test-taking strategies and study skills for the utterly confused.* New York: McGraw Hill; Meyers, J. N. (2000). *The secrets of taking any test.* New York: Learning Express; Ehren, B. J. *Mnemonic devices.* Retrieved from http://onlineacademy.org/modules/a304/support/xpages /a304b0_20600.html; Lloyd, G. (1998–2004). Study skills: Memorize with mnemonics. *Back to College.* Retrieved from http://www.back2college.com/memorize.htm; Raman, M., McLaughlin, K., Violato, C., Rostom, A., Allard, J.P., & Coderre, S. (2010). Teaching in small portions dispersed over time enhances long-term knowledge retention. *Medical Teacher, 32,* 250–255; (b) Willingham, D. T. (2004). Practice makes perfect—but only if you practice beyond the point of perfection. *American Educator.* Retrieved from http://www.aft.org/newspubs/periodicals/ae/spring2004 /willingham.cfm. (c) Raman, M., et al. Teaching in small portions; (d) Tigner, R. B. (1999). Putting memory research to good use: Hints from cognitive psychology. *College Teaching, 47*(4), 149–152; (e) Murdock, B. B., Jr. (1960). The distinctiveness of stimuli. *Psychological Reports, 67,* 16–31; Neath, I. (1993). Distinctiveness and serial position effects in recognition. *Memory & Cognition, 21,* 689–698; (f) Cahill, L. (2003). Similar neural mechanisms for emotion-induced memory impairment and enhancement. *Proceedings of the National Academy of Sciences, 100*(23), 13123–13124. Retrieved from http://www.pnas.org/cgi/content/full/100/23/13123; (g) Bean, J. (1996). *Engaging ideas.* San Francisco: Jossey-Bass; (h) Higbee, *Your memory;* (i) Berk, R. A. (2002). *Humor as an instructional defibrillator.* Sterling, VA: Stylus; Berk, R. A. (2003). *Professors are from Mars®, students are from Snickers®.* Sterling, VA: Stylus. Images: denk creative/Shutterstock.com; Anna_leni/Shutterstock.com; art4all/Shutterstock.com; eatcute/Shutterstock.com; gst/Shutterstock.com; Cienpies Design/Shutterstock.com

TESTING 1, 2, 3...
SHOW WHAT YOU *KNOW*

All the memorizing you do in college leads to one thing—or so it seems—tests. And often tests feel like nothing more than a big hassle. Are they worth it? Exactly what do they prove?

Let's face it, life would be very different without grades in college, time clocks on the job, or performance reviews throughout your career, wouldn't it? You wouldn't have to show up at work if you didn't feel like it, and you'd get a paycheck anyway. You wouldn't have to do a good job because no one would care. And you wouldn't have to write papers, give presentations, or take tests in college. What a wonderful world that would be—or would it? Realistically, it would probably bring total chaos.

accountability understanding and accepting the consequences of doing a good job or a poor one

Life's not like that. Results count. Accountability is the bottom line. Achievement is taken seriously, and exams are actually realistic representations of life's requirements. The experience of taking a test is similar to running a critical meeting or giving a high-stakes presentation on the job. You'll need to walk into the room, ready to show what you know, and answer unanticipated questions. Tests are inevitable; so rather than complain about them, perhaps we should change the way we think about them.

conscientious dedicated to doing your best

The first step of test taking, of course, is to make sure you're prepared. All of the information in this chapter is worthless if you haven't gone to class or read the textbook or taken good notes during lectures. Miracles, by their very definition, are in very short supply. Nothing can substitute for being conscientious about your work. Think about preparing for an exam as you would for running the 26-mile, 385-yard Boston Marathon. You'd have to work for months to develop the stamina you would need to finish successfully. You wouldn't want to just show up for kicks and wing it. If you did, at the very least, you'd probably pull a muscle. At the very worst, they'd carry you away on a stretcher.

The same principle holds true for exams in college. To have the stamina required and avoid the "injury" of not doing well, tests require this same kind of step-by-step, long-term preparation. Using specific test-taking strategies, like the ones discussed in this chapter, improve your test scores, change your attitude about tests, and boost your self-confidence.[8]

Think about taking tests as a three-stage project with a beginning, middle, and end. What do you do *before* the test to get ready? What do you do *during* the test to do your best? What do you do *after* the test to ensure a productive learning experience you can use for future exams?

BEFORE THE TEST:
PREPARE CAREFULLY

As you read the upcoming sections about *before*, *during*, and *after* a test, evaluate how many of these suggestions apply to you. Highlight each item you do regularly in green and highlight the items you could start doing more regularly to improve your test-taking skills in yellow.

1. **Begin preparing for an exam on the first day of class.** Nothing can replace consistent, regular study before and after each class. If you work

Tests, competition, stress. These words describe our lives on a daily basis. If you're an old movie buff, you may remember the 1973 movie *The Paper Chase*. In that movie, new college students received this threatening welcome: "Look to your left, look to your right. One of you won't be here next year." Although times have changed in favor of helping students succeed, it's not impossible to hear this same "wake-up call" on some college campuses today. The meaning behind the message, of course, is that hard work is required here, so you'd better be at the top of your game. While the "threat" could propel you toward excellence, it could also demotivate you before you even start. This "welcome to college" message is all about tests, competition, and endurance, right? Who needs all that stress? *WIIFM? Nothing!* you may be thinking.

But let's be honest: In some ways, every day of your life is a test, and Walt Disney's experience is universal. Competition is a part of each challenge you will face in college and on the job. Will you outscore your classmates on the upcoming biology test? Will you finish your degree or certificate alongside your peers? Or later, will you beat out the competition, eventually, for that job you really want?

Think about this: Even though tests do cause stress, they have an "up" side. Testing your capabilities keeps you sharp, and there's little doubt that competing can be a very good thing. American athletes won 46 gold medals—more than any other country—at the 2016 Olympic competitions in Rio de Janeiro. Authors and journalists vie for Pulitzer Prizes, and notable people from many fields compete for Nobel Prizes in Chemistry, Physics, Physiology or Medicine, and

Literature—and of course, the Nobel Peace Prize. Simply put: When people are put to the test, competition can produce excellence. The magical world Walt Disney created is an example.

But testing and competition have a "dark" side, one that's worth considering. They imply that if there are winners, there must be losers. If your instructor grades the biology test on a curve, some people will do very well, some will do very poorly, and a large block will be in the middle. While some Olympic athletes win medals, others go home empty-handed. And losing isn't fun; hence the term for people who lose badly: "sore losers." Winning and losing can pit people against each other, and instead of creating excitement, they can create a negative environment, potentially. Perhaps the tired, old "Look to your left, look to your right" message should be replaced with this one: "'Look to your left, look to your right: How quickly can you discover the unique talents, knowledge, and expertise that each one of you brings to the table? How quickly can you convey to others what you bring?' How quickly, in short, can we break down the barriers between us—barriers created by fear, competition, jargon, or status—and figure out how to accomplish things together that none of us could accomplish alone?"[9] Now there's a fresh perspective!

While tests are the bane of every college student's existence, here's one reassuring thought: At least when you finish college, you'll be done with them! But is that really true? In the workforce, will you pass the test, literally, to get promoted or to get hired in the first place? Whoa! Tests to get hired or promoted? Yes, it's

> "I have been up against tough competition all my life. I wouldn't know how to get along without it."
>
> ***Walt Disney (1901–1966), American entrepreneur and CEO (reputed to have attended Metropolitan Junior College, Missouri; also took night classes at The Art Institute of Chicago)***

estimated that nearly 60 percent of large organizations use testing to help them make decisions on hiring and promoting employees.[10] "Nowadays, employers are… interested in evaluating your styles, your competencies, your values." Naturally, they want to hire the best person for the job, and some organizations believe that tests of your personality, integrity, emotional intelligence, basic intelligence or a host of other things can help them find winners.[11] In fact, some recent research indicates that testing employees before they even reach the interview stage can actually predict their future performance, and the testing practice can pay off for organizations. Some of the principles you've learned in this chapter can apply![12]

From *your* personal, pragmatic, "WIIFM?" perspective, however, here is what's most important. Ultimately, thinking about life as a test can challenge us, help us reach our goals, do our best, and win the future we want to create. But as four-time Olympic medalist discus thrower Al Oerter once said, "Competition in its best form is a test of self. It has nothing to do with medals. The winner is the person who gets the most out of themselves." That's "What's in it for you"!

"Manuela Schar, of Switzerland, winner of the the Women's Wheelchair Division, 2017"

criteria standards

along the way, then when it comes time for the exam, you will be much more ready and much less in need of last-minute heroics. Keep up with the reading, even if there are things you'd rather be doing, and make a study schedule for yourself leading up to each exam.

2. **Identify the days and times of all your exams for the whole term up front.** At the beginning of the term, record the days and times of all the exams in all your courses—even finals, which will seem very far off—in your planner, cell phone, or online calendar. You'll thank yourself many times over for completing this essential task.

3. **Find out exactly what the test will cover.** There's nothing more terrifying than having a classmate next to you say something like this before the exam begins, "I can't believe this test covers the entire first six chapters," when you thought it only covered the first four chapters. Clarify whether handouts will be included, previous quiz questions—anything you're not sure of. Phone, text, or e-mail other students, or better yet, ask your instructor questions like these: How long will the test be? What material will it cover? Which topics are most important? It's also a good idea to ask about criteria that will be used in grading. Do punctuation and grammar count? Will you be asked to turn in your notes or draft so that the instructor can see your work? Will there be an in-class review? All these questions are usually fair game.

4. **Understand that specific types of preparation are required for specific types of tests.** As described in later sections in this chapter, objective and subjective tests should be approached differently, and online tests require that you know the answers to important questions up front. For example, will the test time out? Must you complete the exam once you start, or can you save your answers and come back to finish later? Should you compose essay answers elsewhere and paste them into the online exam so that you don't lose all your work in case of a technology hiccup?

5. **Begin serious reviewing several days before the test.** The best strategy is paying regular attention to class material, just as you take care of other things you care about, like your car or your dog. After each lecture, work with your notes, revising, organizing, or summarizing them. Then several days before the exam, step up your effort. Divide up the work by days or study blocks. Begin putting your lecture notes and reading notes together. Make flashcards, outlines, charts, summaries, tables, diagrams—whatever works for your learning style preferences and fits the material.

6. **Maximize your memory.** Research indicates that specific techniques, like the ones discussed in this chapter, help transfer information from short-term to long-term memory. Remember to "Make It Stick" (rehearse, overlearn, space it out, separate it, and mind the middle), "Make It Meaningful" (feel, connect, and personalize), "Make It Mnemonic" (spell and locate), "Manipulate It" (mark it up, mark it down, organize, picture, act, produce, and test), and "Make It Funny" (mock it). Go back to Exercise 9.2 and try

using several of the five major memory techniques to master the list. Do some techniques work better than others for you?

7. **Manage your energy so that you're ready to focus and work quickly.** You've heard it before, but if you're exhausted or feverish, you're not as likely to "show what you know" as you will if you're healthy and rested. "All-nighters" are something students brag about, but they catch up with you, and they're a bad habit to get into. According to one expert, "For every hour of sleep we lose, we drop one IQ point."[13] A series of all-nighters during midterms or final exams can seriously impair your intellectual performance. It's also a good idea to get everything ready the night before so that you remove as much hassle as you can from test day, and arrive early, but not too early. Find a good seat and get situated, but don't allow your anxiety to skyrocket while you're waiting.

8. **Don't give in to a nonproductive, negative attitude.** Emotions are contagious. Stay away from other students who are freaked out or pessimistic about the exam. Think—and feel—for yourself. Make sure your self-coaching is productive ("I've studied this section for an hour; if it's on the exam, I'll nail it."), rather than punishing ("I'm so stupid. Why didn't I keep up with the reading?").

9. **Study with other students.** When you teach something to someone else, you must first learn it thoroughly yourself. Why not study with other students? You can take turns teaching one another, comparing class notes, and making practice exams for each other. For most of us, talking things through helps us figure them out as we go. But don't wait to be invited; take responsibility and start a study group yourself. And if you're concerned that a study group of several students may degenerate into a social club, study with just one other person—find a study buddy and commit to doing the work.

"If you would hit the mark, you must aim a little above it."

Henry Wadsworth Longfellow, American poet (1807–1882)

10. **Don't pop pills to stay awake.** You may know students who use Ritalin, Adderall, or Vyvanse as study aids. This is a bad idea. When these drugs are used for the wrong reasons, they can help you stay awake for hours and enter a dreamy state. Usually prescribed for ADHD, these drugs can have serious side effects, such as irregular heartbeat, extremely high body temperature, or even seizures or heart attacks. With such horrible potential health risks staring you in the face, not to mention possible legal sanctions if you obtain these drugs without a prescription, why not make things simple? Just study.[14]

11. **Don't let open-book or take-home tests lull you into a false sense of security.** What could be easier than an open-book test? What could be better than taking a test in the comfort of your own home? Actually, these two types of tests require more preparation than you'd expect. Time is the issue here. If you're unfamiliar with the material, flipping through pages of notes or skipping around in the textbook won't help. Create a reference guide or page tabs for yourself so that you can find various topics in your notes or textbook and use your time efficiently.

12. **Remind yourself of your long-term goals.** Why are you going to college? All this hard work is worth something, or you wouldn't be doing it.

Keep your sights on the finish line! Enjoy the feeling of accomplishing something now that contributes to your goal-oriented success later.

13. **Don't mess with success.** If you're doing well and earning the grades you deserve, don't discard what is working for you. Honestly assess the efficiency and effectiveness of your current practices, and then decide what ideas from this chapter you should add to your test-taking preparation routine.

CRAMMING: DOES "ALL OR NOTHING" REALLY WORK?

Imagine yourself as the actor in the following scenarios. Compare these situations to cramming for tests.

> You haven't called your significant other since last year. Suddenly you appear at her door with candy, flowers, concert tickets, and dinner reservations at the most exclusive restaurant in town. You can't understand why she isn't happier to see you.

> You don't feed your dog for several months. When you finally bring him a plate loaded with ten T-bone steaks to make up for your neglect, you notice he's up and died on you. Oops!

Of course, these situations are ridiculous, aren't they? How could anyone ever neglect such basic necessities of life? There's an important point to be made here. Many things in life require continuous tending. If you ignore them for a time, catching up is next to impossible. Your college courses should be added to the list.

Believe it or not, some students give themselves permission to follow this all-or-nothing principle of cramming in their academic work. They sail along without investing much time or energy in their studies, and then they try to make up for lost time right before an exam by cramming. The word *cram* provokes a distinct visual image, and rightly so. Picture yourself packing for a vacation in a warm, sunny place and hardly being able to close your suitcase because it's crammed full. You can't decide what to bring so you bring everything you can think of.

The same holds for cramming for a test. You try to stuff your brain full of information, including things you won't need. Because you haven't taken the time to keep up with learning as you go, you try to learn everything at the last minute. Cramming is an attempt to overload information into your unreliable working memory. It's only available for a very short time. However, there are other reasons why cramming is a bad idea:

> Your anxiety level will rise quickly.

> Your sleep will suffer.

> Your immune system may go haywire.

> You may oversleep and miss the exam altogether.

Despite the warnings here, most students cram at some time or other while taking college courses, and doing so may even give them a temporary high and make them feel like they're suffering for a cause.[15] But generally, slow and steady wins the race.[16]

TEST TAKING: HIGH ANXIETY?

TEST ANXIETY SURVEY

What is test anxiety? What are the symptoms? Do you have it? Fill out the following informal survey to determine whether you may have test anxiety. For each of the twelve statements, rate your degree of agreement or disagreement.

1	2	3	4	5
Disagree	Disagree	Unsure	Agree	Agree
Completely	Somewhat		Somewhat	Completely

_____ 1. I cringe when I suddenly realize on the day of an exam that a test is coming up.

_____ 2. I obsess about the possibility of failing an upcoming exam.

_____ 3. I often experience disappointment, anger, embarrassment, or some other emotional reaction during an exam.

_____ 4. I think that instructors secretly get enjoyment from watching students squirm over exams.

_____ 5. I experience physical symptoms such as an upset stomach, faintness, hyperventilation, or nausea before an exam.

_____ 6. I tend to zone out during exams; my mind goes blank.

_____ 7. I feel extreme pressure to please others by doing well on exams.

_____ 8. If I'm honest, I'd have to admit that I really don't know how to study for tests.

_____ 9. I'd much rather write a paper or give a presentation than take an exam.

_____ 10. I usually fear that my exam grade will be lower than that of other students.

_____ 11. After taking an exam, I obsess on my performance, going over and over questions that I think I may have missed.

_____ 12. I convince myself that I'm not good at taking exams even though I often do fairly well on them.

_____ TOTAL (add up your score)

If your score equals 49–60, you are a likely candidate for test anxiety. For suggestions on how to manage your anxiety, read on.

If you scored between 37 and 48, you have some signs of anxiety and may need help in managing your stress level.

If you scored 36 or below, you most likely experience a normal amount of anxiety and have already developed coping skills to help you.

Test anxiety—what is it? And more importantly, does it affect you? Although most people think of test anxiety as a negative, the truth is, it's natural to be anxious before, during, and even after an exam. Most everyone is. In fact, some anxiety is useful. The adrenaline rush that accompanies anxiety can keep you alert and focused.

But for some students, like Kevin Baxter, test anxiety takes over and sabotages their efforts. They may say, "I knew it all before the test, but when I saw the questions, everything I knew vanished before my very eyes." These students experience fainting spells or even gastric distress that requires them to make a quick exit from the room. Some of them may be reacting to prior bad experiences with exams. Others may put intense pressure on themselves because they're perfectionists. Clearly, there's evidence from medical science that too

"Positive thinking will let you do everything better than negative thinking will."

Zig Ziglar, motivational speaker and author

cognitive thinking

emotional feeling

behavioral doing

physiological your body reacting with physical symptoms

much anxiety can work against you. Corticosterone, a hormone released during times of extreme stress, can actually hurt your ability to retrieve information from long-term memory.[17] Regardless of the reason, the first part of the solution is understanding exactly what test anxiety is. It has four different, but related, components in terms of what you think, feel, and do, as well as how your body reacts:[18]

> cognitive aspects—nonproductive thoughts that run through your head before, during, and after an exam ("I have to get an A on this test. If I don't, I'll flunk out of school.")

> emotional aspects—negative feelings you experience related to the exam (disappointment, frustration, sadness, and so on)

> behavioral aspects—observable indications of stress (fidgeting, drumming your fingers on the desk, and so on)

> physiological aspects—unhelpful physiological reactions (dry mouth, butterflies in your stomach, your heart pounding in your chest, and so on)

Because you can't expect the tests you take in college to change for your sake—to reduce your anxiety—the possibility for change must come from within *you*. Consider these suggestions as they relate to the four indicators of test anxiety.

Cognitive

> **Understand your testing strengths and challenges, based on your learning style preferences.** Although research indicates that most students prefer multiple-choice tests over essay tests, you have your own strengths and preferences.[19]

> **Don't catastrophize!** Stop yourself from engaging in negative, unproductive self-talk. It's easy to imagine worst-case scenarios: "If I fail this exam, I'll probably fail the exams in all my courses and flunk out of college, and if I don't go to college, I'll probably end up as a homeless person, begging for change on the street." Negative thinking can easily spiral downward, and before you know it, you're thinking about major life catastrophes and the end of the world. Although some exams do have crucial outcomes, it's important to put things in perspective.

Emotional

> **Monitor your moods.** Your emotions change based on many factors; they vary by type, intensity, and timing.[20] If you eat well and get enough sleep before an exam, your moods are more likely to be stable than if you skip meals, give in to sugar highs and lows, and pull all-nighters. An eight-hour sleep debt will cause your mood to take a nosedive.[21]

> **"Park" your problems if you can.** When you go into a store, you leave your car outside in the parking lot and come back to it when you're finished shopping. Think about how that example can relate to taking a test. Park your problems for a while. Focus on your work, and challenge yourself to do your best.

Behavioral

➤ **Relieve some stress with physical activity.** Expend some of that extra, pent-up energy before the exam. Sprint to class or take a walk to clear your head in the hour before the test begins.

➤ **"Step out of your life" by spending time outdoors.** Being in the outdoors is liberating. It's easy to forget that when you're spending large amounts of time in classrooms or at work.

Physiological

➤ **Teach yourself how to relax.** Relaxation training can be used to overcome test anxiety. As simple as it sounds, that may involve learning how to breathe. Watch a new baby sleep, and you'll see instinctive, deep, even breathing in which only the baby's stomach moves up and down. As adults, when we're anxious, we breathe rapidly and shallowly, which doesn't sufficiently oxygenate our brains.

➤ **Seek help from a professional.** An expert who works with anxiety-ridden college students can diagnose your problem and help you visualize success or take steps to overcome your fears.

REDUCE MATH ANXIETY AND INCREASE YOUR TEST SCORES

Let's zero in on a particular type of test anxiety that plagues many college students. Honestly, most people feel some twinge of anxiety about working a complex set of math problems on an exam. But if your level of anxiety interferes with your test success, you may suffer from mild to high math anxiety. One expert estimates that roughly 25 percent of college students are in that category. And some estimates are that as many as 80 percent of community college students experience some degree of math anxiety.[23]

If you're one of them, admitting the problem is the first step. Next, it's important to understand how math anxiety can work against you during exams so that you can do something about it. The most effective strategies to cope are direct and uncomplicated.[24]

Think back; perhaps you can pinpoint where your fears began. It may have been a teacher or a class or a particular test. Experts believe math anxiety is *learned* and that it's up to you to "unlearn" it.

Why and how does math anxiety affect people? Try this experiment: multiply 86×7. To arrive at the answer, you must first multiply 6×7, make note of the 2, and carry the 4. Then you must multiply 7×8 and add the 4 to arrive at 602. Notice the steps involved in this simple math problem. You have to keep certain numbers in your head while you continue to work through it, which is often the case with math. Your working memory allows you to pull it off.

Working memory is your short-term, temporary-storage, limited-space memory. It's the memory you use to hold certain pieces of information—your brain's scratchpad—keeping them available for you to work with and update.[25] A task like multiplying 639×924 would be too much for most people's working memories, but some people have more capacity than others. Here's the kicker: math anxiety actually eats up your working memory.

Why? Managing anxiety takes up working memory space that could be used to solve math problems. When you reduce your anxiety, you have more room to use your working memory productively. Math anxiety also causes people to take longer to do math and to make more mistakes.[26] It's not the case that you use up your working memory because you think and think and think about how to work the problem and get the right answer. Instead, your working memory is hijacked by negative thoughts, causing you to choke.[27]

The solution? Practice for stressful exams under pressure. Set a timer, and tell yourself you must finish before it goes off. Make a game of it: for every question you miss on a practice exam, you must put a quarter in the kitty and pay off your friend, spouse, or mom. In other words, practicing in an equally stressful environment (or nearly so) can help during the actual test.[28] Because math anxiety is a learned fear, it can be unlearned.

As you study for math tests, keep these five suggestions in mind.[29]

1. **Get to know your calculator (like it's your best friend).** If your instructor allows you to use a calculator in class, learn its functions inside and out. Even though today's calculator can do amazing things, it won't help you much during an exam if you don't know how to use it. Your graphic calculator can plot graphs, solve several equations at once, and you can even program it to run customized applications. But it can't do those things on its own; it requires you to run it. So part of your study strategy should be to learn what your calculator can do and become so familiar with it that using it is almost second-nature.

2. **Concentrate on *comprehension*, not *memorization*.** Memorizing formulas or rules is fine, but it won't help you if you don't know how to apply them. This formula, $a^2 + 2ab + b^2 = (a + b)^2$, is a good thing to know about factoring in algebra, but on a test it wouldn't help you factor $w^2 + 8w + 16$ unless you knew exactly how to apply the formula, step by step. Here's a sample practice problem, showing the steps you should learn to feel comfortable with:

   Problem:
   Simplify: $5(a - 4) + 3 = 8$

   Solution:

Step 1: Remove the brackets	Step 2: Isolate variable a
$5a - 20 + 3 = 8$	$5a = 8 - 3 + 20$
	$5a = 25$
	$a = 25/5$
	$a = 5$
	Answer: $a = 5$

3. **Maximize opportunities to practice.** Homework isn't just busywork; it's practice so that you can succeed. Besides homework, you can find countless websites with practice tests online. Here's an example of a question you might encounter on a test:

   Question: There are 2,000 liters of water in a swimming pool. Water is filling the pool at the rate of 100 liters per minute. How much water, in liters, would be in the swimming pool after m minutes?

   Answer: The amount of water added to the pool after m minutes will be 100 liters per minute times m, or $100 \times m$. Because we started with 2,000 liters of water in the pool, we add this to the amount of water added to the pool to get the expression $2,000 + (100 \times m)$.

Having experience reformulating problems like this means that you know how to extract the math from the words used to describe the math. If you can translate a word problem into a mathematical expression, then you can easily plug in any value to get an answer, given a specific value for m. But in order to do that, you need to understand what you're doing. "Practice makes perfect" may be hard to actually accomplish, but it's important to keep practicing in small chunks. Most experts recommend that you take math classes that meet more than once a week, just for the regular practice.

4. **Make flash cards.** The simple act of creating the flashcards will help commit the information to your memory. And if no one is available to help you go through the flash cards, go through them yourself, and write down the answers as you go.

$$\frac{a/c}{b/c} = \frac{a}{b}$$

The act of writing this fact on a flashcard reminds you to look for commonalities in the denominator and numerator.

5. **Hit the "redo" button.** Mistakes are invitations to "do it right" the next time. For example, if you get a homework problem wrong, figure out why, rework the problem, write down a sentence about the right way to solve it, and then work a similar problem to prove to yourself that you understand now. Don't just skip it or convince yourself that you'll probably get it right next time. It's called "self-regulated learning," and it works.[30]

DURING THE TEST:
FOCUS AND WORK HARD

During an exam, the heat is on! Do you use these strategies? If not, which ones can you incorporate to improve your performance? Highlight each item you do regularly in green and highlight the items you could start doing more regularly to improve your test-taking skills in yellow.

1. **Jot down what you don't want to forget right away.** When you first receive your exam, turn it over and jot down everything you want to make sure you remember—mnemonic devices, charts you've created—assuming, of course, that writing on the test is allowed. Some students treat the exam itself as if it were a sacred document, but marking up your exam is usually allowed. Circle key words and strike through answers you eliminate.

2. **Preview the exam.** Just going through all the questions may help you review terms you know. And you'll notice which questions are easier and which are harder right away. It's also likely that reading sample questions will trigger your memory and help you come up with information you need. After the first few minutes, you may relax a bit, and answers will come to you more easily.

3. **Start with what you know.** Make sure you get credit for answers you know; don't waste time early on struggling with the more difficult questions. This strategy will also boost your confidence and help you relax. Studies show that running up against extremely difficult test questions at the beginning of a test can actually hurt your ability to answer simpler questions later on.[31]

"We all have ability. The difference is how we use it."

Stevie Wonder, singer and composer

4. **Weigh your answers.** Allocate your time based on the relative weight of the questions. Don't wrestle with one question for ten minutes when it's only worth one point. Go on to one that's worth more.

5. **Read directions thoroughly.** Misreading or skipping the directions altogether can be a lethal mistake. Remember that your instructor can't read your mind. ("But that's not what I meant!") Slow down and make sure you understand what you're being asked to do.

6. **Read questions carefully.** Sometimes skipping over a word in the sentence (or filling one in where there isn't one) will cause you to jump to a false conclusion. Don't let your eyes (or your brain) play tricks on you!

7. **If the test has a mixed format, complete the multiple-choice questions first.** Often instructors create exams using both *objective* (multiple-choice, true-false) questions and *subjective* questions (fill in the blank, essay). Generally, objective questions ask you to *recognize* answers from several alternatives, and subjective questions ask you to *recall* answers from memory. A multiple-choice question may remind you of something you want to include in an essay. Keep a pad of paper nearby during the exam. Jot down ideas as you answer multiple-choice questions. You'll feel more confident and do a better job if you keep a running list of ideas that occur to you as you go.

8. **Explain your answer to a confusing question in the margin of your test.** You may point out a problem your instructor wasn't aware of or get partial credit.

9. **Change your answers if you're convinced you're wrong.** Despite advice you've probably always received from teachers and classmates alike, changing answers when you're sure you've made a mistake is usually a good idea, not a bad one. In one study, less than 10 percent of students made changes that decreased their scores, whereas 74 percent made changes that increased their scores.[32]

10. **Ask your instructor for clarification.** If the exam appears to have a typo or something seems strange, ask your instructor to clarify for you. Of course, if you ask for the definition of a word that is a clue, you probably won't get an answer, but if you have a legitimate question, don't be afraid to ask.

11. **Pay attention to "aha" moments.** Don't let your "aha" moments turn into "oh, no" moments. If you remember something you couldn't think of earlier, go back to that question and finish it right away.

12. **Don't give in to peer pressure.** If, while you're working away, you look around and see that many students are leaving because they're already finished, don't panic. Take as much of the allowed time as you need. Everyone works at a different rate.

13. **Save time for review.** When you're finished, go back over all your answers. Make sure you've circled the right letter or filled in the correct bubble. Be certain you've made all the points you intended to make in your essay. Look at your work critically, as if you were the instructor. Careless errors can be costly!

14. **Be strategic about taking online tests.** Often tests posted online are timed. If you're taking a distance education course or a classroom course

with an online test component, watch for e-mail announcements that tests have been posted, and note particular instructions. When will the test expire and disappear? Can you reenter the test site and redo answers before you hit the submit button? Can you take tests together with other students? With online tests, of course, the other recommendations in this chapter for true-false or multiple-choice tests apply as well.

TAKING
OBJECTIVE TESTS

Many of the exams you'll take in college will be objective, rather than subjective, tests. Let's examine the best strategies for taking objective tests.

TRUE-FALSE: TRULY A 50–50 CHANCE OF GETTING IT RIGHT?

> Exam questions that test your ability to remember are always more challenging than questions that test your ability to recognize the right answer. T or F?

True-false tests may seem straightforward, but they can be tricky. You assume you have a 50–50 chance of answering correctly. But don't forget, you also have a 50–50 chance of answering incorrectly. Sometimes the wording of the statements makes the *process* of taking true-false tests more challenging than their *content*. Consider these helpful guidelines:

> ➤ **Watch for parts of statements that make the entire statement false.** The statement must be all true to be "true," and a few words may make an otherwise true statement "false." Here's an example:

> Derek Bok, who was president of Harvard University for thirty years, once said, "If you think education is expensive, try ignorance." T or F

The main part of the statement is true; the quotation does belong to Derek Bok. But Bok wasn't president of Harvard for a full thirty years, making the entire statement false.

> ➤ **Assume statements are true until you can prove them false.** Statistically, exams usually contain more true answers than false ones. You have a better than 50 percent chance of being right if you guess "true." But teachers vary; yours may not follow the norm.

> ➤ **Watch for *absolutes*; they often make a statement false.** Words like *always, never,* and *entirely* often make otherwise true statements become false. "You can *always* get an A on an exam if you study for it." Unfortunately, no.

> ➤ **Look for *qualifiers*; they often make a statement true.** On the other hand, words like *sometimes, often,* and *ordinarily* often make statements true. "You can *sometimes* get an A on an exam if you study for it." Fortunately, yes.

> ➤ **Remember that negatives can be confusing.** Is this statement true or false? "Students who don't lack motivation are likely to excel." "Don't lack" really means "have," right?

"I am easily satisfied with the very best."

Winston Churchill, Prime Minister of England (1874–1965)

VARK IT!

Aural: Challenge your test-taking skills. Ask yourself questions that you predict will appear on the exam and answer them aloud. Or do this with a friend or classmate quizzing you.

MULTIPLE *CHOICE* OR MULTIPLE *GUESS*? TAKING THE GUESSWORK OUT

> Which of the following statements is (are) true?
>
> a. Richard Greener, who became Harvard's first African American graduate in 1870, later became a lawyer, educator, and distinguished U.S. consul and diplomat.
>
> b. Elizabeth Blackwell, who graduated from Geneva Medical College in New York, was the first woman in the United States to earn a medical degree.
>
> c. Oberlin College was the first U.S. college to admit women and the last to admit African American students on an equal footing with Caucasians.
>
> d. a and b
>
> e. a, b, and c

Are multiple-choice tests difficult for you? Often what's difficult about multiple-choice tests has more to do with the structure of the test than the content. Studying for these tests requires a particular approach, and if you master the approach, you'll find taking multiple-choice tests to be much easier. You can actually think of them as similar to true-false tests. [The correct answer to the question, by the way, is (d).]

> ➤ **Think of answers on your own before reading your choices.** You may get hung up on the wording of an answer. Answer it on your own so that you can recognize it, no matter how it's worded. You may want to do this by covering up the alternatives first and then going ahead after you know what you're looking for. Sometimes the alternatives will differ by only one or two words. It's easy to become confused.

> ➤ **Line up your test and answer sheet.** This sounds like a simple suggestion, but getting off a line can be very disruptive when you have to erase like crazy and start over!

> ➤ **Determine the TPI (time per item).** Divide the number of questions by the allotted time. If there are seventy-five questions to answer in an hour, you know that you'll need to work faster than one question per minute. Remember to save some time for review and revision at the end, too.

> ➤ **Don't decide answers based on the law of averages.** If you flip a coin three times, and it comes up "heads," most of us assume it's probably time for "tails" to come up next. Likewise, on exams, if you've answered (d) for three questions in a row, you may think it's time for an (a), (b), or (c). It may not be.

> ➤ **Use a process of elimination and guess if there's no penalty.** Some instructors subtract points for wrong answers, but if you do guess, guess wisely. And don't skip questions. Always mark something unless you're penalized for doing so. Take a look at this example:

"Failure is a comma, not a period."

Bonnie McElveen-Hunter, founder and CEO, Pace Communications

Before you write an answer on an essay test, you should do all but the following:

a. Read all the questions.

b. Begin with the hardest question.

c. Look at what the questions are asking you to do, specifically.

d. Underline key words in the question.

You know that you should do (a). Reading all the questions before you start is a must. You know that option (d) makes sense, and so does (c). But you're not quite sure about option (b). You can eliminate (a), (c), and (d), so (b) must be the right answer based on a process of elimination. As you work, eliminate answers that you know are incorrect by marking through them ~~like this~~.

➤ **Look for highly similar pairs.** Sometimes two options will differ by a single word or the order of words. Often one of these is the right choice.

➤ **Look for contradictory answers.** If two statements are complete opposites, one of them is often the right choice.

➤ **Watch out for tricks intended to separate the prepared from the unprepared!** For example, avoid answers that are true in and of themselves, but not true when attached to the first part of the question being asked. For example, imagine this question option on a multiple-choice exam:

Global warming is considered to be a serious issue among some scientists because:

a. Former President Bill Clinton describes global warming as a greater threat to the world than terrorism.

While Clinton did say this in a 2006 speech, it is not the reason for scientists' concern, so (a) isn't the correct answer.[33] Two other tips: generally, when numbers are in each alternative, choose numbers in the middle range. Choosing answers that are longer and more descriptive usually pays off, too.

➤ **Consider each answer as an individual true-false question.** Examine each option carefully, as if you had to decide whether it is true or false, and use that process to decide which answer is correct.

➤ **Be careful about "all of the above" or "none of the above" options.** Although instructors sometimes make these options the correct ones, it's also possible they resort to these options because making up enough possible answers is challenging.

➤ **Watch for terms that have been emphasized.** Look for key terms that appeared in your lecture notes and in chapters of the text. These words may provide links to the correct answer. Remember when taking multiple-choice tests that you are looking for the *best* answer, not simply the *right* one.[34]

> "Knowing is not enough; we must apply. Willing is not enough; we must do."
>
> *Johann Wolfgang von Goethe, German writer and scholar (1749–1832)*

Answer the following multiple-choice questions. After each question, identify which of the principles of test taking from this chapter you are using to identify the correct answer.

1. "I know of no more encouraging fact than the unquestionable ability of man to elevate his life by conscious endeavor." These words were said by:

    a. Bill Clinton
    b. Abraham Maslow
    c. Ronald Reagan
    d. Henry David Thoreau

    _____

2. Which of the following statements about the ACT test is not true?

    a. The ACT includes 215 multiple-choice questions.
    b. ACT results are accepted by virtually all U.S. colleges and universities.
    c. Students may take the ACT test as many times as they like.
    d. None of the above.

    _____

3. Which of the following suggestions about preparing for college is (are) true?

    a. Get involved in co-curricular activities in high school.
    b. Always take challenging courses that show your effort and ability.
    c. Involve your family in your decisions and preparation for college.
    d. Find a mentor, a teacher, or a counselor who can give you good advice.
    e. All of the above.

    _____

[Answer key: (d), (d), (e)]

SHORT-ANSWER, FILL-IN-THE-BLANK, AND MATCHING TESTS

Short-answer tests are like essay tests, which we'll discuss shortly, in many ways. You're required to come up with an organized, thoughtful answer on your own. But instead of a long essay, you only need to write a paragraph or two. Is that easier? It may be, but sometimes it's just as hard or harder to say what you need to say in fewer words. Generally, however, the suggestions for essay tests hold.

For fill-in-the-blank tests, first think the statement through. What does it mean? Try inserting different words. Which one sounds best? Which one was used during lectures or appeared in the textbook? If one word looks awkward, try another one. Although it's not a completely reliable hint, look at the number of words, placement of spaces, and length of the space. If you don't know the exact terminology the question is looking for, insert your own words. You may at least earn partial credit.

Matching tests require particular strategies, too. First of all, you must determine whether items should be used only once or if they can be reused. If it's not clear from the test directions, ask for clarification. Match the items you're certain about first and cross them out if once only is the rule. If you mismatch an item early on, all your subsequent choices will be wrong, too.

TAKING SUBJECTIVE
ESSAY TESTS

Essay Question: Please discuss the value of brain research in relation to our current knowledge of how learning takes place.

Essay questions are difficult for some students because details are required. Rather than being able to *recognize* the correct answer, you must be able to *recall* it totally from your own memory. Here are some recommendations you should consider:

> **Save enough time for essays.** If the test has a mixed format with different types of questions, it's important to save enough time to write well-thought-through essays. Often objective questions such as multiple-choice or true-false only count a point or two, but essay questions often count into the double digits.

> **Read all the questions before you start.** To sharpen your focus and avoid overlap, give yourself an overview of all the questions before you start writing.

> **Make brief notes.** Somewhere on the exam or on scratch paper, write a brief plan for your responses to essay questions. A few minutes of planning may be time well spent. As you plan your answer, keep basic questions in mind—*who, what, when, where,* and *why*—as an organizing framework.

> **State your thesis up front.** How will you handle this question? What's your plan of attack? Your first paragraph should include your basic argument in a thesis statement.

thesis your main point

> **Provide support for your thesis.** Writing an answer to an essay question requires you to make assertions. However, it's not enough that you assert things; you must try to prove that they are true. If your thesis asserts that college students cheat more today than they did when your parents went to college, you must present evidence—statistics, examples, or expert testimony—to demonstrate that what you're asserting is true.

assertions statements you claim to be true

> **Zero in on the verb.** The heart of an essay question is its verb. Take a look at this list and think about how each verb dictates what is required:

Analyze—break into separate parts, and examine or discuss each part

Compare—examine two or more things, and find the similarities and differences (usually you emphasize the similarities)

Contrast—find the differences between two or more things

Critique, criticize, or evaluate—make a judgment, describe the worth of something

Define—provide the meaning (usually requires a short answer)

Describe—give a detailed account, listing characteristics or qualities

Discuss—describe a cause/effect relationship, the significance of something, the pros and cons, or the role played by someone or something

Enumerate—list qualities, characteristics, events, and so on

Explain—similar to discuss

Illustrate—give concrete examples

Interpret—comment on, give examples, provide an explanation for, discuss

Outline—describe the plot, main ideas, or organization of something

Prove—support an argument with evidence from the text or class notes

Relate—show the relationship or connection between two things

State—explain in precise terms

Summarize—give a condensed account of key points, reduce to the essential components

Trace—describe a process or the development of something

EXERCISE 9.5   **UNDERSTANDING "VERB-AGE"**

What would you emphasize in your written response to these essay questions about this chapter, based on the verb used in each question? For each question, write the first several sentences of an answer to demonstrate how you might respond, just like the student's example shown here.

Critique this chapter of *FOCUS* on developing memory and taking tests.

To me, this is the best chapter of FOCUS I've read so far. I never actually realized it before, but I have symptoms of all four aspects of test anxiety. Many students do. I usually think negatively about how well I'll do, feel frustrated, get fidgety, and get an upset stomach. To me, this one section of the chapter makes it worthwhile to read . . .

1. **Summarize** this chapter of *FOCUS* on developing memory and taking tests.

   _____
   _____
   _____
   _____

2. **Outline** this chapter of *FOCUS* on developing memory and taking tests.

   _____
   _____
   _____
   _____

3. **Analyze** this chapter of *FOCUS* on developing memory and taking tests.

   _____
   _____
   _____
   _____

4. **Compare** this chapter of *FOCUS* with an earlier chapter.

   _____
   _____
   _____
   _____

➤ **Use terms from the course.** Perhaps more than any other type of exam, an essay test allows you room to truly display your knowledge. Use the opportunity! Reflect new terms you have learned, and tie your answer directly to course content.

➤ **Rifle your answer, don't shotgun.** Here's an analogy: A shotgun fires many small metal pellets. A rifle fires a single bullet. When writing an essay answer, some students write down everything they know, hoping that something will be correct. You may actually lose points by doing this. It's better to target your answer and be precise.

➤ **Generalize if you're unsure of small, exact details.** You can't quite remember, was it 1884 or 1894? The best idea is to write, "Toward the end of the nineteenth century" instead of choosing one of the two and being wrong.

➤ **Follow all the rules.** When answering an essay question, it's important to be as concise yet thorough as possible. Number your ideas ("There are *three* major . . . "). Avoid slang ("Wordsworth elaborated . . . " not "Wordsworth *jazzed up* the poem."). Refer to researchers or authors or noteworthy people by their last names ("Jung wrote . . . " not "Dr. Carl Jung wrote . . . ").

➤ **Watch your grammar.** The reason why its important, to do this, is because many student's dont and there answers are marked wrong. They wish they would of done better afterward. (You get the point.)

➤ **Write an answer that corresponds to how much the question is worth.** It's important to be concise, but generally, if one essay answer is worth 10 points and another is worth 25 points, your instructor will expect you to write more for the question that's worth more. A more detailed, thorough response is what is called for, but make sure you're adding content, not just padding your answer.

➤ **Put down what you do know.** If you see a question you didn't predict, don't panic. If you've studied, you know *something* that might help give you partial credit even if you don't know the answer in full.

➤ **Proofread and make sure your handwriting can be read.** Although most instructors will count the number of points you covered and use specific standards, grading essays requires instructors to use their own judgment. A good essay answer is taken less seriously if it's littered with mistakes or a real mess to read. This is the real world; neatness counts. Anything you can do to create a positive impression may work in your favor.

➤ **If you run out of time, jot down any remaining points in the time that's left.** You may not get full credit, but partial credit is better than none.

➤ **Include a summary statement at the end.** Your essay answer should read like a real essay with an introduction, a body, and a conclusion. Don't just stop mid-sentence without wrapping things up.[35]

DON'T CHEAT YOURSELF!

What if you were in one of these situations? How would you respond?

> Many students in your math class get through the homework by sharing answers on their Facebook pages. The instructor doesn't know, and the course isn't all that interesting anyway.

> A friend of yours stores all the names and dates she'll need to know for her history exams on her cell phone. With just one click she can call up whatever information she needs. "Try it," she says. "Everyone else does it, and you'll feel cheated if you don't cheat. If you don't do what other students do, you'll graduate with so-so grades, and you'll never be able to compete for the jobs you've always wanted. Besides, getting away with it here just helps prepare you for the business world where things are *really* cutthroat!"

> You hear about an entrepreneurial student who operates an underground paper-writing service. For $20 a page, he will guarantee you the grade you want (based on the grade you already have going in the course so that your paper won't raise the instructor's suspicions), and he "doctors" each sentence so that the source can't be found on the internet. You have four papers, a presentation, and an exam all due the same week, and one or two papers would only run you around $150 to $200. That's not all that much considering the tips you make as a server. Hmm....

Vera Berger/Fancy/Corbis

"For nothing can seem foul to those that win."

**William Shakespeare,
British poet and playwright
(1564–1616)**

How did you respond to these three scenarios? Are you aware of cheating schemes at your school? Could students you know be the ones these scenarios were written about? Notice that these students have practical-sounding reasons for what they are doing. If you want to cheat, it's not hard, and you can always blame someone else. What's the harm? You get better grades, your teachers think they're doing a good job, your school brags about the fine academic record of its students, and you pat yourself on your back for skillfully managing a very busy, demanding life. Everyone wins, right? Wrong.

According to some studies done fifty years ago, one in five college students admitted to cheating. Today's figures range from 75 to 90 percent.[36] Here's some straight talk about cheating:[37]

1. **Remember that cheating snowballs.** What started as secretly pocketing some kid's toy or glancing at your neighbor's reading test in grade school turns into writing a math formula between your fingers or hiding the names of the constellations under your shirt cuff in middle school. Then these violations as a kid turn into full-fledged, sophisticated rule-breaking as students "download their workload" in high school and knowingly violate their school's Academic Integrity Policy in college. Where does it stop?

2. **Instead of saving time, cheating can take time.** Everyone is busy. Most students are working at jobs for pay in addition to taking classes. How can anyone get everything done that needs to get done? But instead of devising elaborate cheating schemes, which take time to design, why not just use that time to study?

3. **If you cheat now, you'll pay later.** Sooner or later, cheating will catch up with you. You may get past your math instructor this time, and you may even get good grades on others' work you turn in as your own. But someday your boss will ask you to write something, do some research, or use a skill a student is expected to have mastered in college, and you won't know where to start.

4. **If you do get caught, cheating may do you in.** Some students cheat because they know other students have gotten away with it. Cheating for them is a thrill, and not getting caught is like winning or beating the system. Roll the dice and see what happens, they say. But you should know that instructors are in the know these days. Academic hallways are abuzz with faculty talk about cheating. If you do get caught, your academic career may come to an abrupt halt.

5. **Cheating is just plain wrong.** You may or may not agree with this point, but it deserves some serious consideration. How would you like to be cheated out of money that's owed you or days off that are due you? The Golden Rule may sound old-fashioned, but the fact that it's been around for a long time with roots in a wide range of world cultures tells you something. "Intellectual Property" and "Academic Integrity" may not be as tangible as money you deserve or eight hours of free time, but they are things that are increasingly protected by every college.

What are your personal ethical standards? Are you willing to cut corners? Would you cheat to achieve top grades in college? What kind of "devil's bargain" would you be willing to strike?

ethical standards agreements about what is right and wrong

Some students today believe that technology is a tool, and using technology to avoid work isn't cheating, it's just plain smart. Some experts call it the "technological detachment phenomenon." These students think: schoolwork is just busywork, so if you download homework answers, buy a paper online, or collaborate with other students over the internet when the assignment calls for your own work, you're just saving valuable time. They think the pervasiveness of technology somehow justifies cheating. But cheating, no matter how you do it, is still cheating—and the person you're cheating most is yourself. One student went to a campus computer lab and happened to find another student's homework saved there. So he changed the name to his own name, and turned the assignment in as his own. But he mistakenly forgot to change the name on one page. Busted.[38]

If you're tempted, remember this. Learning is about *doing*, not figuring out ways *not to do*, and sooner or later, cheating costs you—big time! Don't cheat yourself out of learning what you need to learn in college. Learning is not all about *product*—the exams, papers, grades, and diplomas themselves—it's about *process*, too. The process involves gaining skills that will prepare you for life after college. That's a goal worth working toward.

You can't go through life devising elaborate schemes, hiring someone else to do your work for you, or rationalizing about finding a way to beat the system because you're too busy to do your own work. Cheating in your college classes now just makes it that much easier to risk cheating your employer—and yourself—later on the job. Look through newspapers or watch the evening news to see who's been

Maria Evseyeva/Shutterstock.com

"Non scholae sed vitae discrimus. (We do not learn for school, but for life.)"

—*Lucius Annaeus Seneca, Roman philosopher and statesman (4 B.C.–A.D. 65)*

caught lately. It's a competitive world out there, but more and more companies find that having a good reputation, which comes from being honest, is good business. Integrity starts now: *earn what you learn.*[39]

AFTER THE TEST:
CONTINUE TO LEARN

After you finish an exam and get your results, you may be thrilled or discouraged. Regardless, exams can be excellent learning experiences if you take these steps. As you read, try highlighting each item you do regularly in green and the items you could start doing more regularly to improve your test-taking skills in yellow.

1. **Analyze your results.** Conduct a thorough analysis of your test results. For example, an analysis like this one might tell you what kinds of questions are most problematic for you.

TYPE OF QUESTION	POINTS EARNED/RIGHT	POINTS DEDUCTED/WRONG	TOTAL
Multiple-Choice	32	3	35
Fill-in-the-Blank	15	2	17
True-False	20	8	28
Essay	10	10	20
Total	77	23	100

Or analyze your results by comparing how many lecture questions there were versus textbook questions to find out where to concentrate your efforts on future tests. Or do an analysis by chapter to tell you where to focus your time when studying for the final exam.

2. **Read your instructor's comments and take them to heart.** After an exam, ask yourself: What was the instructor looking for? Was my writing ability part of the issue? Does the test make more sense now than it did while I was taking it? Are there instructor's comments written on the test that I can learn from? What do the results of this exam teach me about preparing differently, perhaps, for the next test?

3. **Explain your grade to yourself.** Where did you go wrong? Did you misread questions? Run out of time? Organize essay answers poorly? Does the grade reflect how much time you studied? If not, why not? Did test anxiety get the better of you? On the other hand, if you studied hard and your grade reflects it, that's an explanation, too!

4. **Be honest.** It's easy to get caught up in the blame game: "I would have gotten a better grade if the exam had been fairer, if the test had been shorter, if the material hadn't been so difficult, if I'd had more time to study...." Your instructors have heard every excuse in the book: "My dog ate my notes," "A relative died," "A family emergency made it impossible to study," "My hard drive crashed"—you name it. Of course, sometimes crises do overtake events. But rather than pointing fingers elsewhere if you're disappointed with your results, take a close look at what you can do differently next time.

5. **Make a specific plan for the next test.** Most courses have more than one exam. You'll probably have an opportunity to apply what you've learned and do better next time.

6. **Approach your instructor politely if you believe your exam has been mismarked.** Sometimes teachers make mistakes. Sometimes they're interrupted while grading and forget to finish reading an essay answer, or the answer key is wrong, or they make a mistake adding up points. Even if the scoring is correct, it may be a good idea to approach your instructor for help about how to improve your next test score.

7. **Reward yourself for good (study) behavior.** After you've worked hard to prepare and the exam is over, reward yourself—take in a movie, go out with friends, do something to celebrate your hard work.

DEEPEN YOUR
LEARNING

The final point this chapter will make about memory and tests is this: in a classic study conducted in the mid-1970s, two Swedish scholars decided to find out the difference between effective and ineffective learners. They gave students this task: read an essay, summarize it, and solve a problem. Then they interviewed the students to find out how they had approached the task.

The interviews revealed two types of learners. One group of students said things like, "I just tried to remember as much as I could" or "I just memorized what I read." Other students said, "I tried to look for the main idea" or "I looked for the point of the article." The professors who conducted the study then characterized the difference between *surface-level processing,* looking at words and numbers alone, and *deep-level processing,* searching beneath the surface for underlying meaning.[40] (See Figure 9.3 for an image to tie to these contrasting ideas.) To become a truly focused learner, you must process information as you go. Dig deep for increased learning, better test results, and greater success!

FIGURE 9.3

Memory Processing: Skipping a Stone versus Deep Sea Diving

Have you ever watched a movie, wondering how *do* actors learn all those lines? Do they have superhuman memory powers?

Actually, what actors are most concerned with is convincing you that they're not playing a role. But actors' contracts require them to be absolutely precise in conforming to the script, so how do they do it? Studying how actors learn their parts with precision has confirmed what learning experts know about memory.[41]

Most actors aren't memory experts, but they do use the memory techniques described in this chapter. They manipulate the lines, elaborate on them to themselves, relate the lines to experiences or feelings of their own, or try writing or saying the lines themselves, rather than just reading them. Four of the techniques used by actors may also be useful to you as you try to commit course material to memory. Maybe you've even tried some of these techniques.

Chunking: Actors chunk their material into beats. For example, an actor might divide a half-page of dialogue into three beats: to flirt, to sweet-talk, and to convince. In other words, the character would first flirt with the other actor, then sweet-talk

him to lower his guard, and then convince him to do something he might not want to do. The results? Three chunks to remember instead of twelve lines of double-spaced text.

Goal Setting: Notice that the chunks are based on goals, a strategy that also works well when you're studying. Actors ask themselves goal-oriented questions such as these: "Should I be flirting with him here?" "Am I trying to sweet-talk him?" "Should I be trying to convince him to do something he doesn't really want to do?" In the same way, you can ask yourself, "Am I trying to learn the underlying formula so that I can work other problem sets?" or "Should I be coming up with my own reasons for why the play is considered to be Shakespeare's best comedy?" When you ask yourself goal-oriented questions while you study, you steer your actions, as actors do, toward learning.

Moving: Going through the motions while rehearsing their lines helps actors memorize them. Imagine the hypothetical actor whose goals were to flirt, to sweet-talk, and to convince, glancing toward the other actor from across the room, moving closer and smiling, and then touching his arm while making the persuasive case. The

actor must know the meanings behind the movements to give meaning to the lines. (She could be glancing across the room to give a dirty look instead of to flirt, for example.) The meanings are tied to the movements, which are tied to the lines, and the lines become committed to memory. When you study, moving around may help you learn. Even if your learning preferences aren't primarily kinesthetic, pieces of information become tied to motions in ways that help you recall information.

Meaning: "Say what you mean" and "mean what you say" was Lewis Carroll's advice in *Alice's Adventures in Wonderland*. When actors concentrate on truly meaning what they're saying, they learn their lines more easily than they do when they simply try to memorize them. As you study course material, do the same thing. Imagine you need to communicate the information to someone you know who needs it. Put emotion into it. In a sense, when you do this, you become an actor, and as a result you "learn your lines."

Do you see how movement could help you learn subject matter that has often been challenging for you? How could becoming "an actor" help you learn?

INSIGHT: *NOW* WHAT DO YOU THINK?

At the beginning of this chapter, Kevin Baxter, a frustrated and discouraged returning adult student, faced a challenge. Now after reading this chapter, would you respond differently to any of the questions you answered about the "FOCUS Challenge Case"? Using what you learned in the chapter, write a paragraph ending to Kevin's case study. What are some of the possible outcomes for Kevin?

1. Which type of test do you find most difficult—multiple-choice, true-false, or essay, for example? Within that particular portion of the chapter, which strategies that you read about will you try on your next exam?

2. Many students have negative attitudes toward tests. What could they do to change their outlook and learn to see tests as opportunities, rather than threats?

3. What piece of helpful information about memorizing or test-taking, based on your own experience, would you add to this chapter? How has it changed the way you prepare for or actually take tests?

CHALLENGE: REALITY CHECK

Can you answer these questions about test taking and studying now that you've read the chapter?

1. What are the three "R's" of remembering?

2. This chapter identifies five major ways to master your memory. Can you identify two of these five ways?

3. What are the four components of test anxiety?

4. Identify three hints to managing your time during tests.

5. How long did it take? _____ hours _____ minutes. Before you began this chapter, you were asked to predict how long it would take you to complete it (total time, even if you read it in more than one sitting). Was your estimate on target, or will you revise it for the next chapter you'll read?_____

Hugo Felix/Shutterstock.com

HOW THIS CHAPTER RELATES TO YOU

1. When it comes to communicating in groups and valuing diversity in college, what do you find most challenging, if anything? Put check marks by the phrases that apply to you or write in your answer.

   ☐ Developing emotional intelligence

   ☐ Communicating productively in groups

   ☐ Appreciating the varied aspects of diversity

   ☐ Developing cultural intelligence

   ☐ Understanding the impact of globalization

   ☐ _____

2. What is most likely to be your response? Put a check mark by it.

   ☐ I'll be open to learning how to improve my skills.

   ☐ I'll see whether this chapter helps me.

   ☐ I'll pay particular attention to these issues in my classes.

   ☐ Eventually, I'll just figure it out on my own.

3. What would you have to do to increase your likelihood of success? Will you do it this quarter or semester?

HOW YOU WILL RELATE TO THIS CHAPTER

1. What are you most interested in learning about? Put check marks by those topics.

   ☐ Whether your emotional intelligence can be improved

   ☐ How to improve communication in groups and with people you care about or work with

   ☐ Why diversity enriches our lives

   ☐ What cultural intelligence is and why it's important

   ☐ How globalization changes our world

YOUR READINESS FACTOR

1. How motivated are you to learn more about communicating in groups and valuing diversity in college? (5 = high, 1 = low)

2. How ready are you to read now? (If something is in your way, take care of it if you can. Zero in and focus.)

3. How long do you think it will take you to complete this chapter? If you start and stop, keep track of your overall time. ____ Hour(s) ____ Minute(s)

Serena Jackson

Hugo Felix/Shutterstock.com

As Professor Arnold read the group members' names aloud for the assigned presentations in "Introduction to Mass Media" on Monday, it was all Serena could do to keep her cool. She listened closely: "Group 1: Jessica Andrews, Jordan Nelson, Cassie Phillips, and Serena Jackson." Even as the names were coming out of Professor Arnold's mouth, Serena could see how it would all play out. Jessica would want to run the group, Cassie wouldn't come through on her part, and Jordan would totally blow off the assignment. *Great,* Serena thought. *A random group of students I don't even know very well will earn 50 percent of* my *grade.* It just didn't seem fair.

They had the last fifteen minutes of class to exchange cell phone numbers and e-mail addresses, which everyone did. There was even some excitement in the room. At least the group presentations would be a break from the weekly lectures. But the very thought of speaking in front of the class made Serena's heart race, and now with these teammates, things were looking grim. She had only earned a B on the first exam, and she desperately needed an A in this class to balance out her likely disappointing algebra grade.

Serena sent off an e-mail to the group on Wednesday, suggesting they meet at the library on Friday morning to decide on a topic and divide up the work. Jessica wrote back immediately, "I work on Friday mornings." Cassie took her time but finally replied on Sunday, "I'm out of town this weekend. Let's wait until next week." Jordan didn't write back at all. "You e-mailed me?" he said,

with a puzzled look on his face in class on Monday. "Oh, I never check my e-mail. I only respond to texts." Serena planned to catch everyone's attention to set a new meeting time as class let out, but Cassie wasn't there, and the other two had bolted by the time she zipped up her backpack.

On Tuesday morning, it was Jessica who texted everyone: "Meeting in UC 213 tomorrow at 2. I know that works for three of us." *Three of us?* Serena asked herself. No one had even checked with her. Were they working around her? Her math class met from 1:15 to 3:30, and she couldn't afford to skip it. She texted back, "I have class then." "No worries," Jessica replied. "We three will get started. Then we can just send a PowerPoint around, and talk through it for the actual presentation." Serena replied, "I could meet at 4. Can you?" "No, Cassie has a doctor's appointment, and I have to babysit for my neighbor." What was the

Source: Youtube/Cengage®

Oleksiy Mark/Photos.com

Intro to Mass Communication

Professor Karen Arnold

group's topic? Who was doing what? Were they trying to exclude her, or did it just seem that way? Sometimes Serena felt isolated as the only minority student in this particular class, which didn't happen very often at her school. Although she was furious inside, the last thing she wanted to do was rock the boat.

Although she didn't want to bother Professor Arnold, Serena finally decided to alert her to the group's issues. But when she dropped by during office hours, her instructor defended the assignment. "I know group projects can be challenging," she said. "But you'll be working through team issues like these in the workplace—and you'll be 'graded' on the team's results. I could step in and try to fix things, but you four should work

through it yourselves. It's good practice for '*the real world*.'" Although Serena knew Professor Arnold was right in the long run, her wisdom didn't help right now.

At least the group had updated her after they met. Jessica's e-mail read, "We only had time for a half-hour meeting, but we decided our presentation would be about the best Super Bowl commercials of all time. Cassie and I will do the research, Jordan will find examples of commercials on the internet, and your job will be doing the PowerPoint slides."

A week before their presentation was due, the group finally managed to agree on a time that everyone could meet—a waste of time, as it turned out. No one was prepared. Jessica spent the meeting time texting her boyfriend. Jordan was on his phone with somebody, and Cassie sat there scarfing down a huge burrito. Somehow they managed to get nothing done in an hour and twenty minutes. The presentation was next Monday, and no one else seemed to be the least bit interested in doing a good job. "Group projects are a pain," Jessica tweeted after class. #hategroup- projects #powerthroughit" What Serena's mother had always told her appeared to be true: "If you want to get something done *right*, do it yourself." But "doing it herself" wasn't an option for Serena's group project, and, most likely, neither was getting an A.

Source: Twitter/Cengage®, Vjom/Shutterstock.com

Intro to Mass Communication
Syllabus

Class: COMM 1015
Instructor: Arnold, Karen **Office:** N507 **Ph:** 867-5309
Bldg: Centennial Hall **Room:** 324 **Days:** M **Time:** 01:40 PM-04:20 PM

Textbook: Biagi, Shirley. *Media Impact: An Introduction to Mass Media*,
12th Ed.
Boston: Cengage Learning
ISBN: 9781305580985

Overview: This survey course will explore mass communication media, its structures, theories, and functions, and how media interacts with modern life. COMM 1015 will also delve into the history of mass media and the future of mass media in the face of new technologies.

Grading:

Assignment:	Points Possible:
Reaction Papers - 10 total	50
Class Participation	50
Exam 1	100
Exam 2	100
Group Project	300
TOTAL:	600

Course Schedule:

Week 1	Course Introduction	
Week 2	Mass Media Theories	Read Ch 1
Week 3	Media Literacy	Read Ch 2 & 3
Week 4	Print Media	Read Ch 5
Week 5	Television and Film	Read Ch 4

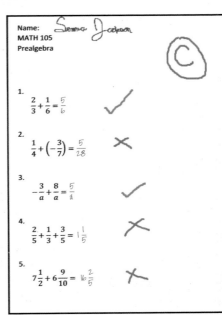

Name: Serena Jackson
MATH 105
Prealgebra

C

1. $\frac{2}{3} + \frac{1}{6} = \frac{5}{6}$ ✓

2. $\frac{1}{4} + \left(-\frac{3}{7}\right) = \frac{5}{28}$ ✗

3. $-\frac{3}{a} + \frac{8}{a} = \frac{5}{a}$ ✓

4. $\frac{2}{5} + \frac{1}{3} + \frac{3}{5} = 1\frac{1}{5}$ ✗

5. $7\frac{1}{2} + 6\frac{9}{10} = 16\frac{2}{5}$ ✗

1. How would you describe Serena's group project experience? Have you ever been in a similar position? What, if anything, should she be doing differently?

2. There's a difference between intelligence quotient (IQ) and emotional quotient (EQ). What EQ skills would Serena need in order to improve this situation? Describe them as best you can.

3. Serena's relationships with her group members are important to her. After all, she may end up in other classes with them in the future. What advice would you give her?

4. Describe Serena's conflict management style. Does she face it head-on, for example, or avoid it? What clues does the case study provide you?

5. Identify three things Serena should do to try for a better group experience and grade.

THE HEART
OF COLLEGE SUCCESS

EXERCISE 10.1   **HOW WOULD YOU RESPOND?**

Read these five scenarios and identify the most emotionally intelligent response.[1]

1. You peer over a classmate's shoulder and notice she has copied your online response from a class blog and submitted it as her paper in the course, hoping the instructor won't notice. What do you do?
   a. Tell the student off to set the record straight, right then and there.
   b. Tell the instructor that someone has cheated.
   c. Ask the student where the research for the paper came from.
   d. Forget it. It's not worth the trouble. Cheaters lose in the end.

2. You're riding on a plane that hits a patch of extreme turbulence. What do you do?
   a. Grab hold of the person in the next seat and hold on for dear life.
   b. Close your eyes and wait it out.
   c. Read something or watch a movie to calm yourself until things improve.
   d. Panic and lose your composure.

3. You receive a paper back in your toughest course and decide that your grade is unacceptable. What do you do?
   a. Challenge the instructor immediately after class to argue for a better grade.
   b. Question whether you're really college material.
   c. Reread the paper to honestly assess its quality and make a plan for improvement.
   d. De-emphasize this course and focus on others in which you are more successful.

4. While kidding around with your friends, you hear one of them tell an offensive, racial joke. What do you do?
   a. Decide to ignore the problem and thereby avoid being perceived as overly touchy.
   b. Report the behavior to your advisor or an instructor.
   c. Stop the group's conversation. Make the point that racial jokes can hurt and that it's important to be sensitive to others' reactions.
   d. Tell your joke-telling friend later that racial jokes offend you.

5. You are working on a group project, and one member is a total slacker. What do you do?
   a. Pick up the slack and do that person's work. That's easier than getting the member to come through for the group.
   b. Call or text the person and express your displeasure. You're busy, too, and it's not fair to the rest of the group.
   c. Generate some strategies with the rest of the group and approach the member with the group's suggestions.
   d. Contact the instructor as soon as possible and ask to be placed in a different group.

Every day, in many ways, you make choices about how you react to situations and other people. College is no exception. It's a time of transition; it can be an emotionally challenging time. Even if you're a returning student who's been on your own for years, college will require you to make some major adjustments in your life. As a new college student, you're on your own, continually adapting to new situations, adjusting your past relationships with friends and family, and forming new ones rapidly.

Here's a fundamental truth: College isn't just about your head. Yes, academics are the reason you're in college, but your heart plays a critical role in your success, too. From friends to family members, to professors, to classmates, how you handle relationships can make or break you academically. Emotional reactions to troubling circumstances have the raw potential to stop you dead in your tracks. Some students, for example, have the *academic* skills required for success, but *nonacademic* issues can interfere.

In college and in life, your EQ (emotional quotient), or *emotional intelligence*, can be just as important as your IQ (intelligence quotient). Studies show that first-year students often feel overwhelmed and lonely. Begin now to refine the emotional skills you'll need to face whatever challenges come your way.

Perhaps you've found yourself in settings such as those described in Exercise 10.1. You might need more actual details to make the best choice in these five scenarios, but according to some experts, choice (c) is the most emotionally intelligent one in each case. Do you agree? How do *you* make decisions such as these? What constitutes an emotionally intelligent response?

WHAT IS
EMOTIONAL INTELLIGENCE?

Many experts believe that intelligence takes many forms. Rather than a narrow definition of intelligence, they believe in Multiple Intelligences: Linguistic, Logical-Mathematical, Spatial, Kinesthetic, Musical, Interpersonal, Intrapersonal, and Naturalistic.[2] Emotional intelligence (or EI) may well be a combination, at least in part, of *intrapersonal* and *interpersonal* intelligences.

Emotional intelligence is a set of skills that determines how well you cope with the demands and pressures you face every day. How well do you understand yourself, empathize with others, draw on your inner resources, and encourage the same qualities in people you care about? Emotional intelligence involves having people skills, a positive outlook, and the capacity to adapt to change. Emotional intelligence can propel you through difficult situations.

The bottom line? New research links emotional intelligence to college success, and learning about the impact of EI in the first year of college helps students stay in school.[3] Or consider this research finding: strong emotional intelligence helps you achieve a higher GPA when you take online courses.[4] In fact, emotional intelligence and learning are related in any context: According to emotional intelligence experts, "Anyone who looks at the brain and how it works knows that your emotional state directly affects how you can use your academic skills. If you're upset, it shrinks your working memory. You can't pay attention to what the teacher's saying. You can't learn."[5]

As you read about the five scales of emotional intelligence, begin thinking about yourself in these areas. As each scale is introduced, ask yourself whether you agree or disagree with the sample statement from a well-known emotional intelligence instrument as it pertains to you.[6]

> "Our emotions are the driving powers of our lives."
>
> *Earl Riney, American clergyman (1885–1955)*

Self-Perception

"I'm aware of how I feel." Agree or disagree?

Are you in tune with your emotions? Do you fully realize when you're anxious, depressed, or thrilled? Or do you just generally feel up or down? Are you aware of layers of emotions? Sometimes we show *anger*, for instance, when what we really feel is *fear*. Are you emotionally strong on your own, rather than depending on others for your happiness? Do you realize that no one else can truly make you happy, that you are responsible for creating your own emotions? How well do you understand yourself and what makes you tick?

Self-Expression

"It's hard for me to describe my feelings." Agree or disagree?

Can you express your feelings to others? Are you assertive about your needs when you need to be? Are you independent, such that you can "speak for yourself," rather than relying on others to speak *for* you?

Interpersonal Skills (Relating to Others)

"I'm aware of how others feel." Agree or disagree?

Are you aware of others' emotions and needs? Do you communicate with sensitivity and work to build positive relationships? Are you a good listener? Are you comfortable with others, and do you have confidence in your relationships with them?

Decision Making

"When I'm really upset, I can't decide what to do." Agree or disagree?

How easy or hard is it for you to solve problems? Can you think of a range of possible solutions? Can you see situations that affect you realistically? Are you able to control your impulses, such that you make good decisions that benefit you?

Stress Management Skills

"I expect things to turn out all right, despite setbacks from time to time." Agree or disagree?

Can you productively manage your emotions so that they work *for* you and not *against* you? Can you control destructive emotions? Can you work well under pressure? Are you in control, even when things get tense and difficult?

Source: From EQ-i:S Post Secondary. Used by permission of Multi-Health Systems Inc.

resilience the ability to bounce back from difficulties

learned optimism a way of thinking that helps you stay optimistic and potentially improves your mental and physical health

Emotional intelligence affects every part of our lives. For example, researchers study related concepts: "hardiness," "resilience," and "learned optimism."[7] Some people are more resistant to stress and illness. Hardy, resilient, optimistic people are confident, committed to what they're doing, feel greater control over their lives, and see hurdles as challenges. Emotional intelligence is part of the reason why.

Emotional intelligence and its five scales are important in all aspects of life, including your future career.[8] When *Harvard Business Review* first published an article on the topic in 1998, it attracted more readers than any article in the journal's previous forty years. When the CEO of Johnson & Johnson read it, he ordered copies for the company's 400 top executives worldwide.[9] Google now puts more than a thousand employees a year through its internal emotional intelligence course with thousands more on a waiting list. Many businesses today are beginning to realize the value of EI to healthy work relationships, better communication, and ultimately, to more employees working for the organization's success and the greater good.[10]

Why? Emotional intelligence is a characteristic of true leaders. Immediately after the first shock of the September 11, 2001, tragedy, the world tuned in to a press conference with New York's Mayor Rudy Giuliani. He was asked to estimate the number of people who had lost their lives in the World Trade Center collapse that day, and his reply was this: "We don't know the exact number yet, but whatever the number, it will be more than we can bear." In that one sentence, Giuliani demonstrated one of the most important principles of true leadership. Leaders inspire by touching the feelings of others.[11]

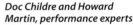

"Managing your emotions is an inside job."

Doc Childre and Howard Martin, performance experts

CAN EMOTIONAL INTELLIGENCE BE IMPROVED?

Everyone wants well-developed emotional intelligence, but how do you get it? Can EI be learned? Although researchers admit that genes definitely play a role, most experts believe that emotional intelligence can be increased. One of the most convincing pieces of evidence is from a study that followed a group of students over seven years. Students assessed their emotional intelligence, selected particular areas to strengthen, and then each created an individual plan to develop them. Seven years later, their competencies remained high.[12]

If you believe what this chapter says about the importance of emotional intelligence and college success, you're probably asking yourself what you can do about it. Are the skills related to emotional intelligence something *you* can work to improve?[13] And if so, how?

Seek honest input from others. It's hard to be objective about yourself. But it is possible to ask for the opinions of others who interact with you regularly. How do they see you? Use other people as coaches to help you see which aspects of your emotional intelligence need strengthening.

Find an EI mentor. A mentor on the job is someone who's older and more experienced than you are and can help you navigate your way through tough problems and manage your college or professional career. Mentors help, and an EI mentor—someone with EI skills you admire—can provide you with important advice about handling challenging emotional situations. Develop a personal relationship with someone whose wisdom you admire, be honest about your problems, and follow the guidance you get.

Complete an assessment tool. Other than just feeling up or down, or thinking back on how you handled problems when they came up, is there a way to know more about your own emotional intelligence? The oldest and most widely used instrument to measure emotional intelligence is the Emotional Quotient Inventory, the EQ-i, from which the sample statements for the five scales we have been discussing come. The instrument asks you to respond to various statements by indicating that they are "very seldom true of me" to "very often true of me," and the results provide you with a self-assessment of your emotional intelligence on each of the five major scales and subscales within them.

As a part of the course for which you're using this text, you may have an opportunity to complete the EQ-i or a similar instrument. Check your college's Counseling Center, too, to see if it offers EI assessment tools for students. You can also locate plenty of informal instruments online. They may not be valid, however, so be cautious about fully trusting their results.

Work with a counselor to learn more. Some areas of emotional intelligence may be too challenging to develop on your own. You may need some in-depth, one-on-one counseling to work on areas that need enrichment. Recognize that doing so isn't a bad thing. Instead, you are taking advantage of the resources available on your campus and working toward the growth that can come during your college years.

Be patient with yourself. Learning to become more sensitive to someone else's emotions in a close relationship isn't something you can get better at overnight, using cookbook techniques. Building emotional skills is a gradual process that involves becoming aware, acting on your new awareness, and noting the results over time.

Keep at it: Developing your emotional intelligence should be a long-term goal. It's safe to say that EI is something all of us can strengthen, if we're willing to work at it. Relationships that are important to us require the best of our emotional intelligence skills. In fact, studies show that the way in which we provide emotional support is strongly related to how satisfied we are with our relationships.[15] Now, let's apply what we've discussed about EI to the topic of working in groups, beginning with Exercise 10.2. What are your views on groupwork now, before reading further?

EXERCISE 10.2 WHAT ARE YOUR VIEWS ON GROUPWORK?

Are you (or will you be) involved in a group project in the class for which you're using this text or another class this term? Consider the following statements and select "yes" if you agree and "no" if you disagree with how groups should operate.

	Yes	No
1. Groups have emotional intelligence, just like individuals do.	___	___
2. Teams should discuss how groups work up front, before the project begins.	___	___
3. Teams should always work to reach agreement.	___	___
4. Teams are generally more productive working face-to-face, as opposed to working online.	___	___
5. A team is only as strong as its weakest link.	___	___
6. When team members all talk at once, it shows great energy for the project.	___	___
7. Group conflict should be avoided whenever possible.	___	___
8. The best teams are the ones in which all the members are friends.	___	___
9. Teams should only meet when all members can be present.	___	___
10. Roles for team members should just come about naturally, not be assigned by an instructor, for example.	___	___

COMMUNICATING IN GROUPS:
SOFT SKILLS ARE HARD!

Emotional intelligence isn't just important for individuals; it plays a role in teamwork. "It unlocks productivity and creativity in a way that nothing else does."[16] Teamwork is a challenge, and not all groups reach a high level of effectiveness.

Think of it this way: A group's IQ isn't the sum total of the IQ of each of its members (Terrance = 110 + Katie = 100 + Jillian = 105 + Brent = 120 for a grand total of 435). High group intelligence—or "collaborative intelligence"—brings a higher level of thinking and more creative ideas. In the same way, a group's emotional intelligence is more than just the sum total of the EI of all its members. It's a new level of productivity that can come when sensitive, tactful people trust one another, believe in their task, use their strengths, and realize that they need one another to do their best.[17]

Sometimes emotional intelligence is referred to as "soft skills." These skills aren't based in hard science, facts, or numbers. Instead, they involve values, judgment, and sensitivity. As a matter of fact, soft skills are hard! It's hard to work with a "difficult" teammate and get good results. It's hard to work under an unreasonable boss and perform at your best, or rebuild a working relationship after a colleague has "backstabbed" you during a meeting. Most anyone can learn new "hard skills," but those who rise to the top of their careers are those with the best soft skills. Interestingly, a survey of Microsoft business leaders rated soft skills as more valuable than academic qualifications![18] Ask anyone who has had a long career: "What are the most difficult issues you have faced over your years on the job?" It's unlikely the answer will have anything to do with the actual job itself ("I just couldn't seem to learn Excel. It totally stumped me!" or "I'll tell you, those cavities in the back molars are really hard to reach!"). Instead, you'll probably hear a story about a coworker who made life difficult until one or the other eventually moved on. Soft skills are tested day in and day out, so learning more about them now, while you're in college, is excellent preparation for upcoming challenges.

WHY GROUPS IN COLLEGE?

In school, the word "group" is used commonly, meaning a collection of people who share a purpose. A random pack of students walking down the hallway of a classroom building on campus wouldn't be defined as a group for our purposes. But students in your history class would qualify as a group because they think of themselves as a group, interact with one another, and all have the same goal—to succeed in your history class. "Teams," on the other hand, are usually found on the playing field or in the workplace. They have assigned roles (pitcher versus shortstop), have fewer members than groups, and share a purpose—to design the most fuel-efficient car of the future, for example. However, in this chapter, we'll use the terms "group" and "team" interchangeably to gain an understanding that will help you engage in group projects productively for all your various classes.[19]

You may have entered college thinking you would need to write papers, submit homework, take tests, and give presentations—by yourself. True enough. But actually, in many ways, "college is a team sport." In addition to the

"What's going on in the inside shows on the outside."

Earl Nightingale, success consultant

"Seventy-five percent of careers are derailed for reasons related to emotional competencies, including inability to handle interpersonal problems; unsatisfactory team leadership during times of difficulty or conflict; or inability to adapt to change or elicit trust."

Center for Creative Leadership

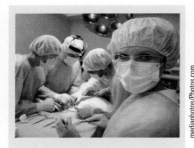

"Contrary to popular belief, there most certainly is an 'I' in 'team.' It is the same 'I' that appears three times in 'responsibility.'"

Amber Harding, sports journalist

harmonious agreement in feeling, attitude, or action

life hack #2

Groups with more personality similarities among members will reach decisions sooner, but groups in which members have more personality differences may reach better decisions since many points of view will have been taken into account.

individual effort you invest in classes, forming relationships with your teachers and classmates will play a major role in your success. Besides papers, presentations, and exams, which you do by yourself, your teachers will also assign group projects—with classmates. You may wonder why. Here's one explanation. When you write a paper, you learn about whatever it is you're writing about, naturally. But you also learn about writing as a practical skill that you can take with you to a job after college. The same thing is true when it comes to group projects. You'll learn about the project's topic. But you'll also learn useful skills about working with people, and if you actually make that part of the project a goal for yourself, you'll leave college with well-developed people skills, which will give you a definite advantage later. There's also evidence that students working in groups retain information better.[20] So, what can you do to ensure a positive group experience for a class or work assignment? Consider the 10 rules presented in Figure 10.1.

But just how important are groups and teams in general? The short answer is: very! If you're under the knife in the OR, you'd better hope that the medical team functions well together. Or if you're on a transatlantic flight, you'd likely have similar hopes for the crew. And for that matter, it helps if they've worked together before. "The National Transportation Safety Board found that 73 percent of the incidents in its database occurred on a crew's first day of flying together, before people had the chance to learn through experience how best to operate as a team—and 44 percent of those took place on a crew's very first flight."[21]

Experience does count, but many of us think that a team of friends works together best; they produce more harmonious results. Actually, however, in a study of symphony orchestras, groups of cranky musicians actually played slightly better than groups of happy ones. Emotions at the end of the concert were more revealing when it came to how well the musicians played than emotions beforehand.[22]

Or perhaps you think things work best when groups are democratic, which can't always be true. (It's silly to think about a team of surgeons debating: "Okay, let's vote. How many of us think the appendix is above the belly button, and how many of us think it's below?") Sometimes, in some types of groups, someone has to be in charge. A leader may emerge naturally, one may be appointed, or one may be the obvious choice (like the surgeon herself), depending on the situation. Or how about this: maybe you've heard that bigger is better when it comes to teams. Actually, that's not quite true, either. Many experts agree that five or seven (no ties when members vote) or six is the magic number for class-based groups, and groups of ten work well in organizations; beyond that, groups may lose interest, find it impossible to coordinate schedules for meetings, and form cliques without even realizing it.

Or finally, consider this commonly held belief. Some students think that online groups are impersonal and boring. There's no doubt that the lack of warm bodies can lower commitment from some members, and that it may take more work to build relationships online. But virtual groups have some advantages, like lessening the problem of conflicting schedules or using the convenience of e-tools like storing the work in Dropbox, building a shared Google Doc, or using a Google Hangout to talk together when members are scattered all across town or even around the globe.

Teamwork—WIIFM? you ask. Good question. Let's start with topics we all know something about: the worlds of sports, music, and movies. In all three, it takes a team. Even lone swimmer Diana Nyad took a team of nutritionists, medics, and navigators in a boat alongside as she became the first person ever to swim from Cuba to Florida without a shark cage. She was sixty-four years old, and the swim took her more than two full days. In the music business, groups like The Beatles have to "get along" despite considerable personality differences, and even famous soloists like Alicia Keys have backup singers and a band as part of their acts. Movies often have a "cast" of hundreds—above and beyond the big-name stars. Sometimes it takes a full five minutes or more to run the credits, showing who all was a part of the movie's production team. In fact, it's safe to say that as important as individual excellence is, much of life is a "team sport," as it turns out.

What about you? You're been developing teamwork skills your entire life. When you were a grade schooler, you probably got As, Bs, and Cs on your report card and comments from your teacher about your behavior in school: "Devin is a good student, but he doesn't play well with others." What does that kind of comment mean, exactly? Was it from whispering too much in class or duking it out with a classmate on the playground? Hopefully, your comments from the teacher were positive. But if you ever did get a negative comment about "playing well with others," you may not have known what your teacher meant for sure; but whatever it was, it probably didn't play well at home.

As an adult, the ability to "play well with others" translates into what is often referred to as "people" or "teamwork" skills—a necessity in the world of work. You can be a whiz at numbers as an accountant, have top-notch talents as a draftsman, or administer expert medical procedures as a nurse. But if your people skills aren't honed, your career is likely to self-destruct or at least stall out.

That's always been true, but now the importance of people skills has resurfaced with a new slant. For digital natives, those for whom technology has always been a part of life, new research suggests that "people skills" can be diluted by many years of spending long hours in front of a computer. In fact, there is evidence that computers actually rewire our brains. "Research on the brain's response to electronic media is fascinating, and not a little disturbing. On the plus side, it suggests that digital natives have higher baseline activity in the part of the brain governing short term memory, the sorting of complex information, and the integration of sensations and thoughts—so, in certain respects, computers make you smarter."[23]

But on the down side, computers don't require you to figure out what they're thinking or interpret their body language. Less interaction with people and more interaction with computers can lead to lower empathy, a reduced ability to read nonverbal cues, a hesitancy to interact socially or maintain eye contact with others, and lower interpersonal skills overall. Some researchers also fear that too much computer interaction keeps the brain from developing the wiring it needs for interaction with people. These characteristics of digital natives, especially if you are one, may be so subtle that you've never even thought about or noticed them.

Okay, so all this is interesting, you say, but WIIFM? Potentially, a great deal, especially if you're a digital native or work with other employees who are. Here's an example.

> "My model for business is The Beatles. They were four guys who kept each other's kind of negative tendencies in check. They balanced each other, and the total was greater than the sum of the parts. That's how I see business: Great things in business are never done by one person, they're done by a team of people."
>
> **Steve Jobs (1955–2011), American entrepreneur and CEO (attended De Anza Community College, Cupertino, California)**

During the 2008 financial collapse, some bright young workers lost their jobs because they didn't empathize with distraught clients who lost everything. Instead of listening to them, the young employees simply sent e-mails saying, "Sorry, we can't help you." So they were let go and replaced with older employees who were willing to meet face-to-face and listen to clients' personal stories of disastrous financial loss. During tough times, people skills counted more than anything else.[24]

Although these characteristics may not apply to every digital native, the most immediate test of your people skills may be during job interviews when you finish college. Your people skills will be on the line. Because interviewers know that interpersonal skills like these are crucial to career success, they may keep an eye on your eye contact during the interview or watch for clues about your willingness to interact socially. When that time comes, you'll want to think through your responses and what they communicate about you. Employers care about your people skills and your ability to work on a team, some say as much as or more than they care about other aspects of your job readiness. The time employees spend working in groups has escalated by 50 percent or more in the last twenty years; in many job fields, three-quarters of employees' days is spent working collaboratively.[25]

Awareness is always the first step to getting better at something. You've left the playground you frequented as a youngster, but "playing well with others" is even more important in the adult world of professional relationships, teamwork, and

the productive communication required in today's organizations. That's crucial to your career success, and that's your answer to the WIIFM question!

WHY GROUPS AT ALL?

Although groups can certainly have their challenges, everyone knows that they can be more effective than a single person. People commonly say things like "the more, the merrier," "two heads are better than one," or "many hands make light work." But besides these remarks we've all heard, think about other specific advantages:

> **Groups have a bigger "knowledge pool" to draw from.** Often, the combined knowledge of the whole group amounts to more than any one member knows. If a class group is tasked with creating the ideal fuel-efficient car of the future, unless there happens to be an automotive engineer around, it's likely a group can do better with the assignment than any one member can. When the situation calls for it, a team can be a better option than an MVP.

> **Groups give individuals a chance to learn from one another.** Chances are that someone in the group knows more about some aspect of the project than you do, and vice versa. Use the opportunity to teach and learn from one another.

> **Groups allow everyone to participate.** If you're an introvert, you may find it easier to talk in a small group than you do in the larger class. If the entire class is split into groups, everyone plays a role during discussions, not just the more outgoing people.

> **Groups can have more influence.** If you're the CEO of a company, the previous statement may not be true. But if you're a first-year student asked to get a student group together to give the faculty input on how to become better teachers, and you invite members representing six different majors on campus—art, general studies, communication, nursing, business, and criminal justice—there's better representation, and the results may be taken more seriously than if you came up with a set of recommendations yourself.

> **Temporary teams or pairs—collaborative learning—can be powerful.** Some instructors will engage you through what's called collaborative learning. Instead of just listening to a lecture as a whole class, you'll be asked to work with one or more partners to solve a problem or find an answer. Actively communicating in small groups can make a big difference in how much you learn.

> **Groups generate more and better ideas through diversity.** Groups are more likely to have representatives with different views. Variety guarantees that good ideas can surface from many diverse points of view.

> "Remember upon the conduct of each depends the fate of all."
>
> **Alexander the Great**

AP Images/Beth A. Keiser

> "Talent wins games, but teamwork and intelligence win championships."
>
> **Michael Jordan, American NBA Basketball Player, widely considered to be the greatest player in the history of the game**

FIGURE 10.1

Quick Study: "The Top 10 Rules of Responsible Group Membership"

THE TOP 10 RULES OF RESPONSIBLE GROUP MEMBERSHIP

1. MAKE SURE THE TASK IS CLEAR TO EVERYONE.
A lack of clarity about the group's task can cause big delays. How much authority do we have? What's our schedule? What's our budget? Or for a class project, what's our assignment, exactly?

2. TALK ABOUT GROUND RULES UP FRONT.
Ever heard of a pre-nup? In case you haven't, it's the "rules" a couple agrees to before marriage. Groups need to talk about things like that in their early meetings, too. For example, one rule might be, "We'll each do our part on time with our best effort." Or "We'll all treat each other with respect and civility." According to a large-scale study launched by Google, equality and sensitivity help groups soar.[A]

FOLLOW THE RULES!

3. REMEMBER THAT TEAMWORK IS AN INDIVIDUAL SKILL.
Sometimes in groups, individual members think, "Oh, well, someone else will do my part. No biggie!" Those people are called "slackers," and they can really put a damper on the group overall.[B] That's one reason why ground rules should be discussed up front.

4. APPOINT A YODA.
Every group needs a Star Wars wise Jedi master. It's Yoda's job to notice who hasn't had a chance to speak yet, who is tromping on someone else's idea, or what needs to be said that hasn't yet been said.[C]

5. COORDINATE THE WORK.
Does the task require that everyone take "a piece of the pie" and work independently for a while? Or does it require that those working on TASK 1 finish before those working on TASKS 2 and 3 can start? Either way, cooperation and collaboration are key.

6. LET ROLES EMERGE.
Usually, different kinds of communicators emerge in groups. Some members are more task-oriented, and some are more people-oriented. Both are needed. Too many task-oriented members can make everyone feel like they're running breathlessly at full speed, and too many people-oriented types can feel like group counseling. Destructive roles, of course, should be checked at the door, and it should be somebody's role (maybe yours) to suggest that.

HELLO I'M A... SUPERHERO

7. CULTIVATE CARING CRITICISM.
Teams can't get anything done if everyone is always "*walking on eggshells*." It's important to be sensitive to people's feelings, but it's also important to be honest. Caring criticism is a balanced approach that breeds openness, not defensiveness.[D]

8. REMEMBER THAT ONGOING GROUPS GO THROUGH STAGES.
Groups start with a *forming* stage, when everyone is getting acquainted. Next comes a *norming* stage as they figure out how to function, according to spoken or unspoken rules. Then they often go through a *storming* stage, where conflict erupts. Finally, they reach a *performing* stage, where they hit optimum productivity.[E] These stages can happen differently in different groups, but going through the four stages is common.

9. CREATE WAYS TO GET UNSTUCK.
Sometimes groups get stuck. They stop making progress because everyone is busy and distractions intervene. Passivity kills groups, so shake things up by asking a tough question, or proposing a crazy idea to shake things loose. Challenge the status quo to get things moving again.

10. USE YOUR SIGNATURE STRENGTHS AND HELP OTHERS FIND THEIRS.
You may think that group work is hard or that you're not particularly good at it. But everyone has a contribution to make. You may know something interesting about the topic, or you may be especially good at injecting positivity or humor. Or your strength may be helping other people find theirs.

IconBunny/Shutterstock.com; Nobelus/Shutterstock.com; rolandtopor/Shutterstock.com; iQoncept/Shutterstock.com; gst/Shutterstock.com; chrisdorney/Shutterstock.com; Nadin3d/Shutterstock.com; Aha-Soft/Shutterstock.com; OLga Shishova/Shutterstock.com; deviyanthi79/Shutterstock.com; Kaer_Stock/Shutterstock.com

Sources: (A) Duhigg, C. (2016, February 25). What Google learned from its quest to build the perfect team. *The New York Times*. Retrieved from https://www.nytimes.com/2016/02/28/magazine/what-google-learned-from-its-quest-to-build-the-perfect-team.html?_r=0; (B) Perron, B. E. (2011). Reducing social loafing in group-based projects. *College Teaching*. Retrieved from http://www.tandfonline.com/doi/full/10.1080/87567555.2011.568021#.UmqlgWSglF8; (C) Ferrazzi, K. (2012, January–February). Candor, criticism, teamwork. *Harvard Business Review*. Retrieved from https://hbr.org/2012/01/candor-criticism-teamwork; (D) Ferrazzi, Candor, criticism, teamwork. (E) Tuckman, B. (1965). Developmental sequence in small groups. *Psychological Bulletin 63*(6): 384–99.

"You are the average of the five people you spend the most time with."

Jim Rohn, entrepreneur, author, and motivational speaker (1920–2009)

VARK IT

Visual: Look back at Serena Jackson's case study. Which of the particular 10 items in this Quick Study would have helped her group? How would *you* have handled her situation?

COMMUNICATING
IN IMPORTANT RELATIONSHIPS

Think of all the kinds of communicating you do—and with whom. And think of all the ways you communicate—by texting, talking face-to-face, or posting a photo of yourself with a few descriptive words online. Not only do you work in groups with classmates, as we've just discussed, but you also have friends you care about. You may think the primary thing friends help you do is fill up your spare time. But new research shows that friends can actually help you fight illness and depression, boost your brain power and even prolong your life. In one study, students were taken to the bottom of a steep hill while wearing a heavy backpack. They were asked to estimate the steepness of the hill. Participants standing next to friends, rather than by themselves, thought the hill looked much less steep, and friends who had known each other longer gave increasingly less steep estimates. Researchers summarized that "People with stronger friendship networks feel like there is someone they can turn to. Friendship is an undervalued resource. The consistent message of these studies is that friends make your life better." If that's true, then how you communicate with them is more important than you may even realize.[26]

Or consider family members. These people make up the core of who you really are. Your kid brother may drive you crazy at times, and a parent may seem to smother you, but generally, these people care about you most. Often we "let it all hang out" with family members, perhaps because we know they'll overlook our flaws. When we're tired or stressed, this is often where we "veg" or vent. But because of the central, long-lasting role they play in our lives, they deserve more quality communication than we sometimes give them.

Classmates and instructors, too, deserve your best communication, even when you disagree with the perspective they're advocating. You may see your instructors as intimidating or helpful, but you'll need to make the first move to get to know them, rather than the other way around. Take the initiative to meet them during their office hours and bring up points from class that you'd like to know more about. It's unlikely a professor will single you out ("John, you looked puzzled when I got to the part of the chapter on pages 160–170. Did you understand what I was talking about?"). You have many classmates, and your instructor may not be able to pay attention to each individual student. It'll be your job to go to your professor to get the clarification you need. Do some of your best communicating with instructors and classmates, and remember that face-to-face communication often works best.

"At the extreme, we are so enmeshed in our connections that we neglect each other."

Sherry Turkle, from Alone Together: Why We Expect More from Technology and Less from Each Other

MANAGING CONFLICT:
LIFE IS NOT A SITCOM

Bad relationships can hurt your job performance, your finances, your physical and mental health—even your life span.[27] Conflict with instructors and classmates, or with anyone you're close to—family or friends, for example—can bring on major stress that affects your academic performance, not to mention your overall happiness.[28]

Unfortunately, movies and television often communicate—subtly or not so subtly—that conflict can be resolved by the end of the show. Just lighten up or settle down and you can resolve almost any problem. And if you can't, just swallow, take a deep breath, and move on. But life isn't like that, nor should it be. Managing the conflict in your life takes time, energy, and persistence. It requires understanding your natural tendencies, considering why you communicate as you do, and making good choices as a communicator.

If you've ever monitored yourself during a particularly heated conflict, you may remember doing something like this: yelling in anger at someone at the top of your lungs, being interrupted by a phone call and suddenly communicating calmly and quietly to the caller, and then returning to the original shouting match after you hang up.

Why? We make *choices* as communicators. Sometimes our choices are productive ones, and sometimes they aren't. It's important to remember that we *do* choose what we say and how we behave. Our choices affect both the *process*—how things go during the conflict—and the *product*—how it turns out in the end. Negative choices produce destructive conflict that includes personal attacks, name calling, an unwillingness to listen, or underhanded strategies. Positive choices are much more likely to bring productive conflict that helps us learn more about ourselves, our partners, and our relationships. To find out more about your own tendencies in conflict situations, take a moment to assess your style, informally, in Exercise 10.3.

"Gettin' good players is easy. Gettin' 'em to play together is the hard part."

Casey Stengel, major league baseball player and manager (1890–1975)

EXERCISE 10.3 **WHAT'S YOUR CONFLICT STYLE?**

For each of the following statements, please rate your response on a scale of 1 to 5, with 1 representing "strongly agree" and 5 representing "strongly disagree."

Strongly Agree	Agree	Not Sure	Disagree	Strongly Disagree
1	2	3	4	5

1. _____ I usually end up compromising in conflict situations. (CO)

2. _____ Someone always loses in a conflict. (CP)

3. _____ I usually let other people "win" in conflicts because I often feel less strongly about the outcome than they do. (AC)

4. _____ When I really care about a relationship, I devote unusual amounts of time and energy into coming up with creative solutions so that each of us can get what we want. (CL)

5. _____ "Don't rock the boat" is a good philosophy. (AV)

6. _____ "Winning" in conflict situations gives me a real "high." (CP)

7. _____ Sacrificing what I want so that someone else can achieve a goal is often worth it. (AC)

8. _____ It's possible for both parties to "win" in conflict situations. (CL)

9. _____ Sometimes you have to settle for "part of the pie." (CO)

10. _____ I try to avoid conflict at all costs. It's not worth it. (AV)

(continued on next page)

Managing conflict: Life is not a Sitcom **273**

People often come at conflicts using differing styles. Not only do you disagree on the topic at hand—whatever it is—but you approach conflict itself differently. This quick quiz is based on a well-known, five-part model of conflict styles (see Figure 10.2). In our version of the model, the horizontal axis is labeled "Concern for Other" (or cooperativeness) and the vertical axis is labeled "Concern for Self" (or assertiveness).[29]

Where are your highest scores? Notice the letters at the end of the ten statements.

If you like to win and care most about your own goals, you compete (CP).

If you care more about the other person's goals, and give in, you accommodate (AC).

If you don't care about your goals or your partner's, you avoid (AV).

If you care somewhat about both and are willing to settle for "part of the pie," you compromise (CO). Strictly speaking, when you compromise, neither of you gets exactly what you want.

If you care about your own goals and your partner's, and you're willing to devote the time and energy required to reach a win–win solution, you collaborate (CL).

What's your style? Do you have a conflict style you're most comfortable with? Do you fall into the habit of using one style, even if it's not productive in particular situations? Flexibility is the key to managing conflicts productively, and if the relationship really counts, collaboration is the ideal.

FIGURE 10.2

Conflict Management Styles

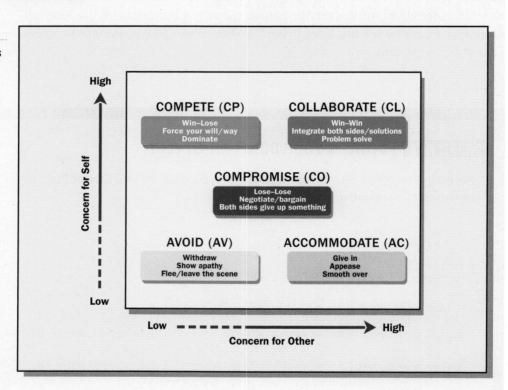

diversity the ways in which people differ from one another

VARK IT

Kinesthetic: Think about a favorite TV show in which two people are often in conflict. Can you determine each person's conflict style?

DIVERSITY MAKES
A DIFFERENCE

Diversity makes the group process potentially rich in terms of *process*—how members communicate—and *product*—the decision they eventually reach or project they create. The ten statements following in Exercise 10.4 are intentionally provocative to stimulate your thinking. They relate to diversity broadly: the differences between human beings based on gender, race, ethnicity, age, culture,

EXERCISE 10.4 YOUR VIEWS ON DIVERSITY

What are your views on diversity? Look at the following ten statements, and indicate the extent to which you agree or disagree.

Strongly Agree 1	Agree 2	Not Sure 3	Disagree 4	Strongly Disagree 5

1. Race is still a factor in hiring decisions today. _____

2. Multiculturalism implies that all cultures have equally valid viewpoints. _____

3. Workforce diversity improves the quality of work. _____

4. The number of male versus female corporate CEOs is nearing the halfway mark in the United States. _____

5. In some situations, sexual orientation is a justifiable basis for discrimination. _____

6. All cultures tend to see the rest of the world through their own cultural lens. _____

7. Feminism is a set of beliefs held by females. _____

8. A global perspective ensures objectivity. _____

9. Religious persecution is a thing of the past. _____

10. There is less racism in the United States today than there was ten years ago. _____

As you the "Diversity Makes a Difference" section of the chapter, search for points relating to these topics. Also, your instructor may wish to use these ten items to begin a discussion online or in class.

physical features and abilities, mental capability, socioeconomic status, religion, politics, sexuality, gender identity, and points of view. Diversity is a fact of life. But consider this: You may think people of your age, religion, race, ethnicity, or gender with characteristics like yours are somehow more "normal" or "better" without even realizing it. But others unlike you may think the same thing about their particular "group" and see you very differently. If you're from a well-to-do family, for example, you may see yourself as "fortunate," but others may see you as "privileged." Perceptions are important in discussions about diversity. They influence our interactions with others, and sometimes perceptions can lead to bias. Take a closer look in Table 10.1.

Each of us is a unique human being. Some of us are taller, some are shorter, some are older, some are younger. Some aspects of our uniqueness are visible. It's not hard to tell the difference between someone who's five feet tall and someone who's seven feet tall or someone who's twenty years old versus someone who's eighty. But other aspects of our uniqueness aren't as obvious. Would people necessarily know your religion, your sexual orientation, or even your race just by looking at you? If you had a stack of photos—a headshot of every student who attends your school—could you sort them by race into the same stacks they'd sort themselves into? Anyone can tell an Asian American from an African American just by looking. Or so they may think.

"I take as my guide the hope of a saint: In crucial things, unity; in important things, diversity; in all things, generosity."

George H. W. Bush, forty-first president of the United States

Table 10.1 • Possible Perceptions of Types of Diversity

TYPES OF DIVERSITY	POSSIBLE PERCEPTIONS	THINGS TO CONSIDER
Age Diversity	"Those youngsters with all the tattoos and piercings! What do they know?"	Trends change, and outward expressions vary from one generation to the next.
	"Older drivers! They're so slow!"	Reaction times slow down, and vision can worsen.
Gender Diversity	"I'm all for women's rights, but a female college president? I'm not sure we're ready for that!"	Actually, 33 percent of community college presidents are women.[30]
	"Why would a guy want to be a nurse? That's a woman's job."	Nursing is a top career field for men or women, now and in the future.
Geographic Diversity	"The South is so backwards."	Southerners are proud of their traditions.
	"Northerners are such snobs."	Regional accents can carry particular stereotypes.
Physical Diversity	"Boy, if I only had a handicapped sticker, I could park anywhere on campus."	Physical challenges warrant access capability.
	"That professional signer in class is really distracting!"	In-class signers help deaf students follow lectures and discussions—like a language translator.
Sexual Orientation Diversity	"Call me homophobic, but all *my* friends are straight."	Homophobia can be a highly negative hidden bias.
	"Transgender? That's just plain weird!"	College is a time to become aware of differences, including things you may never have been exposed to.
Religious Diversity	"Religious people are unthinking."	Religious beliefs are highly personal, and spirituality in some form can bring balance and meaning.
	"I'm glad I was raised believing in the right religion."	Although it can be natural to see your family traditions as "right," realize that others may feel equally strong about theirs.

Race is often the first thing people think of when they hear the word *diversity*. But some experts say race is a relatively modern idea. Centuries ago, people tended to classify other people by status, religion, or language, for example, not by race. Actually, most of us are a blend of ethnicities, and how we perceive ourselves may be different from the way others see us. People may assume that a Pacific Islander with light brown skin, dark hair, and dark eyes, for example, is Hispanic. And a classmate you may assume is white may think of himself as black. Or consider this: If you have a Chinese mother and a white father, you may not know which "race box" to check on standard forms. Should you choose Mom or Dad?[31] Biologists tell us that there's more variation within a race than there is between races. Race isn't biological, they say, but *racism* is real.[32]

Although you or some of your classmates may have grown up in communities with less racial, ethnic, or cultural diversity than others, you have probably experienced the multicultural nature of our society in many different ways, even in terms of food, music, and clothing, for example. The media have introduced you to aspects of diversity, and perhaps you've even traveled to other parts of the United States or the world yourself.

But here's the challenge: Have experiencing diversity and learning about it in school truly made a difference in the way you think and act? Do you choose to diversify your awareness, your relationships, and yourself as a person? Do you think that discrimination no longer exists in our multicultural society?

Many college students today do believe that racial discrimination is no longer a problem. *Been there; done that,* they've concluded. We may think of ourselves as more "highly evolved" than Americans of past decades, but are we? If you see an interracial couple, do you take a second look without even thinking about it? Are we truly bias-free in this day and age?

According to a national survey, "helping to promote racial understanding" was considered "essential" or "very important" by only slightly more than one-third of incoming first-year students.[33] In another study, students were asked to identify the five most critical and two least critical outcomes of a college education from a list of sixteen possibilities. Tolerance and respect for people of other races, ethnicities, and lifestyles were identified as among the least important goals for college learning.[34] Why do you think they responded that way? Do

tolerance a fair, objective attitude toward differences

ethnicities groups of people who share a culture, language, and possibly a religion

---

EXERCISE 10.5   **FACING THE RACE ISSUE**

Take a look at the faces in the photos. Can you categorize them into common racial types: White, Black, Hispanic/ Latino, Native American, or Asian? After you've identified each one, check the answers provided. How accurate were you? Does this activity confirm that although race is used as a common identifier, it isn't an easy or accurate way to classify people?[35]

Answers: (top row): B, H, NA, A, H **and (bottom row):** B, H, H, W, W.

discrimination bias that results in unfair treatment

they think they've already achieved these goals, or do they think they're less important for other reasons?

If you conducted a survey on your campus to find out whether discrimination exists, you might be surprised at the results. Research continues to show that minority students report experiencing discrimination at higher rates than majority students. Many of us downplay the prejudice all human beings harbor to one extent or another. Our brains are "programmed" to group people that are alike and standardize our views about these groups, resulting in stereotypes. Sometimes, we feel safe around others like us and fear those unlike us. Appreciating individuals for what they are, instead of stereotyping, could drastically change the way we think and act. If you open up your thinking to new possibilities, all kinds of new options present themselves. Imagine a band made up of only trombones, a meal with nothing but string beans, a song played on one note, or a world where everyone looks exactly like you. Diversity enriches our lives. Prejudice stunts our thinking.

stereotypes commonly held unfavorable beliefs about people

A University of Michigan study demonstrated that students who had more positive interactions with diverse peers, and in particular took a college course on diversity, were more likely to be academically self-confident, more personally proactive, and more likely to develop better critical thinking skills.[36] Learning to deal effectively with diversity can actually change you as a college student! Prejudice, or looking down on people just because they are different, isn't a good vantage point. If a classmate who's unlike you were the son or daughter of a famous actor, would that change your view? Prejudice sneaks up on us and limits our ability to grow as human beings.

proactive planning ahead, rather than simply reacting

prejudice a general, unfavorable opinion held without specific evidence

APPRECIATE THE
AMERICAN MOSAIC

Ovidiu Hrubaru/Shutterstock.com

"It is time for parents to teach young people early on that in diversity there is beauty and there is strength."

Maya Angelou, American Poet (1928-2014)

It's becoming more and more impossible to draw clear lines between what separates us physically. Actress Jessica Alba has a mother with French and Danish roots and a Mexican-American father; Keanu Reeves is Hawaiian, Chinese, and Caucasian; Mariah Carey is Black, Venezuelan, and Caucasian; and Johnny Depp is Cherokee and Caucasian.[37] The woman in the nearby photo is Naomi Campbell, one of the most successful mixed race (Afro-Chinese and Jamaican) models of all time, host of the reality TV show *The Face*, and philanthropist. Most of us are a blend, but diversity is about more than physical appearance. Each of us is a unique human being.

Actually, college is a perfect time to learn more about diversity—in the classroom and beyond it. Classrooms are becoming more diversely populated; it's true. Diversity in higher education gives you an opportunity to expand your world view and develop empathy for others who have vastly different experiences.

Aside from meeting students who are different from you in college, taking advantage of diversity can help you become a more sophisticated thinker, one who can see problems from multiple perspectives, and a better prepared employee, ready to hit the ground running in today's highly diverse workplace. Appreciating diversity also helps us become better citizens. Diversity is what our society is based on. In a democratic society such as ours, citizens must be able to recognize and endorse creative solutions to complex problems. A former chief justice of the U.S. Supreme Court, Charles Evans Hughes, once said, "When we lose the right to be different, we lose the privilege to be free."

One mistake many college students make is not taking advantage of what diversity offers them. Because people often tend to feel comfortable with others like them they join groups of people just like themselves, based on religion, sexual orientation, or majors, for example. You can choose to belong to the Young Republicans; the Gay, Lesbian, Bisexual, Transgender (GLBT) student group; or the History Honor Society. Joining a group of like students assures you a place where people accept you for who you are, and you feel comfortable. Think about the groups you belong to and what they say about you.

Of course, being comfortable and feeling accepted are important. But instead, imagine choosing to join groups composed of very different types of people. Consider what philosopher and educator John Dewey once said, "Conflict . . . shocks us out of sheep-like passivity," or the words of a famous American lawyer, Louis Nizer, who once put it like this: "Where there is no difference, there is only indifference." Valuing diversity relates directly to your empathy skills and your emotional intelligence. What about stretching ourselves to learn fully what diversity has the potential to teach us?[38]

Imagine you were engaged in a service-learning project for a class, working in your local soup kitchen. It's easy to criticize a homeless person and think, "Why doesn't he just get a job?" But when you actually sit down and share a bowl of soup across the table, you might see things differently. You might hear

EXERCISE 10.6   CIRCLES OF AWARENESS

Each of us has a cultural identity. How do we see ourselves, and how do others see us? Write your name in the center of the drawing, and then label each of the surrounding circles with a word that represents a group you identify with. You may use categories like age, gender, ethnicity, social, political, and so forth. After your drawing is labeled, your instructor will ask you to circulate around the room and find three classmates who have listed at least three of the same subgroups. After that, you will be asked to find three students who listed at least three categories that you did not. In the second group you formed, based on differences, use the activity to discuss diversity, differences among individuals and groups, and how awareness can change behavior. Look over everyone's list, and to diversify your thinking, select one group on someone else's list, but not on yours. Find out more about that group or decide to attend a group meeting to raise your awareness of what you think the group is like, and what it's actually like.[40]

Your Name

stories of personal illness, family tragedy, unbelievable trauma—a list of bad luck coincidences you'd never even think of. Rather than assigning all homeless people to a group with a negative label, learn more about the individuals that make up that group. You might change your views.

One professor says this: "I tell my students to keep in mind that everything they see is a snapshot. That guy drinking from a bottle in a paper bag, he's a photograph. How did he get to where he is? From there, we can share some of the rage at the inherent injustice that awaits so many of our poor children as they grow up. As we examine people, the snapshots become a motion picture that links the past, present, and future—what was, what is, what can be."[39]

injustice · unfair action or treatment

Choose a stereotype you recognize, one you suspect you believe if you're honest, and decide what you can do to test it. Ask yourself whether it affects your thinking and actions. For example, are you aware of these facts about continuing stereotypes in our culture?

> **Sexism is still an issue in corporate America.** As of February of 2016, only 14 of America's Fortune 500 companies were run by a woman, down from 24 in 2014.[41] Further, according to one recent study, women receive between 3 and 30 percent lower salary offers for the same roles, compared to their male counterparts, 69 percent of the time.[42]

> **Racism is still an issue in hiring decisions.** A Gallup poll asked: "Do you feel that racial minorities in this country have job opportunities equal to whites, or not?" Among whites, the answer was 55 percent yes and 43 percent no. (The rest were undecided.) Among African Americans, the answer was 17 percent yes and 81 percent no. You might also be shocked to read about an experiment in which fake applicants of one race were 50 percent more likely to be called for interviews than applicants of another race, based solely on whether their names sounded like they belonged to a particular racial group! As one *Wall Street Journal* reporter noted, "Someday Americans will be able to speak of racial discrimination in hiring in the past tense. Not yet"[43]

> **Discrimination and stereotypes persist.** Students with disabilities report a "chilly classroom climate" for students with disabilities in higher education.[44] According to one college president, "With all [the change in racial demographics], diversity has become the largest issue behind unrest on campus."[45] A study of closeted and out gay and lesbian college students reported that these students perceived unfair treatment and a need to hide their identity from most other students. Both groups reported experiencing a similar amount of antigay attacks.[46] Beyond sexual identity, take a look at all the various kinds of bias that are reported today in Figure 10.3. People still harm one another out of hatred for differences they may not understand.

Diversity makes a difference, and as educator Adela A. Allen once wrote, "We should acknowledge differences, we should greet differences, until difference makes no difference anymore." What can we do about it? Raising awareness is a first step on the road to recognizing the reality and the richness of diversity.

VARK IT!

Read/Write: Write a short paragraph about diversity, using fictitious names, that shows prejudice you've experienced or witnessed.

FIGURE 10.3

Hate Crime Offenses
Source: FBI.gov

Hate in 2015
Here's a breakdown, by category, of why the 7,121
victims of the 5,818 single-bias incidents were targeted:

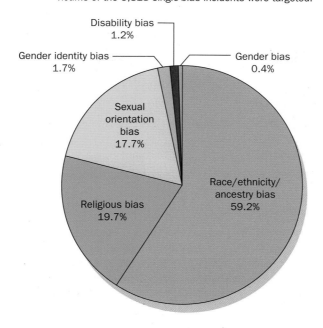

- Disability bias 1.2%
- Gender identity bias 1.7%
- Gender bias 0.4%
- Sexual orientation bias 17.7%
- Religious bias 19.7%
- Race/ethnicity/ancestry bias 59.2%

WHAT'S YOUR CQ?

An advertisement for an international bank gets the point across well. It shows a picture of a grasshopper. Below the grasshopper are these three sentences that describe three different cultural views of grasshoppers: USA—Pest, China—Pet, Northern Thailand—Appetizer.[47] One insect, three cultural perspectives. Americans tend to shoo away pesky grasshoppers. But if you travel to China, be careful of stepping on one that may be someone else's beloved pet. And if you travel to Northern Thailand, try not to look disgusted when you see fried grasshoppers on the appetizer plate.

America   **China**   **Northern Thailand**

iStock.com/diane39; iStock.com/Antagain   iStock.com/jclegg; iStock.com/Antagain   iStock.com/frytka; iStock.com/Antagain

Just as individuals have emotional intelligence, they also have cultural intelligence. Some of us are more naturally sensitive to cultural differences, and we know how to handle ourselves. But all of us can grow our cultural intelligence with training and preparation. EQ relates to self-awareness and relationship skills; CQ relates to awareness and responses to other cultures (and subcultures of our own culture). EQ and CQ are linked.

VARK IT!

Aural: Talk with an international student on your campus about how college life in the United States differs from what a student would experience in his or her home country.

What's your CQ? **281**

DIAGNOSING YOUR CULTURAL INTELLIGENCE

These statements reflect different aspects of cultural intelligence. For each set, add up your scores and divide by four to arrive at an average. As you answer, think about your answers in each category as they compare to the other two categories.

Rate how much you agree with each statement, using this scale:

1 = strongly disagree   2 = disagree   3 = neutral   4 = agree   5 = strongly agree

____ Before I interact with people from a new culture, I think about what I'm going to communicate.

____ If I come up against something unexpected in a new culture, I use the experience to think about how I should respond in other cultures in the future.

____ I plan how I'm going to relate to people from a different culture before I even meet them.

____ When I'm communicating in a new culture, I have a clear sense of whether things are going well or not.

____ Total divided by 4 = ____ COGNITIVE CQ

____ It's easy for me to change my body language (eye contact or posture, for example) to match that used by people from a different culture.

____ I can change my expression when I need to interact with people from another culture.

____ I can modify my speech (for example, accent or tone) when interacting with people from another culture.

____ I can easily change the way I act when a cross-cultural situation seems to require it.

____ Total divided by 4 = ____ PHYSICAL CQ

____ I have confidence that I can deal well with people from another culture.

____ I am certain that I can make friends with people from a culture that's different from mine.

____ I can adapt to the lifestyle of another culture when I need to fairly easily.

____ I am confident that I can deal with a cultural situation, even if it's unfamiliar.

____ Total divided by 4 = ____ EMOTIONAL/MOTIVATIONAL CQ

Generally, an average lower than three identifies an opportunity for improvement, and an average greater than 4.5 identifies a true CQ strength.

Here's a definition: cultural intelligence is an outsider's seemingly natural ability to interpret someone's unfamiliar and ambiguous gestures the way other people of that culture would.[48] CQ has three components that involve your head, your body, and your heart. All three work together to help you interact in a foreign culture—or a subculture that's new to you within your own larger culture. Think, for example, about taking a job in a new culture, either by transferring overseas or by entering an organization with different rules: "Casual Fridays," "Bring Your Dog to Work Day," "Follow Strict Communication Rules and Always Go Through Your Boss," or "Choose Your Own Project to Work on One Day a Week" (if you work for Google). These rules might be different for you, and you'd need good CQ skills to adapt. Or think about entering a subculture you're unfamiliar with: like being "straight" and having a gay best friend, or marrying someone of another ethnicity. CQ can be broken down into three parts, all of which work together:

1. **Cognitive quotient (head):** Do you understand the differences between another culture and your own? Before entering a new culture, do you think before you act? Do you learn about the culture in advance of interacting with its members so that you don't make embarrassing mistakes?

2. **Physical quotient (body):** Do you watch for behaviors that are different in other cultures? Do you mimic the gestures and customs of the people? Do you shake hands correctly? Do you notice whether the culture is "high touch" or "low touch"? Do you adopt their habits so that you earn their trust?

3. **Emotional/motivational quotient (heart):** Do you empathize with people from this culture? Can you imagine what it's like to be a member of this culture? Do you want to connect despite your differences? This aspect of CQ is thought to be most like EQ.

To have good CQ skills, you must be more than a "mimic," simply repeating what you see and hear in another culture. You must be a "chameleon," taking on what it's like to be a member of that culture. You must—through your head, your body, and your heart—prove to others that you have entered their world. Not only are CQ skills important within the American culture, they're also important in today's global society. How culturally intelligent are you? CQ is a natural extension of EQ, and the suggestions for how to improve your EQ apply to strengthening your CQ. If your cognitive quotient is low, read up about other cultures. If your physical quotient is low, watch for differences in gestures or movements and find out what they mean. If your emotional/motivational quotient is low, ask others for input, for example, or find a CQ mentor.

THINK GLOBALLY;
ACT LOCALLY

The 1972 United Nations international conference on the human environment in Stockholm was the origin of the phrase "Think Globally, Act Locally." Perhaps you've heard it. Simply put, it originally meant "Do what you can to 'save the environment.'"

Today the phrase takes on added meaning. True, recycling is becoming the norm, and **sustainability** is the watchword of modern corporations. But beyond environmental concerns, the world is characterized by networks of connections across continents and distances. As citizens of the world, we are all connected, if not geographically, then economically, militarily, socially, financially, and technologically. Google Search now offers an interface in 123 languages, and now only 8.6 percent of all internet users reside in North America.[49] A famous song title once made the claim: "We Are the World."

The education you get now must prepare you to solve the problems of the future. It will require you to look beyond the walls of your classrooms and refine your skills in terms of how relationships work, how diversity impacts our lives, and how to be culturally intelligent. It will require you to think and act both globally *and* locally. The course for which you're using this text is a good place to start.

VARK IT!

Kinesthetic: If you have a Facebook account, look at the pages of three people you know who have traveled to another country. Can you find examples of cultural differences they describe?

"We have not inherited the world from our fore-fathers—we have borrowed it from our children."

Kashmiri proverb

sustainability the practice of meeting our needs now without compromising the ability of future generations to meet theirs (Brundtland Commission of the United Nations, March 20, 1987)

BOX 10.1 **SERVICE-LEARNING: LEARNING BY SERVING**

One of the best ways to learn about diversity in college is by serving others. Instead of spending all your time in a classroom, imagine a class on aging in which you team up with an elder in your community and work together on a project. You might help a senior write her memoirs, for example, or help an elderly man create a family tree for the next generation. You might be wondering, How would that work? What could we possibly have in common—especially if you're an eighteen-year-old teamed up with an eighty-eight-year-old? You might be surprised.

Campus Compact, a national organization with approximately 1100 member two- and four-year colleges, estimates that college student volunteering was worth nearly $3.5 billion to the communities they served in 2014.[50]

Beyond the dollars calculated, college students' community service provides invaluable support. For example, after Tropical Storm Irene, students from six different college and university campuses in Vermont worked on long-term recovery committees and community organizations around the state. Students worked directly with flood survivors, documented changes to local rivers, and improved emergency response plans for future such events.[51]

However, here's an important point: community service and service-learning aren't quite the same thing.[52] Service-learning is specifically about the learning. It's a learning experience in which you connect what you're learning in the classroom for credit with what you're learning in the community. You're applying what you're learning, which may change your perspective. "Service, combined with learning, adds value to each and transforms both."[53] While you're engaged in a

"We make a living by what we get, but we make a life by what we give."

Winston Churchill, Prime Minister of England (1874–1965)

Brand X Pictures/Getty Image

service-learning experience, you'll also be engaged in critical reflection or focused thinking about what you're doing. Critical reflection is like critical thinking, recalling or looking back at the service experience and writing about what you're learning in a continuous, connected, challenging, and contextualized way.[54] That's not the same thing as donating your time for a good cause, as important as that is, in terms of you and your own personal development and the lives of the people you help.

Search out these opportunities to learn and appreciate diversity by serving other people.

CAREER OUTLOOK: MAKE IT PERSONAL

Have you ever been accused of taking things personally? Your Mom looks askance at your new, multitone hair color or your ever-so-stylish "runway" outfit, or your roommate makes a confusing, offhanded comment about something that's dear to your heart. "How dare she?" you think to yourself! When you tell the story to your best friend, she provides a reality check, "Oh,

lighten up. You don't have to take it personally."

People count. We care about what they think of us. But what about the often overlooked reverse point of view? They care, too. People prop us up, validate us (or not), and meet our personal needs—and we do the same for them. Even though we know it, we don't always show it. It explains why some

very intelligent, highly capable people fail and why misunderstandings are common. It's not so much that people always take things personally; it's that they sometimes forget to make things personal.

Consider this scenario: You're on a team with a colleague who's a bear to work with. She may be the hardest worker in the company, have the best ideas, and sport a sales record that no one else can touch. But ultimately, she fails miserably in your organization and moves to another one . . . again. She moves from job to job, and she just can't figure out why she's not seen as successful. But to her, the job is all about the work. The people she works with are invisible to her. She doesn't realize that the people are how the work gets done. According to one career expert, "There's a simple reason for it: we rarely take the time to pause, breathe, and think about what's working and what's not. There's just too much to do and no time to reflect." Making things personal is about listening carefully to the layers of communication and remembering that people count. Actually, it's less about time and more about mindset. Appreciate your differences, explore your commonalities, and above all, remember that work, like the rest of life, is about building productive relationships.[55]

Here's a recommendation: At the end of every workday, take five minutes to reflect not only about the work but also about your coworkers. Ask yourself these three questions:

1. What went well today and what didn't?
2. What lessons from today will help me do a better job tomorrow?
3. Who contributed to my success? Is there someone I should update or thank? If so, do it.[56]

Doing so will not only help you do your best, but it will do the same for others. Remembering to "make it personal" will affect your career more positively than you can possibly imagine now.

Think about a time that you were involved in a college project (a group presentation, for example) when things either did or didn't work well. Which principles you've just read about were (or would have been) important?

INSIGHT: *NOW* WHAT DO YOU THINK?

At the beginning of this chapter, Serena Jackson faced a challenge as a new college student. Now after reading this chapter, would you respond differently to any of the questions you answered about the "FOCUS Challenge Case"? Using what you learned in the chapter, write a paragraph ending to Serena's case study. What are some of the possible outcomes for Serena?

ACTION: YOUR PLANS FOR CHANGE

1. What have your group experiences been like in the past? Do the recommendations about groupwork in this chapter make sense to you? Which one(s) will you try?

2. This chapter asserts that diversity makes a difference. Do you believe that statement? In what ways can learning to appreciate diversity change how you interact with others? How can these communication skills pay off in the future? What will you do to refine them further?

3. Is cultural intelligence something you've ever thought about before? What role might it play in your future personal or professional life?

CHALLENGE: REALITY CHECK

HOW MUCH DID YOU LEARN?

At the beginning of this chapter, you filled out a "Readiness Check" that asked how you thought this chapter would relate to you and how you would relate to it. Now, fill out this "Reality Check" to find out.

1. What is emotional intelligence, and how does it relate to college success?
2. What are the benefits of working in groups?
3. Describe three benefits of valuing diversity.
4. In your own words, define *CQ*.
5. How long did it take? _____ hours _____ minutes. Before you began this chapter, you were asked to predict how long it would take you to complete this chapter (total time, even if you read it in more than one sitting). Was your estimate on target, or will you revise it for the next chapter you'll read?

HOW THIS CHAPTER RELATES TO YOU

1. When it comes to choosing a college major and career what do you find most challenging, if anything? Put check marks by the phrases that apply to you or write in your answer.

   ☐ Knowing how different disciplines connect

   ☐ Choosing a major

   ☐ Choosing a career

   ☐ Understanding my strengths

   ☐ Figuring out what I want to do with my life

   ☐ _____

2. What is most likely to be your response? Put a check mark by it.

   ☐ I'll be open to learning how to make this decision.

   ☐ I'll see whether this chapter helps me.

   ☐ I'll start exploring my options now.

   ☐ Eventually, I'll just figure it out.

3. What would you have to do to increase your likelihood of success? Will you do it this quarter or semester?

HOW YOU WILL RELATE TO THIS CHAPTER

1. What are you most interested in learning about? Put check marks by those topics.

   ☐ Why "college in a box" isn't an accurate view of coursework

   ☐ How the disciplines connect in the Circle of Learning

   ☐ How to choose a major and career

   ☐ How to discover your bliss, conduct research, and take a good look at yourself

   ☐ What a SWOT analysis is

YOUR READINESS FACTOR

1. How motivated are you to learn more about choosing a college major and career? (5 = high, 1 = low)

2. How ready are you to read now? (If something is in your way, take care of it if you can. Zero in and focus.)

3. How long do you think it will take you to complete this chapter? If you start and stop, keep track of your overall time. ____ Hour(s) ____ Minute(s)

VGstockstudio/Shutterstock.com

FOCUS
CHALLENGE CASE

Ethan Cole

One thing was certain: Ethan Cole was unsure. Unsure of his abilities, unsure of which major to choose, unsure of what he wanted to do with his life, unsure of himself. Unsure of almost everything.

Ethan came from a good family, and he actually got along pretty well with his parents. They both had decent jobs, worked long hours, and overall they had been good to him. Compared with many of his friends, he came from a "happy home." But frankly, his parents weren't all that interested in the details of his life. When he announced one day as a high school senior that he wanted to go to the community college in town, they said, "What for?" When he said he didn't know, they replied, "Well, you'll figure it out." And that was that. He enrolled the next day.

The only thing Ethan was sure of was that skateboarding was his life right now. It's all he wanted to do and all he ever thought about. He'd look at a curve on a window frame or an arc in a picture and imagine what skating on it would feel like. All his friends were skateboarders, too, and he read skateboarder magazines and dreamed of the day he might even go pro. He realized not many people make a living at it, but a few really talented athletes did, and maybe—just maybe—he'd be one of them. Recently, he'd found out about the largest concrete skatepark on the globe, SMP Skatepark in Shanghai—182,000

square feet! He'd made a promise to himself to skate there someday. *Life couldn't get much better than that,* he thought.

But school . . . that was a different story. Schoolwork had never captured his attention. In primary school, his physician had diagnosed him with Attention Deficit Disorder (ADD). *No wonder I don't like school,* he remembered thinking then. But finally knowing why he couldn't focus didn't change his attitude. He still hated sitting in a classroom.

Despite these challenges, his parents had always told him he was smart. "You can do anything you want to do," they'd said. "Look at you: you're a good-looking kid with plenty of talents. The world is your oyster!" *What a funny phrase,* he'd always thought when they said that. By the time he finally learned what it meant,

Sino Images/Getty Images

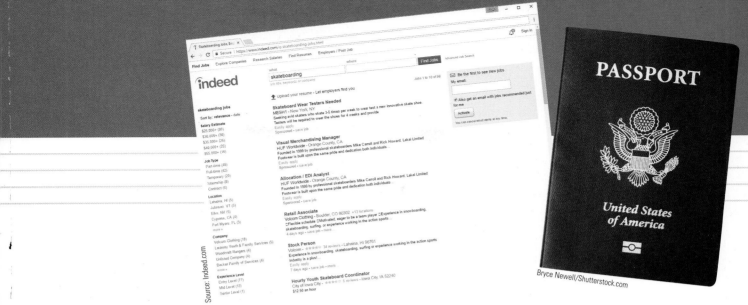

Source: Indeed.com

Bryce Newell/Shutterstock.com

he totally believed it. His life would become whatever he chose to make of it.

The problem was there were too many choices. How could anyone decide what he wanted to be when he was only nineteen? Ethan remembered liking geometry; he was good at creative writing; he played the drums like a real jazz musician; and he was an incredible artist. *But what do you do with* that *combination of skills?* he'd asked himself more than once. What possible college major and career would really fit him? He'd spent plenty of time on career websites to try and figure it out.

He'd managed to pull decent grades his first term—a B average—at the community college close to home. He'd taken Geography, Interpersonal Communication, Drawing 101, and Study Skills, and while he'd done well, none of the course material really sparked a genuine

interest. His instructors didn't take much of an interest in him either. His Study Skills instructor was friendly and tried to get him interested in class, and he knew the material could really help him. But frankly, Ethan just wasn't motivated when it came to school.

Instead, Ethan skateboarded every minute he could. He preferred skateboarding to studying any day of the week, and when it came to actually choosing a major—much less his classes for the next term—he was clueless. The one thing that did interest him was a certificate in entrepreneurship. It was all about starting a business of your own. Now that sounded intriguing. Ethan didn't quite fit any molds, and doing his own thing might just be "his thing!"

But the more he thought about it, dropping out sounded like a good idea, too. He could get a job delivering pizzas, think about his life, and try to figure it all out. He'd have nobody to tell him what to do, nobody to hold him accountable, nobody to pressure him, nobody to force him into making decisions—and plenty of free time to skateboard.

BORTEL Pavel–Pavelmidi/Shutterstock.com

Study Skills (ID 102)
Course Syllabus

INSTRUCTOR: Anna Morgan
OFFICE: 342 Smith Hall
HOURS 9 a.m.-12 p.m. Mon-Thurs

TEXT: *FOCUS on Community College Success* by Constance Staley

COURSE OBJECTIVES: This course is designed to give you the tools to make college easier, more productive, and a more successful learning experience. The goal of this course is to make you a better student by building your study skills and enhancing your learning strategies.

EXPECTATIONS: Students are expected to be respectful of instructors and peers at all times. Assignments should be turned in on time unless you have a valid reason for missing the due date. Please see me if you have any questions.Water bottles are allowed in class, but no food or sugary drinks are permitted. Please turn off your cell phone before you come to class.

GRADING: 100 Possible Points
-Participation: 10 Points.
-Final Presentation: 20 Points.
-Final Exam: 20 Points.
-Assignments(3) and Quizzes (2): 50 Points (10 each)

GRADES: 100-90 = A 89-80 = B 79-70 = C 69-60 = D 59-0 = F

Course Schedule

WEEK 1: Overview and PreTest
WEEK 2: Managing Time and Stress
WEEK 3: Reading Skills
WEEK 4: Test Taking
WEEK 5: Listening and Memory
WEEK 6: Diversity
WEEK 7: Effective Writing

Focus challenge case **289**

1. Do you have anything in common with Ethan? If so, how are you managing the situation so that you can be successful?

2. In your view, what will become of Ethan? What are his prospects for the future? Do you think he'll decide on a career and finish college? Why or why not?

3. Why is Ethan experiencing problems? Are these problems serious? Should they hold him back? List all the problems you can identify.

4. Which majors and careers might Ethan be well suited for? If you were an academic advisor, what advice would you give him?

5. Who would you send Ethan to on your campus for help? What are his options? What do you think he should do at this point?

WHAT'S THE CONNECTION?

College is about becoming an educated person—learning how to think, solve problems, and make decisions. College is much more than the "sum of its tests." It's about developing yourself as a person and becoming well educated. What does it mean to be well educated? Simply put, being well educated is about the pursuit of human excellence.[1]

Colleges help societies *preserve the past* and *create the future*. Studying the history of the U.S. Constitution in a political science course as opposed to studying potential cures for cancer in a cell biology course are concrete examples. Colleges help us look back (preserve the past) and look ahead (create the future).

COLLEGE IN A BOX?

Have you ever thought about the fact that college courses appear to exist in discrete "boxes"? Schools tend to place courses in academic departments, and your class schedule reflects these divisions. For example, your schedule this term might look something like the one in Figure 11.1.

This organizing system helps you keep things straight in your head, and it also helps your school organize a complex institution. Instructors normally work in one department or another. And classes are categorized into particular academic disciplines.

"It takes courage to grow up and become who you really are."

E. E. Cummings, American poet (1894–1962)

academic discipline a branch of learning, instruction, or emphasis

---

VARK IT!

Aural: What courses are you taking this term? How would your "College in a Box" look? As you read this section, talk through the problems with thinking of your college classes as disconnected units.

FIGURE 11.1

Most Schools Compartmentalize Learning

	M	T	W	Th	F
9–10	ENG			COMM	
10–11		MATH			
11–12			PSYCH		PSYCH

But something students often wonder about is how to connect the dots. What's the big picture? Knowledge isn't quite as neat as departments and boxes; it's messy. It overlaps and merges. Despite the divisions and abbreviations colleges use to divide up knowledge, you might be able to take a somewhat similar course in visual art as an art course, a computer science course, or a communication course. You've probably noticed that you sometimes hear something discussed in one of your classes that's also being discussed in another one. Knowledge is interconnected. College in a Box isn't an accurate way of looking at things.

Even though each academic discipline has its own history and identity and way of asking questions and finding answers, the disciplines aren't as distinct as your class schedule might lead you to believe.

HOW DO THE DISCIPLINES CONNECT?

The Circle of Learning (see Figure 11.2) illustrates the interconnectedness of knowledge. Although this circle could be drawn in many different ways, using many different traditional academic disciplines, here is an example to get you thinking.[2]

It works like this. Let's start at the top of the circle with *math,* which is a basic "language" with rules and conventions, just like spoken language. You manipulate numbers and operations and functions, just as you manipulate sounds and words and sentences. Now, move clockwise around the circle.

Math is the fundamental language of *physics,* one branch of which studies atomic and subatomic particles. When atoms combine into molecules, such as carbon dioxide, the academic discipline involved is called *chemistry.* Chemicals combine to create living organisms studied in *biology* courses. Living organisms don't just exist; they think and behave, leading to the study of *psychology.* They

Visual: Circle the subjects on the Circle of Learning chart that you enjoy most. Are they clustered together or at opposite ends of the circle? What could this tell you about choosing a major or career?

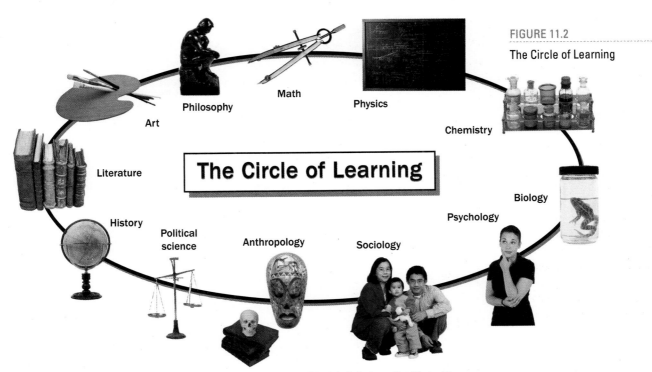

FIGURE 11.2

The Circle of Learning

also interact in groups, families, and societies, which you study in *sociology*. You can also study units of living beings throughout time and across cultures in the discipline of *anthropology*. These units—people—who live and work together are typically governed or govern themselves, leading to *political science*. Let's keep going.

When an account of peoples and countries and their rulers is recorded, you study *history*. These written accounts, sometimes factual or sometimes fictional (for pleasure or intrigue) comprise the study of *literature*. Literature is one way to record impressions and provoke reactions—poetry is a good example—through the use of words. But images and symbols can do the same things—enter *art*. A particular question artists ask is "What is beauty?" otherwise known as aesthetics, which is also a particular topic of study in *philosophy*. Philosophy also includes another subspecialty called number theory, one of the earliest branches of pure mathematics. And now we're all the way around the Circle of Learning, arriving right back at *math*.

That's a quick rundown. Of course, many academic disciplines don't appear on this chart, but they could and should. The point isn't which disciplines are represented. Instead, the Circle of Learning demonstrates that academic disciplines are interconnected because knowledge itself is interconnected.

> "Never mistake knowledge for wisdom. One helps you make a living; the other helps you make a life."
>
> **Sandra Carey, consultant and lobbyist**

EXERCISE 11.1 THE FOUR Ps: PASSION, PURPOSE, PRACTICALITY, PROMISE

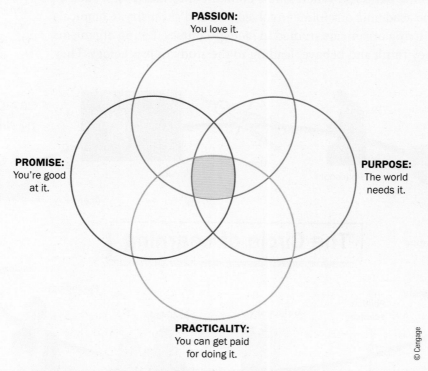

PASSION:
You love it.

PROMISE:
You're good at it.

PURPOSE:
The world needs it.

PRACTICALITY:
You can get paid for doing it.

© Cengage

List potential careers you're interested in within each of the four circles, as well as careers for which the four circles intersect. For example, if you have a *passion* for sushi, should you open a sushi restaurant? Not necessarily. If you show great *promise* as a wrestler, should you go pro? Maybe not. Rather than focusing on one circle, or even two, consider all four "Ps." This graphic, which exists in various formats and is cited in numerous places, can give you new insights about creating your own future. If your instructor wishes, discuss your results in class or online.

Anthropology (understanding people throughout time and across cultures) can provide an important foundation for *political science* (how people are governed or govern themselves), and *history* (a record of peoples and countries and rulers) can easily be the basis for *literature*. Using what you're learning in one discipline can lead to deeper understanding in another, and although some of your instructors will help you connect the dots, putting it all together is basically your responsibility.

In your career, you'll need to use knowledge without necessarily remembering in which course you learned it. You'll be thinking critically and creatively, solving problems, and calling upon all the skills you're developing in all the courses you're studying in college. The bottom line is that connections count. Recognize them, use them, and strengthen them to reinforce your learning.

HOW TO CHOOSE
A MAJOR AND A CAREER

"The self is not something that one finds. It's something one creates."

Thomas Szasz, Professor Emeritus in Psychiatry, State University of New York Health Science Center, Syracuse

Right now, you're in the thick of it. You're going to classes, completing assignments, studying for exams, and most likely holding down a job (or more than one). Growing up, you may have dreamed of becoming a doctor or a teacher or an engineer. At this point, those dreams may still be alive. Or perhaps they've evolved as you've experienced more coursework, found out that a particular subject isn't your strong suit after all, or discovered that something you hadn't even considered is. But at some point in your college career, you'll need to commit to a major, right? In order to do that, the two key questions at the beginning of this text immediately resurface: Who are you, and What do you want? As you've focused on these two questions, you've discovered some answers along the way.

But here's one thing to realize: Times have changed. Your grandfather or grandmother may have had one career over many years at a single company. They may have retired with a celebratory cake and gold watch as rewards for many years of service. The careers of the future will be different, however. Instead of a lifelong commitment, experts now expect that careers will be based on change, opportunity, and resilience. They describe a career as a river and use the concept of "career flow." Your career, like a river, will have a variety of dimensions, and you will be "at the helm." Rather than necessarily being in a single field for your entire career, you will navigate "the waters." Sometimes you'll be moving along smoothly as the river twists and turns peacefully; at other times, you'll be plunging down a waterfall; and at others, you could be stuck in the weeds temporarily or even have to wade to the shoreline and get yourself a new boat.[3] Centuries ago, the philosopher Heraclitus said, "You can't step into the same river twice." Why? Because the river is in constant flux, and because you are always changing. Careers of the future will be filled with exhilaration but also with instability, with opportunities but also occasional challenges. But you will be constantly moving, changing, and growing. College is a great place to prepare for the trip.

Like many students, you probably put great stock in how well college prepares you for a profession.[4] Choosing a college major and directing yourself toward a prospective career can be stressful. Many students feel pressure to make the right decision—and make it right now! You might hear conflicting advice from family members that put a high priority on financial success above

Minerva Studio/Shutterstock.com

other important factors, for example, and feel overwhelmed by the number of possibilities from which to choose.[5] You may know what you want to do with the rest of your life right now—or think you do—but many of your classmates don't, and even if they *say* they do, they may well change their minds. Yes, these decisions are important, but there's evidence that you don't have to have it all figured out right away.[6] Where do you start? The decision-making process should involve these critical steps. If you're still deciding, or even if you think you already have, consider how they apply to you.

STEP 1: DISCOVER YOUR BLISS

You've heard it before. Career advisors often say, "Follow your bliss." And if you don't know what it is, come back when you do.[7] Maybe it's not about following your bliss; maybe it's about discovering it and then building your life accordingly. Maybe it's really about your interests and your strengths. Maybe it's about people other than you—about making an impact.

In an ideal world, which major and career would you choose? Don't think about anything except the actual content you'd be studying. Don't consider career opportunities, requirements, difficulty, or anything else that might keep you from making these choices in an ideal world. What are you passionate about? What do you spend your time thinking about? What would you prefer to do in your spare time? Let's say you have a dream of becoming a famous athlete, for example, a football player, like Tom Brady, or a skateboarder, like Rob Dyrdek, or a tennis player, like Venus Williams. Can you translate your dream into goals and actually become a pro? Perhaps. Some pro athletes like these people are extremely successful. Pro skateboarder Tony Hawk is said to have a net worth of $120 million dollars.[8] Besides practicing your sport by doing wheelies, ollies, pivots, jumps, flips, and fakies, you advertise products for your sponsors—logos on your shirts and your skateboard, for example.[9] If skateboarding is your passion right now, think about which majors might apply. Majoring in physics would help you understand skateboard ascent versus decent, trajectories, spin, and angles. Majoring in landscape architecture would allow you to design skateparks. You would spend time outdoors, build computer and 3-D models of parks, and perhaps even interview other skateboarders about desirable features. Majoring in journalism or video production would put you in a good position to work for a skateboarder magazine, like *Thrasher*. The opportunities *around* your passions are important ways to do what you love—and they're all different.

Like Ethan Cole from the "FOCUS Challenge Case," you may be wondering what to do with your life. Perhaps the *idealist* in you has one potential career in mind and the *realist* in you has another. The $300,000 salary you'd earn as a surgeon may look very compelling until you consider the years of medical school required after college, the time invested in an internship and residency, and the still further years of specialization. It takes long-term commitment, dedication, and resources—yours or borrowed ones—to make that dream come true. Do these factors lessen the appeal? Or perhaps there's conflict between your ideal career and someone else's idea of an ideal career for you. The late comedian Robin Williams once said, "When I told my father I was going to be an actor, he said, 'Fine, but study welding just in case.'"

FIGURE 11.3

Quick Study: "Designing Your Life"

DESIGNING YOUR LIFE

Engage **Energy**

Flow

5. ASK FOR HELP.

Designers rarely work alone. They know it takes a team, and engage in "radical collaboration." Likewise, you don't have to come up with a fantastic design for your life alone. If you brainstorm about what **engages** you, what gives you **energy**, and what puts you in a state of **flow**, then get good ideas from your team about your future. And build more than one plan in case roadblocks come up.

You are here

And where is that, exactly? To figure out where you're going, you have to first know where you are.

START HERE.

- "How do I find a job I like or even love?"
- "How do I build a career with a good living?"
- "How do I balance my career with family?"
- "How can I make a difference in the world?"

LEARN TO THINK LIKE A **DESIGNER**: 5 WAYS TO DO IT.

REFRAME THESE MYTHS.

- My degree will determine my future.
- I should have it all figured out by now.
- My one, true dream is out there.
- It's too late for me.
- I need to find my destiny.
- If I'm successful, I'll be happy.

1. BE CURIOUS.

When you design anything, you have to know what the end user really wants. That's called empathy. In designing your life, the end user is you. How well do you know yourself? What do you really value? What's your purpose in life? What opportunities await you?

2. TRY STUFF.

Designers have a "bias to action." They build prototype after prototype, fail often, and focus on what will happen next, not the final result. When designing your life, try careers via internships, and you'll find out what works for you. Three-quarters of college grads don't end up working in the area of their majors, so trying out options can help you learn more about yourself and about careers.

4. KNOW IT'S A PROCESS.

Life is messy, and so is the process of designing one. You move three steps forward and then two back. That's to be expected. Even designers get stuck at times. But out of the mess of the design process, a well-lived, joyful life can emerge.

No | Oops, that won't work. | X

X | Not quite. | X

NO | no | YES!

3. REFRAME PROBLEMS.

Designers don't get freaked out by mistakes. In fact, they can tweak based on problems or "reframe" an idea to come up with an even better one. Slinkys, Play-Doh, and Sticky Notes were reframed mistakes. You may decide you like nursing but not the frantic pace of the ER, as you expected to. Your nursing major wasn't a mistake; you just need to reframe the problem.

If you find it challenging to get into a state of flow when you're writing a paper, for example, consider trying the app called Flowstate. First, you enter an amount of time you'd like to write, and then you start writing. But if you stop for more than five seconds or quit, you lose what you've accomplished. Sound nerve-wracking? It is, but it can train you to focus yourself into a state of flow![10]

"There's going to be a huge change, comparable to the industrial revolution," Robots and intelligent computer systems "are going to have a far more dramatic impact on the workplace than the internet has."

Jerry Kaplan, Silicon Valley entrepreneur

Or perhaps you just don't know yet. If so, don't panic. Ethan Cole is right: It's hard to have it all figured out from the start.[11] According to *Designing Your Life*, a new best-seller, "For most people, passion comes after they try something, discover they like it, and develop mastery—not before. To put it more succinctly: passion is the result of a good life design, not the cause." The authors, from Stanford University, also write, reassuringly, that "The truth is that all of us have more than one life in us... And if you accept this idea—that there are multiple great designs for your life, though you'll still only get to live one—it is rather liberating."[12]

Wayne Gretzky, called the greatest player in the history of hockey, once said, "God gave me a special talent to play the game... maybe he didn't give me a talent, he gave me a passion." But what if your "bliss" just isn't feasible? You'd give anything to play for the NBA, but you're five foot two and female. You dream of being a rock star, but you can't carry a tune. Then it may be time to set aside the dream and get real. Maybe then it's time to think about what energizes you, what engages you, and what puts you into a state of "flow." When you're in flow, you're so absorbed that you forget where you are and what what's going on around you.[13]

STEP 2: CONDUCT PRELIMINARY RESEARCH

Has it ever occurred to you that you may not have all the facts—accurate ones—about your potential ideal major? Do you know what it *really* takes? Have you gotten your information from qualified sources—or are you basing your opinion on your friend's reaction to one course he took?

Try an experiment. Choose three majors you're considering, one of which is your ideal major, and send yourself on a fact-finding mission. To find out whether you're on target, get the answers to the following ten questions for each of the three possibilities. Go to the physical location (department) where each major is housed, and interview an instructor. The experiment requires legwork; don't just let your fingers do the clicking.

1. What is the major or certificate?
2. Who is the interviewee?
3. What is the name of the academic department where this major is housed? Where are the department offices physically located on campus?
4. Which introductory courses in this major would give you information about your interests and abilities?
5. Which specialized courses in this major interest you? (List three.)
6. What courses do you have to complete before you can major in this subject?
7. How many students major in this discipline on your campus?
8. Which required course in the major do students usually find most challenging? Which is most engaging? Which is most valued? Why?
9. How would the interviewee describe the reputation of this department on campus? What is it known for?
10. From the interviewee's perspective, why should a student major in this discipline?

John Williams RUS/Shutterstock.com

WHAT ARE YOUR JOB PREFERENCES?

Take a good look at yourself and answer the following questions about how you prefer to work. Rank each item 1 or 2 based on your general preference. Although many careers, if not most, require both, your task is to decide which of the two you prefer.

I prefer to work at a job:

1. _____ Alone		_____ With other people	
2. _____ Indoors		_____ Outdoors	
3. _____ With people		_____ With equipment or materials	
4. _____ Directing/leading others		_____ Being directed/led by others	
5. _____ Producing information		_____ Managing information	
6. _____ In an organized, step-by-step way		_____ In a big-idea, big-picture way	
7. _____ Starting things		_____ Completing things	
8. _____ Involving a product		_____ Involving a service	
9. _____ Solving challenging problems		_____ Generating creative ideas	
10. _____ Finding information		_____ Applying information	
11. _____ Teaching/training others in groups		_____ Advising/coaching others one-on-one	

Now look at your eleven first choices. Identify several career fields that come to mind that would allow you to achieve as many of them as possible.

After you complete your interviews, review the facts. Did you change any of your opinions based on what you learned?[14]

STEP 3: TAKE A GOOD LOOK AT YOURSELF

It all comes down to questions this text has been asking you all along: Who are you? And what do you want? If you're unsure of how to proceed in your decision making, follow these recommendations to see whether they help you bring your future into focus.

Send in the SWOT Team! A SWOT analysis is an excellent way to begin taking a good look at yourself in relation to your future. SWOT stands for Strengths, Weaknesses, Opportunities, and Threats. SWOT analyses are typically used in business, but creating one for yourself may be useful when it comes to deciding on a college major and a career. Make a chart with four sections, label each one, and fill them in as objectively as you can.

> **Strengths** are traits that give you a leg up. These are talents you can capitalize on and qualities you can develop.

> **Weaknesses** are traits that currently work against you. You can, however, work to reduce or eliminate them.

> **Opportunities** are conditions or circumstances that work in your favor, like a strong forecast for the future of your prospective career.

"Are you fit company for the person you wish to become?"

Anonymous

VARK IT!

Aural: Discuss your personality, strengths and weaknesses with a close friend. Use this conversation to help inform your decisions about majors and careers.

> **Threats** are conditions that could have bad effects. Some of these factors are beyond your control; however, sometimes you can figure out ways to make them matter less.

As you create your own chart, begin with two basic questions:

What kinds of forces will impact your potential career?

Internal—forces inside you, such as motivation and skill

External—forces outside you that may affect your success: the job market or economy, for example

What kind of influence can these forces exert?

Positive—some forces will give you a boost toward your goals.

Negative—other forces will work against you.[15]

Let's complete a SWOT analysis for Ethan and his dream of becoming a professional skateboarder. Of course, you might say that, technically, he doesn't need an academic degree for that particular career. But if he wants to pursue related, more traditional careers—design a new skatepark or write for a skateboard magazine, for example—he would need knowledge from design and writing to finance and marketing. Besides, college isn't just about jobs, it's about living a fuller life as a well-educated person.

Look back at the "FOCUS Challenge Case," and see whether you agree with the basic SWOT analysis shown in Figure 11.4. What would you conclude? Is professional skateboarding a good career for him? In your view, do the opportunities outweigh the threats? For example, does the possibility of earning big bucks outweigh the risks of possible injuries? If not, could he move toward other potential careers, perhaps some that also involve skateboarding? "Ethan remembered liking geometry, he was good at creative writing, he played the drums like a real jazz musician, and he was an incredible artist." Do you see potential majors for him in college? Sports management? Kinesiology? Architecture? Journalism? Jazz studies? Creative writing? What should Ethan do?

FIGURE 11.4
....
SWOT Analysis

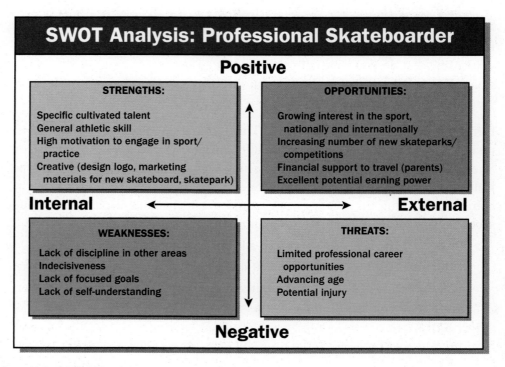

SWOT Analysis: Professional Skateboarder

Positive

STRENGTHS:

Specific cultivated talent
General athletic skill
High motivation to engage in sport/ practice
Creative (design logo, marketing materials for new skateboard, skatepark)

OPPORTUNITIES:

Growing interest in the sport, nationally and internationally
Increasing number of new skateparks/ competitions
Financial support to travel (parents)
Excellent potential earning power

Internal ← → **External**

WEAKNESSES:

Lack of discipline in other areas
Indecisiveness
Lack of focused goals
Lack of self-understanding

THREATS:

Limited professional career opportunities
Advancing age
Potential injury

Negative

SWOT ANALYSIS:

Try doing a SWOT Analysis of a career you're considering. If you have no idea where to begin, choose the career of someone you know—a friend or family member. Carefully analyze the Strengths, Weaknesses, Opportunities, and Threats as you see them. It may help to Google the career for specifics and check information-rich, accurate sites like OOH (Occupational Outlook Handbook), compiled by the U.S. Bureau of Labor Statistics. After you're done, write three conclusions about this career. Is the career you've analyzed worth pursuing in your view?

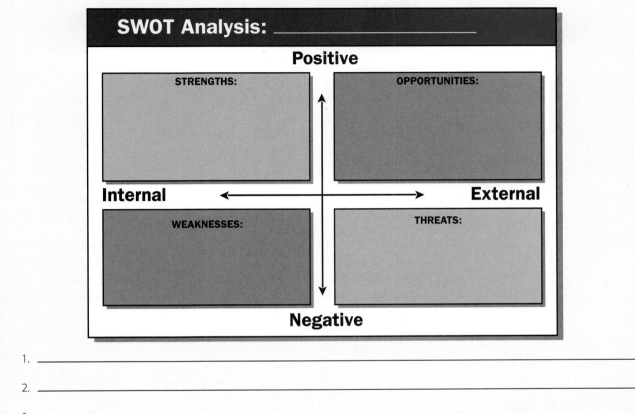

SWOT Analysis: _____

Positive

| STRENGTHS: | OPPORTUNITIES: |

Internal ←————————→ External

| WEAKNESSES: | THREATS: |

Negative

1. _____
2. _____
3. _____

STEP 4: CONSIDER YOUR MAJOR VERSUS YOUR CAREER

Which comes first, the chicken or the egg? The major or the career? Silly question? The obvious answer, of course, is that you must first major or earn a certificate in something in college before you can build a career on it. But the question isn't as straightforward as it seems.

Should you choose a major based on an intended career? Perhaps you know you want to be a science teacher, first and foremost. You don't know whether to get an associate's degree in physical science or an associate of arts degree in teaching. You like all sciences, but teaching is your real interest. If you major in science, which one should you emphasize (see Figure 11.5)?

Or instead, should you choose a major first, and then decide on a career? Say you made a firm decision to major in chemistry when your favorite science teacher did "mad scientist" experiments for the class in eighth grade. But at this point, you're not certain of the professional direction you'd like to pursue. Chemistry is your passion, but should you apply your chemistry degree

VARK IT!

Kinesthetic: Go on a "field trip" to the Career Center on your campus. Collect resources you find there, and bring them to class.

FIGURE 11.5

Which Science Should a Science
Teacher Major In?

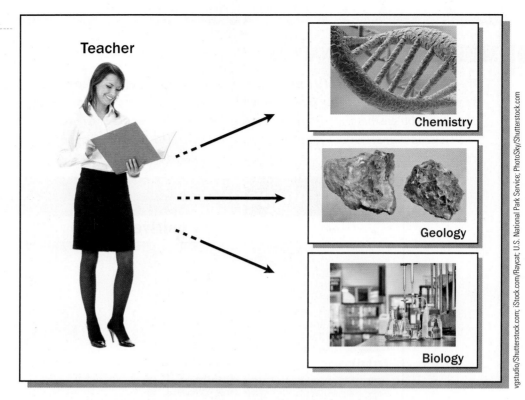

as a forensics expert, a pharmaceutical salesperson, a chemical technician, or a teacher (see Figure 11.6)? You could enter some of these career fields with an associate's degree, but others might require transferring to a four-year school.

So which comes first—major or career? It depends.[16] The answer sounds uncertain, and it's meant to. Although some professional degree programs put you into a particular track right away (nursing, for example), generally either direction can work well. Doors will open and close for you, and as you gain more

FIGURE 11.6

Which Career Should a Chemistry
Major Choose?

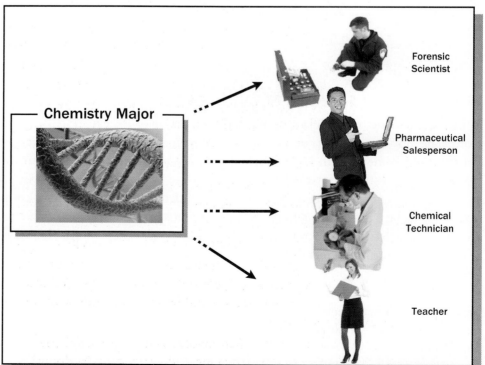

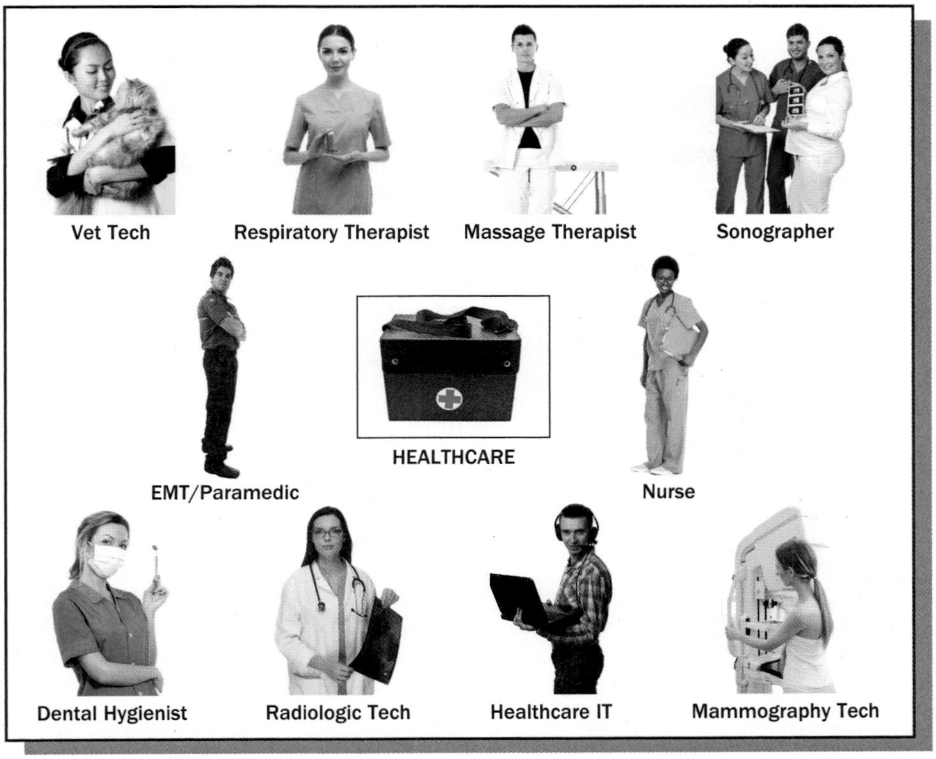

FIGURE 11.7

What Specialty Careers Can a Healthcare Focus Choose From?

Faiz Zaki/Shutterstock.com; Lopolo/Shutterstock.com; Dmitri Mihhailov/Shutterstock.com; Africa Studio/Shutterstock.com; pittawut/Shutterstock.com; Andy Dean Photography/Shutterstock.com; Ostap Davydiak/Shutterstock.com; Tyler Olson/Shutterstock.com; kurhan/Shutterstock.com; Blaj Gabriel/Shutterstock.com; Kamil Macniak/Shutterstock.com

knowledge and experience, you'll narrow your focus. As you learn more about your chosen major, you'll also learn about its specific career tracks. But it's important to remember that a major doesn't have to lock you into one specific career. And you can always narrow or refocus your area of emphasis by earning your bachelor's degree and continuing your education beyond that.[17] If you're attending community college with a specialty career in mind that requires an associate's degree or a certificate, there may be a host of possibilities to choose from as shown in Figure 11.7. In that case, your major and your career may align well.

What's Your Academic Anatomy? Thinking about your academic anatomy is a simple way to begin to get a handle on what you find fulfilling. If you had to rank order the four parts of you listed in Figure 11.8, what would you put in first place? Second, third, and last? To get yourself thinking, ask these questions:

1. Do you find fulfillment by using your *head*? Do you enjoy solving complex problems or thinking through difficult situations? Do you like to reason things out, weigh evidence, and think critically? Someone working toward a paralegal certificate might fit this category.
2. Do you find it satisfying to work with matters of the *heart*? Are you the kind of person others come to with problems because you listen and care? Does trying to make others happy make you happy? A nursing major might be what students with this preference choose, for example.
3. Do you like to create things with your *hands*? Do you enjoy making art? Doing hands-on projects? Building things out of other things? A drafting major who designs and builds models might be what students with this preference choose, for example.
4. Do you excel at physical activities that involve your *whole body*? Are you athletic? Do you like to stay active, no matter what you're doing? A

FIGURE 11.8

What's Your Academic Anatomy?

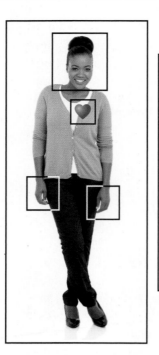

Another way of analyzing your preferences is by considering your "Academic Anatomy." What do you find most satisfying? Working with your

Head?
Heart?
Hands? or
Whole Body?

michaeljung/Shutterstock.com

physical therapy major who goes on to work in a rehabilitation facility helping stroke victims relearn to walk might be what students with this preference choose, for example.

Now look at your academic anatomy rankings. Of course, the truth is that "all of you" is involved in everything you do. And achieving balance is important. But what are your priorities? This type of simple analysis can be one way of informing you about who you are and where you should be headed.

However, no system for choosing a major is perfect. In fact, most are imperfect at best. Here are four things to consider:

1. Sometimes students who don't select a likely major based on their "anatomical preferences" can still be successful. A whole-body person (like Ethan Cole probably is) may decide to major in art (using his hands). But he'll have to find other ways to meet his whole-body needs unless he becomes a sculptor involved in creating large constructed projects.

2. You may intentionally choose an unlikely major. Perhaps art (using your hands) comes so naturally to you that you decide to major in science (using your head). You need the challenge to stay fully involved in getting your education. Although it may sound unlikely, it's been known to happen.

3. You may choose an unlikely major because one particular course turns you on. You had no idea majoring in this subject was even possible, and you didn't know what it entailed. But you find studying it fascinating—so you shift gears to focus all your attention on it.

4. You may be equally engaged, no matter what. You love subjects that require using your head, hands, heart, and whole body. The anatomy of learning is less important to you than other factors—a teacher whose enthusiasm is contagious, for example.[18]

Ethan's rankings would probably go something like this: (1) whole body, (2) hands, (3) heart, and (4) head. And just because "head" is in last place for him doesn't mean he's doomed in college. A career as a financial analyst sitting behind a desk probably wouldn't be his cup of tea, for example. But it may well be yours. As you decide, you may want to consider whether your choice is "anatomically correct."

Whatever major or career you're aiming for—or still looking for—make sure you follow the four steps outlined in this chapter to create the future you want.

WIIFM? 4 MINUTE READ

Newsflash: According to a recent Gallup poll, two-thirds of Americans are not engaged in their work, and many of them are actively disengaged. These actively disengaged "Debbie Downers" resent their work, gripe about it, aren't clear about what their bosses expect, and don't feel their own needs are being met.[19] When and if they get laid off, while their first re-action is shock and disappointment, their second reaction is, "Thank goodness!" As a matter of fact, there are many reasons employees can be dissatisfied, and some of them are downright justified.[20] But underneath it all, the truth is this: Finding the so-called "bliss" that conventional wisdom tells you to follow appears to be a challenge for many people. By contrast, learning how to discover your passion can have momentous consequences as you answer the question, "What's in it for me?"

Why? Because bliss isn't necessarily something you realize during a sudden "aha moment" when you're a new college student. Bliss evolves as you collect life ex-periences. You may have an inkling about your passions now, or you may not. You may need to cultivate them, or you may discover them later. Here's an example: The world-famous chef Julia Child always enjoyed eating. But when she had her first taste of an exquisite French dish—a deli-cate white fish cooked in lemon butter—she said many years later, "The whole experience was an opening up of the soul and spirit for me. I was hooked, and for life, as it turned out." Over time, the more she

cooked, the more she loved to cook. What was it about cooking she loved? Was it the creativity, was it filling her senses with smells and tastes, was it serving or teaching others?[21] Did she just luck into the discovery, or did the experience spark such a powerful response in her that she recognized a passion she could cultivate over the course of her lifetime? Most people don't necessarily think about these questions, but they're worth considering.

To complicate things even more, the un-fortunate truth is that just because you're passionate about something doesn't mean you have what it takes to become an expert. We all need to face issues like these squarely. Or think about the ways in which technology is dramatically changing the career landscape. You may be interested in a career that may be hit hard, like the photo processing business or the travel in-dustry. Some specialists fear that robots will increasingly hijack our future; others claim that humans will adjust by creating new types of work, including jobs that don't even exist now.[22] Rather than fixating on one specific career that may eventually be lost to automation or freelance positions by 2025, think about the *skills* you need to cultivate for the future. Which skills come to mind? Experts say you need technology skills, obviously, and those all-important soft skills we're discussing throughout *FOCUS*. Experts remind us: "It's going to take a long time for robots to be good at soft skills, like social and emotional intel-ligence and cross-cultural competency."[23]

"Your work is going to fill a large part of your life, and the only way to be truly satisfied is to do what you believe is great work. And the only way to do great work is to love what you do. If you haven't found it yet, keep looking. Don't settle."

Steve Jobs (attended De Anza Community College, Cupertino, California)

According to the Bureau of Labor Statistics, today's workers will have ten different jobs by the time they're forty years old, and that number is expected to go up. Rather than focusing narrowly, try thinking broadly about five life-work lessons like these:[24]

1. **You have one life; live it.** People who stay in careers they hate are cheating themselves. You may be thinking, "But I thought I'd like this ca-reer, and my education cost me!" That may be true. That's why internships are important: you can test out careers. At some point, however, you may need to regroup and make a change, even if it requires further education or other preparation. It's your life, after all, and you're in charge. Don't wake up one day and realize you missed the boat.

2. **Diversify**. Generally speaking, your academic preparation should offer you more than one slim career possibility. Skills are transferable, and sometimes all they need is reframing. Or perhaps you can bring your knowledge about one thing to another application. For example, if you're in business, but wellness is a high priority for you, offer a brownbag mini-training event on wellness to your colleagues over lunch. Or consider folding other interests into your primary job: include art in a business career by designing flyers for upcoming training events, for example.

3. **Make the whole world your college, and keep learning**. In many ways, after you finish your college degree or certificate, the *real* learning starts. You get to see your coursework come to life, and that's a fascinating prospect! Make learning a lifelong priority. Change can easily outpace you if you don't keep watching trends and continually enhancing your skills.

4. **Start your success inside**. Don't let silly things derail you, like worries, regrets, or fear of failure or fear of success. Of course, it's true that some things in life are truly worrisome. But happiness is a choice. Allow yourself to choose it!

5. **Make an impact, but remember that doing so takes time**. Many people feel like a cog in a wheel. They have good ideas on the job, but they play such a small role that no one listens or cares. It's easy to expect immediate results, like those we get in other areas of our lives. But making an impact takes time; overnight successes are rare, if they happen at all.

Finally, consider this possibility: "The meaning of life is to find your gifts and the purpose of your success lies in giving it away."[25] If you could master this kind of thinking early in your career, or even at your "mid-life crisis" (if you have one), you'd be in good shape. The answer to the WIIFM question is your success and your happiness.

CAREER OUTLOOK: *ZOOM IN, ZOOM OUT*

Perhaps the most common question asked during hiring interviews is this one: "Where do you see yourself in five years?" Undoubtedly, it's a tough question. In today's fast-changing world, the most honest answer is "Are you kidding—who knows? I'm not even sure what I'll have for dinner tonight." Five years seems like forever. Although your imaginary answer may be the most truthful one, it's not necessarily smart.[26]

One thing that trips up many first-year college students is thinking that they have to have it all figured out—now. They think there should be a linear path between their major and their career.[27] For example, a student should enter college having declared a business major, earn business degree, and then land a good job in the business world. "On a clear day," as the old song goes, "you can see forever." It should be that easy.

Realistically, clarity typically unfolds as you go. Many students don't have a particular major or a career in mind. When things become increasingly foggy during their "trip" through college, they lose their way or maybe even give up. Rather than being linear, the path is often nonlinear. You work toward success by keeping two concurrent perspectives in mind: zooming out on your big-picture goals and zooming in on the "up close and personal" details of managing yourself on a daily basis. While you're in college, you must be able to zoom in on your individual courses and zoom out to your overall degree plan. The same principle definitely holds in your career.[28]

So when the time comes and the interviewer asks you the inevitable question, "Where do you see yourself in five years?" take this advice:

1. Reflect on what you will say beforehand.

2. Figure out what the interviewer is trying to learn about you. Does she expect a full-blown answer, or is she just trying to see how you think?

3. Shorten the time frame so that you can answer: "I'm not really sure how many years it will take, but I do know that I want to join an organization just like this one and work on a highly creative team to learn all I can. Challenges are important to me."

On the other hand, don't:

1. Make up something so far-fetched that even you don't believe what you're saying.

2. Identify the exact job you want in the future. ("Honestly? I'd like your job. Are you planning to retire in the next five years?")

3. Feel obliged to answer the question literally, even if you don't really know for sure. Turn the question into one you can answer, communicating what you want the interviewer to know about you.[29] Although you're being asked to zoom out, instead zoom in on who you are and what you want. It's important to keep both perspectives in mind in your journey toward success.

Think about how you would answer the question identified in this section if you were applying for a job you could get today. When you finish your degree or certificate, would you expect your answer to be different in some ways? Might it be the same in some ways?

At the beginning of this chapter, Ethan Cole, a confused and discouraged student, faced a challenge. Now after reading this chapter, would you respond differently to any of the questions you answered about the "FOCUS Challenge Case"? Using what you learned in the chapter, write a paragraph ending to Ethan's case study. What are some of the possible outcomes for Ethan?

ACTION: YOUR PLANS FOR CHANGE

1. Where are you when it comes to choosing a major or career? If you haven't decided yet, what specific information from this chapter will you use? If you've already decided, had you already taken these suggestions into account? Will you change any of your plans?

2. Do you know someone working in a career field that is disillusioned or disappointed with the choice he or she made? How will you know your decision is a wise one? What can you do to make sure?

CHALLENGE: REALITY CHECK

HOW MUCH DID YOU LEARN?

At the beginning of this chapter, you filled out a "Readiness Check" that asked how you thought this chapter would relate to you and how you would relate to it. Now, fill out this "Reality Check" to find out.

1. What does college in a box mean?
2. What is a SWOT analysis, and how might one help you choose a major and career?
3. What are the four P's that can help in choosing a career?
4. What does the term *academic anatomy* mean?

How long did it take? _____ hours _____ minutes. Before you began this chapter, you were asked to predict how long it would take you to complete this chapter (total time, even if you read it in more than one sitting). Was your estimate on target, or will you revise it for the next chapter you'll read?

CREATING YOUR FUTURE | 12

READINESS CHECK

HOW THIS CHAPTER RELATES TO YOU

1. When it comes to creating a future for yourself, what do you find most challenging, if any? Put check marks by the phrases that apply to you or write in your answer.
   - ☐ Launching a career
   - ☐ Using social media to create my "personal brand"
   - ☐ Writing an impressive résumé
   - ☐ Interviewing successfully
   - ☐ Figuring out what's next for me
   - ☐ _____

2. What is most likely to be your response? Put a check mark by it.
   - ☐ I'll concentrate on learning new skills.
   - ☐ I'll see whether this chapter helps me.
   - ☐ I'll talk with an instructor or advisor.
   - ☐ Eventually, I'll just figure it out on my own.

3. What would you have to do to increase your likelihood of success? Will you do it this quarter or semester?

HOW YOU WILL RELATE TO THIS CHAPTER

1. What are you most interested in learning about? Put check marks by those topics.
   - ☐ How to launch a career
   - ☐ How to write a résumé
   - ☐ How to interview successfully
   - ☐ What to consider if you're thinking of continuing your education
   - ☐ How to put what you've learned in college to good use
   - ☐ How to think about the future

YOUR READINESS FACTOR

1. How motivated are you to learn more about creating your future? (5 = high, 1 = low)

2. How ready are you to read now? (If something is in your way, take care of it if you can. Zero in and focus.)

3. How long do you think it will take you to complete this chapter? If you start and stop, keep track of your overall time. ____ Hour(s) ____ Minute(s)

FOCUS CHALLENGE CASE

Anthony Lopez

Anthony Lopez was average in nearly every sense of the word.
He played T-ball as a kid, but not particularly well. He didn't like school much, but he went when he felt like it. He didn't have many friends except for a few kids that lived in the eight city blocks that made up his neighborhood. He was even sandwiched between two older brothers and two younger sisters. His brothers were successful—one was an attorney and the other a doctor. Somehow, deep inside himself, Anthony knew that measuring up would be hard for him. Maybe that's why he decided to make his mark in his own way.

You could say that Anthony's kid sister, Gina, was his closest friend. Even though she was six years younger, the two of them would pal around the neighborhood. They could laugh over absolutely anything, and their specialty was pulling pranks on all the other neighborhood kids. For a while, the two of them were inseparable. Whenever you saw Gina, you knew that Anthony was close by.

But as Anthony got older, things changed. The trouble started in middle school. His mom, who worked more than one job to keep the family afloat, was worried that he was getting in with the wrong crowd. But Anthony wasn't worried. His friends knew where to get cigarettes and alcohol—even drugs. When he was with them,

he imagined the other kids looked up to him and his tough-guy friends. By the time high school rolled around, Anthony already had a record. Eventually, he dropped out, left home, and basically lived on the streets. When he needed money, he snatched a purse or wallet. He lost contact with his family, and there seemed to be no turning back. Drugs were a way of life for him, and he began sinking deeper and deeper into a life that most people predicted wouldn't turn out well.

But that was then, and this was now. Anthony's life probably would have been headed in the wrong direction entirely, if it hadn't been for several wake-up calls, including seeing his little sister, Gina, on the street one day. He tried to talk with her, but she was so high that she didn't even recognize him. Anthony saw that she was repeating his worst mistakes, which troubled him deeply. The stark realization that he might be ruining her life in addition to his own shocked him back into reality.

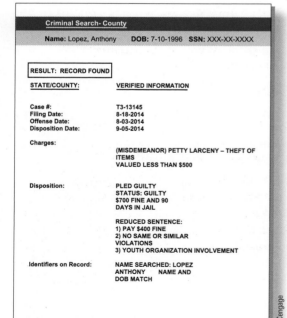

Criminal Search- County

Name: Lopez, Anthony   **DOB:** 7-10-1996   **SSN:** XXX-XX-XXXX

RESULT: RECORD FOUND

STATE/COUNTY:	VERIFIED INFORMATION
Case #:	T3-13145
Filing Date:	8-18-2014
Offense Date:	8-03-2014
Disposition Date:	9-05-2014
Charges:	(MISDEMEANOR) PETTY LARCENY – THEFT OF ITEMS VALUED LESS THAN $500
Disposition:	PLED GUILTY STATUS: GUILTY $700 FINE AND 90 DAYS IN JAIL
	REDUCED SENTENCE: 1) PAY $400 FINE 2) NO SAME OR SIMILAR VIOLATIONS 3) YOUTH ORGANIZATION INVOLVEMENT
Identifiers on Record:	NAME SEARCHED: LOPEZ ANTHONY NAME AND DOB MATCH

© Cengage

Philip Lange/Shutterstock.com

Creatista/Shutterstock.com

Now Anthony was part of an inner-city youth organization for kids like him. The group's leader, Nicky Russo, had once been a gang member himself. He reached out to Anthony, and Anthony responded. Anthony was on a mission to find Gina and get her into the group. Anthony's life was changing, and his life's goal was becoming clear: to help other people like him. He decided to earn his GED and enroll in the best community college he could find to earn an associate's degree in social services. And that's exactly what he did.

As he sat in his favorite class, Urban Social Issues, Anthony realized that he had made the right choice. So much of what he heard his instructor lecturing about had been a part of his own past. As he got deeper into the associate's program, Anthony learned that an associate's degree in social services was a general degree that prepared graduates for many types of jobs. But what if he wanted to be an actual social worker? He learned that the need for social workers was very high, working with young children to older adults. He was taking classes like Racial, Ethnic, and Minority Groups and Sociology of the Family.

Even though the classes were hard, it wasn't long before Anthony was totally engrossed, and he knew he wanted to continue his education. With an associate's degree in social services, he could certainly work more knowledgeably alongside Nicky in the inner city. But what if he transferred to a four-year school for a bachelor's degree in sociology? What if he wanted to earn a master's degree in social work to specialize and become a school or hospital social worker? What if he wanted to conduct research and teach, like his community college instructors? What would getting a Ph.D. require, and should he even be thinking that far ahead? A million questions were forming in his mind.

What did the future hold for Anthony? Right now, he couldn't answer that question. But he did know that his future would be different from the future he might have had without college. What had always been true about Anthony was now true in the best possible sense: Anthony would make his mark.

SOCIAL SERVICES
ASSOCIATE OF ARTS DEGREE

The AA degree with an emphasis in Sociology is designed to provide a better understanding of how humans act and interact in social settings. The program offered provides an excellent foundation for students seeking to continue their education in Sociology, either pursuing a Bachelor's or Master's degree.

First Semester	
ENGL 101 English Composition I	3
SOC 101 Introduction to Sociology	3
Science Elective	3
Humanities Elective	3
Total Credits	12

Second Semester	
ENGL 102 English Composition II	3
SOC 201 Urban Social Issues	3
SOC 225 Cultural & Ethnic Pluralism	3
Quantitative Skills	3
Total Credits	12

Third Semester	
ANTH 206 Cultural Anthropology	3
SOC 240 Sociology of the Family	3
Social Science Elective	3
Humanities Elective	3
Total Credits	12

Fourth Semester	
SOC 340 Indians of North America	3
SOC 355 Cultural & Ethnic Pluralism	3
Science Elective	3
Humanities Elective	3
Total Credits	12

FOURTH EDITION

Cities, Change & Conflict

A POLITICAL ECONOMY OF URBAN LIFE

Nancy Kleniewski • Alexander R. Thomas

1. Do you have anything in common with Anthony? If so, how are you managing the situation so that you can be successful?

2. Anthony appears to be headed toward a life of service. Do you know anyone like him who has turned his or her life around? Describe the situation.

3. What are the pros and cons of continuing his education beyond an associate's degree?

4. In your view, should he continue his education beyond a two-year degree? Why or why not?

VARK IT!

Visual: Draw a mind map that shows the various "forks" in your future. Where might you go, and why? Provide some possibilities and reasons.

"When you come to a fork in the road, take it."

Yogi Berra, baseball player and manager (1925–2015)

WHAT'S THE
NEXT STEP?

You've done it. You've nearly finished your first term of college. Perhaps at this point, you're even jumping ahead to when you finish all of your courses. Then what? Yogi Berra, the once baseball giant, was known for having a way with words. His advice was, "When you come to a fork in the road, take it." *Which one?* you ask. Precisely! (Yogi Berra is said to have been giving directions to his New Jersey home, and both streets worked equally well.)

After you achieve your community college goals—whether you're taking a few targeted classes for a particular reason or earning a certificate or associate's degree—you'll come to a fork in the road. Should you take the fork leading toward pursuing a particular career right away or the fork leading toward continuing your education? This chapter won't answer the question *for* you, but it will give you some things to think about. Just as was the case with Yogi Berra's famous advice, both forks in *your* road will lead you toward the same thing: *your* future. What you decide to do and when you decide to do it will be up to you.

LAUNCHING A CAREER:
PLAN YOUR WORK
AND WORK YOUR PLAN

Let's assume, for now, that you decide to go straight into your chosen career field after community college. You've been focused all along, earned your degree, and now you're ready to find a job that fits your new skills, your personality—*you!* "Fit" is the key word in that last sentence. Where you choose to launch your career and who you work with will be critical factors in your job satisfaction.

The two questions posed early in this text resurface now: "Who are you?" and "What do you want?" Working your way through *FOCUS*, you have learned more about who you are (although this is a lifelong quest). In this final chapter, we'll deal with "What do you want?" The answer to that question can be just as important.

"I arise in the morning torn between a desire to improve the world and a desire to enjoy the world. This makes it hard to plan the day."

E. B. White, American writer (1889–1985)

What do you really want from a career? What's important to you? Even though your views may change over time, it's important to start thinking about them now. Maybe you already prepared for a career once, but something has changed. The field you entered has transformed over time, so that you need to retool. Or a career that attracted you earlier turned out to be much less engaging than you expected. Or your family has grown and you need a career that brings in more resources. That's what community colleges are for. You may be older than the students sitting around you, but you deserve the same educational opportunities. Interestingly, according to research, the most important factor in job satisfaction isn't what you might predict, like money, status, or power. The number one contributor to job satisfaction, statistically speaking, is the quality of your relationship with your boss.[1] Here are some suggestions to help you launch the career you're aiming for.

"I always wanted to be somebody, but I should have been more specific."

Lily Tomlin, comedian

TRY ON A CAREER FOR SIZE

If all your jobs thus far have been just that—*jobs*—to help you pay the bills, how do you know what you want in a *career*? A career is different from a job. It's a profession you've chosen and prepared for. Perhaps you've had more than a string of jobs, and your career is well underway, but now you'd like to go in a different direction. Or perhaps you haven't launched your career yet. Exactly how *do* you launch a new career? You have to start somewhere, so perhaps you'd search online or through actual newspaper job ads. There are plenty of career exploration websites online. Check out the following career mega websites to explore some options:

> CareerBuilder.com

> Monster.com

> Occupational Outlook Handbook (www.bls.gov/ooh/)

> AmericasJobExchange.com/

> Glassdoor.com

> US.jobs (by the National Labor Exchange)

> USAJobs.gov

> LinkedIn

> SimplyHired.com

> ZipRecruiter.com

> Indeed.com

> TheLadders.com

You can Google and surf to your heart's content.

But you may be likely to read something like this: "Opening in . . . (anything). Experience required." Isn't that the way it always goes? You have to *have* experience in order to get a job that will *give* you experience. This problem is one many people face. Sure, you have experience. It's just not the right kind. Perhaps you've bagged fries, mowed yards, bussed tables, and chauffeured pizzas up to this point. If that's not the kind of experience the posted opening is looking for, how do you get the right kind? Or perhaps you're in school to switch career fields. You have

iStock.com/AlbyDeTweede

"Experience is like a comb that life gives you when you are bald."

Navjot Singh Sidhu, former Indian cricketer, politician, and television personality

experience, but it won't help you go in a different direction. The process of job-hunting includes many different steps. Here are some things for you to consider doing during your time in college. One important suggestion is to try a job on for size. Take a look at the three possibilities described in Figure 12.1.

These experiences help you in three ways. First, they allow you to test a potential career field. The actual day-to-day work may be exactly what you expected, or not. They show you whether that particular career field is one you'd really be interested in. *I had no idea this field was so cutthroat, hectic, dull . . . exciting, stimulating, invigorating. . . .* A thumbs-down can be just as informative as a thumbs-up. At least you can remove one option from your list. Second, internships, co-ops, and service-learning opportunities give you experience to list on your résumé. And third, they help you make connections with others in the field, and sometimes they even lead to employment.

The key to successful trial experiences such as internships is the relationship between you and your sponsor in the host organization. If you're not being given enough to do, or not allowed to test your skills in a particular area, speak up. The answer may be put in terms of company policy, or you're "not quite ready for prime time." Nevertheless, you must communicate about these kinds of important issues. No one can read your mind! As you work toward launching your career, keep up with the latest information. Read up

FIGURE 12.1

Three Ways to Try a Job on for Size

	DESCRIPTION: WHAT IS . . .?	WHAT KIND OF EXPERIENCE DO I GET?	WHY WOULD I WANT TO DO IT?	HOW DO I GET INVOLVED?
An Internship	An internship is an opportunity for you to work along-side a professional in a career field of interest to you, and to learn from him or her.	Your supervisor will mentor you, and you'll get a clearer picture of what the career field is like.	You'll gain experience and insights into a job or career field while still in school. Some majors will even require you to complete an internship as a part of your program, for licensure or certification, for example.	Internships may be offered through your academic major department, or through a central office on campus, or sometimes you can pursue one on your own through the internet or personal connections.
A Co-op Program	Co-op programs allow you to take classes and then apply what you've learned on the job, either after or while you take classes.	You may take classes for a term and then work full-time for a term. You can test a career field.	A potential employer can get a sense of your potential, and you can gain practical experience to put on your résumé.	Your advisor will be able to tell you whether your program has co-op opportunities.
Service-Learning	Some classes contain service-learning experiences in which you volunteer your time.	A service-learning component built right into the syllabus can give you valuable, practical experience.	The emphasis is on hands-on learning and connecting what you're learning in class with what you're experiencing out of class. If you take a class on aging, for example, you may work with a senior citizen at an assisted living facility to apply what you're learning in class.	If you're particularly interested in hands-on learning, ask your advisor to recommend classes with service-learning components that will benefit you.

WHAT IF… A CRYSTAL BALL FOR CAREERS?

None of us has a crystal ball that lets us look into our own personal futures. Having one might save us some time and trouble, but we might not always like what we see! But we do have career specialists that look at job trends for the coming years and agencies that make information about those careers readily available. Take a look at their predictions for the top-paying 27 career fields that typically require a two-year degree or less.[2] If you are doing this exercise on your own, randomly choose a number between 1 and 27. Assume the career associated with that number is what your imaginary crystal ball—if you had one—shows you about your own future. Your instructor may also assign you a random career from the list provided. Either way, after your future career is revealed, answer the questions that follow here.

"The magic is inside you. There ain't no crystal ball."

Dolly Parton, American country singer, songwriter, and actress

1. Dental hygienist

2. Diagnostic medical sonographer

3. Registered nurse

4. Web developer

5. Respiratory therapist

6. Cardiovascular technologist

7. Electrician

8. Plumber

9. Commercial diver

10. Paralegal

11. HVAC technician

12. Surgical technologist

13. Heavy equipment operator

14. Licensed practical or vocational nurse

15. Medical laboratory technician

16. Computer programmer

17. Commercial pilot (non-airline)

18. Network systems administrator

19. Multimedia artist (video gaming, entertainment)

20. Electrical or electronics engineering technician

21. Police officer

22. Aircraft mechanic

23. Mechanical engineering technician

24. Architectural drafter

25. Civil engineer

26. Graphic designer

27. Diesel mechanic

1. Why would (or wouldn't) this be a good career choice for you? Identify as many reasons as you can.

2. Do some research on your hypothetical career. What would it take to enter this career in terms of qualifications and education?

3. If the career you've been given randomly doesn't fit, identify one from the list (or one you're actually pursuing) that does. Why did you select the one you chose?

4. What does this activity tell you about yourself? What conclusions can you draw from it?

"It's this simple: You are a brand. You are in charge of your brand. There is no single path to success. And there is no one right way to create the brand called you. Except this: Start today."

Tom Peters, "The Brand Called You," Fast Company

on résumé writing and interviewing, networking, hot career fields, and the latest employment trends. Use the information in this chapter to pique your interest, and search further on your own.

BUILD A PORTFOLIO OF YOUR BEST WORK

Even though it feels good to progress through your degree plan, and move on from one course to another, it's important to keep a record of each class. A potential employer may want to know exactly what you learned in Principles of Web Design, so that she can tell if what you learned matches the way her company does things. An interviewer may ask you about the course you were most successful in. You don't want to stammer and say, "Uh, let me get back to you on that. . . ." You want to sound knowledgeable. Build a portfolio of your best work. Your community college may have a formal way to help you do that through a course management system like Canvas or Moodle or an online electronic portfolio requirement, for example. If not, begin compiling a portfolio of your own. Keep copies of your best papers or other assignments, and write a summary of how each assignment relates to your career goals. If a prospective employer asks you about your writing skills, you can produce a paper on the spot. Or if you bring a laptop with you to an interview, you can access your best PowerPoint presentation or show a website you designed yourself.

BRAND YOURSELF

As business guru Tom Peters put it, "It's a new brand world."[3] It's not a typo; it's true. The coffee mug you may have in your hand right now has a logo on it. So does the tee shirt you're wearing, the phone in your hand, and the flat screen on your wall. Brands are everywhere; they stand for something—for example, quality, consistency, or status. If you're true to a particular brand of coffee, you know you'll get the exact same double mocha latte with nonfat milk in Detroit, Duluth, or Denver. In today's "new brand world," you can use the internet to publicize the brand called <u>you</u>. Think about it: Instead of posting empty status updates ("I'm sitting in my car in the parking lot and …") or, as some people do, putting up photos you wouldn't want everyone to see on the front page of *The New York Times*, why not use the internet to launch your career?[4] If you're just getting a start on the power of social media to build your credibility, follow these steps:

1. **Identify your brand.** Think about famous people. What does Oprah Winfrey stand for? Empowerment? Generosity? Business acumen? What do *you* stand for? What are you known for? What's your reputation? (Hint: You already have one.) What's unique about you? What sets you apart from other job applicants? What do you value? What are your interests? Do you speak another language or two? Have you traveled to other cultures? Have you completed projects that won awards? Internships that gave you experience?

2. **Create a personal branding statement.** Most résumés begin with a wordy, vague objective statement like this, "Objective: To get a job in social media and put my skills to good use." What does that mean, exactly? Instead, put some thought into your personal brand and sum

it up in a pithy, memorable statement: "I'm known for having a head for business and a heart of gold." Then in your résumé, you can describe your entrepreneurial efforts starting "pizza and poli sci" study groups that raised everyone's exam grades (head) and also point out your volunteer work (heart). Or "I see opportunity in every challenge." Then during an interview, you can describe working your way through college by holding down three jobs at once. Or, "I help people plug in and power up their technology skills." Use action verbs; they stand out. People might remember "plug in" and "power up" because you used two verb phrases and created a mental image.

3. **Manage your brand.** Blog passionately about something you care about to increase your visibility, read articles about the career field you'd like to join, or buy a domain that consists solely of your name and build a website that attracts viewers. Update all your brand accounts at least weekly. Use professional sites like LinkedIn and the many functions associated with it by building a complete profile, joining groups, following particular companies, and making connections. LinkedIn is a professional social media site, a virtual online rolodex with 500 million members from more than 200 countries and territories.

4. **Design business cards.** "But wait," you say. "I don't even have a job yet." It doesn't matter; everyone should have a business card with a high-quality headshot, personal brand statement, and contact information. After you create your business card, you can share it virtually via your phone using any one of a number of apps.[5] During interviews, give every interviewer your actual card or an e-version, and you'll demonstrate just how serious you are about the job search. And as you think about possible opportunities based on who you know, consider both "strong ties" (like former bosses and professors) and "weak ties" (your neighbor's colleague's boss).[6]

5. **Leverage social media.** Establishing a personal brand takes time and thought, but social media comprise the best advertising anyone could buy—and it's (mostly) free! Use it to publicize your enthusiasm, your skills, and your energy. It's never too soon to start your job search.[7]

> "Let excellence be your brand… When you are excellent, you become unforgettable. Doing the right thing, even when nobody knows you're doing the right thing will always bring the right thing to you."
>
> *Oprah Winfrey, actress, producer, media host, and philanthropist*

NETWORK, NETWORK, NETWORK!

The old saying is partially true: "It's not *what* you know, it's *who* you know." Who you know *is* important, but what you know is important, too. Another version of the saying, which is more accurate, goes like this: "It's not who you know, it's who you know, knows (and who THEY know)." Career advisors always recommend that you network with both "strong ties" (a professor who knows your work and has contacts in the community) and "weak ties" (your cousin's brother's friend who already works in a related field). But they now also recommend that you capitalize on "workplace ties." In one recent study, more than 60 percent of new hires were selected based on recommendations from former bosses, co-workers, or clients, for example. "The best way to increase the likelihood of getting the job you want later may be to treat your colleagues well at the one you have now."[8] If you use LinkedIn, you can build an online network of contacts, contacts of your contacts, and so forth.

"Don't follow your dreams; chase them."

Richard Dumb

BOX 12.1   DID I REALLY POST THAT?

When you apply for a job, chances are that many other graduates will be applying for the same one, especially if it's a good job. The first thing many employers will do is Google you.[9] When they do, what will pop up? Of course, if nothing pops up at all, that doesn't say much for how seriously you're taking the job search process, at least in terms of establishing a professional presence online. But what if they see all your social media connections, old blogs, websites, posts, photos, Tweets—basically, your

total online life from Day One? You may think your privacy settings will protect you, but employers have ways of getting in, asking you for your Facebook login information (although this practice is illegal in some states) or "shoulder surfing" as they watch *you* log in and see your friends-only posts.[10] Take a look at these four candidates who lost pending job offers, and see if you can derive "principles to post by" that you should adopt, if you haven't already.

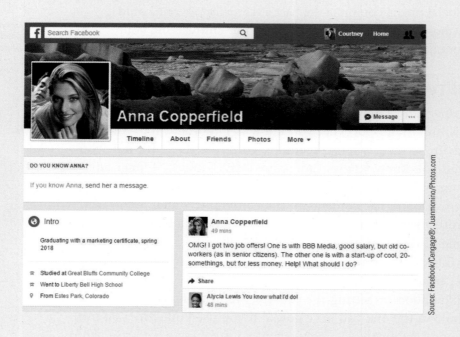

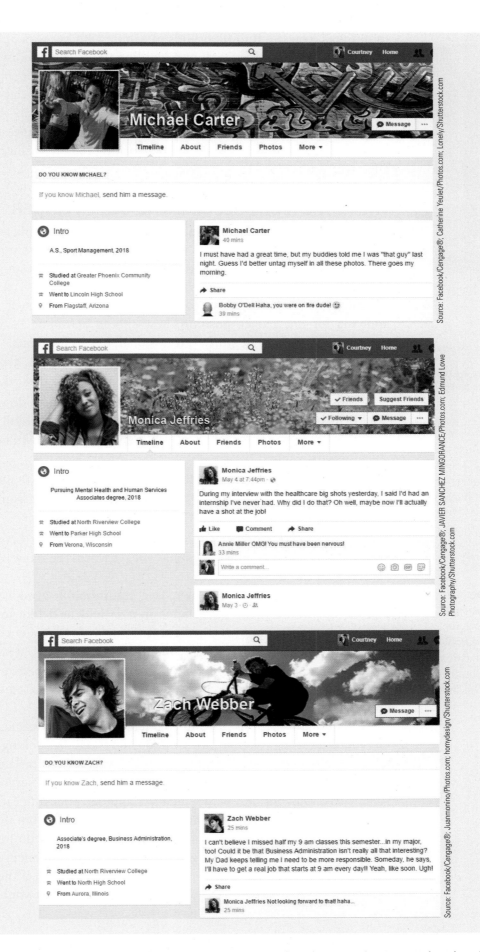

"To dare is to lose one's footing momentarily. To not dare is to lose oneself."

Soren Kierkegaard, Danish philosopher and theologian (1813–1855)

chronological arranging information in time order beginning with the most recent job

In minutes, you can find thousands of people who know people who work in the industry you're interested in. According to the site, you can connect, stay informed about your contacts and industry, and find the people and knowledge you need to achieve your goals. And of course, instead or in addition, you can network with real people in person, too. Ask people you know about who they know that works in your career field, contact these people, meet for coffee, for example, and pursue networking the old-fashioned (but highly effective) way.[11]

WRITE THE RIGHT RÉSUMÉ AND COVER LETTER

Interestingly, today companies may receive hundreds of applications for particular positions. While companies may request and look at your online presence after applying for a job, learning how to write a written résumé is still a vital skill for most of the jobs you might apply for.

In today's competitive world, when literally hundreds of people may be applying for one choice position, how should a résumé be written? Can a résumé be solid, but not stuffy? Professional, but still personal? Thorough, but brief? Actually, there's more than one way to write a résumé, depending on how much experience you have in the career field you'd like to work in.

> **Skills Approach:** If your work experience has little to do with the career field you'd like to enter, but you've learned important skills you could transfer to your new job, use a *skills* approach, as shown in Marcus Brown's résumé.

> **Chronological Approach:** If you have a work history that's relevant, use a chronological approach (that details job by job what you've done), as shown in Jennifer Ortega's résumé.

Take a look to see whether you can detect the differences between these two sample applicants' résumés. Assume they earned the same degree and are applying for the same job.

It's likely that Marcus Brown is a traditionally aged college student. Notice that he has little experience in the field he'd like to work in after getting his certificate in web design. Contrast his résumé with the following one, where Jennifer Ortega has considerable experience working in the IT field. Rather than using a skills approach, her résumé uses a chronological approach that shows everything she's done that's related to the job she's applying for.

You may automatically assume that Jennifer has the advantage over Marcus, but the healthcare company with the opening may be looking for fresh, new talent, and Marcus should capitalize on his web design freelance work or get an actual internship with a professional web designer. Everyone has to start somewhere. Do your best with whichever approach fits you. Finally, remember that you can hire a professional to write a résumé for you, but if you read up on résumé writing and follow the suggestions here, you can do just fine on your own. Hiring a professional or going through an employment agency can be helpful, but they can also be expensive propositions. And if they promise you the moon ("You'll have a new job at the starting salary of your dreams in just one week!"), be wary.

MARCUS BROWN
1234 Aspen Way, Apartment 105
Great Bluffs, CO 89898
(555) 987-6543
mbrown@gbcc.edu

CAREER OBJECTIVE
To obtain a position as a web designer for a large healthcare organization

EDUCATION
Great Bluffs Community College, Great Bluffs, CO
Certificate in Web Design
GPA 3.2/4.0
Personally financed 100% of college tuition by working two jobs

HONORS
Selected for City Council Outstanding Leadership Award (College Division), 2015
Awarded Technology Scholarship, GBCC Foundation

SUMMARY OF ACADEMIC COURSEWORK
Introduction to Web Graphics   Web Development Software
Introduction to Web Multimedia   Electronic Commerce
Principles of Web Design   Emerging Technologies

SKILLS
Technology
Do part-time freelance work, web-page design
Work in Word, PowerPoint, Excel, Access, Macromedia Flash, Dreamweaver, Java, HTML,
    PHP, Adobe Acrobat, and Photoshop
Graphics
Designed flyers and posters for campus events for GBCC Office of Campus Activities
Writing
Wrote columns for GBCC student online newsletter

EMPLOYMENT HISTORY
Server, Pancake Heaven, 2012–2014
Cashier, Toyland, 2014-present
Ticket Taker, Movies at the Mall, 2015-present

REFERENCES (available on request)

Center your name, and use a standard résumé format. Many companies now scan résumés so that they can be read conveniently from one source, so use key words from the job ad.[12] If you submit a hard copy, skip the neon pink paper that you may think helps you stand out from other applicants. Go for a highly professional look.

Make sure your résumé is well organized and cleanly formatted. Research indicates that recruiters in many fields spend approximately six seconds on each résumé. Eye tracking studies show that they spend more time reading highly organized résumés with clear formatting.[13]

Provide numbers whenever you can. Text can be glossed over, but numbers stand out and make your accomplishments more "quantifiable."

Match words used in the job ad. If the ad says, the company is looking for a candidate who has "outstanding leadership skills," make sure those words appear somewhere on your résumé. Don't lie, of course, but most companies now use software that searches for particular terms.[14]

Even if you aren't applying for a job as a web designer, remember that technology is important in today's workplace. Don't underrate your competence. If you're a traditionally aged, younger student who's very tech-savvy, you should realize that many senior employees don't know as much as you do!

If you're able, show that you have worked all through college to demonstrate your commitment to your goal. If you don't have much experience, you may also emphasize volunteer work that you have done, if it relates.

Always obtain preapproval from your references, even if you don't list their names. You may be asked to provide them on a moment's notice.

JENNIFER ORTEGA
789 Breckenridge Court, Apartment C
Great Bluffs, CO 89898
(555) 333-9999
jortega@gbcc.edu

CAREER OBJECTIVE
To obtain a position as a web designer in a large healthcare organization

EMPLOYMENT HISTORY

2016–present   Technology Helpdesk Manager, Central College
· Developed new phone answering system that increased the unit's responsiveness by 50%
· Oversaw a staff of 10 student technology experts
· Installed software and made troubleshooting visits to approximately 15 faculty offices
  per week

2014–2016   IT Supervisor, Great Bluffs School District 1
· Coordinated software maintenance in 12 elementary school administrative offices
· Managed a team of 8 technology employees
· Installed financial software to improve budget management at the K-6 level

2012–2014   Sales staff member, Tech 4 U, Great Bluffs, Colorado
· Earned Salesperson of the Quarter Award, Jan–Mar, 2013
· Recognized with Sales and Service Award, June 2014
· Initiated store display rearrangement

EDUCATION
Great Bluffs Community College, Great Bluffs, CO
Certificate in Web Design
GPA 3.2/4.0
Personally financed 100% of college tuition

HONORS
Selected as the student body representative to GBCC faculty government
Earned a place on the GBCC Dean's Honor Role each term

SUMMARY OF ACADEMIC COURSEWORK

Introduction to Web Graphics	Web Development Software
Introduction to Web Multimedia	Electronic Commerce
Principles of Web Design	Emerging Technologies

SKILLS
Technology
Do part-time freelance work, web-page design
Work in Word, PowerPoint, Excel, Access, Macromedia Flash, Dreamweaver, Java, HTML, PHP,
    Adobe InDesign, Acrobat, and Photoshop
Graphics
Design brochures for local healthcare organizations as a freelancer:
    Forest Hills Rehabilitation Center, Mercy Hospital, and Sunnydale Senior Center
Writing
Write brochure content after consulting with management at these organizations

REFERENCES (available on request)

When writing a chronological resume, list the relevant positions you have held. Include the tasks you performed and skills you developed in each of those positions that might be useful in the job you're applying to.

Numbers are important and memorable! Notice how they stand out.

Providing specific dates and listing tasks, skills, awards, and accomplishments, like Jennifer has, gives you things to discuss with an interviewer.

Note that there are many different ways to say the same thing. Jennifer has noted that she was selected as the student representative. She has chosen particular wording to emphasize that this was an honor.

Start each phrase with a verb to emphasize action, and note that all verbs are in the same tense (past or present).

VARK IT!

Read/Write: Bring a current résumé to class and trade with another Read/Write student. Read the résumé, and give your classmate written feedback.

Take a look at the following cover letter from Marcus Brown and critique it. What has he done right, and what has he done wrong?

---

15 September

To Whom It May Concenr,

I'd like to apply for your opening at Anderson-Wallace Healthcare Industries. I have heard a lot about your company and it sounds great. A friend of mine works there, and he said his starting salary was unbelieveable. What exactly do you do at your company? He's told me a few things, but I'm eager to learn more!

As you can see from my résumé, I don't have much experience. But I have just earned my web design certificate from GBCC, and I did pretty well. I want to start my career at a great company like yours.

I hope to hear from you soon.

Warmly,

Marcus Brown

After finding the mistakes Marcus made, rewrite this letter to bring to class or submit to your instructor.

When you submit a résumé, either in person, through the mail, or online, you should send a well-written cover letter along with it that briefly outlines your qualifications for the job, expresses your interest, and gives the person who reviews your résumé some idea of who you are.

Cover letters are more important than you might think. In fact, they can make or break your résumé, and there are rules about what makes a good one. Consider these suggestions:[16]

1. **Personalize the content.** The cover letter is where you can try to make an actual connection with the reader by highlighting how your skills and background fit the new position. And rather than using a generic greeting, do some Google research and find out the name of the person who's likely to be reading your letter if you can.

2. **Tell a story.** What's the most interesting thing you've done relative to this potential new job? And call out anything about your résumé that's particularly interesting.

3. **Keep it to one page, and use bullet points for impact.** Remember that recruiters are reading dozens, if not hundreds, of cover letters. Do what you can to make it easier for them to understand your message quickly.

4. **Show how you fit the culture.** Employers are all about fit these days, and fit is important for employees to consider, too. Point out that you're a team player if the ad mentions a collaborative environment or talk about your initiative if the ad mentions "self-starters wanted." Cover letters are a good place to talk about your soft skills, too. Show some personality without going overboard.

VARK IT!

Aural: Interview someone in your intended career field. Be prepared to report back to class or e-mail your instructor the results.

FIGURE 12.2

Quick Study: "Interviewing Etiquette"

INTERVIEWING ETIQUETTE

DO

Play up the positive. Interviewers often say, " What's your worst fault?" Have a good answer ready, so that you don't say the first thing that comes to mind. "Oh, that's easy! Oversleeping!" is an example of an "open mouth, insert foot" mistake.

Stay on track. Interviewers often open with, " So, tell me about yourself." Zero in and give job-focused answers. Talk about your career goals, what you liked about your last job, what you can bring to this one, what kind of job experience is important to you, etc.

Get some answers, too. A job interview is like a first date. Ask the interviewer key questions: *"What does this company value?" "What's a typical day like for you?" "How did this position come about?"* The interviewer's answers will tell you a lot about how well you may or may not fit in.

Watch for questions out of left field. Sometimes interviewers ask bizarre questions, like: How many pieces of pizza does the average American eat a year? Unless you're a trivia buff, you won't know—and the interviewer isn't looking for a real answer. She wants to see if you'll get ruffled, and she wants to learn more about how you think.

Know what you're dealing with. Candidates who don't do their homework usually don't get the job. Go online to read up about where you'd like to work. And it goes without saying (although here it is, anyway) that you should arrive early, dress professionally, over prepare, and send a follow-up thank-you note or e-mail—or both.

DON'T

Don't humblebrag. Humblebragging makes you sound like a martyr while at the same time, tooting your own horn: "I should be a better team player, but no one else seems to care as much as I do." Humblebragging actually hurts your chances of getting the job.[a]

Don't engage in "true confessions." Don't go into your family background, your personal problems, or bash a former employer. (The interviewer may worry that you'll bring those problems with you to this new job.) And whatever you do, don't answer a phone call or text during an interview.

Don't start off with salary questions. "So tell me about the salary again? Any way to notch that up a bit?" isn't a good way to start. Of course, you're in it for the money but not just for that. Every job you have will help you prepare for the next one. Don't start negotiating a salary until you've actually been offered a job.

Don't assume you'll just have to talk. Increasingly, interviews involve applying your knowledge as you would on the job. If you're a social media manager candidate, you may have to demonstrate your knowledge. Sample question: "Kanye West just released a new fashion collection. You can see it here. Imagine you had to write a tweet promoting this collection. What would your tweet be?"[b]

Don't negotiate naively. If asked to name a salary figure, be careful. Saying "I could probably live on $40,000" when the interviewer is authorized to start with $45,000, has just given him permission to lower the salary. Instead, ask what the salary range is. Research the salaries of similar jobs, and—even better—have another job offer waiting, so you have choices. Otherwise, you're not negotiating; you're begging.

Sources: (a) Gino, F. (2015, May 20). The right way to brag about yourself. *Harvard Business Review*. Retrieved from https://hbr.org/2015/05/the-right-way-to-brag-about-yourself; Nobel, C. (2015, July 13). 'Humblebragging' is a bad strategy, especially in a job interview. *Forbes*. Retrieved from http://www.forbes.com/sites/hbsworkingknowledge/2015/07/13/humblebragging-is-a-bad-strategy-especially-in-a-job-interview/#271a0dfd538f; (b) Friedman, T. (2013, May 28). How to get a job. *The New York Times*. Retrieved from http://www.nytimes.com/2013/05/29/opinion/friedman-how-to-get-a-job.html?_r=0

5. **End with a question.** Questions are invitations for a response. "Will you be making your selection within the month?" or "When might finalists for the position expect the interviewing to begin?" Without begging, demonstrate your genuine interest.

CONTINUING YOUR
EDUCATION

Like Anthony Lopez, perhaps you're exploring the idea of continuing your education. Typically, the more education you get, the more money you can make, the more you can do, and the more responsibility you have. Figure 12.3 summarizes both earnings and unemployment rates by educational level achieved, but the decision to continue is yours and yours alone. You know yourself and your interests best.

By the end of the "FOCUS Challenge Case," Anthony was considering four alternatives: an associate's degree, a bachelor's degree, a master's degree, and a Ph.D. Each level of these four educational paths has distinct differences he needs to know about. Anthony seems to have "found his bliss," and his heart is in the work. He is convinced that being a social worker is the right career field for him. He is motivated, engaged in what he's learning, and looking forward to a career of service. But at what level? Figure 12.4 lists some basic considerations for Anthony. Can you compare his choices to ones you may be considering?

If Anthony thinks he may wish to take the first step beyond getting his associate's degree, he must begin planning now. Sometimes students who transfer to a four-year institution experience what's called "transfer shock." Courses can be taught differently, classes can be larger, and in a class with several hundred students, the atmosphere can seem more impersonal. According to research, math and science courses, in particular, may seem (and be) harder.[17] The campus itself may have a very different feel to it, and transfer students can feel lost and isolated, which can hurt their academic performance. Anthony must work closely with his community college advisor and an advisor at the school where

AF archive/Alamy Stock Photo

"We can never see past the choices we don't understand."

The Oracle, The Matrix

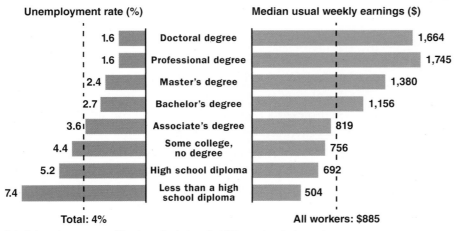

Education Pays

Unemployment rates and earnings by educational attainment, 2016

Unemployment rate (%)		Median usual weekly earnings ($)
1.6	Doctoral degree	1,664
1.6	Professional degree	1,745
2.4	Master's degree	1,380
2.7	Bachelor's degree	1,156
3.6	Associate's degree	819
4.4	Some college, no degree	756
5.2	High school diploma	692
7.4	Less than a high school diploma	504

Total: 4%   All workers: $885

Note: Data are for persons age 25 and over. Earnings are for full-time wage and salary workers.
Source: U.S. Bureau of Labor Statistics, Current Population Survey.

FIGURE 12.3

Education Pays

Source: Bureau of Labor Statistics. (April 20, 2017).
Available at https://www.bls.gov/emp/ep_chart_001.htm/

	ASSOCIATE'S DEGREE IN SOCIAL (HUMAN) SERVICES	BACHELOR'S DEGREE IN SOCIOLOGY(OR A RELATED FIELD)	MASTER'S OF SOCIAL WORK (MSW)	PH.D. IN SOCIOLOGY (OR DOCTOR OF SOCIAL WORK)
Average Time to Complete:	2 years	4–5 years	2 years beyond a bachelor's degree	3–4 years beyond a master's degree
Average Number of Required Courses:	Approximately 20	Approximately 40	10 courses and 900 hours of supervised field experience or internship	10 (plus dissertation)
Type of Work:	Social Service and Human Service Assistant or Aid: work with social workers, pharmacists, psychologists, etc. Varying levels of responsibility. Help people in need.	Social Worker (although an MSW is increasingly required): help clients cope with disabilities (like substance abuse or homelessness). Work in schools, public health agencies, hospitals, etc., and visit clients in their homes.	Social Worker clinical work: supervise other social workers, manage case loads. Must pass state licensure exam. May wish to go into private practice at least part-time. May specialize in such areas as • Child, family, or schools • Medical and public health • Mental health and substance abuse	Professor, High-level administrator, researcher: May teach at the college or university level, conduct research, or run a healthcare or nonprofit organization, for example.
Job Growth:	Faster than average. Expected growth of 11 percent between 2014–2020.	Faster than average. Expected growth of 12 percent between 2014–2020.	Favorable, 10–12 percent, faster than average (varies by type of specialization).	Faster than average, 12 percent for faculty positions (although varies by type of specialization and preference for full- or part-time work).
Median salary:	$31,810 (as of May, 2016)	$46,890 (as of May, 2016)	$46,890 and higher; $64,680 for social and community service managers (as of May, 2016)	$75,430 (as of May, 2016).

FIGURE 12.4

An Educational Career Path[18]

he plans to transfer, to make sure his credits are transferable. His goal should be to make the process as seamless as possible by visiting the new campus now and talking with advisors and professors there. Take control of the situation: Ask for help, if you need it, and get involved in campus life.[19]

The important thing for Anthony—and for you—is to determine what you really want. Many different educational and career paths exist. Don't feel pressure from others to continue your education if you know that decision isn't right for you—or isn't right for you *now*. Think about your goals in life, what you want to achieve, and what kind of work you would find most fulfilling, and then decide which educational level is right for you.

WIIFM?

Isn't the answer to the WIIFM question obvious? "Creating *your* future." It's you we're talking about, after all. It should be obvious, but sometimes when it's *your* future we're talking about, the specifics are hard to uncover. According to motivational speaker Jim Rohn, "If you don't design your own life plan, chances are you'll fall into someone else's plan. And guess what they have planned for you? Not much." *Star Wars* creator George Lucas is now said to have a net worth of over 5 billion dollars. But it took him a summer in the hospital to figure out that his future should start with college and not stay with cars. His attention needed to be redirected in order to get where he really wanted to go.

In terms of creating your future, there's one big idea you need to know. In fact, it's not just big; it's huge. "Whatever captures your attention controls your life." That's a sweeping statement, so where's the evidence?

Here's an example: Several years ago, two consultants were hired to observe infants and toddlers at Disney World. Their task, assigned by park executives, was to find out what most captured children's attention in the theme park. It didn't take long for the consultants to figure out that what captured their attention wasn't the cuddly Disney characters in costume, the wildest rides with the longest lines, or the magical sights and sounds all around them. It was their parents' cell phones, especially while their parents were on them. What the children wanted, it seems, was their parents' attention, and while parents were on their phones, their attention wasn't on their children. Because parents were captivated by these devices, their kids must have wondered what was so very interesting. They wanted to be in on it.[20] The parents probably didn't even realize that what they were doing was affecting their children. After all, they were taking time off and spending money to show their children a good time.

We've all probably been guilty of allowing distractions to control us: texting during an oh-so-romantic dinner, an intimate conversation with a best friend, a class in which the professor is delivering a well-prepared lecture, or a key meeting when we think the boss isn't looking. But the fact that our attention is elsewhere is a dead giveaway that something else is more important at that moment. Being aware of where we're focusing our attention isn't really that easy because our brains become wired, eventually. "Attention shapes the brain," says one expert.[21] The more attention you pay to something, the more neurons your brain builds to pay attention to that thing. That's why your time in college preparing for your future is so important. Devote your attention to it.

And the more you fragment your attention by multitasking, the less you get done. Remember this: "Being busy is not the same as being productive. It's the difference between running on a treadmill and running to a destination. They're both running, but being busy is running in place."[22] It's easy to get stuck. Sometimes students who are in college to create better futures make the mistake of dedicating so much attention to their present dead-end jobs (to help pay for college) that they put their college success at risk. Do you see how that could happen?

What does all this have to do with creating *your* future? As this book has asserted all along: It's about who you are and what you want. Of course, you need to pay attention to your present day-to-day responsibilities. But your future is about the "you" you want to become. So, if you want to be a writer, write. Get up early in the morning and write, even if what comes up on the computer screen reads like gibberish. Do it. If you want to be a teacher, teach a class at your local Boys and Girls Club or volunteer at your child's school for the experience. Do it. Or think of it this way: "You need to spend time

> "I wanted to race cars. I didn't like school, and all I wanted to do was work on cars. But right before I graduated, I got into a really bad car accident, and I spent that summer in the hospital thinking about where I was heading. I decided to take education more seriously and go to a community college."
>
> ***George Lucas, American filmmaker, creator of Star Wars (attended Modesto Junior College, Modesto, California and transferred to the University of Southern California)***

on the future even when there are more important things to do in the present and even when there is no immediately apparent return to your efforts. In other words—and this is the hard part—if you want to be productive, you need to spend time doing things that feel ridiculously *unproductive*."[23] Now there's a paradox!

Steve Jobs once said, "You can't connect the dots looking forward; you can only connect them looking backward. So you have to trust that the dots will somehow connect in your future. You have to trust in something—your gut, destiny, life, karma, whatever. This approach has never let me down, and it has made all the difference in my life." Create your "dots" now, while you're in college, and they will surely connect in *your* future. That's "What's in It for You"!

PUT WHAT YOU'VE LEARNED TO GOOD USE: TEN THINGS EMPLOYERS HOPE YOU WILL LEARN IN COLLEGE

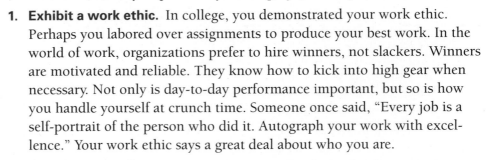

> "Bring your whole self to work. I don't believe we have a professional self Monday through Friday and a real self the rest of the time. It is all professional, and it is all personal."
>
> **Sheryl Sandberg,** *Chief Operating Officer, Facebook*

> "Goals are the fuel in the furnace of achievement."
>
> **Brian Tracy,** *Eat that Frog*

Regardless of which fork in the road you choose—launching a career or transferring to a four-year school—college teaches many lessons, and they're not all about the subject matter in your classes. Much of the academic professionalism you've developed in college can easily translate into career professionalism, with some thought and application on your part. Thanks to having gone to college, you can begin your career with some ready-to-go professional advantages. Here is a set of ten things employers care about, regardless of exactly which college courses you've taken or degree you've worked on. As you evaluate, think about which ones are already in place for you. Employers want you to:

1. **Exhibit a work ethic.** In college, you demonstrated your work ethic. Perhaps you labored over assignments to produce your best work. In the world of work, organizations prefer to hire winners, not slackers. Winners are motivated and reliable. They know how to kick into high gear when necessary. Not only is day-to-day performance important, but so is how you handle yourself at crunch time. Someone once said, "Every job is a self-portrait of the person who did it. Autograph your work with excellence." Your work ethic says a great deal about who you are.

2. **Study up.** In college, you were encouraged to learn deeply, not just memorize facts. Transfer this principle to the workplace. On the job, learn the ins and outs of your industry. If you are an automotive mechanic, know more than just about the nuts and bolts and transmissions of the cars you work on. Learn about the automobile maker's history, what the company stands for, its vision and values, and the reputation it has earned from customers. It's easy to get tunnel vision and lose sight of the bigger picture.

3. **Prove you're a problem solver.** While taking your college classes, you learned problem-solving skills. Some of those problems were personal (*Who can I get to watch my kids at the last minute?*), and some were academic (*Why* was *Edgar Allen Poe so "dark"?*). On the job, everyone values the person who comes up with a workable solution when everyone else is stumped. And your boss will value you more if you come up with solutions yourself. Instead of, *What should I do about X?* say, *We're facing Problem X. Should I do A, B, or C?* You've proven that you've already thought about the problem and generated three possible solutions and demonstrated that you can think on your own.

4. **Speak and write well.** Your college career may have put more emphasis on these skills than any others. In today's world of abbreviated texts and Tweets (TBH = To Be Honest) and empty conversation ("And she's . . . like so . . . you know . . . whatever . . ."), you can become a super star on the job by just speaking and writing well. And in addition to speaking and writing, learn to listen to what's *really* being said and why. With practice, you can listen past the bravado or baloney and get to the *real* message. That's important!

5. **Polish your people skills.** Your college instructors may have assigned group projects in your classes to help you learn teamwork skills. Good

teamwork skills are key to a successful career in anything! People can be difficult to work with, yet *people* are the way work gets done.

6. **Learn the rules of the game.** In school—and throughout your life—you have learned what's sometimes called "The Hidden Curriculum": things everyone knows, more or less, but never learned formally. For example, most people know that it's not polite to tell off-color jokes to people you've just met or smack your gum while giving a speech. In the same way, on the job, the "grapevine," or informal network, is important to understand. To be successful, you must be tuned in. Understand the culture of the organization you work for. What does it value? Who holds the power? Where do you fit in, and what can you contribute?

7. **Know how to gather information and use it.** In college, you're asked to develop your research skills. It's easy to think that each paper for a class is just another assignment to check off the list, when, actually, you're developing skills that will be critical to your success later. You don't just string together pieces of information when you do research for your college classes. You analyze research through the "eyes" of the problem you're trying to address and *your* perspective on it. You weave ideas together to make an argument.

8. **Understand that numbers count.** Unfortunately, math gets a bad rap. Many people approach math classes in college with "fear and loathing," when, actually, math is a key to success in the world of work. If you can understand spreadsheets or figure out the budget, you'll be ahead of the game. Some people de-emphasize the importance of financial skills by referring to them as "bean counting" or "number crunching," but people who know how to apply math on the job are highly sought after.

9. **Go for extra credit.** In some of your courses, your instructors may give extra credit. You could be allowed to do something extra, beyond the requirements on the syllabus, to raise your grade. But what's extra credit in terms of your career? On the job, you have "extra credit" when your abilities stand out. You speak German and no one else does, so when something needs translating, you're the go-to person. Or you're so exceptional at PowerPoint that you're affectionately referred to as the "PowerPoint King."

10. **Manage your time, your attention, and yourself.** College is about self-responsibility. You're in charge of your education; you call the shots. If you manage your time and money, you can focus as you should on your courses. If you "spend" unwisely—in either area—you lose your focus and your performance slips. In your career, the same will be true. Your ability to manage time, your attention, and yourself will affect your personal and professional future.[25]

WHAT IFs

Life is full of "what ifs?" isn't it? What if you had dated someone else? What if you took the other job? What if things were different?

> "When one door closes, another opens. But often we look so long, so regretfully, upon the closed door that we fail to see the one that has opened for us."
>
> *Helen Keller, American author, activist, and lecturer (1880–1968)*

life hack #2

Use these quick suggestions to maximize your productivity:
1. If you can do it in five minutes or less, do it now.
2. Set "blackout" times when your device is off and everyone knows you're unavailable.
3. Remember that dress and posture can improve your confidence.
4. Time your daily routines to cut out waste.
5. Put giant X's on a calendar for every day you focus on something specific you want to get better at, and don't break the chain of X's.[24]

> "Every adversity, every failure, every heartache carries with it the seed of an equal or greater benefit."

Napoleon Hill, author, Keys to Success: The 17 Principles of Personal Achievement *(1883–1970)*

WHAT IF COLLEGE ISN'T RIGHT FOR YOU?

What if you decide, after a term or two, that college isn't right for you? Perhaps your heart just isn't in it, and neither is your head. If so, know that you aren't alone. That realization comes to many students. The important question to ask yourself is whether you're really making the right decision, not just getting discouraged if college seems too challenging. Remember that "College is a team sport," and use all of the campus resources available to you before you abandon your efforts. But something other than college may also be the right decision for you—right now at this particular point in your life. However, this kind of decision is one you shouldn't make lightly.

WHAT IF YOU CAN'T FINISH A DEGREE NOW?

Even though you have dreams and goals, sometimes "life happens." A turn of events changes everything, a new job consumes all of your time and energy, or someone needs you. Don't feel like a failure if that happens. Take time off, regroup, and come back when you can. Going to college expands your thinking and gives you a whole new take on life. Beyond a certificate or diploma, the learning that takes place in college changes you forever—and it's worth the investment in your future.

MY, HOW YOU'VE GROWN!
GOODBYE AND GOOD LUCK!

Remember Aunt Ruth (or whatever her name was)? Every time she visited when you were a kid, she remarked about how much you'd grown. Or when you went to visit her, she'd measure you and mark a notch on the wall to compare your height now to the one from last year's visit. She loved watching you grow, and the fact that she noticed made you feel special.

There's no doubt about it. In this first term of college, you have grown. You have gained new perspectives, new insights, and new ways of thinking about things. Like Aunt Ruth, others may notice. If those close to you are threatened by these changes, reassure them that your newfound knowledge hasn't made you think less of them. Remember the words of writer M. L. Boren, "You should have education enough so that you won't have to look up to people; and then more education so that you will be wise enough not to look down on people." If they are proud of you and your accomplishments, and have supported you along the way, thank them!

The important thing is to keep learning and never stop. Continuing to learn—whether in college or in life—is what will determine who you are and what you will become. Learn new things, update your goals, and reinvent yourself. This text, and the course for which you're reading it, have begun that process. Now the rest is up to you!

> "Success is not final, failure is not fatal: it is the courage to continue that counts."

Winston Churchill, former Prime Minister of the United Kingdom (1874–1965)

CAREER OUTLOOK: KEEP YOUR BALANCE

You're a winner. You're working hard as a highly motivated, ultra-competent employee. Your boss is impressed—so much so that you get promoted. Your new position requires you to work harder, and before you know it, you're promoted again. This cycle keeps repeating itself, and over time, you have success written all over you. You're well on your way to mapping out a great future.

There's an underlying question worth exploring, however. Why are you working so hard? Is it because you're passionate about your work? Perhaps it fuels you, gives you purpose, direction, and fulfillment. You love it.

But what if your success isn't about fulfillment at all? What if it's about moving up, making more money, reveling in the prestige? What if you actually dislike your work? One work-life balance expert asks, why do people "work long hard hours at jobs they hate to enable them to buy things they don't need to impress people they don't like"?[26] Good question. The why of success is fundamentally important.

If you ever lose your professional balance, take charge of your own future. Your company is unlikely to say, "You know what? You've been working far too hard. You need to chill for a few weeks." Although companies are increasingly interested in wellness, corporations won't fix things for you. You must take control and assume responsibility for living the type of life you want to live. For example, make a rule for yourself that evenings are for family or your romantic partner, and stick to it. Or make a pact that you'll only check your e-mail once a day on weekends so that you can let your mind "idle" for a while.

A recent study asked dying people to identify their biggest regrets. "Their most common regret? 'I wish I'd had the courage to live a life true to myself, not the life others expected of me.' Their second most common regret? 'I wish I didn't work so hard.' There are two ways to address these regrets. One, work less hard and spend your time living a life true to yourself, whatever that means. Or two, work just as hard—harder even—on things you consider to be important and meaningful. If you put those two regrets together, you realize that what people really regret isn't simply working so hard, it's working so hard on things that don't matter to them. If our work matters to us, if it represents a life true to us. . . . then we will have lived more fully."[27]

What does balance mean to you as a college student? What will it mean in your anticipated career?

HOW MUCH DID YOU LEARN?

At the beginning of this chapter, you filled out a "Readiness Check" that asked how you thought this chapter would relate to you and how you would relate to it. Now, fill out this "Reality Check" to find out.

1. What is *networking* and how can it help you?

2. Why is it advantageous to build a portfolio of your best work?

3. Why is your continuing your education potentially important?

4. List three of the things employers hope you learn in college.

5. How long did it take? _____ hours _____ minutes. Before you began this chapter, you were asked to predict how long it would take you to complete this chapter (total time, even if you read it in more than one sitting). Was your estimate on target? Have you become more realistic in your estimates over time?

REALITY: FOCUS EXIT INTERVIEW

Although you have not quite completed your first term as a college student, we're interested in your reactions to college so far: how you have spent your time, what challenges you've experienced, and your general views about what college has been like. Please answer thoughtfully.

INFORMATION ABOUT YOU

NAME _____

STUDENT NUMBER _____ COURSE/SECTION _____

INSTRUCTOR _____

GENDER _____ AGE _____

NOTE: Questions 1–10 were asked on the Entrance Interview and need not be repeated here. The numbering below begins with number 11 so that the Entrance and Exit Interview results can be compared, if you or your instructor would like to do that. It may be interesting to see how your original expectations of college compare to your actual experience. Note, too, that the Exit Interview contains several added questions at the end about your future education.

YOUR COLLEGE EXPERIENCE

YOUR REACTIONS TO COLLEGE

11. Which of the following reasons to finish your college degree seem important to you now? (Check all that apply.)

_____ I want to build a better life for myself.

_____ I want to be well-off financially in the future.

_____ My friends are going to college.

_____ It is expected of me.

_____ I want to continue learning.

_____ I am unsure of what I might do instead.

_____ I want to build a better life for my family.

_____ I need a college education to achieve my dreams.

_____ My family is encouraging me to continue.

_____ I want to prepare for a new career.

_____ The career I am pursuing requires a degree.

_____ other (please explain).

12. How did you find you learned best in college? (Check all that apply.)

_____ by looking at charts, maps, graphs

_____ by listening to instructors' lectures

_____ by reading books

_____ by going on field trips

_____ by looking at color-coded information

_____ by listening to other students during in-class discussions

_____ by writing papers

_____ by engaging in activities

_____ by looking at symbols and graphics

_____ by talking about course content with friends or roommates

_____ by taking notes

_____ by actually doing things

13. The following sets of opposite descriptive phrases are separated by five blank lines. Put an X on the line between the two that best represent your response, like this: For me, high school was easy ____:__X__:____:____:____ hard

My first term of college:

challenged me academically	____:____:____:____:____	was easy
was very different from high school	____:____:____:____:____	was a lot like high school
was exciting	____:____:____:____:____	was dull
was interesting	____:____:____:____:____	was uninteresting
motivated me to continue	____:____:____:____:____	discouraged me
was fun	____:____:____:____:____	was boring
helped me feel a part of this campus	____:____:____:____:____	made me feel like an outsider

14. How many total hours per week did you study outside of class for your college courses?

____ 0–5	____ 6–10	____ 11–15	____ 16–20	____ 21–25
____ 26–30	____ 31–35	____ 36–40	____ 40+	

15. Now what do you expect your grade point average to be at the end of your first term of college?

____ A+	____ A	____ A–	____ B+	____ B
____ B–	____ C+	____ C	____ C–	____ D or lower

YOUR STRENGTHS, PERSONALITY, AND INTERESTS

16. Which of these *strengths* or personal characteristics contributed to your college success? (Check all that apply.)

____ a. I am good at building relationships.

____ b. I can usually convince others to follow my plan.

____ c. I like to win.

____ d. I work toward future goals.

____ e. I like to be productive and get things done.

____ f. I have a positive outlook on life.

____ g. I'm usually the person who gets things going.

____ h. I enjoy the challenge of learning new things.

____ i. I am focused.

____ j. I can usually look at a problem and figure out a plan of action.

____ k. I work to keep everyone happy.

____ l. I'm a take-charge kind of person.

____ m. I help other people develop their talents and skills.

____ n. I'm a very responsible person.

____ o. I can analyze a situation and see various ways things might work out.

____ p. I usually give tasks my best effort.

17. How confident are you now in yourself in each of the following areas? (1 = very confident, 5 = not at all confident)

____ overall academic ability

____ mathematical skills

____ leadership ability

____ reading skills

____ public speaking skills

____ study skills

____ technology skills

____ physical well-being

____ writing skills

____ social skills

____ emotional well-being

____ teamwork skills

18. For each of the following pairs of descriptors, which set sounds most like you based on what you've learned about yourself this term? (Choose between the two options on each line and place a check mark by your choice.)

_____ Extraverted and outgoing	or	_____ Introverted and quiet
_____ Detail-oriented and practical	or	_____ Big-picture and future-oriented
_____ Rational and truthful	or	_____ People-oriented and tactful
_____ Organized and self-disciplined	or	_____ Spontaneous and flexible

19. *FOCUS* is about twelve different aspects of college life. Which did you find to be most interesting as they applied to your academic success? (Check all that apply.)

_____ Starting strong, building resilience	_____ Engaging, listening, and note-taking in class
_____ Becoming mindful, setting goals	_____ Reading, writing, and presenting
_____ Learning styles and studying	_____ Developing memory, taking tests
_____ Managing your time, energy, and money	_____ Communicating in groups, valuing diversity
_____ Thinking critically and creatively	_____ Choosing a college major and career
_____ Learning online	_____ Creating your future

YOUR CHALLENGES

20. Of the twelve aspects of college life identified in the previous question, which were most challenging to apply to yourself in your academic work? (Check all that apply.)

_____ Starting strong, building resilience	_____ Engaging, listening, and note-taking in class
_____ Becoming mindful, setting goals	_____ Reading, writing, and presenting
_____ Learning styles and studying	_____ Developing memory, taking tests
_____ Managing your time, energy, and money	_____ Communicating in groups, valuing diversity
_____ Thinking critically and creatively	_____ Choosing a college major and career
_____ Learning online	_____ Creating your future

21. Which one of your current classes was most challenging this term and why?

Which class? (course title *or* department and course number) _____

Why? _____

Did you succeed in this course? _____ yes _____ no _____ Somewhat (please explain): _____

22. Please mark your *top three areas of concern* relating to your first term of college by placing 1, 2, and 3 next to the items you choose (with 1 representing your top concern).

_____ I did not fit in.	_____ I had difficulty making friends.
_____ I was not academically successful.	_____ My grades disappointed my family.
_____ I had difficulty handling the stress.	_____ I had financial problems.
_____ I overextended myself and tried to do too much.	_____ I cut class frequently.
_____ I did not reach out for help when I needed it.	_____ I procrastinated on assignments.
_____ I did not put in enough time to be academically successful.	_____ My professors were hard to communicate with.

_____ I am now tempted to drop out. _____ I was homesick.

_____ I was not organized enough. _____ I was bored in my classes.

_____ I was distracted (for example, spent too much time online). _____ My job(s) outside of school interfered with my studies.

_____ Other (please explain). _____

YOUR FUTURE

23. How certain are you now of the following (1 = totally sure, 5 = totally unsure)?

_____ Finishing your degree

_____ Choosing your major

_____ Deciding on a career

_____ Completing your degree at this school

_____ Transferring to a four-year school

_____ Continuing on to work toward an advanced degree after college

24. What are you most looking forward to after this semester/quarter?

25. Did you achieve the outcomes you were hoping to achieve at the beginning of this first semester/quarter? Why or why not?

You may gain some personal insights if you compare the questions in this "Your College Experience" section of the Exit Interview with the matching questions from the "Your College Expectations" section in the Entrance Interview at the front of the book. Or your instructor may ask you to write about your insights and intended Actions. Now continue on to these final questions about "Your Next Steps."

YOUR NEXT STEPS

26. Looking ahead, how satisfied do you expect to be with your decision to attend this school?

_____ very satisfied   _____ satisfied   _____ somewhat dissatisfied   _____ very dissatisfied   _____ not sure

27. Which of the following statements best reflects your educational intentions?

_____ I plan to stay at this school until I complete my degree.

_____ I plan to transfer to another institution (please identify which one _____).

_____ I plan to stop out of college for a while (to work, for example) and then return to this school.

_____ I plan to drop out of college.

28. If you are thinking about transferring to another institution, why would you do so?

_____ This school does not offer my intended major (which is _____). _____ This school is too small.

_____ This school is too large. _____ This school is too expensive.

_____ I don't feel I fit in. _____ I want to go to a school closer to home.

_____ I want to go to a school further from home. _____ I want to be closer to my boyfriend/ girlfriend /partner/spouse.

_____ I want to be closer to my friends. _____ I will change job locations.

_____ I want to transfer from a two-year to a four-year institution. _____ I want to transfer to a different two-year institution.

_____ other (please explain).

29. What was the biggest difference between what you thought college would be like and what it was actually like for you?

30. How have you changed most over this first semester/quarter? In what ways are you different now that you've been in college? How will this introductory semester/quarter affect or change your future college experience?

NOTES

Chapter 1

1. Paulson, K., & Boeke, M. (2006). *Adult learners in the United States: A national profile.* Washington, DC: American Council on Education.

2. Sellingo, J. J. (2015, June 29). What's wrong with going to a community college? How two-year colleges can be better than four-year universities. *The Washington Post.* Retrieved from https://www.washingtonpost.com/news/grade-point /wp/2015/06/29/whats-wrong-with-going-to-a-community -college-how-two-year-colleges-can-be-better-than-four-year -universities/?utm_term=.92f991e10801; Carey, K. (2007, June). America's best community colleges: Why they're better than some of the "best" four-year universities. *Washington Monthly.* Retrieved from http://www.washingtonmonthly .com/features/2007/0709.careyessay.html

3. Pappas, C. (2013, May 9). The adult learning theory— andragogy—of Malcolm Knowles. *eLearning Industry.* Retrieved from https://elearningindustry.com/the-adult -learning-theory-andragogy-of-malcolm-knowles

4. 2016 Fast fact sheet. (2016, February). A national look at community colleges and the students they serve. *American Association of Community Colleges.* Retrieved from http://www.aacc.nche .edu/AboutCC/Documents/AACCFactSheetsR2.pdf

5. Connick, W. (2016, August 13). What does the expression "WIIFM" in sales mean? *The Balance.* Retrieved from https:// www.thebalance.com/what-is-wiifm-2917381

6. Vista Success. (2016, June 1). 26 Best jobs you can get with an associate's degree. *Vista College.* Retrieved from http:// www.vistacollege.edu/blog/careers/26-best-jobs-you -can-get-with-an-associates-degree

7. Crosby, O. (2002–2003, Winter). Associate degree: Two years to a career or jump start to a bachelor's degree. *Occupational Outlook Quarterly,* 2–13. Retrieved from https://www.bls.gov /careeroutlook/2002/winter/art01.pdf

8. What is the difference between associate's degree programs and certificate programs? *Bestdegreeprograms.org.* Retrieved from http://www.bestdegreeprograms.org/faq /what-is-the-difference-between-associates-degree-programs -and-certificate-programs

9. Bryant & Stratton College Blog Staff. Certificate vs Associate Degree—Make the Right Choice. *Bryant & Stratten College.* Retrieved from https://www.bryantstratton.edu/blog/2015 /april/the-difference-between-associate-degree-programs-and -certificate-programs

10. Different paths for different majors. (2007, January/February). Datanotes: *Achieving the Dream.*

11. Schawbel, D. (2010). *Me 2.0: 4 steps to building your future.* New York: Kaplan Publishing; Driscoll, E. (2012, June 4). What employers want from college grads. *Fox Business.* Retrieved from http://www.foxbusiness.com/personal-finance/2012/06/04 /what-are-employers-want-from-college-grads/

12. Shoenberg, R. (2005). *Why do I have to take this course? A student guide to making smart educational choices.* Association of American Colleges and Universities. Washington, DC: AAC&U.

13. Linda Foltz and the Student Success Center advisors at the University of Colorado at Colorado Springs; Jennifer Sengenberger and Wayne Artis, Pikes Peak Community College; Kocel, K. (2008, March 12). *The Mentor: An Academic Advising Journal.* Retrieved from http:// dus.psu.edu/mentor/old/articles/080312kk.htm;

14. Knight, T. M. (2000, May 17). Planting the seeds of success: Advising college students with disabilities. *The Mentor: An Academic Advising Journal.* Retrieved from http://dus.psu.edu /mentor/old/articles/000517tk.htm

15. The challenges of remedial education: Views of 3 presidents. (2006, October 27). *The Chronicle of Higher Education.* Retrieved from http://chronicle.com/article /The-Challenges-of-Remedial/32361/

16. Developmental education and student success. (2006, September/October). *Datanotes: Achieving the Dream.* Retrieved from http://files.eric.ed.gov/fulltext/ED521317.pdf

17. Crews, D. M., & Aragon, S. R. (2004). Influence of a community college developmental education writing course on academic performance. *Community College Review, 32*(2), 1–18.

18. Settle, J. S. (2011). Variables that encourage students to persist in community colleges. *Community College Journal of Research and Practice, 35,* 281–300.

19. Castellanno, A., & Curry, C. (2013, September 2). Diana Nyad: 'We should never ever give up.' *abcnews.* Retrieved from http:// abcnews.go.com/US/diana-nyad-arrives-key-west-sets -record-cuba/story?id=20133986

20. Vilorio, D. (2016, March). Education matters: Earnings and unemployment rates by educational attainment, 2016. *Bureau of Labor Statistics.* Retrieved from https://www.bls.gov /careeroutlook/2016/data-on-display/education-matters.htm

21. Carnevale, A., Smith, M., & Strohl, J. (2013, June 26). Recovery: Job growth and education requirements through 2020. *Georgetown University Public Policy Institute.* Retrieved from https://cew.georgetown.edu/wp-content/uploads/2014/11 /Recovery2020.ES_.Web_.pdf

22. Crabtree, J. (2016, November 21). College is a much better investment than stocks, BAML analyst says. *CNBC.* Retrieved from http://www.cnbc.com/2016/11/21/college-is-a-much -better-investment-than-stocks-baml-analyst-says.html

23. Leonhardt, D. (2011, June 25). Even for cashiers, college pays off. *The New York Times.* Retrieved from http://www.nytimes .com/2011/06/26/sunday-review/26leonhardt.html

24. Shapiro, D., Dundar, A., Wakhungu, P. K., Yuan, X., Nathan, A., & Hwang, Y. (2015, November). *Completing college: A national view of student attainment rates–Fall 2009 Cohort (Signature Report No. 10).* Herndon, VA: National Student Clearinghouse Research Center.

25. Omara-Otunnu, E. (2006, July 24). Conference examines transition from high school to college. *Advance.* Retrieved from http://www.advance.uconn.edu/2006/060724/06072407.htm

26. Hoachlander, G., Sikora, A. C., Horn, L., & Carroll, C. D. (2003, June). Community college students: Goals, academic preparation and outcomes. *National Center for Education Statistics.* Retrieved from http://nces.ed.gov/pubs2003 /2003164.pdf

27. Pascarella, E. T., Pierson, C. T., Wolniak, G. C., & Terenzini, P. T. (2004). First-generation college students: Additional evidence on college experiences and outcomes. *Journal of Higher Education, 75*(3), 249–284.

28. Tyler, M. D., Johns, K Y. (2009). From first-generation college student to first lady. *Diverse Issues in Higher Education Psychology, 25*(25). Retrieved from http://diverseeducation .com/article/12184/

29. Community college: FAQs. *The College Board.* Retrieved from http://www.collegeboard.com/student/csearch/where -to-start/150494.html; Giang, V. (2011, August 3). The most

famous community college students of all time. *Business Insider.* Retrieved from http://www.businessinsider.com /the-most-famous-people-who-went-to-community-college -2011-7?op=1#ixzz2yDcivQv9; (2014). Notable alumni. *American Association of Community Colleges.* Retrieved from http://www .aacc.nche.edu/AboutCC/alumni/Pages/default.aspx

29. Parents' unexpected divorce can destabilize new college student's life (2006, January 10). *Penn State News.* Retrieved from http://news.psu.edu/story/206200/2006/01/10/parents -unexpected-divorce-can-destabilize-new-college-students-life

30. Brooks, R., & Goldstein, S. (2004). *The power of resilience: Achieving balance, confidence, and personal strength in your life.* Chicago: Contemporary Books, ix.

31. http://dictionary.reference.com/browse/grit.

32. Halvorson, H. G., (2011, February 25). Nine things successful people do differently. *Harvard Business Review.* Retrieved from https://hbr.org/2011/02/nine-things-successful-people#

33. Duckworth, A. L., Peterson, C., Matthews, M. D., & Kelly, D. R. (2007). Grit: Perseverance and passion for long-term goals. *Journal of Personality and Social Psychology 9,* 1087–1101. Retrieved from https://www.sas.upenn.edu/~duckwort /images/Grit%20JPSP.pdf

34. Duckworth, A. (2016). Grit: *The power of passion and perseverance.* New York: Scribner.

35. Achor, S., & Gielan, M. (2016, June 24). Resilience is about how you recharge, not how you endure. *Harvard Business Review.* Retrieved from https://hbr.org/2016/06 /resilience-is-about-how-you-recharge-not-how-you-endure

36. Wise, J. (2010, May 23). Extreme fear: How to thrive under stress. *Psychology Today.* Retrieved from http://www .psychologytoday.com/blog/extreme-fear/201005/how -thrive-under-stress

37. Grierson, B. (2009, May 1). Weathering the storm. *Psychology Today.* Retrieved from http://www.psychologytoday.com /articles/200904/weathering-the-storm

38. Adams, S. (2011, April 9). How to get a real education. *The Wall Street Journal.* Retrieved from https://www.wsj.com /articles/SB10001424052748704101604576247143383496656

39. Di Meglio, F. (2012, May 10). Stress takes its toll on college students. *Bloomberg.* Retrieved from http://www .businessweek.com/articles/2012-05-10/stress-takes-its -toll-on-college-students

40. Goleman, D. (2007). Social intelligence: *The new science of human relationships.* New York: Bantam.

41. Bal, F. T., Zhang, S., & Tachlyama, G. T. (2008). Effects of a self-regulated learning course on the academic performance and graduation rate of college students in an academic support program. *Journal of College Reading and Learning, 39*(1), 54–73; O'Gara, L., Karp, M. M., & Hughes, K. L. (2009). Student success courses in the community college: An exploratory study. *Community College Review, 36*(3), 195–218. Derby, D. C. (2007). Predicting degree completion: Examining the interaction between orientation course participation and ethnic background. *Community College Journal of Research and Practice, 31*(11), 883–894; Duggan, M. H., & Williams, M. R. (2011). Community college student success courses: The student perspective. *Community College Journal of Research and Practice, 35*(1), 121–143.

42. McCarron, G. P., & Inkelas, K. K. (2006). The gap between educational aspirations and attainment for first-generation college students and the role of parental involvement. *Journal of College Student Development, 47*(5), 534–549.

43. Martinez, J. A., Sher, K. J., Krull, J. L., & Wood, P. K. (2009). Blue-collar scholars? Mediators and moderators of university attrition in first-generation college students. *Journal of College Student Development, 50*(1), 87–103; Collier, P. J., & Morgan, D. L. (2008). Is that paper really due today? *Higher Education, 55*(4), 425–446.

44. Cox, R. D. (2009). *The college fear factor: How students and professors misunderstand one another.* Cambridge, MA: Harvard University Press.

45. http://www.counselingcenter.illinois.edu/self-help-brochures /adjustment-to-college-life/first-generation-college-students/

Chapter 2

1. Spielberg finally to graduate. (2002, May 15). *BBC News.* Retrieved from http://news.bbc.co.uk/2/hi/entertainment /1988770.stm

2. Vossa, S. (2016, November 28). Stop meditating alone—for productivity gains, it's a team sport. *Fast Company.* Retrieved from https://www.fastcompany.com/3065488/work-smart /why-group-meditation-might-improve-productivity-at-your -workplace

3. Schulte, B. (2015, June 1). Work interruptions can cost you 6 hours a day. An efficiency expert explains how to avoid them. *The Washington Post.* Retrieved from https://www .washingtonpost.com/news/inspired-life/wp/2015/06/01 /interruptions-at-work-can-cost-you-up-to-6-hours-a-day-heres -how-to-avoid-them/; Hougaard, R., & Carter, J. (2016, March 4). How to practice mindfulness throughout your work day. *Harvard Business Review.* Retrieved from https://hbr.org/2016/03/how-to-practice-mindfulness -throughout-your-work-day

4. Stone, L. (n.d.). Continuous partial attention. *lindastone.net.* Retrieved from https://lindastone.net/qa/continuous-partial -attention/

5. Achor, S., & Gielan, M. (2015, December 18). The busier you are, the more you need mindfulness. *Harvard Business Review.* Retrieved from https://hbr.org/2015/12/the -busier-you-are-the-more-you-need-mindfulness; Bellezza, S., Paharia, N., Keinan, A. (2016, December 15). Research: Why Americans are so impressed by busyness. *Harvard Business Review.* Retrieved from https://hbr.org/2016/12 /research-why-americans-are-so-impressed-by-busyness

6. Wieczner, J. (2016, March 12) Meditation has become a billion-dollar business. *Fortune.* Retrieved from http://fortune .com/2016/03/12/meditation-mindfulness-apps/

7. Adams, J. (N.D.). The ABC of mindfulness. *Mindfulnet.org.* Retrieved from http://www.mindfulnet.org/page2.htm

8. Williams, M., & Penman, D. (2012). *Mindfulness: An eight-week plan for finding peace in a frantic world.* Emmaus, PA: Rodale.

9. Seppala, E. (2015, December 14). How meditation benefits CEOs. *Harvard Business Review.* Retrieved from https://hbr .org/2015/12/how-meditation-benefits-ceos

10. Achor & Gielan, The busier you are.

11. Talbot-Zorn, J., & Edgette, F. (2016, May 2). Mindfulness can improve strategy, too. *Harvard Business Review.* Retrieved from https://hbr.org/2016/05/mindfulness-can-improve-strategy-too

12. Lamb, L. (2016, January 28). How Google and Twitter train their employees to be more mindful. *Fast Company.* Retrieved from https://www.fastcompany.com/3055974/the-future-of -work/how-google-and-twitter-train-their-employees-to-be -more-mindful

13. Schaufenbuel, K. (2015, December 28). Why Google, Target, and General Mills are investing in mindfulness. *Harvard Business Review.* Retrieved from https://hbr.org/2015/12 /why-google-target-and-general-mills-are-investing-in -mindfulness

14. Achor & Gielan, The busier you are.

15. Schaffhauser, D. (2016, January 20). Research: College students more distracted than ever. *Campus Technology.* Retrieved from https://campustechnology.com/articles/2016/01/20 /research-college-students-more-distracted-than-ever.aspx

16. Reitz, M., & Chaskalson, M. (2016, November 4). Mindfulness works but only if you work at it. *Harvard Business Review.* Retrieved from https://hbr.org/2016/11/mindfulness-works-but-only-if-you-work-at-it; Reynolds, G. (2016, February 18). How meditation changes the brain and body. *The New York Times.* Retrieved from http://well.blogs.nytimes.com/2016/02/18 /contemplation-therapy/; What is mindfulness? *Greater Good* Magazine. Retrieved from http://greatergood.berkeley .edu/topic/mindfulness/definition; Schulte, B. (2015, May 26). Harvard neuroscientist: Meditation not only reduces stress, here's how it changes your brain. *The Washington Post.* Retrieved from https://www.washingtonpost.com

/news/inspired-life/wp/2015/05/26/harvard-neuroscientist-meditation-not-only-reduces-stress-it-literally-changes-your-brain; Congleton, C., Hölzel, B. K., & Lasar, S. W. (2015, January 8). Mindfulness can literally change your brain. *Harvard Business Review.* Retrieved from https://hbr.org/2015/01/mindfulness-can-literally-change-your-brain

17. Smith, K. (2012, September 19). Neuroscience: Idle minds. *Nature.* Retrieved from http://www.nature.com/news/neuroscience-idle-minds-1.11440

18. Dweck, C. S. (2000). *Self-theories: Their role in motivation, personality, and development.* New York: Psychology Press, p. 1.

19. Aguilar, L., Walton, G., & Wieman, C. (2014, May). Psychological insights for improved physics teaching. *Physics Today.* Retrieved from http://scitation.aip.org/content/aip/magazine/physicstoday/article/67/5/10.1063/PT.3.2383

20. Brooks, D. (2009, May 1). Genius: The modern view. *The New York Times.* Retrieved from http://www.nytimes.com/2009/05/01/opinion/01brooks.html

21. Duckworth, A. (2016). *Grit: The power of passion and perseverance.* New York: Scribner.

22. Berglas, S., & Jones, E. E. (1978). Drug choice as a self-handicapping strategy in response to noncontingent success. *Journal of Personality and Social Psychology, 36,* 405–417; Jones, E. E., & Berglas, S. (1978). Control of attributions about the self through self-handicapping strategies: The appeal of alcohol and the role of underachievement. *Personality and Social Psychology Bulletin, 4,* 200–206; Dweck, C. S. (2006). *Mindset: The new psychology of success.* New York: Random House.

23. Dweck, *Mindset,* 7.

24. Ibid., 7.

25. Fischer, M. (2007, March-April). Settling into campus life: Differences by race-ethnicity in college involvement and outcomes. *The Journal of Higher Education, 78*(2), 125–161.

26. Dweck, *Self-theories;* Dweck, *Mindset.*

27. Dweck, C. (2016, June 6). Carol Dweck revisits the "Growth Mindset." *The Chronicle of Evidence-Based Mentoring.* Retrieved from http://chronicle.umbmentoring.org/carol-dweck-revisits-the-growth-mindset/

28. Berrett, D. (2012, April 15). Can colleges manufacture motivation? *The Chronicle of Higher Education.* Retrieved from http://chronicle.com/article/Can-Colleges-Manufacture/131564

29. Sei, S. A. (2010, June). Intrinsic and extrinsic motivation: evaluating benefits and drawbacks from college instructors' perspectives. *Journal of Instructional Psychology, 37*(2), 153–160.

30. French, B. F., & Oakes, W. (2003). Measuring academic intrinsic motivation in the first year of college: Reliability and validity evidence for a new instrument. *Journal of the First-Year Experience, 15*(1), 83–102; French, B. F. Executive summary of instruments utilized with systemwide first-year seminars. *Policy Center on the First Year of College;* French, B. F., Immerkus, J. C., & Oakes, W. C. (2005). An examination of indicators of engineering students' success and persistence. *Journal of Engineering Education, 94*(4), 419–425.

31. Deci, E. (2012, August 13). Promoting motivation, health, and excellence. *TEDxTalks.* Retrieved from http://www.youtube.com/watch?v=VGrcets0E6I&feature=youtu.be&hd=1&t=22s

32. Yuhas, D. (2012, November 21). Three critical elements sustain motivation. *Scientific American.* Retrieved from http://www.scientificamerican.com/article.cfm?id=three-critical-elements-sustain-motivation

33. Deci, E. (2012, August 13). Promoting motivation, health, and excellence. *TEDxTalks.*

34. Charyk, C. (2016, April 20). The mental trick you can use to get through any stressful situation. *The Muse.* Retrieved from https://www.themuse.com/advice/the-mental-trick-you-can-use-to-get-through-any-stressful-situation

35. Based on Harrell, K. (2003). *Attitude is everything: 10 life-changing steps to turning attitude into action.* New York: HarperBusiness.

36. Cuddy, A. (2016). *Presence: Bringing your boldest self to your biggest challenges.* New York: Little, Brown and Company.

37. Google Books. Retrieved from https://books.google.com/books/about/Presence_Bringing_Your_Boldest_Self_to_Y.html?id=-VdcCwAAQBAJ

Chapter 3

1. Leamnson, R. (1999). *Thinking about teaching and learning: Developing habits of learning with first year college and university students.* Sterling, VA: Stylus.

2. Maier, J. (2016). The super simple trick that made my mornings way more productive. *The Muse.* Retrieved from https://www.themuse.com/advice/the-super-simple-trick-that-made-my-mornings-way-more-productive.

3. Caine, R. N., & Caine, G. (1994). *Making connections: Teaching and the human brain.* Menlo Park, CA: Addison Wesley.

4. Brandt, R. (1998). *Powerful learning.* Alexandria, VA: Association for Supervision and Curriculum Development, p. 29.

5. Campbell, B. (1992). Multiple intelligences in action. *Childhood Education, 68*(4), 197–201; Gardner, H., & Hatch, T. (1989). Multiple intelligences go to school: Educational implications of the theory of multiple intelligences. *Educational Researcher, 18*(8), 4–9; Gardner, H. (1983). *Frames of mind: The theory of multiple intelligences.* New York: Basic Books.

6. Griggs, L., Barney, S., Brown-Sederberg, J., Collins, E., Keith, S., & Iannacci, L. (2009). Varying pedagogy to address student multiple intelligences. *Human Architecture: Journal of the Sociology of Self Knowledge 7*(1), 55–60.

7. Armstrong, T. (2000). *MI and cognitive skills.* Retrieved from http://www.ascd.org/publications/books/109007/chapters/MI-Theory-and-Cognitive-Skills.aspx

8. Davis, B. (2009). *Tools for teaching,* 2nd ed. San Francisco: Jossey-Bass, p. 273.

9. Fleming, N. D. (1995). I'm different; not dumb: Modes of presentation (VARK) in the tertiary classroom. In A. Zeimer (Ed.), *Research and development in higher education, Proceedings of the 1995 Annual Conference of the Higher Education and Research Development Society of Austral-Asia (HERDSA), HERDSA, 18,* 308–313; Fleming, N. D., & Mills, C. (1992). Not another inventory, rather a catalyst for reflection. *To Improve the Academy, 11,* 137–149. Retrieved from http://onlinelibrary.wiley.com/journal/10.1002/%28ISSN%292166-3327

10. Fleming, I'm different; not dumb.

11. Fleming, N. D. (2005). *Teaching and learning styles: VARK strategies.* Christchurch, NZ: Microfilm Limited.

12. Murphy, M. (2016, April 24). My boss and I have different communication styles, and it's destroying our relationship. *Forbes.* Retrieved from https://www.forbes.com/sites/markmurphy/2016/04/24/my-boss-and-i-have-different-communication-styles-and-its-destroying-our-relationship/#14e2843a38cc

13. Zenger, J., & Folkman, J. (2012, July 16). How damaging is a bad boss, exactly? *Harvard Business Review.* Retrieved from https://hbr.org/2012/07/how-damaging-is-a-bad-boss-exa

14. Harvard Business Review Staff. (2015, July 2). Figure out your manager's communication style. *Harvard Business Review.* Retrieved from https://hbr.org/2015/07/figure-out-your-managers-communication-style

15. Nayar, V. (2014, December 1). Managing three types of bad bosses. *Harvard Business Review.* Retrieved from https://hbr.org/2014/12/managing-3-types-of-bad-bosses&cm_sp=Article-_-Links-_-End%20of%20Page%20Recirculation

16. Gallo, A. (December 4, 2014). The right way to bring a problem to your boss. *Harvard Business Review.* Retrieved from https://hbr.org/2014/12/the-right-way-to-bring-a-problem-to-your-boss

17. Gallo, The right way to bring a problem to your boss; Detert, J. R., & Burris, E. R. (2016, January-February). Can your employees really speak freely? *Harvard Business Review.* Retrieved from https://hbr.org/2016/01/can-your-employees-really-speak-freely

18. Gallo, A. (2014, December 8). Setting the record straight on managing your boss. *Harvard Business Review*. Retrieved from https://hbr.org/2014/12/setting-the-record-straight-on-managing-your-boss

19. Based on DiTiberio, J. K., & Hammer, A. L. (1993). *Introduction to type in college*. Palo Alto, CA: Consulting Psychologists Press.

20. Cortiella, C., & Horowitz, S. H. (2014). *The state of learning disabilities: Facts, trends and emerging issues*. New York: National Center for Learning Disabilities.

21. (2017). College guide for students with learning disabilities. *Bestcolleges.com*. Retrieved from http://www.bestcolleges.com/resources/college-planning-with-learning-disabilities/

22. Strichart, S. S., & Mangrum, C. T. II. (2002). *Teaching learning strategies and study skills to students with learning disabilities, attention deficit disorder, or special needs*, 3rd ed. Boston: Allyn and Bacon; *Learning Disabilities Online*. Retrieved from http://ldonline.org; Sousa, D. A. (2001). *How the special needs brain learns*. Thousand Oaks, CA: Corwin Press.

23. Soldner, L. B. (1997). Self-assessment and the reflective reader. *Journal of College Reading and Learning*, *28*(1), 5–11.

24. VanBlerkom, M. L., & VanBlerkom, D. L. (2004). Self-monitoring strategies used by developmental and non-developmental college students. *Journal of College Reading and Learning*, *34*(2), 45–60.

25. Melchenbaum, D., Burland, S., Gruson, L., & Cameron, R. (1985). Metacognitive assessment. In S. Yussen (Ed.), *The growth of reflection in children*. Orlando, FL: Academic Press, p. 5.

26. Hall, C. W. (2001). A measure of executive processing skills in college students. *College Student Journal*, *35*(3), 442–450; Taylor, S. (1999). Better learning through better thinking: Developing students' metacognitive abilities. *Journal of College Reading and Learning*, *30*(1), 34–45.

27. Learning to learn. *Study Guides and Strategies*. Retrieved from http://www.studygs.net/metacognition.htm

28. Simpson, M. L. (1994/1995). Talk throughs: A strategy for encouraging active learning across the content areas. *Journal of Reading*, *38*(4), 296–304.

29. How Air Traffic Control Works. *How Stuff Works*. Retrieved from http://science.howstuffworks.com/transport/flight/modern/air-traffic-control.htm

30. Glenn, D. (2010, February 7). How students can improve by studying themselves. *The Chronicle of Higher Education*. Retrieved from http://chronicle.com/article/Struggling-Students-Can/64004/

31. Elias, M. (2004, April 5). Frequent TV watching shortens kids' attention spans. *USA Today*. Retrieved from https://usatoday30.usatoday.com/news/nation/2004-04-05-tv-bottomstrip_x.htm

32. Carey, B. (2010, September 6). Forget what you know about good study habits. *The New York Times*. Retrieved from http://www.nytimes.com/2010/09/07/health/views/07mind.html?_r=1&pagewanted=1&ref=homepage&src=me

33. Bol, L., Warkentin, R. W., Nunnery, J. A., & O'Connell, A. A. (1999). College students' study activities and their relationship to study context, reference course, and achievement. *College Student Journal*, *33*(4), 608–622.

34. When students study makes a difference too. (2005, November). *Recruitment & Retention*.

35. Trainin, G., & Swanson, H. L. (2005). Cognition, meta-cognition, and achievement of college students with learning disabilities. *Learning Disability Quarterly*, *28*, 261–272.

36. Guibert, S. (2012, March 23). Learning best when you rest: Sleeping after processing new info most effective. *Science Daily*. Retrieved from http://www.sciencedaily.com/releases/2012/03/120323205504.htm

Chapter 4

1. Sakai, J. (2012, March 15). A wandering mind reveals mental processes and priorities. *Science Daily*. Retrieved from http://www.sciencedaily.com/releases/2012/03/120315161326.htm

2. Coleman, J. (2012, February 22). Faced with distraction, we need willpower. *Harvard Business Review*. Retrieved from https://hbr.org/2012/02/faced-with-distraction-we-need

3. Saunders, F. (2009, November–December). Multitasking to distraction. *American Scientist*, *97*(6), 455.

4. Khawand, P. (2009). *The accomplishing more with less workbook*. On the Go Technologies, LLC.

5. Austin, C. (2010). Go with the flow: Fresh ideas for managing time. *Prezi.com*. Retrieved from http://prezi.com/7gypurup9uke/go-with-the-flow/

6. Rafter, M. V. (2012, February 23). Siri says it's time to get to work. *Workforce.com*. Retrieved from http://www.workforce.com/2012/02/24/siri-says-its-time-to-get-to-work/

7. Choi, J. (N. D.). 4 ways you're lying to yourself about being productive. *The Muse*. Retrieved from https://www.themuse.com/advice/4-ways-youre-lying-to-yourself-about-being-productive

8. Nass, C. (2009). Media multitaskers pay mental price. *YouTube*. Retrieved from https://www.youtube.com/watch?v=2zuDXzVYZ68

9. Fried, J., & Hanson, D. (2010). *Rework*. New York: Crown Business, p. 25.

10. N. A. (2013, September 6). Workaholics may face poor physical and mental well-being, study suggests. *The Huffington Post*. Retrieved from http://www.huffingtonpost.com/2013/09/06/workaholics-well-being-physical-mental-health_n_3795626.html

11. Bradford, H. (2014, November 7). Why being a workaholic is awful for you AND everyone around you. The *Huffington Post*. Retrieved from http://www.huffingtonpost.com/2014/11/07/workaholic-bad_n_6093658.html

12. Saunders, E. G. (2016, March 18). If you dread deadlines, you're thinking about them all wrong. *Harvard Business Review*. Retrieved from https://hbr.org/2016/03/if-you-dread-deadlines-youre-thinking-about-them-all-wrong

13. Fried, J. (2017, January 17). Being tired isn't a badge of honor. *LinkedIn*. Retrieved from https://www.linkedin.com/pulse/being-tired-isnt-badge-honor-jason-fried?trk=eml-email_feed_ecosystem_digest_01-hero-0-null&midToken=AQFh7S3Jb2y6PQ&fromEmail=fromEmail&ut=3SBr9HGG8oJDA1

14. Belvedere, M. J. (2016, April 5). Why Aetna's CEO pays workers up to $500 to sleep. *CNBC*. Retrieved from http://www.cnbc.com/2016/04/05/why-aetnas-ceo-pays-workers-up-to-500-to-sleep.html

15. Eade, D. M. (1998). Energy and success: Time management. *ClinicianNews*, July/August.

16. Loehr, J., & Schwartz, T. (2003). *The power of full engagement: Managing energy, not time, is the key to high performance and personal renewal*. New York: Free Press.

17. Bittel, L. R. (1991). *Right on time! The complete guide for time pressured managers*. New York: McGraw-Hill, p. 16.

18. DeMaio, S. (2009, March 25). The art of the self-imposed deadline. *Harvard Business Review*. Retrieved from http://blogs.hbr.org/demaio/2009/03/the-art-of-the-selfimposed-dea.html

19. Bittel, *Right on time!* p. 16.

20. Loehr, *The power of full engagement*.

21. Allen, D. (2012, March 17). When technology overwhelms, get organized. *The New York Times*. Retrieved from http://www.nytimes.com/2012/03/18/business/when-office-technology-overwhelms-get-organized.html?pagewanted=all

22. Based on Covey, S. R., Merrill, A. R., & Merrill, R. R. (1996). *First things first: To live, to love, to learn, to leave a legacy*. New York: Free Press, 37.

23. Pogue, D. (2013, February). 10 top time-saving tech tips. *Ted Talk*. Retrieved from https://www.ted.com/talks/david_pogue_10_top_time_saving_tech_tips

24. Distractify Staff. (2015, January 7). 30 surprising facts about how we actually spend our time. *Distractify.com*.

25. Hobbs, C. R. (1987). *Time power.* New York: Harper & Row, pp. 9–10.

26. Berglas, S. (2004, June). Chronic time abuse. *Harvard Business Review*. Retrieved from https://hbr.org/2004/06/chronic-time-abuse

27. Solomon, L. J., & Rothblum, E. D. (1984). Academic procrastination: Frequency and cognitive-behavioral correlates. *Journal of Counseling Psychology, 31,* 503–509.

28. Hoover, E. (2005, December 9). Tomorrow I love ya! *The Chronicle of Higher Education, 52*(16), A30–32. Retrieved from http://www.chronicle.com/article/Tomorrow-I-Love-Ya-/10494; Zarick, L. M., & Stonebraker, R. (2009). I'll do it tomorrow: The logic of procrastination. *College Teaching, 57*(4), 211–215.

29. Ferrari, J. R., McCown, W. G., & Johnson, J. (2002). *Procrastination and task avoidance: Theory, research, and treatment.* New York: Springer Publishing.

30. Hoover, Tomorrow I love ya!

31. Khawand, P. (2009). *The accomplishing more with less workbook.* On the Go Technologies, LLC.

32. Sandholtz, K., Derr, B., Buckner, K., & Carlson, D. (2002). *Beyond juggling: Rebalancing your busy life.* San Francisco: Berrett-Koehler Publishers.

33. Adapted from Sandholtz et al., *Beyond juggling*.

34. Farrell, E. F. (2005, February 4). More students plan to work to help pay for college. *The Chronicle of Higher Education, 51*(22), A1. Retrieved from http://chronicle.com/weekly/v51/i22/22a00101.htm

35. Kristof, K. (2011, September 14). Save or spend? Cool tool calculates the cost. *CBS Moneywatch*. Retrieved from http://www.cbsnews.com/news/save-or-spend-cool-tool-calculates-the-cost/; http://www.bills.com/ways-to-save/

36. See FinAid at http://www.finaid.org/loans/studentloandebtclock.phtml

37. Ludlum, M., Tilker, K., Ritter, D., Cowart, T., Xu, W., & Smith, B. C. (2012). Financial Literacy and Credit Cards: A Multi Campus Survey. *International Journal of Business and Social Science, 3*(7), 25–33. Retrieved from http://www.ijbssnet.com/journals/Vol_3_No_7_April_2012/3.pdf; http://moneyland.time.com/2012/04/12/college-students-are-credit-card-dunces/

38. Kantrowitz, M. (2007). *FAQs about financial aid.* FinAid: The Smart Student Guide to Financial Aid. Retrieved from http://www.finaid.org/questions/faq.html; Jevita Rogers, Executive Director of Financial Aid, University of Colorado, Colorado Springs

39. Muller, K. New credit card laws (2009) and students. *ezine@rticles.com*. Retrieved from http://ezinearticles.com/?New-Credit-Card-Laws-(2009)-And-Students&id=2410035; Miranda. (2009, May 21). Credit CARD Act of 2009: How it affects you. *Personaldividends.com*. Retrieved from http://personaldividends.com/money/miranda/credit-card-act-of-2009-how-it-affects-you

40. Staley, C. (2003). "Spending Time." In *50 ways to leave your lectern.* Beverly, MA: Wadsworth, p. 54

41. Nathan, R. (2005). *My freshman year: What a professor learned by becoming a student.* Ithaca, NY: Cornell University Press.

Chapter 5

1. Dishman, L. (2016, May 17). There are the biggest skills that new graduates lack. *Fast Company*. Retrieved from https://www.fastcompany.com/3059940/these-are-the-biggest-skills-that-new-graduates-lack

2. Dishman, L. There are the biggest skills that new graduates lack.

3. Korn, M. (2014, October 21). Bosses seek 'critical thinking,' but what is that? *The Wall Street Journal*. Retrieved from https://www.wsj.com/articles/bosses-seek-critical-thinking-but-what-is-that-1413923730

4. Baldoni, J. (2010, April 7). Three steps to thinking critically the age of distraction. *Fast Company*. Retrieved from https://www.fastcompany.com/1608553/three-steps-thinking-critically-age-distraction; Jackson, M. (2008). *Distracted: The Erosion of Attention and the Coming Dark Age.* Amherst, New York: Prometheus Books.

5. Cole, S. (2014, October 31). Employers want critical thinkers, but do they know what it means? *Fast Company*. Retrieved from https://www.fastcompany.com/3037837/employers-want-critical-thinkers-but-do-they-know-what-it-means

6. Korn, Bosses seek 'critical thinking'; Montini, L. (2014, October 23). The trouble with hiring for 'critical thinking' skills. *Inc.com*. Retrieved from http://www.inc.com/laura-montini/are-you-sure-you-want-to-hire-a-critical-thinker.html

7. Mikel, B. (2017, February 21). Mark Cuban says this will soon be the most sought-after job skill. *Inc.com*. Retrieved from http://www.inc.com/betsy-mikel/mark-cuban-says-this-will-soon-be-the-most-sought-after-job-skill.html

8. Halx, M. D., & Reybold, E. (2005). A pedagogy of force: Faculty perspective of critical thinking capacity in undergraduate students. *The Journal of General Education, 54*(4), 293–315.

9. Walkner, P., & Finney, N. (1999). Skill development and critical thinking in higher education. *Teaching in Higher Education, 4*(4), 531–548.

10. Diestler, S. (2001). *Becoming a critical thinker: A user friendly manual.* Upper Saddle River, NJ: Prentice Hall.

11. Silva, L. (N.D.). 12 things you never knew on how to think effectively. *Life Hack*. Retrieved from http://www.lifehack.org/articles/productivity/12-things-you-never-knew-how-think-effectively.html

12. Van den Brink-Budgen, R. (2000). *Critical thinking for students*, 3rd ed. Oxford: How to Books; Ruggiero, V. R. (2001). *Becoming a critical thinker*, 4th ed. Boston: Houghton Mifflin.

13. Blakey, E., & Spence, S. (1990). Developing metacognition. *ERIC Digest*. Retrieved from http://www.ericdigests.org/pre-9218/developing.htm

14. Florida, R. (2002). *The rise of the creative class: And how it's transforming work, leisure, community and everyday life.* New York: Basic Books, xii.

15. Sternberg. R. J. (2004). Teaching college students that creativity is a decision. *Guidance & Counseling, 19*(4), 196–200.

16. Kim, L. (2015, November 4). 9 ways to dramatically improve your creativity. *Inc*. Retrieved from https://www.inc.com/larry-kim/9-ways-to-dramatically-improve-your-creativity.html

17. Rowe, A. J. (2004). *Creative intelligences: discovering the innovative potential in ourselves and others.* Upper Saddle, NJ: Pearson Education, pp. 3–6, 34.

18. Michalko, M. (2001). *Cracking creativity: The secrets of creative genius.* Berkeley, CA: Ten Speed Press.

19. Adapted from Adler, R., & Proctor, R. F. II (2011). *Looking out/Looking in.* (13th ed.) New York: Holt, Rinehart, and Winston, pp. 110–116.

20. Douglas, J. H. (1977). The genius of everyman (2): Learning creativity. *Science News, 111*(8), 284–288.

21. Harris, R. (2012, April 2). Introduction to creative thinking. *VirtualSalt*. Retrieved from http://www.virtualsalt.com/crebook1.htm

22. Eby, D. Creativity and flow psychology. Retrieved from http://talentdevelop.com/articles/Page8.html

23. Schwartz, T., Gomes, J., & McCarthy, C. (2010). *The way we're working isn't working: The four forgotten needs that energize great performance.* New York: Free Press, 149.

24. Ibid.

Chapter 6

1. Straumsheim, C. (2016, April 13). Stopping stop-outs. *Inside Higher Ed*. Retrieved from https://www.insidehighered.com/news/2016/04/13/study-explores-online-learning-trends-community-colleges

2. Community College FAQs. Community College Research Center. *Columbia University Teachers' College*. Retrieved from http://ccrc.tc.columbia.edu/Community-College-FAQs.html

3. Bollet, R. M., & Fallon, S. (2002). Personalizing e-learning. *Educational Media International, 39*(1), 39–45; Barber, S., in Shank, P. (Ed.) (2011). *The online learning idea book: Proven ways to enhance technology-based and blended learning, vol 2.* San Francisco: Pfeiffer.

4. Guess, A. (2007, September 17). Students' "evolving" use of technology. *Inside Higher Ed*. Retrieved from http://www.insidehighered.com/news/2007/09/17/it; Brooks, D. C. (2016, October). ECAR study of undergraduate students and information technology research report. *Educause*. Retrieved from https://library.educause.edu/~/media/files/library/2016/10/ers1605.pdf

5. Anderson, M. (2015, October 29). The demographics of device ownership. *Pew Research Center*. Retrieved from http://www.pewinternet.org/2015/10/29/the-demographics-of-device-ownership/

6. *Internet World Stats*. Retrieved from http://www.internetworldstats.com/stats.htm

7. Carr, N. (2008, July/August). Is Google making us stupid? *The Atlantic.com*. Retrieved from https://www.theatlantic.com/magazine/archive/2008/07/is-google-making-us-stupid/306868/

8. (N. A.) (2016, September 3). *Statistic Brain*. Retrieved from http://www.statisticbrain.com/computer-virus-statistics/

9. Holson, L. M. (2010, May 8). Tell-all generation learns to keep things offline. *The New York Times*. Retrieved from http://www.nytimes.com/2010/05/09/fashion/09privacy.html

10. (2010, June). Social insecurity. *Consumer Reports: Best and worst computers*, pp. 24–27.

11. New Media Consortium. (2012). *NMC horizon report: 2012 higher education edition*. Retrieved from http://www.nmc.org/publications/horizon-report-2012-higher-ed-edition

12. Schaffhauser, D. (2016, October 18). College students: 'Please personalize my learning.' *Campus Technology*. Retrieved from https://campustechnology.com/articles/2016/10/18/college-students-please-personalize-my-learning.aspx

13. Dahlstrom, E., de Boor, T., Grunwald, P., & Vockley, G. (2011). National study of undergraduate students and technology. *Educause*. Retrieved from http://net.educause.edu/ir/library/pdf/ERS1103/ERS1103W.pdf

14. Mitchell, B. (2017, June 27). Most common internet domain extensions. *Lifewire*. Retrieved from https://www.lifewire.com/most-common-tlds-internet-domain-extensions-817511; Retrieved from http://webfoot.com/advice/email.domain.php

15. Staff, Ratcliff, C. (2016, August). What are the top 10 most popular search engines? *Search Engine Watch*. Retrieved from https://searchenginewatch.com/2016/08/08/what-are-the-top-10-most-popular-search-engines/

16. Massey, T. (2014, September 16). Do college students find their LMS beneficial? *Cengage*. Retrieved from https://blog.cengage.com/do-college-students-find-their-lms-beneficial/

17. Trunk, P. (2008, July/August). Show me the blog. *Wild Blue Yonder*, p. 44.

18. Kelly, R. (2017, January 18). 11 ed tech trends to watch in 2017. *Campus Technology*. Retrieved from https://campustechnology.com/articles/2017/01/18/11-ed-tech-trends-to-watch-in-2017.aspx

19. Kelly, 11 ed tech trends to watch in 2017.

20. Dishman, L. (2016, June 24). The skills it takes to get hired at Google, Facebook, Amazon, and more. *Fast Company*. Retrieved from https://www.fastcompany.com/3061237/the-skills-it-takes-to-get-hired-at-google-facebook-amazon-and-more

21. Dishman. The skills it takes to get hired at Google, Facebook, Amazon, and more.

22. Pratt, M. K. (2016, December 7). 10 hottest tech skills for 2017. *computerworld*. Retrieved from http://www.computerworld.com/article/3147427/it-skills-training/10-hottest-tech-skills-for-2017.html

23. Satell, G. (2014, December 10). The Google way of attacking problems. *Harvard Business Review*. Retrieved from https://hbr.org/2014/12/the-google-way-of-attacking-problems

24. Brown, A. (2016, October 6). Key findings about the American workforce and the changing job market. *Pew Research Center*. Retrieved from http://www.pewresearch.org/fact-tank/2016/10/06/key-findings-about-the-american-workforce-and-the-changing-job-market/

25. Editorial staff. (N. D.). Future proof your career. *Mindtools.com*. Retrieved from https://www.mindtools.com/pages/article/newCDV_81.htm

26. Brick, J. (2013, September 11). 7 life hacks to maximize your productivity. *American Express*. Retrieved from https://www.americanexpress.com/us/small-business/openforum/articles/7-life-hacks-to-maximize-your-productivity/

27. (1998). What is research? *Practical Research* by P. D. Leedy and J. D. Ormrod.

28. Fitzgerald, M. A. (2004). Making the leap from high school to college. *Knowledge Quest, 32*(4), 19–24; Ehrmann, S. (2004). Beyond computer literacy: Implications of technology for the content of a college education. *Liberal Education*. Retrieved from http://www.aacu.org/liberaleducation/le-fa04/le-fa04feature1.cfm; Thacker, P. (2006, November 15). Are college students techno idiots? *Inside Higher Ed*. Retrieved from http://www.insidehighered.com/news/2006/11/15/infolit

29. Christina Martinez, Reference Librarian, University of Colorado, Colorado Springs.

30. Ableson, H. Ledeen, K., & Lewis, H. (2008). *Blown to bits: your life, liberty, and happiness after the digital explosion*. Boston, MA: Pearson Education, Inc.

31. Siu, E. (2016, November 14). 24 eye-popping SEO statistics. *Search Engine Journal*. Retrieved from https://www.searchenginejournal.com/24-eye-popping-seo-statistics/42665/

32. Thacker, P. (2006, November 15). Are college students techno idiots? *Inside Ed*. Retrieved from http://www.insidehighered.com/news/2006/11/15/infolit; Kolowich, S. (2011, August 22). What students don't know. *Inside Higher Ed*. Retrieved from https://www.insidehighered.com/news/2011/08/22/erial_study_of_student_research_habits_at_illinois_university_libraries_reveals_alarmingly_poor_information_literacy_and_skills

33. Based on Wood, G. (2004, April 9). Academic original sin: Plagiarism, the Internet, and librarians. *The Journal of Academic Librianship, 30*(3), 237–242.

Chapter 7

1. Marchand, A. (2010, 29 March). 6 strategies can help entering community-college students succeed. *The Chronicle of Higher Education*. Retrieved from http://chronicle.com/article/6-Strategies-Can-Help-Entering/64871

2. Hattegerg, S. J., & Steffy, K. (2013, September 13). Increasing reading compliance of undergraduates: An evaluation of compliance methods. *Teaching Sociology*. Retrieved from http://journals.sagepub.com/doi/abs/10.1177/0092055X13490752; Hobson, E. H. (2006, January 10). Getting students to read: 14 tips. IDEA Paper #40. *Idea*. Retrieved from http://www.ideaedu.org/Portals/0/Uploads/Documents/IDEA%20Papers/IDEA%20Papers/Idea_Paper_40.pdf

3. Marburger, D. R. (2001). Absenteeism and undergraduate exam performance. *Journal of Economic Education, (32)*, 99–109; Romer, D. 1993. Do students go to class? Should they? *Journal of Economic Perspectives 7*(Summer), 167–174.

4. Credé, M., Roch, S. G., & Kieszczynka, U. M. (2010, June 1). Class attendance in college: A meta-analytic review of the relationship of class attendance with grades and student characteristics. *Review of Educational Research*. Retrieved from http://journals.sagepub.com/doi/abs/10.3102/0034654310362998

5. Perkins, K. K., & Wieman, C. E. (2005). The surprising impact of seat location on student performance. *The Physics Teacher,*

43(1), 30–33. Retrieved from http://scitation.aip.org/content/aapt/journal/tpt/43/1/10.1119/1.1845987

6. Gross-Loh, C. (2016, July 14). Should colleges really eliminate the college lecture? *The Atlantic.* Retrieved from https://www.theatlantic.com/education/archive/2016/07/eliminating-the-lecture/491135/; Gibbs, G. (2013, November 21). Lectures don't work, but we keep using them. *The Times Higher Education.* Retrieved from https://www.timeshighereducation.com/news/lectures-dont-work-but-we-keep-using-them/2009141.article; Lang, J. (2006, September 29). Beyond lecturing. *The Chronicle of Higher Education.* Retrieved from http://www.chronicle.com/article/Beyond-Lecturing/46889

7. Lang, Beyond lecturing.

8. Morreale, S., Staley, C., Stavrositu, C., & Krakowiak, M. (2015). First-year college students' attitudes toward communication technologies and their perceptions of communication competence in the 21st century. *Communication Education, 64,* 107–131.

9. Staley, C. C., & Staley R. S. (1992). *Communicating in business and the professions.* Belmont, CA: Wadsworth, pp. 228–236; Friedman, P. (1978). *Interpersonal communication.* New York: NEA, 84–90.

10. Kiewra, K. A., Mayer, R. E., Christensen, M., Kim, S., & Risch, N. (1991). Effects of repetition on recall and note-taking: Strategies for learning from lectures. *Journal of Educational Psychology, 83,* 120–123.

11. Brock, R. (2005, October 28). Lectures on the go. *The Chronicle of Higher Education, 52*(10), A39–42; French, D. P. (2006). iPods: Informative or invasive? *Journal of College Science Teaching, 36*(1), 58–59; Hallett, V. (2005, October 17). Teaching with tech. *U.S. News & World Report, 139*(14), 54–58; *The Horizon Report.* (2006). Stanford, CA: The New Media Consortium.

12. Adapted from Mackie, V., & Bair, B. Tips for improving listening skills; *International Student and Scholar Services.* University of Illinois at Urbana–Champaign. Retrieved from http://www.isss.illinois.edu/publications/english/englang.html#listen

13. Orginally adapted from *Effective listening skills. Elmhurst College Learning Center.*

14. Pappano, L. (2014, October 31). How to take better lecture notes. *The New York Times.* Retrieved from https://www.nytimes.com/2014/11/02/education/edlife/take-notes-from-the-pros.html?_r=0

15. Schierloh, J. (2005, fall). A Study of the note-taking skills of first-year community college students. *NADE Digest, 1*(2), 14–18.

16. Diluna, A. (2015, October 8). Best way to take notes in class isn't on your laptop, research finds. *NBC News.* Retrieved from http://www.nbcnews.com/feature/freshman-year/best-way-take-notes-class-isnt-your-laptop-research-finds-n416831

17. Cohen, D., Kim, E., Tan, J., and Winkelmes, M. (2013). A note-restructuring intervention increases students' exam scores. *College Teaching, 61* (Summer), 95–99; Haynes, J. M., McCarley, N. G., Williams, J. L. (2015). An analysis of notes taken during and after a lecture presentation. *North American Journal of Psychology, 17*(1), 175–186.

18. Davis, M., & Hult, R. (1997). Effects of writing summaries as a generative learning activity during note taking. *Teaching of Psychology 24*(1), 47–49; Boyle, J. R., & Weishaar, M. (2001). The effects of strategic notetaking on the recall and comprehension of lecture information for high school students with learning disabilities. *Learning Disabilities Research & Practice 16*(3); Kiewra, K. A. (2002). How classroom teachers can help students learn and teach them how to learn. *Theory into Practice 41*(2), 71–81; Aiken, E. G., Thomas, G. S., & Shennum, W. A. (1975). Memory for a lecture: Effects of notes, lecture rate and informational density. *Journal of Educational Psychology, 67,* 439–444; Hughes, C. A., & Suritsky, S. K. (1994). Note-taking skills of university students with and without learning disabilities. *Journal of Learning Disabilities, 27,* 20–24.

19. Prusick, L. (2015, January 8). Simple hearing "life hacks." *Starkey Hearing Technologies.* Retrieved from http://www.starkey.com/blog/2015/01/Simple%20Hearing%20Life%20Hacks

20. Bonner, J. M., & Holliday, W. G. (2006). How college science students engage in note-taking strategies. *Journal of Research in Science Teaching, 43*(8), 786–818.

21. Bui, D. C., Myerson, J., & Hale, S. (2013). Note-taking with computers: Exploring alternative strategies for improved recall. *Journal of Educational Psychology,* 105, 299–309.

22. Pappano, How to take better lecture notes.

23. Doubek, J. (2016, April 7). Attention, students: Put your laptops away. *NPR.* Retrieved from http://www.npr.org/2016/04/17/474525392/attention-students-put-your-laptops-away

24. Weisman, S. (2012, March 5). Five ways to avoid the pitfalls of technology in college. *USA Today College.* Retrieved from http://college.usatoday.com/2012/03/05/five-ways-to-avoid-the-pitfalls-of-technology-in-college/;https://plus.google.com/+evernote/posts/ABvMT7y3fsk#+evernote/posts/ABvMT7y3fsk; Gordon, W. (2013, March 12). *Lifehacker.* Retrieved from http://lifehacker.com/5989980/ive-been-using-evernote-all-wrong-heres-why-its-actually-amazing; Zweig, B. (2012, September 21). Can you go to school with just an iPad? We tried it. *NYU Local.* Retrieved from https://nyulocal.com/can-you-go-to-school-with-just-an-ipad-we-tried-it-cb8da6d2ccfb

25. Sana, F., Weston, T., & Cepeda, N. J. (2013). Laptop multitasking hinders classroom learning for both users and nearby peers. *Computers and Education, 62,* 24–31.

26. Pauk, W. (2000). *How to study in college.* Boston, MA: Cengage Learning.

27. Montis, K. K. (2007). Guided notes: An interactive method of success in secondary and college mathematics classrooms. *Focus on Learning Problems in Mathematics, 29*(3), 55–68.

28. Pardini, E. A., Domizi, D. P., Forbes, D. A., & Pettis, G. V. (2005). Parallel note-taking: A strategy for effective use of Webnotes. *Journal of College Reading and Learning, 35*(2), 38–55. Retrieved from http://editlib.org/p/72385/

29. Yamada-Hosley, H. (2014, December 11). Take notes at work to boost your productivity. *Lifehacker.* Retrieved from http://lifehacker.com/take-notes-at-work-to-boost-your-productivity-1669652836

30. Yamada-Hosley. Take notes at work to boost your productivity.

31. Stillmam, J. (2017, April 7). I'm not texting. I'm taking notes. *The New York Times.* Retrieved from https://www.nytimes.com/2017/04/07/jobs/texting-work-meetings-social-media.html?emc=edit_tnt_20170407&nlid=42590500&tntemail0=y

32. Stull, K. (N. D.). The most important thing you're not doing at work (and how to get started). *The Muse.* Retrieved from https://www.themuse.com/advice/the-most-important-thing-youre-not-doing-at-work-and-how-to-get-started

33. Liu, C. (2017). 5 free note-taking apps that'll help you keep track of everything (and anything). *The Muse.* Retrieved from https://www.themuse.com/advice/5-free-notetaking-apps-thatll-help-you-keep-track-of-everything-and-anything

34. Greenawald, E. (N. D.). The 30-second habit that will change everything. *The Muse.* Retrieved from https://www.themuse.com/advice/the-30second-habit-that-will-change-everything

35. Glenn, D. (2009, May 1). Close the book. Recall. Write it down. *The Chronicle of Higher Education.* Retrieved from http://chronicle.com/article/Close-the-Book-Recall-Write/31819

36. De Simone, C. (2007). Applications of concept mapping. *College Teaching, 55*(1), 33–36.

37. Kiewra, How classroom teachers can help students learn and teach them how to learn.

38. Porte, L. K. (2001). Cut and paste 101. *Teaching Exceptional Children, 34*(2), 14–20.

39. Craik, F. I. M., & Watkins, M. J. (1973). The role of rehearsal in short-term memory. *Journal of Verbal Learning and Verbal Behavior, 12,* 599–607.

40. Based on Staley, *50 ways to leave your lectern,* pp. 80–81.

Chapter 8

1. Rogers, M. (2007, March–April). Is reading obsolete? *The Futurist*, 26–27; Waters, L. (2007, February 9). Time for reading. *The Chronicle of Higher Education*, 53(23), 1B6.

2. Caverly, D. C., Nicholson, S. A., & Radcliffe, R. (2004). The effectiveness of strategic reading instruction for college developmental readers. *Journal of College Reading and Learning*, 35(1), 25–49; Simpson, M. L., & Nist, S. L. (1997). Perspectives on learning history: A case study. *Journal of Literacy Research*, 29(3), 363–395.

3. Community college survey of student engagement. 2016 Benchmark Means Report: Main Survey. *CCSSE*. Retrieved from http://www.ccsse.org/survey/reports/2016/standard_reports/CCSSE_2016_coh_means_stueff_std.pdf

4. Simons, G. F., & Fennig, C. D. (Eds.). 2017. *Ethnologue: Languages of the world*, (20th ed.). Dallas: SIL International. Online version: http://www.ethnologue.com.

5. Learn to pronounce sounds in American English. *Pronuncian.com*. Retrieved from https://pronuncian.com/sounds/

6. Bean, J. C. (1996). *Engaging ideas: The professor's guide to integrating writing, critical thinking, and active learning in the classroom*. San Francisco: Jossey-Bass; Wood, N. V. (1997). College reading instruction as reflected by current reading textbooks. *Journal of College Reading and Learning*, 27(3), 79–95.

7. Saumell, L., Hughes, M. T., & Lopate, K. (1999). Underprepared college students' perceptions of reading: Are their perceptions different than other students? *Journal of College Reading and Learning*, 29(2), 123–125.

8. Smith, B. D. (2006). *Breaking through college reading*. New York: Pearson Education, Inc., p. 351.

9. Paulson, E. J. (2006). Self-selected reading for enjoyment as a college developmental reading approach. *Journal of College Reading and Learning*, 36(2), 51–58.

10. Buzan, T. (1983). *Use both sides of your brain*. New York: E. P. Dutton.

11. Buzan, *Use both sides of your brain*.

12. Sternberg, R. J. (1987). Teaching intelligence: The application of cognitive psychology to the improvement of intellectual skills. In J. B. Baron & R. J. Sternberg (Eds.), *Teaching thinking skills: Theory and practice*. New York: Freeman, pp. 182–218.

13. Glenn, D. (2009, May 1). Close the book. Recall. Write it down. *The Chronicle of Higher Education*. Retrieved from http://chronicle.com/free/v55/i34/34a00101.htm

14. McCarroll, C. (2001). To learn to think in college, write—a lot. *Christian Science Monitor*, 93(177), 20.

15. McGann, K. (2016). 7 simple hacks to get writing when you just can't. *The Write Practice*. Retrieved from http://thewritepractice.com/seven-writing-hacks/; Bram, T. (2016). 5 hacks just for writers. *Life Hacks*. Retrieved from http://www.lifehack.org/articles/communication/5-hacks-just-for-writers.html

16. De Vos, I. (1988, October). Getting started: How expert writers do it. *Training & Development Journal*, 18–19.

17. Bean, *Engaging ideas: The professor's guide to integrating writing, critical thinking and active learning in the classroom*.

18. Portions of this section are based on Staley, C. & Staley, R. (1992). *Communicating in business and the professions: The inside word*. Belmont, CA: Wadsworth.

19. Based on Staley & Staley, *Communicating in business and the professions*.

20. Engleberg, I. N. (1994). *The principles of public presentation*. New York: HarperCollins; Daley, K., & Daley-Caravella, L. (2004). *Talk your way to the top*. New York: McGraw-Hill.

21. Wydro, K. (1981). *Think on your feet: The art of thinking and speaking under pressure*. Englewood Cliffs, NJ: Prentice-Hall.

22. Decker, K. (2012, May 9). Airline-inspired analogies. *Decker Blog*. Retrieved from http://decker.com/airline-inspired-analogies/

23. Decker, Airline-inspired analogies.

24. Clark, D. (2016, March 7). Actually, you should check email first thing in the morning. *Harvard Business Review*. Retrieved from https://hbr.org/2016/03/actually-you-should-check-email-first-thing-in-the-morning?referral=00563&cm_mmc=email-_-newsletter-_-daily_alert-_-alert_date&utm_source=newsletter_daily_alert&utm_medium=email&utm_campaign=alert_date

25. Internet live stats. Retrieved from http://www.internetlivestats.com/twitter-statistics/

26. Omoth, T. (2017). The top five skills employers are looking for in 2017. *Top Resume*. Retrieved from https://www.topresume.com/career-advice/the-top-5-job-skills-that-employers-are-looking-for-in-2017

27. Al-Jarf, R. (2002). Effect of online learning on struggling ESL college writers. NECC 2002 Conference. San Antonio, TX, June 17–19.

Chapter 9

1. Bolla, K. I., Lindgren, K. N., Bonaccorsy, C., & Bleecker, M. L. (1991). Memory complaints in older adults: Fact or fiction? *Archives of Neurology*, 48, 61–64.

2. Higbee, K. L. (2004). What aspects of their memories do college students most want to improve? *College Student Journal*, 38(4), 552–556.

3. Higbee, K. L. (1988). *Your memory: How it works and how to improve it* (2nd ed.). New York: Prentice Hall.

4. Higbee, *Your memory*.

5. Nairine, J. S. (2006). *Psychology: The adaptive mind*. Belmont, CA: Wadsworth/Thomson Learning.

6. Miller, G. A. (1956). The magical number seven plus or minus two: Some limits on our capacity for processing information. *Psychological Review*, 63, 81–97; Raman, M., McLaughlin, K., Violato, C., Rostom, A., Allard, J.P., & Coderre, S. (2010). Teaching in small portions dispersed over time enhances long-term knowledge retention. *Medical Teacher*, 32, 250–255.

7. Narayanan, K. The neurological scratchpad: What is working memory? (2004, July 7). *Brain Connection*. Retrieved from http://brainconnection.positscience.com/the-neurological-scratchpad-looking-into-working-memory/; Kerry, S. (1999–2002). Memory and retention time. *Education Reform.net*. Retrieved from http://www.education-reform.net/memory.htm

8. Dodeen, H. (2008). Assessing test-taking strategies of university students: Developing a scale and estimating its psychometric indices. *Assessment & Evaluation in Higher Education*, 33(4), 409–419.

9. Edmondson, A. C. (2015, June 24). Get rid of unhealthy competition on your team. *Harvard Business Review*. Retrieved from https://hbr.org/2015/06/get-rid-of-unhealthy-competition-on-your-team

10. Chamorro-Premuzic, T. (2015, July 9). Test-taking comes to the office. *Harvard Business Review*. Retrieved from https://hbr.org/ideacast/2015/07/test-taking-comes-to-the-office

11. Martin, W. (2014, August 27). The problem with using personality tests for hiring. *Harvard Business Review*. Retrieved from https://hbr.org/2014/08/the-problem-with-using-personality-tests-for-hiring

12. Bateson, J.; Wirtz, J.; Burke, E.; & Vaughan, C. (2013, November). When hiring, first test, and then interview. *Harvard Business Review*. Retrieved from https://hbr.org/2013/11/when-hiring-first-test-and-then-interview

13. Coren, S. (1996). *Sleep thieves*. New York: Free Press.

14. Brennan, C. (2015, December 16). Popping pills: Examining the use of 'study drugs' during finals. *USA Today*. Retrieved from http://college.usatoday.com/2015/12/16/popping-pills-examining-the-use-of-study-drugs-during-fnals/

15. Brinthaupt, T. M., & Shin, C. M. (2001). The relationship of academic cramming to flow experience. *College Student Journal*, 35(3), 457–472.

16. Tigner, R. B. (1999). Putting memory research to good use: Hints from cognitive psychology. *Journal of College Teaching*, 47(4), 149–152.

17. Small, G. (2002). *The memory bible.* New York: Hyperion.

18. Staff. (2010–2016). Test anxiety. *Anxiety and Depression Association of America.* https://adaa.org/living-with-anxiety/children/test-anxiety

19. Tozoglu, D., Tozoglu, M. D., Gurses, A., & Dogar, C. (2004). The students' perceptions: Essay versus multiple-choice type exams. *Journal of Baltic Science Education, 2*(6), 52–59.

20. Schutz, P. A., & Davis, H. A. (2000). Emotions and self-regulation during test taking. *Educational Psychologist, 35*(4), 243–256.

21. Coren, *Sleep thieves.*

22. Beris, R. (2016). Science says silence is much more important to our brains than we think. *Life Hack.* Retrieved from http://www.lifehack.org/377243/science-says-silence-much-more-important-our-brains-than-thought

23. Adelson, R. (2014, September). Nervous about numbers. *Association for Psychological Science.* Retrieved from https://www.psychologicalscience.org/observer/nervous-about-numbers#.WPupSfnyvb0

24. Perry, A. (2004). Decreasing math anxiety in college students. *College Student Journal, 38*(2), pp. 321–324.

25. Jonides, J., Lacey, S. C., & Nee, D. E. (2005). Processes of working memory in mind and brain. *Current Directions in Psychological Science, 14*(1), 2–5.

26. Ashcraft, M. H., & Kirk, E. P. (2001). The relationships among working memory, math anxiety, and performance. *Journal of Experimental Psychology: General. 130*(2), 224–237.

27. Beilock, S. L., Kulp, C. A., Holt, L. E., & Carr, T. H. (2004). More on the fragility of performance: Choking under pressure in mathematical problem solving. *Journal of Experimental Psychology: General, 133*(4), 584–600.

28. Mundell, E. J. (2005, March 9). Test pressure toughest on smartest. *Healingwell.com.* Retrieved from http://news.healingwell.com/index.php?p=news1&id=524405

29. Based partially on Arem, C. (2003). *Conquering math anxiety,* second edition. Belmont, CA: Brooks/Cole.

30. Glenn, D. (2010, February 7). How students can improve by studying themselves. *The Chronicle of Higher Education.* Retrieved from http://chronicle.com/article/Struggling-Students-Can-Imp/64004/

31. Firmin, M., Hwang, C., Copella, M., & Clark, S. (2004). Learned helplessness: The effect of failure on test-taking. *Education, 124*(4), 688–693.

32. Heidenberg, A. J., & Layne, B. H. (2000). Answer changing: A conditional argument. *College Student Journal, 34*(3), 440–451.

33. Retrieved from http://news.bbc.co.uk/2/hi/uk_news/scotland/glasgow_and_west/4755297.stm

34. Preparing for tests and exams. (2007). *York University.* Retrieved from http://www.yorku.ca/cds/lss/skillbuilding/exams.html#Multiple

35. Taking exams. *Brockport High School.* Retrieved from http://www.frontiernet.net/~jlkeefer/takgexm.html. Adapted from Penn State University; On taking exams. *University of New Mexico.* Retrieved from http://www.unm.edu/~quadl/college_learning/taking_exams.html; Lawrence, J. (2006). Tips for taking examinations. *Lawrence Lab Homepage.* Retrieved from http://cobamide2.bio.pitt.edu/testtips.htm; The multiple choice exam. (2003). *Counselling Services, University of Victoria.* Retrieved from http://www.coun.uvic.ca/learning/exams/multiple-choice.html; General strategies for taking essay tests. *GWired.* Retrieved from http://gwired.gwu.edu/counsel/asc/index.gw/Site_ID/46/Page_ID/14565/; Test taking tips: Guidelines for answering multiple-choice questions. *Arizona State University.* Retrieved from http://neuer101.asu.edu/additionaltestingtips.htm; Landsberger, J. (2007). True/false tests. *Study Guides and Strategies.* Retrieved from http://www.studygs.net/tsttak2.htm; Landsberger, J. (2007). Multiple choice tests. *Study Guides and Strategies.* Retrieved from http://www.studygs.net/tsttak3.htm; Landsberger, J. (2007). The essay exam. *Study Guides and Strategies.* Retrieved from http://www.studygs.net/tsttak4.htm; Landsberger, J. (2007). Short answer tests. *Study Guides and Strategies.* Retrieved from http://www.studygs.net/tsttak5.htm; Landsberger, J. (2007). Open book tests. *Study Guides and Strategies.* Retrieved from http://www.studygs.net/tsttak7.htm; Rozakis, L. (2003). *Test-taking strategies and study skills for the utterly confused.* New York: McGraw-Hill; Meyers, J. N. (2000). *The secrets of taking any test.* New York: Learning Express; Robinson, A. (1993). *What smart students know.* New York: Crown Trade Paperbacks.

36. Schaffhauser, D. (2017, February 23). 9 in 10 students admit to cheating in college, suspect faculty do the same. *Campus Technology.* Retrieved from https://campustechnology.com/articles/2017/02/23/9-in-10-students-admit-to-cheating-in-college-suspect-faculty-do-the-same.aspx

37. *Plagiarism.org.* Retrieved from http://www.plagiarism.org/understanding-plagiarism; A cheating crisis in America's schools. (2007, April 29). *ABC News.* Retrieved from http://abcnews.go.com/Primetime/story?id=132376&page=1

38. Young, J. R. (2010, March 28). High tech cheating abounds, and professors bear some blame. *The Chronicle of Higher Education.* Retrieved from http://chronicle.com/article/High-Tech-Cheating-on-Homew/64857/; Gabriel, T. (2010, August 1). Plagiarism lines blur for students in digital age. *The New York Times.* Retrieved from http://www.nytimes.com/2010/08/02/education/02cheat.html?_r=1&src=me&ref=homepage

39. Caught cheating. (2004, April 29). *Primetime Live,* ABC News Transcript. Interview of college students by Charles Gibson; Zernike, K. (2002, November 2). With student cheating on the rise, more colleges are turning to honor codes. *The New York Times,* p. Q10, column 1, National Desk; Warren, R. (2003, October 20). Cheating: An easy way to cheat yourself. *The Voyager via U-Wire. University Wire (www.uwire.com);* Thomson, S. C. (2004, February 13). Heyboer, K. (2003, August 23). Nearly half of college students say Internet plagiarism isn't cheating. *The Star-Ledger Newark, New Jersey;* Kleiner, C., & Lord, M. (1999).

40. Tagg, J. (2004, March-April). Why learn? What we may really be teaching students. *About Campus,* 2–10; Marton, F., & Säljö, R. On qualitative differences in learning: I-Outcome and process. (1976). *British Journal of Educational Psychology, 46,* 4–11.

41. Noice, H., & Noice, T. (2006). What studies of actors and acting can tell us about memory and cognitive functioning. *Current Directions in Psychological Science, 15*(1), 14–18.

Chapter 10

1. Some situation topics are suggested at Hay Group Transforming Learning EI Quiz. *Haygroup.com.* Retrieved from http://atrium.haygroup.com/us/quizzes/emotional-intelligence-quiz.aspx

2. Gardner, H. (1993). *Multiple intelligences: The theory in practice.* New York: Basic Books; Checkley, K. (1997). The first seven … and the eighth: A conversation with Howard Gardner. Expanded Academic ASAP (online database). Original Publication: *Education,* 116.

3. Parker, J. D. A., Duffy, J. M., Wood, L. M., Bond, B. J., & Hogan, M. J. (2005). Academic achievement and emotional intelligence: Predicting the successful transition from high school to university. *Journal of the First Year Experience & Students in Transition 17*(1), 67–78; Schutte, N. S., & Malouff, J. (2002). Incorporating emotional skills content in a college transition course enhances student retention. *Journal of the First Year Experience & Students in Transition 14*(1), 7–21.

4. Berenson, R., Boyles, G., & Weaver, A. (2008). Emotional intelligence as a predictor for success in online learning. *International Review of Research in Open and Distance Learning, 9*(2), 1–16; Zeidner, M., & Roberts, R. (2010). Coping mediates the relationship between emotional intelligence (EI) and academic achievement. *Contemporary Educational Psychology, 36*(2011), 60–70.

5. Goleman, D. (2015, March 5). Thinking and feeling go hand in hand in the classroom. *LinkedIn Pulse.* Retrieved from https://www.linkedin.com/pulse/thinking-feeling-go-hand-classroom-daniel-goleman

6. EQ-i:S Post Secondary, Multi-Health Systems, Inc. North Tonawanda, NY. Retrieved from http://www.mhs.com. Used with permission. Five scales of emotional intelligence.

7. Turning lemons into lemonade: Hardiness helps people turn stressful circumstances into opportunities. (2003, December 22). *American Psychological Association*. Retrieved from http://www.apa.org/research/action/lemon.aspx; Marano, H. E. (2003). The art of resilience. *Psychology Today*. Retrieved from https://www.psychologytoday.com/articles/200305 /the-art-resilience; Fischman, J. (1987). Getting tough: Can people learn to have disease-resistant personalities? *Psychology Today, 21*, 26–28; Friborg, O., Barlaug, D., Martinussen, M., Rosenvinge, & J. H. Intelligence. *International Journal of Methods in Psychiatric Research, 14*(1), 29–42; Schulman, P. (1995). Explanatory style and achievement in school and work. In G. M. Buchanan & M. E. P. Seligman (Eds.), *Explanatory style* (pp. 159–171). Hillsdale, NJ: Lawrence Erlbaum; American Psychological Association. (1997). Learned optimism yields health benefits. *How Stuff Works*. Retrieved from http://health.howstuffworks.com/mental-health/coping /learned-optimism-health-benefits.htm

8. Cherniss, C. (2000). Emotional intelligence: What it is and why it matters. *Consortium for Research on Emotional Intelligence in Organizations*. Retrieved from http://www.eiconsortium .org/reports/what_is_emotional_intelligence.html

9. Cherniss, *Emotional intelligence.*

10. Giang, V. (2015, March 25). Inside Google's insanely popular emotional-intelligence course. *Fast Company*. Retrieved from http://www.fastcompany.com/3044157/the-future-of -work/inside-googles-insanely-popular-emotional-intelligence -course

11. Goleman, D. (2002, June 16). Could you be a leader? *Parade Magazine*, pp. 4–6.

12. Boyatzis, R. E., Cowan, S. S., & Kolb, D. A. (1995). *Innovation in professional education: Steps on a journey from teaching to learning.* San Francisco: Jossey-Bass.

13. Saxbe, D. (2004, November 1). The socially savvy. *Psychology Today*. Retrieved from http://www.psychologytoday.com /articles/200501/the-socially-savvy

14. Cuddy, A. (2015). *Presence: Bring your biggest self to your boldest challenges.* New York: Little, Brown and Company; Goudreau, J. (2016, January 16). A Harvard psychologist says people judge you based on 2 criteria when they first meet you. *Business Insider*. Retrieved at http://www.businessinsider.com /harvard-psychologist-amy-cuddy-how-people-judge-you-2016-1

15. Knox, D. H. (1970). Conceptions of love at three developmental levels. *The Family Coordinator, 19*(2), 151–157; Fisher, *Why we love;* Cramer, D. (2004). Satisfaction with a romantic relationship, depression, support and conflict. *Psychology and Psychotherapy: Theory, Research and Practice, 77*(4), 449–461.

16. Barth, S. (2001). *3-D chess: Boosting team productivity through emotional intelligence.* Boston: Harvard Business Publishing; (2004). *Teams that click.* Boston: Harvard Business School Press.

17. Barth, *3-D chess.*

18. Tims, A. (2011, March 4). The secret to understanding soft skills. *The Guardian*. Retrieved from http://www.guardian.co .uk/money/2011/mar/05/secret-to-understanding-soft-skills

19. Levi, D. (2014). *Group dynamics for teams.* Thousand Oaks, CA: Sage.

20. Daily Free Press Admin. (2013, February 6). Students working in groups have greater understanding, study suggests. *The Daily Free Press*. Retrieved from http://dailyfreepress .com/2013/02/06/students-working-in-groups-have-greater -understanding-study-suggests/

21. Coutu, D. (2009, May). Why teams don't work: An interview with J. Richard Hackman. *Harvard Business Review*. Retrieved from https://hbr.org/2009/05/why-teams-dont-work

22. Coutu, Why teams don't work.

23. Mullen, J. K. (2012, March 16). Digital natives are slow to pick up nonverbal cues. *Harvard Business Review*. Retrieved from https://hbr.org/2012/03/digital-natives-are-slow-to-pi

24. Mullen, Digital natives are slow to pick up nonverbal cues.

25. Cross, R., Rebele, R., & Grant, A. (2016, January–February). Collaborative overload. *Harvard Business Review*. Retrieved from https://hbr.org/2016/01/collaborative-overload

26. Parker-Pope , T. (2009, April 20). What are friends for? A longer life. *The New York Times*. Retrieved from http://www .nytimes.com/2009/04/21/health/21well.html; Ybarra, O., Burnstein, E., Winkielman, P., Keller, M. C., Manis, M. Chan, E., & Rodriguez, J. (2008). Mental exercising through simple socializing: Social interaction promotes general cognitive functioning. *Personality and Social Psychology Bulletin, 34,* 248–259.

27. Dakss, B. (2006, March 3). Study: Bad relationships bad for heart. *CBS News*. Retrieved from http://www.cbsnews .com/news/study-bad-relationships-bad-for-heart/; Chang. L. (2005, December 5) Unhappy marriage: Bad for your health. *WebMD*. Retrieved from http://www.webmd.com/sex -relationships/news/20051205/unhappy-marriage-bad-for -your-health. Based on Keicolt-Glaser, J. (2005). *Archives of general psychiatry, 62*, 1377–1384.

28. Dusselier, L., Dunn, B., Wang, Y., Shelley, M. C., & Whalen, D. F. (2005). Personal, health, academic, and environmental predictors of stress for residence hall students. *Journal of American College Health, 54*(1), 15–24; Hardigg, V., & Nobile, C. (1995). Living with a stranger. *U.S. News & World Report, 119*(12), 90–91. Nankin, J. (2005). Rules for roomies. *Careers & Colleges, 25*(4), 29.

29. Thomas, K. (1977). Conflict and conflict management. In M. D. Dunnette (Ed.), *Handbook of industrial and organizational psychology*. Chicago: Rand McNally, pp. 889–935; Kilmann, R., & Thomas, K. W. (1975). Interpersonal conflict handling behavior as reflections of Jungian personality dimensions. *Psychological Reports, 37*, 971–980; Rahim, M., & Magner, N. R. (1995). Confirmatory factor analysis of the styles of handling interpersonal conflict: First-order factor model and its invariance across groups. *Journal of Applied Psychology, 80*, 122–132; Wilmot, W. W., & Hocker, J. L. (2001). *Interpersonal conflict* (6th ed.). New York: McGraw Hill; Kilmann, R. H., and K. W. Thomas. (1977). Developing a Forced Choice Measure of Conflict-Handling Behavior: The MODE Instrument, *Educational and psychological measurement, 37*(2), 309–325.

30. N. A. (2015, March 9). Gender gap: Women represent 57% of college students—but just 26% of school leaders. *Education Advisory Board*. Retrieved from https:// www.eab.com/daily-briefing/2015/03/19/one-quarter -of-presidents-are-women

31. Fulbeck, K. (2010). *Mixed: Portraits of multiracial kids.* San Francisco: Chronicle Books.

32. *Race, the power of an illusion. PBS*. California Newsreel. Retrieved from http://www.pbs.org/race/000_General/000 _00-Home.htm

33. Wyer, K. (2007, April 9). Today's college freshmen have family income 60% above national average, UCLA survey reveals. *UCLA News room*. Retrieved from http:// newsroom.ucla.edu/releases/Today-s-College-Freshmen -Have-Family-7831

34. Humphreys, D., & Davenport, A. (2004, Summer/Fall). Diversity and civic engagement outcomes ranked among least important. *AAC&U: Diversity and Democracy*. Retrieved from http://www.diversityweb.org/Digest/vol9no1/humphreys .cfm

35. Based on "Sorting People" activity at http://www.pbs.org/race /002_SortingPeople/002_00-home.htm

36. Laird, T. F. (2005). College students' experiences with diversity and their effects on academic self-confidence, social agency, and disposition toward critical thinking. *Research in Higher Education, 46*(4), 365–387.

37. Bucher, R. D. (2004). *Diversity consciousness: Opening our minds to people, cultures, and opportunities* (2nd ed.). Upper Saddle River, NJ: Pearson Education.

38. Carnes, M. C. (2005). Inciting speech. *Change, 37*(2), 6–11.

39. Lyons, P. (2005, April 15). The truth about teaching about racism. *The Chronicle of Higher Education, 51*(32), B5. Retrieved from http://www.chronicle.com/article/The-Truth-About-Teaching-About/30681

40. Based on Nilsen, L. B. (1998). The circles of awareness. *Teaching at Its Best*. Bolton, MA: Anker Publishing; Bucher, R. D. (2008). *Building cultural intelligence: Nine megaskills*. Upper Saddle River, NJ: Pearson.

41. Bellstrom, K. (2015, December 23). Why 2015 was a terrible year to be a female Fortune 500 CEO. *Fortune*. Retrieved from http://fortune.com/2015/12/23/2015-women-fortune-500-ceos/

42. Santos, M. (2016, April 12). Men get higher salary offers than women 69% of the time. *Working Mother*. Retrieved from http://www.workingmother.com/men-get-higher-salary-offers-than-women-69-percent-time

43. Wessel, D. (2003, September 9). Race still a factor in hiring decisions. *College Journal from the Wall Street Journal*. Retrieved from https://static1.squarespace.com/static/5628e73ae4b0c53c5aff0e81/t/57bb2154893fc0d107 78411d/1471881557163/Wessel.Race.Still.a.Factor.in.Hiring.Decisions.pdf

44. Beilke, J. R., & Yssel, N. (1999). The chilly climate for students with disabilities in higher education. *College Student Journal, 33*(3), 364–372.

45. Parker, P. N. (2006, March–April). Sustained dialogue: How students are changing their own racial climate. *About Campus, 11*(1), 17–23.

46. Gortmaker, V. J., & Brown, R. D. (2006). Out of the college closet: Differences in perceptions and experiences among out and closeted lesbian and gay students. *College Student Journal, 40*(3), 606–619.

47. Earley, P. C., & Mosakowski, E. (2004, October). Cultural intelligence. *Harvard Business Review*, 139–146. Retrieved from https://hbr.org/2004/10/cultural-intelligence; Early, C. P., Ang, S., & Tan, J. (2006) *CQ: Developing cultural intelligence at work*. Stanford, CA: Stanford University Press; Osborn, T. N., (2006). *"CQ": Another aspect of emotional intelligence*.

48. Earley, P. C., & Mosakowski, E. Cultural intelligence.

49. (2017). World internet users and population stats. *Internet World Stats*. Retrieved from http://www.internetworldstats.com/stats.htm

50. Three decades of institutionalizing change: 2014 annual member survey. (2014). *Campus Compact*. Retrieved from http://compact.org/wp-content/uploads/2015/05/2014-CC-Member-Survey.pdf

51. Campus Compact Staff. (2012, June 12). Vermont college and university students to help local communities with long-term recovery. *Campus Compact*. Retrieved from http://compact.org/resource-posts/vermont-college-and-university-students-to-help-local-communities-with-long-term-recovery/

52. Zlotkowski, E. (1999). Pedagogy and engagement. In R. G. Bringle, R. Games, & E. A. Malloy (Eds.). *Colleges and universities as citizens*. Needham Heights, MA: Allyn & Bacon, pp. 96–120.

53. Honnet, E. P., & Poulsen, S. J. (1989). *Principles of good practice for combining service and learning: A Wingspread special report*. The Johnson Foundation.

54. Eyler, J., Giles, Jr., D. E., & Schmiede, A. (1996). *A practitioner's guide to reflection in service learning: Student voices and reflections*. Nashville, TN: Vanderbilt University Press.

55. Bregman, P. (2010, July 21). How to avoid (and quickly recover from) misunderstandings. *Harvard Business Review*. Retrieved from https://hbr.org/2010/07/how-to-avoid-and-quickly-recov.html; Bregman, P. (2011, January 3). The best way to use the last five minutes of the day. *Harvard Business Review*. Retrieved from https://hbr.org/2011/01/the-best-way-to-use-the-last-f.html

56. Bregman, How to avoid (and quickly recover from) misunderstandings; Bregman, The best way to use the last five minutes of the day.

Chapter 11

1. Gregory, M. (2003, September 12). A liberal education is not a luxury. *The Chronicle of Higher Education, 50*(3), B16.

2. Staley, R. S., II. (2003). In C. Staley, *50 ways to leave your lectern* (pp. 70–74). Belmont, CA: Wadsworth.

3. Niles, S. G., Amundson, N. E., & Neault, R. A. (2011). *Career flow: A hope-centered approach to career development*. Boston: Pearson Education, Inc.

4. Farrell, E. F. (2006, December 12). Freshmen put high value on how well college prepares them for a profession, survey finds. *The Chronicle of Higher Education*. Farrell, E. F. (2007, January 5). Report says freshmen put career prep first. *The Chronicle of Higher Education, 53*(18), A32. Retrieved from http://chronicle.com/article/Report-Says-Freshmen-Put-Ca/19260/; Bok, D. (2010, January 31). College and the well-lived life. *The Chronicle of Higher Education*. Retrieved from http://chronicle.com/article/Collegethe-Well-Lived-/63789/

5. Associated Press (2007, January 22). Polls say wealth important to youth. *NewsOK*. Retrieved from http://newsok.com/article/3002446; Schwartz, B. (2004, January 23). The tyranny of choice. *The Chronicle of Higher Education, 50*(20), B6. Retrieved from http://www.chronicle.com/article/The-Tyranny-of-Choice/22622

6. Berrett, D. (2012, June 3). Changing majors is no big deal if the timing is right, studies find. *The Chronicle of Higher Education*. Retrieved from http://chronicle.com/article/Changing-Majors-Is-No-Big-Deal/132105/

7. Burnett, B., & Evans, D. (2016). *Designing your life: How to build a well-lived joyful life*. New York: Alfred A. Knopf.

8. Cramer, R. (2014, September 8). 11 richest professional skateboarders in the world. *The Richest*. Retrieved from http://www.therichest.com/sports/other-sports/11-richest-professional-skateboarders-in-the-world/

9. Professional Skateboarder. (N.D.). *Inside Jobs*. Retrieved from http://www.insidejobs.com/careers/professional-skateboarder

10. Product Hunt. (N.D.). *The Muse*. The best apps for people who get easily distracted at work (so, everyone). Retrieved https://www.themuse.com/advice/the-best-apps-for-people-who-get-easily-distracted-at-work-so-everyone

11. Koeppel, D. (2004, December 5). Choosing a college major: For love or for the money? *The New York Times,* section 10, p. 1, column 4. Retrieved from http://www.nytimes.com/2004/12/05/jobs/choosing-a-college-major-for-love-or-for-the-money.html; Dunham, K. J. (2004, March 2). No ivory tower: College students focus on career. *Wall Street Journal* (Eastern Edition), pp. B1, B8. Retrieved from http://online.wsj.com/article/SB107818521697943524.html

12. Burnett, B., & Evans, D. (2016). *Designing your life: How to build a well-lived, joyful life*. New York: Alfred A. Knopf.

13. Burnett, B., & Evans, *Designing your life*.

14. Based in part on Gordon, V. N., & Sears, S. J. (2004). *Selecting a college major: Exploration and decision making*, 5th ed. Upper Saddle River, NJ: Pearson Education.

15. Based on Hansen, R. S., & Hansen, K. Using a SWOT analysis in your career planning. *Quintessential Careers*. Retrieved from http://www.quintcareers.com/SWOT_Analysis.html

16. Rowh, M. (2003, February–March). Choosing a major. *Career World, 31*(5), 21–23.

17. Ezarik, M. M. (2007, April–May). A major decision. *Career World, 35*(6), 20–22.

18. Rask, K. N., & Bailey, E. M. (2002). Are faculty role models? Evidence from major choice in an undergraduate institution. *The Journal of Economic Education, 33*(2), 99–124.

19. Duckworth, A. (2016). *Grit: The power of passion and perseverance*. New York: Scribner; Robaton, A. (2017, March 31). Why so many Americans hate their jobs. *CBS News: Moneywatch*. Retrieved from http://www.cbsnews.com/news/why-so-many-americans-hate-their-jobs/

20. Ryan, L. (2016, November 29). The top ten reasons people hate their jobs. *Forbes*. Retrieved from https://www

.forbes.com/sites/lizryan/2016/11/29/the-top-ten-reasons
-people-hate-their-jobs/#2bad83551ed9

21. Duckworth, A. (2016). *Grit: The power of passion and persever-ance.* New York: Scribner.

22. Moran, G. (2016, March 31). These will be the top jobs in 2025 (and the skills you'll need to get them). *Fast Company.* Retrieved from https://www.fastcompany.com/3058422/these-will-be-the -top-jobs-in-2025-and-the-skills-youll-need-to-get-them

23. Moran, These will be the top jobs in 2025.

24. Daskal, L. (2017, March 9). 12 important career lessons most people learn too late in life. *Inc.* Retrieved from https://www.inc .com/lolly-daskal/12-important-career-lessons-most-people -learn-too-late-in-life.html

25. Daskal, 12 important career lessons most people learn too late in life.

26. Gallo, A. (2011, March 18). Where Will You Be in Five Years? *Harvard Business Review.* Retrieved from https://hbr .org/2011/03/where-will-you-be-in-five-year.html

27. Brooks, K. (2009). *You majored in what?* New York: Viking.

28. Kanter, R. M. (2011, March). Managing yourself: Zoom in, zoom out. *Harvard Business Review.* Retrieved from http://hbr.org/2011/03/managing-yourself-zoom-in-zoom -out/ar/1

29. Gallo, Where will you be in five years?

Chapter 12

1. Goldhaber, G. M. (1986). *Organizational communication* (4th ed.). Dubuque, IA: Wm. C. Brown, p. 236. In Staley, R. S., II, & Staley, C. C. (1992). *Communicating in business and the pro-fessions: The inside word.* Belmont, CA: Wadsworth; Zenger, J., & Folkman, J. (2012, July 16). How damaging is a bad boss, exactly? *Harvard Business Review.* Retrieved from https:// hbr.org/2012/07/how-damaging-is-a-bad-boss-exa

2. N.A. (2017, May 11). 27 highest-paying jobs that you can pre-pare for in two years or less. *Trade Schools, Colleges, and Univer-sities.* Retrieved from https://www.trade-schools.net/articles /highest-paying-jobs-without-degree.asp

3. Peters, T. (1997, August 31). The brand called you. *FastCompany.* Retrieved from https://www.fastcompany.com/28905/brand -called-you

4. Pan, J. (2012, August 28). Students, here's how to kick-start your personal brand online. *Mashable.* Retrieved from http:// mashable.com/2012/08/28/personal-branding-for-students

5. Johnson, K. (2016, May 15). 5 Business card apps to move your contacts into the digital age. *Business 2 Community.* Retrieved from http://www.business2community.com/mobile -apps/5-business-card-apps-move-contacts-digital-age-01544252# p0GhjEycAXJOL3Ay.97

6. Jay, M. (2013, February). Why 30 is not the new 20. *TedTalk.* Retrieved from https://www.ted.com/talks/meg_jay_why_30 _is_not_the_new_20

7. Schawbel, D. (2010). *Me 2.0: 4 steps to building your future.* New York: Kaplan Publishing.

8. Gershon, I. (2017, June 2). "A Friend of a Friend" is no lon-ger the best way to find a job. *Harvard Business Review.* Retrieved from https://hbr.org/2017/06/a-friend-of-a-friend -is-no-longer-the-best-way-to-find-a-job

9. Pan, Students, here's how to kick-start your personal brand online.

10. White, M. C. (2012, March 9). Can interviewers insist on 'Shoulder Surfing' your Facebook page? *Time.* Retrieved from http://business.time.com/2012/03/09/can-interviewers -insist-on-shoulder-surfing-your-facebook-page/

11. McConnon, A. (2007, August 30). Social networking is graduating—and hitting the job market. *BusinessWeek.* pp. IN 4, IN 6.

12. N.A. (2016, January 2). Is your resume ready for automated screening? *Resume Hacking.* Retrieved from http://www .resumehacking.com/ready-for-automated-resume-screening

13. Giang, V. (2012, April 9). What recruiters look at during the 6 seconds they spend on your resume. *Business Insider.* Retrieved from http://www.businessinsider.com/heres-what -recruiters-look-at-during-the-6-seconds-they-spend-on-your -resume-2012-4

14. N. A., Is your resume ready for automated screening?

15. Gillett, R. (2014, October 30). How to create an infographic resume that doesn't repel hiring managers. *Fast Company.* Retrieved from https://www.fastcompany.com/3037764/how -to-create-an-infographic-resume-that-doesnt-repel-hiring -managers

16. Bahler, K. (2017, April 10). What your cover letter should look like in 2017. *Money.* Retrieved from http://time.com /money/4732891/sample-cover-letter-example-2017/

17. Cedja, B. D., Kaylor, A. J., & Rewey, K. L. (1998). Transfer shock in an academic discipline: The relationship between students' majors and their academic performance. *Community College Review, 26*(3), 1–13.

18. *Occupational Outlook Handbook 2015.* Retrieved from https:// www.bls.gov/ooh/

19. Thurmond, K. (2007). Transfer shock: Why is a term forty years old still relevant? *National Academic Advising Asso-ciation (NACADA).* Retrieved from http://www.nacada.ksu .edu/Resources/Clearinghouse/View-Articles/Dealing-with -transfer-shock.aspx; T. J., Milligan, D. M., & Nelson, L. R. (2000). Alleviating transfer shock: Creating an environment for more successful transfer students. *Community College Journal of Research and Practice, 24,* 443–452.

20. Anderson, K. (2012, June 5). What captures your attention controls your life. *Harvard Business Review.* Retrieved from https://hbr.org/2012/06/what-captures-your-attention-c

21. Hanson, R. (2009). *Buddha's brain: The practical neuroscience of happiness, love, and wisdom.* Oakland, CA: New Harbinger Publications.

22. Bregman, P. (2016, March 28). You need to practice being your future self. *Harvard Business Review.* Retrieved from https://hbr.org/2016/03/you-need-to-practice-being-your -future-self

23. Bregman, P. You need to practice being your future self.

24. DeMers, J. (2015, April 6). 7 life hacks for greater career success. Inc. Retrieved from https://www.inc.com/jayson -demers/7-life-hacks-for-greater-career-success.html

25. Coplin, B. (2003). *10 things employers want you to learn in college.* Berkeley, CA: Ten Speed Press.

26. Marsh, N. (2010, May). How to make work-life balance work. *TedTalks.* Retrieved from https://www.ted.com/talks/nigel _marsh_how_to_make_work_life_balance_work.html

27. Bregman, P. (2010, July 30). Don't regret working too hard. *Harvard Business Review.* Retrieved from https://hbr.org /2010/07/dont-regret-working-too-hard.html

INDEX

Note: Numbers followed by (b) indicate boxes; by (e) indicate exercises; by (f) indicate figures; by (t) indicate tables.